Debating the Democratic Peace

International Security Readers

Strategy and Nuclear Deterrence (1984)

Military Strategy and the Origins of the First World War (1985)

Conventional Forces and American Defense Policy (1986)

The Star Wars Controversy (1986)

Naval Strategy and National Security (1988)

Military Strategy and the Origins of the First World War,
revised and expanded edition (1991)

—published by Princeton University Press

Soviet Military Policy (1989)

Conventional Forces and American Defense Policy, revised edition (1989)

Nuclear Diplomacy and Crisis Management (1990)

The Cold War and After: Prospects for Peace (1991)

America's Strategy in a Changing World (1992)

The Cold War and After: Prospects for Peace, expanded edition (1993)

Global Dangers: Changing Dimensions of International Security (1995)

The Perils of Anarchy: Contemporary Realism and International Security (1995)

Debating the Democratic Peace (1996)

East Asian Security (1996)

—published by The MIT Press

Debating the Democratic Peace

AN *International Security* READER

EDITED BY
Michael E. Brown
Sean M. Lynn-Jones
and Steven E. Miller

THE MIT PRESS
CAMBRIDGE, MASSACHUSETTS
LONDON, ENGLAND

Library of Congress Cataloging-in-Publication Data
  Debating the democratic peace / edited by Michael E. Brown, Sean M. Lynn-Jones,
  and Steven E. Miller.
    p. cm.
  An international security reader
  Includes bibliographical references.
  ISBN 0-262-52213-6 (pbk. : alk. paper)
  1. Peace. 2. Security, International. 3. Democracy. I. Brown, Michael E.
(Michael Edward), 1954–   . II. Lynn-Jones, Sean M. III. Miller, Steven E.
JX1952.D43 1996
327.1'72—dc20   95-44816
                                                            CIP

Contents

The Contributors

MICHAEL E. BROWN is Managing Editor of *International Security* and Associate Director of the International Security Program at the Center for Science and International Affairs, Harvard University.

SEAN M. LYNN-JONES is Editor of *International Security* and Research Associate at the Center for Science and International Affairs, Harvard University.

STEVEN E. MILLER is Editor-in-Chief of *International Security* and Director of the International Security Program at the Center for Science and International Affairs, Harvard University.

MICHAEL W. DOYLE is Professor of Politics and International Affairs at the Center of International Studies, Princeton University.

BRUCE RUSSETT is Dean Acheson Professor of International Relations and Political Science at Yale University.

JOHN M. OWEN is Assistant Professor of Government at Bowdoin College.

CHRISTOPHER LAYNE is a Research Fellow at the Center for Science and International Affairs, Harvard University, and a consultant to the RAND Corporation.

DAVID E. SPIRO is Assistant Professor of Political Science at the University of Arizona.

HENRY S. FARBER is the Hughes Rogers Professor of Economics at Princeton University.

JOANNE GOWA is Professor of Politics at Princeton University.

IDO OREN is Assistant Professor of Political Science at the University of Minnesota.

EDWARD D. MANSFIELD is Associate Professor of Political Science at Columbia University.

JACK SNYDER is Professor of Political Science and Director of the Institute of War and Peace Studies at Columbia University.

Acknowledgments

The editors gratefully acknowledge the assistance that has made this book possible. A deep debt is owed to all those at the Center for Science and International Affairs (CSIA), Harvard University, who have played an editorial role at International Security. We thank Princeton University Press for granting permission for us to reprint chapters from Bruce Russett's *Grasping the Democratic Peace* and for granting us permission to reprint Michael Doyle's article "Kant, Liberal Legacies, and Foreign Affairs" from *Philosophy and Public Affairs*. We are grateful for support from the Carnegie Corporation of New York. Special thanks go to Ann Callahan, Karen Motley, Spencer Rascoff and Meara E. Keegan at CSIA as well as Katy Stenhouse at MIT Press for their invaluable help in preparing this volume for publication.

Preface | *Sean M. Lynn-Jones*

$\mathbf{T}$wo centuries ago, the German philosopher Immanuel Kant predicted that republican states would enjoy a "perpetual peace" with other republics. More recently, many observers have noted that democratic countries virtually never go to war with one another. Since the early 1980s, this apparent pattern has been regarded as one of the most important empirical features of international relations. Jack Levy claims that "the absence of war between democracies comes as close as anything we have to an empirical law in international relations."[1] Bruce Russett believes that "this is one of the strongest nontrivial and nontautological generalizations that can be made about international relations."[2] This absence of war between democracies has come to be known as the "democratic peace."[3]

This volume collects important essays that have advanced and challenged the idea of a democratic peace.[4] The first section of the book presents several seminal essays that argue that the democratic peace exists and is not spurious or epiphenomenal. The authors contend that democracies rarely go to war with one another, and that this democratic peace is the result of characteristics of democracies. These essays also explicate the apparent logic that explains why democracies do not fight one another. In the next section, the critics of the democratic peace have their say. The essays included here argue that the democratic peace is statistically insignificant, and that other factors can explain the apparent absence of war between democratic states. The final section is devoted to debate between the two schools of thought.

The debate over the democratic peace is theoretically important because it represents another round in the ongoing bout between realism and liberalism.[5] The existence of a democratic peace is usually seen as a liberal challenge to

---

1. Jack S. Levy, "Domestic Politics and War," in Robert I. Rotberg and Theodore K. Rabb, eds., *The Origin and Prevention of Major Wars* (Cambridge, U.K.: Cambridge University Press, 1989), p. 88.
2. Bruce Russett, *Controlling the Sword: The Democratic Governance of National Security* (Cambridge, Mass.: Harvard University Press, 1990), p. 123.
3. Most authors refer to peace between democracies, but others argue that liberal states do not fight one another. Immanuel Kant actually focused on what he called republics, not democracies. There is substantial overlap between these categories, but the "liberal peace" may not be identical with the "democratic peace." For convenience, this preface will use "democratic peace" to include the state of peace between liberal states as well as between democracies. The essays in this volume, particularly those by Michael Doyle and John Owen, discuss the differences between liberalism and democracy.
4. Previous *International Security* readers contained only articles that had been published in *International Security*. This volume contains several essays that originally appeared in other publications, because the editors felt that it was important to include essays that made important arguments for the existence and significance of the democratic peace.
5. The democratic peace proposition is not the only liberal challenge to realism. Other strands of liberalism include commercial liberalism, which claims economic interdependence is linked to

realist approaches to international relations.[6] The apparent existence of a democratic peace calls into question two tenets of most realist theories: realist pessimism about the prospects for international peace, and realism's emphasis on systemic factors as explanations of international outcomes.[7]

Realist pessimism does not argue that war is constant and endemic in the international system. Instead, it argues that war is always possible in the absence of a common sovereign, that states must be vigilant and prepare for war, and that no pair of states can count on enjoying peaceful relations indefinitely. In *Leviathan*, Thomas Hobbes presented the classic formulation of this view: "For as the nature of foul weather lieth not in a shower or two of rain; but in an inclination thereto of many days together: so the nature of war, consisteth not in actual fighting; but in the known disposition thereto, during all the time there is no assurance to the contrary." In this volume, Christopher Layne makes similar realist claims, arguing that "in the international system, fear and distrust of other states is the normal state of affairs," and that "in a realist world, survival and security are always at risk, and democratic states will respond no differently to democratic rivals than to non-democratic ones."

The existence of a separate and permanent peace among democracies challenges this realist pessimism, because the democratic peace proposition claims that democracies can indeed enjoy a permanent peace among themselves; they

peace; regulatory liberalism, which examines the role of international institutions; and sociological liberalism, which focuses on transnational relations. See Joseph S. Nye, Jr., "Neorealism and Neoliberalism," *World Politics*, Vol. 40, No. 2 (January 1988), pp. 235–251; and Andrew Moravcsik, "Liberalism and International Relations Theory," Working Paper 92–6, Center for International Affairs, Harvard University, 1992. A revised version of this paper will be published in *International Organization*, forthcoming, 1996. Much of the contemporary realist-liberal debate has been over whether states seek relative or absolute gains, and over the role of international institutions. See David A. Baldwin, ed., *Neorealism and Neoliberalism: The Contemporary Debate* (New York: Columbia University Press, 1993); John J. Mearsheimer, "The False Promise of International Institutions," *International Security*, Vol. 19, No. 3 (Winter 1994/95), pp. 5–49; and the section "Promises, Promises: Can Institutions Deliver?" *International Security*, Vol. 20, No. 1 (Summer 1995), pp. 39–93, in which Mearsheimer debates numerous critics.

6. The two most influential explications of realist theories are Hans J. Morgenthau, *Politics Among Nations: The Struggle for Power and Peace* (New York: Knopf, 1948 and later editions); and Kenneth N. Waltz, *Theory of International Politics* (Reading, Mass.: Addison-Wesley, 1979). For a variety of perspectives on current issues in realism, see Michael E. Brown, Sean M. Lynn-Jones, and Steven E. Miller, eds., *The Perils of Anarchy: Contemporary Realism and International Security* (Cambridge, Mass.: The MIT Press, 1995).

7. It is important to note that the liberal-realist debate over the democratic peace proposition is not a debate between contending theories of war. Neither realist nor liberal theory (at least in the form of the democratic peace proposition) actually says much about the causes of war. Most realist theories claim only that war is likely in international politics; they offer fewer predictions about specific wars. The democratic peace proposition only says that wars between democracies virtually never happen; it offers no predictions about when and where wars do break out.

are not doomed to exist in a state of war. The challenge of the democratic peace is most acute for "offensive realists," who tend to believe that the anarchic nature of the international system gives states strong incentives for aggression and makes war highly probable. Defensive realists, on the other hand, are less likely to be alarmed by the existence of peace between democracies. They contend that the international system often favors peace and cooperation. The separate peace among democracies may exist because systemic conditions favor peace, and because democracies have recognized this fact. Even defensive realists, however, may claim that there are systemic explanations of the peace between democracies and that the connection between democracy and peace is spurious.[8]

The existence of a democratic peace would also undermine a second common tenet of realist theories: the primacy of systemic factors in explaining international politics. Realists traditionally have claimed that the important elements of international politics can be explained without differentiating states by regime type. Systemic factors—especially the condition of anarchy and variations in the distribution of power—cause all states to compete for security, procure arms, form alliances, and fight wars, regardless of whether they are democracies or autocracies.[9] Thus Bruce Russett claims in this volume that "the theoretical edifice of realism will collapse if attributes of states' political systems are shown to have a major influence on which states do or do not fight each other." He contends that realism assumes "that states' internal characteristics are irrelevant to peace."

Complete acceptance of the democratic peace proposition would not deal a fatal blow to realism. Realist propositions would still apply to relations between nondemocracies; liberal-democratic theory remains silent on these matters. Moreover, as Bruce Russett acknowledges in his response to critics of the democratic peace, realist variables like relative power and position in the international system influence the foreign policies of democracies. Thus the

---

8. The distinction between offensive and defensive realists is discussed by Jack Snyder, *Myths of Empire: Domestic Politics and International Ambition* (Ithaca, N.Y.: Cornell University Press, 1991), pp. 10–13 (Snyder labels offensive realists "aggressive" realists); and John J. Mearsheimer, "Back to the Future: Instability in Europe after the Cold War," *International Security*, Vol. 15, No. 1 (Summer 1990), pp. 5–49. Defensive realist views are presented in Charles L. Glaser, "Realists as Optimists: Cooperation as Self-Help," *International Security*, Vol. 19, No. 3 (Winter 1994/95), pp. 50–90; and Stephen Van Evera, *Causes of War*, Vol. 1, *The Structure of Power and the Roots of War* (Ithaca, N.Y.: Cornell University Press, forthcoming, 1997).
9. The *locus classicus* for this argument is Kenneth N. Waltz, *Man, the State, and War: A Theoretical Analysis* (New York: Columbia University Press, 1959).

debate is really about whether an extreme form of philosophically pessimistic realism should be rejected, as well as over how much of international relations can be explained without any reference to second-image factors. Their emphasis on the primacy of systemic causes notwithstanding, virtually all realists— especially Kenneth Waltz—accept that realist (i.e., systemic) theories explain few of the details of international politics and need to be supplemented by other theories.[10] Nevertheless, acceptance of the democratic peace proposition would undermine many common realist arguments.

Because it is logically impossible for either realists or proponents of the democratic peace proposition to prove that democracies have never fought and never will in the future, the liberal-realist debate has focused on other issues. Realists have argued that the apparent fact of the democratic peace does not prove that there is something about democratic regimes that prevents them from fighting one another. They have faulted liberal theorists for failing to identify the causal logic of the democratic peace. Some realist critics have noted that some liberal explanations of the democratic peace also predict that democracies will be more peace-loving in general. For example, if democracies do not fight one another because public opinion always prevents leaders from starting wars, then we should expect to find that democracies are more peaceful than other states. Most empirical studies find, however, that democracies are just as war-prone as other states.[11]

Some realists go beyond challenging the logic of the democratic peace and argue that the existence of the peace is a myth. Such arguments claim that shifting and arbitrary definitions exclude cases of war between democracies, including, for example, the U.S. Civil War, the War of 1812, the Spanish-American War, and Finland's declaration of war against the Western democracies in World War II.

Another realist line of argument does not claim that there have been wars between democracies, but argues that other factors account for the absence of

---

10. See, in particular, Kenneth N. Waltz, "Reflections on *Theory of International Politics*: A Response to My Critics," in Robert O. Keohane, ed., *Neorealism and its Critics* (New York: Columbia University Press, 1986), pp. 322–345.

11. See Melvin Small and J. David Singer, "The War-Proneness of Democratic Regions, 1816–1965," *Jerusalem Journal of International Relations*, Vol. 1, No. 4 (Summer 1976), pp. 50–69; Steve Chan, "Mirror, Mirror on the Wall . . . Are the Freer Countries More Pacific?" *Journal of Conflict Resolution*, Vol. 28, No. 4 (December 1984), pp. 617–648; and Erich Weede, "Democracy and War Involvement," *Journal of Conflict Resolution*, Vol. 28, No. 4 (December 1984), pp. 649–664. For a challenge to the near-consensus that democracies are as war-prone as other types of states, see James Lee Ray, *Democracy and International Conflict: An Evaluation of the Democratic Peace Proposition* (Columbia: University of South Carolina Press, 1995), pp. 17–21.

wars between democracies. These factors include standard realist systemic variables: geographical distance, alliances against common enemies, and a prudent desire to avoid unnecessary wars. According to realist critics of the democratic peace, these factors account for the virtual absence of wars between democracies, with no need to invoke explanations based on shared democratic norms or political institutions.

Finally, realists have argued that there is no guarantee that states will remain or become democracies. Many democracies exist today, but they might revert to nondemocratic forms of government in the future. This argument has two implications. First, it suggests that the democratic peace proposition, even if true, may have little real-world significance in international politics. If there are few or no democracies, any democratic zone of peace will be small, and realist principles will apply to most of international politics. Second, the possibility of democracies' ceasing to be democratic calls into question the theoretical underpinnings of the democratic peace proposition. It becomes much harder for democracies to show mutual respect for one another if they cannot count on democracy's longevity. A democracy that conciliates a fellow democracy today risks being exploited by that state when it becomes a nondemocracy tomorrow. According to realists, this possibility that democratic governments will be replaced compels democratic states to be more vigilant and less cooperative in their mutual relations than liberal theory would suggest.

Proponents of the democratic peace proposition have responded to the realist challenge in four ways. First, they have presented additional quantitative studies that attempt to show that the virtual absence of war between democracies is statistically significant. These studies have controlled for the possible effects of geography, alliances, and levels of development. Second, they have defended their definitions of democracy as careful and reasonable, while also pointing out that the apparent "exceptions" to the democratic peace are few and far between. Third, liberal theorists have attempted to refine and further explicate the causal logic underlying the democratic peace. John Owen's essay in this volume is a recent example of this approach. Finally, they have argued that democracy continues to spread, and that few stable democracies become autocracies.

Apart from the theoretical debate between liberals and realists, the question of the democratic peace also has practical significance. If democracies never go to war with one another, then the best prescription for international peace may be to encourage the spread of democracy. The apparent absence of war between democracies has prompted U.S. policymakers and commentators to argue that promoting democracy should become the basic mission of U.S. grand strategy. Such policies find supporters across the U.S. political and ideological spectrum.[12] The spread of democracy would reduce the likelihood of threats to the United States and expand the democratic zone of peace, as well as having beneficial domestic consequences in the countries that become democratic. If democracy does not cause peace between democratic countries, however, attempting to promote democracy internationally may lead the United States into costly and counterproductive foreign interventions. The historical record of U.S. attempts to spread democracy is mixed at best. Germany and Japan stand as the outstanding examples of states that were democratized from the outside, but major wars and years of occupation were required to bring about these changes.

The first four essays in this volume make the case for the existence of the democratic peace. Each argues that democracies rarely, if ever, fight one another. The essays also spell out several versions of the causal logic that explains the absence of war between democracies.

Michael Doyle's 1983 two-part article, "Kant, Liberal Legacies, and Foreign Affairs," generally is regarded as the seminal work that drew attention to the existence of the democratic peace.[13] It argues that states that adhere to liberal principles enjoy a separate peace among themselves, but are likely to wage war against nonliberal states. Both aspects of liberal practice are explained by liberal principles.

Doyle regards liberalism as "a distinct ideology and set of institutions." Its essential principle is "the importance of the freedom of the individual." Three sets of rights form the foundation of liberalism: freedom from arbitrary authority, which includes freedom of speech, conscience, and the right to own and exchange private property; social and economic rights, including the right to

---

12. The need to promote democracy has been prominent in President Bill Clinton's speeches and his administration's foreign-policy statements. U.S. intervention in Haiti is the most prominent example of the Clinton administration's commitment to spreading democracy. A neoconservative case for spreading democracy is made by Joshua Muravchik, *Exporting Democracy: Fulfilling America's Destiny* (Washington, D.C.: AEI Press, 1991).
13. Doyle's article was not the first to point to the apparent existence of a permanent peace between democracies. Dean Babst, "A Force for Peace," *Industrial Research*, April 1972, pp. 55–58, makes a broadly similar argument. Babst's article originally had been published as "Elective Governments — A Force for Peace," *The Wisconsin Sociologist*, Vol. 3, No. 1 (1964), pp. 9–14. In his five-volume *Understanding Conflict and War* (Los Angeles: Sage, 1975–1981), R.J. Rummel developed the argument that libertarian states tend to be peace-loving and that they do not wage war on one another. See also Peter Wallensteen, *Structure and War: On International Relations 1820–1868* (Stockholm: Raben and Sjogren, 1973). Doyle's work, however, probably did more to stimulate interest in the idea of a democratic peace than these earlier works.

equal opportunity in education, health care, and employment; and the right of democratic participation and representation.

Liberalism is based on four institutions: juridical equality of citizens and freedom of religion and the press; rule by representative legislatures; private property; and a market economy driven by supply and demand. These institutions are shared by the traditions of laissez-faire "conservative" liberalism and social welfare "liberal" liberalism, although the two traditions differ in how much they emphasize each institution.

Internationally, liberalism holds that liberal states should not intervene in the affairs of other liberal states. States in which citizens enjoy liberty respect one another's right to political independence. This mutual respect accounts for the fact that *"constitutionally secure liberal states have yet to engage in war with one another"* (emphasis in original). Such wars may not be impossible, but Doyle argues that they are highly unlikely. He claims that there is a liberal zone of peace whose members are unlikely to even threaten war against one another. Even when liberal states have had conflicting economic interests, they have resolved their differences short of war. And in major wars, liberal states have tended to fight on the same side.

Doyle argues that realist theories cannot explain the liberal peace. He considers and rebuts realist rejoinders to the claim that a democratic peace exists. The realist understanding of international relations holds that all states exist in a state of war, regardless of their domestic institutions. International anarchy renders all states suspicious and competitive toward one another. Liberal states, however, have transcended these circumstances. Even when military technology has given the offense an advantage, liberal states have remained at peace with one another. Only liberal states seem to have maintained a separate peace; states sharing other ideologies or social structures have often fought one another, whether feudal, fascist, or communist.

In Doyle's view, Kant's "Perpetual Peace" provides the best explanation of the liberal peace—and of the tendency of liberal states to wage war against nonliberal states. The liberal peace is not the result of public control over foreign policy or economic interdependence. Instead, Doyle, following Kant, attributes it to the features of republican regimes. Republics are polities with market economies, the legal equality of citizens, and representative governments with a separation of powers. States with republican constitutions find it more difficult to declare war than absolute monarchies. Republics may still go to war, but they are more cautious than autocracies. Liberal states will only fight for liberal reasons. Republics cannot justify war against other republics, which preserve liberal standards of domestic justice. In the longer run, commerce among republics bolsters the liberal peace, because not threatening other republics increases each republic's benefits from economic ties. A liberal, open international economy further reduces incentives for war by removing many economic decisions from the direct realm of state policy.

Liberal principles may create a separate peace among liberal states, but Doyle recognizes that these same principles also cause liberal aggression against nonliberal states. Liberal states often fail to resolve their differences with autocracies peacefully; if war erupts, it often is waged as a crusade to spread liberal values. Liberal interventions in the internal affairs of weak states, however well intentioned, often fail to achieve their objectives and actually make matters worse.

These features of liberal foreign policy are partly attributable to the systemic imperatives that realists see in international politics. Liberal states cannot escape the effects of international anarchy. But liberal principles exacerbate the intensity of system-driven conflicts with nonliberal states. Such states, in the liberal worldview, have no right to be free of foreign intervention because they do not guarantee domestic justice for their citizens. In addition, liberal states are likely to regard nonliberal states as likely aggressors because of their failure to uphold liberal principles at home. Doyle points to U.S. attitudes toward the Soviet Union as a prime example of this pattern. A purely realist explanation cannot account for the way in which U.S. liberal ideology intensified the Cold War.

Doyle concludes with some recommendations for avoiding the failings of liberal foreign policies. He optimistically calculates that the continuing spread of liberal regimes will bring about global peace in the twenty-second century.

Bruce Russett's two chapters from *Grasping the Democratic Peace* attempt to provide a state-of-the-art discussion of the existence and causes of the democratic peace. In "The Fact of Democratic Peace," Russett argues that democracies appear to have adopted the norm against war with one another toward the end of the nineteenth century. It first became evident in Anglo-American relations. Leaders of both countries praised the democratic ideals of the other around the time of the Venezuelan Crisis of 1895–96. Feelings of social and political homogeneity laid the foundations for the "special relationship" between the United States and Britain. Shared liberal and democratic values also catalyzed the Anglo-French Entente before the World War I.

Russett notes that the absence of war between democracies became a prominent feature of international politics as the number of democracies gradually increased in the 1920s and after World War II. By the 1980s, the spread of democracy and the existence of the democratic peace were widely recognized. For Russett, the democratic peace does not mean that democracies have never, used force against one another. He suggests that the proposition should be formulated as stating that democracies very rarely engage in large-scale international war with one another.

Following many other researchers, Russett sets 1,000 battle deaths as the threshold for a "war." He defines a "democracy" as a state "with a voting franchise for a substantial fraction of citizens, a government brought to power in contested elections, and an executive either popularly elected or responsible to an elected legislature." Unlike Doyle, for example, he does not make the existence of civil liberties and economic freedoms a defining feature of a democracy. Russett's definition of democracy is thus more inclusive. If democracies, as defined by Russett, have not fought one another, the fact of the democratic peace becomes even more impressive.

Russett then considers some of the alleged wars between democracies, including the War of 1812 and the Spanish-American War. In virtually every case, at least one of the participants did not meet Russett's criteria for democracy, or the conflict fell short of the 1,000-fatality threshold for war. He points out that most of the alleged wars took place in the nineteenth century, when democratic states were highly imperfect by modern criteria.

As the number of democracies has grown during the twentieth century, the absence of wars between democracies has become more statistically significant. Russett also points out that in dyads of rivals (e.g., Greece and Turkey, India and Pakistan), wars have occurred only when at least one rival is not democratic. In addition, since 1945 democratic dyads have had fewer disputes than nondemocratic or mixed dyads, and they have been less likely to threaten or to use force in their disputes with one another.

In "Why Democratic Peace?" Russett examines potential explanations of the absence of wars between democracies. He notes that realist theories reject the claim that democratic states can enjoy a perpetual peace among themselves. Any theory that can explain the democratic peace might be a powerful alternative to the realist paradigm.

Russett then considers several alternative explanations for why democracies have not fought wars with one another: the role of international institutions and transnationalism; distance; alliances against common threats; wealth; and political stability. None of these explanations, Russett argues, fully accounts for the democratic peace. Democracy itself must be at least part of the explanation.

Russett explicates two ways in which democracy might account for the existence of a democratic peace. The first, which he calls the cultural/normative model, argues that decision-makers in democracies follow norms of peaceful conflict resolution that reflect domestic experiences and values. Because democracies are biased against resolving domestic disputes violently, they try to resolve international disputes peacefully. Democracies also expect that other democracies will share similar preferences. No such expectation exists with regard to nondemocracies. The norm of peaceful conflict resolution thus creates a separate peace among democracies, but does not prevent democracies from fighting nondemocracies.

The second explanation for how democracy causes a democratic peace is the structural/institutional model. It argues that domestic institutional constraints, including checks and balances, separation of powers, and the need for public debate, will slow or constrain decisions to go to war. Leaders in democracies will recognize that other democratic leaders are similarly constrained. As a result, democracies will have more time to resolve disputes peacefully and less fear of surprise attack.

Russett recognizes that it may be difficult to separate the normative/cultural and structural/institutional models. Norms, after all, shape institutions and procedures. In addition, both models depend on whether democracies perceive one another as democracies. Nevertheless, he suggests that it is possible to devise tests that can determine which model appears to be causing democracies to avoid war with one another.

In "How Liberalism Produces Democratic Peace," John Owen refines and explicates the causal mechanism that generates the democratic peace. He shows how liberal principles and democratic processes work together to make war between democracies virtually impossible.

Owen defines a liberal democracy as a state "where liberalism is the dominant ideology and citizens have leverage over war decisions." Liberalism holds that individuals everywhere should have freedom, and that peace is a necessary condition for freedom. Wars should only be fought in the cause of peace and freedom. Liberals believe that other liberal states act to preserve freedom and thus are pacific and trustworthy. Because liberal states have liberal institutional structures that allow for public control of foreign policy, even illiberal leaders will be unable to lead liberal states into war against other liberal states. Owen also points out that these liberal principles and processes only have a chance to operate when a state actually perceives another state as a liberal democracy. Some alleged wars between democracies (e.g., the War of 1812) took place because at least one state did not see the other as a democracy. He also notes that states may be illiberal democracies—they may have representative forms of government without liberal ideologies. Such states will not join the liberal-democratic zone of peace.

Owen deduces several hypotheses from his explanation of how liberalism causes the democratic peace: liberals will trust states they consider liberal and mistrust those they consider illiberal; when liberals observe a foreign state becoming liberal by their own standards, they will expect pacific relations with it; liberals will claim that fellow liberal democracies share their ends, and that illiberal states do not; liberals will not change their assessments of foreign states during crises with those states unless those states change their institutions; liberal elites will agitate for their policies during war-threatening crises; during crises, statesmen will be constrained to follow liberal policy. He then examines four historical cases of troubled relations between liberal states: the Franco-American crisis of 1796–98, and the Anglo-American crises of 1803–12, 1861–65, and 1895–96. The outcomes support Owen's argument. Most Americans believed France in the late 1790s was a democracy, and the naval quasi-war of 1796–98 did not become a real war. When the U.S. leaders failed to perceive Britain as a democracy in 1812, war broke out. In 1863–65, the British government saw the United States as a liberal democracy and adopted a policy of restraint during the U.S. Civil War. In 1895–96, the United States and Britain saw each other as democracies. They avoided war in the Venezuelan Crisis and laid the foundations for the Anglo-American "special relationship." In each case, the process unfolded in accordance with Owen's hypotheses.

Owen replies to realist critics of the democratic peace. To those who claim that neither the normative/cultural or structural/institutional explanation of the democratic peace is adequate, he replies that his integration of the two provides a stronger explanation. He also notes that the existence of threats by one liberal state against another does not invalidate the democratic peace proposition, because such threats are made when liberal states do not recognize one another, or when illiberal leaders are in power. Owen also notes that definitions of democracy are not as malleable in practice as some realists claim. In the crises he examines, American leaders did not suddenly shift their perception of other states and redefine them according to exigencies of national interest.

Owen does not dispute that the international distribution of power matters. But he argues that liberalism has an independent effect that sometimes flies in the face of alleged systemic imperatives. He points out that realist balance-of-threat theory, as proposed by Stephen Walt, is compatible with liberalism.[14] States will use regime type as one criteria in determining whether another state threatens them. Alliances will tend to form against states with regime types that are perceived to be threatening.

The next five articles argue against the democratic peace proposition. Each author adopts a different line of argument, but the articles by Layne, Spiro, and Farber and Gowa collectively conclude that the relationship between democracy and peace is spurious or coincidental. Mansfield and Snyder do not reject the democratic peace proposition, but they find that states in the process of democratization become more likely to engage in war. This finding suggests that the democratic peace may not hold among new democracies.

In "Kant or Cant: The Myth of the Democratic Peace," Christopher Layne argues that the democratic peace proposition does not stand up to empirical scrutiny and is a poor guide for policy. Layne seeks to test the democratic peace by deducing additional, testable hypotheses from its causal logic. He regards the normative variant of the democratic peace proposition as the most promising candidate for further testing. Unlike the structural/institutional explanation, which logically predicts that democracies will be less likely to go to war than other states, the normative explanation only predicts that democracies will not go to war with one another.

To test this normative explanation of the democratic peace, Layne asks which additional predictions can be deduced from its underlying logic. If democratic norms and culture cause democracies to avoid war with one another, Layne argues, then we should expect pairs of democratic states involved in crises with one another to avoid war and resolve these crises peacefully, because these norms constrain their crisis behavior. In other words, Layne tests the democratic peace proposition by asking what it predicts about how democracies will behave in international crises between democracies.[15] He argues that in historical cases of "near misses" of war between democracies the following three indicators should be present: pacific public opinion; an absence of military threats and preparations for such threats; accommodating behavior, including an absence of ultimata, inflexible positions, and coercive diplomacy.

---

14. Stephen M. Walt, *The Origins of Alliances* (Ithaca, N.Y.: Cornell University Press, 1987).
15. In Layne's study, the dependent variable is not whether democracies went to war or not, but how democracies behaved in their diplomatic interactions during crises with one another. These interactions are intervening variables when the democratic-peace hypothesis is used to explain why democracies do not go to war with one another, but they become dependent variables in Layne's study.

Layne selects four crises in which democracies came close to war: the 1861 "*Trent* Affair" between the United States and Great Britain; the 1895–96 U.S.-British Venezuela crisis; the 1898 Fashoda crisis between France and Great Britain; and the 1923 Ruhr crisis between France and Germany. His review of the historical record concludes that in these cases democracies avoided war, but there is no evidence that they did so because they shared democratic norms. The indicators that should have been present were absent. Instead, the democracies behaved in a manner predicted by realism: they acted on the basis of calculations of national interest; paid attention to strategic concerns, particularly the distribution of military capabilities; and used threats when vital interests were jeopardized.

Layne argues that realism provides a better and more parsimonious explanation of why the democracies involved in the crises did not go to war. He suggests that his findings cast doubt on the democratic peace proposition in general. Although proponents of the proposition claim that they have examined many democratic dyads and found no wars, Layne argues that looking at cases where war was possible is a better way to test the proposition.

Layne also questions whether there have been no wars involving democracies. He classifies the War of 1812 and the U.S. Civil War as wars between democratic states. In addition, he argues that Germany in 1914 was as democratic as France and Britain (at least in the making of foreign policy), and that World War I also should be regarded as a war between democracies.

Layne draws several conclusions for policy from his theoretical and empirical analysis. He cautions against making promotion of democracy an aim of U.S. foreign policy. If there is no empirical support for the democratic "zone of peace," it would be a mistake to try to create a democratic world. Attempts to spread democracy to volatile regions would raise risks of war.

David Spiro's "The Insignificance of the Liberal Peace" questions the democratic peace proposition by arguing that the apparent absence of war between democracies is statistically insignificant. Because the chance that any given pair of states will be at war at a given time is very low, he argues, it is not surprising that dyads of democratic states have not gone to war. For most of international history before 1945, there were few democracies and little chance for them to fight one another. The absence of war between democracies could be the result of random chance.

Like Layne, Spiro suggests that structural/institutional explanations of the democratic peace are weak, because institutional constraints on a government's ability to wage war would make democracies less war-prone in general. The

data, however, reveal that democracies frequently go to war against nondemocracies. Spiro thus argues that the normative causes of the democratic peace
should be regarded as the more likely explanation of the apparent absence of
wars between democracies. He claims that few empirical studies of democracy
and war have examined the connection between liberalism and the absence of
inter-democratic wars. Most studies have focused on states with democratic
processes, not those with liberal norms.

Spiro also attacks studies of the democratic peace for failing to define democracy clearly. He claims that many scholars use definitions of democracy
that have little in common with Kant's vision of peaceful republican governments. In addition, different scholars use different definitions of democracy and
thus compile different lists of democracies. It is particularly difficult to apply
modern definitions of liberalism retrospectively.

Spiro suggests that shifting definitions of war also have made the democratic
peace appear more significant than it is. Many studies of the democratic peace
exclude the U.S. Civil War, in which both sides were democracies, as well as
the conflicts between Peru and Ecuador, the 1982 Israeli invasion of Lebanon,
the War of 1812, the Israeli attack on the U.S. naval vessel *Liberty* in 1967, the
Spanish-American War of 1898, and Finland's World War II alliance with the
Axis powers against the Western democracies. Although there may be reasons
for excluding some of these conflicts, Spiro suggests that the number of wars
between democracies is higher than claimed by proponents of the democratic
peace proposition.

Although Spiro is skeptical about the existence of a democratic peace, he
does find that democracies ally with one another more often than random
chance would predict. He suggests that this finding undermines realist insights
that suggest that regime type is irrelevant in alliance choices. Spiro argues that
liberal theory may be supported by the apparent tendency of democracies to
ally with one another, even if it is not confirmed by the absence of wars
between democracies.

In "Polities and Peace," Henry Farber and Joanne Gowa assess the analytical
and empirical foundations of the apparent democratic peace. Farber and Gowa
argue that neither the normative nor structural explanation of the democratic
peace is persuasive. They suggest that the primary norm identified in the
literature on the democratic peace is the norm of peaceful conflict resolution.
This norm, they argue, is not unique to democracies; all types of states are
likely to espouse such a norm, because wars are costly ways of resolving
disputes. The alleged democratic norm against violent conflict is merely a

reflection of a general state interest in avoiding war. Moreover, it is very difficult to measure such norms and their effectiveness.

Farber and Gowa regard the existence of governmental checks and balances as the core of the structural/institutional explanation of the democratic peace. The checks-and-balances argument claims that democracies are less able to wage war because domestic institutional constraints prevent leaders from starting wars. But this explanation is undermined by the well-known propensity of democracies to wage wars against nondemocratic states. In addition, the alleged checks and balances do not prevent democracies from imposing tariffs—a form of hostile behavior short of war.

"Polities and Peace" argues there is not a statistically significant difference in the probability of war between pairs of democracies and between pairs of other types of polities, except in the years since 1945. They argue that the absence of war between democracies during this period reflects their common interest in allying against the Soviet Union, not any peculiar features of their regime type. Farber and Gowa, like many other scholars, also find that democracies are no less likely to be involved in war than other types of states.

Farber and Gowa reach these conclusions by analyzing dyads of countries between 1816 and 1976. In contrast to other researchers, they count a dyad of two warring countries as at war only once, even if the war continued for several years. In addition, they exclude the years of the two world wars from their study on the grounds that general wars cannot be analyzed by looking at dyads. They break down their study into five periods: pre-1914; 1914–18; 1919–38; 1939–45; and 1945–76, but they do not discuss the results for 1914–18 and 1939–45. Farber and Gowa also do not exclude any apparent cases of wars between democracies, such as the Spanish-American War.

Farber and Gowa employ a similar approach to measure how often pairs of democracies were involved in militarized international disputes. They find that before 1914, pairs of democratic states were more likely to engage in disputes short of war than pairs of other types of states. Only after 1945 did pairs of democracies become significantly less dispute-prone. Farber and Gowa argue that the low level of inter-democratic disputes since 1945 reflects the alignment of most democracies against the Soviet Union. This alignment was the result of the tendency of states to balance against threats; any connection to domestic ideology is spurious.

In their conclusions, Farber and Gowa emphasize that the democratic peace seems to be an artifact of the Cold War, and that systemic variables are more important than regime type in explaining the incidence of international conflicts. They suggest that U.S. policies to promote democracy are misguided.

Ido Oren's "The Subjectivity of the 'Democratic' Peace: Changing U.S. Perceptions of Imperial Germany" presents an analysis of how statesmen actually change their definitions of democracy. Oren contends that pairs of countries do not remain at peace because they regard one another as democracies. Instead, countries that have an interest in remaining at peace tend to define one another as democracies. This is a special case of a more general pattern of countries' defining their allies as their "own kind" and labeling their adversaries as different. Oren argues that American leaders have tended to interpret "democracy" to mean "countries like the United States." American leaders have claimed that peace exists among countries that conform to a subjective ideal that has been cast in terms of America's (changing) self-image.

Oren criticizes the literature on the democratic peace for overlooking how the meaning and connotations of "democracy" have changed over the course of U.S. history. Current measures of democracy tend to use "objective" measures that are actually indicators of whether a country resembles the United States or not. But coding and judging regime types is never independent of political relationships.

To illustrate his general argument, Oren focuses on how U.S. scholars and statesmen have classified Imperial Germany. Although current political scientists code pre-1914 Germany as significantly less democratic than Britain, France, and the United States, American observers of the late nineteenth and early twentieth century regarded Germany as a model to be emulated. Few American observers drew a sharp distinction between "autocratic" Germany and the "democratic" United States until after the two countries were at war in 1917. Coding rules reflect norms, which are affected by historical context. Oren argues that the 1917–45 U.S. antagonism with Germany has shaped the definitions of democracy and the coding rules that pervade the democratic peace literature. "In sum," Oren says, "the perception of Imperial Germany imprinted in the present coding rules is grossly colored by hindsight and by contemporary values, which in no small part became our values because of the benefit of hindsight." The U.S. victory over Germany in the two world wars ensured that U.S. values became predominant.

Oren focuses on two prominent U.S. political scientists of the late nineteenth century: John Burgess and Woodrow Wilson. U.S. political scientist John Burgess, who founded the graduate program in political science at Columbia University, admired Germany. He regarded Germany and the United States as the most advanced constitutional governments and the two states that best guaranteed individual liberty. Both ranked higher than France and Britain on this scale. In 1915, Burgess wrote that Germany's "economic system is by far the most efficient, most genuinely democratic, which exists at the present moment in the world, or has ever existed."

Oren points out that Woodrow Wilson, who as president denounced Germany as an autocracy, earlier had lauded German political institutions in his writings as a political scientist. Wilson was an Anglophile, but in his writings he nevertheless expressed his admiration for Bismarck and classified Germany with Britain, the United States, France, and Switzerland as the most advanced constitutional states.

Oren briefly discusses two additional cases: Russia and Japan. He notes that the United States regarded the regimes of these two countries as more similar to the United States whenever U.S. interests called for a closer relationship with Russia/the Soviet Union or Japan. Woodrow Wilson declared that Russia was democratic after the first revolution of 1917. Others expressed admiration for the "democratic" Soviet system when the United States and the Soviet Union jointly opposed fascism. After the Cold War, Russia was again hailed as democratic, but many observers began to doubt Russia's democratic credentials as soon as Russian external behavior became more assertive and sometimes opposed U.S. interests.

U.S. views of Japan have changed in similar ways. Japan is now regarded as a democracy, but Oren predicts that it will lose this status if the United States and Japan ever go to war again.

Oren concludes that "the reason we [the United States] appear not to fight 'our kind' is not that objective likeness substantially affects war propensity, but rather that we subtly redefine 'our kind.'" He argues that realists should not challenge the democratic peace proposition with quibbles over coding decisions and questions of statistical significance. Instead, they should focus on the social construction of ideas about democracy and regime similarity.

In "Democratization and the Danger of War," Edward Mansfield and Jack Snyder present a different type of challenge to the democratic peace proposition. They argue that democratizing states become more likely to go to war. They do not dispute that a democratic peace exists between mature, stable democracies, but they suggest that immature democracies are a force for war, not peace.

Mansfield and Snyder present data indicating that democratizing states are more likely to be involved in war in the years immediately after their democratization begins. This increase becomes greater one, five, and ten years after the start of democratization. When Mansfield and Snyder look at component measures of democratization—competitiveness of participation, executive constraints, and openness of executive recruitment—they find that increases in these measures also increase the probability of war. Compared to states that remain or become autocracies, states that make the transition from autocracy to democratization are more than twice as likely to be in a war during the decade after democratization.

Mansfield and Snyder also note that great powers have become more warlike as they have democratized. During the nineteenth century, liberalizing Britain fought the Crimean War and vastly augmented its overseas empire. Napoleon III's France fought a series of wars until it destroyed itself in the Franco-Prussian War. These wars were intended to establish its domestic legitimacy as mass political participation grew. In Wilhelmine Germany, domestic political struggles resulting from the political rise of the middle class helped to bring on World War I. Japan's democratization in the 1920s prompted the army to devise and implement a program of imperial expansion to win public support.

According to Snyder and Mansfield, there are four reasons why new democracies get into wars. First, elite groups from the old regime often use appeals to nationalism as they compete for domestic power in the new democratic political arena. Second, new elites find it necessary to resort to similar nationalistic appeals. Third, newly mobilized publics are often hard to control. Fourth, if incipient democracy collapses, the return to autocracy increases the chances of going to war. The basic problem of democratizing states is that they lack the stabilizing institutions of mature democracies. This contributes to a political impasse in new democracies: it becomes hard to form stable coalitions that can stay in power and pursue coherent policies. As a result, elites indulge in short-run thinking and reckless policymaking that can lead to war.

Mansfield and Snyder contend that their findings suggest that promoting democratization may not be the best way to build peace. They present several recommendations for reducing the dangers of democratization. Deposed autocratic leaders of emerging democracies should be exiled and given a "golden parachute" so that they have few incentives to try to regain power by adopting aggressive policies. Former military and economic elites should be given a stake in newly liberalized economies. Guaranteeing a free press and a pluralistic security debate can help to reduce the dangers of nationalist mythmaking. The West should foster an independent and aggressive cadre of journalists in democratizing states.

The next five contributions to this volume are rebuttals by advocates of the democratic peace proposition and responses by its critics.

Bruce Russett defends the democratic peace proposition in "The Democratic Peace—And Yet it Moves," his reply to Christopher Layne and David Spiro. He welcomes Layne's attempt to test the democratic peace proposition by performing process-tracing in detailed case studies, but he argues that at least some of the crises can be interpreted differently. For example, factors identified by the democratic peace proposition appear to have operated in the 1895–96 Anglo-American crisis. Russett also suggests that Layne's realist explanation fails to account for why Britain decided to seek an accommodation with the United States instead of Germany. Shared democracy may have made the United States appear more worthy of accommodation. Russett agrees that "power and strategic interest" influence states, as Layne's crises show, but he argues that the democratic peace proposition does not claim that democracy is the only factor that prevents war. The existence of a few cases in which the democratic peace did not operate does not imply that the democratic peace is nonexistent. Russett also notes that dangerous crises between democracies have been rare; shared democracy may explain why this is so.

Russett argues that proponents of the democratic peace proposition have not resorted to supple definitions of democracy and of war. He points out that Layne offers no definition of democracy at all. In response to Spiro's argument that Finland was at war with the Western democracies during World War II, Russett notes that Finland and the allies never engaged in combat after they declared war on one another. Russett also notes that Spiro manipulates the data on other conflicts by excluding wars in which fatalities were low. This has the effect of making the democratic peace seem less significant.

In responding to Spiro's claim that the democratic peace is statistically insignificant, Russett first makes clear that he does not claim that democracies never fight one another, only that wars between democracies are extremely rare. He argues that Spiro's statistical manipulations make it impossible to find statistically significant results. Spiro looks at the probability of war between a given dyad in a given year; his article splits the data into such small parts that the chances of war in a given year are so low that it becomes mathematically impossible to reject the null hypothesis. Russett suggests that a better test of the democratic peace proposition would look at the joint probability of no war between democracies year after year. Russett calculates that the probability of no wars between democracies between 1816 and 1980 is 0.00000000000000000002.

Russett argues that tests that focus on dyads in which war is a real possibility demonstrate that the democratic peace is statistically robust. He claims that, with Zeev Maoz, he has analyzed the years 1946–86, controlling for other variables that tend to cause war. This test found that democratic dyads were much less likely to engage in conflict than dyads in which at least one state was not a democracy.[16]

Russett also presents a new analysis of democratic dyads over the entire period during which both states were democracies. This "lifetime" analysis of "regime-dyads" finds that democratic dyads never engaged in war with one another and were far less likely to use force or to engage in militarized disputes. Finally, he also finds that there is a statistically significant difference between democratic and nondemocratic dyads when one compares their year-by-year propensity to get into disputes or to use force against one another. Contending that he is using Spiro's method of analysis, Russett argues that this difference in frequency of disputes and the use of force is a better indicator of the robustness of the democratic peace, because disputes and uses of force are not nearly as rare as wars. This pattern of democratic behavior is not the result of random chance.

Christopher Layne responds to Russett by reiterating his claim that the democratic peace proposition must be tested by asking whether its causal logic actually explains why democracies did not go to war. If the causal logic is weak, then the proposition rests on nothing more than statistical correlations.

Layne argues that Russett's suggestion that the democratic peace proposition explains the paucity of serious crises between democracies amounts to a claim that the "dogs that didn't bark" support the proposition. Layne rejects this argument, because such non-events cannot be used to test the causal explanations of the democratic peace proposition. He claims that Russett's admission that power and strategic considerations matter is a concession that does indeed "give the game away" to realism.

In "The Liberal Peace—And Yet it Squirms" David Spiro replies to Russett. He argues that his analysis does not "disprove" liberal theory, but demonstrates that the apparent absence of war between democracies is not a statistically significant empirical confirmation of the democratic peace proposition.

---

16. Zeev Maoz and Bruce Russett, "Alliance, Contiguity, Wealth, and Political Stability: Is the Lack of Conflict among Democracies a Statistical Artifact?" *International Interactions*, Vol. 17, No. 3 (1992), pp. 245–267.

Spiro makes four responses to Russett. First, he argues that Russett's conclusions depend on his selective definitions of democracy and war. Thus Russett's criticisms of Spiro's definitional decisions ring hollow. Spiro agrees that there may be grounds for excluding some wars from the sample, but Russett's decisions have the effect of making the democratic peace seem more significant than it is.

Second, Spiro points out that he does not slice up the data on war into such small parts that no statistically significant result is possible. In addition to one-year periods, he examined 5, 10, 20, 30, 40, 50, 60, 70, 80, 90, 100, 110, 120, 130, 140, and 150-year periods between 1816 and 1982. This analysis supported the claim that the virtual absence of wars between democracies is statistically insignificant.

Third, Spiro responds to Russett's claim that only "politically relevant dyads" should be considered. He questions the criteria for determining political relevance, and defends his decisions about which dyads to include as being no more arbitrary than Russett's choices.

Finally, Spiro argues that it is curious that Russett did not present his new data and analysis in his earlier books and articles on the democratic peace. He faults Russett for not presenting more detailed descriptions of the statistical tests that he used.

In the penultimate essay in this volume, Michael Doyle replies to some of the critics of the democratic peace proposition and reflects on the debate. He observes that the ongoing debate reflects the strength of the liberal research program. Few other academic debates generate so much high-quality social science that includes statistical testing as well as case studies.

In response to Layne, Doyle argues that Layne should have compared crises between liberal and nonliberal states, and nonliberal states, as well as between liberal states, to provide a fairer test of liberal theory. He also recommends that future case studies like Layne's draw more on primary sources instead of the secondary literature, and examine not only cabinet decision-making processes, but also parliamentary and public opinion. More generally, Doyle argues that the relative scarcity of crises between liberal states is evidence of the power of the democratic peace proposition, even if there are occasional exceptions.

Regarding statistical tests for the democratic peace proposition, Doyle argues for comparing how states change their foreign policy after liberal revolutions bring new liberal regimes to power. This approach will provide better measures of the significance of liberalism. He calls for examining a broader range of dependent variables other than war, including crises, trade, and alliances.

Other tests might compare how the foreign policies of particular countries changed in liberal and nonliberal periods.

With respect to the nagging question of how to classify Finland's involvement in World War II, Doyle suggest that the 1,000-battle death criterion for war does not resolve the issue. Instead, studies should ask whether Finland was seen as an enemy by the Western allies. If it was not, this case does not undermine the democratic peace.

Doyle concludes that liberal theory needs to be tested against improved versions of its challengers, particularly realism. Theories should not be compared to a statistical residual, but to the most promising alternatives. At present, however, realist theories offer many contradictory theories, making it difficult to put them to head-to-head tests.

In the final essay in this volume, "Michael Doyle on the Democratic Peace—Again," Michael Doyle reminds us that the Democratic Peace proposition has produced a healthy research program. He suggests that future studies should look at the full range of potential international effects of liberalism—not just the democratic peace, but whether liberal states pursue distinctive foreign economic and security policies. Doyle calls for drawing a more careful distinction between liberal and nonliberal republics; not all participatory polities are liberal democracies. He also recommends using process-tracing methods in case studies to determine whether instances of the democratic peace were caused by liberal or nonliberal factors.

Doyle rebuts several of the essays in this volume that question the existence of a democratic peace. He argues that Farber and Gowa fail to justify their decision to segment the data on war and peace into five different periods. Doyle responds to Mansfield and Snyder by pointing out that democratizing regimes may be less likely to go to war if they exist in a liberal international order.

Many debates in the study of international relations have a faddish character. Theoretical struggles are waged with great intensity in the pages of books and academic journals only to suddenly end, leaving the scholarly battlefield deserted as the combatants move on to fight other wars. New policy issues emerge and shape the theoretical agenda, an exciting new methodology diverts attention into areas where it can be applied, or the participants in much-heralded "great debates" tire (or retire).

Based on its progress over the past two decades, the debate over the democratic peace does not deserve such a fate. As Michael Doyle points out in his concluding contributions to this volume, the idea of the democratic peace has produced a progressive research agenda that has engaged scholars who have employed research methods ranging from historical case-studies to sophisticated large-n statistical studies that include data on many countries and conflicts over several centuries. Political theorists and quantitative social scientists have contributed to this literature. There even seems to be some degree of cumulation, as studies replicate or challenge the results of earlier ones.

There remain many promising avenues of research on the democratic peace. First, there is still a need to refine the causal logic that explains the apparent absence of war between democracies. Some of the earlier empirical studies of the relationship between democracy, war, and peace did not develop a theory to explain the democratic peace. More recent studies have begun to address this problem. There is still no consensus, however, on whether liberal principles or democratic institutions and processes (or some combination of the two) cause the democratic peace. For example, liberal states may never go to war because they share liberal norms, but democracies (even illiberal ones) may rarely fight wars because they are prudent enough to recognize that war rarely pays—and that it is even less likely to pay when there is a possibility that nuclear weapons will be used. Owen's contribution to this volume begins to explore some of these issues. A combination of statistical studies and process-tracing in cases might shed further light on this question.

Second, there remains a tremendous opportunity to further test the democratic peace proposition by expanding the number of dependent variables. There are two ways in which such research might proceed. In the first, the logic underlying the democratic peace could be used to deduce additional predictions about the intervening variables that should be present when mutual democracy or shared liberal principles causes two countries to avoid war. The essays by Layne and Owen in this volume contain examples of this approach. Each deduces hypotheses about how democracies should behave when they are embroiled in a crisis with another democracy and then tests these hypotheses by looking at several historical cases.[17] A second approach would expand the number of dependent variables to include other aspects of the international behavior of democracies. The same logic that is held to explain the absence of

---

17. This method is essentially a slightly more formal application of the process-tracing approach developed by Alexander George. See Alexander L. George and Timothy J. McKeown, "Case Studies and Theories of Organizational Decision Making," in *Advances in Information Processing in Organizations*, Vol. 2 (Greenwich, Conn.: JAI Press, 1985), pp. 21–58. See also Gary King, Robert O. Keohane, and Sidney Verba, *Designing Social Inquiry: Scientific Inference in Qualitative Research* (Princeton, N.J.: Princeton University Press, 1994).

war between democracies may also generate other testable hypotheses about patterns of democratic foreign policy.[18] For example, the propensity of democracies to ally with one another that Spiro notes in his contribution to this volume may actually be an additional implication of the same factors that cause the democratic peace. Other implications might be deduced from logic of the democratic peace: the behavior of democracies in crises, rivalries, etc. These implications could be tested with additional case studies or large-n analyses. Both of these approaches depend on further refinement and explication of the causal logic of the democratic peace.

Third, few studies have attempted to distinguish between different types of democracies and to assess the implications of such differences. For example, liberal democracies probably behave differently than illiberal democracies. In addition, democracies with parliamentary systems may behave differently than those with presidential systems.[19]

Fourth, Mansfield and Snyder's claim that democratizing states become more war-prone suggests a need to examine the effects of democratic transitions. In addition to more statistical studies, case studies of the domestic politics and foreign policies of democratizing states could be conducted to determine whether the causal processes identified by Snyder and Mansfield actually operate. Given the number of recent transitions to democracies (and reversals), plenty of potential cases exist, providing ample opportunities for researchers. Even if additional research supports the conclusion that democratizing states become more war-prone, such case studies would contribute to an

---

18. The work of David A. Lake and of Randall L. Schweller exemplifies this type of approach. Lake argues that democracies avoid wars against other democracies, and they are more likely to win wars against nondemocracies. See Lake, "Powerful Pacifists: Democratic States and War," *American Political Science Review,* Vol. 86, No. 1 (March 1992), pp. 24–37. Schweller argues that democracies never initiate preventive wars. See Schweller, "Domestic Structure and Preventive War: Are Democracies More Pacific?" *World Politics,* Vol. 44, No. 2 (January 1992), pp. 235–239. Both authors use what they regard as the logical foundation of the democratic peace to explain another aspect of the behavior of democracies in international politics.

19. Researchers in the field of comparative politics have devoted significant attention to the importance of such distinctions. See, for example, Alfred Stepan and Cindy Skach, "Constitutional Frameworks and Democratic Consolidation: Parliamentarianism vs. Presidentialism," *World Politics,* Vol. 46, No. 1 (October 1993), pp. 1–22. A good overview of this recent literature is Doh Chull Shin, "On the Third Wave of Democratization: A Synthesis and Evaluation of Recent Theory and Research," *World Politics,* Vol. 47, No. 1 (October 1994), pp. 135–170 at 157–161. For recent examinations of the different international behavior of parliamentary and presidential democracies, see Miriam Fendius Elman, "When the Weak Go to War: Domestic Institutional Choices and Their Foreign Policy Legacies," Ph.D. dissertation, Columbia University, 1996; and Elman, "The Foreign Policies of Small States: Challenging NeoRealism in its Own Backyard," *British Journal of Political Science,* Vol. 25, No. 2 (April 1995), pp. 171–217.

understanding of the democratic peace by helping to specify precisely which conditions need to be present for a state to become a democracy that avoids wars with other democracies.

Finally, future research on the democratic peace proposition should do more to integrate national-level and system-level explanations. Most of the existing studies have assumed that explanations at the two levels are in conflict. Few have attempted to specify what systemic factors predict and then layered on a more discriminating set of hypotheses drawn from liberal theory. In effect, realist/systemic and liberal/national-level propositions should be able to work together to present more discriminating explanations of international outcomes. One reason that such studies are rare is that many researchers set up a false dichotomy between systemic and unit-level explanations, instead of considering how they can complement one another. Another reason for the absence of such work is that many existing realist theories do not generate testable hypotheses and predictions. Some realist approaches predict only very general trends and patterns: wars will occur, bipolarity is less war-prone that multipolarity. Other realist approaches tend only to generate *post hoc* explanations; international outcomes are held to be the result of the workings of the balance of power, but the theory does not specify in advance which conditions will lead to which outcomes. Attempts to integrate international and unit-level variables are implicit in some studies that have controlled for wealth, power, contiguity, and opportunity, and are explicit in some expected-utility approaches.[20]

This list of potential further research into the democratic peace almost certainly neglects important projects that are already under way. The vibrancy of the debate over the democratic peace is a sure sign that additional articles on all sides of the question will soon be in print. The editors, who disagree themselves on the existence of the democratic peace, hope that this volume stimulates greater understanding of the current debate and further examination of the relationships between democracy, war, peace, and security policy.

---

20. Bruce Bueno de Mesquita and David Lalman, *War and Reason: Domestic and International Imperatives* (New Haven, Conn.: Yale University Press, 1992).

Part I:
The Case for the Democratic Peace

Kant, Liberal Legacies, and Foreign Affairs

Michael W. Doyle

I

What difference do liberal principles and institutions make to the conduct of the foreign affairs of liberal states? A thicket of conflicting judgments suggests that the legacies of liberalism have not been clearly appreciated. For many citizens of liberal states, liberal principles and institutions have so fully absorbed domestic politics that their influence on foreign affairs tends to be either overlooked altogether or, when perceived, exaggerated. Liberalism becomes either unself-consciously patriotic or inherently "peace-loving." For many scholars and diplomats, the relations among independent states appear to differ so significantly from domestic politics that influences of liberal principles and domestic liberal institutions are denied or denigrated. They judge that international relations are governed by perceptions of national security and the balance of power; liberal principles and institutions, when they do intrude, confuse and disrupt the pursuit of balance-of-power politics.[1]

Although liberalism is misinterpreted from both these points of view, a crucial aspect of the liberal legacy is captured by each. Liberalism is a distinct

Michael W. Doyle is Professor of Politics and International Affairs at the Center of International Studies, Princeton University.

This article has benefited from the extensive criticisms of William Ascher, Richard Betts, William Bundy, Joseph Carens, Felix Gilbert, Amy Gutmann, Don Herzog, Stanley Hoffmann, Marion Levy, Judith Shklar, Mark Uhlig, and the Editors of *Philosophy & Public Affairs*. I have also tried to take into account suggestions from Fouad Ajami, Steven David, Tom Farer, Robert Gilpin, Ernest van den Haag, Germaine Hoston, Robert Jervis, Donald Kagan, Robert Keohane, John Rawls, Nicholas Rizopoulos, Robert W. Tucker, Richard Ullman, and the members of a Special Seminar at the Lehrman Institute, February 22, 1983. The essay cannot be interpreted as a consensus of their views. I would also like to thank the Ford Foundation, whose grant supported some of the research on which this article draws, the Institute for Advanced Study, Exxon, and the National Endowment for the Humanities. The themes of Parts 1 and 2 of this essay were first developed in a paper written in June 1981. That paper drew on a short presentation delivered at the Conference on the Future of American Liberalism, Princeton, New Jersey, 3–4 April 1981.

1. The liberal-patriotic view was reiterated by President Reagan in a speech before the British Parliament on 8 June 1982. There he proclaimed "a global campaign for democratic development." This "crusade for freedom" will be the latest campaign in a tradition that, he claimed, began with the Magna Carta and stretched in this century through two world wars and a cold war. He added that liberal foreign policies have shown "restraint" and "peaceful intentions" and that this crusade will strengthen the prospects for a world at peace (*New York Times*, 9 June 1982). The skeptical scholars and diplomats represent the predominant Realist interpretation of international relations. See notes 4 and 12 for references.

ideology and set of institutions that has shaped the perceptions of and capacities for foreign relations of political societies that range from social welfare or social democratic to laissez faire. It defines much of the content of the liberal patriot's nationalism. Liberalism does appear to disrupt the pursuit of balance-of-power politics. Thus its foreign relations cannot be adequately explained (or prescribed) by a sole reliance on the balance of power. But liberalism is not inherently "peace-loving"; nor is it consistently restrained or peaceful in intent. Furthermore, liberal practice may reduce the probability that states will successfully exercise the consistent restraint and peaceful intentions that a world peace may well require in the nuclear age. Yet the peaceful intent and restraint that liberalism does manifest in limited aspects of its foreign affairs announces the possibility of a world peace this side of the grave or of world conquest. It has strengthened the prospects for a world peace established by the steady expansion of a separate peace among liberal societies.

Putting together these apparently contradictory (but, in fact, compatible) pieces of the liberal legacy begins with a discussion of the range of liberal principle and practice. This article highlights the differences between liberal practice toward other liberal societies and liberal practice toward nonliberal societies. It argues that liberalism has achieved extraordinary success in the first and has contributed to exceptional confusion in the second. Appreciating these liberal legacies calls for another look at one of the greatest of liberal philosophers, Immanuel Kant, for he is a source of insight, policy, and hope.

II

Liberalism has been identified with an essential principle—the importance of the freedom of the individual. Above all, this is a belief in the importance of moral freedom, of the right to be treated and a duty to treat others as ethical subjects, and not as objects or means only. This principle has generated rights and institutions.

A commitment to a threefold set of rights forms the foundation of liberalism. Liberalism calls for freedom from arbitrary authority, often called "negative freedom," which includes freedom of conscience, a free press and free speech, equality under the law, and the right to hold, and therefore to exchange, property without fear of arbitrary seizure. Liberalism also calls for those rights necessary to protect and promote the capacity and opportunity for freedom, the "positive freedoms." Such social and economic rights as equality of opportunity in education and rights to health care and employment, necessary for effective self-expression and participation, are thus among liberal rights. A third liberal right, democratic participation or representation, is necessary to guarantee the other two. To ensure that morally autonomous individuals remain free in those areas of social action where public authority is needed, public legislation has to express the will of the citizens making laws for their own community.

These three sets of rights, taken together, seem to meet the challenge that Kant identified:

To organize a group of rational beings who demand general laws for their survival, but of whom each inclines toward exempting himself, and to establish their constitution in such a way that, in spite of the fact that private attitudes are opposed, these private attitudes mutually impede each other in such a manner that [their] public behavior is the same as if they did not have such evil attitudes.[2]

But the dilemma within liberalism is how to reconcile the three sets of liberal rights. The right to private property, for example, can conflict with equality of opportunity and both rights can be violated by democratic legislation. During the 180 years since Kant wrote, the liberal tradition has evolved two high roads to individual freedom and social order; one is laissez-faire or "conservative" liberalism and the other is social welfare, or social democratic, or "liberal" liberalism. Both reconcile these conflicting rights (though in differing ways) by successfully organizing free individuals into a political order.

The political order of laissez-faire and social welfare liberals is marked by a shared commitment to four essential institutions. First, citizens possess juridical equality and other fundamental civic rights such as freedom of religion and the press. Second, the effective sovereigns of the state are representative legislatures deriving their authority from the consent of the electorate and exercising their authority free from all restraint apart from the requirement that basic civic rights be preserved.[3] Most pertinently for the impact of liberalism on foreign affairs, the state is subject to neither the external authority of other states nor to the internal authority of special prerogatives held, for example,

2. Immanuel Kant, "Perpetual Peace" (1795) in *The Philosophy of Kant*, ed. Carl J. Friedrich (New York: Modern Library, 1949), p. 453.
3. The actual rights of citizenship have often been limited by slavery or male suffrage, but liberal regimes harbored no principle of opposition to the extension of juridical equality; in fact, as pressure was brought to bear they progressively extended the suffrage to the entire population. By this distinction, nineteenth-century United States was liberal; twentieth-century South Africa is not. See Samuel Huntington, *American Politics: the Promise of Disharmony* (Cambridge, Mass.: Harvard University Press, 1981).

by monarchs or military castes over foreign policy. Third, the economy rests on a recognition of the rights of private property, including the ownership of means of production. Property is justified by individual acquisition (for example, by labor) or by social agreement or social utility. This excludes state socialism or state capitalism, but it need not exclude market socialism or various forms of the mixed economy. Fourth, economic decisions are predominantly shaped by the forces of supply and demand, domestically and internationally, and are free from strict control by bureaucracies.

In order to protect the opportunity of the citizen to exercise freedom, laissez-faire liberalism has leaned toward a highly constrained role for the state and a much wider role for private property and the market. In order to promote the opportunity of the citizen to exercise freedom, welfare liberalism has expanded the role of the state and constricted the role of the market.[4] Both, nevertheless, accept these four institutional requirements and contrast markedly with the colonies, monarchical regimes, military dictatorships, and communist party dictatorships with which they have shared the political governance of the modern world.

The domestic successes of liberalism have never been more apparent. Never have so many people been included in, and accepted the domestic hegemony of, the liberal order; never have so many of the world's leading states been liberal, whether as republics or as constitutional monarchies. Indeed, the success of liberalism as an answer to the problem of masterless men in modern society is reflected in the growth in the number of liberal regimes from the

---

4. The sources of classic, laissez-faire liberalism can be found in Locke, the *Federalist Papers*, Kant, and Robert Nozick, *Anarchy, State and Utopia* (New York: Basic Books, 1974). Expositions of welfare liberalism are in the work of the Fabians and John Rawls, *A Theory of Justice* (Cambridge, Mass.: Harvard University Press, 1971). Amy Gutmann, *Liberal Equality* (Cambridge: Cambridge University Press, 1980), discusses variants of liberal thought.

Uncomfortably parallelling each of the high roads are "low roads" that, while achieving certain liberal values, fail to reconcile freedom and order. An overwhelming terror of anarchy and a speculation on preserving property can drive laissez-faire liberals to support a law-and-order authoritarian rule that sacrifices democracy. Authoritarianism to preserve order is the argument of Hobbes's *Leviathan*. It also shapes the argument of right wing liberals who seek to draw a distinction between "authoritarian" and "totalitarian" dictatorships. The justification sometimes advanced by liberals for the former is that they can be temporary and educate the population into an acceptance of property, individual rights, and, eventually, representative government. See Jeane Kirkpatrick, "Dictatorships and Double Standards," *Commentary* (November 1979), pp. 34–45. Complementarily, when social inequalities are judged to be extreme, the welfare liberal can argue that establishing (or reestablishing) the foundations of liberal society requires a nonliberal method of reform, a second low road of redistributing authoritarianism. Aristide Zolberg reports a "liberal left" sensibility among U.S. scholars of African politics that justified reforming dictatorship. (See *One Party Government in the Ivory Coast* [Princeton: Princeton University Press, 1969], p. viii.) And the argument of "reforming autocracy" can be found in J. S. Mill's defense of colonialism in India.

three that existed when Kant wrote to the more than forty that exist today. But we should not be complacent about the domestic affairs of liberal states. Significant practical problems endure: among them are enhancing citizen participation in large democracies, distributing "positional goods" (for example, prestigious jobs), controlling bureaucracy, reducing unemployment, paying for a growing demand for social services, reducing inflation, and achieving large scale restructuring of industries in response to growing foreign competition.[5] Nonetheless, these domestic problems have been widely explored though they are by no means solved. Liberalism's foreign record is more obscure and warrants more consideration.

III

In foreign affairs liberalism has shown, as it has in the domestic realm, serious weaknesses. But unlike liberalism's domestic realm, its foreign affairs have experienced startling but less than fully appreciated successes. Together they

Table 1.

Period	Liberal Regimes and the Pacific Union (By date "liberal")[a]	Total Number
18th century	Swiss Cantons[b] French Republic 1790–1795 the United States[b] 1776–	3
1800–1850	Swiss Confederation, the United States France 1830–1849 Belgium 1830– Great Britain 1832– Netherlands 1848– Piedmont 1848– Denmark 1849–	8
1850–1900	Switzerland, the United States, Belgium, Great Britain, Netherlands Piedmont –1861, Italy 1861– Denmark –1866 Sweden 1864– Greece 1864– Canada 1867– France 1871– Argentina 1880– Chile 1891–	13

5. Fred Hirsch, *The Social Limits to Growth* (Cambridge, Mass.: Harvard University Press, 1977).

Table 1. (Continued)

Period	Liberal Regimes and the Pacific Union (By date "liberal")[a]	Total Number
1900–1945	Switzerland, the United States, Great Britain, Sweden, Canada Greece –1911, 1928–1936 Italy –1922 Belgium –1940; Netherlands –1940; Argentina –1943 France –1940 Chile –1924, 1932 Australia 1901– Norway 1905–1940 New Zealand 1907– Colombia 1910–1949 Denmark 1914–1940 Poland 1917–1935 Latvia 1922–1934 Germany 1918–1932 Austria 1918–1934 Estonia 1919–1934 Finland 1919– Uruguay 1919– Costa Rica 1919– Czechoslovakia 1920–1939 Ireland 1920– Mexico 1928– Lebanon 1944–	29
1945[c]–	Switzerland, the United States, Great Britain, Sweden, Canada, Australia, New Zealand, Finland, Ireland, Mexico Uruguay –1973; Chile –1973; Lebanon –1975 Costa Rica –1948, 1953– Iceland 1944– France 1945– Denmark 1945– Norway 1945– Austria 1945– Brazil 1945–1954, 1955–1964 Belgium 1946– Luxemburg 1946– Netherlands 1946– Italy 1946– Philippines 1946–1972 India 1947–1975, 1977– Sri Lanka 1948–1961, 1963–1977, 1978– Ecuador 1948–1963, 1979– Israel 1949–	49

Table 1.   (Continued)

Period	Liberal Regimes and the Pacific Union (By date "liberal")[a]	Total Number
	West Germany 1949–	
	Peru 1950–1962, 1963–1968, 1980–	
	El Salvador 1950–1961	
	Turkey 1950–1960, 1966–1971	
	Japan 1951–	
	Bolivia 1956–1969	
	Colombia 1958–	
	Venezuela 1959–	
	Nigeria 1961–1964, 1979–	
	Jamaica 1962–	
	Trinidad 1962–	
	Senegal 1963–	
	Malaysia 1963–	
	South Korea 1963–1972	
	Botswana 1966–	
	Singapore 1965–	
	Greece 1975–	
	Portugal 1976–	
	Spain 1978–	
	Dominican Republic 1978–	

[a] I have drawn up this approximate list of "Liberal Regimes" according to the four institutions described as essential: market and private property economies; polities that are externally sovereign; citizens who possess juridical rights; and "republican" (whether republican or monarchical), representative, government. This latter includes the requirement that the legislative branch have an effective role in public policy and be formally and competitively, either potentially or actually, elected. Furthermore, I have taken into account whether male suffrage is wide (that is, 30 percent) or open to "achievement" by inhabitants (for example, to poll-tax payers or householders) of the national or metropolitan territory. Female suffrage is granted within a generation of its being demanded; and representative government is internally sovereign (for example, including and especially over military and foreign affairs) as well as stable (in existence for at least three years).

SOURCES: Arthur Banks and W. Overstreet, eds., *The Political handbook of the World, 1980* (New York: McGraw-Hill, 1980); Foreign and Commonwealth Office, *A Year Book of the Commonwealth 1980* (London: HMSO, 1980); *Europa Yearbook, 1981* (London: Europa, 1981); W. L. Langer, *An Encyclopedia of World History* (Boston: Houghton-Mifflin, 1968); Department of State, *Country Reports on Human Rights Practices* (Washington, DC: Government Printing Office, 1981); and *Freedom at Issue*, no. 54 (Jan.–Feb. 1980).

[b] There are domestic variations within these liberal regimes. For example, Switzerland was liberal only in certain cantons; the United States was liberal only north of the Mason-Dixon line until 1865, when it became liberal throughout. These lists also exclude ancient "republics," since none appear to fit Kant's criteria. See Stephen Holmes, "Aristippus in and out of Athens," *American Political Science Review* 73, no. 1 (March 1979).

[c] Selected list, excludes liberal regimes with populations less than one million.

shape an unrecognized dilemma, for both these successes and weaknesses in large part spring from the same cause: the international implications of liberal principles and institutions.

The basic postulate of liberal international theory holds that states have the right to be free from foreign intervention. Since morally autonomous citizens hold rights to liberty, the states that democratically represent them have the right to exercise political independence. Mutual respect for these rights then becomes the touchstone of international liberal theory.[6] When states respect each other's rights, individuals are free to establish private international ties without state interference. Profitable exchanges between merchants and educational exchanges among scholars then create a web of mutual advantages and commitments that bolsters sentiments of public respect.

These conventions of mutual respect have formed a cooperative foundation for relations among liberal democracies of a remarkably effective kind. *Even though liberal states have become involved in numerous wars with nonliberal states, constitutionally secure liberal states have yet to engage in war with one another.*[7] No one should argue that such wars are impossible; but preliminary evidence does appear to indicate that there exists a significant predisposition against warfare between liberal states. Indeed, threats of war also have been regarded as illegitimate. A liberal zone of peace, a pacific union, has been maintained and has expanded despite numerous particular conflicts of economic and strategic interest.

During the nineteenth century the United States and Britain negotiated the northern frontier of the United States. During the American Civil War the commercial linkages between the Lancashire cotton economy and the American South and the sentimental links between the British aristocracy and the Southern plantocracy (together with numerous disputes over the rights of British shipping against the Northern blockade) brought Great Britain and the North-

---

6. Charles Beitz, *Political Theory and International Relations* (Princeton: Princeton University Press, 1979) offers a clear and insightful discussion of liberal ideas on intervention and nonintervention.
7. There appear to be some exceptions to the tendency for liberal states not to engage in a war with each other. Peru and Ecuador, for example, entered into conflict. But for each, the war came within one to three years after the establishment of a liberal regime, that is, before the pacifying effects of liberalism could become deeply ingrained. The Palestinians and the Israelis clashed frequently along the Lebanese border, which Lebanon could not hold secure from either belligerent. But at the beginning of the 1967 War, Lebanon seems to have sent a flight of its own jets into Israel. The jets were repulsed. Alone among Israel's Arab neighbors, Lebanon engaged in no further hostilities with Israel. Israel's recent attack on the territory of Lebanon was an attack on a country that had already been occupied by Syria (and the P.L.O.). Whether Israel actually will withdraw (if Syria withdraws) and restore an independent Lebanon is yet to be determined.

Table 2. International Wars Listed Chronologically*.

British-Maharattan (1817–1818)
Greek (1821–1828)
Franco-Spanish (1823)
First Anglo-Burmese (1823–1826)
Javanese (1825–1830)
Russo-Persian (1826–1828)
Russo-Turkish (1828–1829)
First Polish (1831)
First Syrian (1831–1832)
Texan (1835–1836)
First British-Afghan (1838–1842)
Second Syrian (1839–1840)
Franco-Algerian (1839–1847)
Peruvian-Bolivian (1841)
First British-Sikh (1845–1846)
Mexican-American (1846–1848)
Austro-Sardinian (1848–1849)
First Schleswig-Holstein (1848–1849)
Hungarian (1848–1849)
Second British-Sikh (1848–1849)
Roman Republic (1849)
La Plata (1851–1852)
First Turco-Montenegran (1852–1853)
Crimean (1853–1856)
Anglo-Persian (1856–1957)
Sepoy (1857–1859)
Second Turco-Montenegran (1858–1859)
Italian Unification (1859)
Spanish-Moroccan (1859–1860)
Italo-Roman (1860)
Italo-Sicilian (1860–1861)
Franco-Mexican (1862–1867)
Ecuadorian-Colombian (1863)
Second Polish (1863–1864)
Spanish-Santo Dominican (1863–1865)
Second Schleswig-Holstein (1864)
Lopez (1864–1870)
Spanish-Chilean (1865–1866)
Seven Weeks (1866)
Ten Years (1868–1878)
Franco-Prussian (1870–1871)
Dutch-Achinese (1873–1878)
Balkan (1875–1877)
Russo-Turkish (1877–1878)
Bosnian (1878)
Second British-Afghan (1878–1880)
Pacific (1879–1880)
British-Zulu (1879)
Franco-Indochinese (1882–1884)
Mahdist (1882–1885)
Sino-French (1884–1885)

Central American (1885)
Serbo-Bulgarian (1885)
Sino-Japanese (1894–1895)
Franco-Madagascan (1894–1895)
Cuban (1895–1898)
Italo-Ethiopian (1895–1896)
First Philippine (1896–1898)
Greco-Turkish (1897)
Spanish-American (1898)
Second Philippine (1899–1902)
Boer (1899–1902)
Boxer Rebellion (1900)
Ilinden (1903)
Russo-Japanese (1904–1905)
Central American (1906)
Central American (1907)
Spanish-Moroccan (1909–1910)
Italo-Turkish (1911–1912)
First Balkan (1912–1913)
Second Balkan (1913)
World War I (1914–1918)
Russian Nationalities (1917–1921)
Russo-Polish (1919–1920)
Hungarian-Allies (1919)
Greco-Turkish (1919–1922)
Riffian (1921–1926)
Druze (1925–1927)
Sino-Soviet (1929)
Manchurian (1931–1933)
Chaco (1932–1935)
Italo-Ethiopian (1935–1936)
Sino-Japanese (1937–1941)
Changkufeng (1938)
Nomohan (1939)
World War II (1939–1945)
Russo-Finnish (1939–1940)
Franco-Thai (1940–1941)
Indonesian (1945–1946)
Indochinese (1945–1954)
Madagascan (1947–1948)
First Kashmir (1947–1949)
Palestine (1948–1949)
Hyderabad (1948)
Korean (1950–1953)
Algerian (1954–1962)
Russo-Hungarian (1956)
Sinai (1956)
Tibetan (1956–1959)
Sino-Indian (1962)
Vietnamese (1965–1975)
Second Kashmir (1965)

Table 2. (Continued)

Six Day (1967)	Vietnamese-Cambodian (1975—)
Israeli-Egyptian (1969–1970)	Timor (1975—)
Football (1969)	Saharan (1975—)
Bangladesh (1971)	Ogaden (1976—)
Philippine-MNLF (1972—)	Ugandan-Tanzanian (1978–1979)
Yom Kippur (1973)	Sino-Vietnamese (1979)
Turco-Cypriot (1974)	Russo-Afghan (1979—)
Ethiopian-Eritrean (1974—)	Irani-Iraqi (1980—)

*Reprinted by permission from Melvin Small and J. David Singer from *Resort to Arms* (Beverly Hills, CA: Sage Publications, 1982), pp. 79–80. This is a partial list of international wars fought between 1816 and 1980. In Appendices A and B of *Resort to Arms*, Small and Singer identify a total of 575 wars in this period; but approximately 159 of them appear to be largely domestic, or civil wars.
This definition of war excludes covert interventions, some of which have been directed by liberal regimes against other liberal regimes. One example is the United States' effort to destabilize the Chilean election and Allende's government. Nonetheless, it is significant (as will be apparent below) that such interventions are not pursued publicly as acknowledged policy. The covert destabilization campaign against Chile is recounted in U.S. Congress, Senate, Select Committee to Study Government Operations with Respect to Intelligence Activities, *Covert Action in Chile, 1963–73*, 94th Congress, 1st Session (Washington, DC: U.S. Government Printing Office, 1975).
The argument of this article (and this list) also excludes civil wars. Civil wars differ from international wars not in the ferocity of combat but in the issues that engender them. Two nations that could abide one another as independent neighbors separated by a border might well be the fiercest of enemies if forced to live together in one state, jointly deciding how to raise and spend taxes, choose leaders, and legislate fundamental questions of value. Notwithstanding these differences, no civil wars that I recall upset the argument of liberal pacification.

ern states to the brink of war, but they never passed over that brink. Despite an intense Anglo-French colonial rivalry, crises such as Fashoda in 1898 were resolved without going to war. Despite their colonial rivalries, liberal France and Britain formed an entente before World War I against illiberal Germany (whose foreign relations were controlled by the Kaiser and the Army). During 1914–15 Italy, the liberal member of the Triple Alliance with illiberal Germany and Austria, chose not to fulfill its obligations under the Triple Alliance to either support its allies or remain neutral. Instead, Italy, a liberal regime, joined the alliance with France and Britain that would prevent it from having to fight other liberal states, and declared war on Austria and Germany, its former allies. And despite generations of Anglo-American tension and British restrictions on American trade, the United States leaned toward Britain and France from 1914 to 1917. Nowhere was this special peace among liberal states more clearly proclaimed than in President Woodrow Wilson's "War Message" of 2 April

1917: "Our object now, as then, is to vindicate the principles of peace and justice in the life of the world as against selfish and autocratic power and to set up amongst the really free and self-governed peoples of the world such a concert of purpose and of action as will henceforth ensure the observance of those principles."[8]

Statistically, war between any two states (in any single year or other short period of time) is a low probability event. War between any two adjacent states, considered over a long period of time, may be somewhat more probable. The apparent absence of war among the more clearly liberal states, whether adjacent or not, for almost two hundred years thus has some significance. Politically more significant, perhaps, is that, when states are forced to decide, by the

---

8. Imperial Germany is a difficult case. The Reichstag was not only elected by universal male suffrage but, by and large, the state ruled under the law, respecting the civic equality and rights of its citizens. Moreover, Chancellor Bismarck began the creation of a social welfare society that served as an inspiration for similar reforms in liberal regimes. However, the constitutional relations between the imperial executive and the representative legislature were sufficiently complex that various practices, rather than constitutional theory, determined the actual relation between the government and the citizenry. The emperor appointed and could dismiss the chancellor. Although the chancellor was responsible to the Reichstag, a defeat in the Reichstag did not remove him nor did the government absolutely depend on the Reihstag for budgetary authority. In practice, Germany was a liberal state under republican law for domestic issues. But the emperor's direct authority over the army, the army's effective independence from the minimal authority of the War Ministry, and the emperor's active role in foreign affairs (including the influential separate channel to the emperor through the military attachés) together with the tenuous constitutional relationship between the chancellor and the Reichstag made imperial Germany a state divorced from the control of its citizenry in foreign affairs.

This authoritarian element not only influenced German foreign policymaking, but also shaped the international political environment (a lack of trust) the Reich faced and the domestic political environment that defined the government's options and capabilities (the weakness of liberal opinion as against the exceptional influence of junker militaristic nationalism). Thus direct influence on policy was but one result of the authoritarian element. Nonetheless, significant and strife-generating episodes can be directly attributed to this element. They include Tirpitz's approach to Wilhelm II to obtain the latter's sanction for a veto of Chancellor Bethmann-Hollweg's proposals for a naval agreement with Britain (1909). Added to this was Wilhelm's personal assurances of full support to the Austrians early in the Sarajevo Crisis and his, together with Moltke's, erratic pressure on the Chancellor throughout July and August of 1914, which helped destroy whatever coherence German diplomacy might otherwise have had, and which led one Austrian official to ask, "Who rules in Berlin? Moltke or Bethmann?" (Gordon Craig, *The Politics of the Prussian Army* [New York: Oxford University Press, 1964], pp. xxviii and chap. 6). For an excellent account of Bethmann's aims and the constraints he encountered, see Konrad H. Jarausch, "The Illusion of Limited War: Chancellor Bethmann-Hollweg's Calculated Risk, July 1914," *Central European History*, Vol. 2. No. 1 (March 1969).

The liberal sources of Italy's decision are pointed out in R. Vivarelli's review of Hugo Butler's *Gaetano Salvemini und die Italienische Politik vor dem Ersten Weltkrieg* in the *Journal of Modern History*, Vol. 52, No. 3 (September 1980), p. 541.

The quotation from President Wilson is from Woodrow Wilson, *The Messages and Papers of Woodrow Wilson*, ed. Albert Shaw (New York: The Review of Reviews, 1924), p. 378.

pressure of an impinging world war, on which side of a world contest they will fight, liberal states wind up all on the same side, despite the real complexity of the historical, economic and political factors that affect their foreign policies. And historically, we should recall that medieval and early modern Europe were the warring cockpits of states, wherein France and England and the Low Countries engaged in near constant strife. Then in the late eighteenth century there began to emerge liberal regimes. At first hesitant and confused, and later clear and confident as liberal regimes gained deeper domestic foundations and longer international experience, a pacific union of these liberal states became established.

The Realist model of international relations, which provides a plausible explanation of the general insecurity of states, offers little guidance in explaining the pacification of the liberal world. Realism, in its classical formulation, holds that the state is and should be formally sovereign, effectively unbounded by individual rights nationally and thus capable of determining its own scope of authority. (This determination can be made democratically, oligarchically, or autocratically.) Internationally, the sovereign state exists in an anarchical society in which it is radically independent; neither bounded nor protected by international "law" or treaties or duties, and hence, insecure. Hobbes, one of the seventeenth-century founders of the Realist approach drew the international implications of Realism when he argued that the existence of international anarchy, the very independence of states, best accounts for the competition, the fear, and the temptation toward preventive war that characterize international relations. Politics among nations is not a continuous combat, but it is in this view a "state of war . . . a tract of time, wherein the will to contend by battle is sufficiently known."[9]

In international relations theory, three "games" explain the fear that Hobbes saw as a root of conflict in a state of war. First, even when states share an interest in a common good that could be attained by cooperation, the absence of a source of global law and order means that no one state can count upon the cooperative behavior of the others. Each state therefore has a rational incentive to defect from the cooperative enterprise even if only to pursue a good whose value is less than the share that would have been obtained from the successful accomplishment of the cooperative enterprise (this is Rousseau's "stag dilemma"). Second, even though each state knows that security is relative to the armaments level of potential adversaries and even though each state

---

9. Thomas Hobbes, *Leviathan* (New York: Penguin, 1980), I, chap. 13, 62; p. 186.

seeks to minimize its arms expenditure, it also knows that, having no global guarantee of security, being caught unarmed by a surprise attack is worse than bearing the costs of armament. Each therefore arms; all are worse off (this is the "security dilemma," a variant of the "prisoner's dilemma"). Third, heavily armed states rely upon their prestige, their credibility, to deter states from testing the true quality of their arms in battle, and credibility is measured by a record of successes. Once a posture of confrontation is assumed, backing down, although rational for both together, is not rational (first best) for either individually if there is some chance that the other will back down first (the game of "chicken").[10]

Specific wars therefore arise from fear as a state seeking to avoid a surprise attack decides to attack first; from competitive emulation as states lacking an imposed international hierarchy of prestige struggle to establish their place; and from straightforward conflicts of interest that escalate into war because there is no global sovereign to prevent states from adopting that ultimate form of conflict resolution. Herein lie Thucydides's trinity of "security, honor, and self-interest" and Hobbes's "diffidence," "glory," and "competition" that drive states to conflict in the international state of war.[11]

Finding that all states, including liberal states, do engage in war, the Realist concludes that the effects of differing domestic regimes (whether liberal or not) are overridden by the international anarchy under which all states live.[12] Thus Hobbes does not bother to distinguish between "some council or one man" when he discusses the sovereign. Differing domestic regimes do affect the quantity of resources available to the state as Rousseau (an eighteenth-century Realist) shows in his discussion of Poland, and Morgenthau (a twentieth-century Realist) demonstrates in his discussion of morale.[13] But the ends that shape the international state of war are decreed for the Realist by the anarchy

10. Robert Jervis, "Cooperation Under the Security Dilemma," *World Politics* Vol. 30, No. 1 (January 1978).

11. Thucydides, *The Peloponnesian Wars*, trans. Rex Warner (Baltimore, Md.: Penguin Books, 1954) I:76; and Hobbes, *Leviathan*, I, chap. 13, 61, p. 185. The coincidence of views is not accidental; Hobbes translated Thucydides. And Hobbes's portrait of the state of nature appears to be drawn from Thucydides's account of the revolution in Corcyra.

12. Kenneth N. Waltz, *Man, the State, and War* (New York: Columbia University Press, 1954, 1959), pp. 120–23; and see his *Theory of International Politics* (Reading, Mass.: Addison-Wesley, 1979). The classic sources of this form of Realism are Hobbes and, more particularly, Rousseau's "Essay on St. Pierre's Peace Project" and his "State of War" in *A Lasting Peace* (London: Constable, 1917), E. H. Carr's *The Twenty Year's Crisis: 1919–1939* (London: Macmillan & Co., 1951), and the works of Hans Morgenthau.

13. Jean-Jacques Rousseau, *The Government of Poland*, trans. Willmoore Kendall (New York: Bobbs-Merrill, 1972); and Hans Morgenthan, *Politics Among Nations* (New York: Alfred A. Knopf, 1967), pp. 132–35.

of the international order and the fundamental quest for power that directs the policy of all States, irrespective of differences in their domestic regimes. As Rousseau argued, international peace therefore depends on the abolition of international relations either by the achievement of a world state or by a radical isolationism (Corsica). Realists judge neither to be possible.

First, at the level of the strategic decisionmaker, Realists argue that a liberal peace could be merely the outcome of prudent diplomacy. Some, including Hobbes, have argued that sovereigns have a natural duty not to act against "the reasons of peace."[14] Individuals established (that is, should establish) a sovereign to escape from the brutalities of the state of nature, the war of all against all, that follows from competition for scarce goods, scrambles for prestige, and fear of another's attack when there is no sovereign to provide for lawful acquisition or regularized social conduct or personal security. "Dominions were constituted for peace's sake, and peace was sought for safety's sake"; the natural duty of the sovereign is therefore the safety of the people. Yet prudent policy cannot be an enforceable right of citizens because Hobbesian sovereigns, who remain in the state of nature with respect to their subjects and other sovereigns, cannot themselves be subjects.

Nevertheless, the interstate condition is not necessarily the original brutality only now transposed to the frontiers. The sovereign is personally more secure than any individual in the original state of nature and soldiers too are by nature timorous. Unlike individuals, states are not equal; some live more expansively by predominance, others must live only by sufferance. Yet a policy of safety is not a guarantee of peace. The international condition for Hobbes remains a state of war. Safety enjoins a prudent policy of forewarning (spying) and of forearming oneself to increase security against other sovereigns who, lacking any assurance that you are not taking these measures, also take them. Safety also requires (morally) taking actions "whatsoever shall seem to conduce to the lessening of the power of foreigners whom they [the sovereign] suspect, whether by slight or force."[15] If preventive wars are prudent, the Realists' prudence obviously cannot account for more than a century and a half of peace among independent liberal states, many of which have crowded one another in the center of Europe.

Recent additions to game theory specify some of the circumstances under which prudence could lead to peace. Experience; geography; expectations of

---

14. Hobbes, "De Cive," *The English Works of Thomas Hobbes* (London: J. Bohn, 1841), 2: 166–67.
15. *Ibid.*, p. 171.

cooperation and belief patterns; and the differing payoffs to cooperation (peace) or conflict associated with various types of military technology all appear to influence the calculus.[16] But when it comes to acquiring the techniques of peaceable interaction, nations appear to be slow, or at least erratic, learners. The balance of power (more below) is regarded as a primary lesson in the Realist primer, but centuries of experience did not prevent either France (Louis XIV, Napoleon I) or Germany (Wilhelm II, Hitler) from attempting to conquer Europe, twice each. Yet some, very new, black African states appear to have achieved a twenty-year-old system of impressively effective standards of mutual toleration. These standards are not completely effective (as in Tanzania's invasion of Uganda); but they have confounded expectations of a scramble to redivide Africa.[17] Geography—"insular security" and "continental insecurity"—may affect foreign policy attitudes; but it does not appear to determine behavior, as the bellicose records of England and Japan suggest. Beliefs, expectations, and attitudes of leaders and masses should influence strategic behavior. A survey of attitudinal predispositions of the American public indicate that a peaceable inclination would be enhanced by having at the strategic helm a forty-five-year-old, black, female, pediatrician of Protestant or Jewish faith, resident in Bethesda, Maryland.[18] Nevertheless, it would be difficult to determine if liberal leaders have had more peaceable attitudes than leaders who lead nonliberal states. But even if one did make that discovery, he also would have to account for why these peaceable attitudes only appear to be effective in relations with other liberals (since wars with nonliberals have not been uniformly defensive).

More substantial contributions have been made in the logic of game theory decision under differing military technologies. These technologies can alter the payoffs of the "security dilemma": making the costs of noncooperation high, reducing the costs of being unprepared or surprised, reducing the benefits of surprise attack, or increasing the gains from cooperation. In particular, Jervis recently has examined the differing effects of situations in which the offense or the defense has the advantage and in which offensive weapons are or are not distinguishable from defensive weapons. When the offense has the advantage and weapons are indistinguishable, the level of insecurity is high, incentives

16. Jervis, "Cooperation Under the Security Dilemma," pp. 172–86.
17. Robert H. Jackson and Carl G. Rosberg, "Why West Africa's Weak States Persist," *World Politics* Vol. 35, No. 1 (October 1982).
18. Interpreted from Michael Haas, *International Conflict* (New York: Bobbs-Merrill, 1974), pp. 80–81, 457–58.

for preemptive attack correspondingly are strong. When offensive weapons do not have an advantage and offensive weapons are distinguishable the incentives for preemptive attack are low, as are the incentives for arms races. Capable of signalling with clarity a nonaggressive intent and of guaranteeing that other states pose no immediate strategic threat, statesmen should be able to adopt peaceable policies and negotiate disputes. But, this cannot be the explanation for the liberal peace. Military technologies changed from offensive to defensive and from distinguishable to nondistinguishable, yet the pacific union persisted and persisted only among liberal states. Moreover, even the "clearest" technical messages appear subject to garbling. The pre-1914 period, which objectively represented a triumph of the distinguishable defense (machine guns, barbed wire, trench warfare) over the offensive, subjectively, as Jervis notes, was a period which appeared to military leaders to place exceptional premiums on the offensive and thus on preemptive war.[19]

Second, at the level of social determinants, some might argue that relations among any group of states with similar social structures or with compatible values would be peaceful.[20] But again, the evidence for feudal societies, communist societies, fascist societies, or socialist societies does not support this conclusion. Feudal warfare was frequent and very much a sport of the monarchs and nobility. There have not been enough truly totalitarian, fascist powers (nor have they lasted long enough) to test fairly their pacific compatibility; but fascist powers in the wider sense of nationalist, capitalist, military dictatorships fought each other in the 1930s. Communist powers have engaged in wars more recently in East Asia. And we have not had enough socialist societies to consider the relevance of socialist pacification. The more abstract category of pluralism does not suffice. Certainly Germany was pluralist when it engaged in war with liberal states in 1914; Japan as well in 1941. But they were not liberal.

---

19. Jervis, "Cooperation Under the Security Dilemma," pp. 186–210, 212. Jervis examines incentives for cooperation, not the existence or sources of peace.
20. There is a rich contemporary literature devoted to explaining international cooperation and integration. Karl Deutsch's *Political Community and the North Atlantic Area* (Princeton: Princeton University Press, 1957) develops the idea of a "pluralistic security community" that bears a resemblance to the "pacific union," but Deutsch limits it geographically and finds compatibility of values, mutual responsiveness, and predictability of behavior among decision-makers as its essential foundations. These are important but their particular content, liberalism, appears to be more telling. Joseph Nye in *Peace in Parts* (Boston: Little, Brown & Co., 1971) steps away from the geographic limits Deutsch sets and focuses on levels of development; but his analysis is directed toward explaining integration—a more intensive form of cooperation than the pacific union.

And third, at the level of interstate relations, neither specific regional attributes nor historic alliances or friendships can account for the wide reach of the liberal peace. The peace extends as far as, and no further than, the relations among liberal states, not including nonliberal states in an otherwise liberal region (such as the north Atlantic in the 1930s) nor excluding liberal states in a nonliberal region (such as Central America or Africa).

At this level, Raymond Aron has identified three types of interstate peace: empire, hegemony, and equilibrium.[21] An empire generally succeeds in creating an internal peace, but this is not an explanation of peace among independent liberal states. Hegemony can create peace by over-awing potential rivals. Although far from perfect and certainly precarious, United States hegemony, as Aron notes, might account for the interstate peace in South America in the postwar period during the height of the cold war conflict. However, the liberal peace cannot be attributed merely to effective international policing by a predominant hegemon—Britain in the nineteenth century, the United States in the postwar period. Even though a hegemon might well have an interest in enforcing a peace for the sake of commerce or investments or as a means of enhancing its prestige or security; hegemons such as seventeenth-century France were not peace-enforcing police, and the liberal peace persisted in the interwar period when international society lacked a predominant hegemonic power. Moreover, this explanation overestimates hegemonic control in both periods. Neither England nor the United States was able to prevent direct challenges to its interests (colonial competition in the nineteenth century, Middle East diplomacy and conflicts over trading with the enemy in the postwar period). Where then was the capacity to prevent all armed conflicts between liberal regimes, many of which were remote and others strategically or economically insignificant? Liberal hegemony and leadership are important (see Section V below), but they are not sufficient to explain a liberal peace.

Peace through equilibrium (the multipolar classical balance of power or the bipolar "cold war") also draws upon prudential sources of peace. An awareness of the likelihood that aggressive attempts at hegemony will generate international opposition should, it is argued, deter these aggressive wars. But

---

21. Raymond Aron, *Peace and War* (New York: Praeger, 1968) pp. 151–54. Progress and peace through the rise and decline of empires and hegemonies has been a classic theme. Lucretius suggested that they may be part of a more general law of nature: "Augescunt aliae gentes, aliae miniuntur/Inque brevis spatio mutantur saecula animantum,/Et quasi cursores vitai lampada tradunt." [Some peoples wax and others wane/And in a short space the order of living things is changed/And like runners hand on the torch of life.] *De Rer. Nat.* ii, 77–79.

bipolar stability discourages polar or superpower wars, not proxy or small power wars. And multipolar balancing of power also encourages warfare to seize, for example, territory for strategic depth against a rival expanding its power from internal growth.[22] Neither readily accounts for general peace or for the liberal peace.

Finally, some Realists might suggest that the liberal peace simply reflects the absence of deep conflicts of interest among liberal states. Wars occur outside the liberal zone because conflicts of interest are deeper there. But this argument does nothing more than raise the question of why liberal states have fewer or less fundamental conflicts of interest with other liberal states than liberal states have with nonliberal, or nonliberal states have with other nonliberals. We must therefore examine the workings of liberalism among its own kind—a special pacification of the "state of war" resting on liberalism and nothing either more specific or more general.

IV

Most liberal theorists have offered inadequate guidance in understanding the exceptional nature of liberal pacification. Some have argued that democratic states would be inherently peaceful simply and solely because in these states

---

22. Kenneth Waltz, *Theory of International Politics*, chap. 8; and Edward Gulick, *Europe's Classical Balance of Power* (New York: Norton, 1967), chap. 3.

One of the most thorough collective investigations of the personal, societal, and international systemic sources of war has been the Correlates of War Project. See especially Melvin Small and J. David Singer, *Resort to Arms* (Beverly Hills, CA: Sage, 1982) for a more comprehensive list and statistical analysis of wars. J. David Singer ("Accounting for International War: The State of the Discipline," *Journal of Peace Research* Vol. 18, No. 1 [1981]) drew the following conclusions: "The exigencies of survival in an international system of such inadequate organization and with so pervasively dysfunctional a culture require relatively uniform response (p. 11). . . . domestic factors are negligible;" war "cannot be explained on the basis of relatively invariant phenomena" (p. 1).

Michael Haas, *International Conflict*, discovers that, at the systemic level, "collective security, stratification, and hegemonization systems are likely to avoid a high frequency in violent outputs" (p. 453); but "no single [causal] model was entirely or even largely satisfactory" (p. 452). At the social level, war correlates with variables such as "bloc prominence, military mobilizations, public perceptions of hostility toward peoples of other countries, a high proportion of gross national product devoted to military expenditures . . ." (p. 461). These variables appear to describe rather than explain war. A cluster analysis he performs associates democracy, development, and sustained modernization with the existence of peaceful countries (pp. 464–65). But these factors do not correlate with pacification during the period 1816–1965 according to M. Small and J. D. Singer, "The War Proneness of Democratic Regimes," *Jerusalem Journal of International Relations* Vol. 1, No. 4 (Summer 1976).

Their conclusions follow, I think, from their homogenization of war and from their attempt to explain all wars, in which a myriad of states have engaged. I attempt to explain an interstate peace, which only liberal regimes, a particular type of state and society, have succeeded in establishing.

citizens rule the polity and bear the costs of wars. Unlike monarchs, citizens are not able to indulge their aggressive passions and have the consequences suffered by someone else. Other liberals have argued that laissez-faire capitalism contains an inherent tendency toward rationalism, and that, since war is irrational, liberal capitalisms will be pacifistic. Others still, such as Montesquieu, claim that "commerce is the cure for the most destructive prejudices," and "Peace is the natural effect of trade."[23] While these developments can help account for the liberal peace, they do not explain the fact that liberal states are peaceful only in relations with other liberal states. France and England fought expansionist, colonial wars throughout the nineteenth century (in the 1830s and 1840s against Algeria and China); the United States fought a similar war with Mexico in 1848 and intervened again in 1914 under President Wilson. Liberal states are as aggressive and war prone as any other form of government or society in their relations with nonliberal states.

Immanuel Kant offers the best guidance. "Perpetual Peace," written in 1795, predicts the ever-widening pacification of the liberal pacific union, explains that pacification, and at the same time suggests why liberal states are not pacific in their relations with nonliberal states. Kant argues that Perpetual Peace will be guaranteed by the ever-widening acceptance of three "definitive articles" of peace. When all nations have accepted the definitive articles in a metaphorical "treaty" of perpetual peace he asks them to sign, perpetual peace will have been established.

The First Definitive Article holds that the civil constitution of the state must be republican. By republican Kant means a political society that has solved the problem of combining moral autonomy, individualism, and social order. A basically private property and market-oriented economy partially addressed that dilemma in the private sphere. The public, or political, sphere was more troubling. His answer was a republic that preserved juridical freedom—the legal equality of citizens as subjects—on the basis of a representative government with a separation of powers. Juridical freedom is preserved because the morally autonomous individual is by means of representation a self-legislator making laws that apply to all citizens equally including himself. And tyranny

---

23. The incompatibility of democracy and war is forcefully asserted by Paine in *The Rights of Man*. The connection between liberal capitalism, democracy, and peace is argued by, among others, Joseph Schumpeter in *Imperialism and Social Classes* (New York: Meridian, 1955); and Montesquieu, *Spirit of the Laws* I, bk. 20, chap. 1. This literature is surveyed and analyzed by Albert Hirschman, "Rival Interpretations of Market Society: Civilizing, Destructive, or Feeble?" *Journal of Economic Literature* Vol. 20 (December 1982).

is avoided because the individual is subject to laws he does not also administer.[24]

Liberal republics will progressively establish peace among themselves by means of the "pacific union" described in the Second Definitive Article of the Eternal Peace. The pacific union is limited to "a treaty of the nations among themselves" which "maintains itself, prevents wars, and steadily expands." The world will not have achieved the "perpetual peace" that provides the ultimate guarantor of republican freedom until "very late and after many unsuccessful attempts." Then right conceptions of the appropriate constitution, great and sad experience, and good will will have taught all the nations the lessons of peace. Not until then will individuals enjoy perfect republican rights or the full guarantee of a global and just peace. But in the meantime, the "pacific union" of liberal republics "*steadily expands* [my emphasis]" bringing within it more and more republics (despite republican collapses, backsliding, and war disasters) and creating an ever expanding separate peace.[25] The pacific union is neither a single peace treaty ending one war nor a world state or state of nations. The first is insufficient; the second and third are impossible or potentially tyrannical. Kant develops no organizational embodiment of this treaty, and presumably he does not find institutionalization necessary. He appears to have in mind a mutual nonaggression pact, perhaps a collective security agreement, and the cosmopolitan law set forth in the Third Definitive Article.[26]

---

24. Two classic sources that examine Kant's international theory from a Realist perspective are Stanley Hoffmann, "Rousseau on War and Peace" in the *State of War* (New York: Praeger, 1965) and Kenneth Waltz, "Kant, Liberalism, and War," *American Political Science Review* Vol. 56, No. 2 (June 1962). I have benefited from their analysis and from those of Karl Friedrich, *Inevitable Peace* (Cambridge, MA: Harvard University Press, 1948); F. H. Hinsley, *Power and the Pursuit of Peace* (Cambridge: Cambridge University Press, 1967), chap. 4; W. B. Gallie, *Philosophers of Peace and War* (Cambridge: Cambridge University Press, 1978), chap. 1; and particularly Patrick Riley, *Kant's Political Philosophy* (Totowa, N.J.: Rowman and Littlefield, 1983). But some of the conclusions of this article differ markedly from theirs.
  Kant's republican constitution is described in Kant, "Perpetual Peace," *The Philosophy of Kant*, p. 437 and analyzed by Riley, *Kant's Political Philosophy*, chap. 5.
25. Kant, "Universal History," *The Philosophy of Kant*, p. 123. The pacific union follows a process of "federalization" such that it "can be realized by a gradual extension to all states, leading to eternal peace." This interpretation contrasts with those cited in n. 24. I think Kant meant that the peace would be established among liberal regimes and would expand as new liberal regimes appeared. By a process of gradual extension the peace would become global and then perpetual; the occasion for wars with nonliberals would disappear as nonliberal regimes disappeared.
26. Kant's "Pacific Union," the *foedus pacificum*, is thus neither a *pactum pacis* (a single peace treaty) nor a *civitas gentium* (a world state). He appears to have anticipated something like a less formally institutionalized League of Nations or United Nations. One could argue that these two institutions in practice worked for liberal states and only for liberal states. But no specifically liberal "pacific

The Third Definitive Article of the Eternal Peace establishes a cosmopolitan law to operate in conjunction with the pacific union. The cosmopolitan law "shall be limited to conditions of universal hospitality." In this he calls for the recognition of the "right of a foreigner not to be treated with hostility when he arrives upon the soul of another [country]," which "does not extend further than to the conditions which enable them [the foreigners] to attempt the developing of intercourse [commerce] with the old inhabitants." Hospitality does not require extending either the right to citizenship to foreigners or the right to settlement, unless the foreign visitors would perish if they were expelled. Foreign conquest and plunder also find no justification under this right. Hospitality does appear to include the right of access and the obligation of maintaining the opportunity for citizens to exchange goods and ideas, without imposing the obligation to trade (a voluntary act in all cases under liberal constitutions).[27]

Kant then explains each of the three definitive articles for a liberal peace. In doing so he develops both an account of why liberal states do maintain peace among themselves and of how it will (by implication, has) come about that the pacific union will expand. His central claim is that a natural evolution will produce "a harmony from the very disharmony of men against their will."[28]

The first source derives from a political evolution, from a *constitutional law*. Nature (providence) has seen to it that human beings can live in all the regions where they have been driven to settle by wars. (Kant, who once taught geography, reports on the Lapps, the Samoyeds, the Pescheras.) "Asocial sociability" draws men together to fulfill needs for security and material welfare as it drives them into conflicts over the distribution and control of social products. This violent natural evolution tends toward the liberal peace because "asocial sociability" inevitably leads toward republican governments and republican governments are a source of the liberal peace.

Republican representation and separation of powers are produced because they are the means by which the state is "organized well" to prepare for and meet foreign threats (by unity) and to tame the ambitions of selfish and

---

union" was institutionalized. Instead liberal states have behaved for the past 180 years as if such a Kantian pacific union and treaty of Perpetual Peace had been signed. This follows Riley's views of the legal, not the organizational, character of the *foedus pacificum*.

27. Kant, "Perpetual Peace," pp. 444–47.

28. Kant, the fourth principle of "The Idea for a Universal History" in *The Philosophy of Kant*, p. 120. Interestingly, Kant's three sources of peace (republicanism, respect, and commerce) parallel quite closely Aristotle's three sources of friendship (goodness, pleasure or appreciation, and utility). See *Nicomachean Ethics*, bk. 8, chap. 3, trans. J.A.K. Thomson (Baltimore, Md: Penguin, 1955).

aggressive individuals (by authority derived from representation, by general laws, and by nondespotic administration). States which are not organized in this fashion fail. Monarchs thus cede rights of representation to their subjects in order to strengthen their political support or to obtain tax revenue. This argument provides a plausible, logical connection between conflict, internal and external, and republicanism; and it highlights interesting associations between the rising incidence of international war and the increasing number of republics.

Nevertheless, constant preparation for war can enhance the role of military institutions in a society to the point that they become the society's rulers. Civil conflict can lead to praetorian coups. Conversely, an environment of security can provide a political climate for weakening the state by constitutional restraints.[29] Significantly, the most war-affected states have not been liberal republics.[30] More importantly, the argument is so indistinct as to serve only as a very general hypothesis that mobilizing self-interested individuals into the political life of states in an insecure world will eventually engender pressures for republican participation. Kant needs no more than this to suggest that republicanism and a liberal peace are possible (and thus a moral obligation). If it is possible, then sometime over the course of history it may be inevitable. But attempting to make its date of achievement predictable—projecting a steady trend—he suggests, may be asking too much. He anticipates backsliding and destructive wars, though these will serve to educate the nations to the importance of peace.[31]

Kant shows how republics, once established, lead to peaceful relations. He argues that once the aggressive interests of absolutist monarchies are tamed and once the habit of respect for individual rights is engrained by republican government, wars would appear as the disaster to the people's welfare that he and the other liberals thought them to be. The fundamental reason is this:

If the consent of the citizens is required in order to decide that war should be declared (and in this constitution it cannot but be the case), nothing is more natural than that they would be very cautious in commencing such a poor game, decreeing for themselves all the calamities of war. Among the latter

---

29. The "Prussian Model" suggests the connection between insecurity, war, and authoritarianism. See *The Anglo-American Tradition in Foreign Affairs,* ed. Arnold Wolfers and Laurence Martin (New Haven: Yale University Press, 1956), "Introduction," for an argument linking security and liberalism.
30. Small and Singer, *Resort to Arms,* pp. 176–79.
31. Kant, "The Idea for a Universal History," p. 124.

would be: having to fight, having to pay the costs of war from their own resources, having painfully to repair the devastation war leaves behind, and, to fill up the measure of evils, load themselves with a heavy national debt that would embitter peace itself and that can never be liquidated on account of constant wars in the future. But, on the other hand, in a constitution which is not republican, and under which the subjects are not citizens, a declaration of war is the easiest thing in the world to decide upon, because war does not require of the ruler, who is the proprietor and not a member of the state, the least sacrifice of the pleasure of his table, the chase, his country houses, his court functions, and the like. He may, therefore, resolve on war as on a pleasure party for the most trivial reasons, and with perfect indifference leave the justification which decency requires to the diplomatic corps who are ever ready to provide it.[32]

One could add to Kant's list another source of pacification specific to liberal constitutions. The regular rotation of office in liberal democratic polities is a nontrivial device that helps ensure that personal animosities among heads of government provide no lasting, escalating source of tension.

These domestic republican restraints do not end war. If they did, liberal states would not be warlike, which is far from the case. They do introduce Kant's "caution" in place of monarchical caprice. Liberal wars are only fought for popular, liberal purposes. To see how this removes the occasion of wars among liberal states and not wars between liberal and nonliberal states, we need to shift our attention from constitutional law to international law, Kant's second source.

Complementing the constitutional guarantee of caution, *international law* adds a second source—a guarantee of respect. The separation of nations that asocial sociability encourages is reinforced by the development of separate languages and religions. These further guarantee a world of separate states—an essential condition needed to avoid a "global, soul-less despotism." Yet, at the same time, they also morally integrate liberal states "as culture progresses and men gradually come closer together toward a greater agreement on principles

---

32. Immanuel Kant, "Perpetual Peace" in *The Enlightenment*, ed. Peter Gay (New York: Simon & Schuster, 1974), pp. 790–92.

Gallie in *Philosophers of Peace and War* criticizes Kant for neglecting economic, religious, nationalistic drives toward war and for failing to appreciate that "regimes" make war in order to enhance their domestic political support. But Kant holds that these drives should be subordinated to justice in a liberal society (he specifically criticizes colonial wars stimulated by rapaciousness). He also argues that *republics* derive their legitimacy from their accordance with law and representation, thereby freeing them from crises of domestic political support. Kant thus acknowledges both Gallie's sets of motives for war but argues that they would not apply within the pacific union.

for peace and understanding."[33] As republics emerge (the first source) and as culture progresses, an understanding of the legitimate rights of all citizens and of all republics comes into play; and this, now that caution characterizes policy, sets up the moral foundations for the liberal peace. Correspondingly, international law highlights the importance of Kantian publicity. Domestically, publicity helps ensure that the officials of republics act according to the principles they profess to hold just and according to the interests of the electors they claim to represent. Internationally, free speech and the effective communication of accurate conceptions of the political life of foreign peoples is essential to establish and preserve the understanding on which the guarantee of respect depends. In short, domestically just republics, which rest on consent, presume foreign republics to be also consensual, just, and therefore deserving of accommodation. The experience of cooperation helps engender further cooperative behavior when the consequences of state policy are unclear but (potentially) mutually beneficial.[34]

Lastly, *cosmopolitan law*, adds material incentives to moral commitments. The cosmopolitan right to hospitality permits the "spirit of commerce" sooner or later to take hold of every nation, thus impelling states to promote peace and to try to avert war.

Liberal economic theory holds that these cosmopolitan ties derive from a cooperative international division of labor and free trade according to comparative advantage. Each economy is said to be better off than it would have been under autarky; each thus acquires an incentive to avoid policies that would lead the other to break these economic ties. Since keeping open markets

---

33. Kant, *The Philosophy of Kant*, p. 454. These factors also have a bearing on Karl Deutsch's "compatibility of values" and "predictability of behavior" (see n. 20).

34. A highly stylized version of this effect can be found in the Realist's "Prisoner's Dilemma" game. There a failure of mutual trust and the incentives to enhance one's own position produce a noncooperative solution that makes both parties worse off. Contrarily, cooperation, a commitment to avoid exploiting the other part, produces joint gains. The significance of the game in this context is the character of its participants. The "prisoners" are presumed to be felonious, unrelated apart from their partnership in crime, and lacking in mutual trust—competitive nation states in an anarchic world. A similar game between fraternal or sororal twins—Kant's republics—would be likely to lead to different results. See Robert Jervis, "Hypotheses on Misperception," *World Politics* Vol. 20, No. 3 (April 1968), for an exposition of the role of presumptions and "Cooperation Under the Security Dilemma," for the factors Realists see as mitigating the security dilemma caused by anarchy.

Also, expectations (including theory and history) can influence behavior, making liberal states expect (and fulfill) pacific policies toward each other. These effects are explored at a theoretical level in R. Dacey, "Some Implications of 'Theory Absorption' for Economic Theory and the Economics of Information" in *Philosophical Dimensions of Economics*, ed. J. Pitt (Dordrecht, Holland: D. Reidel, 1980).

rests upon the assumption that the next set of transactions will also be determined by prices rather than coercion, a sense of mutual security is vital to avoid security-motivated searches for economic autarky. Thus avoiding a challenge to another liberal state's security or even enhancing each other's security by means of alliance naturally follows economic interdependence.

A further cosmopolitan source of liberal peace is that the international market removes difficult decisions of production and distribution from the direct sphere of state policy. A foreign state thus does not appear directly responsible for these outcomes; states can stand aside from, and to some degree above, these contentious market rivalries and be ready to step in to resolve crises. Furthermore, the interdependence of commerce and the connections of state officials help create crosscutting transnational ties that serve as lobbies for mutual accommodation. According to modern liberal scholars, international financiers and transnational, bureaucratic, and domestic organizations create interests in favor of accommodation and have ensured by their variety that no single conflict sours an entire relationship.[35]

No one of these constitutional, international or cosmopolitan sources is alone sufficient, but together (and only where together) they plausibly connect the characteristics of liberal polities and economies with sustained liberal peace. Liberal states have not escaped from the Realists' "security dilemma," the insecurity caused by anarchy in the world political system considered as a whole. But the effects of international anarchy have been tamed in the relations among states of a similarly liberal character. Alliances of purely mutual strategic interest among liberal and nonliberal states have been broken, economic ties between liberal and nonliberal states have proven fragile, but the political bond of liberal rights and interests have proven a remarkably firm foundation for mutual nonaggression. A separate peace exists among liberal states.

V

Where liberal internationalism among liberal states has been deficient is in preserving its basic preconditions under changing international circumstances, and particularly in supporting the liberal character of its constituent states. It has failed on occasion, as it did in regard to Germany in the 1920s, to provide

---

35. Karl Polanyi, *The Great Transformation* (Boston: Beacon Press, 1944), chaps. 1–2, and Samuel Huntington and Z. Brzezinski, *Political Power: USA/USSR* (New York: Viking Press, 1963, 1964), chap. 9. And see Richard Neustadt, *Alliance Politics* (New York: Columbia University Press, 1970) for a detailed case study of interliberal politics.

international economic support for liberal regimes whose market foundations were in crisis. It failed in the 1930s to provide military aid or political mediation to Spain, which was challenged by an armed minority, or to Czechoslovakia, which was caught in a dilemma of preserving national security or acknowledging the claims (fostered by Hitler's Germany) of the Sudeten minority to self-determination. Farsighted and constitutive measures have only been provided by the liberal international order when one liberal state stood preeminent among the rest, prepared and able to take measures, as did the United States following World War II, to sustain economically and politically the foundations of liberal society beyond its borders. Then measures such as the British Loan, the Marshall Plan, NATO, GATT, the IMF, and the liberalization of Germany and Japan helped construct buttresses for the international liberal order.[36]

Thus, the decline of U.S. hegemonic leadership may pose dangers for the liberal world. This danger is not that today's liberal states will permit their economic competition to spiral into war, but that the societies of the liberal world will no longer be able to provide the mutual assistance they might require to sustain liberal domestic orders in the face of mounting economic crises.

These dangers come from two directions: military and economic. Their combination is particularly threatening. One is the continuing asymmetry of defense, with the United States (in relation to its GNP) bearing an undue portion of the common burden. Yet independent and more substantial European and Japanese defense establishments pose problems for liberal cooperation. Military dependence on the United States has been one of the additional bonds helpful in transforming a liberal peace into a liberal alliance. Removing it, without creating a multilaterally directed and funded organization among the liberal industrial democracies, threatens to loosen an important bond. Economic instabilities could make this absence of a multilateral security bond particularly dangerous by escalating differences into hostility. If domestic economic collapses on the pattern of the global propagation of depressions in the 1930s were to reoccur, the domestic political foundations of liberalism could fall. Or, if international economic rivalry were to continue to increase, then consequent attempts to weaken economic interdependence (establishing closed trade and currency blocs) would break an important source of liberal accom-

---

36. Charles Kindleberger, *The World in Depression* (Berkeley: University of California Press, 1973); Robert Gilpin, *U.S. Power and the Multinational Corporation* (New York: Basic Books, 1975); and Fred Hirsch and Michael Doyle, "Politicization in the World Economy" in Hirsch, Doyle and Edward Morse, *Alternatives to Monetary Disorder* (New York: Council on Foreign Relations/McGraw-Hill, 1977).

modation.[37] These dangers would become more significant if independent and substantial military forces were established. If liberal assumptions of the need to cooperate and to accommodate disappear, countries might fall prey to a corrosive rivalry that destroys the pacific union.

Yet liberals may have escaped from the single, greatest, traditional danger of international change—the transition between hegemonic leaders. When one great power begins to lose its preeminence and to slip into mere equality, a warlike resolution of the international pecking order becomes exceptionally likely. New power challenges old prestige, excessive commitments face new demands; so Sparta felt compelled to attack Athens, France warred Spain, England and Holland fought with France (and with each other), and Germany and England struggled for the mastery of Europe in World War I. But here liberals may again be an exception, for despite the fact that the United States constituted Britains greatest challenger along all the dimensions most central to the British maritime hegemony, Britain and the United States accommodated their differences.[38] After the defeat of Germany, Britain eventually, though not without regret, accepted its replacement by the United States as the commercial and maritime hegemon of the liberal world. The promise of a peaceable transition thus may be one of the factors helping to moderate economic and political rivalries among Europe, Japan, and the United States.

Consequently, the quarrels with liberal allies that bedeviled the Carter and Reagan Administrations should not be attributed solely to the personal weaknesses of the two presidents or their secretaries of state. Neither should they be attributed to simple failures of administrative coordination or to the idiosyncracies of American allies. These are the normal workings of a liberal alliance of independent republics. There is no indication that they involve a dissolution of the pacific union; but there is every indication that, following the decline in American preponderance, liberal states will be able to do little

---

37. Robert Gilpin, "Three Models of the Future," *International Organization* Vol. 29, No. 1 (Winter 1975).

38. George Liska identifies this peaceful, hegemonic transition as exceptional in *Quest for Equilibrium: America and the Balance of Power on Land and Sea* (Baltimore, Md: The Johns Hopkins University Press, 1977), chap. 4, p. 75. Wilson's speeches, including his "War Message," suggest the importance of ideological factors in explaining this transition: "Neutrality is no longer feasible or desirable where the peace of the world is involved and the freedom of its peoples, and the menace to that peace and freedom lies in the *existence* [emphasis supplied] of autocratic governments backed by organized force which is controlled wholly by their will, not by the will of their people." This quotation is from *The Messages and Papers of Woodrow Wilson*, p. 378. Ross Gregory in *The Origins of American Intervention in the First World War* (New York: Norton, 1971) offers an interpretation along these lines, combining commercial, financial, strategic, and ideological factors in his account of the policy which brought the United States onto a collision course with Germany.

to reestablish the union should the international economic interdependence that binds them dissolve and should the domestic, liberal foundations of its central members collapse. But should these republican foundations and commercial sources of interdependence remain firm, then the promise of liberal legacies among liberal regimes is a continuing peace, even when the leadership of the liberal world changes hands.

When in *The Snows of Kilimanjaro*, Julian (F. Scott Fitzgerald) tells his friend (Hemingway), "The very rich are different from you and me," his friend replies, "Yes, they have more money." But the liberals are fundamentally different. It is not just, as the Realists might argue, that they have more or less resources, better or worse morale. Their constitutional structure makes them—realistically—different. They have established peace among themselves. But the very features which make their relations to fellow liberals differ from the state of war that all other states inhabit also make their relations with nonliberals differ from the prudent, strategic calculation that Realists hope will inform the foreign policies of states in an insecure world. These failings are the subject of the second part of this article.

VI

Even though liberalism has achieved striking success in creating a zone of peace and, with leadership, a zone of cooperation among states similarly liberal in character, liberalism has been equally striking as a failure in guiding foreign policy outside the liberal world. In these foreign relations, liberalism leads to three confusing failings: the first two are what Hume called "imprudent vehemence" and, conversely, a "careless and supine complaisance";[39] the third is

---

39. David Hume, "Of the Balance of Power" in *Essays: Moral, Political, and Literary* (1741–1742) (Oxford University Press, 1963), pp. 346–47. With "imprudent vehemence," Hume referred to the English reluctance to negotiate an early peace with France and the total scale of the effort devoted to prosecuting that war, which together were responsible for over half the length of the fighting and an enormous war debt. With "complaisance," he referred to political exhaustion and isolationism. Hume, of course, was not describing fully liberal republics as defined here; but the characteristics he describes, do seem to reflect some of the liberal republican features of the English eighteenth century constitution (the influence of both popular opinion and a representative [even if severely limited] legislature). He contrasts these effects to the "prudent politics" that should govern the balance of power and to the special but different failings characteristic of "enormous monarchies," which are prone to strategic overextension, bureaucratic, and ministerial decay in court intrigue, praetorian rebellion (pp. 347–48). These failings are different from those of more, even if not fully, republican regimes. Indeed just as the eighteenth century English failings illuminate aspects of contemporary liberal diplomacy, the failings of his universal monarchy seem to be reflected in some aspects of the contemporary authoritarian and totalitarian predicament.

the political uncertainty that is introduced by the moral ambiguity of the liberal principles which govern the international distribution of property.

Imprudent vehemence is the most familiar failing. In relations with powerful states of a nonliberal character, liberal policy has been characterized by repeated failures of diplomacy. It has often raised conflicts of interest into crusades; it has delayed in taking full advantage of rivalries within nonliberal alliances; it has failed to negotiate stable mutual accommodations of interest. In relations with weak states of a nonliberal character, liberal policy has succumbed to imperial interventions that it has been unable to sustain or to profit from. Its interventions, designed to create liberal societies by promoting the economic development and political stability of nonliberal societies, have frequently failed to achieve their objects. Confusion, drift, costly crusades, spasmodic imperialism are the contrasting record of liberal foreign policy *outside* the liberal world. A failure to negotiate with the powerful and a failure to create stable clients among the weak are its legacies.[40] Why?

These failures mainly flow from two sources. First, outside the pacific union, liberal regimes, like all other states, are caught in the international state of war Hobbes and the Realists describe. Conflict and wars are a natural outcome of struggles for resources, prestige, and security among independent states; confusion is an unsurprising accompaniment in a state of war without reliable law or organization.

Second, these failures are also the natural complement of liberalism's success as an intellectual guide to foreign policy among liberal states. *The very constitutional restraint, shared commercial interests, and international respect for individual rights that promote peace among liberal societies can exacerbate conflicts in relations between liberal and non-liberal societies.*

If the legitimacy of state action rests on the fact that it respects and effectively represents morally autonomous individuals, then states that coerce their citi-

---

40. A careful statistical analysis that has just appeared, R. J. Rummel, "Libertarianism and International Violence" *Journal of Conflict Resolution* Vol. 27, No. 1 (March 1983), empirically demonstrates that "libertarian" states engaged neither in war nor in other forms of conflict with each other in the period 1946–1980. (But his definition of libertarian appears to be more restrictive than my definition of liberal states.) He also finds that between 1946 and 1980 libertarian states were less likely to engage in any form of conflict than were states of any other domestic political regime. The extensive history of liberal imperialism and the liberal role in conflicts and wars between liberal and nonliberal states for the longer period from the 1790s that I survey lead me to conclusions which differ from his second point. Both George Kennan's *American Diplomacy* (New York: Mentor, 1951) and Hans Morgenthau's *Politics Among Nations* (New York: Alfred A. Knopf, Inc., 1973), esp. p. 147, are cogent criticisms of the impact of American liberalism. Different but related analyses of the impact of liberal principles and institutions on U.S. foreign policy are made by Stanley Hoffmann, *Gulliver's Troubles* (New York: McGraw-Hill, 1968), esp. pp. 114–43.

zens or foreign residents lack moral legitimacy. Even Kant regarded the attitude of "primitive peoples" attached to a lawless liberty as "raw, uncivilized, and an animalic degradation of humanity."[41] When states reject the cosmopolitan law of access (a rejection that authoritarian or communist states, whether weak or powerful, can often find advantageous and, indeed, necessary for their security), Kant declares that they violate natural law:

The inhospitable ways of coastal regions, such as the Barbary Coast, where they rob ships in the adjoining seas or make stranded seamen into slaves, is contrary to natural law, as are the similarly inhospitable ways of the deserts and their Bedouins, who look upon the approach of a foreigner as giving them a right to plunder him.[42]

Nevertheless, Kant rejects conquest or imperial intervention as an equal wrong. The practice of liberal states, which in many cases only applies liberal principles in part, has not been so forbearing.

According to liberal practice, some nonliberal states, such as the United States' communist rivals, do not acquire the right to be free from foreign intervention, nor are they assumed to respect the political independence and territorial integrity of other states. Instead conflicts of interest become interpreted as steps in a campaign of aggression against the liberal state. Of course, powerful authoritarian or totalitarian states, such as Nazi Germany or the Soviet Union, sometimes wage direct or indirect campaigns of aggression against liberal regimes. And totalitarian diplomacy is clouded by the pervasive secrecy these societies establish. But part of the atmosphere of suspicion can be attributed to the perception by liberal states that nonliberal states are in a permanent state of aggression against their own people. Referring to fascist states, Cordell Hull concluded, "their very nature requires them to be aggressive."[43] Efforts by nonliberal states at accommodation thus become snares to trap the unwary. When the Soviets refuse to negotiate, they are plotting a world takeover. When they seek to negotiate, they are plotting even more insidiously. This extreme lack of public respect or trust is one of the major features that distinguishes relations between liberal and nonliberal societies from relations among liberal societies.

---

41. Kant, "Perpetual Peace," in Friedrich, ed. p. 442.
42. Ibid., p. 446.
43. Cordell Hull, Radio Address, 9 April 1944, excerpted in Norman Graebner, *Cold War Diplomacy* (New York: Van Nostrand, 1977), p. 172.

At the same time, lack of public trust constrains social and economic exchanges. Commercial interdependence can produce conflict as well as welfare when a society becomes dependent on foreign actions it cannot control. Among liberal societies the extent and variety of commercial exchanges guarantee that a single conflict of interest will not shape an entire relationship. But between liberal and nonliberal societies, these exchanges, because they are limited for security considerations, do not provide a counterweight to interstate political tension nor do they offer the variety that offsets the chance that a single conflict of interest will define an entire relationship.

Furthermore, the institutional heritage of liberal regimes—representation and division of powers—opens avenues for special interests to shape policy in ways contrary to prudent diplomacy. As George Kennan has noted, this form of government "goes far to rule out the privacy, the flexibility, and the promptness and incisiveness of decision and action, which have marked the great imperial powers of the past and which are generally necessary to the conduct of an effective world policy by the rulers of a great state."[44] And these features may be compounded by the incentives for exaggerated claims that competitive electoral politics tend to encourage. The loss of these attributes is not harmful to interliberal relations (in fact, their absence is more likely to be beneficial), but the ills of ready access to foreign policy created by representation and the division of power multiply when a lack of trust is combined with the limited economic and social connection of extra-liberal relations. Together they promote an atmosphere of tension and a lobby for discord that can play havoc with both strategic choice and moral intent.

These three traits affect liberal relations both with powerful nonliberal states and with weak nonliberal societies, though in differing ways.

In relations with *powerful* nonliberal states the consequences of these three features have been missed opportunities to pursue the negotiation of arms reduction and arms control when it has been in the mutual strategic interest and the failure to construct wider schemes of accommodation that are needed to supplement arms control. Prior to the outbreak of World War I, this is the charge that Lord Sanderson levelled against Sir Eyre Crowe in Sanderson's response to Crowe's famous memorandum on the state of British relations with Germany.[45] Sanderson pointed out that Crowe interpreted German demands

---

44. George F. Kennan, *A Cloud of Danger* (Boston: Little, Brown & Co., 1977), p. 4.
45. Memoranda by Mr. Eyre Crowe, 1 January 1907, and by Lord Sanderson, 25 February 1907, in G. P. Gooch et al., eds., *British Documents on the Origins of the War, 1898–1914*, 3 (London: His Majesty's Stationery Office [HMSO], 1928), pp. 397–431.

to participate in the settlement of international disputes and to have a "place in the sun" (colonies), of a size not too dissimilar to that enjoyed by the other great powers, as evidence of a fundamental aggressiveness driving toward world domination. Crowe may well have perceived an essential feature of Wilhelmine Germany, and Sanderson's attempt to place Germany in the context of other rising powers (bumptious but not aggressively pursuing world domination) may have been naive. But the interesting thing to note is less the conclusions reached than Crowe's chain of argument and evidence. He rejects continued accommodation (appeasement) with Germany not because he shows that Germany was more bumptious than France and not because he shows that Germany had greater potential as a world hegemon than the United States, which he does not even consider in this connection. Instead he is (legitimately) perplexed by the real uncertainty of German foreign policy and by its "erratic, domineering, and often frankly aggressive spirit" which accords with the well-known personal characteristics of "the present ruler of Germany."

Similar evidence of fundamental suspicion appears to characterize U.S. diplomacy toward the Soviet Union. In a fascinating memorandum to President Wilson written in 1919, Herbert Hoover (then one of Wilson's advisers), recommended that the President speak out against the danger of "world domination" the "Bolsheviki"—a "tyranny that is the negation of democracy"—posed to free peoples. Rejecting military intervention as excessively costly and likely to "make us a party in reestablishing the reactionary classes in their economic domination over the lower classes," he proposed a "relief program" designed to undercut some of the popular appeal the Bolsheviks were garnering both in the Soviet Union and abroad. Although acknowledging that the evidence was not yet clear, he concluded: "If the militant features of Bolshevism were drawn in colors with their true parallel with Prussianism as an attempt at world domination that we do not stand for, it would check the fears that today haunt all men's minds." (The actual U.S. intervention in the Soviet Union was limited to supporting anti-Bolshevik Czechoslovak soldiers in Siberia and to protecting military supplies in Murmansk from German seizure.)[46]

---

46. Herbert Hoover to President Wilson, 28 March 1919, excerpted in *Major Problems in American Foreign Policy*, ed. Thomas Paterson (Lexington, MA: D.C. Heath and Co., 1978), Vol. 2, p. 95.

Fear of Bolshevism may have been one of the factors precluding a liberal alliance with the Soviet Union in 1938 against Nazi aggression. But the connection liberals draw between domestic tyranny and foreign aggression may also operate in reverse. When the Nazi threat to the survival of liberal states did require a liberal alliance with the Soviet Union, Stalin became for a short period the liberal press's "Uncle Joe."

In the postwar period, and particularly following the Korean War, U.S. diplomacy equated the "international Communist movement" (all communist states and parties) with "Communist imperialism" and with a domestic tyranny in the U.S.S.R. that required a cold war contest and international subversion as means of legitimizing its own police state. John Foster Dulles most clearly expressed this conviction, together with his own commitment to a strategy of "liberation," when he declared: ". . . we shall never have a secure peace or a happy world so long as Soviet communism dominates one third of all the peoples that there are, and is in the process of trying at least to extend its rule to many others."[47]

Liberalism has also encouraged a tendency to misread communist threats in the Third World. Since communism is seen as inherently aggressive, Soviet military aid "destabilizes" parts of Africa in Angola and the Horn; the West protects allies. Thus the People's Republic of China was a "Soviet Manchukuo" while Diem was the "Winston Churchill of Asia." Both the actual (and unstable) dependence of these regimes on their respective superpowers and anticolonialism, the dominant force of the region, were discounted.

Most significantly, opportunities for splitting the Communist bloc along cleavages of strategic national interest were delayed. Burdened with the war in Vietnam, the United States took ten years to appreciate and exploit the strategic opportunity of the Sino-Soviet split. Even the signal strategic, "offensive" success of the early cold war, the defection of Yugoslavia from the Soviet bloc, did not receive the wholehearted welcome that a strategic assessment of its important would have warranted.[48] Both relationships, with Yugoslavia and

---

47. U.S. Senate, *Hearings Before the Committee on Foreign Relations on the Nomination of John Foster Dulles, Secretary of State Designate*, 15 January 1953, 83rd Congress, 1st Session (Washington, D.C.: United States Government Printing Office [USGPO], 1953), pp. 5–6.

48. Thirty-three divisions, the withdrawal of the Soviet bloc from the Mediterranean, political disarray in the Communist movement: these advantages called out for a quick and friendly response. An effective U.S. ambassador in place to present Tito's position to Washington, the public character of the expulsion from the Cominform (June 1948), and a presidential administration in the full flush of creative statesmanship (and an electoral victory) also contributed to Truman's decision to rescue Yugoslavia from the Soviet embargo by providing trade and loans (1949). Nonetheless (according to Yugoslav sources), this crisis was also judged to be an appropriate moment to put pressure on Yugoslavia to resolve the questions of Trieste and Carinthia, to cut its support for the guerrillas in Greece, *and* to repay prewar (prerevolutionary) Yugoslav debts compensating the property owners of nationalized mines and land. Nor did Yugoslavia's strategic significance exempt it from inclusion among the countries condemned as "Captive Nations" (1959) or secure most-favored-nation trade status in the 1962 Trade Expansion Act. Ideological anticommunism and the porousness of the American political system to lobbies combined (according to Kennan, ambassador to Yugoslavia at that time) to add these inconvenient burdens to a crucial strategic relationship. (John C. Campbell, *Tito's Separate Road* [New York: Council on Foreign

China, become subject to alternating, largely ideologically derived, moods: visions of exceptionalism (they were "less ruthless," more organic to the indigenous, traditional culture) sparred with bouts of liberal soul-searching ("we cannot associate ourselves with a totalitarian state"). And these unresolved tensions continue to affect the strategic relationship with both communist independents.

A purely Realist focus on the balance of power would lead one to expect the hostility between the two superpowers, the United States and the Soviet Union, that emerged preeminent after the defeats of Nazi-Germany and Japan. Furthermore, a bipolar rivalry raises perceptions of zero-sum conflict (what one gains the other must lose) and consequently a tendency toward overreaction. And liberalism is just one of many ideologies prone to ideological crusades and domestic "witch hunts."[49] But, Realists have no reason to anticipate the hesitation of the United States in exploiting divisions in the Communist bloc and in forming strategic relationships with the USSR's communist rivals. U.S. cold war policy cannot be explained without reference to U.S. liberalism. Liberalism creates both the hostility to communism, not just to Soviet power, and the crusading ideological bent of policy. Liberals do not merely distrust what they do; we dislike what they are—public violators of human rights. And to this view, laissez faire liberals contribute antisocialism and social democratic liberals add a campaign for democracy.

One would think this confused record of policy would have produced a disaster in the East-West balance of forces. Squandered opportunities to negotiate East-West balances of interest and erratic policy should have alienated the United States' allies and dissipated its strategic resources. But other factors mitigated liberal confusion and crusades. Communist nuclear weapons and state power dictated prudence, and mutual survival has called for detente. The liberal alliance was deeply rooted in the pacific union and almost impervious

Relations/Harper and Row, 1967], pp. 18–27; Suctozar Vukmanovic-Tempo, in Vladimir Dedijer, *The Battle Stalin Lost* [New York: Viking, 1970], p. 268; George F. Kenna, *Memoirs, 1950–1963* [Boston: Little, Brown & Co., 1972], chap. 12.)
49. Like the *original* crusades (an earlier instance of transcendental foreign policy), the first were expeditions that created strategic littorals (Lithuania, Estonia, Latvia, and Poland in 1918 to 1920 for Antioch and Jerusalem): the second and third (1947 to 1949 for the crusades of the monarchs) new logistical reinforcements, or anticommunism in Europe; the fourth (the crossing of the 38th Parallel for Constantinople) was a strategic diversion. A McCarthyite (Albigensian) crusade at home followed. The fifth and sixth crusades extended the range of the conflict to the Third World (for Damietta); and later crusades were excuses for reequipping armies.

to occasional crises over alliance policy toward the Soviet Union. And the productivity of market economies provided resources that could be mobilized to sustain the strategic position of the liberal West despite a confusion of aims and strategy.

Dilemmas and disasters are also associated with liberal foreign policy toward *weak*, nonliberal states; no greater spirit of accommodation or tolerance for noninterventionist sovereignties informs liberal policy toward the many weak, nonliberal states in the Third World. Indeed, liberalism's record in the Third World is in many respects worse than in East-West relations, for here power is added to confusion. This problem affects both conservative liberals and welfare liberals, but the two can be distinguished by differing styles of intervention.[50]

Both liberal strains appear congenitally confused in analyzing and in prescribing for situations of intervention. The liberal dictum in favor of nonintervention does not hold. Respecting a nonliberal state's state rights to noninterference requires ignoring the violations of rights they inflict on their own populations. Addressing the rights of individuals in the Third World requires ignoring the rights of states to be free of foreign intervention. Bouts of one attitude replace bouts of the other; but since the legitimacy of the nonliberal state is discounted, the dominant tendency leads toward interventionism.

A liberal imperialism that promotes liberalism neither abroad nor at home was one result of this dilemma. Protecting "native rights" from "native" oppressors, and protecting universal rights of property and settlement from local transgressions, introduced especially liberal motives for imperial rule. Kant's right of universal hospitality justifies nothing more than the right to visit and exchange. Other liberals have been prepared to justify much more. Some argue that there is a universal right of settlement under which those who cannot earn a living in their own countries have a right to force others—particularly nomads and tribal hunters—to cede parts of their territory for more intensive settlement. J. S. Mill justifies even more coercive treatment of what he calls the "barbarous nations." They do not have the rights of civilized nations, "except a right to such treatment as may, at the earliest possible period, fit them for becoming one." He justifies this imperial education for "barbarous" nations,

---

50. See Robert A. Packenham, *Liberal America and the Third World* (Princeton: Princeton University Press, 1973), for an interesting analysis of the impact of liberal ideology on American foreign and policy, esp. chaps. 3 and pp. 313–23.

while requiring nonintervention among "civilized" nations, because the former are not capable of reciprocating in the practice of liberal rights, and reciprocity is the foundation of liberal morality.[51]

Ending the slave trade destabilized nineteenth-century West African oligarchies, yet encouraging "legitimate trade" required protecting the property of European merchants; declaring the illegitimacy of suttee or of domestic slavery also attacked local cultural traditions that had sustained the stability of indigenous political authority. Europeans settling in sparsely populated areas destroyed the livelihood of tribes that relied on hunting. The tribes, quite defensively, retaliated in force; the settlers called for imperial protection.[52] The protection of cosmopolitan liberal rights thus bred a demand for imperial rule that violated the equality of American Indians, Africans, and Asians. In practice, once the exigencies of ruling an empire came into play, liberal imperialism resulted in the oppression of "native" liberals seeking self-determination in order to maintain imperial security: to avoid local chaos and the intervention of another imperial power attempting to take advantage of local disaffection.

Thus nineteenth-century liberals, such as Gladstone, pondered whether Egypt's protonationalist Arabi rebellion (1881–82) was truly liberal nationalist (they discovered it was not) before intervening to protect strategic lifelines to

---

51. See Hobbes, *Leviathan*, Pt II, chap. 30, and Pt I, chap. 15. This right is discussed in Michael Walzer, *Spheres of Justice* (New York: Basic Books, 1983), p. 46. Mill's remarks on colonialism are in "A Few Words on Nonintervention," pp. 377–79, and in "Civilization" he distinguishes "civilized" nations from "barbarous" nations, not on racial or biological grounds but on the basis of what our contemporary scholars now call socioeconomic modernization or development. Mill declared, "Their minds are not capable of so great an effort [as reciprocity], nor their will sufficiently under the influence of distant motives." Both essays are in J. S. Mill, *Essays on Literature and Society*, ed. with an introduction by J. B. Schneewind (New York: Collier, 1965). Perhaps the most interesting memorial to liberal imperialism is the inscription, written by Macaulay, on the base of Lord William Bentinck's statue in Calcutta: "He abolished cruel rites; he effaced humiliating distinctions; he gave liberty to the expression of public opinion; his constant study was to elevate the intellectual and moral character of the natives committed to his charge" (cf. Mill). It is excerpted in Earl Cromer, *Ancient and Modern Imperialism* (London: Longmans, 1910), p. 67.

52. Alexis de Tocqueville, *Democracy in America*, vol. I (New York: Vintage, 1945), p. 351. De Tocqueville describes how European settlement destroys the game; the absence of game reduces the Indians to starvation. Both then exercise their rights to self-defense. But the colonists are able to call in the power of the imperial government. Palmerston once declared that he would never employ force to promote purely private interests—commercial or settlement. He also declared that he would faithfully protect the lives and liberty of English subjects. In circumstances such as those de Tocqueville described, Palmerston's distinctions were meaningless. See Kenneth Bourne, *Palmerston: The Early Years* (New York: Macmillan, 1982), pp. 624–26. Other colonial settlements and their dependence on imperial expansion are examined in Ronald Robinson, "Non-European Foundations of Imperialism," in Roger Owen and Bob Sutcliffe, eds., *Studies in the Theory of Imperialism* (London: Longmans, 1972).

India, commerce, and investment.[53] Britain's Liberal Party faced similar dilemmas in managing Ireland; they erratically oscillated between coercion and reform. These foreign disasters contributed to the downfall of the Liberal Party as Parliament in 1886 chose to be ruled by a more aristocratic and stable Conservative Party. The Conservatives did pursue a steadier course of consistent coercion in Ireland and Egypt, yet in their effort to maintain a paramountcy in southern Africa they too were swept away in a campaign to protect the civic and property rights of British settlers (*uitlanders*) in the Boer's theocratic republics. These dilemmas of liberal imperialism are also reflected in U.S. imperialism in the Caribbean where, for example, following the Spanish-American War of 1898, Article III of the Platt Amendment gave the United States the "right to intervene for the preservation of Cuban independence, the maintenance of a government adequate for the protection of life, property, and individual liberty. . . ."[54]

The record of liberalism in the nonliberal world is not solely a catalogue of disasters. The North American West and the settlement colonies—Australia and New Zealand—represent a successful transplant of liberal institutions, albeit in a temperate, underpopulated, and then depopulated environment and at the cost of Indian and aborigine rights. Similarly, the twentieth-century expansion of liberalism into less powerful nonliberal areas has also had some striking successes. The forcible liberalization of Germany and Japan following World War II and the long covert financing of liberal parties in Italy are the

---

53. Gladstone had proclaimed his support for the equal rights of all nations in his Midlothian Speeches. Wilfrid Scawen Blunt served as a secret agent in Egypt keeping Gladstone informed of the political character of Arabi's movement. The liberal dilemma—were they intervening against genuine nationalism or a military adventurer (Arabi)—was best expressed in Joseph Chamberlain's memorandum to the Cabinet, 21 June 1882, excerpted in J. L. Garvin and J. Amery, *Life of Joseph Chamberlain* (London: Macmillan & Co., 1935) 1, p. 448. And see Peter Mansfield, *The British in Egypt* (New York: Holt, Rinehart and Winston, 1971), chaps. 2–3; Ronald Hyam, *Britain's Imperial Century: 1815–1914* (London: Batsford, 1976), chap. 8; and Robert Tignor, *Modernization and British Colonial Rule in Egypt* (Princeton: Princeton University Press, 1966).

54. On Ireland and its relation to British parties, Conor Cruise O'Brien, *Parnell and His Party, 1880–1890* (Oxford: Clarendon Press, 1964); on South Africa, G.H.L. LeMay, *British Supremacy in South Africa 1899–1907* (London: Oxford University Press, 1965). A good representative of liberal attitudes on force and intervention is the following comment by Vice Admiral Humphrey Smith:

"I don't think we thought much about war with a big W.. We looked on the Navy more as a World Police Force than as a war-like institution. We considered that our job was to safeguard law and order throughout the world—safeguard civilization, put out fires on shore, and act as guide, philosopher, and friend to the merchant ships of all nations." Vice Admiral Humphrey Smith, *A Yellow Admiral Remembers* (London, 1932), p. 54 in Donald C. Gordon, *The Dominion Partnership in Imperial Defence: 1870–1914* (Baltimore, Md.: The Johns Hopkins University Press, 1965), p. 47.

The Platt Amendment is excerpted in *Major Problems in American Foreign Policy*, ed. Paterson, Vol. 1, p. 328.

more significant instances of successful transplant. Covert financing of liberalism in Chile and occasional diplomatic démarches to nudge aside military threats to noncommunist democratic parties (as in Peru in 1962, South Korea in 1963, and the Dominican Republic in 1962[55] and again in 1978) illustrate policies which, though less successful, were directed toward liberal goals. These particular postwar liberal successes also are the product of special circumstances: the existence of a potential liberal majority, temporarily suppressed, which could be reestablished by outside aid or unusually weak oligarchic, military, or communist opponents.[56]

Elsewhere in the postwar period, when the United States sought to protect liberals in the Third World from the "communist threat," the consequences of liberal foreign policy on the nonliberal society often became far removed from the promotion of individual rights. Intervening against "armed minorities" and "enemies of free enterprise" meant intervening for other armed minorities, some sustaining and sustained by oligarchies, others resting on little more than U.S. foreign aid and troops. Indigenous liberals simply had too narrow a base of domestic support.

To the conservative liberals, the alternatives are starkly cast: Third World authoritarians with allegiance to the liberal, capitalist West or "Communists" subject to the totalitarian East (or leftist nationalists who even if elected are but a slippery stepping stone to totalitarianism).[57] Conservative liberals are prepared to support the allied authoritarians. The communists attack property in addition to liberty, thereby provoking conservative liberals to covert or overt intervention, or "dollar-diplomacy" imperialism. The interventions against Mossadegh in Iran, Arbenz in Guatemala, Allende in Chile, and against the Sandinistas in Nicaragua appear to fall into this pattern.[58]

---

55. During the Alliance for Progress era in Latin America, the Kennedy Administration supported Juan Bosch in the Dominican Republic in 1962. See also William P. Bundy, "Dictatorships and American Foreign Policy," *Foreign Affairs* Vol. 54, No. 1 (October 1975).

56. See Samuel Huntington, "Human Rights and American Power," *Commentary*, September 1981, and George Quester, "Consensus Lost," *Foreign Policy* Vol. 40 (Fall 1980), for argument and examples of the successful export of liberal institutions in the postwar period.

57. Jeane Kirkpatrick, "Dictatorships and Double Standards," pp. 34–45. In 1851 the liberal French historian Guizot made a similar argument in a letter to Gladstone urging that Gladstone appreciate hat the despotic government of Naples was the best guarantor of liberal law and order then available. Reform, in Guizot's view, meant the unleashing of revolutionary violence. (Philip Magnus, *Gladstone* [New York: Dutton, 1964], p. 100.)

58. Richard Barnet, *Intervention and Revolution: The United States in the Third World* (New York: Meridian, 1968), chap. 10; and on Nicaragua, see *The New York Times*, 11 March 1982, for a description of the training, direction, and funding ($20 million) of anti-Sandinista guerrillas by the United States.

To the social welfare liberals, the choice is never so clear. Aware of the need to intervene to democratize the distribution of social power and resources, they tend to have more sympathy for social reform. This can produce on the part of "radical" welfare liberals a more tolerant policy toward the attempts by reforming autocracies to redress inegalitarian distributions of property in the Third World. This more complicated welfare-liberal assessment can itself be a recipe for more extensive intervention. The large number of conservative oligarchs of military bureaucracies with whom the conservative liberal is well at home are not so congenial to the social welfare liberal; yet the communists are still seen as enemies of liberty. They justify more extensive intervention first to discover, then to sustain, Third World social democracy in a political environment that is either barely participatory or highly polarized. Thus Arthur Schlesinger recalls President Kennedy musing shortly after the assassination of Trujillo (former dictator of the Dominican Republic), "There are three possibilities in descending order of preference, a decent democratic regime, a continuation of the Trujillo regime [by his followers] or a Castro regime. We ought to aim at the first, but we can't really renounce the second until we are sure we can avoid the third." Another instance of this approach was President Carter's support for the land reforms in El Salvador, which was explained by one U.S. official in the following analogy: "There is no one more conservative than a small farmer. We're going to be breeding capitalists like rabbits."[59]

Thus liberal policy toward the Third World state often fails to promote individual rights. Its consequences on liberalism at home may also be harmful. As Hobson pointed out in his study of imperialism, imperial security and imperial wars may enhance in the short run the position of nonliberal domestic forces, such as the military, and introduce in the longer run issues into the political debate, such as security, that raise the role of nonliberal coalitions of conservative oligarchy or technocracy.[60]

One might account for many of these liberal interventions in the Third World by geopolitical competition, the Realists' calculus of the balance of power, or by the desire to promote the national economic interests of the United States. The attempt to avoid Third World countries coming under the hegemony of the USSR or to preserve essential sources of raw materials are alternative

---

59. Arthur Schlesinger, *A Thousand Days* (Boston, MA: Houghton Mifflin, 1965), p. 769, and quoted in Barnet, *Intervention and Revolution*, p. 158. And for the U.S. official's comment on the Salvadoran land reform, see L. Simon and J. Stephen, *El Salvador Land Reform 1980–1981* (Boston, MA: Oxfam-America, 1981), p. 38. See Zolberg, *One Party Government in the Ivory Coast.*
60. John Hobson, *Imperialism: A Study* (Ann Arbor: University of Michigan Press, 1965), pp. 145–47.

interpretations of much of the policy attributed to liberalism which on their face are plausible. Yet these interventions are publicly justified on the first instance as attempts to preserve a "way of life": to defend freedom and private enterprise. The threat has been defined as "Communism," not just "Sovietism" or "economic nationalism." Expectations of being punished electorally, should they abandon groups they had billed as democratic allies contributed to the reluctance of U.S. politicians to withdraw from Vietnam. The consistent policy of seeking a legitimating election, however unpromising the circumstances for it (as in Vietnam), reflects the same liberal source.[61] Moreover, few communist or socialist Third World states actually do seek to cordon off their markets or raw materials from the liberal world economy. And the radical movements, first and foremost anticolonialist, against which the United States has intervened, have not been simple proxies for the Soviet Union.

Furthermore, by geopolitical considerations alone, the large interventions may have been counterproductive. The interventions have confirmed or enhanced the coherence of the Soviet bloc as the Chinese Civil War (U.S. logistical support for the KMT) and the drive to the Yalu of the Korean War, the Vietnam War, and the Angolan War served to increase the dependence of the PRC, Vietnam, and Angola on the USSR. In each of these interventions, U.S. geopolitical interests might have been served best by supporting the communist side and encouraging its separation from the Soviet bloc. But because the United States failed to distinguish communism from Soviet power, this separation was impossible. Had the Soviet Union been a capitalist authoritarian superpower, geopolitical logic also would have led the United States to intervene against the expansion of its bloc.[62] But the United States intervenes against the expansion of communism regardless of geopolitical considerations just as it (along with Britain) did against Soviet communism following World War I.[63]

---

61. Leslie Gelb and Richard Betts, *The Irony of Vietnam* (Washington, D.C.: Brookings, 1979). Frances Fitzgerald, *Fire in the Lake* (New York: Vintage/Random House, 1972), chap. 11, portrays the elections of 1967 in this way. Allan Goodman, *Politics in War* (Cambridge, Mass.: Harvard University Press, 1973), disagrees, but does find that the elections of 1971 fit this description.
62. Robert W. Tucker, *The Radical Left and American Foreign Policy* (Baltimore, Md: The Johns Hopkins University Press, 1971).
63. Although geopolitical anti-Sovietism and the effects of the two liberalisms complemented each other throughout the postwar period and together usually led to intervention; less-frequently, geopolitics and liberalism worked together to restrain intervention. Once recognized, the defection of *established* Communist regimes such as Yugoslavia and China was welcomed, though neither defection was fully exploited. Both the geopolitical interest and the prospects of increased trade or development were served by Yugoslav and Chinese separation from the Soviet bloc. In other instances this particular complementary restraint may have had less welcome effects. The most serious harm to American national economic interests inflicted in the postwar period was the OPEC

Is the United States anticommunist because communism is the ideology adopted by the Soviet Union; or are liberals anti-Soviet because the Soviet Union is the headquarters of communism? In encouraging intervention, the imprudent vehemences of geopolitics and the liberalisms cannot be clearly separated in a bipolar contest between a communist and a liberal superpower. Nonetheless, liberalism does appear to exacerbate intervention against weak nonliberals and hostility against powerful nonliberal societies.

VII

A second manifestation of international liberalism outside the pacific union lies in a reaction to the excesses of interventionism. A mood of frustrated withdrawal—"a careless and supine complaisance"—affects policy toward strategically and economically important countries. Just as interventionism seems to be the typical failing of the liberal great power, so complaisance characterizes declined or not quite risen liberal states.[64] Representative legislatures may become reluctant to fund the military establishment needed to play a geopolitical role. Rational incentives for "free riding" on the extended defense commitments of the leader of the liberal alliance also induce this form of complaisance. During much of the nineteenth century, the United States informally relied upon the British fleet for many of its security needs. Today, the Europeans and the Japanese, according to some American strategic analysts, fail to bear their "fair" share of alliance burdens.

A different form of complaisance is charged by Realists who perceive ideologically based policies as self-indulgent. Oligarchic or authoritarian allies in the Third World do not find consistent support in a liberal policy that stresses human rights. They claim that the security needs of these states are neglected, that they fail to obtain military aid or more direct support when they need it (the Shah's Iran, Humberto Romero's El Salvador, Somoza's Nicaragua, and South Africa). Equally disturbing from a Realist point of view, communist regimes are shunned even when a detente with them could further United

---

embargo and price revolution of 1973–74. Geopolitical factors dictated no intervention because the Iranian "regional policeman" needed funds to purchase its arms. Conservative liberals rightly perceived no substantial attack on U.S. oil corporations. Welfare liberals had come to believe in improving the terms of trade for Third World exports, and oil appeared a good place to begin. None of these sources of restraint appear in quite the same light in 1982.

64. Robert Gilpin, *War and Change in World Politics* (New York: Cambridge University Press, 1981), discusses the sources of change in the foreign policies of rising and declining hegemonies.

States strategic interests (Cuba, Angola). Welfare liberals particularly shun the first group, while laissez faire liberals balk at close dealings with the second. In both cases the Realists note that our economic interests or strategic interests are slighted.[65]

VIII

Lastly, both variants of liberalism raise dilemmas in North-South economic relations and particularly in the international distribution of property or income. Not expecting to have to resolve whether freedom of enterprise should extend to doing business with the followers of Marx and Lenin, conservative, laissez faire liberals have become incensed over the attractiveness to American and European corporations of profits made in the communist world. And the commitment of liberals—both social welfare and laissez faire liberals—to the efficiency and the political advantages of international free trade is severely tested by the inflow of low-cost imports from newly industrializing countries of the Third World. These imports threaten domestic industries, which tend to be politically active and affiliated with the extremes of conservative or welfare liberalism. Some of these have strongly resisted domestic, union organization (for reasons of cost) and thus strongly support domestic laissez faire, conservative liberalism (among these, most prominent are some textile firms). The welfare liberals face similar political dilemmas in their association with well-organized labor in related industries (for example, the garment industry) or in industries just recently threatened by imports (for example, steel or autos).[66]

In addition, the welfare liberal faces international moral and domestic political dilemmas. If the disadvantaged are rightly the objects of social welfare, redistribution should be directed toward the vast preponderance of the world's

---

65. Kirkpatrick points out our neglect of the needs of the authoritarians, see *Dictatorships and Double Standards*. Theodore Lowi argues that Democratic and Republican policies toward the acquisition of bases in Spain reflected this dichotomy; "Bases in Spain" in *American Civil-Military Decisions*, ed. Harold Stein (University: The University of Alabama Press, 1963), p. 699. In other cases where both the geopolitical and the domestic orientation of a potential neutral might be influenced by U.S. aid, liberal institutions (representative legislatures) impose delay or public constraints and conditions on diplomacy that allow the Soviet Union to steal a march. Warren Christopher has suggested that this occurred in U.S. relations with Nicaragua in 1979. Warren Christopher, "Ceasefire Between the Branches," *Foreign Affairs*, Vol. 60 No. 5 (Summer 1982), p. 998.
66. On economic policy, and pressure groups, see J. J. Pincus, "Pressure Groups and the Pattern of Tariffs," *Journal of Political Economy* Vol. 83 No. 4 (August 1975), pp. 757–778; and L. Salamon and J. Siegfried, "Economic Power and Political Influence," *American Political Science Review* Vol. 71 No. 3 (September 1977), pp. 1026–1043.

poor who are in the Third and Fourth Worlds. Three arguments reveal facets of the moral and political problems welfare liberals face.

First, there is the obligation of humanitarian aid. Peter Singer has argued that the humanitarian obligation an individual has to rescue a drowning child from a shallow pool of water (when such a rescue would not require a sacrifice of something of comparable moral importance, for example, one's own life) should be extended to international aid to famine victims and the global poor.[67] Recently, Brian Barry has provided a strong defense against skepticism concerning this obligation.[68] But he concludes that, while it is hard to doubt that .25 percent of national income (the U.S. figure for foreign aid) is too low, there does not seem to be a clear limit on how much aid of the enormous amount needed is obligatory. One should add that since this aid is required by needy individuals (mostly) in the Third and Fourth Worlds and not clearly owed to their states, the logistics of distributing humanitarian aid will prove difficult. And since this aid is due from individuals in the wealthy North, a limitless personal obligation to the world's poor threatens a form of tyrannical morality. Nor is the burden easily shifted to liberal governments in the North. Political obstacles to taxing rich liberal societies for humanitarian aid are evident. The income of the American poor places them among the world's more advantaged few. But the demand for redistributing income from the United States to the world's poor meets two domestic barriers: the United States poor *within* the United States are clearly disadvantaged, and our democratic politics places the needs of disadvantaged voting citizens above those of more disadvantaged but foreign people.

The second and third problems arise with respect to claims to international redistribution based on obligations of justice. Both establishing a just global society and justly distributing resources in an unjust international society raise apparently insuperable barriers.

In cases of extreme inequality and political recalcitrance within a country, the welfare liberals find justifiable a developmental, redistributing dictatorship to equalize opportunity as a necessary foundation for a just liberal society.[69] The liberal justification for such a dictatorial redistribution on a national scale

---

67. Peter Singer, "Famine, Affluence, and Morality," *Philosophy & Public Affairs* Vol. 1, No. 3 (Spring 1972): pp. 229–43.
68. Brian Barry, "Humanity and Justice in Global Perspective" in *Ethics, Economics, and the Law; Nomos XXIV*, ed. J. Roland Pennock and John W. Chapman (New York: New York University Press, 1982), chap. 11.
69. Rawls, *A Theory of Justice*, pp. 352–53.

is that without it authentically democratic liberal politics and social economy are rendered ineffective. The enormous social inequalities of the international order might—however implausibly—suggest the same prescription should apply to the international order. But extended to global scale, this prescription runs up against a fundamental liberal constraint. It is not clear that an effective global, liberal polity can be formed. Kant regarded global sovereignty, whether liberal in aim or not, as equivalent to global tyranny due to the remoteness of the representation it would entail. If the maximum effective size of a legislature is about 500, a global constituency would have to be of the order of 8 million persons. Confederal solutions that mix direct and indirect elections further attenuate the political life of the citizen or they create the grounds for serious conflict between the local government and the remote confederation. In short, the redistribution that can be justified on liberal grounds does not stretch beyond liberal government. Since modern states may already be too large for effectively liberal politics, global government cannot be a liberal aim. Yet without the prospect of moral autonomy through representative government this form of international redistribution is not justified on liberal grounds.

The dilemma of justly redistributing income in an international society of independent states is addressed by Brian Barry. After rejecting "just requitals" (just prices) for past exploitation as being inadequate justice for poor societies lacking any resources whatsoever and after rejecting justice as "fair play" (reciprocal obligations) for being ill-suited to the minimally integrated international economy, he settles on justice as equal rights.[70] He follows Hart's argument that special rights (to property) presuppose general rights (to property) and that natural resources (or inherited endowments) cannot be justly acquired without consent. Without consent, all have an equal right to global resources. The contemporary rich countries, therefore, owe a share of their income or resources to poor countries. Moreover, they owe this share without the requirement that it be directed to the poorest in the poor countries, because the rich have no right to impose conditions on income or property to which all have an equal right. If rich countries can dispose of global income autonomously, poor countries should have the same right.[71]

---

70. Barry, "Humanity and Justice," p. 234. For an exposition of the implications of a Rawlsian argument ("fair play") concerning international justice, see Charles Beitz, *op. cit.*, Part III. And for a criticism of the extension of Rawls's arguments to international justice, see Christopher Brewin, "Justice in International Relations," in *The Reason of States*, ed. Michael Donelan (London: George Allen and Unwin, 1978), pp. 151–52.
71. Barry, "Humanly and Justice," p. 248.

There are two objections that I think should be made against accepting Barry's principle of indiscriminate interstate justice. First, if justice is determined by the equal rights of individuals to global resources or inheritances, then rich *countries* only acquire income justly when they acquire it justly from individuals (for example, by consent). Only just countries have rights over the autonomous disposition of national income. An unjust rich state has no right to dispose or hold income. A just rich country, conversely, has the right to dispose autonomously of national income, provided that national income represents its just share of global income. Any surplus is owed to *individuals* who are poor or to (just) poor states that have acquired a right to dispose of income or resources by the consent of their citizens. Neither unjust poor states nor unjust rich states should (by the argument of equal rights of individuals) have rights over global income. If there were justice among "thieves," it might call for distribution without condition from unjust rich states to unjust poor states. But there is no reason why that scheme should apply to the surplus of just rich states beyond that which they distribute to just poor states. Some form of trust for the global poor (for present lack of such an institution, perhaps the World Bank or UNICEF) seems a better recipient than an unjust poor state. An obligation of equal justice that requires, say, Norway or Sweden to tax its citizens to provide direct transfers to a Somoza or a Duvalier in preference to funding the IDA of the World Bank or UNICEF is morally bizarre.[72]

The second objection reflects the residual insecurity of the contemporary order. As long as there is no guarantee of security, indiscriminate obligations of justice to redistribute income and resources (including redistribution to potential security threats) cannot be justified. Obliging Israel to tax itself for Syria, or Japan for China, or even the United States for Cuba threatens the rights of individuals within these states to promote their territorial integrity and political independence.

These two objections to the application of just redistribution should not apply within the pacific union. States within the liberal union do rest on consent and do not constitute threats to one another. Between the union's rich and poor members, obligations of justice to distribute global resources and

---

72. None of the points raised in the first objection to Barry's argument of international distribution devalue the right of nationality or justify liberal imperialism. Both nationality and property are national-state rights derived from the equal rights of individuals, but they are different. Nationality can only be enjoyed collectively, property can retain an individual form of appropriation. No international scheme of provision a global affiliation can substitute for nationality when the nation is the accepted center of loyalty; international provision of income to individuals can substitute for or bypass a corrupt state.

income supplement humanitarian obligations applicable globally to aid the poor. (Of course, obstacles are daunting. Among them are how to raise international revenue in a just fashion; how to distribute this revenue in an efficient manner; and how to persuade democratic citizens to support a lengthy program when some mismanagement is likely and when strategic ties to authoritarian allies make competitive demands on the revenues they have become accustomed to raise for foreign purposes. These obstacles may even make a public recognition of the obligation unlikely, but that does not mean it should not be recognized.)

To counterbalance these costly dilemmas in relations between liberal and nonliberal states, liberalism has had two attractive programs. One is a human rights policy that counters the record of colonial oppression and addresses the ills of current domestic oppression in the Second and Third Worlds. The other is a policy of free trade and investment. But neither has had the impact it might have. The attraction of human rights has been tarnished by liberal practice in supporting dictatorships; complementarily, human rights holds little attraction to dictatorial governments in the Third World. The market has been tarnished by unequal bargaining, and now that the bargaining has become more equal, by a mounting "new protectionism."

Liberal principles and economic institutions retain their attractive potential even though they alone cannot satisfy Third World needs such as creating national unity or reducing social inequalities. Releasing this potential from the burden of liberal practice is a feat the liberal world has yet to accomplish.

Thus liberalism has achieved extraordinary success in relations among liberal states as well as exceptional failures in relations between liberal and nonliberal states. Both tendencies are fundamentally rooted in the operation of liberalism within and across national borders. Both are liberalism's legacy in foreign affairs.

IX

No country lives strictly according to its political ideology and few liberal states are as hegemonically liberal as the United States.[73] Even in the United States, certain interests and domestic actors derive their sense of legitimacy from sources other than liberalism. The state's national security bureaucracy reflects

---

73. Louis Hartz, *The Liberal Tradition in America* (New York: Harcourt, Brace, and World, 1953). The United States is one of the few liberal states both of whose leading political fractions (parties) are liberal. Others have shared or competitive fractions: aristocratic or statist-bureaucratic fractions contesting more centrally liberal fractions.

an approach to politics among nations that focuses on other states, particularly threatening states. Its policies correspondingly tend to fall into the Realist, national interest frame of reference. Certain of the West European states and Japan have more syncretic and organic sources of a "real" national interest. But in the United States, and in other liberal states to a lesser degree, public policy derives its legitimacy from its concordance with liberal principles. Policies not rooted in liberal principles generally fail to sustain long term public support. I have argued that these principles are a firm anchor of the most successful zone of international peace yet established; but also a source of conflicted and confused foreign policy toward the nonliberal world. Improving policy toward the nonliberal world by introducing steady and long-run calculations of strategic and economic interest is likely to require political institutions that are inconsistent with both a liberal policy and a liberal alliance: for example, an autonomous executive branch or a predominance of presidential and military actors in foreign policy so as to obtain flexible and rapid responses to changes in the strategic and economic environment. In peacetime, such "emergency" measures are unacceptable in a liberal democracy. Moreover, they would break the chain of stable expectations and the mesh of private and public channels of information and material lobbying that sustain the pacific union. In short, completely resolving liberal dilemmas may not be possible without threatening liberal success.

Therefore, the goal of concerned liberals must be to reduce the harmful impact of the dilemmas without undermining the successes. There is no simple formula for an effective liberal foreign policy. Its methods must be geared toward specific issues and countries. But liberal legacies do suggest guidelines for liberal policy making that contrast quite strikingly with the Realists' advocacy of maximizing the national interest.

First, if "publicity" makes radically inconsistent policy impossible in a liberal republic, then policy toward the liberal and the nonliberal world should be guided by general liberal principles. Liberal policies thus must attempt to promote liberal principles abroad: to secure basic human needs, civil rights, and democracy, and to expand the scope and effectiveness of the world market economy. Important among these principles, Kant argued, are some of the "preliminary articles" from his treaty of perpetual peace: extending nonintervention by force in internal affairs of other states to nonliberal governments and maintaining a scrupulous respect for the laws of war.[74] These, as J. S. Mill

---

74. See Kant's "Preliminary Articles," pp. 431–36; and for a contemporary application of liberal views that shares a number of positions with the policies suggested here, see Richard Ullman,

argued, imply a right to support states threatened by external aggression and to intervene against foreign intervention in civil wars.[75] Furthermore, powerful and weak, hostile and friendly nonliberal states must be treated according to the *same* standards. There are no special geopolitical clients, no geopolitical enemies other than those judged to be such by liberal principles. This policy is as radical in conception as it sounds. It requires abandoning the national interest and the balance of power as guidelines to policy. The interests of the United States must be consistent with its principles. We must have no liberal enemies and no unconditional alliances with nonliberal states.

Second, given contemporary conditions of economic interdependence, this policy could employ economic warfare to lead a liberal crusade against communism and against Third World authoritarians of the left or the right. It could also lead to a withdrawal into isolationism and a defense of only one principle: the right of the United States to territorial integrity and political independence. Both of these policies are consistent with liberal principles, but neither promotes security in a nuclear age nor enhances the prospects for meeting the needs of the poor and oppressed. To avoid the extremist possibilities of its abstract universalism, U.S. liberal policy must be further constrained by a geopolitical budget. Here the Realists' calculus of security provides a benchmark of survival and prudence from which a liberal policy that recognizes national security as a liberal right can navigate. This benchmark consists of prudent policies toward the most significant, indeed the only, strategic threat the United States faces—the USSR. Once the Realists set a prudent policy toward the USSR, the liberals can then take over again, defining more supportive and interdependent policies toward those countries more liberal than the USSR, and more constraining and more containing policies toward countries less liberal than the USSR.[76]

"The Foreign World and Ourselves: Washington, Wilson, and the Democratic Dilemma," *Foreign Policy* (Winter 75/76); and Stanley Hoffmann, *Duties Beyond Borders* (Syracuse: Syracuse University Press, 1981), chaps. 2–4. Michael Walzer in *Just and Unjust Wars* (New York: Basic Books, 1977), has reformulated and revised the major liberal propositions concerning the justice of wars and justice in wars.

75. Interestingly, even a liberal imperialist of a Millian persuasion would now accept that the right to nonintervention should extent to the contemporary Third World. Since the criteria set forth in "Civilization" (commercialization, security) are now met by all nations, Mill would find that we no longer have "barbarous nations" requiring imperial rule.

76. These points benefited from comments by Fouad Ajami, Thomas Farer, and Richard Ullman. For a recent example of a prudential argument for detente, see Stanley Hoffmann, "Detente Without Illusions," *New York Times*, 7 March 1983. And for a coherent exposition of a liberal foreign policy which has helped inform my views on this entire question, Marshall Cohen, "Toward a Liberal Foreign Policy," which will appear in *Liberalism Reconsidered*, ed. by D. MacLean and C. Mills (Totowa, NJ: Rowman and Littlefield, 1983).

And third, specific features of liberal policy will be influenced by whether voting citizens choose to be governed by a laissez faire or by a social democratic administration. But both of these liberalisms should take into account more general guidelines to a prudent, liberal foreign policy—such as those that follow.

In relations with the USSR, a prudent set of policies calls for a frank acceptance of our political incapacity to sustain a successful reforming crusade. Instead mutually beneficial arrangements should be accepted to the extent they do not violate liberal principles or favor long-run Soviet interests over the long-run interests of the United States and the liberal world. Arms control would be central to this as would the expansion of civilian trade. We would encounter difficulties when our liberal allies can gain economic benefits from trade deals (for example, the sale of computer technology) that might in the long run favor the USSR. These situations may be exceptionally difficult to resolve diplomatically since assessments of strategic advantage tend to be uncertain and since the particular nature of the benefits (say, sales of grain as opposed to sales of computers) can influence the assessment of the strategic risks entailed. Liberals will also need to ensure that ties of dependence on the USSR (such as the gas pipeline) are not a major constraint on liberal foreign policy by providing alternative sources (for example, uranium) for allies or by equalizing the import costs of energy and by assuring alternative sources in an emergency. Given the Soviet Union's capacity to respond to bottlenecks imposed by the West, there will be few occasions (fortunately for the coherence of the liberal alliance) when it can be clearly shown that an embargo would unambiguously hamper the Soviet Union and help the liberal alliance.[77]

In relations with the People's Republic of China, similar liberal principles permit trade that includes arms sales to a state no more restrictive of its subjects' liberty but much less restrictive of the liberty of foreign peoples than is the USSR. But strategic temptations toward a further alliance should be curbed. Such an alliance would backfire, perhaps disastrously, when liberal publics confront policymakers with the Chinese shadows of antiliberal rule.

Arms control, trade, and accommodation toward nonliberal Third World nations must first be measured against a prudent policy toward the Soviet Union and then should reflect the relative degrees of liberal principle that their domestic and foreign policies incorporate. Although our policy should be

---

77. *The Economist Study* of Soviet technology, June 1981, and an extensive literature on the use of economic sanctions, including F. Holtzman and R. Portes, "Limits on Pressure," *Foreign Policy* (Fall 1978) No. 32, pp. 80–90.

directed by liberal principles, it should free itself from the pretension that by acts of will and material benevolence we can replicate ourselves in the Third World. The liberal alliance should be prepared to have diplomatic and commercial relations as it does with the USSR with every state that is no more repressive of liberal rights than is the USSR. For example, North Korea and Mozambique might receive PRC level relations; Vietnam, with its foreign incursions, and Angola, with its internal ethnic conflict, Soviet-level relations. Being one of the few states that deny the legal equality of its subjects, South Africa should be treated as Amin's Uganda and Pol Pot's Khmer Republic should have been, in a more containing fashion than is the USSR. No arms should be traded, investment should be restricted with a view to its impact on human rights, and trade should be limited to humanitarian items that do not contribute to the longevity of *apartheid*.

Elsewhere, the liberal world should be prepared to engage in regular trade and investment with all Third World states no more restrictive of liberty than is the PRC, and this could include the sale of arms not sensitive to the actual defense of the liberal world in regard to the USSR. Furthermore, the liberal world should take additional measures of aid to favor Third World states attempting to address the basic needs of their own populations and seeking to preserve and expand the roles of the market and democratic participation. Much of the potential success of this policy rests on an ability to preserve a liberal market for Third World growth; for the market is the most substantial source of Third World accommodation with a liberal world whose past record includes imperial oppression. To this should be added mutually beneficial measures designed to improve Third World economic performance. Export earnings insurance, export diversification assistance, and technical aid are among some of these. (And social democrats will need to take steps that begin to address the humanitarian obligations of international aid and the limited obligations of international justice rich countries have to poor individuals and to [just] poor countries.)

Liberals should persevere in attempts to keep the world economy free from destabilizing, protectionist intrusions. Although intense economic interdependence generates conflicts, it also helps to sustain the material well-being underpinning liberal societies and to promise avenues of development to Third World states with markets that are currently limited by low income. Discovering ways to manage interdependence when rapid economic development has led to industrial crowding (at the same time as it retains massive numbers of the world's population in poverty) will call for difficult economic adjustments at home and institutional innovations in the world economy. These innovations may even require more rather than less explicit regulation of the domestic economy and more rather than less planned dis-integration of the international economy. Under these circumstances, liberals will need to ensure that those suffering losses, such as from market disruption or restriction, do not suffer a permanent loss of income or exclusion from world markets. Furthermore, to prevent these emergency measures from escalating into a spiral of isolationism, liberal states should undertake these innovations only by international nego-tiation and only when the resulting agreements are subject to a regular review by all the parties.[78]

Above all, liberal policy should strive to preserve the pacific union of simi-larly liberal societies. It is not only currently of immense strategic value (being the political foundation of both NATO and the Japanese alliance); it is also the single best hope for the evolution of a peaceful world. Liberals should be prepared, therefore, to defend and formally ally with authentically liberal, democratic states that are subject to threats or actual instances of external attack or internal subversion.

Strategic and economic Realists are likely to judge this liberal foreign policy to be either too much of a commitment or too little. The Realists may argue that through a careful reading of the past we can interpret in a clear fashion a ranked array of present strategic and economic interests. Strategically beneficial allies, whatever their domestic system, should be supported. The purposes of our power must be to maximize our present power. Global ecologists and some on the left claim an ability to foresee future disasters that we should be preparing for now by radical institutional reforms.

But liberals have always doubted our ability to interpret the past or predict the future accurately and without bias. Liberalism has been an optimistic ideology of a peculiarly skeptical kind. Liberals assume individuals to be both self-interested and rationally capable of accommodating their conflicting inter-ests. They have held that principles such as rule under law, majority rule, and the protection of private property that follow from mutual accommodation among rational, self-interested people are the best guide to present policy. These principles preclude taking advantage of every opportunity of the pre-sent. They also discount what might turn out to have been farsighted reform.

---

78. These and similar policies can be found in Fred Hirsch and Michael Doyle, and in C. Fred Bergsten et al, "The Reform of International Institutions," and Richard N. Cooper et al., "Towards a Renovated International System" (Triangle Papers 11 and 14), both in *Trilateral Commission Task Force Reports: 9–14* (New York: New York University Press, 1978).

The implicit hope of liberals is that the principles of the present will engender accommodating behavior that avoids the conflicts of the past and reduces the threats of the future. The gamble has not always paid off in the past (as in accepting a Sudeten separatism). It certainly is not guaranteed to work in the future (for example, in controlling nuclear proliferation or pollution). But liberalism cannot *politically* sustain nonliberal policies. Liberal policies rest upon a different premise. They are policies that can be accepted by a liberal world in good faith and sustained by the electorates of liberal democracies.

In responding to the demands of their electorates, liberal states must also ascribe responsibility for their policies to their citizenry. The major costs of a liberal foreign policy are borne at home. Not merely are its military costs at the taxpayers' expense, but a liberal foreign policy requires adjustment to a less controlled international political environment—a rejection of the status quo. The home front becomes the front line of liberal strategy. Tolerating more foreign change requires a greater acceptance of domestic change. Not maintaining an imperial presence in the Persian Gulf calls for a reduction of energy dependence. Accepting the economic growth of the Third World may require trade and industrial adjustment. The choice is one between preserving liberalism's material legacy of the current world order at the cost of liberal principles or of finding ways of adjusting to a changing world order that protect liberal principles.

FIRST ADDITION

Kant argued that the natural evolution of world politics and economics would drive mankind inexorably toward peace by means of a widening of the pacific union of liberal republican states. In 1795 this was a startling prediction. In 1981, almost two hundred years later, we can see that he appears to have been correct. The pacific union of liberal states has progressively widened. Liberal states have yet to become involved in a war with one another. International peace is not a utopian ideal to be reached, if at all, in the far future; it is a condition that liberal states have already experienced in their relations with each other. Should this history sustain a hope for global peace?

Kant did not assume that pacification would be a steady progress; he anticipated many setbacks. Periods of history since 1795, among them the Napoleonic Wars and the two World Wars, have fully justified his pessimism. The future may have more fundamental setbacks in store.

First, human beings have been driven into forming liberal republics by the pressures of internal and external war. Discord has thus created the essential institutions on which liberal pacification rests. But the Kantian logic of war may find itself supplanted by a nuclear logic of destruction. However persuasive a moral foundation for peace a global wasteland might make, it would make a poor material foundation for its survivors. Indeed, the erratic and lengthy process of educative wars that Kant anticipated appears impossible under nuclear conditions. Long before the nations completed their process of graduation into republicanism, a nuclear wasteland might well have reduced them to barbarism. Yet nuclear logic also calls forth a sense of caution (the balance of terror) that could accelerate the process of graduation into peace even before republics established a homogeneous governance of the world.[79]

Second, Kant assumed that republics formed an endpoint of political evolution: "the highest task nature has set mankind." The increasing number, the longevity, the spread of republics to all continents and to all cultures that are free from foreign domination lend credence to his judgment. Nonetheless, a great and long depression or a runaway inflation could create the condition that lead to authoritarian or totalitarian regimes. Having access to the new technology of surveillance to root out domestic dissidents, such regimes might prove difficult for their populations to dislodge. And nuclear deterrence might provide them with external security.[80]

Third, Kant relied upon international commerce to create ties of mutual advantage that would help make republics pacific. But past technological progress that lowered the costs of transport and that developed rapidly and unevenly—together encouraging international trade—could change direction. Instead, a trade-saving path of technical progress such as emerged in the Roman Empire could reemerge. If the technological progress of transportation develops less quickly than the spread of manufacturing technology, if current trends toward resource-saving technology continue, if economic development tends to equalize capital-labor ratios, or if states choose economic stability over growth and prefer domestic manufacturing, agriculture and services to trade, then world trade could decline even as global economic development continued. The educative force of international exchange would thereby decline.[81]

---

79. For a thorough survey of these issues see Michael Mandelbaum, *The Nuclear Question* (New York: Cambridge University Press, 1979).
80. Gilpin, *War and Change*, p. 229. Senate Judiciary Committee, *Committee Print: Surveillance Technology* (Washington, D.C.: GPO, 1976).
81. In this connection, an interesting hypothesis that either a frontier, a rapidly growing industrial sector, or an improved educational system are the only hopes for preserving an essential foundation for modern democracies has been advanced by Marion Levy, "A Revision of the Gemeinschaft-Gesellschaft Categories and Some Aspects of the Interdependencies of Minority and Host Systems," in *Internal War*, ed. Harry Eckstein (London: Collier-Macmillan, 1964), p. 261.

But, if we assume that these setbacks do not emerge and that, as Kant argued, a steady worldwide pressure for a liberal peace continues, can the past record of liberalism's expansion lead us to any sense of when it might ultimately triumph?

SECOND ADDITION

EXTRAPOLATING NATURE'S SECRET DESIGN. Kant's argument implies two dynamic paths toward peace: one transnational, the other international. The first operates through the ties of trade, cultural exchange, and political understanding that together both commit existing republics to peace and, by inference, give rise to individualistic demands in nonrepublics whose resolution requires the establishment of republican government. The second operates through the pressure of insecurity and of actual war that together engender republican governments—the domestic constitutional foundations of peace. While the second appears fundamental, the first is not merely dependent. The transnational track conveys the impression of a global society expanding from one country to the next, encompassing an ever larger zone of peace, and yet working on each society in an independent even though connected and similar fashion. The international track—war—is basically a set of epidemics become, in the larger perspective, endemic to the international state of war. It operates conjointly, on one because it is operating on another. It is inherently relational and interdependent.

In all likelihood, the past rate of progress in the expansion of the pacific union has been a complex and inseparable combination of the effects of both tracks. But if we imagine that progress had been achieved solely by one track or the other, we can deduce the outer limits of the underlying logics of the transnational and international progresses toward peace.

The second row represents the transnational track of an underlying arithmetic widening of the zone of peace accomplished by linking republics together and creating pressures, incentives, and ideals leading more nations to become

Table 3. The Pacific Union.

	1800	1800–1850	1850–1900	1900–1945	1945–(1980)
Number of Liberal Regimes	3	8	13	29	49
Transnational Track		+5	+5	+16	+20
International Track		>2x	<2x	>2x	<2x

republican. An expanding rate of absolute progress reveals itself as the base develops each century—in the nineteenth adding 5 per 50 years, in the twentieth more than tripling to approximately 18 (i.e., $(16 + 20)/2$) per 50 years. Thus if the rate triples again in the twenty-first century to approximately 50 liberal states per 50 years and if the state order remains fixed at roughly 150 states, the pacific union will not become global until, at the earliest, the year 2101. The third row, a geometric progression that corresponds to the interdependent logic of war, may be the better indicator of Kantian progress. There republics more than double in number during warlike periods such as 1800 to 1850 or 1900 to 1950, less than double in more pacific times (1850–1900 or perhaps 1945–2000, when there have so far been many wars, but no "great" or world wars involving many states akin to the Napoleonic War or World Wars I and II). Thus if we assume continuing preparation for war and petty wars—akin to the period 1850 to 1900—and a similar ratio of expansion (13/8) then global peace should be anticipated, at the earliest, in 2113.[82]

Of course, this pacific calculus further assumes that, as Kant required in his "Second Supplement," a "Secret Article" be included in the treaty for a Perpetual Peace: "The maxims of the philosophers concerning the conditions of the possibility of public peace shall be consulted by the states which are ready to go to war." To this proviso, we need add that the greater complexity of international relations today calls for economists, political scientists, sociologists, and psychologists as well as natural scientists to add their advice to that of the philosophers. This increase in the costs of consultation would, however, be fully justified if even a small war or two were thereby indefinitely delayed, wars being so much more destructive than they were in Kant's day.

---

82. In the last sentence of "Perpetual Peace," Kant expressed a hope for a similar rate of expansion of the pacific union. "It is to be hoped that the periods in which equal progress is achieved will become shorter and shorter." Kant, "Perpetual Peace," in Friedrich, p. 476.

The Fact of Democratic Peace

Bruce Russett

$\mathbf{W}$e have no quarrel with the German people. . . . It was not upon their impulse that their government acted in entering this war. It was not with their previous knowledge or approval. It was a war determined upon as wars used to be determined upon in the old unhappy days when peoples were nowhere consulted by their rulers and wars were provoked and waged in the interest of dynasties or of little groups of ambitious men who were accustomed to use their fellow men as pawns and tools. Self-governed nations do not fill their neighbor states with spies or set the course of intrigue to bring about some critical posture of affairs which will give them an opportunity to strike and make conquest. . . . Cunningly contrived plans of deception or aggression, carried, it may be from generation to generation, can be worked out and kept from the light only within the privacy of courts or behind the carefully guarded confidences of a narrow and privileged class.

—*Woodrow Wilson's war message to Congress,*
April 2, 1917

Scholars and leaders now commonly say "Democracies almost never fight each other." What does that mean? Is it true? If so, what does it imply for the future of international politics? Would the continued advance of democracy introduce an era of relative world peace? Can policymakers act so as to make that kind of peaceful world more likely, and, if so, how? Does the post-Cold War era represent merely the passing of a particular adversarial relationship, or does it offer a chance for fundamentally changed relations among nations?

During the Cold War, Soviet-American hostility was overdetermined. The very different political systems of the two superpowers, with their built-in ideological conflict, ensured a deadly political and military rivalry. So too did the systemic stresses of two great powers, each leading a big alliance in a bipolar confrontation, which ensured that each would resist any enhancement of the other's strength as a threat to its own security. But the end of the Cold War destroyed both those sources of hostility. The ideological conflict dissolved with the end of communism, and the bipolar confrontation collapsed with that of the Soviet alliance system and of the Soviet Union itself. Given the revolutionary changes both in the global system and in the states that comprise it, the old bases for evaluating the character of international relations have also collapsed.

The end of ideological hostility matters doubly because it represents a surrender to the force of Western values of economic and especially political

Bruce Russett is Dean Acheson Professor of International Relations and Political Science at Yale University.

This essay was originally published as chapter 1 of his *Grasping the Democratic Peace* (Princeton, N.J.: Princeton University Press, 1993).

58

Clearly the British prime minister, Lord Salisbury, misjudged the American government's determination, and he was not willing to fight a war. Of Cleveland's intention we cannot be certain, but his actions look more like that of a poker player who expected his bluff to work, and not to be called. Both sides "blinked" in some degree—especially the British, at a time when their relations with Germany were deteriorating and they did not need another enemy.

Although important in preventing an Anglo-American war over this bagatelle, British strategic interests do not deserve all the credit for avoiding war. Stephen Rock, who has examined this and other international relationships during this time, has some illuminating comments on the public and official discourse. Describing the milieu of the Anglo-American relations—both during the crisis and over the next few years as the participants stepped back from the brink and considered what they might have done—he explains that "The reform bills of 1867 and 1884, which extended the franchise in England, had largely dissolved" the American image of England as feudal and aristocratic. "Anglo-Saxonism emerged as a major force" in relations between two nations toward the end of the nineteenth century, and burst forth in the war crisis. Feelings of Anglo-Saxon kinship contained strong elements of racialism and social Darwinism, but they held a serious political component as well. Richard Olney, Cleveland's secretary of state during the Venezuelan crisis, declared in 1896, "If there is anything they [Americans] are attached to, it is to ideals and principles which are distinctly English in their origin and development. . . . Nothing would more gratify the mass of the American people than to stand . . . shoulder to shoulder with England."[5] Consider how different these sentiments were from what Americans were saying about Spain in 1898.

From the other side, British Colonial Secretary Joseph Chamberlain had already praised the "common laws and common standards of right and wrong" of the two countries. Later he declared that Americans' "laws, their literature, their standpoint on every question are the same as ours; their feeling, their interest, in the cause of humanity and the peaceful development of the world, are identical with ours." Arthur Balfour claimed that America's "laws, its language, its literature, and its religion, to say nothing of its constitution are essentially the same as those of English-speaking peoples elsewhere, [and] ought surely to produce a fundamental harmony—a permanent sympathy." According to Rock, this feeling of homogeneity of societal attributes

---

5. Stephen R. Rock, *Why Peace Breaks Out: Great Power Rapprochement in Historical Perspective* (Chapel Hill: University of North Carolina Press, 1989), pp. 49–56.

lay behind the initial outpouring of pacifist sentiment during the Venezuelan boundary controversy and was a central element in popular and official desires for the settlement of that and other issues. . . . First, it colored the perceptions of both Englishmen and Americans, causing them to underestimate the importance of the conflict of geopolitical and economic interests between the two countries and to discount the significance of the concessions necessary to achieve an understanding. Second, it led many persons to conclude that the benefits of avoiding a fratricidal war with "racial" kin outweighed the costs of the sacrifices required for this to be accomplished.[6]

In effect, an Anglo-American security community was becoming established; "the last serious threat of war between the two powers passed."[7] H. C. Allen concludes that "the British public never looked like accepting war, the American public after the first fine careless rapture drew back from the prospect of making it."[8] In the Spanish-American war shortly thereafter, British sympathies were overwhelmingly with the United States.[9]

Meanwhile and subsequently, British and then American relations with Germany deteriorated, and ended ultimately in war. Paul Kennedy contrasts Britain's attitudes toward Germany with its new "special relationship" with the United States.[10] Rock declares, "These effects were devastatingly absent—or reversed—in the Anglo-German and German-American cases."[11]

While turn-of-the-century Britain was an industrial-capitalist, liberal, parliamentary democracy, imperial Germany was an autocratic, bureaucratic, authoritarian state. . . . These differences were appreciated, and even exaggerated, on both sides of the North Sea, and they colored the attitudes and perceptions of important segments of popular opinion as well as governmental leaders themselves. Englishmen, who could agree on practically nothing else, were in fact almost unanimous in their distaste for the German political system, its ideology, and its methods. . . . Both of these nations [Germany and the United States] were rising imperial powers with growing navies. Both threatened British interests in various regions of the globe. Yet Britons, while they detested and feared Germany, almost universally admired the United States and felt minimal apprehension at her ambitions. Part of this was geographic.

---

6. Ibid., pp. 49–56.
7. Bruce Russett, *Community and Contention: Britain and America in the Twentieth Century* (Cambridge, Mass.: MIT Press, 1963), p. 5.
8. H.C. Allen, *Great Britain and the United States: A History of Anglo-American Relations (1783–1952)* (New York: St. Martin's, 1955), p. 540.
9. Charles S. Campbell, *Anglo-American Understanding, 1898–1903* (Baltimore: Johns Hopkins University Press, 1957), chap. 2.
10. Paul Kennedy, *The Rise of Anglo-German Antagonism* (London: Allen and Unwin, 1980), esp. p. 399.
11. Rock, *Why Peace Breaks Out*, p. 56.

. . . But a large portion was ideological and cultural as well. Imbued as they were with a sense of Anglo-Saxon solidarity, the vast majority of Englishmen simply did not believe that Americans could wish or do them serious harm.[12]

The Fashoda crisis of 1898, however, which pitted Britain against France, poses a harder case. British and French interests had been advancing toward the Sudan, with Britain increasingly determined to control the area as protection for its major stake in Egypt. But French forces occupied the small fortress of Fashoda before the British could get there. When a much larger British force arrived, government leaders had to decide what to do. The French were in no position to fight. Their forces at Fashoda were far weaker, they had their hands full on the Continent with Germany, and Britain held unquestioned naval superiority. The premier, Théophile Delcassé, admitted that "the problem is how to combine the demands of honor with the necessity of avoiding a naval war which we are absolutely incapable of carrying through."[13] Thus he offered compromise in several forms, ultimately offering to quit the area in return for commercial concessions. The British, however, would have none of it. They refused to negotiate so long as French forces were in the area, and the British prime minister, Lord Salisbury, seemed ready to go to war if the French would not concede totally. Ultimately they did.

The most recent scholarly work on the crisis concludes that "there is really no evidence in the archives in London and Paris that either government seriously considered going to war over Fashoda."[14] The French gave in because of their military weakness and the need to avoid isolation in their far graver quarrel with Germany. In addition, their hand was weakened by governmental instability resulting from the Dreyfus affair.[15] Salisbury wanted good relations with France to counter the growing threat he felt from Germany, and generally preferred diplomacy to force. In this crisis Salisbury was the poker player. He had to play a "two-level game"[16] with imperialist hawks in domestic politics as well as with the French. While he might have been willing to fight if he had to, he did not want war and knew how weak the French really were.

---

12. Ibid., pp. 86–87.
13. G.N. Sanderson, *England, Europe, and the Upper Nile, 1882–1899: A Study in the Partition of Africa* (Edinburgh: Edinburgh University Press, 1965), p. 359.
14. Darrell Bates, *The Fashoda Incident of 1898: Encounter on the Nile* (New York: Oxford University Press, 1984), p. 153.
15. René Albrecht-Carrié, *Britain and France* (Garden City, N.Y.: Doubleday, 1970).
16. Robert Putnam, "Diplomacy and Domestic Politics: The Logic of Two-Level Games," *International Organization*, Vol. 42, No. 3 (Summer 1988), pp. 427–460.

Considerations of any norm that these two nations should not fight each other were well in the background on both sides; war was avoided primarily for other reasons. Nevertheless, sober reflection on the crisis brought the norms forward: "Both Britain and France possessed a commitment to liberalism and representative government and were opposed to autocracy and absolutism. During the period of reconciliation, numerous references were made to this effect, and to the role of this similarity in drawing the two countries together." A Liberal party leader, H. C. G. Matthew, said: "Most Liberals regarded the Entente with France as the natural result of common democratic impulses." Though they played little role in settling the crisis itself, these feelings were catalyzed by Fashoda and fed directly into the emerging Anglo-French entente.[17]

Thus the feeling of common liberal and democratic values played its part in moderating power conflicts between the United States and Britain, and Britain and France. Between the United States and Germany, on the other hand, the feelings were very different. The German and American political-economic systems involved "two essentially different conceptions of the state: that of the economically liberal laissez-faire state, in which one from the German side saw only disorder, egoism, and corruption, and the half-absolutist, neofeudalistic, bureaucratic state, which in American eyes destroyed the freedom of the individual and lacked democratic legitimation through the 'voice of the people.'"[18] For Americans, an earlier vision of Germany became "replaced by the picture of an increasingly repressive, militaristic, authoritarian, and autocratic society."[19] Such views were strengthened by the subsequent German war with Britain. Relationships based on type of political system reinforced strategic considerations. The ground was prepared for Wilson's vision of a world that could be at peace if and only if it were democratic.

The Spread of Democratic Peace

At the time of Kant, and even of Wilson, the hope for a world of democratic nation states was merely that: a hope, a theory perhaps, but without much

---

17. Rock, *Why Peace Breaks Out*, pp. 117–118.
18. Horst Christof, "Deutsch-amerikanische Entfremdung: Studien zu den deutsch-amerikanischen Beziehungen von 1913 bis zum Mai 1916" (Ph.D. dissertation, Julius-Maximilians-Universität, Warzburg, 1975), quoted in Rock, *Why Peace Breaks Out*, p. 141.
19. Rock, *Why Peace Breaks Out*, p. 143.

empirical referent. Certainly in Kant's time, Europe was hardly an area in which republics flourished. By the time of Wilson's Fourteen Points there were more, in the New World as well as the Old, but the dozen or so democracies of that time still were substantially in a minority.

Wilsonian "idealism" was widely regarded as discredited by the outbreak of World War II. True, the principles of collective security, as embodied in the League of Nations, failed to contain aggression by the Axis powers. In that sense, the element of international law in the Kantian and Wilsonian vision failed. But the elements of trade and democracy were never given a fair chance. International trade was damaged first by the imposition of war reparations on defeated Germany—with some of the effects forecast by John Maynard Keynes[20]—and then by the round of "beggar my neighbor" trade restraints imposed with the collapse of the world economy in the Great Depression.[21] Not coincidentally, democracy also was lost in many countries; first in Russia, then Italy, Germany, Central Europe, Japan, and elsewhere. Thus the Kantian prescription once again had little basis on which to work.

Largely unnoticed, however, was the empirical fact that democracies had rarely if ever gone to war with each other during this period. Since there were few democracies, often at a distance from each other, it is hardly surprising that their failure to fight each other was little noticed. States need both an opportunity and a willingness[22] to go to war with each other. Noncontiguous democracies, unless one or both were great powers, had little opportunity to fight each other. States cannot fight unless they can exert substantial military power against each others' vital territory. Most states, if not great powers with "global reach" (large navies in this era[23]) could exert such power only against contiguous states or at least near neighbors. Furthermore, the willingness of states to fight depends in large part on issues over which they have conflicts of interest. Territorial disputes (over borders, or rights of ethnic groups whose presence is common to both) are rare in the absence of proximity.[24] Since relatively few of the democracies bordered each other in the 1920s and 1930s,

20. John Maynard Keynes, *The Economic Consequences of the Peace* (London: Macmillan, 1919).
21. Charles Kindleberger, *The World in Depression: 1929–1939* (Berkeley: University of California Press, 1973).
22. Benjamin Most and Harvey Starr, *Inquiry, Logic, and International Politics* (Columbia: University of South Carolina Press, 1989).
23. George Modelski and William R. Thompson, *Sea Power in Global Politics, 1494–1993* (Seattle: UNiversity of Washington Press, 1988).
24. Paul F. Diehl and Gary Goertz, *Territorial Changes and International Conflict* (London: Routledge, 1992).

it is not surprising that they generally avoided war with each other. Thus the empirical fact of little or no war between democracies up to this time could be obscured by the predominance of authoritarian states in the international system, and the frequent wars involving one or more such authoritarian states. One could still see the international system as not only anarchic, but in principle threatening the "war of all against all."

Following World War II the situation changed, again, ironically, with a vision of war prevention geared primarily to the last war. The post-World War II era began with the founding of the United Nations, dedicated—as was the League—to the general principle of collective security as carried out by Franklin Roosevelt's "four (ultimately five) policemen" with the power of permanent representatives on the Security Council. But with the Cold War and Soviet-American deadlock in the Security Council arising almost immediately, attention shifted to the more traditional means of collective security through alliance. Despite rhetorical statements like the Universal Declaration of Human Rights and the fact that most—but not all—members of the newly formed North Atlantic Treaty Organization were democracies, democracy was seen more as a binding principle of the Cold War coalition against communism than as a force actively promoting peace among democracies themselves. Moreover, many members of the wider Western alliance system (in Latin America, the Middle East, and Asia) certainly were not democratic.

But by the 1970s, with the increasing numbers of democracies in the international system, the empirical fact of peace among democracies became harder to ignore. There were at one time by various counts thirty-five or so democratic states, and more of them were proximate to one another. Still there was little war, or even serious threats of war, to be found in relationships among those democracies. And more clearly than before, the phenomenon of democratic peace extended beyond the North Atlantic area, and beyond merely the rich industrialized countries belonging to the OECD. The phenomenon began then to be more widely recognized, and by the end of the 1980s it had been widely accepted in the international relations literature, though not so easily explained. This research result is extremely robust, in that by various criteria of war and militarized diplomatic disputes, and various measures of democracy, the relative rarity of violent conflict between democracies still holds up.[25] By early 1992

---

25. This finding is sometimes attributed to Michael Doyle, "Kant, Liberal Legacies, and Foreign Affairs, part 1," *Philosophy and Public Affairs*, Vol. 12, No. 3 (Summer 1983), pp. 205–235; Michael Doyle, "Kant, Liberal Legacies, and Foreign Affairs, part 2," *Philosophy and Public Affairs*, Vol. 12, No. 4 (1983), pp. 323–353; and Michael Doyle, "Liberalism and World Politics," *American Political*

it even had passed into popular political rhetoric, with the international zone of "democratic peace" invoked in speeches by then Secretary of State James Baker and President George Bush, and by Bill Clinton during his presidential campaign.[26]

Wide recognition is not, however, synonymous with universal acceptance. It became confused with a claim that democracies are *in general*, in dealing with all kinds of states, more peaceful than are authoritarian or other nondemocratically constituted states. This is a much more controversial proposition than "merely" that democracies are peaceful in their dealings with each other, and

---

Science Review, Vol. 80, No. 4 (December 1986), pp. 1151–1161. The first empirical reports were Dean Babst, "Elective Governments—A Force for Peace," *The Wisconsin Sociologist*, Vol. 3, No. 1 (1964), pp. 9–14; Dean Babst, "A Force for Peace," *Industrial Research* (April 1972), pp. 55–58; Peter Wallensteen, *Structure and War: On International Relations 1820–1968* (Stockholm: Raben & Sjogren, 1973); and Melvin Small and J. David Singer, "The War-Proneness of Democratic Regimes," *Jerusalem Journal of International Relations*, Vol. 1, No. 4 (Summer 1976), pp. 50–69). Early theoretical contributions, later empirical reports, and reviews include R.J. Rummel, *Understanding Conflict and War*, Vol. 2, *The Conflict Helix* (Los Angeles: Sage, 1976); R.J. Rummel, *Understanding Conflict and War*, Vol. 4, *War, Power, and Peace* (Los Angeles: Sage, 1979); R.J. Rummel, *Understanding Conflict and War*, Vol. 5, *The Just Peace* (Los Angeles: Sage, 1981); R.J. Rummel, "Libertarianism and International Violence," *Journal of Conflict Resolution*, Vol. 27, No. 1 (March 1983), pp. 27–71; R.J. Rummel, "A Catastrophe Theory Model of the Conflict Helix, with Tests," *Behavioral Science*, Vol. 32, No. 4 (1987), pp. 241–266; Bruce Russett and Harvey Starr, *World Politics: The Menu for Choice*, 1st ed. (New York: W.H. Freeman, 1981), chap. 15; Steve Chan, "Mirror, Mirror on the Wall . . . Are the Freer Countries More Pacific?" *Journal of Conflict Resolution*, Vol. 28, No. 4 (December 1984), pp. 617–648; Erich Weede, "Democracy and War Involvement," *Journal of Conflict Resolution*, Vol. 28, No. 4 (December 1984), pp. 649–664; Klaus Jürgen Gantzel, "Is Democracy a Guarantor against War-Making Policy?" Working Paper No. 14, University of Hamburg, Institute of Political Science, Center for the Study of Wars, Armaments, and Development, 1987; William Domke, *War and the Changing Global System* (New haven, Conn.: Yale University Press, 1988); Jean-Baptiste Duroselle, "Western Europe and the Impossible War," *Journal of International Affairs*, Vol. 41, No. 2 (1988), pp. 345–361; Zeev Maoz and Nasrin Abdolali, "Regime Types and International Conflict," *Journal of Conflict Resolution*, Vol. 33, No. 1 (March 1989), pp. 3–35; Francis Fukuyama, "The End of History?" *The National Interest*, Vol. 16, No. 3 (Summer 1989), pp. 3–18; Bruce Russett, *Controlling the Sword: The Democratic Governance of National Security* (Cambridge, Mass.: Harvard University Press, 1990), chap. 5; Stuart A. Bremer, "Dangerous Dyads: Conditions Affecting the Likelihood of Interstate War, 1816–1965," *Journal of Conflict Resolution*, Vol. 36, No. 2 (1992), pp. 309–341; Bruce Bueno de Mesquita and David Lalman, *War and Reason* (New Haven, Conn.: Yale University Press, 1992); and Zeev Maoz and Bruce Russett, "Alliance, Contiguity, Wealth, and Political Stability: Is the Lack of Conflict between Democracies a Statistical Artifact?" *International Interactions*, Vol. 17, No. 3 (1992), pp. 245–268. James Lee Ray, *Global Politics*, 4th ed. (Boston: Houghton Mifflin, 1990), p. 240, concurs with Jack S. Levy, "Domestic Politics and War," *Journal of Interdisciplinary History*, Vol. 18, No. 3 (1988), pp. 653–673, that this constitutes "as close as anything we have to an empirical law in international relations"; also see Nils Petter Gleditsch, "Democracy and Peace," *Journal of Peace Research*, Vol. 29, No. 4 (1992), pp. 369–376. For a general statement on the importance of studying international relations at the level of pairs of states, rather than at the state or system level, see Most and Starr, *Inquiry, Logic, and International Politics*.

26. The Baker and Bush statements are quoted in Russett, *Grasping the Democratic Peace*, chapter 6; pp. 127–129. Clinton's emerged prominently in his speech to the Los Angeles World Affairs Council, August 13, 1992, *New York Times*, August 14, 1992, p. A15.

one for which there is little systematic evidence.[27] Especially in the Vietnam era of U.S. "imperial overreach," it was a politically charged and widely disbelieved proposition. In that light, both academic observers and policymakers refused to accept even the statement that democracies are peaceful toward each other as a meaningful empirical generalization without some kind of theoretical explanation indicating that it was not merely a coincidence or accident.

Furthermore, some variants of the proposition took the form of statements like "democracies never go to war with each other," or even "democracies never fight each other." The latter statement, applied to relatively low-level lethal violence, is demonstrably wrong as a law-like "never" statement even for the modern international system. The former, limiting the statement to the large-scale and typically sustained form of organized international violence commonly designated as war, nonetheless tempts the historically minded reader to come up with counterexamples. And, especially with the key terms still largely undefined, it is not hard to identify candidate counterexamples.

Democracy, War, and Other Ambiguous Terms

This book will establish the following: First, democratically organized political systems in general operate under restraints that make them more peaceful in their relations with other democracies. Democracies are not necessarily peaceful, however, in their relations with other kinds of political systems. Second, in the modern international system, democracies are less likely to use lethal violence toward other democracies than toward autocratically governed states or than autocratically governed states are toward each other. Furthermore, there are no clearcut cases of sovereign stable democracies waging war with each other in the modern international system. Third, the relationship of rela-

---

27. Virtually all the authors cited in note 25 agree that democracies are not in general markedly less likely to go to war than are other states. The principal dissenter is Rummel, "Libertarianism and International Violence," and R.J. Rummel, "Libertarian Propositions on Violence within and between Nations," *Journal of Conflict Resolution*, Vol. 27, No. 1 (March 1985), pp. 419–455. But Rummel's empirical analysis ("Libertarianism and International Violence") is limited to 1976–80—a period that omits, among others, the Vietnam War and most post-colonial wars—and his literature review ("Libertarian Propositions on Violence within and between Nations") has been overtaken and corrected by subsequent empirical analyses. Other work, such as Bremer, "Dangerous Dyads," and Stuart A. Bremer, "Are Democracies Less Likely to Join Wars?" paper presented at the annual meeting of the American Political Science Association, Chicago, September 1992, suggests a mixed and still muddy picture; i.e., democracies are less likely to originate wars with all kinds of states, but more likely to join ongoing wars being fought by other states.

tive peace among democracies is importantly a result of some features of democracy, rather than being caused exclusively by economic or geopolitical characteristics correlated with democracy. Exactly what those features are is a matter of theoretical debate, which we shall explore.

At the risk of boring the reader, further discussion requires some conceptual precision. Without it everyone can—and often does—endlessly debate counter-examples while by-passing the phenomenon itself. We need to define what we mean by democracy and war, so as to be able to say just how rare an occasion it is for two democracies to go to war with each other. When we do so it will be evident that those occasions virtually never arise. We then shall spend the rest of the book trying to understand the reasons for that rarity, and its implications for international politics in the post-cold war era.

INTERSTATE WAR

War here means large-scale institutionally organized lethal violence, and to define "large-scale" we shall use the threshold commonly used in the social scientific literature on war: one thousand battle fatalities.[28] The figure of one thousand deaths is arbitrary but reasonable. It is meant to eliminate from the category of wars those violent events that might plausibly be ascribed to:

1. "Accident" (e.g., planes that may have strayed across a national boundary by mistake, and been downed).
2. Deliberate actions by local commanders, but not properly authorized by central authorities, as in many border incidents.
3. Limited, local authorized military actions not necessarily intended to progress to large-scale violent conflict but undertaken more as bargaining moves in a crisis, such as military probes intended to demonstrate one's own commitment and to test the resolve of the adversary.
4. Deliberate military actions larger than mere probes, but not substantially resisted by a usually much weaker adversary. The Soviet invasion of Czechoslovakia in 1968, which was met with substantial nonviolent resistance but not force of arms and resulted in less than a score of immediate deaths, is such an example, and contrasts with the Soviet invasion of Hungary in 1956, which produced roughly seventeen thousand Hungarian and Soviet dead.

---

28. Melvin Small and J. David Singer, *Resort to Arms: International and Civil Wars, 1816–1929* (Los Angeles: Sage, 1982).

A threshold of one thousand battle deaths rather neatly cuts off the above kinds of events while leaving largely intact the category of most conflicts that intuitively satisfies the commonsense meaning of war. (Not, of course such rhetorical examples as the "war on poverty" or "war on drugs," or for that matter the boat seizures and very limited exchange of gunfire [no casualties or intent to inflict casualties[29]] between Britain and Iceland in the 1975 "Cod War" over fishing rights.) It is also convenient that the one thousand-battle-death threshold provides a neat empirical break, with few conflicts between nation states very near it on either side. The most questionable case is probably that between Britain and the Argentine military dictatorship in 1982, over the Falkland Islands/Islas Malvinas. The battle-death count is customarily given as about 950, or just below our numerical threshold. But not to count it would be splitting hairs. It was deliberate, authorized, and involved some fierce land, naval, and air engagements and two invasions (first by Argentina, and then when the British returned to expel the Argentine invaders). It should count as a war, without apology.

The U.K.-Argentine war was unusual in that it inflicted very few civilian casualties. Most wars are not so limited, with civilian deaths frequently far outnumbering those of combatants. Deaths from hunger and disease may also far outnumber battle-inflicted casualties, as surely happened in many nineteenth-century wars and may well have been the case with the Iraqis after Operation Desert Storm. But the number of such deaths may be difficult or impossible to estimate reliably and may be as much a consequence of inadequate medical and public-health capabilities as of military actions. Without minimizing the human consequences of such civilian deaths, it is simply less ambiguous to limit the definition to battle deaths. Similarly, the definition omits wounded and military personnel missing in action, figures commonly included in "casualty" totals but of lower reliability.

A related problem is that of deciding which political units are to be listed as fighting in a war. Sometimes in coalition warfare most or all of the deaths in a particular coalition will be borne by one or a few members with other members formally but not practically engaged in combat. For the latter, especially in circumstances where a nominal combatant suffers few or *no* identifiable deaths, it seems forced to include it among war participants. Small and Singer use a criterion requiring a state either to commit at least one thousand

---

29. William Mark Habeeb, *Power and Tactics in International Negotiations: How Weak Nations Bargain with Strong Nations* (Baltimore: Johns Hopkins University Press, 1988), chap. 6.

troops to battle, or to suffer at least one hundred battle fatalities, in order to count as a participant.[30]

This definition also excludes, on theoretical grounds, covert actions in which one government secretly undertakes activities, including the use of lethal violence and the support of violent actors within the other government's territory, either to coerce or to overthrow that government. Such activities may not involve deaths on the scale of "wars," and when they do the foreign intervention is by its very covert nature hard to document (though one can often, if perhaps belatedly, discover the metaphoric "smoking gun"). But these activities, precisely because they are denied at the time by the government that undertakes them, imply very different political processes than does a war publicly and officially undertaken. Because they may be undertaken under circumstances when overt war is not acceptable they will, however, receive attention at a later point in the book.

For purposes of theoretical precision in argument yet another qualification is required, and that is a definition of "interstate" war. Here that term means war between sovereign "states" internationally recognized as such by other states, including by major powers whose recognition of a government typically confers de facto statehood. Some such definition focusing on organized independent states is common in the social science literature, and is important for the analysis of this book. It is meant to exclude those "colonial" wars fought for the acquisition of territory inhabited by "primitive" people without recognized states, as practiced by nineteenth-century imperialism, or for the twentieth-century liberation of those people. War it may certainly be, but interstate it is not unless or until both sides are generally recognized as having the attributes of statehood. Applying this definition may well display a Western cultural bias, but it is appropriate to the behavior of states which, in the period, also are defined as "democratic" by the admittedly Western standards spelled out below. Nonstate participants would not meet those standards.

Wars of liberation—with one or both parties not yet recognized as a state—are in this respect similar to those civil wars in which one or both parties to the conflict fights precisely so as to be free of sharing statehood with the other. Such wars are fought to escape from the coercive institutions of a common state, and to include them would confuse rather than clarify the generalization that democracies rarely go to war with each other. As will be clear in the next chapter, a crucial element in that generalization often depends upon the role

---

30. Small and Singer, *Resort to Arms*, chap. 4.

of democratic institutions and practices in promoting peaceful conflict resolution within states. Intrastate conflicts that become so fierce that lethal violence is common often indicate that the institutions of the state have become the problem rather than the solution. For example, the United Kingdom and the Republic of Ireland have lived in peace with each other, as separate states, since 1922; the conflict in Northern Ireland arises precisely because many people there emphatically do not wish to be governed as part of the existing common political structure. Democracies are only slightly less likely than other kinds of states to experience civil war.[31]

DEMOCRACY

For modern states, democracy (or polyarchy, following Dahl[32]) is usually identified with a voting franchise for a substantial fraction of citizens, a government brought to power in contested elections, and an executive either popularly elected or responsible to an elected legislature, often also with requirements for civil liberties such as free speech.[33] Huntington uses very similar criteria of "a twentieth-century political system as democratic to the extent that its most powerful collective decision makers are selected through fair, honest, and periodic elections in which candidates freely compete for votes and in which virtually all the adult population is eligible to vote."[34] In addition, he identifies a free election for transfer of power from a nondemocratic government as "the critical point in the process of democratization." Ray similarly requires that the possibility for the leaders of the government to be defeated in an election and replaced has been demonstrated by historical precedent.[35]

A simple dichotomy between democracy and autocracy of course hides real shades of difference, and mixed systems that share features of both. Moreover, the precise application of these terms is to some degree culturally and temporally dependent. As we shall see, democracy did not mean quite the same to

---

31. Bremer, "Are Democracies Less Likely to Join Wars?"
32. Robert A. Dahl, *Polyarchy: Participation and Opposition* (New Haven, Conn.: Yale University Press, 1971).
33. With some variations in the mix and in the precise empirical applications, these elements are common in the cross-national literature. By the middle to late twentieth century the requirement for a responsible executive becomes largely redundant to the other conditions; see Tatu Vanhanen, *The Process of Democratization: A Comparative Study of 147 States, 1980–88* (New York: Crane Russak, 1990), but it certainly is not for the nineteenth century. A good measurement is Richard L. Merritt and Dina A. Zinnes, "Democracies and War," in Alex Inkeles, ed., *On Measuring Democracy: Its Consequences and Concomitants* (New Brunswick, N.J.: Transaction, 1991), pp. 207–234.
34. Samuel P. Huntington, *The Third Wave: Democratization in the Late Twentieth Century* (Norman: University of Oklahoma Press, 1991), pp. 7,9.
35. James Lee Ray, "Wars between Democracies: Rare or Non-Existent?" *International Interactions*, Vol. 18, No. 3 (1993), pp. 251–276.

the ancient Greeks as it does to people of the late twentieth century. Even in the modern era the yardstick has been rubbery. Nineteenth century democracies often had property qualifications for the vote and typically excluded women, while the United States—democratic by virtually any standard of the day—disenfranchised blacks. Britain, with its royal prerogatives, rotten boroughs, and very restricted franchise before the Reform Act of 1832, hardly could be counted as a democracy. Even that reform brought voting rights to less than one-fifth of adult males, so one might reasonably withhold the "democracy" designation until after the Second Reform Act of 1867, or even until the secret ballot was introduced in 1872. By then, at the latest, Britain took its place with the relatively few other states commonly characterized as democratic in the parlance of the era. But if, before the late nineteenth century, we admit countries with as few as 10 percent of all adults eligible to vote as democratic (a criterion used by Small and Singer[36]; Doyle uses a cutoff of 30 percent of all males[37]), by the middle to late twentieth century nothing less than a substantially universal franchise will suffice.

The term "contested elections" admits similar ambiguities, but in practice it has come to require two or more legally recognized parties. States with significant prerogatives in military and foreign affairs for nonelected agents (e.g., monarchs) should be excluded as having nonresponsible executives, even in the nineteenth century.

By the middle to late twentieth century the matter of guaranteed and respected civil rights, including rights to political organization and political expression, also become a key element in any commonsense definition of democracy.[38] The exercise of such civil rights tends to be highly correlated with the existence of democratic institutions as just elaborated, but not perfectly so. The institutions may be found without the regular widespread exercise of the rights; the opposite (civil liberties assured, but not democratic institutions) is rarer. For purposes of the discussion here we will nevertheless not use civil liberties per se as a defining quality, and we shall also ignore the matter of free-market economic liberties. While there is very likely a causal nexus between economic liberties and secure political freedom, the relationship is complex and, unlike some authors,[39] I will not build it into the definition.

---

36. Small and Singer, "The War-Proneness of Democratic Regimes."
37. Doyle, "Kant, Liberal Legacies, and Foreign Affairs, part 1."
38. Robert A. Dahl, *Democracy and Its Critics* (New Haven, Conn.: Yale University Press, 1989).
39. Rummel, "Libertarianism and International Violence"; and Doyle, "Kant, Liberal Legacies, and Foreign Affairs, part 1."

In not including civil rights and economic liberty as defining qualities of democracy we are lowering the standards by which a country can be labeled a democracy. That is highly relevant to our next topic, an examination of conflicts alleged by some scholars to be wars between democracies. By lowering the standards we are making it more likely that some events will be labeled wars between democracies—events that I and many other writers contend are, a most, exceedingly rare.

Theoretical precision, however, requires one further qualification: some rather minimal stability or longevity. Huntington emphasizes stability or institutionalization as "a central dimension in the analysis of any political system."[40] To count a war as one waged by a democracy Doyle requires that representative government be in existence for at least three years prior to the war.[41] Perhaps that is a bit too long, yet some period must have elapsed during which democratic processes and institutions could become established, so that both the citizens of the "democratic" state and its adversary could regard it as one governed by democratic principles. Most of the doubtful cases arise within a single year of the establishment of democratic government.

By application of these criteria it is impossible to identify unambiguously *any* wars between democratic states in the period since 1815. A few close calls exist, in which some relaxation of the criteria could produce such a case. But to have no clearcut cases, out of approximately 71 interstate wars involving a total of nearly 270 participants, is impressive. Even these numbers are deceptively low as representing total possibilities. For example, as listed by Small and Singer, 21 states count as participating on the Allied Side in World War II, with 8 on the Axis side.[42] Thus in that war alone there were 168 pairs of warring states. Allowing for other multilateral wars, approximately 500 pairs of states went to war against each other in the period. Of these, fewer than a handful can with any plausibility at all be considered candidates for exceptions to a generalization that democracies do not fight each other.

Some Alleged Wars between Democracies

To see what these criteria produce, consider the list in Table 1.1 of wars that have sometimes been suggested as exceptions to the generalization that democracies do not go to war with each other.

---

40. Huntington, *The Third Wave*, p. 11.
41. Doyle, "Kant, Liberal Legacies, and Foreign Affairs, part 1."
42. Small and Singer, *Resort to Arms.*

Table 1.1   Some "Candidate" Wars between Democracies.

War of 1812, U.S. and Great Britain
Roman Republic (Papal States) vs. France, 1849
American Civil War, 1861
Ecuador-Colombia, 1863
Franco-Prussian War, 1870
Boer War, 1899
Spanish-American War, 1898
Second Philippine War, 1899
World War I, Imperial Germany vs. western democracies 1914/17
World War II, Finland vs. western democracies 1941
Lebanon vs. Israel, 1948
Lebanon vs. Israel, 1967

Four should be dismissed because they fall outside the criteria established even for any kind of interstate war in the period. The first, the War of 1812, is easy to dismiss simply because it precedes the beginning date—1815—of the best-known compilation of all wars.[43] That may seem like a cheap and arbitrary escape, but it is not. There simply were very few democracies in the international system before that date, and as we discussed with the British case above, though Britain had moved quite far from royal absolutism it just did not fit the criteria either of suffrage or of fully responsible executive.

The American Civil War and the Second Philippine War are also readily eliminated as plausible candidates by straightforward use of the definitions. Whatever it may be called below the Mason-Dixon line, the Civil War is rightly named, in that the Confederacy never gained international recognition of its sovereignty; as a war for separation or to prevent separation it comes under our rubric of wars induced by the frictions of sharing common statehood. The Philippine War of 1899 was a colonial war, in which the United States was trying to solidify control of a former Spanish colony it had acquired. The Philippine resistance constituted an authentic war of resistance against colonialism, but not on the part of an elected democratic government. This is not in any way to denigrate the resistance, but merely to insist on a distinction that will be important throughout the book: especially by the standards of Western ethnocentric attitudes at the time, the Philippine resistance was not widely regarded as "democratic" in a way that would induce either normative or institutional constraints on the United States.

43. Ibid.

The Boer War, begun in 1899, also fails to fit the requirements for an interstate war. Small and Singer identify it as an extrasystemic war because the South African Republic—by far the larger of the two Boer combatants, the other being the Orange Free State—was not generally recognized as an independent state.[44] Britain recognized only its internal sovereignty, retaining suzerainty and requiring it to submit all treaties to the British government for approval. This, too, is properly an unsuccessful war for independence. Moreover, the two Boer republics strained the definition of democracy, then as for almost a century subsequently. Not only was suffrage restricted to the white male minority (roughly 10 percent of the adult population) in the South African Republic, but the electorate was further reduced, perhaps by half, by a property qualification and long-term residence requirements.[45]

Two other conflicts can be dismissed because they fall short of the casualty levels required for a "war." These are Finland's participation in World War II on the "wrong" side and Lebanon's involvement in the Six-Day War of 1967. Finland was actively at war only with the Soviet Union, in an attempt to wrest back the territory taken from it in the Winter War of 1939–40. Although it was nominally at war with the Western allies, there is no record of combat or casualties between Finland and democratic states that would even approach the rather low threshold specified above. In the Six-Day War of 1967 Lebanon (then still an at least marginally democratic state, as it was not when invaded by Israel in 1982) participated in "combat" only by sending a few aircraft into Israeli airspace; the planes were driven back with, apparently, no casualties at all.

In the remaining six cases one or both of the participants fails the test for democracy. Lebanon's participation in the 1948 war was well above the criterion used for a belligerent. Israel, however, had not previously been independent, and had not yet held a national election. While the authenticity of Israel's national leadership was hardly in question, Lebanon—itself not fully democratic—could not have been expected to accredit it as a democratic state.

---

44. Ibid.
45. Robert Lacour-Gayet, A History of South Africa (New York: Hastings House, 1978), pp. 168, 170, 182, 194. Robert L. Rotberg, Suffer the Future: Policy Choices in Southern Africa (Cambridge, Mass.: Harvard University Press, 1980), p. 30, further reports that voters had to be "approved by the elders of the Dutch Reformed Church," but the constitutional provision requiring a voter to be a member of the church was repealed immediately after its passage in 1858. See G.W. Eybers, Select Constitutional Documents Illuminating South African History, 1795–1910 (London: Routledge, 1918), pp. 368–369.

The 1863 war between Ecuador and Colombia also fits the criteria for war, but neither regime meets any reasonable requirement for democratic stability. Both governments came to power through revolution. Colombia's president governed with a new federal constitution promulgated only in May 1863; Ecuador's Gabriel García Moreno became president two years earlier, but is described as heading an "autocratic regime"[46] and governing "with absolute authority."[47] As for France against the Roman Republic, both parties were but ephemerally democratic. Following the revolution of early 1848, presidential elections took place under the new French constitution only in December of that year. The notion of a democratic Papal States sounds oxymoronic. The pope introduced a constitution with an elective council of deputies in 1848, but reserved veto power to himself and the College of Cardinals. After an insurrection in November, he fled and the Roman Republic was proclaimed in February 1849. Within two months the republic was at war with France.

The Franco-Prussian War can be eliminated simply by looking at France. Reforms ratified in the plebiscite of May 1870 could be interpreted as making the empire into a constitutional monarchy, but war began a mere two months later. In Prussia/Germany the emperor appointed and could dismiss the chancellor; a defeat in the Reichstag did not remove the chancellor from office. The emperor's direct authority over the army and foreign policy deprives the state of the democratic criterion of "responsible executive" on war and peace matters; Volker Berghahn calls the constitutional position of the monarchy "almost absolutist."[48] Doyle rightly excludes Imperial Germany from his list of liberal states.[49] Such a decision removes World War I from the candidate list.

The most difficult case is the Spanish-American War of 1898. Spain after 1890 had universal male suffrage, and a bicameral legislature with an executive nominally responsible to it. But the reality was more complex. The ministry was selected by the king, who thus remained the effective ruler of the state. Nominally competitive elections were really manipulated by a process known as *caciquismo*. By mutual agreement, the Liberal and Conservative parties rotated in office; governmental changes preceded rather than followed elections. Through extensive corruption and administration procedures the king and politicians in Madrid controlled the selection of parliamentary candidates and their election. Election results were often published in the press before

---

46. George C. Kohn, *Dictionary of Wars* (Garden City, N.Y.: Doubleday, 1986), p. 150.
47. William L. Langer, *An Encyclopedia of World History* (Boston: Houghton Mifflin, 1972), p. 852.
48. Volker Berghahn, *Germany and the Approach of War in 1914* (New York: St. Martin's, 1973), p. 9.
49. Doyle, "Kant, Liberal Legacies, and Foreign Affairs, part 1."

polling day. The meaningless elections were thus manipulated by the king and his close advisers; the system lacked the democratic quality of a responsible executive.[50] Ernest May describes the system as "preserving the appearance of a parliamentary democracy with none of its suspected dangers."[51] None of the published large-scale analyses of the question of democracies fighting each other puts Spain among the democratic countries[52] nor do most major long-term political surveys.[53]

It seems, therefore, best to treat it as a close call but probably not a refutation even of the strong statement that democracies *never* make war on each other. Equally important, as we shall see later in the book, is the matter of perceptions. The Spanish political situation was at best marginal enough that key United States decisionmakers could readily persuade themselves and their audiences that it was not democratic. Consider, for example, the remarks of the two Republican senators from Massachusetts. Senator Henry Cabot Lodge: "We are there because we represent the spirit of liberty and the spirit of the new time, and Spain is over against us because she is mediaeval, cruel, dying." Senator George Hoar: "The results of a great war [on which the U.S. was embarking] are due to the policy of the king and the noble and the tyrant, not the policy of the people."[54]

Subsequent to my writing the above, Ray has presented a thorough review of these and other alleged cases of wars between democracies, and concludes that the generalization of no wars between democracies remains true.[55] Whether or not one holds to the lawlike "never" statement may not really be very important. Almost all of the few near misses are in the nineteenth century. Since that was an era of generally very imperfect democracy by modern criteria, it is no surprise to find most of the near misses then.

Depending on the precise criteria, only twelve to fifteen states qualified as democracies at the end of the nineteenth century. The empirical significance of

---

50. Raymond Carr, *Modern Spain 1875–1980* (Oxford: Oxford University Press, 1980), pp. 10–15.
51. Ernest R. May, *Imperial Democracy: The Emergence of America as a Great Power* (New York: Harcourt, Brace & World, 1961), p. 97.
52. Small and Singer, "The War-Proneness of Democratic Regimes"; Doyle, "Kant, Liberal Legacies, and Foreign Affairs, part 1;" Chan, "Mirror, Mirror on the Wall"; Maoz and Abdolali, "Regime Types and International Conflict"; and Bremer, "Dangerous Dyads."
53. Tatu Vanhanen, *The Emergence of Democracy: A Comparative Study of 119 States, 1850–1979* (Helsinki: Finnish Society of Sciences and Letters, 1984), Arthur S. Banks, *Cross-Polity Time-Series Data* (Cambridge, Mass.: MIT Press, 1971), and Ted Robert Gurr, Keith Jaggers, and Will Moore, *Polity II Handbook* (Boulder: University of Colorado Press, 1989), code it as sharing democratic and autocratic characteristics.
54. *Congressional Record,* April 13, 1898, p. 3783; and *Congressional Record,* April 14, 1898, p. 3831.
55. Ray, "Wars between Democracies."

the rarity of war between democracies emerges only in the first half of the twentieth century, with at least twice the number of democracies as earlier, and especially with the existence of perhaps sixty democracies by the mid-1980s. Since the statistical likelihood of war between democracies is related to the number of pairs of democracies, the contrast between the two centuries is striking: by a very loose definition, possibly three or four wars out of roughly sixty pairs before 1900, and at most one or two out of about eighteen hundred pairs thereafter.[56] As twentieth-century politics unfold, the phenomenon of war between democracies becomes impossible or almost impossible to find.

Even with the differing definitions of democracy and of war, this generalization is exceedingly robust. Long-term rival states, with many conflicts of interest between them, have gone to war or had substantial fatal clashes only when one or both of them was not governed democratically. For example, in the case of the Greek-Turkish dispute over Cyprus, by far the worst violence erupted in 1974 under the most dictatorial government either country experienced since 1945, when the Greek colonels overthrew the elected Cypriot government of Archbishop Makarios. Faced with the prospect of forcible *enosis* between Greece and Cyprus, Turkey replied by invading the island and occupying nearly a third of its territory. By contrast, the 1963–64 clashes—when democratic Greek and Turkish governments supported their protégés during outbreaks on the islands—were much more easily contained, largely by an American warning and UN peacekeeping action. And confrontations later in the 1970s, between democratic governments, were restrained short of any fatalities.[57] India and Pakistan have of course fought repeatedly and sometimes bloodily during their history as independent states. Yet no fatalities are recorded in disputes between them during Pakistan's most democratic periods of 1962–64 and 1988–92.[58]

Even the kind of crisis bargaining that uses military force in a threatening manner becomes, in the twentieth century, rare between democracies, even if

---

56. The formula for calculating the number of possible pairs is $N(N-1)/2$. Systematic statistical analyses appear in *Grasping the Democratic Peace*. The data here and for Table 1.2 are from the compilation of Militarized International Disputes discussed in chapter 4 of *Grasping the Democratic Peace*.

57. Kyriacos Markides, *The Rise and Fall of the Cyprus Republic* (New Haven, Conn.: Yale University Press, 1977); Dankwart A. Rustow, *Turkey: America's Forgotten Ally* (New York: Council on Foreign Relations, 1987); and Monteagle Stearns, ed., *Entangled Allies: U.S. Policy toward Greece, Turkey, and Cyprus* (New York: Council on Foreign Relations, 1992).

58. S.M. Burke, *Pakistan's Foreign Policy: An Historical Analysis* (London: Oxford University Press, 1973); Raju C. Thomas, *Indian Security Policy* (Princeton, N.J.: Princeton University Press, 1986); and Herbert K. Tillema, *International Conflict Since 1945: A Bibliographic Handbook of Wars and Military Interventions* (Boulder, Colo.: Westview Press, 1991).

Table 1.2. Dispute Behavior of Politically Relevant Interstate Dyads, 1946–1986.

Highest Level of Dispute	Both States Democratic	One or Both Nondemocratic	Total Dyads
No dispute	3,864	24,503	28,367
Threat of force	2	39	41
Display of force	4	116	120
Use of force	8	513	521
War	0	32	32
Totals	3,878	25,203	29,081
Escalation Probabilities			
To threat of force	0.05%	0.16%	
To display of force	85.7%	94.4%	
To use of force	57.1%	77.9%	
To war	0.0%	4.6$	

SOURCES: See chapter 4 for sources and definitions.

not quite absent. And if there is crisis bargaining, it does not escalate to the point of war.

Table 1.2 illustrates these facts in data on all militarized diplomatic disputes over the period from 1946 to 1986. "Dyad" means a pair of states; for the table we count each year of existence separately, thus Britain and France in 1946 constitute one observation, and another in 1947. The highest level of conflict reached in the dispute between that pair of states is identified. (Disputes that spill over into two or more years are counted only in the year they began or were escalated to a higher level.) The phrase "politically relevant dyads" refers to all pairs of states that are contiguous or at least fairly close to each other, or where one of the states in the pair is a major power and hence has military "global reach." This recognizes, as noted above, that the majority of states in the international system lack the means or the interest to engage in militarized disputes with each other, and hence are irrelevant to a serious analysis. Further information on definitions and sources can be postponed for much more detailed analysis in chapter 4.

The information in this simple table has several rich theoretical implications, and we shall return to it in subsequent chapters. There were no wars between democracies, and even though the number of democratic dyads is relatively small, if they had fought wars as frequently with each other as one finds in the second column, there would have been five wars between democracies. Note also that in this period there were only fourteen instances of disputing pairs involving the threat, display, or use of military force by one democracy against another. The odds that any pair of politically relevant democratic states would have a militarized dispute, at any level, in a year during this period were only 1 in 276. By contrast, if one or both states in the pair was not a democracy, the odds were as short as 1 in 36—eight times greater. Surely this is a very dramatic difference in behavior. The actual use of military force involved trivial occasions like the "Cod War"; very minor fire by Israel against Britain during the 1956 Suez intervention, in which the British and Israelis were in fact accomplices; brief conflict between British and Turkish forces during a 1963 peacekeeping operation on Cyprus; and Turkish sinking of a Greek boat in 1978.

One can also use the tabular information to calculate "escalation probabilities" for militarized disputes that do occur. For democracies, the chances that any militarized dispute would progress up the scale of force were consistently lower, at every level, than for pairs in which one or both states were not democracies. For example, only a little more than half of the few disputes between democracies resulted in the actual use of force, whereas nearly 80 percent of all disputes by other kinds of pairs of states escalated at least to the use of force. For earlier periods (the nineteenth century, and 1900–1945) the relationships for conflict-proneness and escalation appear to be in the same direction—democratic pairs of states dispute less—but much weaker than in the post-1945 era.[59]

It is tempting to believe that a norm against the use of force between democracies, and even the threat of use of force, has emerged and strengthened over time. To pursue the matter of norms, however, becomes a subject for much further analysis. The emergence of norms against democracies fighting each other is traceable, and by many theories it did indeed become a powerful restraint. Other theories, however, attribute the relative absence of lethal violence between democracies to many other influences. The next chapter lays out these partly competing, partly complementary theories in detail.

---

59. Maoz and Abdolali, "Regime Types and International Conflict"; and Bremer, "Dangerous Dyads."

Why Democratic Peace?

Bruce Russett

When democratic states were rare, the Kantian perspective had little practical import, and power politics reigned. But if the Kantian perspective is correct, recent events replacing authoritarian regimes with democratic values and institutions in much of Asia, Eastern Europe, and Latin America[1] may have profound implications not just for governmental practices within states, but for worldwide peace among states. It may be possible in part to supersede the "realist" principles (anarchy, the security dilemma of states) that have dominated practice to the exclusion of "liberal" or "idealist" ones since at least the seventeenth century.

Politics within a democracy is seen as largely a nonzero-sum enterprise; by cooperating, all can gain something even if all do not gain equally, and the winners are restrained from crushing the losers. Indeed, today's winners may, as coalitions shift, wish tomorrow to ally with today's losers. If the conflicts degenerate to physical violence, either by those in control of the state or by insurgents, all can lose. In most international politics—the anarchy of a self-help system with no overall governing authority—these norms and practices are not the same. "Realists" remind us of the powerful norms of legitimate self-defense and the acceptability of military deterrence, norms much more extensive internationally than within democratic states. Politics among nations takes on a more zero-sum hue, with the state's sovereign existence at risk.

The principles of anarchy and self-help in a zero-sum world are most acute in "structural realist" theories of international relations. The nature of states' internal systems of government is seen as nearly irrelevant; their overall behavior is basically determined by the structure of the international system and

Bruce Russett is Dean Acheson Professor of International Relations and Political Science at Yale University.

This essay includes parts of chs. 2 and 6 of his Grasping the Democratic Peace (Princeton, N.J.: Princeton University Press, 1993).

1. The trend to democratic government has been documented worldwide up to 1988 by Raymond Gastil, Freedom in the World: Political Rights and Civil Liberties, 1988–1989 (New York: Freedom House, 1989), and later by Freedom House, i.e., R. Bruce McColm, et al., Freedom in the World: Political Rights and Civil Liberties, 1991–92 (New York: Freedom House, 1992), and traced back to the eighteenth century by George Modelski, Is America's Decline Inevitable? (Wassenaar: Netherlands Institute for Advanced Study, 1988), and Ted Robert Gurr, Keith Jaggers, and Will Moore, "The Transformation of the Western State: The Growth of Democracy, Autocracy, and State Power since 1800," in Inkeles, On Measuring Democracy. Also see Harvey Starr, "Democratic Dominoes: Diffusion Approaches to the Spread of Democracy," Journal of Conflict Resolution, Vol. 35, No. 2 (June 1991), pp. 356–381; and Samuel P. Huntington, The Third Wave: Democratization in the Late Twentieth Century. (Norman: University of Oklahoma Press, 1991).

their position in that structure. "Peace" is a fleeting condition, dependent upon deterrence and eternal vigilance. By this structural realist understanding the kind of stable peace that exists among democracies cannot last, because eventually democracies would be compelled, by the structure of the international system and their eternal security dilemma, to enter a state of war or at best of military deterrence.[2] Realism has no place for an expectation that democracies will not fight each other. To the degree we establish that peace between democracies is a fact, and are able to explain it theoretically, we build an alternative view of the world with great import for expectations and for policy. We begin with the theories.

If scholars are near consensus that democratically governed states rarely go to war with each other or even fight each other at low levels of lethal violence, this does not mean there is anything like consensus on why the phenomenon occurs. Nor can the same generalization be supported for relations among other kinds of political systems (for example, military or other dictatorships). Sharing common forms of political structure and political culture in general does not prevent war between independent states.[3] If similarity of form of government in general were enough, then we would have seen peace between the Soviet Union and China, between the Soviet Union and its formerly communist East European neighbors, and between China and Vietnam. Despite important differences in political values and organization among the communist countries, they were much more like one another in values and ideology than like the democracies or even like right-wing dictatorships. Yet war between these countries, and disputes that threatened to erupt in war, were commonplace.

Certainly some kinds of differences, if politically salient, can cause conflict. But that becomes virtually tautological unless one can specify what differences

---

2. Kenneth Waltz, *Theory of International Relations* (Reading, Mass.: Addison-Wesley, 1979); and John Mearsheimer, "Back to the Future: Instability in Europe after the Cold War," *International Security*, Vol. 15, No. 1 (Summer 1990), pp. 5–56.
3. Spencer Weart, *Never at War: Why Don't Democracies Fight One Another?* (forthcoming), suggests that certain types of oligarchies rarely have fought each other in various historical eras, but Stuart A. Bremer, "Dangerous Dyads: Conditions Affecting the Likelihood of Interstate War, 1816–1965," *Journal of Conflict Resolution*, Vol. 36, No. 2 (1992), pp. 309–341, finds no evidence for this in the modern world. Previous analyses of very broad measures of social and cultural similarity have produced mixed results. See Lewis Frye Richardson, *Statistics of Deadly Quarrels* (Chicago: Quadrangle, 1961); David Wilkinson, *Deadly Quarrels: Lewis F. Richardson and the Statistical Study of War* (Berkeley and Los Angeles: University of California Press, 1980), chap. 9; Bruce Russett, *International Regions and International System: A Study in Political Ecology* (Chicago: Rand McNally, 1967), chap. 11; and R. J. Rummel, *Understanding Conflict and War*, Vol. 4, *War, Power, and Peace* (Los Angeles: Sage, 1979), chap. 16.

will be salient. For sixteenth-century Europe religious differences between Catholics and Protestants provided politically salient ideological reasons for killing each other; by the twentieth century those differences were irrelevant to violent conflict save in isolated pockets like Northern Ireland. Thus it seems likely that the reasons for "democratic peace" are either rooted somehow in the nature of democracy itself, or are correlated in the modern world with the phenomenon of democracy.

Some scholars vigorously question the causal inference that democracies are at peace with each other simply because they are democratic. They point instead to other influences that are correlated with democracy and hence create a spurious relation between democracy itself and general peace between democratic states. Without going into the vast range of hypotheses about the causes of war and peace, we need to consider some of the most important ones that might specifically account for the relationship between democratic states.

Alternative Explanations

Alternative hypotheses to explain the phenomenon include the following.

TRANSNATIONAL AND INTERNATIONAL INSTITUTIONS MAKE PEACE

The states in question are peaceful toward each other because they are bound by common ties in a network of institutions crossing national boundaries. Democracies often do share many common institutions. Analysts may emphasize the role of the European Community (EC), for example, and certainly one of the major motivations of the founders of the institutions that evolved into the EC was to bind together previously hostile states so that they would be unable to make war on each other. Some international organizations clearly have this intention. Others, not primarily addressed to war prevention, help to resolve many troublesome conflicts of interest that might feed suspicion and hostility. But states and ethnic groups typically share common institutions just because they have major interests in conflict as well as in common; institutions are supposed to provide a means to resolve those conflicts peacefully. If the common institutions cannot do so, or if one party is coerced into unwillingly sharing common institutions with another, the institutions exacerbate conflict and may become the occasion for civil war.[4] Hence the existence of common

---

4. Russett, *International Regions and the International System*, chap. 12, finds that, if anything, states sharing membership in international organizations are more likely to be involved in violent conflict with each other.

intergovernmental or supranational institutions cannot so plausibly be invoked as a prior reason for the absence of war. Peaceful relations must in some degree precede the institutions.

An influential variant of the institutional approach focuses on transnationalism: individual autonomy and pluralism within democratic states foster the emergence of transnational linkages and institutions—among individuals, private groups, and governmental agencies. Those linkages can serve to resolve transnational conflicts peaceably and, by forming transnational alliances into other states, inhibit their national governments from acting violently toward each other. This perspective derives from classics both of international integration theory and of bureaucratic politics and foreign policy.[5] It is not, however, completely separable from the matter of democracy. Democracies foster, and are fostered by, the pluralism arising from many independent centers of power and influence; autocracies do not. Democracies are open to many private and governmental transnational linkages; autocracies rarely are. (Recall the late and unlamented Iron Curtain.) Thus transnationalism cannot easily be considered separately from the distinction between democracies and other kinds of states. Since it is substantially correlated with the "open" institutions of democratic politics, it cannot be treated analytically or empirically as an independent cause.

DISTANCE PREVENTS WAR

Most wars are fought between physically adjacent states, thanks to their combination of capability and willingness (reasons) to fight neighbors.[6] Likewise, individuals are most likely to be murdered by friends and close relatives with whom they are are in constant contact. But until after World War II democracies

---

5. See, for example, Karl W. Deutsch, et al., *Political Community and the North Atlantic Area* (Princeton, N.J.: Princeton University Press, 1957), and I.M. Destler, H. Sato, P. Clapp, and H. Fukui, *Managing an Alliance: The Politics of U.S.-Japanese Relations* (Washington, D.C.: Brookings, 1976), esp. chap. 5. A milestone in the transnational relations literature is Robert O. Keohane and Joseph S. Nye, *Power and Interdependence: World Politics in Transition* (Boston: Little, Brown, 1977), with institutions defined less as formal organizations than as "recognized patterns of practice around which expectations converge," Oran R. Young, "International Regimes: Problems of Concept Formation," *World Politics*, Vol. 32, No. 3 (April 1980), pp. 331–356, see p. 337, and as facilitators of communication. An important look at transnational relations is Thomas Risse-Kappen, *Cooperation among Democracies: Norms, Transnational Relations, and the European Influence on U.S. Foreign Policy* (Princeton: Princeton University Press, 1995).

6. First established by Richardson, *Statistics of Deadly Quarrels*, corroborated in reviews by Wilkinson, *Deadly Quarrels*, chap. 5; J. David Singer, "Accounting for International War: The State of the Discipline," *Journal of Peace Research*, Vol. 18, No. 1 (1981), pp. 1–18; and Paul Diehl, "Geography and War: A Review and Assessment of the Empirical Literature," *International Interactions*, Vol. 17, No. 1 (1991), pp. 11–27, and confirmed as an independent influence by Bremer, "Dangerous Dyads."

tended to be relatively few and far between. Hence the absence of murderous quarrels between democracies was not too surprising, and may need—at least for the pre-1945 era—little further explanation. Even for much of the post-1945 period, the rarity of contiguous democratic states outside of Western Europe might explain much of the absence of violent conflict between democracies.[7] Yet the more recent one's snapshot of the international system, with many contiguous democracies in Europe and the Western Hemisphere, the less conclusive the distance argument seems.

ALLIANCES MAKE PEACE

Allies may be presumed to choose each other because of their common interests, and hence to be already peacefully inclined toward each other. Moreover, their common interests are likely to concern security against a common enemy. If so, they are not likely to fight each other. Many democracies have shared common interests in presenting a unified alliance front. NATO and the Western alliance system provide the most recent example, but in both world wars the democracies found themselves ranged together (with some nondemocracies alongside, to be sure) against the nondemocratic Central/Axis powers.[8] So of course democracies won't fight each other.

One trouble with this hypothesis is that it begs the question. Did they not fight each other because they were allied, or did they ally because they feared a common foe (and hence did not fight each other)? And if the latter, did they fear a common foe because they were united in a desire to preserve their common democratic institutions? If the latter, then democracy, not alliance, accounts for the peace among them.

A related hypothesis accounts for peace among members of multilateral alliances not by the alliance per se, but by the active policy of a dominant major power to keep peace within the alliance. Such a hegemonic power may make it very clear to the small powers that in the interest of common security against a major power rival it simply will not tolerate violence among them. Surely in

---

7. Samuel P. Huntington, "No Exit: The Errors of Endism," *The National Interest*, Vol. 17, No. 1 (Fall 1989), pp. 3–11, expressed great skepticism about democratic peace on this ground, and even Small, Melvin, and J. David Singer, "The War-proneness of Democratic Regimes, 1816–1965." *Jerusalem Journal of International Relations*, Vol. 1, No. 4 (Summer 1976), pp. 50–69, strongly implied that their pioneering results on the absence of war between democracies were only an effect of distance.
8. Randolph Siverson and Juliann Emmons, "Birds of a Feather: Democratic Political Systems and Alliance Choices," *Journal of Conflict Resolution*, Vol. 35, No. 2 (June 1991), pp. 285–306, confirm a generalization, stronger since World War II than before it, that democracies are more likely to ally with each other than with nondemocracies. Bueno de Mesquita, Bruce, and David Lalman, *War and Reason: Domestic and International Imperatives* (New Haven, Conn.: Yale University Press, 1992), chap. 5, do not confirm that over the long period they analyze.

the Western Hemisphere (Rio Pact) and in NATO the United States played such a role, with threats to withhold economic and military assistance to the culprits.[9]

The trouble with this variant of the hypothesis, however, is that as a generalization it is empirically backward. Repeated systematic analyses, beginning with Bruce Bueno de Mesquita's,[10] affirm that allies are in general more likely to fight each other, even while still formally allied, than are nonallies. Again, the reasons are not so mysterious: the apparently "common" interests may be enforced by a big power with the capability and will to keep straying allies in the fold. Military action by the Soviet Union against Hungary in 1956 provides an example. Consistent with this interpretation, Stuart Bremer finds allied states likely to fight each other when both states are militarized.[11] But democratic allied states are different; they are not likely to have violent conflicts with each other.[12]

WEALTH MAKES PEACE

Since democracies are often wealthy, it can be hard to separate their effects. Several variants of this argument persist. One is that for politically stable, economically advanced, and rapidly growing countries the cost/benefit ratio of any war fought on or near their home territories with another advanced state looks extraordinarily unpromising. Historically many wars have been fought to acquire territory; the value of acquiring as war booty the territory of an advanced industrial country would rarely compensate for the costs of wartime destruction and the problems of pacifying newly incorporated peoples.[13] The disincentives would be magnified for highly interdependent economies, which suffer even from damage inflicted on each other's territory that destroys investments, markets, or sources of imports. Interdependence also creates groups with vested interests in continuing economic exchanges.[14]

9. Erich Weede, "Extended Deterrence by Superpower Alliance," *Journal of Conflict Resolution,* Vol. 27, No. 2 (1983), pp. 231–254, attributed peace among states of the Western alliance system to the U.S. hegemonic role. Recently (1992), however, he has acknowledged that mutual democracy provides a better explanation.
10. Bruce Bueno de Mesquita, *The War Trap* (New Haven, Conn.: Yale University Press, 1981).
11. Bremer, "Dangerous Dyads."
12. Siverson and Emmons, "Birds of a Feather"; and Bueno de Mesquita and Lalman, *War and Reason,* pp. 166–167.
13. John Mueller, *Retreat from Doomsday: The Obsolescence of Major War* (New York: Basic, 1989); and W. Geoffrey Shepherd, *The Ultimate Deterrent* (New York: Praeger, 1986).
14. Richard Rosecrance, *The Rise of the Trading State* (New York: Basic, 1986); and Helen Milner, *Resisting Protectionism* (Princeton, N.J.: Princeton University Press, 1988).

The wealth-makes-peace argument is thus closely related to the one that transnational interests of trade and investment make peace. Writers as various as the nineteenth-century liberal Richard Cobden, the Marxist Karl Kautsky, and Joseph Schumpeter argued that the web of economic interdependence would promote international peace. Yet Lenin and other theorists of imperialism opined otherwise. Economic interdependence, for example between the United States and Japan, provides both glue and friction. Even where a relationship between trade and peace can be demonstrated, there may be a chicken-and-egg problem. Weak economic ties within the industrialized world during the Depression help explain the political tensions that produced World War II, but after that war peaceful relations were largely established before high levels of economic interdependence were reached in the 1970s.[15] Some systematic evidence indicates that trade diminishes political conflict, with the party receiving greater benefits from trade acting on greater incentives.[16] But if one party perceives the benefits as markedly asymmetrical against it, the effects are not pacific. Trade between rich and poor states may concentrate on raw materials, with the threat of military action by the rich state in the background or forefront. Other research points the primary causal arrow from political relations to economic ones ("trade follows the flag") rather than the other way.[17] As with other generalizations, the conclusions are often context-dependent or indeterminate.[18]

Yet another variant of the wealth-makes-peace view emphasizes growth. Many democracies have experienced fairly consistent rapid economic growth during the past half-century. Rapidly growing states may generally be less inclined to initiate conflict. The reasons are similar to those regarding the connection between wealth and lack of conflict. A special case, however, may be made regarding growth in democracies. States often engage in international conflict to divert attention and anger from domestic problems.[19] Democratic

15. Bruce Russett and Harvey Starr, World Politics: The Menu for Choice, 4th ed. (New York: W.H. Freeman, 1992), pp. 385–392.
16. Mark Gasiorowski and Solomon Polachek, "Conflict and Interdependence: East-West Trade and Linkages in the Era of Détente," Journal of Conflict Resolution, Vol. 26, No. 4 (1982), pp. 709–729; and Solomon Polachek, "Conflict and Trade," Journal of Conflict Resolution, Vol. 24, No. 1 (1980), pp. 55–78.
17. Brian Pollins, "Does Trade Still Follow the Flag?" American Political Science Review, Vol. 83, No. 2 (1989), pp. 465–480; and Brian Pollins, "Conflict, Cooperation, and Commerce: The Effect of International Political Interactions on Bilateral Trade Flows," American Journal of Political Science, Vol. 33, No. 3 (1989), pp. 737–761.
18. Russett, International Regions and the International System; and Bueno de Mesquita and Lalman, War and Reason, p. 289.
19. Jack S. Levy, "The Diversionary Theory of War: A Critique," in Manus Midlarsky, ed., Handbook of War Studies (Boston: Unwin Hyman, 1989), pp. 259–288.

governments are not immune to such temptations. They often initiate international disputes during economic slowdowns or recessions, or if in economic difficulty respond more aggressively when others initiate disputes.[20] But rapidly growing democracies would not have such an incentive for conflict between them.

POLITICAL STABILITY MAKES PEACE
The diversionary effects of economic instability are related to those of political instability. States with stable and durable political systems will lack incentives to externalize domestic discontent into conflict with foreign countries. They will be even more reluctant to engage in conflict against other states that are politically stable. If they see the government of the would-be opponent as possessing substantial legitimacy, they will expect the population at large, and those sectors of society that have ensured domestic stability, to back it in international conflict.[21] Unstable governments have more to gain from scapegoating and diversion, and are more likely to do so when they confront an adversary that faces substantial domestic political problems.

If stable governments are less likely to initiate international disputes, especially against other stable governments, it is important to note that twentieth-century European and Anglo-American democracies were generally more stable—more durable and adaptable—than were nondemocracies.[22] The more years a given type of political system lasts, the better its odds of surviving another year. Perhaps the inherent stability that characterizes many democratic political systems accounts for their low rate of conflict with other democracies. In fact, the combination of variables denoted as stable democracy becomes a component of the theory to be developed and tested in this book.

Conceptually and empirically the competing explanations overlap somewhat and reinforce each other. Some of them are quite plausible. The network of

20. Charles W. Ostrom and Brian Job, "The President and the Political Use of Force," *American Political Science Review*, Vol. 80, No. 2 (1986), pp. 541–566; Russett, *Controlling the Sword: The Democratic Governance of National Security* (Cambridge, Mass.: Harvard University Press, 1990); Bruce Russett and Gad Barzilai, "The Political Economy of Military Actions: Israel and the United States," in Alex Mintz, ed., *The Political Economy of Military Spending in the United States* (London: Unwin Hyman, 1991); and Alex Mintz and Bruce Russett, "The Dual Economy and Israeli Use of Force," in Steve Chan and Alex Mintz, eds., *Defense, Welfare, and Growth* (London: Routledge, 1992), pp. 179–197.
21. Paul Huth and Bruce Russett, "General Deterrence between Enduring Rivals: Testing Three Competing Models," *American Political Science Review*, Vol. 87, No. 1 (1993), pp. 61–73; and Zeev Maoz, "Joining the Club of Nations: Political Development and International Conflict, 1816–1976," *International Studies Quarterly*, Vol. 33, No. 2 (1989), pp. 199–231.
22. Ted Robert Gurr, "Persistence and Change in Political Systems," *American Political Science Review*, Vol. 68, No. 4 (1974), pp. 1482–1504.

international institutions has been strongest in the past half-century among the democratic, allied, prosperous, and politically stable states of Western Europe. Yet counterexamples can be cited for each proffered explanation. There have not been wars even between poor but democratic states, yet World War II is an obvious example of a war pitting advanced capitalist states against each other. Argentina and Britain fought in 1982 despite their common alliance with the United States. The Soviet Union, after achieving apparent stability by the early 1920s, nevertheless fought four wars. Later we will analyze the incidence of wars and less violent conflicts between states in the post-1945 era, with proper statistical controls to test many of the above alternative hypotheses. Even when controls for physical distance, alliance, wealth, economic growth, and political stability are incorporated into the analysis, an independent explanatory role for democracy remains.[23] Nevertheless, no merely empirical relationship can be compelling without a powerful theoretical explanation. Nor can it be clear how widely, in different historical and cultural contexts, the relationship may apply. Two kinds of theories, one stressing norms and the other stressing political structures, offer explanations to which we now turn.

Democratic Norms and Culture?

We should begin with the common assertion that democracies are *inherently* more peaceful or "dovish" internationally because of the political culture favoring the peaceful resolution of disputes, or because democratic processes produce restraint by the general populace which will have to pay the price of war in blood and money.[24] Individual examples of the operation of these factors can easily be found. Over the course of a long war democratic governments may experience seriously eroding domestic support for the war effort, and may feel constrained, if they do go to war, to pursue strategies designed to minimize their own costs, especially in casualties. (U.S. strategy against Iraq in 1991 immediately comes to mind.)

---

23. Also see Bremer, "Dangerous Dyads," and Stuart A. Bremer, "Democracy and Militarized Interstate Conflict, 1816–1965," *International Interactions*, Vol. 18, No. 3 (1993), pp. 231–250, for the effect of democracy even with other controls for relative power, great power status, hegemony, and militarization.

24. Joseph Schumpeter, *Imperialism and Social Classes* (Cleveland, Ohio: World Publishing, 1955); and Jack Snyder, *Myths of Empire: Domestic Politics and International Ambition* (Ithaca, N.Y.: Cornell University Press, 1991).

This is a strong assertion, however, and, overall, the evidence for it as a generalization is not very compelling.[25] It ignores the evidence for the familiar "rally 'round the flag effect" typically induced by the threat or use of force by democracies against other countries. Hostility especially to certain kinds of foreigners—those seen as governed autocratically—can often be mobilized to support military actions by democracies.[26] Elites can even feel impelled by popular pressures to act militarily.[27] Also, so long as this explanation focuses on the characteristics of single states, it cannot explain the consistent evidence that democracies are about as war-prone and disputatious in general (not toward other democracies) as are other kinds of states.[28] Nor can it explain the pattern of nineteenth- and twentieth-century imperialism by democracies.[29] And it would have us believe that the United States was regularly on the defensive, rarely on the offensive, during the Cold War. Though there are elements of plausibility in the argument that democracies are inherently peaceful, it contains too many holes, and is accompanied by too many exceptions, to be usable as a major theoretical building block.

A more plausible theoretical strain, however, yields a more limited assumption. It focuses on powerful norms within democratic states against the use of lethal force under certain conditions—namely, "dovishness" in relations between democracies, though not necessarily in their relations with other kinds of states. Several authors offer a perspective emphasizing social diversity, perceptions of individual rights, overlapping group memberships, cross-pressures, shifting coalitions, expectations of limited government, and toleration of dissent by a presumably loyal opposition. The basic norm of democratic theory is that disputes can be resolved without force through democratic political

---

25. Bueno de Mesquita and Lalman, *War and Reason*, p. 155, find that by their measure the mean domestic costs to democracies of using force are greater than for nondemocracies, but the difference is small. Bremer, "Dangerous Dyads," and Bremer, "Democracy and Militarized Interstate Conflict," suggests a mixed picture; i.e., democracies are less likely to originate wars with all kinds of states, but more likely to join wars being fought by other states.

26. Nehemia Geva, Karl DeRouen, and Alex Mintz, "The Political Incentive Explanation of the 'Democratic Peace' Phenomenon: Evidence from Experimental Research," *International Interactions*, Vol. 18, No. 3 (1993), pp. 215–229; and Alex Mintz and Nehemia Geva, "Why Don't Democracies Fight Each Other? An Experimental Assessment of the 'Political Incentive' Explanation," *Journal of Conflict Resolution*, Vol. 37, No. 3 (1993).

27. Russett, *Controlling the Sword*, chap. 2.

28. Maoz and Abdolali, "Regime Types and International Conflict"; Bremer, "Dangerous Dyads"; and Russett, *Grasping the Democratic Peace*, ch. 4.

29. On Snyder's effort, *Myths of Empire*, see Fareed Zakaria, "Realism and Domestic Politics: A Review Essay," *International Security*, Vol. 17, No. 1 (Summer 1992), pp. 177–198.

processes that in some balance ensure both majority rule and minority rights. A norm of equality operates both as voting equality and certain egalitarian rights to human dignity. Democratic government rests on the consent of the governed, but justice demands that consent not be abused. Resort to organized lethal violence, or the threat of it, is considered illegitimate, and unnecessary to secure one's "legitimate" rights. Dissent within broad limits by a loyal opposition is expected and even needed for enlightened policy-making, and the opposition's basic loyalty to the system is to be assumed in the absence of evidence to the contrary.[30]

All participants in the political process are expected to share these norms. Even though all these images may be founded to a large extent on myth as well as on reality, they may operate as powerful restraints on violence between such systems. In practice the norms do sometimes break down, but the normative restraints on violent behavior—by state and citizens—are fully as important as the state's monopoly on the legitimate use of force in keeping incidents of the organized use of force rare. The norms themselves may be more important than any particular institutional structure (two-party/multiparty, republican/parliamentary) or formal constitutional provision. If institutions precede the development of norms in the polity, the basis for restraint is likely to be less secure.

By this hypothesis, the *culture, perceptions, and practices* that permit compromise and the peaceful resolution of conflicts without the threat of violence within countries come to apply across national boundaries toward other democratic countries. In short, if people in a democracy perceive themselves as autonomous, self-governing people who share norms of live-and-let-live, they will respect the rights of others to self-determination if those others are also perceived as self-governing and hence not easily led into aggressive foreign policies by a self-serving elite. The same structures and behaviors that "we" assume will limit our aggression, both internally and externally, may be expected similarly to limit similarly governed people in other polities. Those who claim the principle of self-determination for themselves are expected to extend it to others. Within a transnational democratic culture, as within a democratic nation, others are seen as possessing rights and exercising those rights in a spirit of enlightened self-interest. Acknowledgment of those rights allows us to mitigate our fears that they will try to dominate us. That acknowledgment

---

30. Most of the authors cited in "The Fact of Democratic Peace," note 25 write predominantly from this perspective.

also prevents us from wishing to dominate them; a norm that it would be wrong to do so in effect raises the "costs" to us of doing so.

By contrast, these restraints do not apply toward a country governed by very different and nondemocratic principles. According to democratic norms, authoritarian states do not rest on the proper consent of the governed, and thus they cannot properly represent the will of their peoples—if they did, they would not need to rule through undemocratic, authoritarian institutions. Rulers who control their own people by such means, who do not behave in a just way that respects their own people's rights to self-determination, cannot be expected to behave better toward peoples outside their states. "Because nonliberal governments are in a state of aggression with their own people, their foreign relations become for liberal governments deeply suspect. In short, fellow liberals benefit from a presumption of amity; nonliberals suffer from a presumption of enmity."[31] The essence of America's Cold War ideology was that it had no quarrel with the Russian people, but only with the atheistic communist elites who repressed them. A vision of the other people as not in self-governing control of their own destiny justified a hostile policy. Authoritarian states are expected to aggress against others if given the power and the opportunity. By this reasoning, democracies must be eternally vigilant and may even need to engage in defensively motivated war or preemptive action anticipating an immediate attack.

Whereas wars against other democratic states are neither expected nor considered legitimate, wars against authoritarian states may often be both. Thus an international system composed of both democratic and authoritarian states will include both zones of peace (actual and expected, among the democracies) and zones of war or at best deterrence between democratic and authoritarian states. And by this reasoning democracies may fight wars and other lethal conflicts as often as authoritarian states do—which is what most of the systematic empirical evidence indicates. They just will not fight each other.

The presumption of enmity from and toward nondemocracies was exemplified by American determination to root out aggressive fascism and Nazism in Japan and Germany after World War II, and to establish the basis for democratic government there. It took more dubious forms in many Cold War interventions (including covert operations, which we shall consider later) and in the 1989 invasion of Panama. Elihu Root's wartime rhetoric, in his presiden-

---

31. Doyle, Michael W. "Liberalism and World Politics." *American Political Science Review*, Vol. 80, No. 4 (December 1986), pp. 1151–1169.

tial address to the American Society of International Law, expressed the tradition vividly:

So long as military autocracy continues, democracy is not safe from attacks, which are certain to come, and certain to find it unprepared. The conflict is inevitable and universal; and it is *à l'outrance*. To be safe democracy must kill its enemy when it can and where it can. The world can not be half democratic and half autocratic. It must be all democratic or all Prussian. There can be no compromise. If it is all Prussian, there can be no real international law. If it is all democratic, international law honored and observed may well be expected as a natural development of the principles which make democratic self-government possible.[32]

These assumptions lead to the following propositions about democracies' external relations. The norms of regulated political competition, compromise solutions to political conflicts, and peaceful transfer of power are externalized by democracies in their dealing with other national actors in world politics. On the other hand, nondemocracies may not externalize these norms. Hence, when two democracies come into a conflict of interest, they are able to apply democratic norms in their interaction, and these norms prevent most conflicts from mounting to the threat or use of military force. If they do go that far, at least they will not go to all-out war. By contrast, when a democracy comes into conflict with a nondemocracy, it will not expect the nondemocratic state to be restrained by those norms. It may feel obliged to adapt to the harsher norms of international conduct of the latter, lest it be exploited or eliminated by the nondemocratic state that takes advantage of the inherent moderation of democracies. Similarly, conflict between nondemocracies may be dominated by the norm of forceful conduct and search for decisive (noncompromise) outcome or elimination of the adversary.

Robert Axelrod's work on the evolution of cooperation and norms shows how norms of behavior depend heavily on the environment in which they are applied.[33] When a player employing a conditionally cooperative strategy like tit-for-tat is confronted by someone playing a consistently noncooperative

---

32. Elihu Root, "The Effect of Democracy on International Law," presidential address to the annual meeting of the American Society of International Law, Washington, D.C., April 26, 1917.
33. Robert Axelrod, *The Evolution of Cooperation* (New York: Basic, 1984); Robert Axelrod, "An Evolutionary Theory of Norms," *American Political Science Review*, Vol. 80, No. 4 (December 1986), pp. 1095–1112; also Roy Behr, "Nice Guys Finish Last . . . Sometimes," *Journal of Conflict Resolution*, Vol. 25, No. 2 (1980), pp. 289–300; and Raymond Dacey and Norman Pendergraft, "The Optimality of Tit-for-tat," *International Interactions*, Vol. 15, No. 1 (1988), pp. 45–64.

strategy, noncooperation dominates. Short of teaching cooperation to "meanies"—which takes a long time—noncooperative strategies typically force cooperative strategies to become noncooperative.[34]

Legal systems in democratic states seem to make distinctions between democratic and authoritarian states when deciding whether to enforce in their own courts the laws of other nations. Other democratic states are recognized as within a "zone of law," a legal community defined by various institutional and ideological similarities. Courts in democracies share enough common values to recognize and enforce each other's law in accord with pluralist principles of tolerance and reciprocity. They do not, however, recognize the legal systems of nondemocratic states as equal partners; they are seen as lacking the political autonomy of democratic legal systems, and hence not appropriate as providing norms for conflict resolution.[35]

Governments and political institutions can change rapidly after a revolution, but norms take time to develop. Laws can change faster than the practices in which norms are embedded. Formal norms such as one of nonrecourse to war can be written into a constitution, but become effective only with the repeated practice of bargaining and conciliation.[36] Thus if violent conflicts between democracies do occur, we would expect them to take place between democratic states that are relatively young in terms of the tenure of the democratic regime. That is, they would occur between states in at least one of which democratic norms have not matured to a degree that is expressed in moderate and dependable strategies of peaceful conflict management. Democratic governments in which democratic norms are not yet fully developed are likely to be unstable, or to be perceived by other states as unstable, so they may be unable to practice norms of democratic conflict resolution internationally. Equally important, the democratic states with whom they develop conflicts of interest may not perceive them as dependable in their practices. Newness and instability cloud others' perceptions.

Of course, democracies have not fought wars only out of motivations of self-defense, however broadly one may define self-defense to include anticipation of others' aggression or to include "extended deterrence" for the defense

---

34. I owe this argument to Zeev Maoz.
35. Anne-Marie Burley, "Law among Liberal States: Liberal Internationalism and Act of State Doctrine," *Columbia Law Review,* Vol. 92, No. 8 (1992), pp. 1907–1996.
36. Friedrich Kratochwil, *Rules, Norms and Decisions* (London: Cambridge University Press, 1991).

of allies and other interests. Many of them have also fought imperialist wars to acquire or hold colonies, or to retain control of states formally independent but within their spheres of influence. Here is another aspect of perception and misperception, of cases where democracies have fought against people who on one ground or another could be characterized as not self-governing.

The nineteenth-century objects of colonial expansion were peoples who in most instances were outside the European state system. They were in most instances not people with white skins, and whose institutions of government did not conform to the Western democratic institutional forms of their coloniz-ers. Europeans' ethnocentric views of those peoples carried the *assumption* that they did not have institutions of self-government. Not only were they available for imperial aggrandizement, they could be considered candidates for better-ment and even "liberation"—the white man's burden, or *mission civilatrice*. They could be brought the benefits not only of modern material civilization, but of Western principles of self-government. If they did not have such insti-tutions already, then by definition they were already being exploited and repressed. Their governments or tribal leaders could not, in this ethnocentric view, be just or consensual, and thus one need have few compunctions about conquering these legitimate candidates for "liberal" imperialism.[37] Later, when Western forms of self-government did begin to take root on a local basis in many of the colonies, the extremes of pseudo-Darwinian racism lost their legitimacy. Decolonization came not only because the colonial governments lost the power to retain their colonies, but because in many cases they lost confi-dence in their normative right to rule.

We can now summarize all this discussion about restraints on violent conflict among democracies in a set of propositions as follows.

The Cultural/Normative Model

1. In relations with other states, decisionmakers (whether they be few or many) will try to follow the same norms of conflict resolution as have been developed within and characterize their domestic political processes.
2. They will expect decisionmakers in other states likewise to follow the same norms of conflict resolution as have been developed within and characterize those other states' domestic political processes.

---

37. As shown in chap. 5 of Russett, *Grasping the Democratic Peace*, in fact "preindustrial" peoples often had participatory forms of government that shared many democratic attributes.

A. Violent conflicts between democracies will be rare because:

3. In democracies, the relevant decisionmakers expect to be able to resolve conflicts by compromise and nonviolence, respecting the rights and continued existence of opponents.
4. Therefore democracies will follow norms of peaceful conflict resolution with other democracies, and will expect other democracies to do so with them.
5. The more stable the democracy, the more will democratic norms govern its behavior with other democracies, and the more will other democracies expect democratic norms to govern its international behavior.
6. If violent conflicts between democracies do occur, at least one of the democracies is likely to be politically unstable.

B. Violent conflicts between nondemocracies, and between democracies and nondemocracies, will be more frequent because:

7. In nondemocracies, decisionmakers use, and may expect their opponents to use, violence and the threat of violence to resolve conflict as part of their domestic political processes.
8. Therefore nondemocracies may use violence and the threat of violence in conflicts with other states, and other states may expect them to use violence and the threat of violence in such conflicts.
9. Democratic norms can be more easily exploited to force concessions than can nondemocratic ones; to avoid exploitation democracies may adopt nondemocratic norms in dealing with nondemocracies.

The numbered propositions are part of the deductive structure, and whereas it will be useful further to illustrate their application and plausibility, we will not subject most of them to rigorous empirical testing. The basic empirical statements A and B, however, will be so tested, in the form that *violent conflicts between democracies should be observed much less frequently than between democracies and nondemocracies.* Indeed, because of the susceptibility of democratic norms to exploitation, we may well find *violent conflicts between democracies and at least some kinds of nondemocracies to be more frequent than would be expected* if conflicts were distributed around the international system totally by chance. Proposition 6, that *if violent conflicts do arise between democracies at least one of the democracies is likely to be politically unstable,* also is empirically testable. As such, it can provide some extra empirical content to the basic hypothesis about the relative frequency of violent conflict of democracies with other democracies and with nondemocracies.

Propositions 5 and 6 therefore incorporate into the cultural/normative theoretical structure the point about political stability that was initially treated as one of several alternative perspectives on the phenomenon of peace between democracies. They do not yet, however, indicate just why force might be used when one democracy in a pair is politically unstable.

As noted in the discussion about the possible role of economic growth or its absence, increasing evidence is accumulating that democracies are more likely to use or threaten to use military force, in general, when the economy has been doing badly. Most of the studies cited there also indicate that democracies are more likely to use or threaten to use military force in the year or months immediately preceding an election.[38] The motivation, of diverting hostility toward foreigners and of producing a "rally 'round the flag" effect for the party in power, is similar. If we expand the notion of political instability to include domestic political threats to the government because of its economic policy shortcomings, or competition in a close election, this gives us a temporal context for the possible use of military force by democracies. It suggests that the "unstable" state will initiate, or escalate, the use of force in a diplomatic dispute. But it does not tell us against whom it may direct that force.

To do that, we can elaborate the hypothesis as suggesting that the threat or use of *force will be directed against states that a democracy perceives as politically unstable.* At least two possible reasons for this come to mind: The state may see an unstable democratic regime as under these political pressures, and hence as a real danger needing to be forcibly constrained or deterred. Alternatively, an unstable democratic regime may seem a publicly more legitimate and acceptable object for diverting hostility and provoking a rally effect. That is, the government may truly feel itself threatened in some degree by such a regime, or, if not, it may believe that the public will at least accept perception of a threat. If the adversary is perceived as a stable democracy, by contrast, the cultural/normative argument suggests little political benefit in trying to invoke a rally against it. Thus instability may work both as encouraging the use or threat of force by the "unstable" regime, and in selecting an "unstable" object for the exercise of force.

Empirically it will be very difficult to sort out the mechanism systematically. Even in the 1946–86 period with many democracies in the international system,

---

38. They are not, however, more likely just before elections to engage in the full-scale use of military force known as war; if anything they are more likely to go to war during the year just after the election has passed. See Kurt Taylor Gaubatz, "Election Cycles and War," *Journal of Conflict Resolution*, Vol. 35, No. 2 (1991), pp. 212–244.

Table 1.2 showed only fourteen militarized disputes between democracies. In their manifestation of threat or use of force all of them were extremely localized, typically an air incursion or shelling in the general direction of a boat lasting a single day. None were reciprocated uses of military force, in which the attacked party made any military reprisal, and nearly all of them were bloodless. Most could plausibly have been unauthorized acts by local commanders. In most instances it is hard to show that they were deliberate and considered governmental acts of the sort plausibly included under the rubric of politically motivated incidents just discussed. And while one can identify who actually used force or first threatened to use it, it is not so easy to say which side played the greater role in provoking the incident. Thus one should not expect to find a systematic pattern of motivation in such low-level incidents. In near-wars, however—where the level of violence may be greater, and the degree of central control and deliberate act may be stronger—we may find some such evidence.

We should also, by extension, expect such events to occur *between states where one or both states' status as a democracy leaves some basis for doubt.* Perceptions of instability may be based on the recency and immaturity of experience with democratic processes and norms: a new democracy will not yet have developed wide experience in practices of democratic conflict resolution. Perceptions of instability may also be based on a high degree of violent opposition to the democratic government: a democracy under siege of domestic terrorism, insurgency, or civil war is one in which the ostensible norms of peaceful conflict resolution simply are not working well. If a government's practice of democratic forms of government is very recent and subject to violent domestic challenge, or its practice of democracy is incomplete or imperfect by the standards of the day, it may be imperfectly constrained by the norms of democratic government that are supposed to keep conflict nonviolent. Or uncertainty about the commitment to democratic norms by the state with which one has a conflict of interest may lead to perceptions and expectations that it will practice those norms imperfectly.

The list of numbered propositions above often implies a dichotomy between democratic and nondemocratic states. But in the real world such a dichotomy masks degrees of democratic practice. Therefore if we find militarized disputes between democracies we should typically find that one party or both is only recently democratic, is subject to violent domestic challenge, or is toward the center of a democratic to nondemocratic continuum. We should also, in a revised version of proposition 6, look for evidence that one party, correctly or not, *perceives* the other as not really democratic.

Structural and Institutional Constraints?

As with the normative and cultural argument, it is best to avoid assuming that democracies are dovish or peaceful in all their relations. Rather, a plausible argument can be constructed on the strategic principles of rational action; that is, about how states, in interactions of threat and bargaining, behave in anticipation of how their bargaining adversaries will behave. Decisionmakers develop images of the government and public opinion of other countries. They regard some governments or peoples as slow to fight, or as ready and eager to do so. In forming these images leaders look for various cues: in other leaders' and countries' past behavior in diplomatic or military disputes, and in other countries' form of government. Perhaps other governments will see a democracy as culturally (normatively) dovish on the above grounds, but Kant's own view argued that *institutional constraints*—a structure of division of powers, checks and balances—would make it difficult for democratic leaders to move their countries into war.

Democracies are constrained in going to war by the need to ensure broad popular support, manifested in various institutions of government. Leaders must mobilize public opinion to obtain legitimacy for their actions. Bureaucracies, the legislature, and private interest groups often incorporated in conceptualizations of the "state" must acquiesce. The nature and mix of institutions vary in different kinds of states (for example, "strong" states and "weak" states, parliamentary and presidential systems) but it is complex. Popular support in a democracy can be built by rhetoric and exhortation, but not readily compelled.

The complexity of the mobilization process means that leaders will not readily embark on an effort to prepare the country for war unless they are confident they can demonstrate a favorable ratio of costs and benefits to be achieved, at acceptable risk.[39] Moreover, the complexity of the process requires time for mobilization, as the leaders of various institutions are convinced and formal approval is obtained. Not only may it take longer for democracies to

---

39. David Lake, "Powerful Pacifists: Democratic States and War," *American Political Science Review*, Vol. 86, No. 1 (1992), pp. 24–37, (also Mark R. Brawley, "Regime Types, Markets and War: The Importance of Pervasive Rents in Foreign Policy," paper presented at the annual meeting of the International Studies Association, Atlanta, April 1992) makes a structural argument that democracies with broad franchises are inherently less imperialistic than are autocratic states, and while democracies may fight to resist autocracies, the conjuncture of two democracies with low imperialist drive makes them unlikely to fight each other. His empirical test is indirect, however, of a derived proposition that democracies will win wars in which they engage more often than will

gear up for war, the process is immensely more public than in an authoritarian state. Democratic governments can respond to sudden attack by using emergency powers, and by the same powers can even strike preemptively in crisis. But in normal times they are ill suited to launching surprise attacks.[40] Apparently for these reasons, major-power democracies seem never to have launched preventive war (a deliberate attack not under immediate provocation) against another major power.[41] The greater the scale, cost, and risk of using violence, the more effort must be devoted to preparations in public, and of the public.

Even if two states were totally ignorant of each other's form of government, structural delays in the process of mobilization for war in both states would provide time to elapse for negotiation and other means of peaceful conflict resolution. Yet perceptions matter here too. If another nation's leaders regard a state as democratic, they will anticipate a difficult and lengthy process before the democracy is likely to use significant military force against them. They will expect an opportunity to reach a negotiated settlement if they wish to achieve such a settlement. Perhaps most importantly, a democracy will not fear a surprise attack by another democracy, and thus need not cut short the negotiating process or launch a preemptive strike in anticipation of surprise attack.

If democratic leaders generally consider other democracies to be reluctant and slow to fight because of institutional constraints (and possibly because of a general aversion of the people to war), they will not fear being attacked by another democracy. Two democratic states—each constrained from going to war and anticipating the other to be so inhibited—likely will settle their conflicts short of war. Bruce Bueno de Mesquita and David Lalman provide a deductive argument that two such states, each with perfect information about the other's constraints, will always settle their conflicts by negotiation or by retaining the status quo.[42] In the real world perfect information is lacking, but the presence of democratic institutions provides a visible and generally correct signal of "practical dovishness"—restraints on war in the form of institutional

---

autocracies. The latter can alternatively be attributed to democracies' greater ability to motivate their citizens and to superior information-processing capability. See Russett, *Controlling the Sword*, p. 150.

40. Ben Hunt has suggested, in a personal communication, that the degree of elites' control by public opinion may be the key variable, and that, while it is highly correlated with democracy, the correlation is not perfect—some democracies' elites may be less constrained than are others by public opinion, and some autocracies more so than others.

41. Randall L. Schweller, "Domestic Structure and Preventive War: Are Democracies More Pacific?" *World Politics*, Vol. 44, No. 2 (1992), pp. 235–269.

42. Bueno de Mesquita and Lalman, *War and Reason*, chap. 4.

constraint if not of inherent disposition. Reading that sign, democracies will rarely if ever go to war with each other.

Leaders of nondemocratic states may also anticipate that a democratic country will be slow to go to war. But if they are themselves aggressive, they may be more likely to threaten or bully a democracy to make concessions. In turn, that would raise the threshold of provocation facing the democracy, and perhaps overcome its initial inhibition against fighting. That would explain why the overall frequency of war fighting by democracies is no different from that of nondemocratic states.[43] But leaders of two nondemocratic states, neither encumbered by powerful structural constraints, are more likely than two democratic states to escalate to war.

This argument can be summarized as follows.

The Structural/Institutional Model:

A. Violent conflicts between democracies will be infrequent because:

1. In democracies, the constraints of checks and balances, division of power, and need for public debate to enlist widespread support will slow decisions to use large-scale violence and reduce the likelihood that such decisions will be made.

2. Leaders of other states will perceive leaders of democracies as so constrained.

3. Thus leaders of democracies will expect, in conflicts with other democracies, time for processes of international conflict resolution to operate, and they will not fear surprise attack.

B. Violent conflicts between nondemocracies, and between democracies and nondemocracies, will be frequent because:

---

43. In chapter 5 of *War and Reason*, Bueno de Mesquita and Lalman present this hypothesis and some confirming evidence. (Similar reasoning goes back at least to Quincy Wright, *A Study of War* [Chicago: University of Chicago Press, 1942], pp. 842–845; and Harvey Starr, "Democracy and War: Choice, Learning, and Security Communities," *Journal of Peace Research*, Vol. 29, No. 2 [1992], pp. 207–213, Harvey Starr, "Why Don't Democracies Fight One Another? Evaluating the Theory-Findings Feedback Loop," *Jerusalem Journal of International Relations*, Vol. 14, No. 4 [Spring 1992], pp. 41–59, extends the insight that forms of government signal a state's likely international behavior.) Bueno de Mesquita and Lalman reject (pp. 152–155) the argument that "the political culture of democracies leads to an abhorrence of violence" in general, and build their theory on the assumption that democratic leaders "face a greater political cost for using force." In context they treat this as an institutional constraint, though in a personal communication Bueno de Mesquita suggested that democratic norms may similarly raise the costs.

4. Leaders of nondemocracies are not constrained as leaders of democracies are, so they can more easily, rapidly, and secretly initiate large-scale violence.

5. Leaders of states (democracies and nondemocracies) in conflict with nondemocracies may initiate violence rather than risk surprise attack.

6. Perceiving that leaders of democracies will be constrained, leaders of nondemocracies may press democracies to make greater concessions over issues in conflict.

7. Democracies may initiate large-scale violence with nondemocracies rather than make the greater concessions demanded.

Distinguishing the Explanations

The cultural/normative and institutional/structural explanations are not neatly separable. Institutions depend on norms and procedures. For example, stability, which we treated as a measure of normative acceptance of democratic processes, is also an institutional constraint if political structures are not subject to overthrow. States may also consider the dominant norms in other states, as well as their institutions, as signals; thus both explanations also depend in part on perceptions. Great emphasis on reading signals of the other's intention, however, slights the importance of self-constraint. Institutions may slow or obstruct one's own ability to fight. Perhaps more importantly, a norm that it is somehow not "right" to fight another democracy raises the moral and political cost, and thus limits one's own willingness to do so. Bueno de Mesquita and Lalman neglect this,[44] as well as the opposition a democratic government might find among its own population against fighting another *democratic government*.[45] Within democracies, structural impediments to using force are less strong than within autocracies; normative restraints must bear the load. So we should not assume that normative constraints are unimportant in relations between democracies. Both norms and institutions may contribute to the phenomenon of peace between democracies; they are somewhat complementary and overlapping. But they are also in some degree distinctive and competing explanations, allowing us to look for greater impact of one or another in various contexts.

Other influences, such as trade and the network of international law and organizations as suggested by Kant, likely also play a role in directly supple-

---

44. Bueno de Mesquita and Lalman, *War and Reason.*
45. Geva, DeRouen, and Mintz, "The Political Incentive Explanation."

menting and strengthening that of democracy. Further elaboration of the theoretical arguments is probably needed. Certainly, detailed empirical work is necessary on how institutions operate, and on how perceptions toward other countries evolve, so as to make it possible to weigh the relative power of institutional and normative explanations. So too is the creation and application of systematic empirical tests to differentiate between the two kinds of explanations for violence in the modern interstate system.

Another way of differentiating between the two is to look for other hypotheses that may be derived from either, and tested. One such hypothesis for the normative model is represented in work by William Dixon.[46] He postulates that *democracies, with norms of using third-party intervention for peaceful and non-coercive resolution of conflicts internally, will carry those norms into management of their international conflicts with other democracies.* Dixon then looks at how international conflicts have been settled in the post-World War II era. Not only does he confirm our results from Table 1.2 that conflicts between democracies are much less likely to escalate to lethal violence and to be settled peacefully, but he finds that they are much more likely to be settled by some means of third-party conflict management, such as the use of good offices, mediation, and intervention. Also, all conflicts between democracies were ended either by agreement or by stalemate; none terminated in a settlement imposed by one of them or by a third party. Such a pattern is much more readily explicable by common norms than by characteristics of internal democratic institutions acting as constraint. Russell Leng similarly infers support for the normative argument from evidence that in interstate crises democracies are much more likely to use strategies of reciprocating the escalatory or de-escalatory moves of other states than are authoritarian regimes.[47] He argues that reciprocation is an engrained democratic norm, as contrasted with behavior like bullying, appeasing, or stonewalling.

Another test can be derived from the patterns of strategic interaction as discussed in the model of structural constraints. By that argument, two democracies engaged in a conflictual bargaining process with each other can reasonably expect each other not to escalate the dispute to the point of war or serious

---

46. William Dixon, "Democracy and the Management of International Conflict," *Journal of Conflict Resolution*, Vol. 37, No. 1 (1993), pp. 42–68; also William Dixon, "Democracy and the Peaceful Settlement of International Conflict," paper presented at the annual meeting of the American Political Science Association, Chicago, September 1992.

47. Russell Leng, "Reciprocating Influence Strategies and Success in Interstate Crisis Bargaining," *Journal of Conflict Resolution*, Vol. 37, No. 1 (1993), pp. 3–41.

violence. Therefore, many bargaining models predict there would be few strategic restraints on escalating the conflict up to, but not beyond, the point of an exchange of lethal violence. In fact, each state might have strong incentives to go that far for the purpose of showing resolve; perhaps even escalating to the first (limited) use of force in confidence that the other would be unlikely to reply in any substantial military manner. Such behavior is implicit in the bargaining "game" of chicken, which is widely applied to crisis negotiation.[48] This reasoning, therefore, leads to the prediction that disputes between democracies should commonly escalate to the display and even limited use of force, though not to war. But as Table 1.2 showed, that is not the case. Democracy/democracy pairs are less likely to enter into militarized disputes at all than are other pairs of states, and less likely to escalate them at any level up the escalation ladder—not just at the top to war.[49]

Rather, this suggests that *to use or threaten to use force is not usually normatively acceptable behavior in disputes between democracies,* even in the form of symbolic, ritualized bargaining behavior. Relations between democracies therefore fit into the category of "stable peace"[50] or a "security community"[51] in which states not only do not fight each other, they do not expect to fight each other, or significantly prepare to fight each other. In such relationships disputes are routinely settled without recourse to threat and military deterrence. Dependent as the definition of security community has been on expectations, it has been a difficult phenomenon to observe reliably; here, in the relative absence of militarized dispute and escalation, is a reasonably objective measure.

The Future of the Democratic Peace

Compared with their actions toward other kinds of states, democracies in the modern world are unlikely to engage in militarized disputes with each other.

---

48. Steven J. Brams and D. Marc Kilgour, *Game Theory and National Security* (Oxford: Basil Blackwell, 1988); Steven J. Brams, *Negotiation Games: Applying Game Theory to Bargaining and Arbitration* (London: Routledge, 1990); and William Poundstone, *Prisoner's Dilemma* (New York: Doubleday, 1992).
49. James Fearon, "Audience Costs, Learning, and the Escalation of International Disputes," manuscript, Political Science Department, University of Chicago, 1992, argues from the structural tradition that escalation represents a costly signal especially for democratic leaders who risk being forced to back down in front of their powerful domestic audience. If so, disputes between democracies should indeed show less escalation, but the initiation of disputes between democracies would not necessarily be less frequent.
50. Kenneth Boulding, *Stable Peace* (Austin: University of Texas Press, 1979).
51. Deutsch, et al., *Political Community and the North Atlantic Area.*

When they do get into disputes with each other, they are less likely to let the disputes escalate. They rarely fight each other even at low levels of lethal violence, and never (or almost never) go to war against each other. They are not in any of these respects markedly more peaceful toward authoritarian states than authoritarian states are toward each other. But democracies' relatively peaceful relations toward each other are well established, and are not spuriously caused by some other influence such as sharing high levels of wealth or rapid economic growth or ties of alliance. Peace among democracies was not maintained simply by pressure from a common adversary in the Cold War, and it is outlasting that threat. The more democratic each state is, the more peaceful their relations are likely to be.

The phenomenon of democratic peace can be explained by the pervasiveness of normative restraints on conflict between democracies. That explanation extends to the international arena the cultural norms of live-and-let-live and peaceful conflict resolution that operate within democracies. The phenomenon of democratic peace can also be explained by the role of structural restraints on democracies' decisions to go to war. Those restraints ensure that in a conflict of interest with a democracy another state can expect ample time for conflict-resolution processes to be effective, and virtually no risk of incurring surprise attack.

Evidence supports both of these explanatory models. The debate between their proponents is not settled, nor should it be seen entirely as a debate. They are not fully separable in theory or in practice. Both make a contribution, and the two kinds of influences reinforce each other to produce the phenomenon of democratic peace.

Nevertheless, some evidence suggests that the normative model is the more powerful. Norms, as measured by the absence of violence in domestic politics and the duration of democratic regimes, were somewhat more strongly associated with peace between democracies than was our measure of structural/institutional constraints. When democracies do have serious diplomatic disputes, they are unlikely to escalate them—as a normative explanation would predict, contrary to common structural models. They are more likely to reciprocate each other's behavior, to accept third party mediation or good offices in settling disputes, and to settle disputes peacefully. The spread of democratic norms and practices in the world, if consolidated, should reduce the frequency of violent conflict and war. Where normative restraints are insufficient, institutionalized restraints on foreign policy decision-making may be a second-best influence. Yet in democracies with institutional constraints but weak normative ones (due to recency of democracy, or violence or instability), charismatic or adventurous leaders may override the institutional limits.

In the world of ancient Greece the institutions that could be expected to restrain the resort to force by democracies were almost entirely lacking, and the norms that democracies should not fight each other were nascent and weak. But there was some evidence of restraint attributable to norms. In most of the wars that did occur between democracies, perception of political instability in the adversary state, and misperception of its democratic nature, played an important role in instigating the war.

Nonindustrial societies, as studied by anthropologists, also provide an opportunity to look for restraints on warfare among democratically organized polities that typically lack the institutional constraints of a modern state. Yet despite that absence, democratically organized units evince significantly less warfare with each other than do nondemocratically organized units. Moreover, political stability (or its absence) again proves an important influence on the resort to violence by those democratically organized units. These findings, more than those about ancient Greece, support the proposition that democracies are in general relatively peaceful toward each other. Though the relationship is not quite so strong and consistent as that which emerges in the modern international system, to find it at all in nonindustrial societies shows that the phenomenon of democratic peace is not limited to contemporary Western democracies.

Strengthening Democracy and Its Norms

The literature on the "prerequisites" of democracy is vast, and much of it is deeply flawed—ethnocentric and too enamoured of economic preconditions. Yet some things have been learned, and stated with some modesty, in recent analyses. Among several good efforts,[52] the most prominent may be Samuel Huntington's book, *The Third Wave: Democratization in the Late Twentieth Cen-*

---

52. Dahl, *Democracy and Its Critics*; Guillermo O'Donnell, Philippe Schmitter, and Laurence Whitehead, *Transitions from Authoritarian Rule* (Baltimore, Md.: Johns Hopkins University Press, 1986); Larry Diamond, Juan Linz, and Seymour Martin Lipset, eds., *Democracy in Developing Countries* (Boulder, Colo.: Lynne Rienner, 1989); Giuseppe DiPalma, *To Craft Democracies: An Essay on Democratic Transitions* (Berkeley: University of California Press, 1990); Dietrich Rueschmeyer, Evelyne Huber, Stephens, and John D. Stephens, *Capitalist Development and Democracy* (Chicago: University of Chicago Press, 1992); and also the review in Graham T. Allison and Robert P. Beschel, "Can the United States Promote Democracy?" *Political Science Quarterly*, Vol. 107, No. 1 (1992), pp. 81–98.

tury.[53] Since it reviews most of the earlier literature a summary of its conclusions should suffice. Nor do its conclusions depart markedly from those of most other recent analyses. Huntington begins by identifying five changes in the world that played significant parts in *producing* the latest wave of recent transitions to democracy: (1) deepening legitimacy problems of authoritarian governments unable to cope with military defeat and economic failure; (2) economic growth that has raised living standards, educational levels, and urbanization—raising expectations and the ability to express them; (3) changes in religious institutions that made them less defenders of the status quo than opponents of governmental authoritarianism; (4) changes in the policies of other states and international organizations, to promote human rights and democracy; and (5) "snowballing" or demonstration effects, enhanced by international communication, as transitions to democracy in some states served as models for their neighbors.

Later in the book, Huntington lists conditions that have favored or are favoring the *consolidation* of new democracies: (1) experience of a previous effort at democratization, even if it failed; (2) a high level of economic development; (3) a favorable international political environment, with outside assistance; (4) early timing of the transition to democracy, relative to a worldwide "wave," indicating that the drive to democracy derived primarily from indigenous rather than exogenous influences; (5) experience of a relatively peaceful rather than violent transition; and (6) the number and severity of the problems confronted.[54]

Such lists do not lead to simple diagnosis or prescription, with "necessary" or "sufficient" conditions, but they do offer a helpful focus for discussion. Most importantly, they single out both internal and external influences on the process of democratization. Internal influences are certainly prominent, especially in the consolidation list. It is hard to imagine a successful consolidation of democracy without many or most of them. But the list of international conditions is impressive also. Favorable international conditions may not be essential (either alone or in combination) in every case, but they can make a difference, and sometimes a crucial one when the internal influences are mixed. The United States and its allies have made a difference—for the defeated Axis powers after World War II, and sometimes in other cases since that time.

---

53. Huntington, *The Third Wave*, pp. 45–46.
54. Ibid., pp. 270–279.

Currently, with economic conditions so bad in much of the Third World, Eastern Europe, and the former Soviet Union, and the consequent dangers to the legitimacy of new democratic governments, external assistance—technical and financial—is especially important. Rather small amounts—but more than have been forthcoming to date—could make a difference. As a stick, aid can surely be denied to governments that regularly violate human rights, for example of ethnic minorities. Clear anti-democratic acts, such as a military coup or an aborted election, can be punished by suspending aid. As to the carrot of extending aid on a conditional basis, broader goals of developing democratic institutions require creation of a civil society, and are less easily made conditional. Recipients may see multilateral aid, with conditions of democratic reform attached, as a less blatant invasion of their sovereignty than aid from a single country.[55] Without exaggerating the prospects for success, it would be a terrible loss if the United States and other rich democracies did not make serious efforts. It would be a loss, as the Bush-Baker rhetoric claims, to themselves as well as to the peoples of the struggling democracies.

A special complication, one hardly unique to the current era but felt acutely now, is nationalism in the quilt of ethnicities left behind from the former Soviet Empire. Nationalism, with its combination of inclusion and exclusion, readily conflicts with the quasi-universalistic ethos of "democracies don't fight each other." Hatreds, long suppressed, emerge to bedevil any effort to build stable, legitimate government. They bring border conflicts to liberate or incorporate "oppressed" minorities, and civil wars. Civil wars often are contests between ethnic groups for exclusive control of the central coercive institutions of the state. The conflict then becomes one over the right of some minority ethnic groups to secede from the control of those institutions, and in doing so frequently to take with them other ethnic groups who may in turn consider themselves oppressed by their new government. Neither the institutions nor the experience of "live and let live" may exist.

An irony is that the initial creation of democratic institutions may contribute to the explosion of ethnic conflicts, by providing the means of free expression, including expression of hatred and feelings of oppression. That does not mean, however, that the solution lies in less democracy. Rather, it likely lies in devising institutions, and nurturing norms and practices, of democratic government with respect for minority rights. It may also require allowing the secession of

---

55. Joan M. Nelson with Stephanie Eglinton, *Encouraging Democracy: What Role for Conditioned Aid?* (Washington, D.C.: Overseas Development Council, 1992).

groups who are not satisfied that their rights and interests can be sufficiently respected under a single government. A consolation may be that nationalism in a democratic era probably dooms any substantial effort of imperialism that would incorporate into a larger political unit different ethnic groups against their will. The will of acquired peoples to separation can be repressed only at great cost and risk. Nationalism need not be inconsistent with respect for human rights.[56] The creation of institutions, norms, and practices to protect minorities has never been easy. But it presents the fundamental challenge of world political development in this era.

Again recall the requirement, for a democratic peace, of stability of democracy and perceptions of stability. For the near future, at least, that condition is likely to be in short supply in much of the world. If one's neighbor has vast unsolved economic problems, is it politically stable? Has it experienced democracy long enough, with some success in managing its problems, to be stable? If it is "democratic" for some, even a majority, of its citizens, but forcibly represses its minorities, is it "stable?" Many of the new states of the old Soviet Union fail these and other tests. Some have not yet had a real democratic transition.

Georgia, for example, did elect, by reasonably democratic procedures, Zviad Gamsakhurdia as president when it was still a republic in the Soviet Union. But on independence, he seized dictatorial powers. In January 1992 he was finally overthrown in bitter fighting, and replaced (but not by election) by Eduard Shevardnadze, who fought of a subsequent coup attempt. Meanwhile, severe ethnic violence continued in the secessionist region of Abkhazia. Elections to confirm Shevardnadze's status as democratic leader were not held until October. Georgia in 1992 may have been an aspiring democracy or a nascent democracy, but it was not yet a stable democracy nor, by any reasonable international standard, even just a "democracy." Until its democracy is established, it should surprise no one if Georgia or states like it get into war with their neighbors. Nor would such a war invalidate a "democracies don't go to war with each other" generalization.

Another threat to the theory and the reality of "democracies don't go to war with each other" lurks in the Middle East. Save for Turkey much of the time, and Lebanon for a while, Israel has been the only stable democracy in that part of the world. Israel's democracy is surely flawed by the treatment of its Arab subjects, but in most respects it has well earned the label of democracy. If an

---

56. Yael Tamir, *Liberal Nationalism* (Princeton, N.J.: Princeton University Press, 1993).

Arab state should achieve an equivalent degree of democracy, and then go to war with Israel, we would have a blatant exception to the proposition.

Unless one categorically rules that "Arab democracy" is an oxymoron—and I do not—such an event is imaginable. A Muslim fundamentalist movement might achieve power in the name of democracy. We will never know what might have been in Algeria had the military not seized power after the elections of 1991. But, conceivably, such a regime could have been both stable and somewhat democratic; i.e., while promoting Islamic values of a majority it might have respected minority rights and tolerated the expression of secular opposition under domestic and international pressures. Such a government probably would not be seen as a major security threat to nonfundamentalist neighboring regimes. Would such a fundamentalist government fight Israel if the military situation seemed propitious? Perhaps, as part of an alliance with other Islamic states. Certainly the normative restraints on democracies not fighting each other would be sorely stressed by the entrenched normative roots of Arab-Israeli hostility. But such a state might be less likely itself to initiate a war, thanks to structural as well as possible normative constraints.

Can a Wider Democratic Peace Be Built?

Understanding that democracies rarely fight each other, and why, has great consequence for policy in the contemporary world, as well as for theoretical debates of "realists" vs. "idealists" or "liberal transnationalists." It should affect the kinds of military preparations believed to be necessary, and the costs one would be willing to pay to make them. It should encourage peaceful efforts to assist the emergence and consolidation of democracy. But a misunderstanding of it could encourage war-making against authoritarian regimes, and efforts to overturn them—with all the costly implications of preventive or hegemonic military activity such a policy might imply. Not all authoritarian states are necessarily aggressive. In fact, at any particular time, the great majority are not.

Recollection of the post-1945 success with defeated adversaries can be both instructive and misleading. It is instructive in showing that democracy could supplant a thoroughly discredited totalitarian regime, at a time when authoritarianism in general was not held in high esteem globally. It can be misleading if one forgets how expensive it was (Marshall Plan aid, and important economic concessions to Japan), and especially if one misinterprets the political conditions of military defeat. The United States and its allies utterly defeated the old regimes. To solidify democratic government the allies conducted vast (if incomplete) efforts to remove the former elites from positions of authority. But they had something to build on, in the form of individuals and institutions from previous experiences with democracy. The model of "fight them, beat them, and then make them democratic" is irrevocably flawed as a basis for contemporary action. It probably would not work anyway, and no one is prepared to make the kind of effort that would be required. A crusade for democracy is not in order.

External military intervention, even against the most odious dictators, is a dangerous way to try to produce a "democratic world order." Sometimes, with a cautious cost-benefit analysis and with the certainty of substantial and legitimate internal support, it may be worthwhile—that is, under conditions when rapid military success is likely *and* the will of the people at issue is clear. Even so, any time an outside power supplants any existing government the problem of legitimacy is paramount. The very democratic norms to be instilled may be compromised. At the least, intervention should not be unilateral. It must be approved, publicly and willingly, by some substantial international body like the UN or the OAS. Under most circumstances, even such international bodies are better used as vehicles to promote democratic processes at times when the relevant domestic parties are ready. Peacekeeping operations to help provide the conditions for free elections, monitor those elections, and advice on the building of democratic institutions are usually far more promising than is military intervention. The UN, newly strengthened with the end of the Cold War, has emerged as a major facilitator of peaceful transitions and democratic elections in such places as Cambodia, Namibia, El Salvador, and Nicaragua.[57]

Perhaps most important, understanding the sources of democratic peace can have the effect of a self-fulfilling prophecy. Social scientists sometimes create reality as well as analyze it. Insofar as norms do guide behavior, repeating those norms helps to make them effective. Repeating the norms as descriptive principles can help to make them true. Repeating the proposition that democracies should not fight each other helps reinforce the probability that democracies will not fight each other. It is an empirical fact that democracies rarely fight

---

57. See Bruce Russett and James S. Sutterlin, "The U.N. in a New World Order," *Foreign Affairs*, Vol. 70, No. 2 (1991), pp. 69–83, on UN peacekeeping in a broad sense. One possible hybrid form of peacekeeping might be an agreement, by all parties in advance, that the international agency would have the right (but not an obligation) to intervene if a government, elected in a process certified by the agency as fair and democratic, were subsequently overthrown. Morton H. Halperin and David J. Scheffer with Patricia L. Small, *Self-Determination in the Modern World* (Washington, D.C.: Carnegie Endowment for International Peace, 1992) call such agreements "prior consent" to intervention.

each other. They do not need to fight each other because they can employ alternative methods of conflict resolution, and at less cost than through violent conflict. A norm that democracies should not fight each other thus is prudentially reinforced, and in turn strengthens the empirical fact about infrequent violent conflict.

Norms may be violated and break down. Nevertheless, norms do constrain behavior, both by affecting what one wants to do and what one may be able to persuade others to do or not to do. The discourse of ethics, and of politics, is for instrumental as well as moral reasons largely a normative one. For example, the wrenching abortion debate is overwhelmingly a normative conflict ("respect life" versus "respect choice") for the control of public policy. In a world where democracy has become widespread, understanding the fact of the "democratic peace" proposition will help to make it true. So too will wider acceptance of the norm.

In turn, a stable and less menacing international system can permit the emergence and consolidation of democratic governments. Harold Lasswell's dire warnings of "a world of garrison states"[58] may have been extreme, and some of the charges about a "military-industrial complex" a quarter of a century ago were shrill and exaggerated. Nevertheless, it is hard to refute the argument that international threats—real or only perceived—strengthen the forces of secrecy and authoritarianism in the domestic politics of states involved in "protracted conflict."[59] Relaxation of international threats to peace and security reduces both the need, and the excuse, for repression of democratic dissent. Democracy and the expectation of international peace can feed on each other to mitigate both the real and the perceived dangers of a still anarchic international system. An evolutionary process may even be at work. Because of the visible nature and public costs of breaking commitments, democratic leaders may be better able to persuade leaders of other states that they will keep the agreements they enter into.[60] Democracies more often win their wars than do authoritarian states,[61] whether because they are more effective in

---

58. Harold D. Lasswell, "The Garrison State," *American Journal of Sociology*, Vol. 96, No. 4 (1941), pp. 455–468.
59. Ted Robert Gurr, "War, Revolution and the Growth of the Coercive State," *Comparative Political Studies*, Vol. 21, No. 1 (1988), pp. 45–65.
60. Fearon, "Audience Costs, Learning, and the Escalation of International Disputes"; and Kurt Taylor Gaubatz, "Democratic States and Commitment in International Relations," paper presented at the annual meeting of the American Political Science Association, Chicago, September 1992.
61. Lake, David A. "Powerful Pacifists: Democratic States and War." *American Political Science Review*, Vol. 86, No. 1 (March 1992), pp. 24–37.

marshaling their resources or are more accurate and efficient information processors.[62] And the government of the loser of a war is much more likely to be overthrown subsequently[63] and may be replaced by a democratic regime.

Perhaps major features of the international system can be socially constructed from the bottom up; that is, norms and rules of behavior internationally can become extensions of the norms and rules of domestic political behavior. The modern international system is commonly traced to the Treaty of Westphalia and the principles of sovereignty and noninterference in internal affairs affirmed by it. In doing so it affirmed the anarchy of the system, without a superior authority to ensure order. It also was a treaty among princes who ruled as autocrats. Our understanding of the modern anarchic state system risks conflating the effects of anarchy with those stemming from the political organization of its component units. When most states are ruled autocratically—as in 1648 and throughout virtually all of history since—then playing by the rules of autocracy may be the only way for any state, democracy or not, to survive in Hobbesian anarchy. Alexis de Tocqueville's doubts about democracies' ability to pursue stable and enlightened foreign policies are well known.[64] But Tocqueville was writing in 1835, mindful of a realist anarchic system in which the vast majority of states were still autocracies. A democracy which tried to operate by democratic norms was at a great disadvantage, and might well shift policy unstably in trying to adjust to the risks.

The emergence of new democracies with the end of the Cold War presents an opening for change in the international system more fundamental even than at the end of other big wars—World Wars I and II and the Napoleonic Wars. For the first time ever, in 1992 a virtual majority of states (91 of 183)[65] approximated the standards we have employed for democracy. Another 35 were in some form of transition to democracy. Democracy in many of these states may not prove stable. This global democratic wave may crest and fall back, as earlier ones have done. But if the chance for wide democratization can be grasped and consolidated, international politics might be transformed.

---

62. Karl W. Deutsch, *The Nerves of Government: Models of Political Communication and Control* (New York: Free Press, 1963).

63. Arthur Stein and Bruce Russett, "Evaluating War Outcomes and Consequences," in Ted Robert Gurr, ed., *Handbook of Political Conflict* (New York: Free Press, 1990); and Bruce Bueno de Mesquita, Randolph Siverson, and Gary Woller, "War and the Fate of Regimes: A Comparative Analysis," *American Political Science Review*, Vol. 86, No. 3 (1992), pp. 639–646.

64. Alexis de Tocqueville, *Democracy in America*, 2 vols. (New York: Knopf, 1945), esp. part I, ch. 13.

65. McColm, et al., *Freedom in the World*, p. 47.

A system composed substantially of democratic states might reflect very different behavior than did the previous one composed predominantly of autocracies. If, after winning the Cold War at immense cost, the alliance of industrial democracies should now let slip a chance to solidify basic change in the principles of international order at much lower cost, our children will wonder. If history is imagined to be the history of wars and conquest, then a democratic world might in that sense represent "the end of history." Some autocratically governed states will surely remain in the system. But if enough states become stably democratic in the 1990s, then there emerges a chance to reconstruct the norms and rules of the international order to reflect those of democracies in a majority of interactions. A system created by autocracies centuries ago might now be recreated by a critical mass of democratic states.

How Liberalism Produces Democratic Peace | *John M. Owen*

The proposition that democracies seldom if ever go to war against one another has nearly become a truism. The "democratic peace" has attracted attention for a number of reasons. It is "the closest thing we have to an empirical law in the study of international relations," reports one scholar.[1] It poses an apparent anomaly to realism, the dominant school of security studies. And it has become an axiom of U.S. foreign policy. "Democracies don't attack each other," President Clinton declared in his 1994 State of the Union address, meaning that "ultimately the best strategy to insure our security and to build a durable peace is to support the advance of democracy elsewhere." Clinton has called democratization the "third pillar" of his foreign policy.[2]

The democratic peace proposition is vulnerable in at least three ways, however. First, it contains two inherent ambiguities: How does one define democracy? What counts as a war? The slipperiness of these terms provides a temptation to tautology: to define them so as to safeguard the proposition. Indeed, some challengers to the proposition claim that democracies have been at war with each other several times.[3] A second challenge is that the

John M. Owen is a fellow at the Center for International Security and Arms Control at Stanford University.

This article was written under the auspices of the Center for International Affairs at Harvard University. The author wishes to thank the Olin Institute for Strategic Studies for its generous support. He also wishes to thank Robert Art, Michael Desch, Gil Merom, Daniel Philpott, Randall Schweller, and David Spiro for comments on a previous draft.

1. Jack S. Levy, "Domestic Politics and War," in Robert I. Rotberg and Theodore K. Rabb, *The Origin and Prevention of Major Wars* (New York: Cambridge University Press, 1989), p. 88. See also Bruce Russett, *Grasping the Democratic Peace: Principles for a Post–Cold War World* (Princeton: Princeton University Press, 1993), pp. 3–23; and James Lee Ray, "Wars between Democracies: Rare or Nonexistent?" *International Interactions*, Vol. 18, No. 3 (Spring 1988), pp. 251–276.
2. "Excerpts from President Clinton's State of the Union Message," *New York Times*, January 26, 1994, p. A17; "The Clinton Administration Begins," *Foreign Policy Bulletin*, Vol. 3, No. 4/5 (January–April 1993), p. 5.
3. See for example Christopher Layne, "Kant or Cant: The Myth of the Democratic Peace," *International Security*, Vol. 19, No. 2 (Fall 1994), pp. 5–49; Kenneth N. Waltz, "The Emerging Structure of International Politics," *International Security*, Vol. 18, No. 2 (Fall 1993), p. 78; Jack Vincent, "Freedom and International Conflict: Another Look," *International Studies Quarterly*, Vol. 31, No. 1 (March 1987), pp. 102–112; and Henry S. Farber and Joanne Gowa, "Polities and Peace," unpublished manuscript, Princeton University, January 11, 1994. Claiming that democracies have never fought one another is Ray, "Wars between Democracies."

International Security, Vol. 19, No. 2 (Fall 1994), pp. 87–125
© 1994 by the President and Fellows of Harvard College and the Massachusetts Institute of Technology.

lack of wars among democracies, even if true, is not surprising. Wars are so rare that random chance could account for the democratic peace, much as it could account for an absence of war among, say, states whose names begin with the letter K.[4] A third critique points out that the democratic peace lacks a convincing theoretical foundation. No one is sure why democracies do not fight one another and yet do fight non-democracies.[5] That we do not really know the causal mechanism behind the democratic peace means we cannot be certain the peace is genuine. It may be an epiphenomenon, a by-product of other causal variables such as those suggested by realist theories of international politics.[6]

In this article I defend the democratic peace proposition by attempting to remedy the last problem. I do not rebut the argument that the proposition is tautological, although it is worth noting that most democratic peace theorists are meticulous in their definitions, and that their critics are also susceptible to the tautological temptation. I also leave aside the "random chance" argument, except to point out with its proponents that democracies also appear more likely to align with one another. Rather, I argue that liberal ideas cause liberal democracies to tend away from war with one another, and that the same ideas prod these states into war with illiberal states. I derived the argument by testing propositions from existing democratic peace theories[7] on historical cases, then using the results to formulate a new theory.

---

4. David Spiro, "The Insignificance of the Liberal Peace," *International Security*, Vol. 19, No. 2 (Fall 1994), pp. 50–86; John J. Mearsheimer, "Back to the Future: Instability in Europe after the Cold War," *International Security*, Vol. 15, No. 1 (Summer 1990), p. 50. Spiro does not believe random chance accounts for war; he also argues that liberal states do tend to align with one another.
5. Melvin Small and J. David Singer, "The War-proneness of Democratic Regimes," *Jerusalem Journal of International Relations*, Vol. 1, No. 4 (Summer 1976), pp. 50–69. R.J. Rummel maintains that democracies are *generally* less prone to war. Rummel, "Libertarianism and International Violence," *Journal of Conflict Resolution*, Vol. 27, No. 1 (March 1983), pp. 27–71.
6. Mearsheimer, "Back to the Future," pp. 48–51; Farber and Gowa, "Polities and Peace," pp. 3–8. See also Michael Desch, "War and State Formation, Peace and State Deformation?" unpublished manuscript, Olin Institute for Strategic Studies, Harvard University, November 1993.
7. See Immanuel Kant, "Perpetual Peace, a Philosophical Sketch," in *Perpetual Peace and Other Essays*, trans. Ted Humphrey (Indianapolis: Hackett Publishing Company, 1983), pp. 107–143; Michael Doyle, "Kant, Liberal Legacies, and Foreign Affairs, Part I," *Philosophy and Public Affairs*, Vol. 12, No. 3 (Summer 1983), pp. 205–235; Doyle, "Liberalism and World Politics," *American Political Science Review*, Vol. 80, No. 4 (December 1986), pp. 1151–1169; Russett, *Grasping the Democratic Peace*; Bruce Bueno de Mesquita and David Lalman, *War and Reason: Domestic and International Imperatives* (New Haven: Yale University Press, 1992), chap. 5; David A. Lake, "Powerful Pacifists: Democratic States and War," *American Political Science Review*, Vol. 86, No. 1 (March 1992), pp. 24–37; Randall L. Schweller, "Domestic Structure and Preventive War: Are

The cases are war-threatening crises involving the United States from the 1790s through World War I.[8]

I define a liberal democracy as a state that instantiates liberal ideas, one where liberalism is the dominant ideology and citizens have leverage over war decisions. That is, liberal democracies are those states with a visible liberal presence, and that feature free speech and regular competitive elections of the officials empowered to declare war. I argue that liberal ideology and institutions work in tandem to bring about democratic peace. Liberals believe that individuals everywhere are fundamentally the same, and are best off pursuing self-preservation and material well-being. Freedom is required for these pursuits, and peace is required for freedom; coercion and violence are counter-productive. Thus all individuals share an interest in peace, and should want war only as an instrument to bring about peace. Liberals believe that democracies seek their citizens' true interests and that thus by definition they are pacific and trustworthy. Non-democracies may be dangerous because they seek other ends, such as conquest or plunder. Liberals thus hold that the national interest calls for accommodation of fellow democracies, but sometimes calls for war with non-democracies.

When liberals run the government, relations with fellow democracies are harmonious. When illiberals govern, relations may be rockier. Even then, if war is threatened with a state that the liberal opposition considers a fellow democracy, liberals agitate to prevent hostilities using the free speech allowed them by law. Illiberal leaders are unable to rally the public to fight, and fear that an unpopular war would lead to their ouster at the next election. On the other hand, if the crisis is with a state believed to be a non-democracy, the leaders may be pushed toward war.

This argument improves on previous accounts of the democratic peace in several ways. First, it grounds liberal ideology in an Enlightenment concept of self-interest. Second, it opens the "black box" of the state to show how democratic structures translate liberal preferences into policy even when

Democracies More Pacific?" *World Politics*, Vol. 44, No. 2 (January 1992), pp. 235–269; T. Clifton Morgan and Sally Howard Campbell, "Domestic Structure, Decisional Constraints, and War: So Why Kant Democracies Fight?" *Journal of Conflict Resolution*, Vol. 35, No. 2 (June 1991), pp. 187–211; R.J. Rummel, *Understanding Conflict and War*, Vol. 4 (Beverly Hills: SAGE Publications, 1974).
8. The crises on which I tested the explanations were: U.S.-Britain 1794–96, U.S.-France 1796–98, U.S.-Britain 1803–12, U.S.-Britain 1845–46, U.S.-Mexico 1845–46, U.S.-Britain 1861–63, U.S.-Spain 1873, U.S.-Chile 1891–92, U.S.-Britain 1895–96, U.S.-Spain 1898, U.S.-Mexico 1914–16, and U.S.-Germany 1916–17. See John M. Owen, "Testing the Democratic Peace: American Diplomatic Crises, 1794–1917," Ph.D. dissertation, Harvard University, 1993.

statesmen are themselves illiberal. Third, it takes into account the importance of perceptions. For my argument to hold, liberals must consider the other state democratic. My argument also answers several criticisms of the democratic peace thesis. It shows that the inadequacy of either democratic structures or norms alone to explain democratic peace does not prove that the democratic peace is spurious. It shows how illiberal leaders of democracies can make threats against one another and yet still be domestically constrained from attacking one another. It explains several supposed exceptions to the democratic peace by taking account of actors' perceptions; for example, the War of 1812 was fought at a time when almost no Americans considered England a democracy.

I begin by briefly reviewing previous theories of democratic peace and attempts to test them. I then summarize the foundations of liberalism and the foreign policy ideology it produces. In so doing, I explore the perceptual aspect of the causal mechanism. Next I describe how democratic institutions make it likely that liberal ideology will influence policy during a war-threatening crisis. I then illustrate the argument in four historical cases: the Franco-American crisis of 1796–98, and the Anglo-American crises of 1803–12, 1861–63, and 1895–96. I answer realist critics of the democratic peace proposition, and suggest possible ways to synthesize realism and liberalism. I conclude by cautioning that although democratic peace is real, threats to liberalism itself mean that it is not a certain precursor to perpetual peace.

Previous Attempts to Explain Democratic Peace

Typically, theories of the democratic peace are divided into *structural* and *normative* theories. Structural accounts attribute the democratic peace to the institutional constraints within democracies. Chief executives in democracies must gain approval for war from cabinet members or legislatures, and ultimately from the electorate. Normative theory locates the cause of the democratic peace in the ideas or norms held by democracies. Democracies believe it would be unjust or imprudent to fight one another. They practice the norm of compromise with each other that works so well within their own borders.[9]

---

9. Some explanations, including those of Kant, Doyle, and Rummel (fn. 7), contain both structural and normative elements. However, these writers disagree as to what constitutes a democracy and why they forgo wars against one another; they do not take perceptions into account; and they underspecify how democratic structures work.

On balance, statistical tests of these two theories have yielded no clear winner.[10] Moreover, although quantitative studies provide a necessary part of our evaluation of these theories by identifying correlations, by their nature they cannot tell us the full story. First, they often must use crude proxy variables that are several steps removed from the phenomena being measured.[11] Second, they infer processes from statistical relationships between these variables, but do not examine those processes directly. Overcoming these limitations requires looking at the actual processes in historical cases, or "process tracing."[12] Joseph Nye writes that democratic peace "need[s] exploration via detailed case studies to look at what actually happened in particular instances."[13] One way to carry out such tests is to ask: If the theory is true, then what else should we expect to observe happening?[14]

In carrying out such process-tracing on a dozen cases, I uncovered problems in both structural and normative accounts. I found that democratic structures were nearly as likely to drive states to war as to restrain them from it. Cabinets, legislatures, and publics were often more belligerent than the government heads they were supposed to constrain. I found that the normative theory neglected to take perceptions into account. Often states which today's researchers consider democratic did not consider each other democratic. Thus the anticipated normative check on war was frequently absent.[15]

---

10. Studies favoring some form of structural theory include Bueno de Mesquita and Lalman, *War and Reason;* and Morgan and Campbell, "So Why Kant Democracies Fight?" Favoring normative theory are Zeev Maoz and Bruce Russett, "Normative and Structural Causes of Democratic Peace, 1946–1986" *American Political Science Review,* Vol. 87, No. 3 (September 1993), pp. 624–638; and William J. Dixon, "Democracy and the Peaceful Settlement of Conflict," *American Political Science Review,* Vol. 88, No. 1 (March 1994), pp. 14–32.

11. For example, Maoz and Russett infer democratic norms from regime stability and from levels of internal social and political violence. Maoz and Russett, "Normative and Structural Causes," p. 630.

12. Alexander George and Timothy J. McKeown, "Case Studies and Theories of Organizational Decision Making," in *Advances in Information Processing in Organizations,* Vol. 2 (Greenwich, Conn.: JAI Press, 1985); see also David Dessler, "Beyond Correlations: Toward a Causal Theory of War," *International Studies Quarterly,* Vol. 35, No. 3 (September 1991), pp. 337–345; James Lee Ray, *Democracy and International Conflict: An Evaluation of the Democratic Peace Proposition* (Columbia: University of South Carolina Press, 1995), chapter 4.

13. Joseph S. Nye, Jr., *Understanding International Conflicts* (New York: HarperCollins, 1993), p. 40.

14. See Gary King, Robert O. Keohane, and Sidney Verba, *Designing Social Inquiry: Scientific Inference in Qualitative Research* (Princeton: Princeton University Press, 1994).

15. See Owen, "Testing the Democratic Peace." For a summary of the findings, see Owen, "Is the Democratic Peace a Matter of Luck?" paper presented at the annual meeting of the American Political Science Association, Washington, D.C., September 1993.

These findings do not kill the democratic peace thesis. Logically, that neither structures nor norms by themselves explain the democratic peace does not imply that the two in tandem cannot do so. The structure/norms typology used by the literature is used merely for analytic convenience. If in trying to determine whether an automobile will run I separate its gasoline from its engine, then find that neither component by itself suffices to run the automobile, I cannot then conclude that the car will not run. It could still be that liberal ideology motivates some citizens against war with a fellow democracy, and democratic institutions allow this ideology to affect foreign policy.

Some of the cases suggest such a synergy, I found, but only when the actors' perceptions are taken into account. For example, most Americans in the nineteenth century thought in terms of *republics* and *monarchies* rather than *democracies* and *non-democracies*. When in 1873 the United States nearly went to war with Spain during the *Virginius* affair, many Americans, including the secretary of state, explicitly argued for peace precisely because Spain was at the time a republic.[16] Again in 1892, when President Benjamin Harrison asked Congress to declare war on Chile after the *Baltimore* affair, many Americans expressed opposition based on the fact that Chile was a republic.[17]

These considerations combine with quantitative evidence to suggest that democratic peace is a genuine phenomenon that simply needs a better explanation. Multivariate analysis indicates that it is not the product of some omitted variable. In separate studies, Bremer and Maoz and Russett found that democracy as an independent variable still had explanatory power after controlling for an impressive array of competitors. Variables suggested by realism such as relative power, alliance status, and the presence of a hegemon did not erase the effects of democracy.[18]

---

16. See especially the attitude of Hamilton Fish, the U.S. secretary of state, in Allan Nevins, *Hamilton Fish: The Inner History of the Grant Administration* (New York: Dodd, Mead, 1936), pp. 668–674. The fullest treatment of the crisis is in Richard H. Bradford, *The "Virginius" Affair* (Boulder: Colorado Associated University Press, 1980).
17. E.g., in opposing Harrison, Representative William Breckinridge of Kentucky told Congress: "War . . . is only the last resort, especially so when the war must be with a republic like our own, anxious for liberty, desiring to maintain constitutional freedom, seeking progress by means of that freedom." 52d Congress, 1st sess., *Congressional Record*, Vol. 23 (January 26, 1892), p. 550. See also Joyce S. Goldberg, *The "Baltimore" Affair* (Lincoln: University of Nebraska Press, 1986).
18. Stuart Bremer, "Democracy and Militarized Interstate Conflict, 1816–1965," *International Interactions*, Vol. 18, No. 3 (Spring 1993), pp. 231–249; Zeev Maoz and Bruce Russett, "Alliances, Contiguity, Wealth, and Political Stability: Is the Lack of Conflict between Democracies a Statistical Artifact?" *International Interactions*, Vol. 17, No. 3 (Spring 1992), pp. 245–267.

As explained at the end of this article, however, I do not argue that power politics has no force in determining the foreign policies of liberal democracies. Rather, I describe a second force—liberalism—which prods democracies toward peace with each other, and toward war with non-democracies. In looking within the state, I suggest domestic foundations for those studies that have explored the international systemic aspects of the democratic peace.[19]

Liberalism as the Cause of Democratic Peace

Liberal ideas are the source—the independent variable—behind the distinctive foreign policies of liberal democracies. These ideas give rise to two intervening variables, liberal ideology and domestic democratic institutions, which shape foreign policy. Liberal ideology prohibits war against liberal democracies, but sometimes calls for war against illiberal states. Democratic institutions allow these drives to affect foreign policy and international relations.[20]

LIBERAL IDEAS

Liberalism is universalistic and tolerant. Liberal political theory, such as that of Hobbes, Locke, Rousseau, and Kant, typically begins with abstract man in a state of nature in which he is equal to all other men. Although beliefs and cultures may differ, liberalism says, all persons share a fundamental

---

19. On the level of the international system, this model is compatible with others which essentially present democracies as constrained (for various reasons) to prevent disputes among themselves from turning into wars. For Bruce Bueno de Mesquita and David Lalman, for example, democracies know each other to be prevented by domestic checks and balances from initiating war. This knowledge makes cooperation the rational choice in the "international interactions game." At the same time, democracies know that non-democracies, which are unconstrained, have the same knowledge and are prone to exploit them for that reason. Democracies thus may find it rational pre-emptively to attack non-democracies for fear of being taken advantage of. See Bueno de Mesquita and Lalman, *War and Reason*, chap. 5; see also William J. Dixon, "Democracy and the Peaceful Settlement"; and D. Marc Kilgour, "Domestic Political Structure and War Behavior: A Game-Theoretic Approach," *Journal of Conflict Resolution*, Vol. 35, No. 2 (June 1991), pp. 266–284.

20. See Judith Goldstein and Robert O. Keohane, *Ideas and Foreign Policy: Beliefs, Institutions, and Political Change* (Ithaca: Cornell University Press, 1993), pp. 13–17. See also Spiro, "Insignificance," for the importance of liberal conceptions of national interest.

interest in self-preservation and material well-being.[21] There is thus a harmony of interests among all individuals. To realize this harmony, each individual must be allowed to follow his or her own preferences as long as they do not detract from another's freedom. People thus need to cooperate by tolerating one another and forgoing coercion and violence.[22] Since true interests harmonize, the more people are free, the better off all are. Liberalism is cosmopolitan, positing that all persons, not just certain subjects of one's own state, should be free. The spread of liberalism need not be motivated by altruism. It is entirely in the individual's self-interest to cooperate.[23] In sum, liberalism's ends are life and property, and its means are liberty and toleration.

Liberals believe that not all persons or nations are free, however. Two things are needed for freedom. First, persons or nations must be themselves enlightened, aware of their interests and how they should be secured.[24] Second, people must live under enlightened political institutions which allow their true interests to shape politics.[25] Liberals disagree over which political institutions are enlightened. Kant stressed a strict separation of the executive from the legislative power.[26] For most Americans in the nineteenth century,

---

21. John Locke, for example, writes: "The great and *chief end* therefore, of Mens uniting into Commonwealths, and putting themselves under Government, *is the Preservation of their Property.*" Locke, *Second Treatise of Government*, chap. 9, para. 124. Locke says "property" includes one's "Life, Liberty, and Estate"; ibid., chap. 7, para. 87. In Locke, *Two Treatises of Government*, ed. Peter Laslett (New York: Cambridge University Press, 1988), pp. 350–351, 323.
22. Immanuel Kant, who deduced a zone of peace among republics in the 1790s, argues that over time, the devastation of conflict teaches them that it is best to cooperate with others so as to realize their full capacities. See for example Kant, "Idea for a Universal History with a Cosmopolitan Intent," in *Perpetual Peace*, pp. 31–34. See also Locke, *Second Treatise*, chap. 2, para. 5, p. 270. By "harmony," I do not imply that uncoordinated selfish action by each automatically results in all being better off (a "natural" harmony). All individuals are interested in peace, but enlightenment, the right institutions, and cooperation are necessary to bring peace about. On the distinction between uncoordinated harmony and cooperation, see Robert O. Keohane, *After Hegemony: Cooperation and Discord in the World Political Economy* (Princeton: Princeton University Press, 1984), pp. 49–64.
23. Kant says a republic is possible "even for a people comprised of devils (if only they possess understanding)." Kant, *Perpetual Peace*, p. 124. See also Alexis de Tocqueville, "How the Americans Combat Individualism by the Doctrine of Self-interest Properly Understood," *Democracy in America*, ed. J.P. Mayer, trans. George Lawrence (New York: Harper and Row, 1988), part 2, chap. 8, pp. 525–528.
24. See Kant, "An Answer to the Question: What Is Enlightenment?" in Kant, *Perpetual Peace*, pp. 41–48.
25. For a brief history of the view that selfish rulers rather than ordinary people are responsible for war, see Michael Howard, *War and the Liberal Conscience* (New Brunswick, N.J.: Rutgers University Press, 1978), pp. 14–18.
26. Kant, "Perpetual Peace," pp. 112–115. Kant calls such states "republics," but by his definition monarchies may be republics.

only republics (non-monarchies) were "democracies" or "free countries."[27] Today, Westerners tend to trust states that allow meaningful political competition. Central to all these criteria is the requirement that the people have some leverage over their rulers. That is, nineteenth-century republics and today's liberal democracies share the essential liberal goal of preventing tyranny over individual freedom.

LIBERAL FOREIGN POLICY IDEOLOGY

Liberalism gives rise to an ideology that distinguishes states primarily according to regime type: in assessing a state, liberalism first asks whether it is a liberal democracy or not.[28] This is in contrast to neorealism, which distinguishes states according to capabilities. Liberalism, in looking to characteristics other than power, is similar to most other systems of international thought, including communism, fascism, and monarchism.[29]

Liberalism is, however, more tolerant of its own kind than these other systems. Once liberals accept a foreign state as a liberal democracy, they adamantly oppose war against that state. The rationale follows from liberal premises. *Ceteris paribus*, people are better off without war, because it is costly and dangerous. War is called for only when it would serve liberal ends—i.e., when it would most likely enhance self-preservation and well-being. This can only be the case when the adversary is not a liberal democracy. Liberal democracies are believed reasonable, predictable, and trustworthy, because they are governed by their citizens' true interests, which harmonize with all individuals' true interests around the world. Liberals believe that they understand the intentions of foreign liberal democracies, and that those intentions are always pacific toward fellow liberal democracies.

---

27. See for example David M. Fitzsimons, "Tom Paine's New World Order: Idealistic Internationalism in the Ideology of Early American Foreign Relations," unpublished manuscript, University of Michigan, 1994.
28. I have benefited from conversations with Sean Lynn-Jones on many of these points. For an attempt to reformulate liberal international relations theory based on distinctions among domestic political orders, see Andrew Moravcsik, "Liberalism and International Relations Theory," Working Paper, Center for International Affairs, Harvard University, 1992.
29. Traditional realists such as E.H. Carr and Hans Morgenthau, ancient Greeks, medieval Muslims, and communists all see state-level distinctions as important. Carr, *The Twenty Years' Crisis* (London: Macmillan, 1946), p. 236; Morgenthau, *Politics among Nations*, 3d ed. (New York: Alfred A. Knopf, 1965), p. 131; Sohail Hashmi, "The Sixth Pillar: Jihad and the Ethics of War and Peace in Islam," Ph.D. dissertation, Harvard University, 1994; Robert Jervis, "Hypotheses on Misperception," *World Politics*, Vol. 20, No. 3 (April 1968), p. 467.

Again, it is not necessary that liberals be motivated by justice, only by self-interest.[30]

Illiberal states, on the other hand, are viewed *prima facie* as unreasonable, unpredictable, and potentially dangerous. These are states either ruled by despots, or with unenlightened citizenries. Illiberal states may seek illiberal ends such as conquest, intolerance, or impoverishment of others. Liberal democracies do not automatically fight all illiberal states in an endless crusade to spread freedom, however. Usually, they estimate that the costs of liberalizing another state are too high, often because the illiberal state is too powerful.[31] Liberal democracies do not fully escape the imperatives of power politics.

THE IMPORTANCE OF PERCEPTIONS. That a state has enlightened citizens and liberal-democratic institutions, however, is not sufficient for it to belong to the democratic peace: if its peer states do not believe it is a liberal democracy, they will not treat it as one. History shows many cases where perceptions tripped up democratic peace. For example, as Christopher Layne demonstrates, the French after World War I did not consider Germany a fellow liberal democracy, even though Germans were governed under the liberal Weimar constitution. The salient fact about Germany, in the French view of 1923, was not that it had a liberal constitution, but that it was peopled by Germans, who had recently proven themselves most unenlightened and were now reneging on reparations agreements.[32]

Thus, for the liberal mechanism to prevent a liberal democracy from going to war against a foreign state, liberals must consider the foreign state a liberal democracy. Most explanations of democratic peace posit that democracies recognize one another and refuse to fight on that basis; but the researchers never test this assumption.[33] In fact, often it does not hold. The refusal to

---

30. Here my argument differs from that of Michael Doyle, who writes that "domestically just republics, which rest on consent, presume foreign republics to be also consensual, just, and therefore deserving of accommodation." Doyle, "Kant, Part I," p. 230.

31. Compare this with the Union's attitude toward Britain in the Civil War, described below. For explanations that see democratic prudence as more central to the democratic peace, see Schweller, "Democracy and Preventive War"; and Lake, "Powerful Pacifists."

32. See Layne, "The Myth of the Democratic Peace." More research needs to be done on the question of how a state with democratic institutions comes to be regarded by its peers as liberal.

33. For example, Bueno de Mesquita and Lalman assert: "The presence of the constraint is not alone sufficient to ensure cooperation or harmony. However, it is common knowledge whether a given state is a liberal democracy." In *War and Reason*, p. 156. The same assumption is used (less explicitly) by Doyle, "Liberalism and World Politics"; Russett, *Grasping the Democratic Peace*; Ray, "Wars between Democracies"; Lake, "Powerful Pacifists"; Schweller, "Domestic Structure and Preventive War"; and Rummel, "Libertarianism and International Violence."

take this into account keeps the democratic peace literature from understanding apparent exceptions to democratic peace, such as the War of 1812, the American Civil War, and the Spanish-American War.[34] My argument explains these apparent exceptions. As shown below, most Americans did not consider England democratic in 1812 because England was a monarchy. In 1861, Southern slavery prevented liberals in the Union from considering the Confederacy a liberal democracy.[35] Almost no Americans considered Spain a democracy in 1898. To determine which states belong to the pacific union, we must do more than simply examine their constitutions. We must examine how the liberals themselves define democracy.

Skeptics would immediately counter that the subjectivity inherent in terms such as "democracy" and "despotism" means that these concepts have no independent causal force. When leaders want war, they simply define the rival state as despotic; when they want peace, they define the friend as democratic. Thus Joseph Stalin became "Uncle Joe" when Americans needed to justify fighting alongside the Soviet Union against Germany in World War II.

In fact, however, democracy and despotism are not wholly subjective. Liberals have relatively stable conceptions of what a democracy looks like. In the nineteenth century, most Americans applauded when other states became republican, and anticipated friendly relations with those states. More recently, the attitude of the Western democracies toward Russia shows the independent power that liberalization has on expectations of hostility. The failed August 1991 coup and subsequent breakup of the Soviet Union did not cause the vast Soviet nuclear arsenal to disappear. Yet James Baker, then U.S. secretary of state, announced on February 5, 1992:

The Cold War has ended, and we now have a chance to forge a democratic peace, an enduring peace built on shared values—democracy and political and economic freedom. The strength of these values in Russia and the other

---

34. Kenneth Waltz asserts that the War of 1812 and the Civil War were fought between democracies; Waltz, "Emerging Structure," p. 78. David Lake, who argues for the democratic peace proposition, calls the Spanish-American War a war between democracies. Lake, "Powerful Pacifists," p. 33.

35. As the nineteenth century reached its midpoint, slavery came to be seen by such Southern figures as John C. Calhoun as "the most safe and stable basis for free institutions in the world." It mattered a great deal to Northerners that the South was illiberal. Thus the *New York Tribune* in 1855 could write: "We are not one people. We are two peoples. We are a people for Freedom and a people for Slavery. Between the two, conflict is inevitable." See Eric Foner, *Politics and Ideology in the Age of the Civil War* (New York: Oxford University Press, 1980), pp. 40–41, 52–53.

new independent states will be the surest foundation for peace—and the strongest guarantee of our national security—for decades to come.[36]

ILLIBERAL DEMOCRACIES. The importance of liberal ideology is evident from other supposed exceptions to democratic peace. It has been considered a puzzle, for example, that ancient Greek democracies waged war against one another.[37] But Thucydides reveals that the ancient Athenians were not liberal. They valued heroism and conquest over self-preservation and well-being. The Corinthians tell the oligarchical Spartans that they are more sluggish than the Athenians, who "are adventurous beyond their power, and daring beyond their judgment, and in danger they are sanguine. . . . Their bodies they spend ungrudgingly in their country's cause . . . and to them laborious occupation is less of a misfortune than the peace of a quiet life."[38] The Athenian good life consisted in what Charles Taylor calls the warrior ethic.[39] In this world view, all persons are not fundamentally the same, and there is no harmony of interests among them.[40] Ancient democracy as a result is a restive, adventurous, conquering regime, to be trusted by no one.

A similar illiberalism is evident in many "democracies" today. Balkan peoples live in popularly-governed polities; yet they define themselves primarily not as abstract individuals, but according to religious categories: Serbs are Orthodox Christian, Croats are Roman Catholic, and Bosnians are Muslim. The lack of commonality means no democratic peace among these peoples. Iranians live in a state with universal adult suffrage and vigorous parliamentary debate, yet they do not view the world through a liberal lens, where all

---

36. On April 21, 1992, Baker declared, "Real democracies do not go to war with each other." Quoted in Russett, *Grasping the Democratic Peace*, pp. 128–129.
37. See Bruce Russett and William Antholis, "The Imperfect Democratic Peace of Ancient Athens," in Russett, *Grasping the Democratic Peace*, pp. 43–71.
38. Thucydides, *The Peloponnesian War* I, 70, ed. T.E. Wick, trans. Richard Crawley (New York: Random House, 1982), p. 40.
39. "There is . . . a warrior (and later warrior-citizen) morality, where what is valued is strength, courage, and the ability to conceive and execute great deeds, and where life is aimed at fame and glory, and the immortality one enjoys when one's name lives for ever on men's lips." This ethic, dominant in the era of Homer, was still very much alive at the time of Pericles, as evidenced by Plato's arguments against it. Charles Taylor, *Sources of the Self: The Making of the Modern Identity* (Cambridge: Harvard University Press, 1987), pp. 115–118.
40. As Russett and Antholis write, "the citizens of most democratic cities probably did not think of democracy as a trans-Hellenic project, at least at the outset of the Peloponnesian War. The individual liberties central to liberal democracy were not so universalized in the ancient world." Russett, *Grasping the Democratic Peace*, p. 45. See Aristotle, *The Politics*, trans. Carnes Lord (Chicago: University of Chicago Press, 1984), Book I, chaps. 4–6, pp. 39–43 on how certain persons are slaves by nature.

individuals are best off cooperating to pursue self-preservation and well-being. Other new democracies, such as those arising from the ruins of the Soviet Union, may be illiberal as well. If so, democratic peace will not emerge in that area of the world.

DEMOCRATIC INSTITUTIONS

The domestic structures that translate liberal preferences into foreign policy are likewise a product of liberal ideas. Liberalism seeks to actualize the harmony of interests among individuals by insuring that the freedom of each is compatible with the freedom of all. It thus calls for structures that protect the right of each citizen to self-government. Most important for our purposes are those giving citizens leverage over governmental decision makers. Freedom of speech is necessary because it allows citizens to evaluate alternative foreign policies. Regular, competitive elections are necessary because they provide citizens with the possibility of punishing officials who violate their rights. Liberalism says that the people who fight and fund war have the right to be consulted, through representatives they elect, before entering it.[41]

DEMOCRATIC INSTITUTIONS. When those who govern hold the liberal ideology prohibiting war against fellow liberal democracies, then the role of democratic institutions is limited simply to putting these liberals in office. Liberal American presidents have included Thomas Jefferson and Woodrow Wilson. These men sought to implement liberal foreign policies, including harmonious relations with those states they considered liberal and confrontation with those they considered illiberal.

Not everyone in every liberal democracy, however, necessarily holds the liberal ideology. Some may instead be political realists, who view power as more important than freedom. Some others may simply want good relations with economic partners, regardless of regime type.[42] When such illiberals govern liberal democracies, they may lead the nation into disputes with fellow liberal democracies. They can do so because the general public pays little attention to everyday foreign policy.

41. "If . . . the consent of the citizenry is required in order to determine whether or not there will be war, it is natural that they consider all its calamities before committing themselves to so risky a game." Kant, "Perpetual Peace," p. 113.
42. An explanation of why not everyone in a regime necessarily holds the dominant ideology is beyond the scope of this article. Here I simply take it as empirically obvious that not all citizens of liberal democracies are liberal, just as not all citizens of communist states are communist.

ELITES AND EVERYDAY FOREIGN POLICY. Day-to-day foreign policy is mostly the province of elites. Ordinary citizens have good reason for ignoring relations with other nations. Since relations with most nations have little perceptible impact on the individual citizen, the expected payoff to each is not worth the time investment.[43] This collective-action problem means that normal foreign policy is delegated to representatives.

In making everyday foreign policy, the main domestic influences on these representatives are elites. Together, representatives and elites form what James Rosenau calls *opinion leaders:* people "who occupy positions which enable them regularly to transmit, either locally or nationally, opinions about any issue to unknown persons outside of their occupational field or about more than one class of issues to unknown professional colleagues." They include "government officials, prominent businessmen, civil servants, journalists, scholars, heads of professional associations, and interest groups."[44] In liberal democracies, these include staunch liberals who always desire to see good relations with fellow liberal democracies, and often desire confrontation with those states they consider illiberal. Without the leverage provided by public attention, the liberal elite has no special advantage over other elites, such as special interests.[45] The state may thereby fall into a crisis with a fellow liberal democracy.

WHEN WAR IS THREATENED: LIBERAL ELITES AND THE PUBLIC. At the point where war is threatened, however, it becomes in the interest of each citizen to pay attention. War costs blood and treasure, and these high costs are felt throughout society. It also requires public mobilization. Those statesmen and elites who want war must persuade public opinion that war is necessary. In democracies, this persuasion typically includes arguments that the adversary state is not democratic. When the prior liberal consensus is that the adversary *is* a liberal democracy, however, these illiberal statesmen find that they cannot mobilize the public.

This is in part because they face strong opposition from liberal opinion leaders. Using the tools allowed them by domestic institutions—the media,

---

43. This reasoning follows that of Anthony Downs, *An Economic Theory of Democracy* (New York: Harper and Row, 1957), pp. 207–276.
44. James Rosenau, *Public Opinion and Foreign Policy: An Operational Formulation* (New York: Random House, 1961), pp. 35–39; Michael Leigh, *Mobilizing Consent: Public Opinion and American Foreign Policy, 1937–1947* (Westport, Conn.: Greenwood Press, 1976), pp. 4–5.
45. For a theory of how special interests can "hijack" foreign policy, see Jack Snyder, *Myths of Empire: Domestic Politics and International Ambition* (Ithaca: Cornell University Press, 1991), pp. 31–55.

public speeches, rallies, and so on—liberal elites agitate against war with fellow liberal democracies. They prevent illiberal elites from persuading the public that war is necessary.[46] Illiberal statesmen find that war with a liberal democracy would be extremely unpopular. Moreover, they begin to fear electoral ouster if they go to war against a fellow liberal democracy. Even illiberal statesmen are then compelled to act as liberals and resolve the crisis peacefully.[47]

Alternatively, there may be times when liberals desire war with an illiberal state, yet illiberal statesmen oppose such a war. Using the same institutions of free discussion and the threat of electoral punishment, liberals may force their leaders into war. Such was the case in the Spanish-American War.[48]

This part of my argument conforms to recent research on public opinion and foreign policy, which indicates a dialectic among elites, the general public, and policy makers. A number of studies indicate that opinion changes precede policy changes, suggesting that the former cause the latter rather than vice versa.[49] Moreover, a recent work finds that in the 1970s and 1980s the greatest influences on aggregate shifts in U.S. public opinion were television news commentators and experts. For example, television commentators' statements on crises in Vietnam in 1969 and the Middle East in 1974–75 and 1977–78 evidently swayed public opinion. Often these media commentators opposed official governmental policy.[50] Together, these findings suggest that, at least in the United States, an opinion elite at times shapes public positions on issues, thus constraining foreign policy.

Figure 1 illustrates the argument. Liberal ideas form the independent variable. These ideas produce the ideology which prohibits war with fellow liberal democracies and sometimes calls for war with illiberal states. The ideas also give rise to democratic institutions. Working in tandem, the ideology and institutions push liberal democracies toward democratic peace.

---

46. On the importance of free speech to democratic peace, see Stephen Van Evera, "Primed for Peace: Europe After the Cold War," *International Security*, Vol. 15, No. 3 (Winter 1990/91), p. 27.
47. Works that have used the assumption that elected officials value re-election above all else include Downs, *Economic Theory;* and David R. Mayhew, *Congress: The Electoral Connection* (New Haven: Yale University Press, 1974).
48. See John L. Offner, *An Unwanted War: The Diplomacy of the United States and Spain over Cuba, 1895–1898* (Chapel Hill: University of North Carolina Press, 1992).
49. For a summary, see Lawrence R. Jacobs and Robert Y. Shapiro, "Studying Substantive Democracy," *PS*, Vol. 27, No. 1 (March 1994), pp. 9–10.
50. Popular presidents had strong effects, while unpopular ones had little effect. Interestingly, special interest groups usually caused public opinion to move in a *contrary* direction. Benjamin I. Page, Robert Y. Shapiro, and Glenn R. Dempsey, "What Moves Public Opinion," *American Political Science Review*, Vol. 81, No. 1 (March 1987), pp. 23–43.

Figure 1. Causal Pathways of Liberal Democratic Peace.

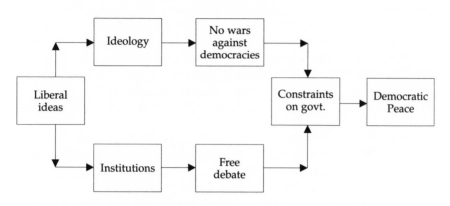

Hypotheses on Democratic Peace

To reiterate, I define liberal democracies as those states that are dominated by liberal ideology, and that feature, in both law and practice, free discussion and regular competitive elections. Signs that a state is dominated by liberalism may be institutional, such as equality of all citizens before the law. Or they may be informal, such as the predominance of appeals to personal freedom, self-preservation, and prosperity in debates about public life. Some states with liberal elements may be undemocratic, such as Great Britain before the 1832 Great Reform Act. Some democratic states may be illiberal, such as the Confederate States of America during the Civil War. Not all liberal democracies will forgo war with one another. A liberal democracy will only avoid war with a state that *it believes to be liberal.*

A causal mechanism such as I describe may be logically coherent yet empirically false. I now turn to the search for clues that this liberal mechanism really exists and works. As I did with previous theories of democratic peace, I ask: If this argument were valid, what would we expect to observe in the foreign policy processes in liberal democracies? I check these expectations or hypotheses against real historical cases. If the hypotheses are falsified—if history does not bear out my expectations—then my argument is like its predecessors inadequate.[51] The hypotheses are:

Liberals will trust states they consider liberal and mistrust those they consider illiberal. I argue that liberal ideology divides the world's states into liberal democracies and illiberal states. Because they share the enlightened ends of self-preservation, material well-being, and liberty, liberal democracies are seen as trustworthy and pacific. States ruled by despots and those populated by unenlightened citizens seek illiberal ends, and are believed potentially dangerous.

When liberals observe a foreign state becoming liberal by their own standards, they will expect pacific relations with it. Although definitions of democracy vary across time and space, these definitions are relatively stable rather than arbitrary. If a state once thought despotic adopts the right institutions, or comes to be dominated by liberals, liberals in other states will begin to trust it more.

Liberals will claim that fellow liberal democracies share their ends, and that illiberal states do not. Specifically, liberals will say that liberal democratic states seek the preservation and well-being of their citizens, that they love peace and freedom, and that they are cooperative. They will say of illiberal states that they seek conquest to the detriment of their citizens' true interests, disdain peace, and are treacherous.

Liberals will not change their assessments of foreign states during crises with those states unless those states change their institutions. When a liberal democracy is embroiled in a dispute with a state it considers a fellow liberal democracy, its liberals will not switch to viewing the state as illiberal. Similarly, when a liberal democracy is in a dispute with a state it considers illiberal, its liberals will not suddenly decide that the state is liberal after all, unless its domestic institutions change. (If this hypothesis is not borne out, the democratic peace is illusory, because power politics or some other force would actually be determining what label liberals attached to foreign states.)

Liberal elites will agitate for their policies during war-threatening crises. In a crisis with a fellow liberal democracy, liberals will use the news media and other fora to persuade leaders and the public to resolve the crisis peacefully. In a crisis with an illiberal state, liberals may agitate in favor of war if they believe it would serve liberal ends.

---

51. See King, Keohane, and Verba, *Designing Social Inquiry.*

During crises, statesmen will be constrained to follow liberal policy. When officials are themselves liberal, they will simply find a way to defuse crises with liberal democracies, or they may escalate them if the other state is illiberal. When officials are not liberal, they will still be pressured by public opinion, which has been aroused by a liberal elite, to forgo war with a liberal democracy; or, if the foreign state is illiberal, they may be spurred into war.

Four Cases

Four historical cases illustrate the argument: Franco-American relations in 1796–98, and Anglo-American relations during 1803–12, 1861–63, and 1895–96. These are four of the twelve cases from which I derived the argument.[52] I chose the twelve original cases because, first, they hold the identity of one state, the United States, constant. The United States has throughout its history been dominated by liberalism and featured free elections. Second, the cases allow the perceptions and governmental systems of the other state in each crisis to vary. In some crises, liberal Americans had previously considered the foreign state liberal; in others, they had not; in still others, opinion was divided. Moreover, in some of the cases the other state was dominated by liberalism and had free elections, and in others it did not. Third, choosing cases from before 1945 allows me to rule out the effects of bipolarity and nuclear weapons, two powerful confounding factors.

I chose these four cases because they have been written about extensively, and my claims are easily tested. The causal factors in my argument also vary across the four. I do not consider France in 1796–98 or Britain in 1803–12 liberal-democratic; but I do consider Britain in 1861–63 and 1895–96 to be so. These cases also point up the importance of perceptions to democratic peace. Most Americans did not consider Britain liberal-democratic in either 1803–12 or 1861–63; and most British did not consider the Union liberal in 1861, but they changed their minds in the fall of 1862. In addition, the three Anglo-American cases have all been cited as evidence *against* democratic peace.[53]

Strictly speaking, one cannot test an argument on the very cases from which it was derived. Such a "test" would be biased in favor of the argument.

---

52. The cases are listed in fn. 8.
53. On the War of 1812, see Waltz, "Emerging Structure"; on 1861 and 1895–96, see Layne, "Kant or Cant."

A true test involves fresh cases. Thus I use the following four cases to illustrate the argument rather than provide a crucial trial of its validity.

FRANCO-AMERICAN RELATIONS, 1796-98
In 1798 the United States initiated what became known as the Quasi-War with France, in which the two nations fought a series of naval battles in the Caribbean Sea. The American action was in response to French seizures of U.S. merchant vessels on the high seas, and to the "XYZ Affair" in which the French government attempted to extort thousands of dollars from three U.S. envoys in Paris. The French, then at war with England, had taken these actions in retaliation for the Jay Treaty, in which the Americans promised the British not to trade with France.[54] Here I argue that liberal ideology in the form of republican solidarity prevented France and the United States from engaging in full-scale war.

The United States in the late 1790s qualifies as a liberal democracy. Although suffrage in most states was limited to white males who owned property, regular elections were mandated by law, and Republican opposition to the Federalist government was lively. Republicans held to liberal tenets. They considered only republics—non-monarchies—to be liberal states, and they viewed France as a sister republic.[55]

They did so even though France does not qualify by my definition as a liberal democracy. The Constitution of the Year III (1795) mandated regular elections, and the French press was free, but the Executive in effect destroyed any institutional claim France had to democracy. In September 1797 and again in March 1798, radicals in the Directory ordered *coups d'état* expelling members of the executive and legislature who opposed them.[56] French foreign policy making is therefore not of direct interest here. Instead, I only

---

54. Accounts of the origins of the conflict may be found in Alexander DeConde, *The Quasi-War: The Politics and Diplomacy of the Undeclared War with France 1797–1801* (New York: Charles Scribner's Sons, 1966); Albert Hall Bowman, *The Struggle for Neutrality: Franco-American Diplomacy during the Federalist Era* (Knoxville: University of Tennessee Press, 1974); William C. Stinchcombe, *The XYZ Affair* (Westport, Conn.: Greenwood Press, 1980); E. Wilson Lyon, "The Directory and the United States," *American Historical Review*, Vol. 43, No. 3 (April 1938), pp. 514–532; and James A. James, "French Opinion as a Factor in Preventing War between France and the United States, 1795–1800," *American Historical Review*, Vol. 30, No. 1 (October 1924), pp. 44–55.
55. See for example Bowman, *Struggle for Neutrality*, pp. 25–30.
56. Georges Lefebvre, *The Thermidoreans and the Directory*, trans. Robert Baldick (New York: Random House, 1964), pp. 176–179; R.R. Palmer, *The Age of the Democratic Revolution* (Princeton: Princeton University Press, 1964), pp. 214–217, 255–259.

show that processes in the United States conform to the hypotheses derived from my argument.

U.S. REPUBLICANS TRUSTED FRANCE AND MISTRUSTED GREAT BRITAIN. Even after the French maritime depredations and the XYZ Affair, the Republicans forgave the French even as they excoriated the British. Their rationale was that France remained a sister republic, and England remained a monarchy. One Republican newspaper averred: "There is at present as much danger of an invasion from the French, as from the inhabitants of Saturn."[57] Thomas Jefferson, vice president and leader of the Republicans, applauded rumors of a pending French invasion of Britain, because it would "republicanize that country" so that "all will be safe with us."[58]

REPUBLICANS HAD CHEERED THE FRENCH REVOLUTION AND EXPECTED PACIFIC RELATIONS WITH THEIR SISTER REPUBLIC. In 1789, American support for the French Revolution had been nearly unanimous. With the execution of Louis XVI and establishment of the First Republic in 1793, Federalists turned against the French, but most Republicans remained staunch supporters. One historian writes:

Democratic papers commenced a calculated program of justifying those in power in Paris. This practice was consciously pursued throughout the remainder of the decade and must be acknowledged in order to assess the part of foreign relations in the political propaganda of the period. A defense was found for every French action, from Robespierre's Feast of the Supreme Being to the seizures of American ships.[59]

Republicans did not simply decide in 1798 to oppose war with France and invent an ideological justification for that position; they had been well disposed toward France since 1789.

REPUBLICANS CLAIMED THAT THE FRENCH SHARED THEIR ENDS, AND THAT THE BRITISH DID NOT. The Republicans saw the Anglo-French struggle as one between the principles of monarchy and republicanism more than between two European powers, and thus as part and parcel of the same struggle they had themselves fought only a decade before.[60] During the debate over the

---

57. *Independent Chronicle* (Boston), March 4, 1798, quoted in Donald H. Stewart, *The Opposition Press of the Federalist Period* (Albany: State University of New York Press, 1969), pp. 442–443.
58. Stinchcombe, *XYZ Affair*, p. 118.
59. Stewart, *Opposition Press*, p. 120.
60. See Jerald Combs, *The Jay Treaty* (Berkeley: University of California Press, 1970), pp. 110–111; Samuel Flagg Bemis, *Jay's Treaty: A Study in Commerce and Diplomacy* (New York: Macmillan, 1923; repr. ed., Westport, Conn.: Greenwood Press, 1975), pp. 95–96.

Jay Treaty in 1796, one Virginian told his fellow Congressmen: "As it has not been in the power of the United States to assist their Republican allies, *when fighting in fact their battles,* the least they can do . . . must be, that they will not put the enemies [the British] of those allies into a better condition than they were."[61]

REPUBLICANS DID NOT CHANGE THEIR FAVORABLE ASSESSMENT OF FRANCE DURING THE CRISIS, DESPITE FEDERALIST EFFORTS. Much American public opinion of France had soured after the XYZ Affair, but Republican elites stood by France against England. One newspaper declared that "'our Pharaohs' still wishfully looked for the downfall of the Republic and were ready to 'lend a hand to effect it'." Another said of the Federalists: "The tory faction will endeavour to torture fact, in order to excite our feelings against the cause of liberty and the revolution. . . . Let us be calm."[62]

REPUBLICANS AGITATED AGAINST WAR WITH FRANCE. In Congress, the party of Jefferson used all its energy to stave off a war declaration. Accusing President Adams of trying to declare war by himself, they introduced resolutions stating that "it is not expedient for the United States to resort to war against the French Republic."[63] The Republican press shrieked in protest against the possibility of a Franco-American war.[64]

THE PRESIDENT AND THE CONGRESSIONAL FEDERALISTS WERE CONSTRAINED BY THE REPUBLICANS FROM DECLARING WAR ON FRANCE. In the spring of 1798, Adams wanted war with France. In March he drafted a war message to Congress saying, "All men will think it more honorable and glorious to the national character when its existence as an independent nation is at stake that hostilities should be avowed in a formal Declaration of War."[65] Yet the president never presented the message to Congress. He could not do so, because he knew he did not have the votes to obtain a war declaration. Not everyone in Congress opposed Adams: the "high Federalists" had wanted war long before he had. It was the Republicans and the moderate Federalists who would not vote for war.

The Republican motivation is already clear. The moderate Federalists opposed war in part because the nation was so divided—i.e., because Republican opposition was so adamant. Believing only a united effort would enable

---

61. 4th Cong., 1st sess., *Annals of Congress* (April 20, 1796), Vol. 5, p. 1099. Emphasis added.
62. Stewart, *Opposition Press,* p. 286.
63. 5th Cong., 2d sess., *Annals of Congress* (March 27, 1798), Vol. 2, p. 1329.
64. Stewart, *Opposition Press,* pp. 289–290.
65. DeConde, *Quasi-War,* pp. 66–68.

the nation to fight France effectively, the moderates were in effect constrained by a liberal ideology they did not even hold. As one moderate put it after the defeat of a test vote in the House of Representatives in July 1798, "we should have war; but he did not wish to go on faster to this state of things than the people of this country, and the opinion of the world would justify."[66]

ANGLO-AMERICAN RELATIONS, 1803–12

Another Anglo-French war, begun in 1803, likewise entangled the U.S. merchant marine. Both the British and French were again humiliating the United States by seizing U.S. cargoes, and the British were impressing American sailors into service as well. Ultimately, under the presidency of James Madison, the United States went to war.[67] The War of 1812 is often cited by critics of the democratic peace proposition as an example of two democracies at war.[68] By my definition, however, Britain cannot be considered a liberal democracy.[69] Moreover, even a cursory examination of the events leading up to the war shows that very few Americans, and virtually no British, considered Great Britain a democracy at the time. Here again, Republicans in the United States act as my argument would predict.

REPUBLICANS MISTRUSTED ENGLAND, AND SOME STILL TRUSTED NAPOLEONIC FRANCE. Thomas Jefferson, president from 1801 to 1809, wrote privately to a friend in 1810 that the nature of the British government rendered England unfit "for the observation of moral duties," and that it would betray any agreement with the United States. Napoleon, on the other hand, was safe: "A *republican* Emperor, from his affection to republics, independent of motives of expediency, must grant to ours the Cyclops' boon of being the last devoured."[70]

---

66. Ibid., p. 106.
67. See Reginald Horsman, *The Causes of the War of 1812* (Philadelphia: University of Pennsylvania Press, 1962); Roger H. Brown, *The Republic in Peril: 1812* (New York: Norton, 1971); Bradford Perkins, *Prologue to War* (Berkeley: University of California Press, 1961).
68. See for example Waltz, "Emerging Structure," p. 78.
69. Elections in pre-reform Britain were uncompetitive. Many seats in the House of Commons represented tiny boroughs where one patron determined who was elected; other towns were entirely disenfranchised. Votes in the Commons were effectively bought and sold in an open market. The House of Lords, an unelected body, could veto legislation. Moreover, the cabinet, which possessed war powers, was responsible to the king rather than to parliament. See E.L. Woodward, *The Age of Reform 1815–1870* (Oxford: Clarendon Press, 1938), pp. 18–28.
70. Robert W. Tucker and David C. Hendrickson, *Empire of Liberty: The Statecraft of Thomas Jefferson* (New York: Oxford University Press, 1990), pp. 329–330.

REPUBLICANS CLAIMED THAT ENGLAND DID NOT SHARE THEIR ENDS. With few exceptions, Republicans blasted England for opposing the cause of liberty.[71] One Congressman exclaimed that "the standard of freedom had never been raised in any country without [England's] attempting to pull it down."[72] Republicans believed England was trying to wipe republicanism from the face of the earth. One newspaper asserted:

Not only the rights of the nation, but the character of the government, are involved in the issue. . . . The deliberations of Congress "at this momentous era," will perhaps, do more to stamp the character of genuine republican governments, than has been effected in this respect since the creation of the world.

Republicans feared that continued foreign humiliation would lead to a Federalist government which would align the United States with England and set up a monarchy.[73]

REPUBLICANS DEFINED ENGLAND AS NON-DEMOCRATIC BEFORE AND DURING THE CRISIS. Far from changing their views of the British to suit the moment, Jeffersonians had consistently hated the mother country since before the American Revolution. In 1806 one Congressman rhetorically asked if his colleagues could tolerate "that same monarch [George III] . . . who, instead of diminishing, has added to the long and black catalogue of crimes set forth in our Declaration of Independence."[74]

REPUBLICANS AGITATED FOR WAR. Both Jefferson and James Madison, Republican president from 1809 to 1817, preferred economic sanctions to war. But the 1811 War Hawk Congress decided with Madison that force had to be used to punish the British. Henry Clay, John C. Calhoun, and other young Republican Congressmen demanded war, as did the Republican press.[75]

STATESMEN FOLLOWED REPUBLICAN IDEOLOGY. Since Republicans controlled the executive and Congress, they did not need to be forced by democratic institutions to initiate war. Public support for war was certainly not unanimous; New England in particular was vehemently opposed. But Madison and the War Hawks declared war anyway. One biographer writes of Madison:

71. One prominent exception was John Randolph, the eccentric Virginian, who agreed with Federalists that England rather than France was fighting for the liberties of the world. See Brown, *Republic in Peril*, pp. 151–155.
72. 12th Cong., 1st sess., *Annals of Congress*, Vol. 23 (January 6, 1812), p. 688.
73. Brown, *Republic in Peril*, pp. 74–84.
74. 9th Cong., 1st sess., *Annals of Congress*, Vol. 15 (March 7, 1806), pp. 609–610.
75. Horsman, *Causes of the War of 1812*, chapter 13.

To have submitted to [Britain's] unilateral decrees, her discriminatory trade regulations, or her naval outrages would have . . . ratified unjust principles in international law and emboldened antirepublican forces in Britain and the United States, thus threatening, in Madison's opinion, the survival of free government anywhere in the world.[76]

Realists at the time opposed the War of 1812, and in fact realists ever since have had difficulty accounting for it. Morgenthau calls it "the sole exception" to the rule that the United States has followed realist tenets in dealing with Europe.[77] In their 1990 book, Robert Tucker and David Hendrickson chide Jefferson for throwing America's lot in with France rather than Britain during the Napoleonic Wars. The United States would have avoided trouble, had it

publicly recognized that England was in truth engaged in a contest for public liberty and international order, and that by virtue of its own stance against Napoleon Britain protected the United States from the peculiar menace that Bonaparte embodied. . . . Jefferson would not say this because he did not believe it.[78]

That is, the Republican conception of the national interest ultimately required war because Britain was a monarchy.

ANGLO-AMERICAN RELATIONS, 1861–63

Fifty years later, Americans still mainly saw the world's nations as republics and monarchies.[79] Britain remained a monarchy and therefore a despotism. At several points during the American Civil War, Britain and the Union teetered on the brink of war. In none of these crises did liberal affinity for England play much of a role in keeping the Union from attacking Britain. And in the first, the *Trent* affair,[80] British liberal affinity for the Union was

---

76. Ralph Ketcham, *James Madison* (New York: Macmillan, 1971), p. 530.
77. Hans J. Morgenthau, *In Defense of the National Interest* (New York: Knopf, 1951), p. 5.
78. Tucker and Hendrickson, *Empire of Liberty*, pp. 226–227.
79. Sources on this case include Ephraim Douglass Adams, *Great Britain and the American Civil War*, 2 vols. (New York: Longmans, Green and Co., 1925); Brian Jenkins, *Britain and the War for the Union*, 2 vols. (Montreal: McGill-Queen's University Press, 1974 and 1980); Howard Jones, *Union in Peril: The Crisis over British Intervention in the American Civil War* (Chapel Hill: University of North Carolina Press, 1992); Norman B. Ferris, *The "Trent" Affair: A Diplomatic Crisis* (Knoxville: University of Tennessee Press, 1977); Martin P. Claussen, "Peace Factors in Anglo-American Relations, 1861–1865," *Mississippi Valley Historical Review*, Vol. 26 (March 1940), pp. 511–522.
80. The crisis occurred when a Union ship seized the British mail packet *Trent* as it carried two Southern emissaries to London to try to negotiate formal recognition of the Confederacy. The British were almost unanimously outraged, and clearly would have declared war had Lincoln not apologized and returned the emissaries. See Ferris, *Trent*.

rather weak as well, which in turn fed Union hostility toward England. The resolution of the *Trent* crisis can be explained without reference to democratic peace theory: the administration of Abraham Lincoln backed down to a British ultimatum because it could not afford war with such a powerful foe over such an issue.[81] With the Union fighting for its life against the Confederacy, Lincoln and his cabinet prudently decided that no liberal purpose would be served by an Anglo-American war.

By my definition, Britain in the 1860s was a liberal democracy. The 1832 Reform Act had made elections fairer, and had made the cabinet responsible to parliament rather than to the Crown. This meant the executive was ultimately responsible to the electors, giving the public leverage over war decisions.[82]

British liberal sympathy for the Union was weak during *Trent* because most British took Lincoln at his word that the Civil War was about restoring the Union—a cause uninspiring to the British—rather than abolition.[83] British of all classes had supported the abolition of slavery since the 1830s. Then in September 1862, Lincoln issued the preliminary Emancipation Proclamation, declaring that as of January 1, 1863, all slaves in the rebellious states would be free. Although it was condemned by pro-Confederates as likely to provoke a slave insurrection, the Proclamation cause British opinion to shift to the Union side. This shift helped prevent Britain from intervening in the Civil War. Christopher Layne's account of Anglo-American relations in this time misses this because he only looks at the *Trent* affair.

BRITISH LIBERALS TRUSTED THE UNION. Even before the Emancipation Proclamation, the Union had its staunch supporters among the Philosophical Radicals, notably John Bright and Richard Cobden. Bright told Parliament in early 1862, "there probably never has been a great nation in which what is familiarly termed mob law is less known or has had less influence. . . . Understand, I confine my observations always to the free States of the

---

81. See Layne, "The Myth of the Democratic Peace," Again, I do not argue that liberals will continually seek war against states they consider illiberal. Liberalism determines the ends, but power politics may circumscribe the means.

82. The shift in cabinet responsibility was *de facto* rather than *de jure*; since 1832, no monarch has ever dismissed a ministry. See Robert Livingston Schuyler and Corinne Comstock Weston, *British Constitutional History since 1832* (Princeton: D. Van Nostrand, 1957), pp. 26–44.

83. In his first inaugural address, Lincoln said: "I have no purpose, directly or indirectly to interfere with the institution of slavery in the States where it exists. I believe I have no lawful right to do so, and I have no inclination to do so." Quoted in Adams, *Great Britain and the Civil War*, Vol. 1, p. 50.

North."[84] Bright's view gained wide acceptance after the Proclamation, because abolitionists viewed slaveholding states as aggressive by nature.[85]

AFTER THE EMANCIPATION PROCLAMATION, LIBERALS WANTED BETTER RELATIONS WITH THE UNION, AND BELIEVED THE UNION SHARED LIBERAL ENDS. Britain's *Morning Star* newspaper summarized the change in October: "The inevitable has come at last. Negro emancipation is formally and definitively adopted as the policy in war and peace of the United States."[86] The *Daily News* predicted that now "the most audacious Secessionists" in England would shy away from proposing recognition of the "confederated Slave States." All through the war the Union had blockaded the Confederacy, preventing cotton from reaching England and causing extreme distress in the Lancashire textile region. Yet after the Proclamation, England's working class newspapers shifted over to the Union's side, proclaiming that the Union's cause, liberation of the masses, was their cause. One paper said the most dangerous problem facing Britain was now "the recognition of the slaveholding Confederate States, and, as an almost necessary consequence, an alliance with them against the Federal States of America."[87]

LIBERALS AGITATED AGAINST INTERVENTION AFTER THE PROCLAMATION. As the Proclamation energized evangelical Christian and other emancipation groups in Britain, Bright stated that the "anti-slavery sentiment" of his country was finally being "called forth."[88] One historian writes that "there took place meeting after meeting at which strong resolutions were passed enthusiastically endorsing the issue of the emancipation proclamation and pledging sympathy to the cause of the North."[89] In Manchester, a rally at the end of 1862 approved a missive to Lincoln congratulating him for the "humane and righteous course" he had taken in furthering America's founding concept that "all men are created equal." In London during the spring of 1863, a rally of 2,500 or more workers pledged themselves "to use their 'utmost efforts' to prevent the recognition of any government 'founded on human slavery'."[90]

THE BRITISH CABINET WAS CONSTRAINED BY LIBERALISM FROM INTERVENING IN THE CIVIL WAR. Shortly after the Proclamation, the cabinet was considering

---

84. *Hansard's Parliamentary Debates* (Commons), 3d Ser., Vol. 165 (February 17, 1862), col. 382.
85. See, e.g., the remarks of Goldwin Smith in the Venezuelan crisis, below.
86. Jenkins, *Britain and the War*, Vol. 2, p. 152.
87. Ibid., p. 216; Philip Foner, *British Labor and the American Civil War* (New York: Holmes and Meier, 1981), p. 69.
88. Jenkins, *Britain and the War*, Vol. 2, pp. 209–211.
89. Adams, *Great Britain and the Civil War*, Vol. 2, p. 107.
90. Foner, *British Labor*, pp. 41, 61.

a French proposal to offer joint mediation to end the Civil War. All knew that the Union would almost certainly refuse, and armed intervention would have to follow to enforce mediation. Advocates of intervention, including Lord John Russell and William Gladstone, wanted to end the Union blockade of the South. They were also sickened at the brutality of the war, and supported the Southerners' right to self-determination.[91] Other advocates also argued that a permanently divided and weakened America was in long-term British interests.[92] Viscount Palmerston, the prime minister, had at times supported intervention as well.[93] But in late October, he soured on the prospect.

Palmerston gave many reasons, but significantly, his main obstacle seems to have been the shift in public opinion caused by the Emancipation Proclamation. In October, Palmerston wrote privately to Russell that slavery was now England's "great difficulty" in trying to put together peace terms. Could the cabinet, he asked, "without offence to many People here recommend to the North to sanction Slavery and to undertake to give back Runaways, and yet would not the South insist upon some such Conditions after Lincoln's Emancipation Decree"? The French were readier to intervene, he wrote, because they were freer from the "Shackles of Principle and of Right & Wrong on these Matters, as on all others than we are."[94]

To be sure, Palmerston heard other arguments against intervention. His secretary for war, George Cornewall Lewis, was primarily concerned that British recognition of the Confederacy would set a bad international legal precedent. Lewis also argued that the European powers would have difficulty forcing the Union to accept terms. Also on Palmerston's mind was the progress of the war itself, which had recently not gone well for the South.[95] But as Palmerston had said to the Russian ambassador to London in 1861, there were "two Powers in this Country, the government & public opinion, and that both must concur for any great important steps."[96]

---

91. Jones, *Union in Peril*, pp. 178–179, 184–185, 203; Adams, *Great Britain and the Civil War*, Vol. 1, pp. 212–215; Jenkins, *Britain and the War*, Vol. 2, pp. 168–169.
92. For example, William Lindsay, a member of Parliament, said he desired intervention because he "desired the disruption of the American Union, as every honest Englishman did, because it was too great a Power and England sh'd not let such a power exist on the American continent." Jones, *Union in Peril*, p. 134.
93. Ibid., pp. 150–151.
94. Ibid., pp. 191, 206.
95. Ibid., pp. 210–217.
96. Ferris, *Trent*, p. 158.

After the autumn of 1862, public opinion rendered British intervention impossible. Russell himself stopped Britain from selling ironclad warships to the Confederacy in the spring of 1863, writing privately to a colleague: "If we have taken part in interventions, it has been in behalf of the independence, freedom and welfare of a great portion of mankind. I should be sorry, indeed, if there should be any intervention on the part of this country which could bear another character."[97] Even Gladstone argued against intervention during the summer: "A war with the United States . . . ought to be unpopular on far higher grounds, because it would be a war with our own kinsmen for slavery."[98]

ANGLO-AMERICAN RELATIONS, 1895–96

Just over thirty years later, Britain and the United States were again close to war.[99] President Grover Cleveland and Richard Olney, his secretary of state, saw a boundary dispute between British Guiana and Venezuela as an opportunity to assert U.S. power in the New World. Cleveland and Olney demanded U.S. arbitration in the dispute, arguing that England was violating the Monroe Doctrine by trying to expand its territory in the New World. After Lord Salisbury, British prime minister and foreign minister, told Cleveland that it was no affair of the United States', Congress voted unanimously in December 1895 to fund an American commission to decide the boundary, with its recommendations to be enforced by whatever means necessary. War fever was loose for a few days in America. But the crisis was resolved peacefully over the next few months, and never again would these two nations seriously consider war with each other.

Because both states were liberal democracies, and sizable populations in each state considered the other liberal, I consider the foreign policy processes in both.

AMERICANS HAD OBSERVED BRITAIN DEMOCRATIZING IN THE 1880S AND HAD BEGUN TO EXPECT BETTER RELATIONS. Many Americans in the 1890s still

---

97. Jenkins, *Britain and the War*, Vol. 2, p. 241.
98. *Hansard's Parliamentary Debates* (Commons), 3d ser., Vol. 171 (June 30, 1863), cols. 1805–1806.
99. Accounts of this crisis are found in Ernest R. May, *Imperial Democracy: The Emergence of America as a Great Power* (Chicago: Imprint Publications, 1991); Allen, *Great Britain and the United States;* Dexter Perkins, *The Monroe Doctrine 1867–1907* (Baltimore: Johns Hopkins University Press, 1937); A.E. Campbell, *Great Britain and the United States 1895–1903* (Westport, Conn.: Greenwood Press, 1960); and Marshall Bertram, *The Birth of Anglo-American Friendship: The Prime Facet of the Venezuelan Boundary Dispute* (Lanham, Md.: University Press of America, 1992).

viewed Britain mainly as a monarchy and thus not democratic. But others had begun to challenge this old view after the Third Reform Act in 1884 enormously expanded the franchise in Britain. Andrew Carnegie then proclaimed, "Henceforth England is democratic," and predicted that "British democracy is to be pacific, and that the American doctrine of non-intervention will commend itself to it."[100] On the eve of the Venezuelan crisis, Joseph Pulitzer, publisher of the *New York World*, decried a senator's proposal that the United States align with Russia and wage war against England:

Russia represents the worst despotism that civilization has permitted to survive, except possibly that of Turkey. England represents Anglo-Saxon liberty and progress only in less degree than does our own government. We have much in common with the English. We have nothing whatever in common with Russia.[101]

A liberal elite desired good relations with England precisely because the nation had democratized.

MOST BRITONS NOW SAW THE UNITED STATES AS TRUSTWORTHY. One reason was the end of slavery. The scholar Goldwin Smith wrote during the crisis, "I am firmly convinced that since the abolition of slavery there prevails among them no desire for territorial aggrandizement."[102] Another was democratization in Britain itself. A historian writes, "Anti-Americanism, traditionally associated with a disappearing social order, had long been on the wane . . . Thus in all the tensions of the period, and particularly in the Venezuela dispute, the most important influence for amity and peace was the new English democracy." Fear of Russia and Germany influenced this desire for American friendship, but the point is that the new Britain was more inclined than the old to choose America as friend.[103] William Vernon Harcourt, Liberal leader in the House of Commons, often referred to "we semi-Americans" when writing to his friend Joseph Chamberlain, the Liberal colonial secretary.[104] On both sides of the Atlantic, Anglo-Saxon chauvinism played a strong role in this affinity.[105]

---

100. Andrew Carnegie, "Democracy in England," *North American Review*, Vol. 142, No. 1 (January 1886), p. 74.
101. *Public Opinion*, November 21, 1895, p. 21. One publicist called England "the Crowned Republic." Moncure D. Conway, "The Queen of England," *North American Review*, Vol. 145, No. 2 (August 1887), p. 121.
102. *New-York Times*, December 25, 1895, p. 3.
103. Allen, *Great Britain and the United States*, p. 525.
104. A.G. Gardiner, *The Life of Sir William Vernon Harcourt* (London: Constable and Co., 1923), Vol. 2, pp. 396–397.
105. Campbell, *Great Britain and the United States*, pp. 9–10.

AMERICAN LIBERALS CONTINUED TO SEE ENGLAND AS LIBERAL DURING THE CRISIS. Neither Cleveland nor Olney was part of the liberal pro-British elite in the United States, and much of the American public wanted war at the beginning of the crisis. But the U.S. ambassador to London, Thomas F. Bayard, was a pro-British liberal who viewed the United States and Great Britain as the "two guardians of civilization." During the crisis, Bayard stressed his well-known views that England was to be trusted because, unlike Venezuela, it was governed by law.[106] In Congress, Senator Edward O. Wolcott of Colorado declared Venezuela one of South America's "so-called republics" in which the "rulers are despots and suffrage a farce." He hoped the Venezuelan mines would be governed by "English common law" with its "certainty of enforcement."[107]

Most pro-British liberals were found outside government, however. Prominent among these was Pulitzer, whose *New York World* said on December 21:

There is not a hothead among the jingoes who does not know that England is more likely to become a republic than the United States are to revert to monarchism. The entire trend of government for the past fifty years has been toward democracy. . . . Observe the working of the leaven of democracy in England.[108]

"In a word," commented the *Nation*, "the American Secretary of State's references to Venezuelan republicanism and friendship and English monarchy and hostility have no more to do with the facts than with the planet Jupiter."[109]

BRITISH LIBERALS CONTINUED TO SEE THE UNITED STATES AS LIBERAL THROUGH THE CRISIS. The British press expressed general revulsion at the prospect of war with the United States. The *Standard* gave a typical opinion:

We feel confident that a vast majority of the Americans will soon be profoundly sorry for what Mr. Cleveland has done. He has travestied and damaged a principle that they hold dear, and has made the Republic which we have all honored on account of its supposed attachment to peace and

---

106. Charles Callan Tansill, *The Foreign Policy of Thomas F. Bayard* (New York: Fordham University Press, 1940), p. 716.
107. 54th Cong., 1st sess., *Congressional Record* (December 20, 1895), Vol. 28, Pt. 1, pp. 859–860.
108. John L. Heaton, *The Story of a Page* (New York: Harper and Bros., 1913), p. 114.
109. *The Nation*, January 2, 1896, p. 5.

non-intervention, figure in the eyes of Europe as a gratuitously aggressive and reckless champion of war.[110]

The *Daily Telegraph* calmly stated, "We are perfectly satisfied to rely upon the straightforward, high-bred simplicity of Lord Salisbury's diplomacy and the good sense, widespread honesty, intelligence, and kindliness of the American people."[111]

AMERICAN LIBERALS AGITATED FOR PEACE. Pulitzer led the peace movement, sending cablegrams to influential British asking their opinions on the crisis. On Christmas Day the *World*'s front page featured a selection of responses under the headline "PEACE AND GOOD WILL," expressing horror at the thought of an Anglo-American war.[112] There was, moreover, an interactive effect as Americans observed this British good will. In January 1896 the *Philadelphia Press* asserted, "Nothing in the succession for a month past of discussion, declaration and feeling, personal and public, private and National, has so moved the American Nation as a whole as the sudden revelation which has been made of English horror of war with this country."[113]

BRITISH LIBERALS AGITATED FOR PEACE. Not only the British press, but also Joseph Chamberlain, the colonial secretary who had originally agreed with Salisbury to rebuff Cleveland and Olney, "determined to move heaven and earth to avert conflict between the two English-speaking peoples," one biographer writes.[114] In a speech in Birmingham, Chamberlain proclaimed:

War between the two nations would be an absurdity as well as a crime. . . . The two nations are allied more closely in sentiment and in interest than any

---

110. Quoted in the *New York Times*, December 21, 1895, p. 6. It is also interesting to note that the London *Review of Reviews* took great pains to counter those Americans who claimed England was not democratic. "The superstition that the United States is in a peculiar sense Republican, whereas we are Monarchical, is being utilized for all it is worth in order to bolster up the case for intervention in Venezuela. If British subjects in Guiana would but repudiate their allegiance to the British Empire, and set up in business as a British republic, no American citizen would object to them eating their way into the heart of Venezuela. All the difficulty arises from the prejudice against the monarchy—a prejudice that is as old as George III., and ought to have been buried with him." *Review of Reviews* (London), December 14, 1895, pp. 484–485.
111. *New-York Times*, December 19, 1895, p. 3.
112. Heaton, *The Story of a Page*, p. 114; W.A. Swanberg, *Pulitzer* (New York: Charles Scribner's Sons, 1967), p. 199. This is in stark contrast to Pulitzer's behavior two years later in the crisis with Spain, a country few if any Americans considered democratic. In agitating for war, the *World* declared, "War waged on behalf of freedom, of self-government, of law and order, of humanity, to end oppression, misrule, plunder and savagery, is a holy war in itself." Heaton, *Story of a Page*, p. 162.
113. *Public Opinion*, Vol. 20 (January 23, 1896), p. 107.
114. J.L. Garvin, *The Life of Joseph Chamberlain*, Vol. 3 (London: Macmillan, 1934), p. 67.

other nations on the face of the earth. . . . I should look forward with pleasure to the possibility of the Stars and Stripes and the Union Jack floating together in defence of a common cause sanctioned by humanity and justice.[115]

His friend Harcourt made it clear that he would make the crisis a major issue in the upcoming session of Parliament. He urged Chamberlain to grant the Americans all they wanted.[116]

RESOLUTION OF THE CRISIS. Especially in the United States, liberals had a difficult task. Not only were Cleveland and Olney unimpressed by British democratization, but much of the American public, especially Irish-Americans, roared its approval at this "tweaking of the lion's tail." One cannot prove what drove officials on either side of the Atlantic defuse the crisis. What can be said is that on January 2, 1896, Cleveland appointed a distinguished commission to adjudicate the Venezuelan-British Guianan border, with only one member who could be construed as anglophobic. Since the president could have appointed a much more inflammatory commission, this must be seen as a conciliatory step.

The British cabinet voted on January 11, over the objections of Salisbury, to accept the U.S. commission's jurisdiction. It was the liberals on the cabinet, led by the pro-American Chamberlain, who favored the settlement. Salisbury, a realist with no affinity for American democracy, would have accepted war, and he nearly resigned in protest when the cabinet outvoted him.

The resolution of the Venezuelan border crisis was the beginning of the apparently permanent Anglo-American friendship. Today, realists argue that Britain appeased the Americans here and elsewhere because it could no longer sustain its "splendid isolation" in the face of rising threats from Germany and Russia.[117] That argument begs the question of why the British aligned with the United States rather than with Germany. Germany threatened British interests in Africa, but the United States threatened British interests in the New World. Liberalism offers an answer: British liberals trusted the democratic United States more than imperial Germany. During the Venezuelan crisis, the German emperor sent the infamous Krüger telegram congratulating the Boers in southern Africa for repelling the British Jameson raid. In a striking contrast to its calm reaction to Cleveland and

---

115. May, *Imperial Democracy*, pp. 44–45, 53–54.
116. Ibid., p. 49; Gardiner, *Life of Harcourt*, pp. 396–397; Garvin, *Chamberlain*, p. 161; Bertram, *Anglo-American Friendship*, p. 83. Harcourt had always admired the United States, and argued vigorously against British intervention in the U.S. Civil War.
117. Layne, "The Myth of the Democratic Peace."

Olney's provocations, the British public was outraged. One historian writes, "when 'Yankee Doodle' was cheered and 'Die Wacht am Rhein' hissed in London, it demonstrated clearly how utterly different was popular feeling towards the two countries."[118]

Appeasement of the United States was no arbitrary choice. Now that Britain was more democratic than ever, its government and people trusted democratic America more than ever.[119]

Democratic Peace and the Realist Challenge: The Liberal Response

Many realists have declared democratic peace a fantasy. Permanent peace between mutually recognized liberal democracies, they argue, is not possible. Liberal states, like all others, must base foreign policy on the imperatives of power politics. Some realists argue that there is no theoretically compelling causal mechanism that could explain democratic peace. Others claim that even if there were, the foreign policy processes of democracies show that such a "mechanism" is empirically impotent.[120] Realist skeptics make a number of claims:

First, they claim that if neither democratic structures nor norms alone can explain the democratic peace, then there is no democratic peace.[121] I have already pointed out the logical fallacy behind this claim. The structural/normative distinction is epistemological, not ontological. I argue that structure and norms work in tandem: liberal ideas proscribe wars among democracies, and democratic institutions ensure that this proscription is followed.

Realists claim that if there were a democratic peace, then liberal democracies would never make threats against one another.[122] The claim is that the logic of the democratic peace proposition implies that liberal democracies will never try to coerce one another. But of course, there is no inherent

---

118. Allen, *Great Britain and the United States*, p. 354.
119. Stephen Rock writes: "Englishmen, who could agree on practically nothing else, were in fact almost unanimous in their distaste for the German political system, its ideology, and its methods. . . . Both [Germany and the United States] were rising imperial powers with growing navies. . . . Yet Britons, while they detested and feared Germany, almost universally admired the United States and felt minimal apprehension at her ambitions." Rock, *Why Peace Breaks Out: Great Power Rapprochement in Historical Perspective* (Chapel Hill: University of North Carolina Press, 1989), pp. 86–87.
120. See Mearsheimer, "Back to the Future"; Waltz, "Emerging Structure"; Layne, "The Myth of the Democratic Peace"; Farber and Gowa, "Polities and Peace."]
121. Layne, "Kant or Cant."
122. Ibid.

"logic" of democratic peace independent of an explicit argument about how it works. My argument answers realism in two ways. First, liberal democracies do not always consider each other liberal. What a scholar in 1994 considers democratic is not always what a statesman in 1894 considered democratic. Second, liberal democracies are sometimes governed by illiberal leaders who are somewhat autonomous in implementing foreign policy. Such leaders may make threats; they are simply unable to mobilize the nation for war, due to the constraints of democratic institutions.

Realists claim that if there were democratic peace, then public opinion in liberal democracies would never want war with a fellow liberal democracy.[123] Like the previous claim, this one makes two assumptions: that all citizens of liberal democracies are liberal, and that they agree on which foreign states are also liberal. Neither assumption is true, and neither is necessary for democratic peace to occur. All that is necessary for statesmen to be constrained is that they believe war would be too unpopular. For this, a nation's population need not all be liberal.

Realists claim that when power politics requires war with a democracy, liberals will redefine that state as a despotism; when power politics requires peace with a non-democracy, they will redefine that state as a democracy.[124] That is, ideological labels are sugar-coating to make otherwise bitter policies easier to swallow. Statesmen's public rationales for foreign policy are solely rhetorical; one must look at their confidential statements to understand their true motives. In this article, however, I have shown that in crises liberals hang fast to the ideological labels they previously gave foreign states. Republicans stood by France after the XYZ Affair. They mistrusted England from the time of the American Revolution up to the end of the War of 1812 (and beyond). Many Americans began to see England as democratic in the 1880s, and continued to do so during the Venezuelan crisis. Britons began admiring the United States well before the rise of Germany "forced" them to make friends in the late 1890s. The one case where liberals changed their opinion of a foreign state during a crisis was in the Civil War. There, British opinion shifted to the Union side after the Emancipation Proclamation. The cause of this shift was not power politics, but the Emancipation Proclamation,

---

123. Ibid.
124. This is implied in Hans Morgenthau's argument that Woodrow Wilson led the United States into World War I "not to make the world safe for democracy," but because "Germany threatened the balance of power. . . . Wilson pursued the right policy, but he pursued it for the wrong reason." Morgenthau, *National Interest*, pp. 25–26.

which signified that the Union was fighting for abolition, a liberal cause the British had long supported.

Realists claim that "strategic concerns and the relative distribution of military capabilities . . . should crucially—perhaps decisively" affect the outcomes of crises between liberal democracies, and moreover that "broader geopolitical considerations pertaining to a state's position in international politics should, if implicated, account significantly for the crisis's outcome."[125] I do not contest the relevance of power politics to the foreign policies of liberal democracies. These realist hypotheses, however, imply that during a crisis, statesmen will be able either to ignore liberals or to persuade them to change their minds. But liberal ideology and institutions clearly had independent power in 1798, when John Adams could not ask Congress for war against France due to staunch Republican opposition. In 1862, Palmerston privately admitted to being constrained by pro-Union opinion from intervening in the Civil War. Realism would and did counsel the British to work to keep the United States divided and weak, but they passed up the opportunity. In 1895–96, war would clearly have been highly unpopular, especially in England, and Salisbury was thwarted by Liberals in his own cabinet from confronting the United States.

Realists claim that states that view each other as liberal-democratic will still balance against each other.[126] Realists who posit that states balance solely against capabilities must explain why Britain conciliated the United States rather than Germany. As explained below, a more nuanced realism, such as balance-of-threat theory, could account for this outcome. In assessing whether a foreign states is a threat, liberals such as Chamberlain look at, among other things, the state's regime type.

Realists claim that Wilhelmine Germany was a democracy, and therefore democracies fought one another in World War I.[127] There is not the space to address this claim fully, but two things may briefly be said. First, even before the war, most British and Americans saw Germany as undemocratic. The British abhorred German ideology, and although many Americans admired Germany's progressive social policies, most viewed the country as politically backward. "Germany is mediæval," said one magazine in 1912. "'Divine

---

125. Layne, "Kant or Cant."
126. Waltz, "Emerging Structure," pp. 66–67, predicts that Japan and Germany will acquire nuclear capabilities to balance against the United States.
127. Layne, "The Myth of the Democratic Peace."

Rights' is written on the brow of the Kaiser. . . . This is the trinity that rules Germany: a mediæval king, a feudal aristocracy, and the pushing parvenus of coal dust and iron filings."[128] Second, the chancellor was responsible to the Emperor William rather than the legislature. The electorate had little leverage over war decisions. The press was not wholly free, as illustrated when William suppressed an antiwar book in 1913. The emperor also controlled the upper chamber of the legislature, the Bundesrat, which had veto power over the legislation of the lower house.[129] Thus, by neither the standards of its time nor those of this study can Germany be called a liberal democracy in 1914.

IS A REALIST-LIBERAL SYNTHESIS POSSIBLE?

Both realists and liberals who have written about democratic peace have been loath to cede any ground to the opposing side. Yet my argument and evidence suggest that both camps are describing real forces in international politics, namely, power politics and liberal ideas. It is conceivable that these two forces sometimes push in different directions in a particular case, yielding a weak effect in favor of one or the other. Jon Elster discusses such dynamics in a very different context: suppose a weak aggregate tendency was discovered for people to donate more to charity when others do so. The weak tendency may well be due to the existence of two different types of people with opposite tendencies: one, slightly dominant, that gives much more when observing others give (following a norm of reciprocity), and one that gives less (following a utilitarian norm). The combined effect conceals two strong mechanisms working at cross purposes.[130] Similarly, it could be that *Realpolitik* pushes policy into one direction and liberalism in another, and that the combined effect weakly favors one or the other. Consistent with this, my cases indicate that some actors are realist, some liberal.

A key to synthesizing the two theories would seem to be that liberals define national interest in such a way that cooperation with fellow liberal

128. *World's Work*, June 1912, p. 146.
129. John L. Snell, *The Democratic Movement in Germany, 1789–1914* (Chapel Hill: University of North Carolina Press, 1976), pp. 165, 212–219, 237–238, 343, 366; *Literary Digest*, June 14, 1913, pp. 1332–1333. For an argument that the German political system contributed to the coming of war, see Paul Kennedy, "The Kaiser and German *Weltpolitik*," in J. Rohl and N. Sombert, eds., *Kaiser Wilhelm II: New Interpretations* (Cambridge: Cambridge University Press, 1982), pp. 143–168.
130. Jon Elster, *Political Psychology* (Cambridge: Cambridge University Press, 1993), pp. 2–7. I thank David Dessler for bringing this source to my attention.

democracies is required. Given this premise, two synthetic approaches seem promising. First, the balance-of-threat theory of Stephen Walt could incorporate states' estimates of regime type. Walt writes that a state's alliance decisions are based not only on the aggregate and offensive power and geographic proximity of foreign states, but also on how aggressive their intentions are. He cites the Eyre Crowe memorandum of 1907, which stated that the British welcomed the growth of German power *per se*, but were concerned about German intentions.[131] My argument holds that liberals judge foreign states' intentions in part based on whether those states are liberal democracies. Had Eyre Crowe considered Germany liberal, he would not have been so worried.

A second approach would use the ideational framework of Alexander Wendt, David Lumsdaine, and others. Essentially, this approach postulates that international anarchy does not necessarily lead to self-help and power politics. Rather, these features are derivative of states' practices, particularly the ways they define themselves and their interests. That is, even absent a world sovereign, states must hold certain beliefs about each other before they fear each other.[132] Neorealism posits that these beliefs are always a product of power factors and thus not an independent variable. But the evidence that there is democratic peace and that it is a product of liberal ideas suggests neorealism is wrong. Power would not drop out of a framework that claims ideational sources of national interest. It would simply be one of several forces, filtered through an ideational lens.

Conclusion

That no one has directly observed a causal mechanism preventing democracies from going to war against one another has damaged the democratic peace thesis. In this article, I have argued that there is indeed such a mechanism. Fundamentally it is the liberal ideas undergirding liberal democracies. Liberalism says that all persons are best off pursuing self-preservation and material well-being, and that freedom and toleration are the best means to

---

131. Stephen M. Walt, *The Origins of Alliances* (Ithaca: Cornell University Press, 1987), pp. 21–25.
132. See Alexander Wendt, "Anarchy Is What States Make of It: The Social Construction of Power Politics," *International Organization*, Vol. 46, No. 2 (Spring 1992), pp. 391–425; and David Halloran Lumsdaine, *Moral Vision in International Politics: The Foreign Aid Regime, 1949–1989* (Princeton: Princeton University Press, 1993), pp. 3–29.

these ends. The liberal commitment to individual freedom gives rise to foreign policy ideology and governmental institutions that work together to produce democratic peace.

Ideologically, liberals trust those states they consider fellow liberal democracies and see no reason to fight them. They view those states they consider illiberal with suspicion, and sometimes believe that the national interest requires war with them. In different countries at different times, liberals have differed on the form of a liberal democracy, but the essential ideology is the same. Institutionally, liberalism brings about democratic structures that give citizens leverage over governmental decisions. Sometimes liberals run the government and simply implement their view of the national interest. Even when they do not, the institutions of free speech and regular, competitive elections allow liberal elites to force even illiberal leaders of democracies to follow liberal ideology. When a liberal democracy is in a war-threatening crisis with a state it considers liberal-democratic, its liberal elites agitate against war. Illiberal leaders find they cannot persuade the public to go to war, and moreover fear they will lose the next election if they do go to war. By the same process, they may be goaded into war with states that liberals believe to be illiberal.

This model was illustrated in four war-threatening crises involving the United States. In three of these, liberalism helped to prevent war. In one (Anglo-American relations from 1803–12), liberalism helped bring on war. Among other things, these cases illustrate the importance of perceptions.

Although I argue that realists are wrong in denying the existence of the democratic peace, I do not argue that power politics has no role in liberal-democratic foreign policy. The balance of power matters to liberals as well as to realists, but liberals view it as part of a larger picture of international politics. It appears that a synthesis of realism and liberalism is possible, as least concerning democratic peace.

The democratic peace provides strong evidence that ideas matter in international relations, both as shapers of national interest and as builders of democratic institutions. Thomas Paine claimed that the American Revolutionaries "have it in our power to begin the world all over again."[133] He may have been overreaching: the hostile relations between France and the United States in the 1790s, sister republics of the first democratic peace, show how

---

133. In "Common Sense," January 1776, quoted in Michael H. Hunt, *Ideology and U.S. Foreign Policy* (New Haven: Yale University Press, 1987), p. 19.

the world of power politics can stymie the harmonious plans of liberals. Yet it looks as though a force does rise up within liberal democracies capable of steering conflict off of its usual trajectory.

Still, this study does not show that the democratic peace necessarily leads to perpetual peace. Threats to liberalism itself should engender caution. Historically, one threat has come from liberalism's inability to fulfill the material expectations it raises. When peace does not bring prosperity, as in Weimar Germany, war begins to look more attractive and liberalism may collapse. A second threat may lie in liberalism's tendency to destroy traditional ways of life and sources of meaning. Islamic fundamentalists, for example, simply reject the individualism that undergirds the democratic peace, and there are signs that many within the West itself reject it also.[134] Despite its stunning recent successes,[135] and arguments that it has triumphed over its philosophical competitors,[136] it is not at all clear that liberalism has brought an end to History.

---

134. For a synopsis of threats to liberalism and thus to democratic peace, see Samuel P. Huntington, "No Exit: The Errors of Endism," *The National Interest*, No. 17 (Fall 1989), pp. 3–11.

135. For a theoretical treatment of the spread of democracy, see Samuel P. Huntington, *The Third Wave: Democratization in the Late Twentieth Century* (Norman: University of Oklahoma Press, 1991).

136. See Francis Fukuyama, *The End of History and the Last Man* (New York: The Free Press, 1992).

Part II:
The Case Against the Democratic Peace

Kant or Cant

The Myth of the Democratic Peace

Christopher Layne

$\mathbf{T}$he theory of the "Democratic Peace" raises important theoretical issues:[1] the contention that democratic states behave differently toward each other than toward non-democracies cuts to the heart of the international relations theory debate about the relative salience of second-image (domestic politics) and of third-image (systemic structure) explanations of international political outcomes. Democratic peace theory has also come to have a real-world importance as well: Policymakers who have embraced democratic peace theory see a crucial link between America's security and the spread of democracy, which is viewed as the antidote that will prevent future wars. Indeed some democratic peace theorists, notably Bruce Russett, believe that in an international system comprising a critical mass of democratic states, "It may be possible in part to supersede the 'realist' principles (anarchy, the security dilemma of states) that have dominated practice to the exclusion of 'liberal' or 'idealist' ones since at least the seventeenth century."[2] Because of its theoretical claims and

Christopher Layne of Los Angeles is an unaffiliated scholar. He is presently a consultant to the government contracts practice group of the law firm of Hill, Wynne, Troop and Meisinger, which represents major firms in the defense industry.

I am extremely grateful to the following colleagues who reviewed various drafts of this paper and offered helpful criticisms: John Arquilla, Ted Galen Carpenter, Kerry Andrew Chase, Jeffry Frieden, John Mearsheimer, Benjamin C. Schwarz, Jack Snyder, Stephen Walt, and Kenneth Waltz. I also thank Stephen Van Evera and David Spiro for providing me copies of, and permission to quote from, their unpublished works.

1. I use the term "democratic peace theory" because it is a convenient shorthand term. However, strictly speaking, the claim that democracies do not fight democracies is a proposition, or hypothesis, rather than a theory. Democratic peace "theory" proposes a causal relationship between an independent variable (democratic political structures at the unit level) and the dependent variable (the asserted absence of war between democratic states). However, it is not a true theory because the causal relationship between the independent and dependent variables is neither proven nor, as I demonstrate in this article, adequately explained. See Stephen Van Evera, "Hypotheses, Laws and Theories: A User's Guide," unpub. memo, Department of Political Science, MIT.
2. Bruce Russett, *Grasping the Democratic Peace: Principles for a Post–Cold War World* (Princeton: Princeton University Press, 1993), chap. 7; and Russett, "Can A Democratic Peace Be Built?" *International Interactions*, Vol. 18, No. 3 (Spring 1993), pp. 277–282.

International Security, Vol. 19, No. 2 (Fall 1994), pp. 5–49

policy implications, the democratic peace theory merits careful examination.[3] In this article, I focus primarily on a critique of the persuasiveness of democratic peace theory's causal logic and ask whether democratic peace theory or realism is a better predictor of international outcomes. I then briefly assess the robustness of democratic peace theory's empirical evidence in light of my conclusions about the strength of its explanatory power.

I begin by reviewing the explanations of the Democratic Peace advanced by democratic peace theorists. There are two strands to the theory's causal logic. One attributes the absence of war between democracies to institutional constraints: the restraining effects of public opinion, or of the checks and balances embedded in a democratic state's domestic political structure. The other posits that it is democratic norms and culture—a shared commitment to the peaceful adjudication of political disputes—that accounts for the absence of war between democratic states. As I demonstrate, the institutional-constraints argument fails to provide a compelling explanation for the absence of war between democracies. Thus, democratic peace theory's explanatory power rests on the persuasiveness of the contention that democratic norms and culture explain why, although democratic states fight with non-democracies, they do not go to war with each other.

This article's centerpiece is a test of the competing explanations of international outcomes offered by democratic peace theory and by realism. This test is based on case studies of four "near misses"—crises where two democratic states almost went to war with each other. These four cases are well-documented instances of democratic great powers going to the brink of war without going over it. As such, they present an opportunity to determine which of the competing hypotheses advanced respectively by democratic peace theory and realism best account for international political outcomes.[4]

---

3. In this article, I build upon and expand the criticisms of democratic peace theory found in John J. Mearsheimer, "Back to the Future: Instability in Europe After the Cold War," *International Security*, Vol. 15, No. 1 (Summer 1990), pp. 5–56; and Kenneth N. Waltz, "America as Model for the World? A Foreign Policy Perspective," *PS* (December 1991), pp. 667–670.

4. Other cases of crises between democratic great powers that might be studied include Anglo-French relations during the Liberal *entente cordiale* of 1832–48, Franco-Italian relations during the late 1880s and early 1890s and, if Wilhelmine Germany is classified as a democracy, the Moroccan crises of 1905–06 and 1911 and the Samoan crises of 1889 and 1899. These cases would support my conclusions. For example, from 1832 to 1848, the Foxite legacy disposed England's Whigs to feel a strong commitment to France based on a shared liberal ideology. Yet Anglo-French relations during this period were marked by intense geopolitical rivalry over Belgium, Spain, and the Near East, and the threat of war was always a factor in the calculations of policymakers in both London and Paris. Foreign Minister Lord Palmerston profoundly distrusted French ambitions and constantly urged that England maintain sufficient naval power to defend its

Moreover, they present an easy case for democratic peace theory and a hard case for realism. The selected cases favor democratic peace theory because, in each, the pacifying effect of democratic norms and culture was bolstered by complementary factors (e.g., economic interdependence, or special ties linking the disputants). I deduce, from both the democratic norms and culture argument and from realism, sets of indicators—testable propositions— that should be present if a crisis's outcome is explained by either of the two theories. Using a process-tracing approach, I examine each crisis in detail.

I conclude that realism is superior to democratic peace theory as a predictor of international outcomes. Indeed, democratic peace theory appears to have extremely little explanatory power in the cases studied. Doubts about the validity of its causal logic suggest that the empirical evidence purporting to support democratic peace theory should also be revisited. Democratic peace theorists contend that the theory is validated by a large number of cases. However, a powerful argument can be made that the universe of cases from which it can be tested is actually quite small. This is a crucial issue, because if the theory's empirical support is based on a small-N universe, this magnifies the importance of possible exceptions to the rule that democracies do not fight each other (for example, World War I, the War between the States, the War of 1812). I conclude by discussing democratic peace theory's troublesome implications for post–Cold War American foreign policy.

The Case for a Democratic Peace: Its Claims and its Logic

Democratic peace theory does not contend that democratic states are less war-prone than non-democracies; they are not. The theory does, however, make two important claims, first, that democracies never (or rarely; there is

interests against a French challenge. See Kenneth Bourne, *Palmerston: The Early Years, 1784–1841* (New York: Macmillan, 1982), p. 613. Also see Roger Bullen, *Palmerston, Guizot and the Collapse of the Entente Cordiale* (London: Athlone Press, 1974); and Sir Charles Webster, *The Foreign Policy of Palmerston*, Vol. I: *1830–1841, Britain, The Liberal Movement and The Eastern Question* (London: G. Bell & Sons, 1951). Italy challenged France for Mediterranean ascendancy although the two nations were bound by liberalism, democracy, and a common culture. The two nations engaged in a trade war and came close to a real war. France apparently was dissuaded from attacking Italy in 1888 when the British Channel Fleet was sent to the Italian naval base of La Spezia. Italy was prevented from attacking France by its military and economic weakness. See C.J. Lowe and F. Marzari, *Italian Foreign Policy, 1870–1940* (London: Routledge & Kegan Paul, 1975), chap. 4; C.J. Lowe, *The Reluctant Imperialists: British Foreign Policy 1879–1902* (London: Routledge & Kegan Paul, 1974), Vol. I, pp. 147–150; John A.C. Conybeare, *Trade Wars: The Theory and Practice of International Commercial Rivalry* (New York: Columbia University Press, 1987), pp. 183–188.

a good deal of variation about this) go to war with other democracies.[5] As Jack S. Levy observes, the "absence of war between democracies comes as close as anything we have to an empirical law in international relations."[6] Second, when democracies come into conflict with one another, they only rarely threaten to use force, because it is "illegitimate" to do so.[7] Democratic peace theory explicitly holds that it is the very nature of democratic political systems that accounts for the fact that democracies do not fight or threaten other democracies.

THE CAUSAL LOGIC

Democratic peace theory must explain an anomaly: democracies are no less war-prone than non-democratic states. Yet, while they will readily threaten and fight non-democracies, they do not threaten or fight other democracies. The key challenge for the theory, then, is to identify the special characteristics of democratic states that restrain them from using coercive threats against, or actually going to war with, other democracies. The theory advances two alternative explanations: (1) institutional constraints; and (2) democratic norms and cultures.[8]

There are two major variants of the institutional constraints argument. Michael Doyle, building on Immanuel Kant, explains that democratic governments are reluctant to go to war because they must answer to their

---

5. Melvin Small and J. David Singer first observed the pattern of democracies not fighting democracies in a 1976 article: Small and Singer, "The War-proneness of Democratic Regimes, 1816–1865," *Jerusalem Journal of International Relations*, Vol. 1, No. 4 (Summer 1976), pp. 50–69. Their finding has been the subject of extensive further empirical testing which has produced a consensus around the propositions stated in the text. See Stuart A. Bremer, "Dangerous Dyads: Conditions Affecting the Likelihood of Interstate War, 1816–1865," *Journal of Conflict Resolution*, Vol. 36, No. 2 (June 1992), pp. 309–341; Steve Chan, "Mirror, Mirror on the Wall . . . Are the Freer Countries More Pacific?" *Journal of Conflict Resolution*, Vol. 28, No. 4 (December 1984), pp. 617–648; Zeev Maoz and Nasrin Abdolali, "Regime Type and International Conflict," *Journal of Conflict Resolution*, Vol. 33, No. 1 (March 1989), pp. 3–35; R.J. Rummel, "Libertarianism and International Violence," *Journal of Conflict Resolution*, Vol. 27, No. 1 (March 1983), pp. 27–71; Erich Weede, "Democracy and War Involvement," *Journal of Conflict Resolution*, Vol. 28, No. 4 (December 1984), pp. 649–664.
6. Jack S. Levy, "Domestic Politics and War," in Robert I. Rotberg and Theodore K. Rabb, eds., *The Origin and Prevention of Major Wars* (Cambridge: Cambridge University Press, 1989), p. 88.
7. Russett, *Grasping the Democratic Peace*, p. 33; Michael W. Doyle, "Kant, Liberal Legacies and Foreign Affairs," Part I, *Philosophy and Public Affairs*, Vol. 12, No. 3 (Summer 1983), p. 213.
8. This is the terminology employed by Russett, *Grasping the Democratic Peace*; also see Bruce Russett and Zeev Maoz, "Normative and Structural Causes of Democratic Peace," *American Political Science Review*, Vol. 87, No. 3 (September 1993), pp. 624–638. Russett points out (pp. 40–42) that, although analytically distinct, these two explanations are intertwined.

citizens.[9] Citizens pay the price for war in blood and treasure; if the price of conflict is high, democratic governments may fall victim to electoral retribution. Moreover, in democratic states, foreign policy decisions carrying the risk of war are debated openly and not made behind closed doors, which means that both the public and policymakers are sensitized to costs of fighting. A second version of the institutional constraints argument focuses on "checks and balances"; it looks at three specific features of a state's domestic political structure: executive selection, political competition, and the pluralism of the foreign policy decisionmaking process.[10] States with executives answerable to a selection body, with institutionalized political competition, and with decisionmaking responsibility spread among multiple institutions or individuals, should be more highly constrained and hence less likely to go to war.

The democratic norms explanation holds that "the *culture, perceptions, and practices* that permit compromise and the peaceful resolution of conflicts without the threat of violence *within countries* come to apply across national boundaries toward other democratic countries."[11] Democratic states assume both that other democracies also subscribe to pacific methods of regulating political competition and resolving disputes, and that others will apply these norms in their external relations with fellow democracies. In other words, democratic states develop positive perceptions of other democracies. Consequently, Doyle says, democracies, "which rest on consent, presume foreign republics to be also consensual, just and therefore deserving of accommodation."[12] Relations between democratic states are based on mutual respect

---

9. Doyle, "Kant, Liberal Legacies, and Foreign Affairs," pp. 205–235. See also Doyle, "Liberalism and World Politics," *American Political Science Review*, Vol. 80, No. 4 (December 1986), pp. 1151–1169; Russett, *Grasping the Democratic Peace*, pp. 38–40.

10. T. Clifton Morgan and Sally H. Campbell, "Domestic Structure, Decisional Constraints and War: So Why Kant Democracies Fight?" *Journal of Conflict Resolution*, Vol. 35, No. 2 (June 1991), pp. 187–211; and T. Clifton Morgan and Valerie L. Schwebach, "Take Two Democracies and Call Me in the Morning: A Prescription for Peace?" *International Interactions*, Vol. 17, No. 4 (Summer 1992), pp. 305–420.

11. Russett, *Grasping the Democratic Peace*, p. 31 (second emphasis added).

12. Doyle, "Kant, Liberal Legacies, and Foreign Affairs," p. 230. It is also argued that the predisposition of democratic states to regard other democracies favorably is reinforced by the fact that liberal democratic states are linked by mutually beneficial ties of economic interdependence. Democracies thus have strong incentives to act towards each other in a manner that enhances cooperation and to refrain from acting in a manner that threatens their stake in mutually beneficial cooperation. Ibid., pp. 230–232; Rummel, "Libertarianism and International Violence," pp. 27–28. For the "interdependence promotes peace" argument see Richard Rosecrance, *The Rise of the Trading State* (New York: Basic Books, 1986). In fact, however, for great powers economic interdependence, rather than promoting peace, creates seemingly important

rooted in the fact that democracies perceive each other as dovish (that is, negotiation or the status quo are the only possible outcomes in a dispute). This perception, it is argued, is based on a form of learning. Democratic states benefit from cooperative relations with one another and they want to expand their positive interactions. In turn, this desire predisposes them to be responsive to the needs of other democratic states, and ultimately leads to creation of a community of interests. As democracies move towards community, they renounce the option to use (or even to threaten to use) force in their mutual interactions.[13]

The democratic ethos—based on "peaceful competition, persuasion and compromise"—explains the absence of war and war-like threats in relations between democratic states.[14] Conversely, the absence of these norms in relations between democracies and non-democracies, it is said, explains the paradox that democracies do not fight each other even though in general they are as war-prone as non-democracies: "When a democracy comes into conflict with a nondemocracy, it will not expect the nondemocratic state to be restrained by those norms [of mutual respect based on democratic culture]. It may feel obliged to adapt to the harsher norms of international conduct of the latter, lest it be exploited or eliminated by the nondemocratic state that takes advantage of the inherent moderation of democracies."[15] Thus it is a fundamental postulate of democratic peace theory that democracies behave in a qualitatively different manner in their relations with each other than they do in their relations with non-democracies.

The Realist Case: The Same Things Over and Over Again

If history is "just one damn thing after another," then for realists international politics is the same damn things over and over again: war, great power security and economic competitions, the rise and fall of great powers, and the formation and dissolution of alliances. International political behavior is characterized by continuity, regularity, and repetition because states are con-

---

interests that must be defended by overseas military commitments (commitments that carry with them the risk of war). See Christopher Layne and Benjamin C. Schwarz, "American Hegemony—Without an Enemy," *Foreign Policy*, No. 92 (Fall 1993), pp. 5–23.

13. Doyle, "Kant, Liberal Legacies, and Foreign Affairs"; and Harvey Starr, "Democracy and War: Choice, Learning and Security Communities," *Journal of Peace Research*, Vol. 29, No. 2 (1992), pp. 207–213.

14. Maoz and Russett, "A Statistical Artifact?" p. 246.

15. Russett, *Grasping the Democratic Peace*, p. 33.

strained by the international system's unchanging (and probably unchangeable) structure.

The realist paradigm explains why this is so.[16] International politics is an anarchic, self-help realm. "Anarchy," rather than denoting chaos or rampant disorder, refers in international politics to the fact that there is no central authority capable of making and enforcing rules of behavior on the international system's units (states). The absence of a rule-making and enforcing authority means that each unit in the system is responsible for ensuring its own survival and also that each is free to define its own interests and to employ means of its own choice in pursuing them. In this sense, international politics is fundamentally competitive. And it is competitive in a manner that differs crucially from domestic politics in liberal societies, where the losers can accept an adverse outcome because they live to fight another day and can, therefore, ultimately hope to prevail. In international politics, states that come out on the short end of political competition face potentially more extreme outcomes, ranging from constraints on autonomy to occupation to extinction.

It is anarchy that gives international politics its distinctive flavor. In an anarchic system, a state's first goal is to survive. To attain security, states engage in both internal and external balancing for the purpose of deterring aggressors, and of defeating them should deterrence fail. In a realist world, cooperation is possible but is hard to sustain in the face of the competitive pressures that are built into the international political system's structure. The imperative of survival in a threatening environment forces states to focus on strategies that maximize their power relative to their rivals. States have powerful incentives both to seek the upper hand over their rivals militarily and to use their edge not only for self-defense but also to take advantage of others. Because military power is inherently offensive rather than defensive in nature, states cannot escape the security dilemma: measures taken by a state as self-defense may have the unintended consequence of threatening others. This is because a state can never be certain that others' intentions are benign; consequently its policies must be shaped in response to others' capabilities. In the international system, fear and distrust of other states is the normal state of affairs.

---

16. Classic explications of realism are Kenneth N. Waltz, *Theory of International Politics* (Reading, Mass.: Addison-Wesley, 1979) and Hans J. Morgenthau, rev. by Kenneth W. Thompson, *Politics Among Nations: The Struggle for Power and Peace*, 6th ed. (New York: Knopf, 1985).

Here democratic peace and realism part company on a crucial point. The former holds that changes within states can transform the nature of international politics. Realism takes the view that even if states change internally, the structure of the international political system remains the same. As systemic structure is the primary determinant of international political outcomes, structural constraints mean that similarly placed states will act similarly, regardless of their domestic political systems. As Kenneth Waltz says: "In self-help systems, the pressures of competition weigh more heavily than ideological preferences or internal political pressures."[17] Changes at the unit level do not change the constraints and incentives imbedded at the systemic level. States respond to the logic of the situation in which they find themselves even though this may result in undesirable outcomes, from the breakdown of cooperation to outright war. States that ignore the imperatives of a realist world run the risk of perishing. In a realist world, survival and security are always at risk, and democratic states will respond no differently to democratic rivals than to non-democratic ones.

Testing Democratic Peace Theory

Institutional constraints do not explain the democratic peace. If democratic public opinion really had the effect ascribed to it, democracies would be peaceful in their relations with all states, whether democratic or not. If citizens and policymakers of a democracy were especially sensitive to the human and material costs of war, that sensitivity should be evident whenever their state is on the verge of war, regardless of whether the adversary is democratic: the lives lost and money spent will be the same. Nor is democratic public opinion, *per se*, an inhibitor of war. For example, in 1898 it was public opinion that impelled the reluctant McKinley administration into war with Spain; in 1914 war was enthusiastically embraced by public opinion in Britain and France. Domestic political structure—"checks and balances"— does not explain the democratic peace either. "This argument," as Morgan and Schwebach state, "does not say anything directly about the war-proneness of democracies," because it focuses on an independent variable—decisional constraints embedded in a state's domestic political structure—that is associated with, but not exclusive to, democracies.

---

17. Kenneth N. Waltz, "A Reply to My Critics," in Robert O. Keohane, ed., *Neorealism and Its Critics* (New York: Columbia University Press, 1986), p. 329.

Because these explanations fall short, the democratic norms and culture explanation must bear the weight of the democratic peace theory's causal logic. It is there we must look to find that "something in the internal makeup of democratic states" that explains the democratic peace.[18]

Democratic peace theory not only predicts a specific outcome—no war between democracies—but also purports to explain why that outcome will occur. It is thus suited to being tested by the case study method, a detailed look at a small number of examples to determine if events unfold and actors act as the theory predicts. The case study method also affords the opportunity to test the competing explanations of international political outcomes offered by democratic peace theory and by realism. To test the robustness of democratic peace theory's causal logic, the focus here is on "near misses," specific cases in which democratic states had both opportunity and reason to fight each other, but did not.

The case studies in this article use the process-tracing method (opening up the "black box") to identify the factors to which decisionmakers respond, how those factors influence decisions, the actual course of events, and the possible effect of other variables on the outcome.[19] As Stephen Van Evera says, if a theory has strong explanatory power, process-tracing case studies provide a robust test because decisionmakers "should speak, write, and otherwise behave in a manner consistent with the theory's predictions."[20]

Democratic peace theory, if valid, should account powerfully for the fact that serious crises between democratic states ended in near misses rather than in war. If democratic norms and culture explain the democratic peace, in a near-war crisis, certain indicators of the democratic peace theory should be in evidence: First, public opinion should be strongly pacific. Public opinion is important not because it is an institutional constraint, but because it is an indirect measure of the mutual respect that democracies are said to have for each other. Second, policymaking elites should refrain from making military threats against other democracies and should refrain from making preparations to carry out threats. Democratic peace theorists waffle on this point by

18. Maoz and Russett, "Normative and Structural Causes," p. 624.
19. Alexander L. George and Timothy J. McKeown, "Case Studies and Theories of Organizational Decision Making," in Robert F. Coulam and Richard A. Smith, eds., *Advances in Information Processing in Organizations*, Vol. 2 (Greenwich, Conn.: JAI Press, 1985), p. 35.
20. Stephen Van Evera, "What Are Case Studies? How Should They Be Performed?" unpub. memo, September 1993, Department of Political Science, MIT, p. 2.

suggesting that the absence of war between democracies is more important than the absence of threats. But this sets the threshold of proof too low. Because the crux of the theory is that democracies externalize their internal norms of peaceful dispute resolution, then especially in a crisis, one should not see democracies threatening other democracies. And if threats are made, they should be a last-resort option rather than an early one. Third, democracies should bend over backwards to accommodate each other in a crisis. Ultimata, unbending hard lines, and big-stick diplomacy are the stuff of *Realpolitik*, not the democratic peace.

A realist explanation of near misses would look at a very different set of indicators. First, realism postulates a ratio of national interest to democratic respect: in a crisis, the more important the interests a democracy perceives to be at stake, the more likely that its policy will be shaped by realist imperatives rather than by democratic norms and culture. When vital interests are on the line, democracies should not be inhibited from using threats, ultimata, and big-stick diplomacy against another democracy. Second, even in a crisis involving democracies, states should be very attentive to strategic concerns, and the relative distribution of military capabilities between them should crucially—perhaps decisively—affect their diplomacy. Third, broader geopolitical considerations pertaining to a state's position in international politics should, if implicated, account significantly for the crisis's outcome. Key here is what Geoffrey Blainey calls the "fighting waterbirds' dilemma," involving concerns that others watching from the sidelines will take advantage of a state's involvement in war; that war will leave a state weakened and in an inferior relative power position *vis-à-vis* possible future rivals; and that failure to propitiate the opposing state in a crisis will cause it to ally with one's other adversaries or rivals.[21]

I have chosen to study four modern historical instances in which democratic great powers almost came to blows: (1) the United States and Great Britain in 1861 ("the *Trent* affair"); (2) the United States and Great Britain in 1895–96 (the Venezuela crisis); France and Great Britain in 1898 (the Fashoda crisis); and France and Germany in 1923 (the Ruhr crisis).[22] I focus on great

---

21. Geoffrey Blainey, *The Causes of War*, 3rd ed. (South Melbourne: Macmillan Co. of Australia, 1988), pp. 57–67. As the parable goes, while the waterbirds fight over the catch, the fisherman spreads his net.

22. My classification of the United States in 1861 and 1895 and of Germany in 1923 as great powers might be challenged. By the mid-nineteenth century British policymakers viewed the United States, because of its size, population, wealth, and growing industrial strength (and

powers for several reasons. First, international relations theory is defined by great powers: they are the principal components of the international system, and their actions—especially their wars—have a greater impact on the international system than do those of small powers.[23] Moreover, while democratic peace theory should apply to both great and small powers, realist predictions about great power behavior are not always applicable to small powers, because the range of options available to the latter is more constrained.[24] Crises between democratic great powers are a good head-to-head test because democratic peace theory and realism should both be applicable.[25]

The cases selected should favor democratic peace theory for more than the obvious reason that none of them led to war. In each crisis, background factors were present that should have reinforced democratic peace theory's predictions. In the two Anglo-American crises, a common history, culture and language, and economic interdependence were important considerations.[26] In the Fashoda crisis, the factors that led to the 1904 Anglo-French entente were already present and both countries benefited significantly from their economic relations.[27] The Franco-German Ruhr crisis tested both the Wilsonian prescription for achieving security in post–World War I Europe and the belief (increasingly widespread among French and German business elites, and to a lesser extent the political elites) that the prosperity of both states hinged on their economic collaboration.

---

latent military power), as "a great world power," notwithstanding the fact that it was not an active participant in the European state system. Ephraim Douglass Adams, *Great Britain and the American Civil War* (New York: Russell and Russell, 1924), Vol. I, p. 10. In 1895 the perception of American power had heightened in Britain and in other leading European powers. In 1923, Germany, although substantially disarmed pursuant to Versailles, remained Europe's most economically powerful state. As most statesmen realized, it was, because of its population and industry, a latent continental hegemon. Democratic peace theorists have classified all eight states as having been democracies at the time of their involvement in the crises under discussion. See Doyle, "Kant, Liberal Legacies, and Foreign Affairs," part I, pp. 214–215. Russett, *Grasping the Democratic Peace*, pp. 5–9, briefly discusses the Venezuela and Fashoda crises, but his bibliography has few historical references to these two crises (and related issues), and omits most standard sources.

23. Waltz, *Theory of International Politics*, pp. 72–73.
24. See Robert L. Rothstein, *Alliances and Small Powers* (New York: Columbia University Press, 1968), especially chap. 1.
25. As noted above, other such crises also support my argument.
26. For a brief discussion of the cultural, social, and economic bonds between Britain and the United States during the mid-nineteenth century, see Martin Crawford, *The Anglo-American Crisis of the Mid-Nineteenth Century: The Times and America, 1850–1862* (Athens: University of Georgia Press, 1987), pp. 39–55.
27. Stephen R. Rock, *Why Peace Breaks Out: Great Power Rapprochement in Historical Perspective* (Chapel Hill: University of North Carolina Press, 1989), pp. 91–119.

ANGLO-AMERICAN CRISIS I: THE *TRENT* AFFAIR, 1861

In 1861, tensions arising from the War Between the States brought the Union and Britain to the brink of war. The most important causes of Anglo-American friction stemmed from the Northern blockade of Confederate ports and the consequent loss to Britain of the cotton upon which its textile industry depended. The immediate precipitating cause of the Anglo-American crisis, however, was action of the *USS San Jacinto* which, acting without express orders from Washington, intercepted the British mail ship *Trent* on November 8, 1861. The *Trent* was transporting James M. Mason and John Slidell, the Confederacy's commissioners-designate to Great Britain and France; they had boarded the *Trent*, a neutral vessel, in Havana, Cuba, a neutral port. A boarding party from the *San Jacinto*, after searching the *Trent*, placed Mason and Slidell under arrest. The *Trent* was allowed to complete its voyage while the *San Jacinto* transported Mason and Slidell to Fort Warren in Boston harbor, where they were incarcerated.

When word was received in Britain, the public was overcome with war fever. "The first explosion of the Press, on receipt of the news of the *Trent*, had been a terrific one."[28] An American citizen residing in England reported to Secretary of State William H. Seward, "The people are frantic with rage, and were the country polled I fear 999 men out of 1000 would declare for war."[29] From Edinburgh, another American wrote, "I have never seen so intense a feeling of indignation in my life."[30]

The British government was hardly less bellicose than the public and the press. Fortified by legal opinions holding that Mason and Slidell had been removed from the *Trent* in contravention of international law, the Cabinet adopted a hard-line policy that mirrored the public mood. Prime Minister Lord Palmerston's first reaction to the news of the *Trent* incident was to write to the Secretary of State for War that, because of Britain's "precarious" relations with the United States, the government reconsider cuts in military expenditures planned to take effect in 1862.[31] At the November 29 Cabinet meeting, Palmerston reportedly began by flinging his hat on the table and

---

28. Adams, *Britain and the Civil War*, Vol. I, p. 216.
29. Quoted in Gordon H. Warren, *Fountain of Discontent: The Trent Affair and Freedom of the Seas* (Boston: Northeastern University Press, 1981), p. 105.
30. Quoted in Adams, *Britain and the Civil War*, Vol. I, p. 217.
31. Quoted in Norman B. Ferris, *The Trent Affair: A Diplomatic Crisis* (Knoxville: University of Tennessee Press, 1977), p. 44.

declaring to his colleagues, "I don't know whether you are going to stand this, but I'll be damned if I do!"[32]

The Cabinet adopted a dual-track approach towards Washington: London used military threats to coerce the United States into surrendering diplomatically, while on the diplomatic side, Foreign Secretary Lord John Russell drafted a note to the Union government in which, while holding firm to the demand that Mason and Slidell be released, he offered Washington an avenue of graceful retreat by indicating that London would accept, as tantamount to an apology, a declaration that the *San Jacinto* had acted without official sanction. Nevertheless, the note that was actually transmitted to Washington was an ultimatum. Although the British minister in Washington, Lord Lyons, was instructed to present the communication in a fashion calculated to maximize the chances of American compliance, his charge was clear: unless within seven days of receipt the Union government unconditionally accepted Britain's demands, Lyons was to ask for his passports and depart the United States. As Russell wrote to Lyons: "What we want is a plain Yes or a plain No to our very simple demands, and we want that plain Yes or No within seven days of the communication of the despatch."[33]

Although some, notably including Russell, hoped that the crisis could be resolved peacefully, the entire Cabinet recognized that its decision to present an ultimatum to Washington could lead to war. The British believed that there was one hope for peace: that Washington, overawed by Britain's military power and its readiness to go to war, would bow to London's demands rather than resisting them.[34] As the Undersecretary of State for Foreign Affairs stated, "Our only chance of peace is to be found in working on the fears of the Government and people of the United States."[35]

Driven by the belief that Washington would give in only to the threat of force, London's diplomacy was backed up by ostentatious military and naval preparations. Anticipating a possible conflict, the Cabinet embargoed the export to the United States of saltpeter (November 30) and of arms and ammunition (December 4). Underscoring the gravity of the crisis, for only

---

32. Ibid., p. 109; Howard Jones, *Union in Peril: The Crisis Over British Intervention in the Civil War* (Chapel Hill: University of North Carolina Press, 1992), pp. 84–85.
33. Quoted in Jones, *Union in Peril*, p. 85.
34. Jenkins, *War for the Union*, p. 214.
35. Quoted in Kenneth Bourne, *Britain and the Balance of Power in North America, 1815–1908* (Berkeley: University of California Press, 1967), p. 219.

the fourth time in history the Cabinet created a special war committee to oversee strategic planning and war preparations. Urgent steps were taken to reinforce Britain's naval and military contingents in North America. Beginning in mid-December, a hastily organized sealift increased the number of regular British army troops in Canada from 5,000 to 17,658, and Royal Navy forces in North American waters swelled from 25 to forty warships, with 1,273 guns (compared to just 500 before the crisis).[36] These measures served two purposes: they bolstered London's diplomacy and, in the event diplomacy failed, they positioned Britain to prevail in a conflict.

London employed big-stick diplomacy because it believed that a too-conciliatory policy would simply embolden the Americans to mount increasingly serious challenges to British interests.[37] Moreover, British policymakers believed that England's resolve, credibility, and reputation were at stake internationally, not just in its relations with the United States. The comments of once and future Foreign Secretary Lord Clarendon were typical: "What a figure . . . we shall cut in the eyes of the world, if we lamely submit to this outrage when all mankind will know that we should unhesitatingly have poured our indignation and our broadsides into any weak nation . . . and what an additional proof it will be of the universal . . . belief that we have two sets of weights and measures to be used according to the power or weakness of our adversary."[38] Thus "the British were prepared to accept the cost of an Anglo-American war . . . rather than sacrifice their prestige as a great power by headlong diplomatic defeat."[39]

London's hard-line policy was fortified by its "general optimism about the ultimate outcome" of an Anglo-American war.[40] Queen Victoria said a war would result in "utter destruction to the North Americans" and Secretary of

36. The figures are from Warren, *Fountain of Discontent*, pp. 130, 136. For an overview of British military and naval activities during the Trent crisis see Kenneth Bourne, "British Preparations for War with the North, 1861–1862," *English Historical Review*, Vol. 76, No. 301 (October 1961), pp. 600–632.

37. Ferris, *Trent Affair*, p. 56; Wilbur Devereux Jones, *The American Problem in British Diplomacy, 1841–1861* (London: Macmillan, 1974), p. 203. In international relations theory terms, London's view of Anglo-American relations was based on a deterrence model rather than a spiral model. See Robert Jervis, *Perception and Misperception in International Politics* (Princeton: Princeton University Press, 1976), pp. 58–111. Coexisting uneasily with the positive view of an Anglo-American community was the British image of the United States as a vulgar "mobocracy" that, unless firmly resisted, would pursue a rapacious and bullying foreign policy. Warren, *Fountain of Discontent*, pp. 47–51.

38. Quoted in Bourne, *Balance of Power*, p. 247.

39. Bourne, "British Preparations," p. 631.

40. Bourne, *Balance of Power*, p. 247.

State for War George Cornewall Lewis said "we shall soon *iron the smile* out of their face."[41] Palmerston was therefore untroubled by the discomfiture imposed on the Union by London's uncompromising policy. In his view, regardless of whether the crisis was resolved peacefully or resulted in war, Britain's interests would be upheld. He wrote to Queen Victoria:

If the Federal Government comply with the demands it will be honorable to England and humiliating to the United States. If the Federal Government refuse compliance, Great Britain is in a better state than at any former time to inflict a severe blow upon, and to read a lesson to the United States which will not soon be forgotten.[42]

In late 1861, the war against the Confederacy was not going well for Washington and the one major engagement, the first Battle of Manassas, had resulted in a humiliating setback for the Union army. Whipped up by Secretary of State Seward, who was a master at "twisting the lion's tail" for maximum domestic political effect, Northern opinion was hostile in London and resented especially Queen Victoria's May 1861 neutrality proclamation, which Northerners interpreted as *de facto* British recognition of Southern independence. News of the seizure of Mason and Slidell had a double effect on Northern public opinion. First, it was a tonic for sagging Northern morale. Second, it was seen as a warning to Britain to refrain from interfering with the Union's prosecution of the war against the Confederacy. Thus, although some papers (notably the *New York Times* and the *New York Daily Tribune*) urged that Washington should placate the British, public opinion strongly favored a policy of standing up to London and refusing to release Mason and Slidell.[43] In response to Britain's hard line, "a raging war cry reverberated across the Northern states in America."[44] Charles Francis Adams, Jr., whose father was U.S. minister in London at the time, wrote later of the affair: "I do not remember in the whole course of the half-century's retrospect . . . any occurrence in which the American people were so completely swept off their feet, for the moment losing possession of their senses, as during the weeks which immediately followed the seizure of Mason and Slidell."[45]

41. Quoted in ibid., pp. 245–246, emphasis in original.
42. Quoted in Jenkins, *War for the Union*, p. 216.
43. Ferris, *Trent Affair*, pp. 111–113.
44. Norman B. Ferris, *Desperate Diplomacy: William H. Seward's Foreign Policy, 1861* (Knoxville: University of Tennessee, 1976), p. 194.
45. Quoted in Adams, *Britain and the Civil War*, Vol. I, p. 218.

The Lincoln administration was aware of the strength of anti-British sentiment among the public and in Congress (indeed, in early December, Congress passed a resolution commending the *San Jacinto's* captain for his action). There is some evidence that in order to placate public opinion, President Lincoln was inclined toward holding on to Mason and Slidell, notwithstanding the obvious risks of doing so.[46] Nevertheless, after first toying with the idea of offering London arbitration in an attempt to avoid the extremes of war or a humiliating climb-down, the United States elected to submit to Britain's demands. Given that Washington "could not back down easily," it is important to understand why it chose to do so.

The United States bowed to London because, already fully occupied militarily trying to subdue the Confederacy, the North could not also afford a simultaneous war with England, which effectively would have brought Britain into the War Between the States on the South's side.[47] This was clearly recognized by the Lincoln administration when the cabinet met for two days at Christmas to decide on the American response to the British note. The cabinet had before it two critical pieces of information. First, Washington had just been informed that France supported London's demands (ending American hopes that Britain would be restrained by its own "waterbird" worries that France would take advantage of an Anglo-American war).[48] Second, Washington had abundant information about the depth of the pro-war sentiment of the British public. The American minister in London, Charles Francis Adams, wrote that the English "were now all lashed up into hostility" and that: "The leading newspapers roll out as much fiery lava as Vesuvius is doing, daily. The Clubs and the army and the navy and the people in the streets generally are raving for war."[49] Senator Charles Sumner passed on to the Lincoln administration letters from the noted Radical members of parliament, Richard Cobden and John Bright. While deploring their government's policy and the tenor of British public opinion, both Cobden and Bright

---

46. Warren, *Fountain of Discontent*, pp. 184–185; Adams, *Britain and the Civil War*, p. 231. Howard Jones, however, suggests that Lincoln probably intended to give up Mason and Slidell and that he may have been posturing in order to shift to other members of his cabinet the onus of advancing the argument for surrendering them. Jones, *Union in Peril*, pp. 91–92.
47. Ferris, *Trent Affair*, pp. 177–182; Jenkins, *War for the Union*, pp. 223–226; Warren, *Fountain of Discontent*, pp. 181–182.
48. See Jenkins, *War for the Union*, pp. 225–226.
49. Quoted in Ferris, *Trent Affair*, pp. 154, 147 and see also pp. 66–67, 139–141; Jones, *Union in Peril*, p. 89.

stressed that war would result unless the United States gave in to London. Cobden observed:

Formerly England feared a war with the United States as much from the dependence on your cotton as from a dread of your power. *Now* the popular opinion (however erroneous) is that a war would give us cotton. And we, of course, consider your power weakened by your Civil War.[50]

Facing the choice of defying London or surrendering to its demands, Washington was compelled to recognize both that Britain was serious about going to war and that such a war almost certainly would result in the Union's permanent dissolution. During the cabinet discussions, Attorney General Edward Bates suggested that Britain was seeking a war with the United States in order to break the Northern blockade of Southern cotton ports and he worried that London would recognize the Confederacy. The United States, he said, "cannot afford such a war." He went on to observe, "In such a crisis, with such a civil war upon our hands, we cannot hope for success in a . . . war with England, backed by the assent and countenance of France. We must evade it—with as little damage to our own honor and pride as possible."[51] Secretary of State Seward concurred, stating that it was "no time to be diverted from the cares of the Union into controversies with other powers, even if just causes for them could be found."[52] When the United States realized that Britain's threat to go to war was not a bluff, strategic and national interest considerations—the "waterbird dilemma"—dictated that Washington yield to Britain.

The *Trent* affair's outcome is explained by realism, not democratic peace theory. Contrary to democratic peace theory's expectations, the mutual respect between democracies rooted in democratic norms and culture had no influence on British policy. Believing that vital reputational interests affecting its global strategic posture were at stake, London played diplomatic hardball, employed military threats, and was prepared to go to war if necessary. Both the public and the elites in Britain preferred war to conciliation. Across the Atlantic, public and governmental opinion in the North was equally bellicose. An Anglo-American conflict was avoided only because the Lincoln admin-

---

50. Quoted in ibid., p. 172 (emphasis in original). Bright's letter warned: "If you are resolved to succeed against the South, *have no war with England.*" Quoted in Adams, *Britain and the Civil War*, p. 232 (emphasis in original).
51. Quoted in ibid., p. 182.
52. Quoted in Jenkins, *War for the Union*, p. 224.

istration came to understand that diplomatic humiliation was preferable to a war that would have arrayed Britain with the Confederacy and thus probably have secured the South's independence.

ANGLO-AMERICAN CRISIS II: VENEZUELA, 1895–96

In 1895–96, the United States and Great Britain found themselves embroiled in a serious diplomatic confrontation arising out of an obscure long-standing dispute between London and Caracas over the Venezuela–British Guiana boundary. By 1895, Caracas was desperately beseeching Washington to pressure London to agree to arbitrate the dispute. The Cleveland administration decided to inject the United States diplomatically into the Anglo-Venezuelan disagreement, but not out of American solicitude for Venezuela's interests or concern for the issue's merits.[53] For the United States, the Anglo-Venezuelan affair was part of a larger picture. By 1895, American policymakers, conscious of the United States's status as an emerging great power, were increasingly concerned about European political and commercial intrusion into the Western Hemisphere.[54] For Washington, the controversy between London and Caracas was a welcome pretext for asserting America's claim to geopolitical primacy in the Western hemisphere. It was for this reason that the United States provoked a showdown on the Anglo-Venezuelan border dispute.[55]

The American position was set forth in Secretary of State Richard Olney's July 20, 1895, note to the British government.[56] The United States stated that its "honor and its interests" were involved in the Anglo-Venezuelan dispute, "the continuance of which it cannot regard with indifference." Washington demanded that London submit the dispute to arbitration. In grandiloquent terms, Olney asserted that the Monroe Doctrine not only gave the United

---

53. Walter LaFeber demonstrates that the United States injected itself into the crisis to protect its own interests, not Venezuela's. LaFeber, *The New Empire: An Interpretation of American Expansion, 1860–1898* (Ithaca: Cornell University Press, 1963), chap. 6.
54. The relationship between security concerns and American foreign and strategic policy is discussed in Richard D. Challener, *Admirals, General and Foreign Policy, 1898–1914* (Princeton: Princeton University Press, 1973) and J.A.S. Grenville and George B. Young, *Politics, Strategy, and American Diplomacy: Studies in American Foreign Policy, 1873–1917* (New Haven: Yale University Press, 1966).
55. Walter LaFeber, "The Background of Cleveland's Venezuelan Policy: A Reinterpretation," *American Historical Review*, Vol. 66 No. 4 (July 1961), p. 947; Ernest R. May, *Imperial Democracy: The Emergence of America as a Great Power* (New York: Harcourt, Brace and World, 1961), p. 34.
56. The full text of the note can be found in *Foreign Relations of the United States, 1895* (Washington, D.C.: U.S. Government Printing Office), Vol. I, pp. 542–576.

States the right to intervene in the Venezuela affair but also a more general right to superintend the affairs of the Western hemisphere.

In challenging Britain, President Grover Cleveland and his secretary of state realized they were taking a serious step. Although they almost certainly hoped to score a peaceful diplomatic victory, their strategy was one that could have led instead to an armed confrontation. Olney's July 20 note (praised by Cleveland as "the best thing of the kind I have ever read") was deliberately brusque and, as Henry James pointed out, under prevailing diplomatic custom, London could justifiably have regarded it as an ultimatum.[57] Moreover, Washington intended Olney's note for publication. Olney and Cleveland believed that their strong language would get London's attention and that, by using the Monroe Doctrine as a lever, the United States could ram a diplomatic settlement down Britain's throat.[58] Cleveland and Olney expected London to back down and agree to arbitration and they hoped that Britain's positive response could be announced when Congress reconvened in December.

To the administration's consternation, however, London refused to give in to Washington's demands. British Prime Minister and Foreign Secretary Salisbury's unyielding reply prompted Cleveland's December 17, 1895, message to Congress. While acknowledging that the prospect of an Anglo-American war was an unhappy one to contemplate, the president declared there was "no calamity which a great nation can invite which equals that which follows a supine submission to wrong and injustice and the consequent loss of national self-respect and honor beneath which are shielded and defended a people's safety and greatness." Cleveland strongly defended the validity of the Monroe Doctrine, which he described as vital to America's national security and to the integrity of its domestic political institutions. He asserted that London's exercise of jurisdiction over any territory that the United States determined to belong properly to Venezuela was "willful aggression upon [America's] rights and interests."

In taking this position, Cleveland declared that he was "fully alive to the responsibility incurred and keenly realize[d] all the consequences that may follow." Notwithstanding his strong rhetoric, however, Cleveland did leave

---

57. Henry James, *Richard Olney and His Public Service* (New York: DaCapo Press, 1971, reprint ed.), p. 109. President Cleveland quoted in May, *Imperial Democracy*, p. 40.
58. Gerald C. Eggert, *Richard Olney: Education of a Statesman* (University Park: Pennsylvania State University Press, 1974), pp. 202, 212–213.

the British with some maneuvering room. Before acting against Britain, he said, the United States would set up a commission to investigate the Anglo-Venezuelan dispute and Washington would take no steps until the commission's report was made and accepted. Nevertheless, the import of Cleveland's message was clear: the United States was willing to fight Britain if necessary in order to establish America's primacy in the Western hemisphere.[59]

As Kenneth Bourne points out, during the Venezuela crisis the risk of war was quite real.[60] Salisbury flatly rejected the terms for resolving the crisis set out in Olney's July 20 note. J.A.S. Grenville wrote: "nothing could be plainer than Salisbury's rejoinder to Olney: the United States had no business interfering in the dispute, the Monroe Doctrine had no standing as an international treaty and did not in any case apply to the controversy; the British government would accordingly continue to refuse arbitration of the Venezuelan claims as a whole."[61] Salisbury understood the risk that Washington would maintain its stance and that the crisis would escalate. But as Grenville points out, he was willing to run this risk because "he did not believe the danger to Britain would be serious. The country and empire would have united in defence of British possessions, and in the face of their determination he believed the United States would give way."[62] Either Washington would understand the significance of the disparity between its military power and Britain's, or the United States would be defeated.

In late 1895 Britain and the United States clearly were on a collision course, and conflict almost certainly would have occurred had Britain held fast to the policy line adopted by Salisbury in November 1895. London did not do so, however, and by late January 1896 London and Washington had embarked upon a diplomatic process that culminated in November 1896 in an amicable settlement of Anglo-American differences. The crucial question is, why did Britain suddenly reverse course at the beginning of 1896?

---

59. Both Walter LaFeber and Ernest May come to this conclusion. See LaFeber, *The New Empire*, p. 268 and May, *Imperial Democracy*, p. 42.
60. Kenneth Bourne, *Balance of Power*, p. 319. It should be noted that not all historians agree with Bourne. For example, J.A.S. Grenville has argued that the Venezuelan crisis was synthetic and that there was no real risk of war during the crisis; Grenville, *Lord Salisbury and Foreign Policy at the Close of the Nineteenth Century* (London: Athlone Press, 1964), p. 55. However, in later work, Grenville wrote: "Given the mood of the British Cabinet . . . a serious Anglo-American conflict seemed inevitable." Grenville and Young, *Politics, Strategy and American Diplomacy*, p. 169.
61. Grenville, *Lord Salisbury*, p. 63.
62. Ibid., p. 65.

Although there is no "smoking gun," compelling circumstantial evidence supports the historians' consensus opinion that Britain was constrained from going to war in 1896 by an unfavorable distribution of military capabilities *vis-à-vis* the United States and by a deteriorating international situation. London, Lord Salisbury excepted, had become concerned about the outcome of an Anglo-American war because of Britain's inability, due to threats elsewhere, to spare warships to reinforce its naval presence in North American waters; fears that Canada would be conquered by the United States; and fears that in a prolonged war, the United States would be able to force a stalemate and possibly even prevail because of its enormous economic strength.[63] Moreover, between November 1895 and mid-January 1896, Britain's international position took a sharp turn for the worse: "England stood completely isolated at the beginning of 1896. Her position was scarcely endurable."[64] Anglo-German relations had been plunged into crisis by the Krueger telegram that Kaiser Wilhelm II had dispatched in the wake of the Jameson raid on the Transvaal. Elsewhere, the threats from Britain's main rivals, Russia and France, seemed only slightly less menacing.

Britain concluded that it must settle with Washington because it could not afford yet another enemy. At the critical January 11, 1896, Cabinet meeting, Salisbury remained steadfastly committed to his November "no negotiations" policy, but his colleagues decided to resolve the crisis with Washington peacefully. As Grenville and Young point out: "In November they believed that Britain held all the trump cards [but] the mood was no longer confident. The Cabinet was now inclined to cut Britain's losses in a world which appeared to have become suddenly hostile."[65] Overruled by the Cabinet, Salisbury—who believed that eventual war with the United States was "some-

---

63. See Bourne, *The Balance of Power in North America*, p. 340–341; A.E. Campbell, *Britain and the United States*, pp. 29–40; Eggert, *Richard Olney*, pp. 232–233; Paul Kennedy, *The Realities Behind Diplomacy: Background Influences on British External Policy, 1865–1980* (London: George Allen & Unwin, 1981), pp. 107–109; Arthur J. Marder, *The Anatomy of British Sea Power: A History of British Naval Policy in the Pre-Dreadnought Era, 1880–1905* (New York: Knopf, 1940), pp. 254–257. In an early January 1896 letter to Theodore Roosevelt, Lord Bryce said that nothing could be farther from his countrymen's minds than interfering with America's rights or the hemispheric balance of power because: "Our hands are more than sufficiently full elsewhere." Quoted in A.E. Campbell, *Britain and the United States*, pp. 59–60.
64. Marder, *Anatomy of British Sea Power*, p. 257.
65. Grenville and Young, *Politics, Strategy and American Diplomacy*, p. 170; Grenville, *Lord Salisbury*, pp. 67–69.

thing more than a possibility"—apparently considered resigning the premiership.[66]

There is virtually no evidence that supports a democratic peace theory explanation of the Venezuela crisis's outcome. Although the crisis ended before either London or Washington could make war-like threats, both the United States and Britain began planning militarily for a possible conflict.[67] This suggests that both British and American policymakers considered that war, or at least the preparation for it, was a legitimate component of their diplomatic strategies.

It does not appear, either, that public opinion affected policy on either side of the Atlantic. In Britain, the Cleveland administration's demands initially were greeted with hostility. Nevertheless, even before January 1896, British public opinion overwhelmingly favored a peaceful settlement of the Anglo-American crisis. There is, however, no evidence in the historical record that public opinion had any effect on the Cabinet's January 11 decision to resolve the crisis peacefully. Indeed, during the Venezuela crisis, Britain's policy-making elite had a different view of Anglo-American relations than did the British public. At the time of the Venezuela crisis there was still "an enormous gulf" between the advocates of an Anglo-American rapprochement based on racial kinship "and the hard-headed realism of the school of professional politicians and strategists headed by Salisbury."[68]

On the American side of the Atlantic, Cleveland's bellicose December 17 message elicited widespread public support. As Walter LaFeber notes, "Expansionist-minded Americans heartily endorsed the President's message, though most of them also fully shared his hopes that no war would result."[69] However the public's enthusiasm rather quickly subsided, and important groups, especially the churches and some elements of the financial and manufacturing sectors, recoiled at the prospect of an Anglo-American war. Nevertheless, if war had occurred, the public would probably have united behind the Cleveland administration. American public opinion viewed the prospect of war with England "not with enthusiasm but as, though regret-

---

66. See J.L. Garvin, *Life of Joseph Chamberlain* (London: Macmillan, 1934), Vol. III, p. 161; Salisbury quoted in Bourne, *The Balance of Power in North America*, p. 339.
67. Both London and Washington planned for a North American war during early 1896. American planning focused on invading Canada, Britain's on defending it. See Bourne, *The Balance of Power in North America*, pp. 319–331.
68. Bourne, *Balance of Power*, p. 340. Marder, *Anatomy of British Sea Power*, pp. 254–255, shows that Britain's national security elites took a very hard-line stance during the Venezuela crisis.
69. LaFeber, *New Empire*, p. 270.

table, necessary if there were no other way of establishing the paramount position of the United States in the western hemisphere."[70]

Recent generations have come to regard the Anglo-American "special relationship" as an immutable fact of international life. Indeed, in some ways it is considered an archetype of relations between democratic states. The "great rapprochement" upon which the special relationship was built was the epilogue to the Venezuelan crisis. But whatever Anglo-American relations arguably have become, the impetus for the rapprochement between London and Washington (like the impetus for the settlement of the Venezuelan crisis itself) was, as C.S. Campbell points out, rooted in geostrategic concerns and not in the considerations that underlie democratic peace theory.[71]

By 1898, the effects of Britain's by then not-so-splendid isolation were being painfully felt, and London's overtures to Washington must be viewed as part of the dramatic "end of isolation" process of strategic and diplomatic readjustment that London undertook after the Boer War.[72] The British did not welcome the rapid expansion of American power; rather they reconciled themselves to something they could not prevent and which, unlike the German, Russian and French challenges, did not seem immediately threatening to vital British interests. The Anglo-American rapprochement was possible because on every issue in dispute between them, London yielded to Washington's demands. As Bourne dryly observes, "All this was not simply or even perhaps at all significant of any special goodwill towards the United States."[73] Britain could not afford to make any more enemies, and least of all could London afford to incur the enmity of the United States, with which the British knew they could no longer compete geopolitically. For London, the "special relationship" was a myth devised "to enable Britain

---

70. A.E. Campbell, *Britain and the United States*, p. 41.
71. Charles S. Campbell, *Anglo-American Understanding, 1898–1903* (Baltimore: Johns Hopkins University Press, 1957), pp. 8–24. Kenneth Bourne and Paul Kennedy both point out that many of the same non-strategic factors underlying the Anglo-American rapprochement ("Anglo-Saxonism," economic interdependence) had been strongly present since at least 1850. They did not, however, noticeably mitigate Anglo-American hostility. These factors only came into play *after* the changing international situation forced London to reassess its grand strategy. Bourne, *Balance of Power*, p. 343; Kennedy, *Realities Behind Diplomacy*, p. 118.
72. There is strong consensus on this point among diplomatic historians. Bourne, *Balance of Power*, pp. 409–410; A.E. Campbell, *Britain and the United States*, pp. 208; C.S. Campbell, *Anglo-American Understanding*, p. 346, 184–185; Bradford Perkins, *The Great Rapprochement: England and the United States, 1895–1914* (New York: Atheneum, 1968) pp. 156–157; Kennedy, *Realities Behind Diplomacy*, pp. 118–119.
73. Bourne, *Balance of Power*, p. 343.

to withdraw gracefully" from those areas where British interests clashed with Washington's, and its function was to make the "pill" of appeasing the United States "more palatable to swallow."[74]

The outcome of the Venezuelan crisis is better explained by realism than by democratic peace theory. Consistent with realist expectations, both Britain and the United States began planning for war. Although, as democratic peace theory would predict, there was no war fever in either Britain or the United States, there is no evidence that public opinion played any role in London's decision-making process. It was London's decision to reverse its initially uncompromising stance and instead seek an amicable diplomatic solution with Washington that allowed Britain and the United States to avoid war. All available evidence supports the realist explanation that London made this decision solely for strategic reasons.

THE ANGLO-FRENCH STRUGGLE FOR CONTROL OF THE NILE: FASHODA, 1898

The Fashoda crisis marked the culmination of the Anglo-French struggle for supremacy over Egypt and the headwaters of the Nile.[75] Until 1882 Egypt, although nominally part of the Ottoman Empire, had been administered by an Anglo-French condominium. In 1882, Britain intervened unilaterally to suppress a nationalist revolt. Because the Suez canal was the vital artery linking Britain with India and its other far eastern imperial interests, strategic considerations overrode London's initial inclination to withdraw quickly from Egypt after the 1882 intervention. By the early 1890s, Lord Salisbury and other British policymakers had determined that in order to safeguard Egypt, Britain had to exert control over the Nile's source and its entire valley.

For France, Britain's post-1882 Egyptian primacy was an affront and, spurred by France's colonial party, Paris periodically looked for ways in which it could compel London to honor its pledge to withdraw from Egypt.

---

74. Ronald Hyam, *Britain's Imperial Century, 1815–1914: A Study of Empire and Expansion* (London: B.T. Batsford, 1976), pp. 202, 205; C.J. Lowe and M.L. Dockrill, *The Mirage of Power: British Foreign Policy, 1902–1914*, Vol. I (London: Routledge and Kegan Paul, 1972), p. 99.
75. For accounts of the Fashoda crisis and its background, the following are excellent sources: William L. Langer, *The Diplomacy of Imperialism, 1890–1902*, 2d ed. (New York: Knopf, 1965), pp. 101–144, 259–302; Ronald Robinson and John Gallagher with Alice Denny, *Africa and the Victorians: The Official Mind of Imperialism* (London: Macmillan, 1981, rev. ed.), pp. 76–159, 290–306; G.N. Sanderson, *England, Europe, and the Upper Nile, 1882–1899* (Edinburgh: Edinburgh University Press, 1965), chaps. 12–15; and Sanderson, "The Origins and Significance of the Anglo-French Confrontation at Fashoda," in Prosser Gifford and William Roger Louis, eds., *France and Britain in Africa: Imperial Rivalry and Colonial Rule* (New Haven: Yale University Press, 1971), pp. 285–332.

The immediate impetus for the French expedition to Fashoda appears to have come from a January 1893 talk given by the hydraulic engineer Victor Prompt at the Egyptian Institute in Paris, which suggested that the flow of water to Egypt could be restricted by damming the Upper Nile. After reviewing Prompt's speech, President of the French Republic Sadi Carnot exclaimed, "we must occupy Fashoda!"[76]

The plan to advance on Fashoda was eagerly embraced by Theophile Delcassé during his 1893–95 tenure first as undersecretary and then as minister for colonies. As a journalist and as a politician, he had been obsessed by the Egyptian question. For Delcassé and other French colonialists, France's prestige and its Mediterranean interests required an end to Britain's occupation of Egypt.[77] In 1896, a plan by marine captain Jean-Baptiste Marchand for an overland expedition to establish French control at Fashoda was approved by Foreign Minister Gabriel Hanotaux and Colonial Minister Emile Chautemps. They did not seek to precipitate an armed confrontation with Britain; they favored an eventual Anglo-French rapprochement and entente. However, they were convinced that French opinion would not accept an entente unless the two powers could reach settlement on the points of dispute between them, including Egypt. Thus, for Hanotaux and Delcassé, the Fashoda expedition was conceived as a lever to force the British to negotiate the Egyptian question and thus to increase France's great-power prestige.

In September 1898, Delcassé was foreign minister. As the conflict loomed, he hoped that it might be averted by Marchand's failure to reach his objective or, if the French expedition did run into British forces, by an agreement that the crisis would be settled diplomatically by London and Paris, not militarily by the opposing forces at Fashoda. Apparently relying on Salisbury's reputation for making "graceful concessions," Delcassé hoped to defuse the crisis by exchanging Marchand's withdrawal for Britain's agreement to reopen the Egyptian question and to discuss giving France an outlet on the Nile.[78] The British, however, had no intention of negotiating. London's position was simple: "Marchand should go, without quibbles or face saving."[79]

76. Quoted in A.J.P. Taylor, "Prelude to Fashoda: The Question of the Upper Nile, 1894–5," *English Historical Review*, Vol. 65, No. 254 (January 1950), p. 54.
77. Christopher Andrew, *Theophile Delcassé and the Making of the Entente Cordiale: A Reappraisal of French Foreign Policy, 1898–1905* (New York: Macmillan, 1968), pp. 21–25.
78. Ibid., p. 100; Roger Glenn Brown, *Fashoda Reconsidered: The Impact of Domestic Politics on French Policy in Africa* (Baltimore: Johns Hopkins University Press, 1970), pp. 92–93.
79. Robinson and Gallagher, *Africa and the Victorians*, p. 371.

French policymakers "deluded themselves" into thinking that by taking Fashoda they could force London to negotiate the Egyptian issue.[80] As early as March 1895, when London had its first intimations about French designs on the upper Nile, Sir Edward Grey, then parliamentary undersecretary for foreign affairs, had stated bluntly that such a move "would be an unfriendly act and would be so viewed in England."[81] In spring 1898, responding to reports that France was driving on the upper Nile, London decided on an all-out reconquest of Sudan.

After victory at Khartoum, Field Marshal Lord Kitchener was ordered to advance to Fashoda and instructed, in the event he encountered French forces, to do nothing that "would in any way imply a recognition on behalf of Her Majesty's Government of a title on behalf of France . . . to any portion of the Nile Valley."[82] On September 19, 1898, Kitchener's forces reached Fashoda, where they were greeted by Marchand's band. Although the opposing forces treated each other with elaborate military courtesy, their meeting plunged London and Paris into a deep diplomatic crisis. The Anglo-French "quarrel was not about Fashoda, or about the fate of the Sudan, or even about the security of the Nile waters and of Egypt; it was about the relative status of France and Britain as Powers."[83]

Once the crisis began, Delcassé quickly recognized that France was in an untenable position. The British ambassador in Paris reported that Delcassé was "prepared to retreat . . . if we can build him a golden bridge."[84] Delcassé believed his maneuvering room was seriously circumscribed by the potentially volatile domestic political situation in France stemming from the Dreyfus affair. To accept a humiliating diplomatic defeat would probably mean the Brisson cabinet's fall and, it was widely feared, even a military coup.[85] Delcassé reportedly begged London, "Do not drive me into a corner."[86] On October 11, he told the British ambassador that if London made it easy for

---

80. Langer, *Diplomacy of Imperialism*, pp. 550–551.
81. Quoted in James Goode, *The Fashoda Crisis: A Survey of Anglo-French Imperial Policy on the Upper Nile Question, 1882–1899* (Ph.D. diss., North Texas State University, 1971), p. 150; and Darrell Bates, *The Fashoda Incident of 1898: Encounter on the Nile* (New York: Oxford University Press, 1984), p. 24.
82. Lord Salisbury's instructions quoted in Robinson and Gallagher, *Africa and the Victorians*, p. 368.
83. Sanderson, "Origins and Significance of Fashoda," p. 289.
84. Quoted in Sanderson, *The Upper Nile*, p. 346.
85. Brown, *Fashoda Reconsidered*, pp. 99–100, 127.
86. Quoted in T.W. Riker, "A Survey of British Policy in the Fashoda Crisis," *Political Science Quarterly*, Vol. 44, No. 1 (March 1929), p. 63.

him "in form he would be conciliatory in substance."[87] On October 27 the French ambassador to London, telling Salisbury that Marchand would soon leave Fashoda, pleaded for Britain to make some concession in return.[88]

Meanwhile, notwithstanding both the pleading tone of French diplomacy and the possible repercussions of Britain's stance on French internal politics, London adamantly refused to give Paris an alternative to the bleak choice of ordering Marchand's humiliating withdrawal or going to war. On September 18, the British ambassador in Paris told Delcassé "categorically" that London would not consent to any compromise of the Fashoda dispute.[89] On September 30, responding to Delcassé's statement that France would fight rather than submit to a British ultimatum, the British ambassador reiterated that there could be no discussions until Marchand withdrew from Fashoda. Salisbury was determined "to compel, rather than persuade, the French to withdraw."[90]

London's hard-line diplomacy was overwhelmingly supported by bellicose public opinion. Even before Fashoda, because of the tensions engendered by the Anglo-French colonial rivalry, "war with France was not exactly desired in England, but it would be accepted without hesitation if the occasion arose."[91] Once the crisis began, the press overwhelmingly supported the government's decision to refuse negotiations with France, and during the crisis "the British popular press indulged in an orgy of scurrility."[92] "There was plenty of warlike spirit in the country," and British public opinion was "aggressively jingoistic" over Fashoda.[93] "The unequivocal expression of British opinion" was solidly behind the Cabinet's hard-line policy.[94] This no doubt was true because the British public believed England's prestige was at stake and consequently was "in a mood to respond vigorously" to the French challenge.[95]

The public mood was matched by that of Britain's political elite. As Chancellor of the Exchequer Michael Hicks Beach said on October 19, "The country

87. Quoted in Keith Eubank, "The Fashoda Crisis Re-examined," *The Historian*, Vol. 22, No. 2 (February 1960), p. 152.
88. Quoted in ibid., p. 154.
89. Quoted in Robinson and Gallagher, *Africa and the Victorians*, p. 370.
90. Sanderson, *The Upper Nile*, p. 334.
91. Ibid., p. 372.
92. Ibid.; Riker, "British Policy in the Fashoda Crisis," pp. 65–67; Sanderson, *The Upper Nile*, p. 348.
93. Robinson and Gallagher, *Africa and the Victorians*, p. 376; Sanderson, *The Upper Nile*, p. 354.
94. Riker, "British Policy in the Fashoda Crisis," pp. 66–67.
95. Sanderson, "Origins and Significance of Fashoda," pp. 295, 300.

has put its foot down."[96] The government's uncompromising stance was supported strongly by the opposition Liberal Imperialists, notably Lord Rosebery, H.H. Asquith, and Sir Edward Grey.[97] Rosebery, a former prime minister and foreign secretary, recalled that his Cabinet had warned the French away from the Upper Nile in 1895 and declared that any Cabinet that showed signs of conciliating Paris over Fashoda would be replaced within a week. Indeed when, in the crucial October 27 Cabinet meeting, Salisbury left the impression in some minds that he was leaning towards compromise with Paris, the majority of ministers quickly poured cold water on that idea and the Admiralty was ordered to put the navy on a war footing.

The British knew that if Paris did not capitulate, armed conflict would ensue. London regarded that prospect with equanimity and, indeed, confidence. Because they believed both Britain's credibility and its reputation as a great power to be at stake, the British felt they had no alternative to forcing a showdown with the French: "Had Britain followed a less intransigent policy in the circumstances of October 1898, there would certainly have been a temptation, not only in Paris but also in St. Petersburg and Berlin, to write her off as a Power who would never risk a war, however great the provocation."[98]

In October 1898 the British navy enjoyed a decisive superiority over the French fleet in both numbers and quality, and the outcome of an Anglo-French war was a foregone conclusion.[99] London manifested no reluctance in pressing its strategic advantage. During October, the Royal Navy made preparations for a war with France.[100] On October 15, the Channel fleet was assembled. By October 26, the Royal Navy had drawn up detailed war plans. On October 28 the reserve squadron was activated and concentrated at Portland; soon the Channel fleet was deployed to Gibraltar and the Mediterranean fleet was moved to Malta. As these measures became known in Paris from intelligence reports and stories in the British press, they made a strong impression on French policymakers.

There is no question that France was finally compelled to accept a crushing diplomatic defeat because of its military inferiority *vis-à-vis* Britain. The Royal

---

96. Quoted in Langer, *Diplomacy of Imperialism*, p. 553.
97. Langer, *Diplomacy of Imperialism*, pp. 552–553; Robinson and Gallagher, *Africa and the Victorians*, pp. 376–378; Riker, "British Policy in the Fashoda Crisis," p. 67; Sanderson, *The Upper Nile*, p. 347.
98. Sanderson, "Origin and Significance of Fashoda," pp. 301–302.
99. On the Royal Navy's advantages and London's confidence in British sea power, see Marder, *Anatomy of British Sea Power*, pp. 320–331; Langer, *Diplomacy of Imperialism*, pp. 559–560.
100. Marder, *Anatomy of British Sea Power*, pp. 321–328.

Navy's power contrasted sharply with the numerical and qualitative deficiencies, and unpreparedness, of the French fleet. When Paris calculated the prevailing Anglo-French military balance, an embarrassing diplomatic climbdown emerged as a more attractive alternative than decisive defeat in a war.[101] As Delcassé admitted, he and President of the Republic Fauré were compelled to order Marchand's withdrawal by "the necessity of avoiding a naval war which we are absolutely incapable of carrying on, even with Russian help."[102] In the end, "Delcassé had no real alternative but to yield; except as an irrational gesture of defiance, war with England was not a possible choice."[103] The Fashoda crisis's outcome was, as Grenville says, "a demonstration of British power and French weakness."[104]

The outcome of the Fashoda crisis is explained by realism, not by democratic peace theory. Believing that vital strategic and reputational interests were at stake, the British ruled out diplomatic accommodation with Paris notwithstanding Delcassé's pleas to be given a face-saving way to extricate France from the crisis. Britain's intransigence runs directly counter to democratic peace theory's expectation that relations between democratic states are governed by mutual respect based on democratic norms and culture. Backed strongly by public and elite opinion, London adopted a policy that left Paris with two stark choices: diplomatic humiliation or military defeat in a war. Counter to democratic peace theory's expectations, but consistent with those of realism, Britain made, and was prepared to carry out, military threats against France. Paris caved in to British demands rather than fight a war it could not win.

FRANCO-GERMAN CRISIS: THE RUHR, 1923

The Ruhr occupation, culmination of the post-1918 cold peace, "practically amounted to the renewal of war."[105] The occupation arose from the collision

---

101. Two other factors weighed heavily in Britain's favor: First, Kitchener had an enormous local superiority over Marchand on the ground at Fashoda. Second, France's Russian ally made it clear that it would not support Paris and, in any event, even if St. Petersburg had wanted to intervene there was little the Russian navy could do to offset Britain's maritime superiority. See Langer, *Diplomacy of Imperialism*, pp. 559–563; Marder, *Anatomy of British Sea Power*, pp. 323, 328–329. As Paul Kennedy observes, "all the best cards were in Britain's hands." Kennedy, *Realities Behind Diplomacy*, pp. 112–113.
102. Quoted in Andrew, *Theophile Delcassé*, pp. 102–103. Fauré's reaction to Britain's naval preparations is described in Brown, *Fashoda Reconsidered*, pp. 115–116.
103. Sanderson, *The Upper Nile*, p. 362.
104. Grenville, *Lord Salisbury*, p. 218.
105. Royal J. Schmidt, *Versailles and the Ruhr: Seedbed of World War II* (The Hague: Martinus Nijhoff, 1968), p. 17; Marshall M. Lee and Wolfgang Michalka, *German Foreign Policy, 1917–1933:*

of France's policy of security and Germany's policy of seeking revision of the Versailles Treaty system. The reparations issue was the immediate cause of the Ruhr occupation, but although it had economic significance in itself, its true importance was that Paris and Berlin regarded it as symbolic of the geopolitical competition between them.[106]

For Paris, compelling Germany to adhere strictly to its reparations obligations was seen as crucial to maintaining the Versailles system. Moreover reparations were, as the Ruhr occupation demonstrated, a lever for France to revise Versailles in its favor by imposing political and territorial sanctions on Germany when Berlin defaulted on its payments. For Germany, obtaining modification of reparations was a wedge to open the issue of revising the entire Versailles framework. The "fulfillment" policies adopted by Berlin were designed to force revision by demonstrating that strict compliance with reparations obligations was beyond Germany's capacity and would lead inevitably to Germany's financial and economic collapse.[107]

Although Germany had been defeated and its short-term power constrained by the Versailles settlement, the underlying sources of its geopolitical strength—its industrial base and population—remained intact. French policymakers were obsessed about the resurgence of a German security threat and determined to prevent it by imposing military, territorial and economic restrictions on Germany.

France's postwar German policy was rooted in the aims that Paris had pursued during the war. As early as 1915, Foreign Minister Delcassé had envisioned breaking up the German Reich into a number of small states, coupled with annexation by France, Holland, and Belgium of the Rhine's left bank.[108] By late 1917, Paris had decided to leave a truncated Reich intact while annexing Alsace-Lorraine and the Saar, and creating an independent

---

Continuity or Break? (Leamington Spa, U.K.: Berg, 1987), p. 47; Detlev J.K. Peukert, *The Weimar Republic: The Crisis of Classical Modernity,* trans. Richard Deveson (New York: Hill and Wang, 1992), p. 61; Hermann J. Rupieper, *The Cuno Government and Reparations, 1922–1923: Politics and Economics* (The Hague: Martinus Nijhoff, 1979) p. 96.
106. Peukert, *Weimar Republic,* p. 55; Marc Trachtenberg, *Reparation in World Politics: France and European Economic Diplomacy, 1916–1923* (New York: Columbia University Press, 1980), p. 122; Stephen A. Schuker, *The End of French Predominance in Europe: The Financial Crisis of 1924 and the Adoption of the Dawes Plan* (Chapel Hill: University of North Carolina Press, 1976), p. 6.
107. On Berlin's strategy of seeking revision through fulfillment, see David Felix, *Walther Rathenau and the Weimar Republic: The Politics of Reparations* (Baltimore: Johns Hopkins University Press); and Rupieper, *The Cuno Government.*
108. D. Stevenson, *French War Aims Against Germany, 1914–1919* (Oxford: Clarendon Press, 1982), pp. 26–27.

French satellite state in the Rhineland.[109] France's military and economic security would be enhanced by imposing reparations on Germany and by giving France control of the iron and coal that were crucial to West European industrial supremacy.

After the war, France's objectives did not change. Paris sought military security, reparations, and the establishment of France as Europe's leading steel producer. At Versailles, to avoid alienating Britain and the United States, France abandoned its annexationist aspirations in the Rhineland; however, throughout the period from the Armistice to the Ruhr occupation, Paris covertly supported Rhenish separatism while continuing to harbor hopes of controlling the left bank.[110] Even while appearing to abandon France's territorial claims in the Rhineland, French Premier Clemenceau had achieved much of their essence by coupling the reparations and security issues: under the Versailles Treaty's provisions, as long as Germany remained in default on reparations, French troops could remain in the Rhineland.

The government's German policy was strongly supported by the French public. French public opinion had demanded a peace settlement that would "impose the greatest possible restrictions on Germany's influence and power," and the French public's Germanophobia carried over into the postwar period.[111] Public and policymakers alike believed that Germany should be forced to pay all of the costs France had sustained in connection with the war (including reconstruction of German-occupied French territory), and official and public opinion were mutually reinforcing. Indeed, French public opinion, which French Prime Minister Poincaré had done much to shape, was so anti-German in late 1922 that it is doubtful that he would have survived politically had he not moved to occupy the Ruhr.[112]

The French military invasion of the Ruhr was prompted by Paris's mounting frustration with Germany's campaign to obtain a significant reduction of its reparations obligations. Although there is some disagreement as to the exact nature of Poincaré's objectives in occupying the Ruhr, the balance of

---

109. On French war aims see Walter A. McDougall, *France's Rhineland Diplomacy, 1914–1924: The Last Bid for a Balance of Power in Europe* (Princeton: Princeton University Press, 1978), p. 25; Schmidt, *Versailles to the Ruhr*, pp. 22–23; Stevenson, *French War Aims*, pp. 38–39.

110. Stevenson, *French War Aims*, pp. 195–196. The definitive account of France's Rhenish policy is McDougall, *Rhineland Diplomacy*.

111. Stevenson, *French War Aims*, pp. 135–136. Leaders such as Poincaré actively promoted anti-German attitudes, not a particularly difficult task. See Schmidt, *From Versailles to the Ruhr*, p. 231.

112. Rupieper, *The Cuno Government*, pp. 88, 96; Schmidt, *From Versailles to the Ruhr*, p. 52.

opinion is that the Ruhr occupation was undertaken in an attempt to advance France's goals of revising the Versailles system in its favor. The Ruhr occupation clearly was intended to bolster French security by crippling Germany's economy while simultaneously enabling Paris to realize its ambition of establishing France as Europe's leading economic power. At a minimum, Paris hoped that the Ruhr occupation would inflame Rhenish separatism and lead the Rhineland to break away from the Reich; there is some evidence that the Ruhr occupation was undertaken specifically to advance the French aims of annexing the Rhineland and dissolving the Reich.[113] Once the Ruhr crisis commenced, France actively abetted the Rhenish separatists.

In the Ruhr crisis, France did not hesitate to use military force against democratic Weimar Germany in pursuit of French security interests. Indeed, what leaps out from histories of the period between 1915 (when French policymakers began to think seriously about their war aims) and 1923 is the repeated French rejection of "second image" arguments that France's postwar security position would be enhanced if Germany were transformed into a democracy. Unlike the British, who soon after the war came to believe a democratic Germany was the key to maintaining the peace in Europe, France preferred to put German democracy at risk rather than abandon its strategy of protecting its security with tangible guarantees. As Walter McDougall observes:

The Quai d'Orsay perceived little connection between forms of government and foreign policies. The Wilsonian idea that democracies choose peaceful foreign policies, while authoritarian regimes are aggressive, found few disciples in the French government and military . . . . A strong united Germany, whether monarchist or republican, would pose a threat to France and surely come to dominate the economies of the Danubian and Balkan regions.[114]

The French military occupation of the Ruhr provoked a major crisis—if not a Franco-German war, at least a quasi-war. A real war was avoided only because Germany lacked the capabilities to wage it. Still the Germans resisted the occupation fiercely. If anything united the fractious Germans of the

---

113. McDougall argues that Rhenish separation from the Reich was Poincaré's hope but not his specific goal in the Ruhr operation. McDougall, *Rhineland Diplomacy*, pp. 247–249. Schmidt argues that Poincaré undertook the Ruhr occupation for the specific purpose of gaining permanent territorial control of the Ruhr and Rhineland and promoting the Reich's disintegration. Schmidt, *From Versailles to the Ruhr*, pp. 232–233.
114. McDougall, *Rhineland Diplomacy*, p. 114.

Weimar Republic, it was hatred for the Versailles system and a determination to overturn it. The Germans believed that the French move was designed to bring about the dissolution of the Reich. Because of Germany's military weakness, the Reichswehr ruled out a policy of active resistance to the French occupation; however, steps were taken to facilitate military resistance in the event the French attempted to advance beyond the Ruhr.[115] Although unable to oppose France militarily, the Berlin government did adopt a policy of resistance to the French occupation, based on the noncooperation of German workers, civil servants, and railway personnel with French occupation authorities. The resistance was not entirely passive; the Reichswehr coordinated an active campaign of sabotage against the French occupation forces.[116] To sustain the resistance, the Berlin government provided the Ruhr population with food and unemployment subsidies. Passive resistance was financed by printing money, a practice that triggered Germany's financial collapse (due to hyperinflation and the concomitant collapse of the mark); this ultimately compelled Berlin to abandon its resistance to the Ruhr occupation. Over the long term, the Ruhr occupation had even more important effects on German domestic politics and public opinion: France's hard line policies strengthened the position of the right-wing nationalist parties in Germany and served to discredit the Weimar democracy.

The Ruhr crisis strongly disconfirms democratic peace theory. In World War I's aftermath, both the public and the elites in France perceived Germany as a dangerous threat to France's security and its great power status, even though Weimar Germany was a democracy. What mattered to the French was Germany's latent power, not its domestic political structure. Contrary to democratic peace theory's predictions, French policy toward democratic Germany reflected none of the mutual respect based on democratic norms and culture that democracies are supposed to display in their relations with each other. On the contrary, driven by strategic concerns, the French used military power coercively to defend the Versailles system upon which they believed their safety depended, rather than entrust their national security to

---

115. See F.L. Carsten, *The Reichswehr and Politics, 1918 to 1933* (Oxford: Clarendon Press, 1966) pp. 154–155. German preparations included mobilization of reserve units (whose existence was illegal under the terms of Versailles), the purchase of fighter aircraft from Holland and seaplanes from Sweden, and the training of secret units to conduct guerrilla operations behind the lines of any French advance beyond the Ruhr.
116. Ibid., pp. 154–155.

the hope that Germany's postwar democratic institutions would mitigate the geopolitical consequences flowing from the underlying disparity between German and French power.

Theoretical Conclusions

Proponents have made sweeping theoretical claims for, and have drawn important policy conclusions from, democratic peace theory. These claims rest on a shaky foundation, however. The case studies presented above subject both democratic peace theory and realism to a robust test. It is striking that in each of these four cases realism, not democratic peace theory, provides the more compelling explanation of why war was avoided. Indeed, the democratic peace theory indicators appear not to have played *any* discernible role in the outcome of these crises.

In each of these crises, at least one of the democratic states involved was prepared to go to war (or, in the case of France in 1923, to use military force coercively) because it believed it had vital strategic or reputational interests at stake. In each of these crises, war was avoided only because one side elected to pull back from the brink. In each of the four crises, war was avoided not because of the "live and let live" spirit of peaceful dispute resolution at democratic peace theory's core, but because of realist factors. Adverse distributions of military capabilities explain why France did not fight over Fashoda, and why Germany resisted the French occupation of the Ruhr passively rather than forcibly. Concerns that others would take advantage of the fight (the "waterbirds dilemma") explain why Britain backed down in the Venezuela crisis, and the Union submitted to Britain's ultimatum in the *Trent* affair. When one actually looks beyond the *result* of these four crises ("democracies do not fight democracies") and attempts to understand *why* these crises turned out as they did, it becomes clear that democratic peace theory's causal logic has only minimal explanatory power.

Although democratic peace theory identifies a correlation between domestic structure and the absence of war between democracies, it fails to establish a causal link. Because democratic peace theory's deductive logic lacks explanatory power, a second look at the theory's empirical support is warranted to see if the evidence is as strong as is commonly believed. The statistical evidence that democracies do not fight each other seems impressive but in fact, it is inconclusive, because the universe of cases providing empirical support for democratic peace theory is small, and because several important cases of wars between democratic states are not counted for reasons that are not persuasive.

QUANTITATIVE SUPPORT FOR THE THEORY: HOW BIG AN N?
Democratic peace theory purports to be validated by a large number ("N") of cases. A large N is achieved by aggregating the number of possible democratic dyads. Thus Switzerland and Sweden, or Austria and Israel, count as democratic dyads validating democratic peace theory. The result is the appearance of a large number of interactions with little or no conflict between democracies. Notwithstanding the theory's claim, however, the universe of supporting cases is small. There are three reasons why this is so. First, between 1815 and 1945 there were very few democracies (and the N would shrink further if only dyads involving democratic great powers are considered). Second, the possibility of *any* dyad (whether democratic, mixed, or non-democratic) becoming involved in a war is small, because wars are a relatively rare occurrence. States, even great powers, do not spend most of their time at war.[117] As David Spiro points out, if all nations are unlikely to fight wars, the claim that democracies do not fight each other loses much of its power. He states that if nations are rarely at war, and liberal dyads are a small proportion of all possible pairings of nation-states, then perhaps we should be surprised if democracies ever do go to war, but not at the absence of wars among democracies.[118]

Third, not all dyads are created equal. For the purposes of testing democratic peace theory, a dyad is significant only if it represents a case where there is a real possibility of two states going to war. To fight, states need both the *opportunity* (that is, the ability to actually project their power to reach an opponent) and a *reason* to do so. Only dyads meeting these preconditions are part of the appropriate universe of cases from which democratic peace theory can be tested.

---

117. On the striking decline in the frequency of great power war during the past two centuries see Jack S. Levy, *War and the Modern Great Power System, 1495–1975* (Lexington: University Press of Kentucky, 1983), chap. 6.
118. David E. Spiro, "The Insignificance of the Liberal Peace," *International Security*, Vol. 19, No. 2 (Fall 1994), pp. 50–86. Spiro concludes that the statistical evidence for the liberal peace is weak: either the data are ambiguous, or random chance would predict the absence of wars between democracies. Spiro is sympathetic to the democratic peace theory. He suggests that the tendency of liberal states to ally with, instead of opposing, each other is important and probably is rooted in liberal norms.

WARS BETWEEN DEMOCRACIES: BIG EXCEPTIONS IN A SMALL-N WORLD. The size of the N is an important question. If the effective universe of cases from which democratic peace theory can be tested is a small N, the importance of exceptions to the rule that democracies do not fight each other is heightened. Here, by their own admissions, democratic peace theorists are on thin ice. For example, referring specifically to the classification of the War of 1812 as one not involving two democracies, Bruce Russett acknowledges that this decision "may seem like a cheap and arbitrary escape" but asserts it is not.[119] It is only intellectual suppleness—the continual tinkering with definitions and categories—that allows democratic peace theorists to deny that democratic states have fought each other.[120]

An important example of this is the War Between the States, which the democratic peace theorists generally rule out on the grounds that it was an internal conflict within a state rather an international conflict between sovereign states.[121] Yet the events of 1861–65 seem especially relevant because the theory is based explicitly on the premise that the norms and culture that operate within democracies are externalized by them in their relations with other democratic states.[122] Democratic peace theory itself makes relevant the

---

119. Russett, *Grasping the Democratic Peace*, p. 16. However, sometimes things *are* exactly as they seem. Russett excludes the War of 1812 on the grounds that, prior to the Reform Bill of 1832, Britain was not a democracy. Yet, until the "revolution" that followed Andrew Jackson's 1828 election to the presidency, the United States was not appreciably more democratic than Britain. *The Federalist* and the Constitution itself, in its provision for an Electoral College and indirect election of senators, reflect the desire of the framers to circumscribe egalitarian democratic impulses. In early nineteenth-century America, suffrage was significantly restricted by property and other qualifications imposed at the state level. See Clinton Williamson, *American Suffrage: From Property to Democracy, 1750 to 1860* (Princeton: Princeton University Press, 1960); Paul Kleppner, et al., *The Evolution of American Electoral Systems* (Westport, Conn.: Greenwood Press, 1981).
120. A good example is James L. Ray, "Wars Between Democracies: Rare, or Nonexistent?" *International Interactions*, Vol. 18, No. 3 (1993), pp. 251–276. After readjusting the definition of democracy, Ray takes a brief look at five of the nineteen alleged exceptions to the rule that democratic states do not fight each other and concludes that over the last 200 to 250 years there are no exceptions to the rule.
121. Russett's comments (*Grasping the Democratic Peace*, p. 17) notwithstanding, after secession the War Between the States did take on the cast of an international conflict between two sovereign democratic entities. It certainly was so regarded by contemporaneous observers (and had the Confederacy prevailed, it certainly would be so regarded today). For example, no less a figure than Prime Minister William Gladstone, the arch-apostle of British Liberalism, observed that: "Jefferson Davis and other leaders of the South have made an army; they are making, it appears, a navy; and they have made what is more than either: they have made a nation." Quoted in James M. McPherson, *Battle Cry of Freedom: The Civil War Era* (New York: Oxford University Press, 1988), p. 552.
122. Democratic peace theory "*extends to the international arena* the cultural norms of live-and let-

issue of whether democratic norms and culture do, in fact, result in the peaceful resolution of disputes within democracies. The War Between the States cuts to the heart of the democratic peace theory's causal logic: if democratic norms and culture fail to prevent the outbreak of civil war within democracies, what reason is there to believe that they will prevent the outbreak of interstate wars between democracies?

In the case of the Union and the Confederacy, the characteristics at the heart of democratic peace theory—the democratic ethos of respect for other democracies, a political culture that emphasizes the non-violent dispute resolution, the shared benefits of cooperation, the restraining effect of open debate and public opinion—failed conspicuously to assure a peaceful result. Indeed, if a democracy as tightly knit—politically, economically, culturally—as the United States was in 1861 could split into two warring successor states, we should have little confidence that democracy will prevent great power conflicts in an anarchic, competitive, self-help realm like international politics.

An even more important example is the issue of whether Wilhelmine Germany was a democracy. Even if World War I were the only example of democracies fighting each other, it would be so glaring an exception to democratic peace theory as to render it invalid. As even Michael Doyle concedes, the question of whether Wilhelmine Germany was a democracy presents a "difficult case."[123] Indeed, it is such a difficult case that, in a footnote, Doyle creates a new category in which to classify Wilhelmine Germany—that of a bifurcated democracy: pre-1914 Germany was, he says, democratic with respect to domestic politics but not in the realm of foreign policy.[124] Doyle does not consider Imperial Germany to have been a democracy for foreign policy purposes because the executive was not responsible to the Reichstag and, consequently, the foreign policy making process remained, he argues, autocratic.

---

live and peaceful conflict resolution that operate *within* democracies." Ibid., p. 19 (emphasis added).

123. Doyle, "Kant, Liberal Legacies and Foreign Affairs," part I, p. 216, fn 8.

124. Ibid. I do not address the issue of whether any state can in fact have such a tightly compartmentalized political system that it can be democratic in domestic politics but not in foreign policy. I know of no other example of a bifurcated democracy. If this concept of bifurcated democracy were accepted, proponents of democratic peace theory could defend their argument by asserting that, while democratic in the realm of domestic policy, in 1914 Britain and France, like Wilhelmine Germany, also were non-democratic in terms of foreign policy.

In fact, however, with respect to foreign policy, Wilhelmine Germany was as democratic as France and Britain. In all three countries, aristocratic or upper-middle-class birth and independent wealth were prerequisites for service in the diplomatic corps and the key political staffs of the foreign office.[125] In all three countries, foreign policy was insulated from parliamentary control and criticism because of the prevailing view that external affairs were above politics.

In democratic France, the Foreign Minister enjoyed virtual autonomy from the legislature, and even from other members of the cabinet.[126] As Christopher Andrew notes, "On the rare occasions when a minister sought to raise a question of foreign policy during a cabinet meeting, he was accustomed to the remark: 'Don't let us concern ourselves with that, gentlemen, it is the business of the foreign minister and the President of the Republic.'"[127] Treaties and similar arrangements were ratified by the president of the Republic (that is, by the cabinet) and the legislature played no role in the treaty making process (although the Senate did have the right to ask to be informed of treaty terms insofar as national security permitted).[128] Notwithstanding the formal principle of ministerial responsibility, the French legislature possessed no mechanisms for effectively supervising or reviewing the government's conduct of foreign policy.[129] Even in democratic France, the executive enjoyed unfettered power in the realm of foreign policy. This concentration of foreign policy-making power in the executive had a profound effect on the chain of events leading to World War I. The terms of the Franco-Russian alliance and military convention—the "fateful alliance" that ensured that an Austro-Russian war in the Balkans could not remain localized—were kept secret from the French legislature, public, and press.[130]

In democratic Britain, too, as in France and Germany, crucial foreign policy decisions were taken without consulting Parliament. Notwithstanding the

---

125. See Lamar Cecil, *The German Diplomatic Service, 1871–1914* (Princeton: Princeton University Press, 1976); Paul Gordon Lauren, *Diplomats and Bureaucrats: The First Institutional Responses to Twentieth Century Diplomacy in France and Germany* (Stanford: Hoover Institution Press, 1976), pp. 27–29; Frederick L. Schuman, *War and Diplomacy in the French Republic: An Inquiry into Political Motivations and the Control of Foreign Policy* (New York: Whittlesy House, 1931); Zara S. Steiner, *The Foreign Office and Foreign Policy, 1898–1914* (Cambridge: Cambridge University Press, 1969); and Steiner, "The Foreign Office under Sir Edward Grey," in F.H. Hinsley, ed., *British Foreign Policy Under Sir Edward Grey* (Cambridge: Cambridge University Press, 1977), pp. 22–69.
126. Schuman, *War and Diplomacy*, pp. 21, 28–32.
127. Andrew, *Theophile Delcassé*, p. 64.
128. Ibid., p. 22; Lauren, *Diplomats and Bureaucrats*, p. 29.
129. Lauren, *Diplomats and Bureaucrats*, p. 29.
130. Schuman, *War and Diplomacy*, p. 143.

profound implications of the Anglo-French staff talks, which began in January 1906, Foreign Secretary Sir Edward Grey and Prime Minister H.H. Asquith did not inform the Cabinet of their existence.[131] Grey and Asquith feared (and rightly so) that a Cabinet majority would oppose the staff talks and indeed the very idea of more intimate Anglo-French strategic relations. When questioned in Parliament in 1910, 1911, and 1913 about the Anglo-French military discussions, Grey and Asquith consistently gave false or evasive answers that kept hidden both the nature and the implications of the strategic agreements between London and Paris.[132] Even when Grey and Asquith had to account to the Cabinet, after it learned in November 1911 of the existence of staff talks, they left their colleagues with the incorrect impression that London had undertaken no binding obligations to France.[133] Notwithstanding Grey's and Asquith's constant reiteration (to the French, to Cabinet, and to Parliament) that London retained unimpaired freedom of maneuver, they had, in fact, undertaken a portentous commitment through a constitutionally doubtful process. In the Cabinet's debates about whether Britain should go to war in August 1914, Grey's argument that the Entente, and the concomitant military and naval agreements, had morally obligated Britain to support France proved decisive.[134]

It is apparent that before World War I, the most important and consequential grand strategic decisions made by both Paris (on the Russian alliance) and London (on the entente and military arrangements with France) were made without any legislative control or oversight, notwithstanding both countries' democratic credentials. Form should not be confused with substance. In the realm of foreign policy, France and Britain were no more and no less democratic than the Second Reich.[135]

---

131. See Samuel R. Williamson, *The Politics of Grand Strategy: Britain and France Prepare for War, 1904–1914* (Cambridge: Harvard University Press, 1969).
132. Ibid., pp. 134, 137–138, pp. 202–204, 330–331.
133. Ibid., pp. 198–200.
134. Grey threatened to resign from the Cabinet unless it agreed to take Britain into the war on France's side. Grey's resignation threat was determinative because the non-interventionist Cabinet Radicals realized that their refusal to declare war would lead to the Cabinet's replacement either by a Conservative-Unionist government or by a coalition between the Conservatives and the Liberal Imperialists. See K.M. Wilson, "The British Cabinet's Decision for War, 2 August 1914," *British Journal of International Studies*, Vol. 1, No. 2 (July 1975), pp. 148–159.
135. The classification of Wilhelmine Germany as a democracy is also supported by an analysis of the foreign policy making process of its successor, the Weimar Republic. Although the Weimar Republic invariably is classified as a democracy, in crucial respects, it closely resembled the Second Reich. During the Weimar Republic, the Foreign Office and the Army collaborated to ensure that the processes of formulating foreign policy and grand strategy were insulated from

The case of Wilhelmine Germany suggests that democratic great powers indeed have gone to war against one another (and could do so again in the future). Yet the prevailing view that the Second Reich was not a democracy has powerfully influenced the international relations–theory debate both on the broad question of how domestic political structure affects international outcomes and the specific issue of whether there is a "democratic peace." However, the received wisdom about pre–World War I Germany has been badly distorted by a combination of factors: the liberal bias of most Anglo-American accounts of German history between 1860–1914; the ideologically tinged nature of post-1960 German studies of the Wilhelmine era; and the residual effects of Allied propaganda in World War I, which demonized Germany.[136] The question of whether Wilhelmine Germany should be classified as a democracy is an important one and it deserves to be studied afresh.

AN ALTERNATIVE HYPOTHESIS: THE SECOND IMAGE REVERSED

From a realist perspective, democratic peace theory has mistakenly reversed the linkage between international systemic constraints and domestic political institutions. Otto Hintze made the realist argument that a state's internal political structure is highly influenced by external factors.[137] This creates a selection process that explains why some states become democracies while others do not. States that enjoy a high degree of security, like Britain and the United States at the beginning of the twentieth century, can afford the more minimalist state political structures of classical Anglo-American liber-

---

the Reichstag's oversight and control. The leading study is Gaines Post, Jr., *The Civil-Military Fabric of Weimar Foreign Policy* (Princeton: Princeton University Press, 1973). Post observes (p. 358) that the Weimar Republic stands as a "model for the virtual exclusion of the parliamentary or legislative level from politico-military activity in a representative system of government." If Weimar Germany is considered to be a democracy, then how can Wilhelmine Germany be classified as a non-democracy?

136. For a discussion of the leftist ideological biases that color the writings of Fritz Fischer's disciples and a critique of Fischer, Berghahn, Kehr, and Wehler, see Wolfgang J. Mommsen, "Domestic Factors in German Foreign Policy before 1914," *Central European History*, Vol. 6, No. 1 (March 1973), pp. 4–18. An insightful critique of the "failure of liberalism" school is Klaus P. Fischer, "The Liberal Image of German History," *Modern Age*, Vol. 22, No. 4 (Fall 1978), pp. 371–383.

137. This thesis is developed in Otto Hintze, "The Formation of States and Constitutional Development: A Study in History and Politics"; Hintze, "Military Organization and the Organization of the State"; and Hintze, "The Origins of the Modern Ministerial System: A Comparative Study," in Felix Gilbert, ed., *The Historical Essays of Otto Hintze* (New York: Oxford University Press, 1975).

alism, because there is no imminent external threat that necessitates a powerful governmental apparatus to mobilize resources for national security purposes. States that live in a highly threatening external environment are more likely to choose either more statist forms of democracy or even authoritarian structures, precisely because national security concerns require that the state have available to it the instruments for mobilizing national power resources.[138] The greater the external threat a state faces (or believes it does), the more "autocratic" its foreign policymaking process will be, and the more centralized its political structures will be.

If this hypothesis is true, it suggests that democratic peace theory is looking through the wrong end of the telescope. States that are, or that believe they are, in high-threat environments are less likely to be democracies because such states are more likely to be involved in wars, and states that are likely to be involved in wars tend to adopt autocratic governmental structures that enhance their strategic posture.[139] Thus, as realist theory would predict, international systemic structure is not only the primary determinant of a state's external behavior but may also be a crucial element in shaping its domestic political system. This hypothesis may provide a more useful approach than democratic peace theory to investigating the links between domestic structure and foreign policy.

Policy Conclusions: Why It Matters

The validity of democratic peace theory is not a mere academic concern. Democratic peace theory has been widely embraced by policymakers and foreign policy analysts alike and it has become a lodestar that guides Amer-

---

138. This argument is developed in Brian M. Downing, *The Military Revolution and Political Change: Origins of Democracy and Political Change* (Princeton: Princeton University Press, 1992).
139. There is another way of visualizing this phenomenon. The more threatened a state is (or believes it is) the more it will move toward more centralized domestic structures. A state may move so far that it ceases to be democratic and becomes autocratic. This hypothesis conforms with the experience of liberal democratic great powers in this century. In both World Wars, the exigencies of conflict resulted in such a concentration of state power in both the United States and Britain that, for a time, arguably, both became autocratic. The Cold War, similarly, impelled the United States to become a "national security state," still a democracy but one where the power of the state was vastly enhanced and the executive's predominance over the legislature in the sphere of foreign policy was decisively established. Quincy Wright came to a similar conclusion about the effect of external environment on domestic political structure and observed that "autocracy, at least in the handling of foreign affairs, has been the prevailing constitutional form." Wright, *A Study of War* (Chicago: University of Chicago Press, 1964, abridged ed.), p. 158.

ica's post–Cold War foreign policy. Michael Doyle's 1983 conception of a democratic "zone of peace" is now routinely used in both official and unofficial U.S. foreign policy pronouncements. Following the Cold War, a host of commentators have suggested that the export or promotion of democracy abroad should become the central focus of American's post–Cold War foreign policy.[140] From Haiti to Russia, America's interests and its security have been identified with democracy's success or failure. National Security Adviser Anthony Lake said that America's post–Cold War goal must be to expand the zone of democratic peace and prosperity because, "to the extent democracy and market economics hold sway in other nations, our own nation will be more secure, prosperous and influential."[141]

Those who want to base American foreign policy on the extension of democracy abroad invariably disclaim any intention to embark on a "crusade," and profess to recognize the dangers of allowing policy to be based on excessive ideological zeal.[142] These reassurances are the foreign-policy version of "trust me." Because it links American security to the nature of other states' internal political systems, democratic peace theory's logic inevitably pushes the United States to adopt an interventionist strategic posture. If democracies are peaceful but non-democratic states are "troublemakers" the conclusion is inescapable: the former will be truly secure only when the latter have been transformed into democracies, too.

Indeed, American statesmen have frequently expressed this view. During World War I, Elihu Root said that, "To be safe democracy must kill its enemy when it can and where it can. The world cannot be half democratic and half autocratic."[143] During the Vietnam War, Secretary of State Dean Rusk claimed that the "United States cannot be secure until the total international environment is ideologically safe." These are not isolated comments; these views reflect the historic American propensity to seek absolute security and to

---

140. See for example Joshua Muravchik, *Exporting Democracy: Fulfilling America's Destiny* (Washington, D.C.: AEI Press, 1991); and Larry Diamond, "Promoting Democracy," *Foreign Policy*, No. 87 (Summer 1992), pp. 25–46.

141. "Remarks of Anthony Lake," Johns Hopkins School of Advanced International Studies, Washington, D.C., September 21, 1993 (Washington, D.C.: National Security Council Press Office).

142. Lake stated that the Clinton administration does not propose to embark on a "democratic crusade." Both Doyle and Russett acknowledge that democratic peace theory could encourage democratic states to pursue aggressive policies toward non-democracies, and both express worry at this. Doyle, "Kant, Liberal Legacies, and Foreign Affairs," part II; Russett, *Grasping the Democratic Peace*, p. 136.

143. Quoted in Russett, *Grasping the Democratic Peace*, p. 33.

define security primarily in ideological (and economic) terms. The political culture of American foreign policy has long regarded the United States, because of its domestic political system, as a singular nation. As a consequence, American policymakers have been affected by a "deep sense of being alone" and they have regarded the United States as "perpetually beleaguered."[144] Consequently, America's foreign and defense policies have been shaped by the belief that the United States must create a favorable ideological climate abroad if its domestic institutions are to survive and flourish.[145]

Democratic peace theory panders to impulses which, however noble in the abstract, have led to disastrous military interventions abroad, strategic overextension, and the relative decline of American power. The latest example of the dangers of Wilsonianism is the Clinton administration's Partnership for Peace. Under this plan, the asserted American interest in projecting democracy into East Central Europe is advanced in support of NATO security guarantees and eventual membership for Poland, Hungary, and the Czech Republic (and some form of U.S. security guarantee for Ukraine). The underlying argument is simple: democratic governments in these countries will guarantee regional peace in the post–Cold War era, but democracy cannot take root unless these countries are provided with the "reassurance" of U.S. or NATO security guarantees.

In fact, however, East Central Europe is bound to be a highly volatile region regardless of whether NATO "moves east." The extension of NATO guarantees eastward carries with it the obvious risk that the United States will become embroiled in a future regional conflict, which could involve major powers such as Germany, Ukraine, or Russia. There is little wisdom in assuming such potentially risky undertakings on the basis of dubious assumptions about the pacifying effects of democracy.[146]

---

144. William Appleman Williams, *Empire As A Way of Life: An Essay on the Causes and Character of America's Present Predicament Along With a Few Thoughts About An Alternative* (New York: Oxford University Press, 1980), p. 53.

145. Lloyd C. Gardner, *A Covenant With Power: America and World Order from Wilson to Reagan* (New York: Oxford University Press, 1984), p. 27. For an excellent critique of the notion that America's domestic ideology must be validated by its foreign policy, see Michael H. Hunt, *Ideology and U.S. Foreign Policy* (New Haven: Yale University Press, 1987).

146. It could be argued that if Hintze's argument is correct (that secure states are more likely to become, or remain, democratic), then extending security guarantees to states like Ukraine, or preserving extant alliances with states like Germany, Japan, and South Korea, is precisely what the United States should do. Indeed, the Bush and Clinton administrations have both subscribed to a worldview that holds that the United States, as the sole remaining superpower, must take responsibility for maintaining regional power balances in Europe and East Asia. By

Democratic peace theory is dangerous in another respect, as well: it is an integral component of a new (or more correctly, recycled) outlook on international politics. It is now widely believed that the spread of democracy and economic interdependence have effected a "qualitative change" in international politics, and that war and serious security competitions between or among democratic great powers are now impossible.[147] There is therefore, it is said, no need to worry about future great power challenges from states like Japan and Germany, or to worry about the relative distribution of power between the United States and those states, unless Japan or Germany were to slide back into authoritarianism.[148] The reason the United States need not be concerned with the great-power emergence of Japan and Germany is said to be simple: they are democracies and democracies do not fight democracies.

Modern-day proponents of a liberal theory of international politics have constructed an appealing vision of perpetual peace within a zone of democracy and prosperity. But this "zone of peace" is a peace of illusions. There is no evidence that democracy at the unit level negates the structural effects of anarchy at the level of the international political system. Similarly, there is no evidence that supports the sister theory: that economic interdependence leads to peace. Both ideas have been around for a long time. The fact that they are so widely accepted as a basis for international relations theory shows that for some scholars, "theories" are confirmed by the number of real-world tests that they fail. Proponents of liberal international relations theory may contend, as Russett does, that liberal approaches to international politics have not failed, but rather that they have not been tried.[149] But this is what disappointed adherents of ideological worldviews always say when belief is overcome by reality.

---

preventing the "renationalization" of other states' security policies and by foreclosing the possibility of regional power vacuums, the United States, it is argued, can preserve the kind of international environment that is conducive to the spread of democracy and economic interdependence. For critiques of this policy see Christopher Layne, "The Unipolar Illusion: Why New Great Powers Will Rise," *International Security*, Vol. 17, No. 4 (Spring 1993), pp. 5–51; Layne, "American Grand Strategy After the Cold War: Primacy or Blue Water?" in Charles F. Hermann, ed., *American Defense Annual* (New York: Lexington Books, 1994); and Layne and Schwarz, "American Hegemony."

147. Robert Jervis, "The Future of World Politics: Will It Resemble the Past?" *International Security*, Vol. 16, No. 3 (Winter 1991/92), pp. 39–73.

148. For an example of this argument see James M. Goldgeier and Michael McFaul, "A Tale of Two Worlds: Core and Periphery in the Post–Cold War Era," *International Organization*, Vol. 46, No. 3 (Spring 1992), pp. 467–491.

149. Russett, *Grasping the Democratic Peace*, p. 9, says that Kantian and Wilsonian principles have not been given a real chance to operate in international politics.

If American policymakers allow themselves to be mesmerized by democratic peace theory's seductive—but false—vision of the future, the United States will be ill prepared to formulate a grand strategy that will advance its interests in the emerging world of multipolar great power competition. Indeed, as long as the Wilsonian worldview underpins American foreign policy, policymakers will be blind to the need to have such a grand strategy, because the liberal theory of international politics defines out of existence (except with respect to non-democracies) the very phenomena that are at the core of strategy: war, the formation of power balances, and concerns about the relative distribution of power among the great powers. But in the end, as its most articulate proponents admit, liberal international relations theory is based on hope, not on fact.[150] In the final analysis, the world remains what it always has been: international politics continues to occur in an anarchic, competitive, self-help realm. This reality must be confronted, because it cannot be transcended. Given the stakes, the United States in coming years cannot afford to have either its foreign policy, or the intellectual discourse that underpins that policy, shaped by theoretical approaches that are based on wishful thinking.

---

150. Russett, *Grasping the Democratic Peace*, p. 136, argues that, "understanding the sources of democratic peace can have the effect of a self-fulfilling prophecy. Social scientists sometimes create reality as well as analyze it. Insofar as norms do guide behavior, repeating those norms helps to make them effective. *Repeating the norms as descriptive principles can help to make them true.*" (Emphasis added.)

The Insignificance of the Liberal Peace

David E. Spiro

Ever since Michael Doyle's 1983 essay pointed out that no liberal democracy has ever fought a war with another liberal democracy,[1] scholars have treated pacifism between democracies as "the closest thing we have to a law in international politics,"[2] and the field is nearly at the point where this "law" is accepted without question.[3] The purpose of this article is to raise critical questions about this newly rediscovered law of peace among democracies.

The primary question I address is whether the statistic that democracies never (or rarely) fight wars with each other is significant. Doyle supported his argument by showing that since 1816 no nations he considered to be liberal had fought wars with each other. Although he used a computerized database on interstate wars, he did not perform any probability analyses to show that zero is statistically significant.[4] Zero is a powerful statistic, which

David E. Spiro is an Assistant Professor of Political Science at the University of Arizona in Tucson. He is the author of Hegemony Unbound: Petrodollar Recycling and the De-Legitimation of American Power *(Ithaca: Cornell University Press, forthcoming 1995).*

The author thanks Edward D. Mansfield for the many discussions that motivated this study; and he is grateful for comments from Robert Art, Michael Doyle, John Matthews, John Owen, and Randall Schweller. This article was written partly under the auspices of the Institute for International Economic Studies, Tokyo, Japan.

1. Michael Doyle, "Kant, Liberal Legacies, and Foreign Affairs," Parts I and II, *Philosophy and Public Affairs*, Vol. 12, No. 3 (Summer 1983), pp. 205–235; and No. 4 (Fall 1983), pp. 323–353. The argument is summarized in Michael Doyle, "Liberalism and World Politics," *American Political Science Review*, Vol. 80, No. 4 (December 1986), pp. 1151–1169. The absence of wars among liberal democracies was noted before Doyle's article, but it was not seen as confirmation of any particular theory. See Peter Wallenstein, *Structure and War: On International Relations 1820–1968* (Stockholm: Raben and Sjogren, 1973); and Melvin Small and J. David Singer, "The War-Proneness of Democratic Regimes," *The Jerusalem Journal of International Relations*, Vol. 1, No. 1 (Summer 1976), pp. 50–69.
2. Jack S. Levy, "Domestic Politics and War," *Journal of Interdisciplinary History*, Vol. 18, No. 4 (1988), pp. 653–673.
3. See, for example, David Lake, "Powerful Pacifists: Democratic States and War," *America Political Science Review*, Vol. 86, No. 1 (March 1992), pp. 24–37. One exception, not yet published, is Joanne Gowa, "Democracies, Autocracies, and Foreign Policy," mimeo, Princeton University, 1993. See also John Owen, "How Liberalism Produces Democratic Peace," *International Security*, Vol. 19, No. 2 (Fall 1994), pp. 87–125; and Christopher Layne, "Kant or Cant: The Myth of the Democratic Peace," ibid., pp. 5–49.
4. The computerized data set is from the Inter-university Consortium for Political and Social

International Security, Vol. 19, No. 2 (Fall 1994), pp. 50–86
© 1994 by the President and Fellows of Harvard College and the Massachusetts Institute of Technology.

seems beyond debate or refutation, but as John Mearsheimer observed, "democracies have been few in number over the past two centuries, and thus there have not been many cases where two democracies were in a position to fight each other."[5]

As an example of how zero can be statistically insignificant, consider that people win million-dollar lotteries in the United States every day of the week, but not one single member of my immediate family has ever won one. Something can happen all of the time, and still the fact that it never happens to a certain group of individuals does not mean anything. No one needs to explore what it is about the nature of my family that prevents winning lotteries, because zero is not a significant result. It is predicted by random chance.

If the absence of wars between democracies is predicted by random chance, this is not to say that chance is a good explanation for war. It does mean that an explanation we know to be untrue—random chance—predicts the absence of war between democracies better than liberal theories of international relations, and therefore the absence of wars should not be considered as confirming evidence of those theories. And if the absence of wars between democracies is not surprising, then there is no puzzle to explain, and this "liberal legacy" does not challenge realist understandings of why nations do or do not go to war.

I will argue that the absence of wars between liberal democracies is not, in fact, a significant pattern for most of the past two centuries. Studies that do claim significance for the absence of wars between democracies are based on analyses that are highly sensitive to the ways that they select definitions of the key terms of democracy and war, and to the methods they choose for statistical analysis.[6] I argue that much of the quantitative literature on democracy and war has little to do with the theories it seeks to confirm, and that the results rest on methods and operationalization of variables that undergo contortions before they yield apparently significant results.

The brief section that follows summarizes the liberal theories predicting peace among democracies. Then I consider how to define "democracy" and

---

Research (ICPSR), Study I9044, J. David Singer and Melvin Small, "Wages of War, 1816–1980: Augmented with Disputes and Civil War Data" (Winter 1984).
5. John Mearsheimer, "Back to the Future: Instability in Europe After the Cold War," *International Security*, Vol. 15, No. 1 (Summer 1990), pp. 50–51.
6. See, for examples, Bruce Russett, *Grasping the Democratic Peace* (Princeton: Princeton University Press, 1993); and Rudolph J. Rummel, "Libertarianism and International Violence," *Journal of Conflict Resolution*, Vol. 27, No. 1 (March 1983), pp. 27–51.

"war." The core of this article consists of a probability analysis showing that the absence of wars between liberal democracies is not statistically significant except for a brief period during World War I. I conclude by arguing that this analysis casts doubts on two major studies that attempt to argue in favor of the statistical significance of the liberal peace, and I suggest that future research should focus on why democracies ally with one another rather than why they never fight.

The Liberal Legacy

Immanuel Kant first suggested that constitutional republics would be pacifist. Although "peace among men living side by side is not the natural state," the checks and balances of republican constitutions would prevent adventurous rulers from committing their nations to war, and the submission of each republican government to international law would obviate the impetus for wars.[7] In a time when wars over dynastic succession were fought with mercenaries, Kant thought that if the consent of citizens were required for the declaration of war, none would be declared because citizens would be cautious about having to fight, paying the costs of war, having to repair the devastation of the fighting, and "loading themselves with a heavy national debt that would embitter peace itself and that can never be liquidated on account of constant wars in the future." Under a constitution that is not republican, on the other hand, the war would not require sacrifice of the ruler. "He may, therefore, resolve on war as on a pleasure party for the most trivial reasons, and with perfect indifference leave the justification which decency requires to the diplomatic corps who are ever ready to provide it."[8] Checks and balances should make constitutional republics more pacific toward all nations, not just toward like governments.

Kant's reasoning about popular consent does not lead us to expect a complete absence of wars between constitutional republics. Indeed, while the monarchs Kant had in mind seemed unconstrained in their ability to fight short and limited wars with mercenaries, modern leaders even of autocracies are rarely free of societal constraints. Even though they lack democratic checks and balances, modern autocrats cannot remain in power for

---

7. Immanuel Kant, *Perpetual Peace* (Indianapolis: Liberal Arts Press, 1957 [first published 1795]), p. 10.
8. Kant, *Perpetual Peace*, p. 13.

long if they do not respond to societal pressures.[9] Conversely, every democracy contains a state with some degree of autonomy, and leaders can and do mobilize public opinion for wars that the leaders wish to initiate. Leaders in modern democracies may be more constrained than leaders in autocracies in their ability to prosecute unpopular wars, but the constraints are a matter of degree.

This element of democratic-peace theory, which Maoz and Russett call the "structural" element, yields a prediction that democracies will be more pacific toward all states (not just toward other democracies), yet many studies have shown that democracies are just as war-prone as other types of regimes.[10] In any case, the absence of wars between democracies would not be a confirmation of this theory, unless we were also able to prove that democracies fought fewer wars with non-democracies.

The complete absence of wars between democracies can only be confirmation of what Maoz and Russett have called the "normative" elements of democratic-peace theory.[11] Kant predicted that societies governed by civil constitutions would submit to a binding international law of peace.[12] He thought that these states would be more peaceful than others, and that they would develop a "law of nations founded on a federation of free states." The absence of wars between liberal regimes would be supporting evidence that they have formed a pacific union, in which war with each other is deemed illegitimate.[13]

Doyle argues that there is indeed a "pacific union" among liberal regimes. The union consists of liberal nations, which have upheld three sets of rights: freedom from arbitrary authority, protection and promotion of freedom, and democratic participation. "Even though liberal states have become involved

---

9. Gowa, "Democracies, Autocracies, and Foreign Policy."
10. Small and Singer, "The War Proneness of Democratic Regimes"; David Garnham, "War-Proneness," *Journal of Peace Research*, Vol. 23, No. 3 (September 1986), pp. 279–289; and Zeev Maoz and Nasrin Abdolali, "Regime Types and International Conflict, 1816–1976," *Journal of Conflict Resolution*, Vol. 29, No. 1 (March 1989), pp. 3–35.
11. Zeev Maoz and Bruce Russett, "Normative and Structural Causes of Democratic Peace, 1946–1986," *American Political Science Review*, Vol. 87, No. 3 (September 1993), which is reprinted as Russett, *Grasping the Democratic Peace*, chapter 4 and parts of chapter 1.
12. See John M. Owen, "Testing the Democratic Peace: American Diplomatic Crises, 1794–1917," PhD dissertation, Harvard University, 1993, chapter 1.
13. Kant called theorists such as Grotius, Pufendorf, and Vattel "irritating comforters" because they held to the possibility that some wars could be legitimate. He wrote that, "there is no instance on record that a state has ever been moved to desist from its purpose because of arguments backed up by the testimony of such great men." Kant, *Perpetual Peace*, p. 17.

in numerous wars with nonliberal states," writes Doyle, "constitutionally secure liberal states have yet to engage in war with one another."[14] Doyle argues that representative states recognize the legitimacy of other liberal states' independence of action. In liberal theory, the individual is the seat of moral value, and a polity that represents autonomous individuals therefore enjoys the right to liberty of action.[15] A liberal and representative state recognizes this liberty, and does not interfere with the policies of other liberal nations. It is the illegitimacy of war against other liberal states, Doyle argues, that has led to the mutual pacifism of democracies.

Calling Kantian theory "a source of insight, policy, and hope," Doyle makes persuasive arguments against realist explanations of the liberal peace, and suggests that the absence of wars must be explained by examining "the workings of liberalism among its own kind."[16] Yet Doyle's work did not go beyond suggesting what empiricists might look for, and empiricists have done surprisingly little to show that elements of liberalism and democracy are causal influences on peace.

Bruce Russett, for instance, concedes that before World War II democracies were too scarce and far apart to have been likely to fight, and "hence the absence of murderous quarrels between democracies was not too surprising, and may need—at least for the pre-1945 era—little further explanation."[17] He lists several other factors that have influenced peace between nations since World War II (alliances, wealth, political stability), and he confines his argument about the effects of democracy on peace to the very recent past. These caveats would seem to argue against the efficacy of liberal theory for explaining international relations, yet the core thesis of Russett's book *Grasping the Democratic Peace* is that democracies do not fight one another. And despite the very limited role that democracy plays in Russett's empirical results, he nonetheless concludes that "the realist top-down, outside-in view . . . misses a great deal."[18]

Defining the Variables

Russett and other scholars argue that Kant's liberal legacy is true, the evidence notwithstanding. In their quest to confirm the liberal worldview, these

---

14. Doyle, "Kant, Liberal Legacies, and Foreign Affairs," Part I, p. 213 (original emphasized).
15. John A. Hall, *Liberalism: Politics, Ideology and the Market* (London: Paladin, 1987).
16. Doyle, "Kant, Liberal Legacies, and Foreign Affairs," Part I, pp. 206 and 224.
17. Russett, *Grasping the Democratic Peace*, p. 26.
18. Russett, *Grasping the Democratic Peace*, p. 93.

authors ignore their own arguments, and they selectively adopt definitions of key variables so that data analysis yields the results they seek.

DEMOCRACY

Democracy is the key concept in theories of the liberal peace, yet it is surprisingly difficult to define and operationalize. How it is defined determines what nations are included in the analysis of whether they are likely to fight one another, and that in turn determines the significance of the liberal peace. Kant quite vehemently differentiated the peaceful republican government from democracy. He saw democracy as a form of tyranny, wherein the majority executed laws despotically against the minority. What Kant called democracy, however, is quite different from modern definitions of liberal democracy. Republicanism, for Kant, was a principle of separating administration of law from legislative power. A republican constitution entailed freedom of the members of society, who were subject to a single legislation, and who were equal by law as citizens. What Kant meant by republicanism applies to nations that Doyle categorizes as liberal regimes.[19] Yet most other authors use definitions of democracy so different from the republics described by Kant that their results cannot bear on his theory, and it is entirely unclear to what theories of democracy and peace their results do pertain.

If there is something about the checks and balances of a constitutional republic, or of a pluralist democracy, or of a liberal regime, that prevents war, then we should expect to observe that democracies fight less than other types of regimes. Since every study (save for that of Rudolph J. Rummel, discussed below) agrees that this structural theory is not validated empirically, the definition of democracy used in empirical tests needs to have some basis in a normative theory of democratic peace.[20] A majority of studies, however, use a data set coded by Ted Gurr ("Polity II") that measures elements of the democratic process, and says nothing about liberal norms. Gurr's variables include competitiveness of participation, regulation of participation, competitiveness of executive recruitment, openness of executive

---

19. It is important to differentiate between Kantian republics, Doyle's liberal regimes, and the democratic processes that are studied by most other scholars. This essay tends to interchange the terms, but the analysis is primarily based on Doyle's liberal regimes.
20. Studies supporting the normative theory include William Dixon, "Democracy and the Management of International Conflict," *Journal of Conflict Resolution*, Vol. 37, No. 1 (March 1993), pp. 42–68; Dixon, "Democracy and the Peaceful Settlement of Conflict," *American Political Science Review*, Vol. 88, No. 1 (March 1994), pp. 14–32; and Maoz and Russett, "Normative and Structural Causes."

recruitment, and constraints on the chief executive.[21] Because these variables are rated on an 11-point scale, researchers using the data must arbitrarily pick a number above which states are democratic, and below which they are not.

The list of democracies compiled by Zeev Maoz (using Polity II) disagrees with Doyle's list of liberal regimes for two-thirds of the nations that either or both list as democratic. For the period 1946–82 they agree on nineteen nations, while they disagree over the years for which eighteen nations were democratic and completely disagree about the nature of twenty-one nations. Using Maoz's cutoff criteria on Gurr's data, France (for example) is not considered democratic after 1981 but El Salvador is, and Belgium was not a democracy until 1956, but for 1946 Columbia, Guatemala, and Turkey are coded as democracies. Gurr's coding results in Argentina, Burma, Cyprus, Czechoslovakia, Guatemala, South Korea, Laos, and Mauritius counting as democracies (for certain years, not for the whole period); and Doyle is alone in considering Bolivia, Brazil, the Dominican Republic, Ecuador, Honduras, Lebanon, Mexico, Nigeria, Philippines, Senegal, Singapore, Sri Lanka, and Trinidad/Tobago to be liberal regimes at various times.[22]

To get at the normative aspect of liberalism, Maoz and Russett used two other variables as proxies. One was stability, which simply meant the number of years that Gurr coded the nation as a democracy. For this reason, Wilhelmine Germany is excluded as a democracy—otherwise World War I would count as a war among democracies.[23] How deeply entrenched must democratic processes be? It is a reasonable guess that nations with entrenched democratic processes are likely to have liberal norms, but societal norms do not necessarily result from entrenched political processes.

---

21. Many studies use democracy variables from ICPSR Study I9263, Ted Robert Gurr, "Polity II: Political Structures and Regime Change, 1800–1986," including Maoz and Russett, "Normative and Structural Causes"; and Dixon, "Democracy and the Management of International Conflict."
22. Maoz and Russett, "Normative and Structural Causes," appendix, reprinted as Russett, *Grasping the Democratic Peace*, p. 94; and Doyle, "Liberalism and World Politics," appendix.
23. Imperial Germany is not in the period that Maoz and Russett study, but Doyle does consider imperial Germany quite carefully, and gives a well-reasoned argument that "the emperor's active role in foreign affairs . . . together with the tenuous constitutional relationship between the chancellor and the Reichstag made imperial Germany a state divorced from the control of its citizenry in foreign affairs." The argument is nonetheless an *ex post facto* description of outcomes rather than a set of *a priori* deductive reasons for why a republic such as imperial Germany should be excluded from the list of liberal states. Doyle, "Kant, Liberal Legacies, and Foreign Affairs," Part I, pp. 216–17, fn. 8.

A second proxy variable for democratic norms was political deaths, as compiled in the Conflict and Peace Data Bank (COPDAB) data set.[24] If a nation's government did not kill its citizens, then it was considered to be a liberal regime. Governments that are violently repressive are not liberal, so the converse is probably (but not necessarily) true. By defining democracy this way, what Maoz and Russett actually find is that an entrenched government that does not kill its own citizens is unlikely to inflict violence on another entrenched government that does not kill its own citizens. This does not contradict the liberal thesis, and it suggests that the liberal thesis is correct, but it is by no means definitive confirmation.

Doyle chose his list of liberal regimes according to whether they had private market-based economies, external sovereignty, citizens with juridical rights, and republican representative governments. These qualifications emphasize liberal norms rather than democratic procedures. Though Doyle's list does not involve quantifying liberal norms, his procedures for selecting nations as liberal are just as rigorous as the coding in Gurr's data set, and they better reflect liberal explanations for why democracies should not fight. Yet this definition of liberalism is so strongly rooted in the present that historical analyses of past centuries may yield us little insight.

To illustrate this point, consider Doyle's categorization of the United States and Switzerland as liberal in the eighteenth century, even though neither permitted women to vote, and the United States permitted slavery. (Indeed, it is open to question whether the United States had a representative government before Jacksonian democracy).[25] Doyle categorizes nations as liberal if they granted female suffrage within a generation of its being demanded. Yet Doyle excludes ancient republics from consideration because "none appear to fit Kant's criteria."[26] Russett argues that ancient democracies tended to ally with one another, but because the state was relatively autonomous, those ancient societies do not provide a test of liberal theory.[27] The question of how much a republic can vary from modern understandings of liberalism

---

24. ICPSR Study I7767, Edward E. Azar, "Conflict and Peace Data Bank (COPDAB), 1948–1978: Daily Events File."
25. I thank Professor Samuel Huntington for suggesting this point.
26. Doyle, "Kant, Liberal Legacies, and Foreign Affairs," Part I, p. 212.
27. Bruce Russett, *Controlling the Sword* (Cambridge: Harvard University Press, 1990), p. 123. See also Bruce Russett and William Antholis, "Democracies Rarely Fight Each Other? Evidence from the Peloponnesian War," *Journal of Peace Research*, Vol. 29, No. 4 (1992), reprinted as Russett, *Grasping the Democratic Peace*, chapter 3.

seems to depend upon the degree of difference rather than a qualitative threshold.

If the form of government is what matters, then it is far from clear why Doyle excludes warlike Athens from Kant's criteria, particularly if standards for liberalism depend upon the contemporaneous prejudices in each historical period. If, as Doyle stresses, the normative aspects of liberalism are important, then the question of when illiberalism can be ignored seems to depend on the extent to which we tolerate the disenfranchisement of individuals other than wealthy white males at various points in recent history. It is disingenuous to claim that societies are liberal if unempowered groups are able to vote sometime after they get around to asking for it.

On the other hand, there will always be a wide gap between the ideal-type of equality among citizens and the reality of socioeconomic, racial, and gender-based inequalities. Indeed, perhaps a defining characteristic of liberal societies should be that groups constantly challenge and contest the system, because this would indicate true freedom of thought, and a true evolution of individual empowerment.

The advantage of using contemporaneous standards is that they provide a threshold for deciding which nations are liberal. Maoz and Russett reported that their analyses did not change very much when they changed their cutoff points for democracy using Gurr's scaling. Because they restricted their analysis to the period from 1946–86, one would not expect that contemporaneous conceptions of liberalism would have changed much. The shifting threshold is much more of a problem for studies that consider longer sweeps of history. The importance of democratic thresholds goes beyond academic debates. It is also the most policy-relevant question for this body of literature as waves of democratization and liberalization sweep the globe, though not necessarily in synchrony.

Perhaps the most useful solution is offered by John Owen, who studies public and elite opinion on whether or not a potential adversary is democratic.[28] What matters for Owen is not how analysts define democracy, but rather how the populace that is supposed to be sharing liberal norms understands the character of other regimes. Although this is an innovative contribution to case studies of democratic dyads, it is not yet possible to apply it to every dyad in the world between 1816 and the present, which puts this approach out of reach for studies such as this one.

---

28. Owen, "Testing the Democratic Peace."

WAR

Edward D. Mansfield has demonstrated quite convincingly that how an analyst chooses data sets on war determines the conclusions yielded by the data analysis.[29] The problems for studies of democracies and war include what we consider as war, whether we include civil wars, and how we treat possible exceptions to the "rule" that democracies never fight. This study is concerned only with interstate wars, which excludes lower levels of international conflict and civil wars. Civil wars are excluded because we need to distinguish between domestic violence and interstate conflict.

This exclusion has the unfortunate consequence of removing from consideration one of the bloodiest conflicts in history, the American Civil War, while very low-level conflicts, such as the 1969 "Football War" between El Salvador and Honduras, meet the definition of interstate war. Excluding the American Civil War is also disturbing because it may provide a good example of what is wrong with liberal theory. During that war, both sides were democracies, and yet we can understand completely why democracies would fight over something so vital as the concept of national identity. In some cases it may be possible that a conflict of interests is so deep and abiding that nations fight despite the fact that they are both liberal democracies. This would suggest that the clash of national interests at the systemic level remains our primary tool for understanding international conflict.

In a study of exceptions to the rule that democracies never fight one another, James Lee Ray argues that the Confederacy was not truly democratic.[30] Its president, Jefferson Davis, was elected to a provisional first term of one year by representatives from secession conventions. Because the Confederacy lost, it never had time to establish the democratic precedent that one party would step down if it lost. (Japan did not establish that precedent either until very recently.) And what is most telling to Ray is that women and slaves, accounting for well over half of the population, were excluded from elections.

These reasons for excluding the Civil War are not specific to the Confederacy, but Ray does not apply them to other democracies that fought only with non-democracies. The constitution and constitutional practices of the

---

29. Edward D. Mansfield, "The Distribution of Wars Over Time," *World Politics*, Vol. 41, No. 1 (October 1988), pp. 21–51.
30. James Lee Ray, "Wars Between Democracies: Rare, or Nonexistent?" *International Interactions*, Vol. 18, No. 3 (1993), pp. 251–276.

North and South were nearly identical: women and slaves did not vote in the Union either. What prevents the South from now being considered a democracy is that it did not win the war.

Other authors have cited many possible interstate wars between liberal democracies, always finding reasons for exceptions. Doyle mentions in a footnote that Peru and Ecuador engaged in armed conflict while both were liberal regimes, but "the war came within one to three years after the establishment of a liberal regime, that is, before the pacifying effects of liberalism could become deeply ingrained."[31] The Israeli invasion of Lebanon in 1981 might also count as a war between democracies, but Lebanon's government was in shambles and the armies of Syria and the PLO were already operating on its territory. Because the War of 1812 between the United States and Great Britain came before the start (1816) of the Singer and Small data set, Doyle's study does not consider it. In any case, Doyle classifies Great Britain as illiberal before the electoral reforms of 1832. He also excludes covert interventions, such as the efforts by the United States to destabilize Chile after Allende was democratically elected.

Rummel, who examined levels of interstate conflict less violent than warfare, suggests that the Israeli attack on the American intelligence gathering ship *USS Liberty* in 1967 might count as an exception to the rule. He dismisses this example because Israel was "only partially free" due to its mixed capitalist-socialist economy.[32] David Lake cites the Spanish-American War of 1898 and the Finnish alliance with the Axis powers in World War Two as examples of wars between democracies. By Doyle's definition, Spain only became a liberal regime in 1978, but Lake's article, making use of the Polity II data set, codes Spain as democratic in 1898.[33] Maoz and Russett are careful to say that democracies "rarely" go to war with each other, because of these findings, which they term "borderline cases." (They themselves find *no* incidence of wars between democracies.)[34]

In Ray's examination of possible exceptions to the rule that democracies never fight one another, he finds that all can be explained away. The Second Philippines War of 1899, in which the United States defeated a democratic

---

31. Doyle, "Kant, Liberal Legacies, and Foreign Affairs," Part I, p. 213.
32. Rummel, "Libertarianism and International Violence," pp. 29–30.
33. Lake, "Powerful Pacifists," pp. 28, 33, and 35.
34. Zeev Maoz and Bruce Russett, "Alliances, Distance, Wealth, and Political Stability: Is the Lack of Conflict among Democracies a Statistical Artifact?" *International Interactions*, Vol. 17, No. 3 (1992), p. 264, fn. 2.

republic, does not count because the Philippines did not have time to hold elections before it lost to the United States. Because Hitler suspended the constitution in 1933, it does not matter that he had been elected or that the suspension was legal.[35] When Israel invaded democratic Lebanon in 1948 it was a new state, and had not yet held elections.

We might dismiss each of these examples as a trivial exception, except for the case of Finland in World War II. Although Lake calls this "an easily explained exception," explanation is not the same as disqualification.[36] Because Finland, which had been a liberal democracy since 1919, fought to avoid annexation by the Soviet Union, it joined the alliance of fascist powers from 1941 to 1944. There were no attacks by Finnish troops on the armies of liberal democracies, but the fact that it joined the opposing alliance and fought against one of the central powers in the alliance technically puts Finland at war with five liberal regimes from 1941–44, and also France in 1944. The data set used by Doyle lists Finland as opposing the Allies, but it is not mentioned in his essays.

Ray explains that although Finland was democratic, "there was never any direct military conflict between Finland and Great Britain," and it was not officially at war with the United States or France.[37] In fact, Finland refused an offer of assistance from the Allied forces against Germany in return for a peace treaty with the USSR in 1940. This decision was carried out with the full knowledge of the popularly elected parliament, and the policy was continued after a peaceful transfer of power between Presidents Kallio and Ryti in December 1940.[38] Great Britain did bomb Finland at least once, on July 30, 1941.[39] Faced with a choice of surrendering to the USSR in June 1944 or allying with Germany to ensure military supplies, President Ryti decided to bind with Germany. This was contrary to the preferences of the Parliament,

---

35. I do not mean to imply that Nazi Germany should be coded as democratic, but it is disturbing that this regime came about as the result of a democratic election. What is the utility of a theory predicting the absence of wars between democracies if a democratically elected leader can legally suspend the constitution, quickly change the regime to a fascist one, and then initiate a global war?
36. Lake, "Powerful Pacifists," p. 28.
37. Ray, "Wars Between Democracies: Rare, or Nonexistent?" p. 271.
38. I thank Gina Marie Finan for her research assistance on Finland. For further analysis of this period, see R. Michael Berry, *American Foreign Policy and the Finnish Exception: Ideological Preferences and Wartime Realities* (Helsinki: Suomen Historiallinen Seura, 1987); D.G. Kirby, *Finland in the Twentieth Century* (London: C. Hurst and Company, 1979); and Henrik S. Nissen, ed., *Scandinavia During the Second World War* (Minneapolis: University of Minneapolis Press, 1983).
39. Nissen, *Scandinavia During the Second World War*, p. 85.

and two months later Ryti was replaced in elections by Mannerheim, who began peace negotiations with the USSR. Thus, in a democratic state, a leader who pursued an alliance with fascists and who declared war on democracies was not re-elected, and his successor chose a different policy; democratic checks and balances led to Mannerheim's election. They did not, however, prevent Ryti from allying with fascists. The fact that Mannerheim pursued peace with the USSR should prove it was possible for Presidents Kallio and Ryti to have made different choices before 1944.

These exceptions point to a weakness in the claim for a liberal peace, because they illustrate that it is possible for different researchers to code liberalism and democracy differently. If the claim is to be an absolute one, as Rummel suggests, the implication is that there must be a threshold of democratization or of liberalism that prevents wars against nations that are also beyond the threshold. Furthermore, because the literature on democracy and war is highly empirical, it is important to remember that the subjective judgments by which variables are coded in data sets have significant and important effects on the results yielded by analysis of those data.

Testing for the Significance of Zero Wars

Obviously, the probability that two nations will go to war is determined by many factors. Although students of international relations do not know precisely how to explain past wars, we are certain that they are not due to random chance: societies do not flip coins to decide whether and against whom to commit acts of organized violence. In statistical analysis, the measure of the significance of a relationship between variables is usually compared to the "null hypothesis" of random chance. If we cannot reject the null hypothesis of random chance, it does not mean we must accept random chance as an explanation, but it does mean that we should reject the hypothesis being tested.

In evaluating whether the absence of war between liberal democracies confirms a liberal theory of international relations, we should at least be able to say that the outcome "zero wars" is different from what random chance would predict. Or, to go back to the analogy of playing a lottery, we need to know whether it is puzzling that no one in a particular family ever wins a lottery. If it is natural and expected that no one win a lottery in one family, then there is no reason to spend a lot of time researching what it is about the family that prevents it from winning. The question then, is whether the absence of an event is likely and expected by chance alone. Random chance is not the reason that nations do or do not fight. But if the distribution of wars among democracies is not statistically different from that which is generated by random chance, then the democratic peace is not confirming evidence for liberal theory.

We need to consider pairings, or dyads, of nations because the question is not whether a particular nation was likely to have fought a war, but rather whether pairings of nations were likely to have been at war.[40] This emphasis on pairings of nations, or dyads, significantly changes the way we think about the likelihood of war between democracies. Consider this example: in 1980, there were 156 nation-states in the world, of which 40 were liberal regimes.[41] There were two interstate wars (Russia in Afghanistan, and Iran-Iraq), involving four countries. This implies that 26 percent of all nations were liberal democracies (40/156), and the absence of wars between them seems striking. A consideration of dyadic relationships, however, gives a much different picture.

Given nations A, B, and C, there are three nations and three dyads; but a fourth nation gives a total of six dyads (AB, AC, AD, BC, BD, CD), and seven nations constitute twenty-one dyads. For 1980, the 156 nations in the world made 12,090 possible dyads, of which 780 were dyads of liberal democracies, and only 2 dyads were at war. Put this way, only 6 percent of the possible one-on-one pairings of nations were liberal, and the dyads at war were two one-hundredths of 1 percent of the total. It no longer seems so striking that democracies were not at war, because dyads at war were extremely rare in 1980.[42]

---

40. Benjamin Most and Harvey Starr, *Inquiry, Logic, and International Politics* (Columbia: University of South Carolina Press, 1989). Studies that emphasize the use of dyadic relationships include Steve Chan, "Mirror, Mirror on the Wall . . .: Are the Freer Countries More Pacific?" *Journal of Conflict Resolution*, Vol. 28, No. 4 (December 1984), pp. 617–648; Maoz and Abdolali, "Regime Types and International Conflict"; Randoph M. Siverson and Juliann Emmons, "Birds of a Feather," *Journal of Conflict Resolution*, Vol. 35, No. 2 (June 1991), pp. 285–306; Maoz and Russett, "Normative and Structural Causes," appendix; and Stuart A. Bremer, "Dangerous Dyads: Conditions Affecting the Likelihood of Interstate War, 1816–1965," *Journal of Conflict Resolution*, Vol. 36, No. 2 (June 1992), pp. 309–342.
41. The figure for existing nation-states is from ICPSR Study I9044, Singer and Small, "Wages of War," and the data on liberal democracies is adapted from Doyle, "Liberalism and World Politics."
42. Randall Schweller points out that by such logic, 1914 would appear to be a peaceful year because only 18 out of a total of 946 dyads (less than 2 percent) were at war. This would seem to be a powerful argument against measuring the proportion of all dyads at war, but rather than rejecting the "peace of 1914" as ridiculous, perhaps we should pay attention to the numerical

To consider the significance of zero wars between liberal democracies, I computed the probability that zero wars was different from what we could expect to find given a random distribution of wars among dyads. The method of computation is the same as comparing the make-up of a sample to the entire population, where the probability that the sample is like the entire population has what is known as a "hypergeometric distribution."[43] In essence, the question I asked was, given a certain number of nation-dyads at war in one year, and given a certain number of democratic dyads (call the number d), if d dyads were selected at random, what would be the probability of finding none of them at war?

Imagine a bin full of balls, some of which are plain and some of which are red. If there are 50 plain balls and 50 red ones (thoroughly mixed), and we draw a number of balls from the bin, then what is the probability that the sample we drew has a certain mix of plain and red? Over a very large number of trials, the average proportion of plain to red balls in the samples should be the same as the 50–50 proportion in the general population. Each individual sample, however, is likely to differ slightly from the general population.

In this example, the probability of finding 5 red and 5 plain balls in a 10-ball sample is only 26 percent. (The likelihood of finding 4 red and 6 plain, or 6 red and 4 plain, is 0.41; 3–7 or 7–3 is 0.22; 2–8 or 8–2 is 0.08; and 1–9 or 9–1 is 0.01). Zero would be a very striking statistic in this example, because the probability of drawing 10 balls that are all one color is only six one-hundredths of one percent. The probability distribution of finding different mixes of colors is said to be hypergeometric.[44]

Now imagine that the bin is filled with all of the possible nation-state dyads for a given year. The balls are either "at war (red)" or "not at war (white)." We choose a sample, the number of which equals the number of

---

evidence: 1914 was, indeed, a terribly violent year for white men in Europe, but the global majority of nations, people, and territory were not, in fact, at war.

43. Explaining probability theory is far beyond the scope of this article. A lucid explanation of probabilities with special distributions is in Morris H. DeGroot, *Probability and Statistics* (Reading, Mass.: Addison-Wesley, 1986).

44. The distribution is hypergeometric because when each ball in the sample is drawn without replacement, its color affects the likelihood that the next ball will be of the same color—the proportion of red to plain balls in the bin changes slightly as each ball is removed. The probability is determined as follows, with n being the number of balls in the bin, m the number of balls of type 1 (so that n − m are type 2), s the number chosen without replacement from the bin, and x the number of balls of type 1 drawn:

$$\text{probability} = \frac{(m!/x!)/(m\text{-}x)! * (n - m)!/(s - x)!/((n - m) - (s - x))!}{(n!/s!)/(n - s)!}$$

democratic dyads during that year. What is the probability that the sample contains no dyads "at war"? In 1980, for example, there were 12,090 dyads among nations, and 3 of those dyads were at war; so fewer than 2/100 of one percent of the dyads were at war. Democracies formed 780 dyads (6.5 percent of the total). If war dyads were completely evenly distributed among all nations, then we would expect to find 0.2 wars among democratic dyads (2/100 of one percent of 780 dyads). The chance of taking any 780 dyads and finding 0 at war in 1980 is 82.9 percent. Thus the odds are over 8 in 10 that we will not find any wars among democracies for that year, if war is distributed randomly. Therefore, zero is not significant.

I tested the probability of finding zero liberal dyads at war for each year from 1816 to 1980.[45] To give the liberal thesis as much of a chance as possible, if a nation was at war for part of a year, no matter how short a time, it was considered to be at war during that year. Similarly, nations that became liberal regimes at any point during a year were counted as liberal for the whole year.[46]

WALKING THROUGH THE RESULTS

The results of the computations for each year 1816–1980 are presented in the Appendix. Column 7 lists the number of liberal dyads that were at war in each year, which was zero for all years but 1941–45 (discussed below). Column 8, "Random Probability of 7," shows the likelihood that zero wars is due to random chance. (For 1941–45 the statistic shows the random chance of finding 4–5 liberal dyads at war.) Where the probability is one, there is a 100 percent likelihood of finding zero liberal dyads at war (or, conversely, a zero likelihood of finding any liberal dyads at war). In other words, Column 8 is the probability that zero wars is due to random chance.

The figure for "Wars Expected Among Liberals" (Column 9) is computed by applying the ratio of all dyads at war to the number of liberal dyads. If

---

45. I am indebted to Professor Gary King, who does not endorse the use of a random null hypothesis in this case, for providing the Gauss program for hypergeometric distributions. I rewrote the program in QBasic so that it will run on most IBM-compatible computers. For a copy of the program and the data, send e-mail to dspiro@arizona.edu.
46. The only changes made to the Singer and Small data set were for Germany in 1918 (since it was liberal for part of the year, unmodified data would have resulted in five liberal dyads at war), and for France in 1940 (I made 1939 the last year it was liberal, because it entered war dyads as an illiberal regime in 1940). Two other modifications to the data are discussed below.

half of all dyads were at war, and there were 10 liberal dyads, then we would expect to find 5 liberal dyads at war. Column 10 is the standard deviation.[47]

The data for the probabilities are depicted graphically in Figure 1. Each bar on the graph is the probability of finding zero wars between liberal democracies for the year indicated below the X axis. For those years where the bar reaches to the top of the graph (i.e., the probability is 1.0), it means that there is *no chance at all* that there could be wars between liberal democracies. Only for those years where the bars drop below 0.2 is there any possible statistical significance to finding zero liberal dyads at war. The bars are consistently high throughout the nineteenth century, up until World War I, which means that the absence of wars between democracies is strongly predicted by random chance (an exception, though not a significant one, is 1866, which is discussed below). From 1914 to 1918, where the bars are quite short, the absence of wars between democracies is not due to random chance, and this period requires explanation. During World War II the short bars also indicate statistical significance, but what is significant is that liberal dyads were, in fact, at war. More than one dozen bars in the postwar period are between 0.4 and 0.6, which means that the probability of finding no democracies at war is between 40 and 60 percent. Although these probabilities are less striking than those for other years, they indicate nonetheless that the liberal peace does not differ significantly from a null hypothesis of random chance.

Even Kant saw "the natural state" as warlike. Yet the results of the probability analysis show that all-out war is not a very common occurrence. Singer and Small identified 67 interstate wars from 1816 to 1980, and Chan reported that nations were involved in an average of 0.032 wars per year over the same period.[48] (He also pointed out that the four nations involved in the highest numbers of wars per year, Israel, India, France, and the United Kingdom, are democracies.) Of the 176 states that existed at some point from 1816 to 1980, more than half were never involved in a war.

During the nineteenth century, the absence of wars between democracies is not significant, and does not require explanation: from 1816 to 1829, there was only one liberal dyad, between the United States and the Swiss Confederation. In 1830 and 1831 the number of liberal dyads rose to six, when

---

47. For those who do not know what standard deviation means, skip column 10.
48. Chan, "Mirror, Mirror on the Wall . . . : Are the Freer Countries More Pacific?" pp. 627–628.

Figure 1. Random Probability of Zero Wars Between Liberal Dyads.

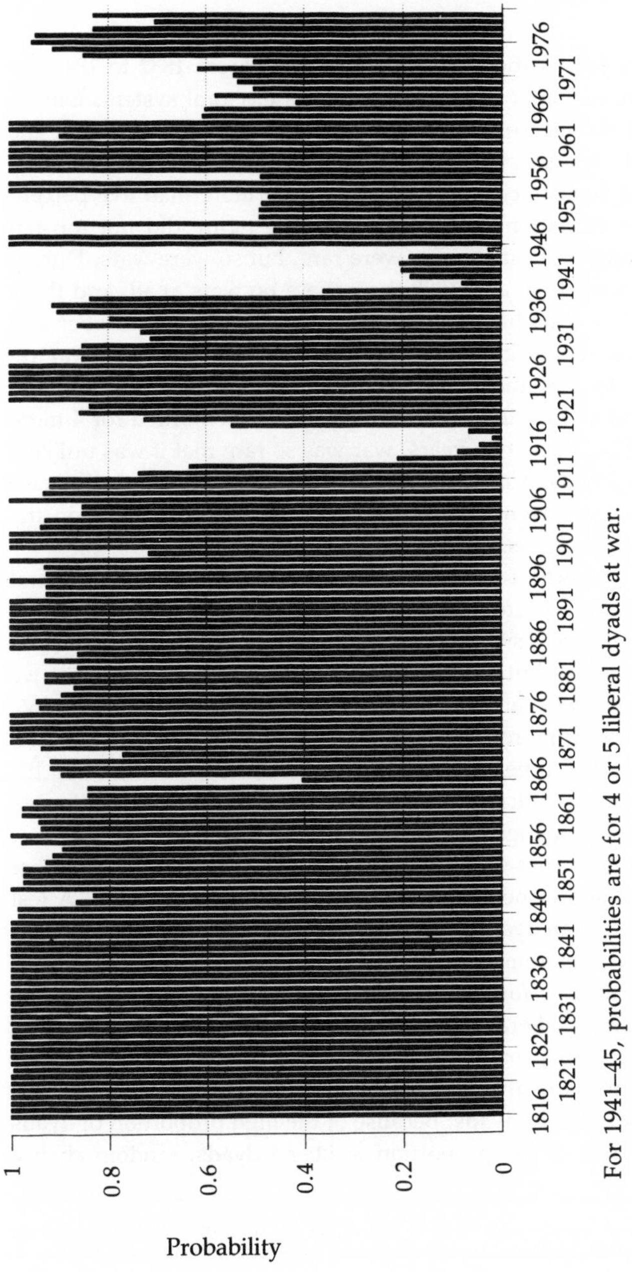

For 1941–45, probabilities are for 4 or 5 liberal dyads at war.

Belgium and France joined the club of democracies. From 1832 to 1847 the number rose to ten, as Great Britain reformed its electoral system. During this time the total number of dyads nearly doubled, which lowered the proportion of liberal dyads in the international system.

Until 1871, liberal democracies did not account for more than five percent of the total number of nation-state dyads, and the figure did not top ten percent until this century. Democracies were rare, but so were wars. During 44 of the years between 1816 and 1899 there were no wars at all, and there was only one dyad at war during 21 of the years. While the number and percentage of liberal dyads grew during the nineteenth century, war remained infrequent. In 1866 the Seven Weeks War added 21 to the number of dyads at war, and in 1870 the Franco-Prussian War accounted for 4 more war dyads. Aside from those two years, war was so rare that it was unlikely for any dyad to be involved in conflict. For the nineteenth century, peace was too common an occurrence to require explanation by variation in the number of liberal democracies.

If we apply the proportion of all dyads at war to the number of liberal dyads, the result is the expected random distribution of wars for the liberal population. From 1816 to 1899, we would expect fewer than 0.10 liberal dyads to be at war for all but eleven of the years. The probability that we would find no liberal dyads at war is quite high for each year, except 1866, discussed below. During more than half of the years, no dyad was at war, so the probability in those years of finding no liberal dyads at war is 100 percent. The probability of drawing zero liberal dyads at war from the bin of all dyads is consistently high for the rest of the century.

The number of democracies grew in the twentieth century, but the number of democratic dyads shows no correlation with the number of wars. A test of the relationship between dyads at war and liberal dyads over time indicates that this relationship is extremely weak.[49]

The tests of probabilities for the twentieth century also suggest that the absence of wars between liberal states is by and large random. This century has been much more war-prone than the last, with an absence of dyads at war for only 22 years, and the wars that have occurred were longer and involved a greater number of dyads. Because of the high proportion of dyads at war, and the growth of the proportion of liberal dyads, random chance

---

49. I did an Ordinary Least Squares regression on war dyads as a function of liberal dyads from 1816 to 1980. The correlation coefficient is very small, and the adjusted R-squared is 0.001.

would lead us to expect many more liberal dyads at war for the twentieth century. By contrast with the previous century, there are only 32 years after 1900 for which the expected number of liberal dyads at war is less than 0.10. The periods for which one would expect the greatest number of liberal dyads at war are not surprising: the years of World Wars I and II, and the Korean conflict.

What is most interesting is that 1940–1944 are five of the six years for which we would expect the highest number of wars between liberal regimes in the 167-year sample (the other is 1917). During those years, when random chance predicts that there should have been liberal regimes at war, there were indeed liberal regimes at war.

During the Second World War, Finland was not at war in 1940 and in 1945, and the low probabilities for those two years suggest that the absence of war between liberal regimes is noteworthy. On the other hand, because there was a conflict involving Finland for four of the six years, the results for 1940 and 1945 hardly serve to confirm liberal theory. For the war as a whole, we find as many liberal dyads at war as would be predicted by chance.

World War I is a different story. Unless one really wants to make the argument that imperial Germany was a liberal democracy (and I do not), the results for 1914–18 suggest that the absence of wars between liberal states is significant. This period is an exception to the overall findings. For this brief period, we need to explain why no democracies fought one another. World War I is the only conflict that raises a question about why democracies did not fight. For every other year since the end of the Napoleonic Wars (which is when the data set began), there is no puzzle that requires (or supports) liberal theories of peace.

MODIFICATIONS TO THE DATA SETS

For the Seven Weeks War in 1866 and the Korean Conflict, the absence of conflict among liberal dyads would have been more significant had I not modified the data set. My modifications, however, were quite minor, and the significance would have depended upon counting very small-scale participation in wars by inconsequential actors. For the sake of simplicity and continuity with other published results, I used the Singer and Small list of international wars (which excludes civil wars), from 1816 to 1980.[50] It defines

---

50. ICPSR I9044, Singer and Small, "Wages of War."

an interstate war as a series of armed conflicts between at least two sovereign nations, involving at least 1000 battle deaths. The list of nations that existed in each year also comes from this data set, which excludes countries with populations of less than 500,000 (e.g., Andorra or Vanuatu).

In using this data set, I treated all wars and all participants in wars equally, so long as more than 1000 troops in total died on battle-fields. But many small wars in the data set inflate the number of dyads that are counted as "at war." Between July 14 and 18, 1969, El Salvador and Honduras fought the "Football War," and a total of 1900 troops died (700 from El Salvador). During World War II, according to the data set, a total of 15,171,226 soldiers from 29 participating nations died on battlefields. In the probability analysis I did for this study, El Salvador and Honduras make one dyad at war, just as the Soviet Union and Nazi Germany during World War II make one dyad at war. The relative importance and destructiveness of wars is not considered.[51]

I include smaller and relatively less important wars in the analysis because the effect of such inclusion is to bias the results toward making zero wars between democracies more significant. With more "at war" dyads in the bin of balls, it is more likely that the sample we choose (of democratic dyads) should have some "at war" dyads. Therefore, the finding of zero should be more difficult to explain as coming from a random distribution.

Minor modification to the data set is necessary because for certain years the number of dyads at war is inflated by minimal or token participation of nations in coalitions. In 1866, for example, there were four wars involving 19 different nations. The Franco-Mexican War lasted from 1862 to 1867 with 20,000 casualties; the Lopez War from 1864 to 1870 involved Paraguay against Argentina and Brazil with 310,000 casualties; and the Spanish-Chilean War from late October 1865 to May 1866 involved Chile and Peru against Spain with 1,000 casualties.[52] Together these three wars comprise five dyads. Given a total of 861 total nation-state dyads in 1866, this does not make a large proportion of dyads at war. The Seven Weeks War, however, involved 11 nations, many of them suffering only minimal casualties. Prussia, Italy, and Mecklenburg-Schwerin fought against Austro-Hungary, Saxony, Bavaria,

---

51. The data set does distinguish major power wars, and it contains enough data to differentiate between wars of various magnitudes, which is why the problem lies with my use of the data set, and not the data set itself.

52. Argentina did not join the Lopez War until March 5, 1865, and Peru joined the Spanish-Chilean War for only four months beginning in January 1866.

Hanover, Wuerttemburg, Electoral Hesse, and Grand Ducal Hesse; this makes for an additional 24 dyads at war. During this short conflict, 36,100 men died on the battlefield, and 34,000 (or 94 percent) of those deaths were suffered by Austro-Hungary, Prussia, and Italy. If we were to exclude the other eight participants from the data set, the Seven Weeks War would account for only two dyads at war. Even if we were to include all of the participants except for Mecklenburg-Schwerin, which suffered 100 casualties, there would be 8 fewer dyads at war in 1866. Mecklenburg-Schwerin (which existed for 24 years from 1843 to 1867) just barely made the Singer and Small data set, because its population is the smallest of any nation. Had the arbitrary cut-off point for a nation's population been 600,000 rather than 500,000 Mecklenburg-Schwerin's participation would have been considered "extrasystemic," and it would have been grouped with colonial or imperial wars.

These are important considerations, because with 29 dyads at war in 1866 among a total population of 861 nation-state dyads, the probability that we would find zero wars among 36 democratic dyads is only 28 percent. This figure is still above the confidence levels that are commonly employed by social scientists, but it does suggest that the difference between the number of wars (1.21) random chance leads us to expect among democratic dyads, and the absence of wars between democratic dyads bears further examination. When we exclude Mecklenburg-Schwerin from the Seven Weeks War (and let us be honest—how many readers had even heard of the place before now?) so that the number of dyads at war is reduced to 21 for 1866, then the probability of finding zero wars among democracies rises to 40 percent. This figure still suggests that a finding of zero wars may not be due to random chance, but the significance of zero is quite open to question. Finally, if we consider the Seven Weeks War to be a conflict of Prussia and Italy against Austro-Hungary, then only 7 dyads were at war in 1866, and the probability of finding zero wars among democracies rises to 74 percent. In this last case, it is very difficult to argue for the significance of zero wars. As a compromise, I included all of the participants in the Seven Weeks War except for Mecklenburg-Schwerin.

The analysis is similarly affected by the number of participants in the Korean conflict. The United Nations forces that battled China and North Korea included not only South Korea and the United States, but also Turkey, the UK, Canada, France, Australia, Greece, Colombia, Ethiopia, Thailand, Holland, Belgium, and the Philippines. An average of 44 Belgians died each year on Korean battlefields which, although sad, is less than the number of

Belgians who died in 1953 because they fell off of ladders.[53] Perhaps this low number of fatalities should not qualify as adding two war dyads to the international system for 1951–53.

The United States suffered 54,000 fatalities in Korea, and nearly 2 million Koreans and Chinese died. The other twelve nations who joined the side of the United Nations lost a little over 3,100, or 0.16 percent of the total casualties. When we count all 28 dyads involved in the Korean conflict, the probability of finding no wars among democracies is 0.2 percent, or one in five hundred.[54] If, however, the Korean Conflict is analyzed as consisting of war between four nations (and involving four dyads), the probability that we would find no liberal dyads at war in 1950–53 is around 40 percent. The results are not significant in either direction. The figure of four dyads at war during the Korean Conflict is used in the probability analysis.

The Seven Weeks War and the Korean Conflict are the only two wars for which the results are affected by a wide divergence in the participation of coalition partners. It is tempting to censor out all war participants that suffered disproportionately low casualties compared to the war's total. Yet this would result in omitting all wars for which one side enjoyed a preponderance of force (the United States in the Gulf War, for instance). Another rule of thumb might be to expunge those coalition partners with much smaller losses than the dominant member of the coalition (e.g., Mecklenberg-Schwerin suffered 100 dead, compared to 10,000 for Prussia and 4,000 for Italy). But this would not be entirely proper because we are looking at the democratic nation as a unit of analysis, not the individual in a democracy. Mecklenberg-Schwerin lost 0.17 percent of its population in the war, which is precisely the same proportion as for Italy (indeed the ratios are so similar as to make the figures suspect). The problem can be solved by comparing the battle casualties per month of fighting per million population among the different members of a coalition. For the United Nations forces in Korea, the figures

---

53. I thank Brad Joseph for research assistance on this statistic, which is from the World Health Organization.
54. The results are:

Year	Probability	Expected liberal dyads at war	Standard deviation
1950	0.056	2.594	1.450
1951	0.002	5.512	2.094
1952	0.003	5.231	2.053
1953	0.002	5.407	2.080

In 1950 China had not joined the war, so the number of dyads at war was half that of 1951–53.

are presented in Table 1. If we arbitrarily set the cut-off for the ratio some-where between one fifth of one percent and 1.75 percent, then South Korea and the United States are included in the Korean Conflict, but the other twelve nations are not. This rule of thumb does not, however, work to simplify 1866.

I also made one other adjustment to the analysis, which differs from some of the literature on democracy and war, but is in keeping with the Singer and Small data. According to the data sets, Finland was a democracy and it was at war with the Allied powers during World War II. Although it did not deploy troops against the allies, Finland did save Germany from worrying about another front, and it confronted Soviet troops who otherwise would have been contributing to the Allied effort. In any event, the Singer and Small data set does not specify that troops from a nation must be in con-frontation with troops from every nation of the opposing alliance in order to be considered as a participant in the conflict. To be consistent, we need to count Finland as a democracy at war with other democracies, which means that for 1941 to 1944, the results measure the probability of finding 4 liberal dyads at war (5 in 1944).

I have included Finland's alliance with the Axis powers for three reasons. The first is that the data analysis in the literature usually follows the coding

Table 1. The Distribution of Casualties Among the United Nations Forces in the Korean Conflict.

	Battle deaths	Battle deaths per month of fighting per million population	Ratio compared to South Korea
South Korea	415,000	547	100 %
United States	54,000	9.6	1.77%
Turkey	720	1.0	0.19%
United Kingdom	670	0.4	0.07%
Canada	310	0.7	0.13%
France	290	0.2	0.04%
Australia	281	1.1	0.20%
Greece	170	0.7	0.14%
Colombia	140	0.5	0.09%
Ethiopia	120	0.3	0.05%
Thailand	110	0.2	0.03%
Netherlands	110	0.4	0.07%
Belgium	100	0.4	0.07%
Philippines	90	0.1	0.02%

in data sets, without *ad hoc* changes for cases that contradict the authors' hypotheses. Singer and Small coded Finland as at war with the liberal alliance during World War II, and so should studies that use the data set. The second reason is that war dyads were not pared down to exclude nations that did not actually fight one another, even though they were on opposing sides. If this were done for the present study, the "observation" of no liberal dyads at war from 1941 to 1944 would require explanation, but the number of war dyads for other years would drop substantially, and that would make the random probability of finding no liberal dyads at war much higher. Finally, for the reasons outlined in the section above, I believe that Finland should be counted as a liberal democracy that threw in its lot with those of fascist powers against other liberal democracies, and the inclusion of this conflict is not a mere technicality.[55]

TESTING MULTI-YEAR PERIODS

In his 1983 essay, Doyle was quick to point out that war between any two nations is a low-probability event for a short period of time. Because war between adjacent states is more probable over a longer timeframe, however, he argued that "the absence of war among the more clearly liberal states, whether adjacent or not, for almost two hundred years thus has some significance."[56] Elsewhere, Doyle suggested that the type of analysis presented in this article should be applied to periods of longer than one year.[57]

The problem with doing such an analysis is that very few states were continuously liberal for longer periods, and by the same token, very few states that participated in wars were extant for long periods. Only 12 nations were continuously in existence for the 150-year period 1833–1982, and only 3 of them were liberal. It is easier to study shorter periods, but the question

---

55. If the figures are changed so that no liberal dyads were at war, the results would be as follows:

Year	Probability	Expected liberal dyads at war	Standard deviation
1941	0.183	5.32	2.17
1942	0.141	3.56	1.79
1943	0.172	4.16	1.93
1944	0.145	4.72	2.05

56. Doyle, "Kant, Liberal Legacies, and Foreign Affairs," Part I, p. 217.
57. Comments during the panel "Do Democracies Fight?" annual meeting of the American Political Science Association, Chicago, 1992.

becomes how to select the length of the period that is both long enough to satisfy Doyle's critique, and short enough to provide data.

Rather than making that decision, I analyzed all of the possible periods from 1816 to 1982 of 5 years, 10 years, 20 years, and then in 10-year increments up to 150 years. I only included nations that existed for the entire period and liberal regimes that were liberal for the entire period. If two nations were at war for at least one day of the entire period, then they counted as one war dyad.[58] The results are not at all what one would expect.

For the shorter five and ten-year periods, the probability of democracies going to war is low, just as in the one-year periods used above. For the twenty-year periods beginning and ending in the nineteenth century, the likelihood of finding liberal regimes at war is still low, but slightly higher than for one-year periods. The twenty-year periods that included World War I indicate that the absence of wars between liberal regimes was significant. The other significant values for the twentieth century are for periods in which Finland was at war with the Allied powers. Though they were not below significant confidence levels, the probabilities for many of the other twenty-year periods of the twentieth century are below fifty percent; that is, the chance that the absence of liberal-liberal wars is random is less than fifty percent.

The probabilities found during thirty and forty-year periods are also low for those that include World War I and the periods in which Finland fought. The remainder of these lengths of periods have much higher probabilities. As the periods get longer, the analysis indicates that the absence of wars between liberal regimes is predicted by random chance. Only for twenty, thirty, and forty year periods do the results yield significant findings, and then only for World War I. In the analysis of single-year periods, World War I was also an exception to the insignificance of the liberal peace. Liberal theory would predict that longer periods should demonstrate what is unusual and unexpected about the absence of wars between democracies. Yet it is the shorter periods that are consistent with the analysis of single years, while the longer periods confirm that the absence of wars between democracies is

---

58. They do not count for more than one dyad, no matter how many years they were at war. Henry S. Farber and Joanne Gowa, "Polities and Peace," mimeo, Princeton University, January 11, 1994, argue that liberal theory predicts that wars *will not break out* between democracies, so observations of continued wars between non-democratic or mixed dyads is irrelevant. The numerical results and the program used to produce them is available on internet. Send a request to dspiro@arizona.edu.

no different from random chance. Thus the analysis of longer periods is strong confirmation of the analysis of single years. As expected, the average probability levels decrease for longer periods, but they are still far above any confidence level for significance. Only for the shorter periods do we find significant probabilities, and they are for the timespans that include World War I.

Conclusions and Implications

These statistical findings seem to confirm Mearsheimer's speculation that "democracies have been few in number over the past two centuries, and thus there have not been many cases where two democracies were in a position to fight each other."[59] Yet there is a wide and vigorous empirical literature that has supported the claims of liberal theorists that democracies do not fight.[60] How are we to reconcile these findings?

The strongest claim for liberal theory was made by Rummel, in a series of papers on libertarianism and pacifism.[61] Rummel tested the relationship between what he calls "freedom" and pacifism. By Rummel's definition, people are less free in Sweden, Denmark, and Israel because "such centralized, semi-socialist governments introduce a considerable measure of coercion that contributes to foreign violence."[62]

Rummel's results are significant, but only for a very limited time period (1976 to 1980). He found that libertarian states did not act violently toward one another, and that the more libertarian a state, the less likely it was to use violence in its foreign policy. The results would have been less significant given two changes. First, he used a logarithmic scale to code conflict, and

---

59. John Mearsheimer, "Back to the Future: Instability in Europe After the Cold War," *International Security*, Vol. 15, No. 1 (Summer 1990), pp. 50–51.
60. Many studies, however, have shown that there is, at best, a very weak correlation between democracy and peace. Erich Weede, "Democracy and War Involvement," *Journal of Conflict Resolution*, Vol. 28, No. 4 (December 1984), pp. 649–664; Chan, "Mirror, Mirror on the Wall . . .: Are the Freer Countries More Pacific?"; and William J. Dixon, "Political Democracy and War: A New Look at an Old Problem," prepared for the International Studies Association meeting, London, March 28–April 1, 1989.
61. Rudolph J. Rummel, *Understanding Conflict and War*, Vols. 1–4 (Beverly Hills: SAGE, 1976–1981); Rummel, "Libertarianism and International Violence"; Rummel, "Libertarian Propositions on Violence Within and Between Nations," *Journal of Conflict Resolution*, Vol. 29, No. 3 (September 1985), pp. 419–55; and Rummel, "Power Kills: Democracy as a Method of Nonviolence," mimeo, Haiku Institute of Peace Research, Hawaii, 1994.
62. Rummel, "Libertarianism and International Violence," p. 30.

found a total of 121 dyads in violent conflict each year summed over the five years. No "free" nations were in violent conflict. If instead he had simply counted dyads in an interstate war, the five-year total of conflict-dyad-years would have totaled 12, rather than 121. Given 12 war dyads, there is an 83 percent likelihood of finding no wars among free dyads.

Second, Rummel selected a very short period, and during that period a number of dictatorships went to war with each other. His findings show that for this period, these states were more likely to be at war (especially with each other) than other types of regimes. Although these states are at the opposite end of the spectrum from classical liberalism, to show that underdeveloped dictatorships go to war is not to say that free nations do not go to war. Rummel's findings do not stand scrutiny for any period other than 1976–80.[63] Rummel tested a very limited period using questionable definitions. The results are not as significant as he makes them out to be.

The work of Maoz and Russett provides the strongest empirical evidence that liberal democracy is an important factor in why nations do not fight. They examine two separate theses for why democracies are supposed not to fight, and analyze the importance of variables given other possibly relevant explanations such as wealth, economic growth, and alliance membership. The two separate theses are structural and normative—the structural thesis being variations on the "checks and balances" explanation, and the normative thesis being similar to Doyle's claim that citizens in democracies respect the political legitimacy of other democracies and do not support violence against them.

Maoz and Russett found weak support for the structural thesis, and much stronger results confirming the normative one. They did not test dyads before the end of World War II because "the global spread of democracy was not substantial prior to that period," and presumably because they suspected that democracy would not be statistically significant. The finding that dyads sharing democratic norms were less likely to fight from 1946–86 runs counter to my analysis. There are several reasons for this discrepancy.

The biggest reason is that Maoz and Russett employed a pooled time series. What this means is that they collected dyadic observations for each year, 1946–86, and then pooled them all together. The logic for using a pooled time series is not at all clear. A dyad such as the United States and Canada

---

63. See Weede, "Democracy and War Involvement."

counts as 41 separate observations in the pooled time series, because it was a democratic dyad in each of the years from 1946–86. This has the effect of enlarging the number of observations many-fold. As the number of balls in a bin increases, so too does the probability that the characteristics of a drawn sample will match the whole population. If there are 40,000 balls, of which 40 are red, and we draw a sample of 4000, then there is only a very small chance (around 2 percent) that we would find no red balls in the sample. Now let us consider smaller numbers; let us divide everything by 40. If we have 1000 balls in a bin, of which only 1 is red, and we draw 100, there is a 90 percent likelihood of drawing no red balls. Just as the chances of finding no red balls went from 2 percent to 90 percent in the example above, Maoz and Russett are sure of finding significant results where they aggregate forty years of observations into a pooled time series.

Another problem with their analysis is that in the type of statistical analysis they perform, it is a fundamental assumption that the observations are independent of one another, but as Maoz and Russett point out, their observations are not independent.[64] This goes beyond a technical issue of collinearity, because Maoz and Russett are comparing a static explanation with a historical explanation. They argue that the static one (type of regime) is more significant than path-dependent explanations (variables that are related to their own past, such as balance of power), but this conclusion rests on an analysis that removes the variables from their historical context.

Another reason their results contradict mine may have to do with the data sets they used as proxies for the variables of war and of democratic norms. They studied militarized international disputes, rather than interstate war (although Russett proposed to study the latter in his introductory chapter). A militarized international dispute is "a set of interactions between or among states involving threats to use military force, displays of military force, or actual uses of force."[65] This choice of data has two consequences. It makes a threat by Senegal to use military force against the Gambia equivalent to the American use of nuclear weapons against Japan. It also inflates dramatically the number of dyadic disputes to 978 for the period (versus 154 conflictual-dyad-years for 1946–82 in the Singer and Small data set). If Maoz and Russett

64. Maoz and Russett, "Normative and Structural Causes," reprinted in Russett, *Grasping the Democratic Peace*, fn. 13, pp. 146–147.
65. Charles Gochman and Zeev Maoz, "Militarized Interstate Disputes, 1816–1975," *Journal of Conflict Resolution*, Vol. 29, No. 4 (Winter 1984), p. 586.

had used data for interstate conflict, as they said they would, and had they counted dyads over time rather than pooling one-year observations, they would have reported 2145 total dyads, of which 7 were at war, and 18 were liberal (with no liberal dyads at war).[66] The probability of finding zero liberal dyads at war with these figures is 59 percent, which is not significant.

Doyle's work has been successful in leading to a research program that allows disagreement and falsification, and that is an accomplishment that few other scholars of international relations can claim. The focus of the literature has been on why liberal regimes rarely fight one another, and it has also drawn upon Kant's prediction that in a constitutional republic the populace prevents the ruler from starting wars. This has led to an interesting body of work on how representative governments with checks and balances place constraints on leaders.[67] A few studies suggest that interesting questions about the effects of democracy on conflict management remain to be studied.[68] Very little of the literature has focused on the question of whether (or why) liberal regimes ally with one another, which the data analysis presented above suggests should be the question. Siverson and Emmons found that during the two World Wars, democracies allied with one another more than chance would predict, and Siverson and Starr found that alliances were likely to change after the nature of participant's regimes changed.[69] Thus, while the nature of regimes does little to explain when and with whom they go to war, it is an important variable in understanding the composition of alliances.

Future research ought to pay more attention to why democracies have allied with one another. The probability analysis in this study shows that the absence of wars between democracies is not a puzzle that requires further thought. But the one exception to this conclusion is World War I, a war of democratic allies against illiberal regimes. World War I does not raise the

---

66. The data sets I used end in 1982.
67. Carol Ember, Melvin Ember, and Bruce Russett, "Peace Between Participatory Polities," *World Politics*, Vol. 44, No. 4 (July 1992); Clifton T. Morgan and Sally Howard Campbell, "Domestic Structure, Decisional Constraints, and War: So Why Kant Democracies Fight?" *Journal of Conflict Resolution*, Vol. 35, No. 2 (June 1991), pp. 187–211; Clifton T. Morgan and Valerie Schwebach, "Take Two Democracies and Call Me in the Morning: A Prescription for Peace?" *International Interactions*, Vol. 17, No. 3 (1992).
68. Examples are Dixon, "Democracy and the Peaceful Settlement of Conflict"; and Stuart A. Bremer, "Are Democracies Less Likely to Join Wars?" paper presented at the annual meeting of the American Political Science Association, Chicago, 1992.
69. Siverson and Emmons, "Birds of a Feather"; and Siverson and Starr, "Regime Change and the Restructuring of Alliances."

question of why democracies refrained from attacking each other so much as it poses the puzzle of why they allied with one another. The question for future research should be whether the normative basis for liberal democracy leads regimes to join one another in waging war on non-believers.

That the nature of regimes would affect the composition of alliances runs counter to the predictions of realism, particularly the variant of realism taught by Kenneth Waltz. Liberal theory is not confirmed by the absence of wars between democracies, but it may be bolstered if the nature of regimes is important for alliance formation. Yet classical realism, with its emphasis on state interests, may also have much to contribute.

If the reason for liberal alliances has to do with representative government, then future research must take into account differences in the relative autonomy of liberal states. Kant viewed democracy as a form of despotism precisely because he took the classical view that pluralist governments were completely permeable to popular interests. The tyranny of mob rule gives us little reason to think that liberal regimes would never go to war with other liberal regimes. On the other hand, Kant's republican governments, which resemble modern notions of relatively autonomous states, have the capacity to mobilize the masses for war. In 1991 the democratically elected president of the United States likened the president of Iraq to Hitler in order to garner popular support for the commitment of 500,000 troops to the defense of a feudal desert monarchy with whom the United States had no history of alliance or even friendship. Checks and balances may make America less war-prone, but there is nothing intrinsic about its form of government to prevent it from ever going to war with one another democracy. Liberal regimes can incite their populace to foolish wars just as easily as illiberal regimes.

Realism may have much to offer our understanding of why democracies have tended to ally with one another (at least during two very important periods in modern history). One of the many aspects of John Owen's work that is interesting is his study of how the populace perceives the nature of other regimes. Similarly, the subjective definition of state interests is not inconsistent with classical realism, but it is left by the wayside in Waltzian theory. It is plausible that interests are based on intersubjective understandings about what constitutes "them and us," just as Hegel suggested that our notions of sovereignty developed from an alienation between the "self" and the "other." A more full-bodied realist theory that takes into account such subjectivity would have no problem in explaining how a liberal normative framework affects the choice of alliance partners.

Democratic alliances are not a reason for liberal and realist theorists to end their debate; indeed, they are an interesting new ground for the debate to continue. There is little about democracy that helps us to deduce why one would never fight with another, but there is clearly something to the notion that liberal regimes fight to protect (i.e., to spread) the values of democracy and freedom, and this might imply that like nations would ally in the liberal cause. What leads them to speak peace with one another is, according to Michael Howard, the "liberal conscience."[70] Yet it is this liberal conscience that leads to proselytizing the rest of the world by war, and to the justification of such wars as moral.[71] Regimes that agree on the "conditions of universal hospitality" are likely to define their interests in a similar manner, and to ally to fight for the same causes. This is not, as Kant suggested, due to the liberal nature of the conditions of universal hospitality, but rather to power and interests, subjectively conceived.

---

70. Michael Howard, *War and the Liberal Conscience*, 2nd ed. (New Brunswick, N.J.: Rutgers University Press, 1986).
71. Michael Walzer, *Just and Unjust Wars*, 2nd ed. (New York: Basic Books, 1992), chapter 3.

Appendix. The Random Chance of Finding Zero Wars Between Democracies.

1 Year	2 Total nations	3 Total dyads between nations	4 Dyads at war	5 Liberal nations	6 Dyads between liberal nations	7 Liberal dyads at war	8* Random probability of 7	9 Wars expected between liberals	10 Standard deviation between liberals
1816	23	253	0	2	1	0	1	0	0
1817	23	253	0	2	1	0	1	0	0
1818	23	253	0	2	1	0	1	0	0
1819	23	253	0	2	1	0	1	0	0
1820	23	253	0	2	1	0	1	0	0
1821	23	253	0	2	1	0	1	0	0
1822	23	253	0	2	1	0	1	0	0
1823	23	253	1	2	1	0	0.996	0.004	0.063
1824	23	253	0	2	1	0	1	0	0
1825	24	276	0	2	1	0	1	0	0
1826	25	300	0	2	1	0	1	0	0
1827	25	300	0	2	1	0	1	0	0
1828	26	325	1	2	1	0	0.997	0.003	0.055
1829	26	325	1	2	1	0	0.997	0.003	0.055
1830	27	351	0	4	6	0	1	0	0
1831	29	406	0	4	6	0	1	0	0
1832	29	406	0	5	10	0	1	0	0
1833	29	406	0	5	10	0	1	0	0
1834	29	406	0	5	10	0	1	0	0
1835	29	406	0	5	10	0	1	0	0
1836	29	406	0	5	10	0	1	0	0
1837	29	406	0	5	10	0	1	0	0
1838	31	465	0	5	10	0	1	0	0
1839	32	496	0	5	10	0	1	0	0
1840	32	496	0	5	10	0	1	0	0
1841	34	561	0	5	10	0	1	0	0
1842	35	595	0	5	10	0	1	0	0
1843	36	630	0	5	10	0	1	0	0
1844	36	630	0	5	10	0	1	0	0
1845	36	630	0	5	10	0	1	0	0
1846	37	666	1	5	10	0	0.985	0.015	0.122
1847	38	703	1	5	10	0	0.986	0.014	0.118
1848	39	741	5	7	21	0	0.866	0.142	0.370
1849	40	780	5	8	28	0	0.832	0.179	0.415

Appendix. The Random Chance of Finding Zero Wars Between Democracies (continued).

1 Year	2 Total nations	3 Total dyads between nations	4 Dyads at war	5 Liberal nations	6 Dyads between liberal nations	7 Liberal dyads at war	8* Random probability of 7	9 Wars expected between liberals	10 Standard deviation
1850	40	780	0	7	21	0	1	0	0
1851	41	820	1	7	21	0	0.974	0.026	0.158
1852	41	820	1	7	21	0	0.974	0.026	0.158
1853	41	820	1	7	21	0	0.974	0.026	0.158
1854	42	861	3	7	21	0	0.928	0.073	0.267
1855	44	946	4	7	21	0	0.914	0.089	0.294
1856	44	946	5	7	21	0	0.894	0.111	0.329
1857	44	946	1	7	21	0	0.978	0.022	0.147
1858	44	946	0	7	21	0	1	0	0
1859	45	990	3	7	21	0	0.938	0.064	0.249
1860	47	1081	3	7	21	0	0.942	0.058	0.239
1861	43	903	1	7	21	0	0.977	0.023	0.151
1862	42	861	1	7	21	0	0.975	0.024	0.154
1863	42	861	2	9	36	0	0.952	0.049	0.218
1864	42	861	4	9	36	0	0.843	0.167	0.400
1865	42	861	4	9	36	0	0.843	0.167	0.400
1866	42	861	21	9	36	0	0.404	0.878	0.907
1867	40	780	3	8	28	0	0.896	0.108	0.322
1868	37	666	2	8	28	0	0.918	0.084	0.284
1869	37	666	2	8	28	0	0.918	0.084	0.284
1870	37	666	6	9	36	0	0.772	0.252	0.490
1871	34	561	1	9	36	0	0.936	0.064	0.245
1872	33	528	0	9	36	0	1	0	0
1873	33	528	0	9	36	0	1	0	0
1874	33	528	0	9	36	0	1	0	0
1875	34	561	0	9	36	0	1	0	0
1876	35	595	1	9	36	0	0.939	0.061	0.238
1877	35	595	1	9	36	0	0.946	0.054	0.226
1878	37	666	2	9	36	0	0.895	0.108	0.320
1879	37	666	2	10	45	0	0.869	0.135	0.355
1880	37	666	1	10	45	0	0.928	0.071	0.258
1881	36	630	1	10	45	0	0.928	0.071	0.258
1882	36	630	1	10	45	0	0.928	0.071	0.258
1883	36	630	2	10	45	0	0.862	0.143	0.364

Appendix. The Random Chance of Finding Zero Wars Between Democracies (continued).

1 Year	2 Total nations	3 Total dyads between nations	4 Dyads at war	5 Liberal nations	6 Dyads between liberal nations	7 Liberal dyads at war	8* Random probability of 7	9 Wars expected between liberals	10 Standard deviation between liberals
1884	36	630	1	10	45	0	0.928	0.071	0.258
1885	36	630	2	10	45	0	0.862	0.143	0.364
1886	36	630	0	10	45	0	1	0	0
1887	38	703	0	10	45	0	1	0	0
1888	39	741	0	10	45	0	1	0	0
1889	38	703	0	10	45	0	1	0	0
1890	38	703	0	10	45	0	1	0	0
1891	38	703	0	11	55	0	1	0	0
1892	39	741	0	11	55	0	1	0	0
1893	39	741	0	11	55	0	1	0	0
1894	39	741	1	11	55	0	0.926	0.074	0.262
1895	39	741	1	11	55	0	0.926	0.074	0.262
1896	39	741	0	11	55	0	1	0	0
1897	39	741	1	11	55	0	0.926	0.074	0.262
1898	40	780	1	11	55	0	0.930	0.071	0.256
1899	41	820	0	11	55	0	1	0	0
1900	42	861	5	11	55	0	0.718	0.319	0.546
1901	42	861	5	11	55	0	1	0	0
1902	42	861	0	11	55	0	1	0	0
1903	42	861	0	11	55	0	1	0	0
1904	42	861	0	11	55	0	0.936	0.064	0.245
1905	43	903	1	12	66	0	0.927	0.073	0.260
1906	42	861	2	12	66	0	0.852	0.153	0.376
1907	42	861	2	12	66	0	0.852	0.153	0.376
1908	43	903	0	12	66	0	1	0	0
1909	44	946	1	12	66	0	0.930	0.070	0.255
1910	44	946	1	13	78	0	0.917	0.082	0.275
1911	44	946	1	13	78	0	0.917	0.082	0.275
1912	43	903	4	12	66	0	0.738	0.292	0.520
1913	43	903	6	12	66	0	0.633	0.439	0.636
1914	44	946	18	13	78	0	0.209	1.484	1.156
1915	44	946	28	13	78	0	0.087	2.309	1.435
1916	44	946	36	13	78	0	0.042	2.968	1.619
1917	43	903	44	13	78	0	0.017	3.801	1.818

Appendix. The Random Chance of Finding Zero Wars Between Democracies (continued).

1	2	3	4	5	6	7	8*	9	10
Year	Total nations	Total dyads between nations	Dyads at war between nations	Liberal nations at war	Dyads between liberal nations	Liberal dyads at war	Random probability of 7	Wars expected between liberals	Standard deviation between liberals
1918	47	1081	36	13	78	0	0.064	2.598	1.527
1919	50	1225	4	19	171	0	0.548	0.558	0.692
1920	59	1711	2	23	253	0	0.726	0.296	0.502
1921	60	1770	1	23	253	0	0.857	0.143	0.350
1922	61	1830	1	25	300	0	0.836	0.164	0.370
1923	61	1830	0	24	276	0	1		
1924	61	1830	0	24	276	0	1		
1925	62	1891	0	23	253	0	1		
1926	63	1953	0	23	253	0	1		
1927	64	2016	0	23	253	0	1		
1928	64	2016	1	25	300	0	0.851	0.149	0.356
1929	64	2016	0	25	300	0	1		
1930	64	2016	1	25	300	0	0.851	0.149	0.356
1931	64	2016	2	26	325	0	0.713	0.313	0.513
1932	65	2080	2	25	300	0	0.732	0.288	0.497
1933	65	2080	1	25	300	0	0.860	0.140	0.347
1934	66	2145	2	22	231	0	0.796	0.215	0.438
1935	66	2145	1	21	210	0	0.902	0.098	0.297
1936	66	2145	1	20	190	0	0.911	0.089	0.284
1937	67	2211	2	20	190	0	0.836	0.172	0.396
1938	66	2145	11	20	190	0	0.359	0.974	0.940
1939	63	1953	31	18	153	0	0.078	2.429	1.485
1940	56	1540	84	14	91	4	0.183*	4.964	2.102
1941	54	1431	56	14	91	4	0.201*	3.561	1.791
1942	53	1378	56	14	91	4	0.205*	3.698	1.821
1943	58	1653	75	15	105	5	0.185*	4.764	2.064
1944	65	2080	42	19	171	5	0.026*	3.453	1.763
1945	67	2211	0	25	300	0	1		
1946	69	2346	0	26	325	0	1		
1947	73	2628	5	28	378	0	0.460	0.719	0.784
1948	76	2850	1	28	378	0	0.867	0.133	0.339
1949	76	2850	4	31	465	0	0.490	0.653	0.739
1950	76	2850	4	31	465	0	0.490	0.653	0.739

Appendix. The Random Chance of Finding Zero Wars Between Democracies (continued).

1 Year	2 Total nations	3 Total dyads between nations	4 Dyads at war	5 Liberal nations	6 Dyads between liberal nations	7 Liberal dyads at war	8* Random probability of 7	9 Wars expected between liberals	10 Standard deviation
1952	78	3003	4	32	496	0	0.485	0.661	0.742
1953	79	3081	4	33	528	0	0.471	0.685	0.753
1954	83	3403	0	33	528	0	1	0	0
1955	85	3570	0	35	595	0	1	0	0
1956	88	3828	4	36	630	0	0.487	0.658	0.741
1957	90	4005	0	36	630	0	1	0	0
1958	91	4095	0	37	666	0	1	0	0
1959	90	4005	0	38	703	0	1	0	0
1960	108	5778	0	38	703	0	1	0	0
1961	112	6216	0	38	703	0	1	0	0
1962	118	6903	1	38	703	0	0.896	0.102	0.302
1963	120	7140	0	41	820	0	1	0	0
1964	123	7503	0	40	780	0	1	0	0
1965	125	7750	5	39	741	0	0.607	0.478	0.657
1966	130	8385	5	41	820	0	0.602	0.489	0.664
1967	131	8515	9	41	820	0	0.415	0.867	0.885
1968	133	8778	6	40	780	0	0.581	0.533	0.697
1969	133	8778	8	39	741	0	0.503	0.675	0.786
1970	134	8911	8	38	703	0	0.535	0.631	0.762
1971	139	9591	8	38	703	0	0.544	0.586	0.737
1972	139	9591	7	36	630	0	0.616	0.460	0.655
1973	141	9870	11	35	595	0	0.503	0.663	0.789
1974	143	10153	3	33	528	0	0.849	0.156	0.385
1975	150	11175	2	34	561	0	0.911	0.100	0.309
1976	151	11325	1	33	528	0	0.954	0.047	0.211
1977	152	11476	1	34	561	0	0.947	0.049	0.216
1978	154	11781	3	37	666	0	0.829	0.170	0.400
1979	155	11935	5	39	741	0	0.704	0.310	0.540
1980	156	12090	3	40	780	0	0.829	0.194	0.425

*The random probability of finding zero (or in 1941–45, 4 to 5) liberal dyads at war.

Polities and Peace

Henry S. Farber and Joanne Gowa

In recent months, the Clinton administration has begun to advocate a replacement for the doctrine of containment that drove U.S. foreign policy during the Cold War. According to Anthony Lake, the Assistant to the President for National Security Affairs, the leading candidate to succeed containment is "a strategy of enlargement—enlargement of the world's . . . community of market democracies."[1] President Clinton concurs, noting that a strategy of enlargement serves U.S. interests because "democracies rarely wage war on one another."[2]

Several empirical analyses suggest that the Clinton administration's advocacy of enlargement is well-grounded. They conclude that democratic states do pursue distinctive foreign policies. Perhaps the most intriguing among their findings is that democratic states rarely, if ever, wage war against other democratic states. Indeed, some observers consider this finding to be "as close as anything we have to an empirical law in international relations."[3]

Yet doubts remain about whether the observed association reflects a causal relationship.[4] In this paper, we attempt to resolve these doubts. In order to do so, we reexamine both the logic and the empirical basis of the claim central to

Henry S. Farber is the Hughes Rogers Professor of Economics at Princeton University. Joanne Gowa is Professor of Politics at Princeton University.

For comments on earlier versions of this paper, we are grateful to Henry S. Bienen, William J. Dixon, George W. Downs, Robert Gilpin, Gene Grossman, Peter B. Kenen, John Londregan, Edward D. Mansfield, Walter Mattli, Robert Powell, Bruce M. Russett, Howard Rosenthal, and seminar participants at Princeton University and the University of Chicago. For excellent research assistance, we are grateful to Jacqueline Berger, Deborah Garvey, and Matthias Kaelberer. Financial support for this research was provided by the Industrial Relations Section at Princeton University. Joanne Gowa also acknowledges the financial support of the Center of International Studies at Princeton University.

1. Anthony Lake, "From Containment to Enlargement," U.S. Department of State, Bureau of Public Affairs, *Dispatch*, Vol. 4, No. 39 (September 1993), p. 3.
2. William Clinton, "Confronting the Challenges of a Broader World," U.S. Department of State, Bureau of Public Affairs, *Dispatch*, Vol. 4, No. 39 (September 1993), p. 3.
3. Jack S. Levy, "Domestic Politics and War," *Journal of Interdisciplinary History*, Vol. 18, No. 4 (Spring 1988), pp. 653–673.
4. T. Clifton Morgan notes, for example, that he and many others "have long had nagging suspicions that the conclusions we have drawn from the empirical tests are spurious. It may well be that alliance patterns, power distributions, contiguity, or any of a number of other variables could be confounding our observed relationship." T. Clifton Morgan, "Democracy and War: Reflections on the Literature," *International Interactions*, Vol. 18, No. 3 (1993), p. 200.

International Security, Vol. 20, No. 2 (Fall 1995), pp. 123–146

the "democratic peace" literature: that is, that members of pairs of democratic states are far less likely to wage war against or engage in serious disputes with each other than are members of other pairs of states.[5]

We first review the analytic foundations of the democratic peace literature. We conclude that these foundations are tenuous. Then we examine the evidence. We analyze the period before World War I and the period after World War II separately. The results that emerge differ markedly from those of previous studies.

First, we find that there is *no* statistically significant relationship between democracy and war before 1914. In the case of disputes short of war, we find that the probability that these disputes will occur is significantly higher between members of pairs of democratic states than between members of other pairs of states in the same period. Our analysis shows that it is only after 1945 that the probability of war or serious disputes is significantly lower between democratic states than between members of other pairs of states.

This pattern of cross-temporal variation contradicts the central claim of the democratic peace literature that dispute rates are consistently lower between democracies than between members of other pairs of states. It also suggests that the Cold War results may be a product of common interests, rather than of common polities.

Although extrapolating the results of any analysis is often problematic, our findings suggest that whether or not democratic polities become more common may not affect U.S. security interests strongly. Thus, although the evolution of democracy in the former Soviet bloc countries may be desirable on other grounds, the analysis presented here suggests that it will not affect an issue of

---

5. See, e.g., Stuart Bremer, "Dangerous Dyads: Conditions Affecting the Likelihood of Interstate War," *Journal of Conflict Resolution*, Vol. 36, No. 2 (June 1992), pp. 309–341; Stuart Bremer, "Democracy and Militarized Interstate Conflict," *International Interactions*, Vol. 18, No. 3 (1993), pp. 231–249; Steve Chan, "Mirror, Mirror on the Wall . . . Are the Freer Countries More Pacific?" *Journal of Conflict Resolution*, Vol. 28, No. 4 (December 1984), pp. 616–648; Steve Chan, "Democracy and War: Some Thoughts on Future Research Agenda," *International Interactions*, Vol. 18, No. 3 (1993), pp. 205–214; William Dixon, "Democracy and the Peaceful Settlement of International Conflict," *American Political Science Review*, Vol. 88, No. 1 (March 1994), pp. 14–32; Michael Doyle, "Liberalism and World Politics," *American Political Science Review*, Vol. 80, No. 4 (December 1986), pp. 1151–1169; Zeev Maoz and Nasrin Abdolali, "Regime Types and International Conflict," *Journal of Conflict Resolution*, Vol. 33, No. 1 (March 1989), pp. 3–35; Zeev Maoz and Bruce M. Russett, "Normative and Structural Causes of Democratic Peace, 1946–86," *American Political Science Review*, Vol. 87, No. 3 (September 1993), pp. 624–638; Bruce M. Russett, *Grasping the Democratic Peace: Principles for a Post–Cold War World* (Princeton: Princeton University Press, 1993); Melvin Small and J. David Singer, "The War-Proneness of Democratic Regimes," *Jerusalem Journal of International Relations*, Vol. 1, No. 4 (Summer 1976), pp. 50–68.

central importance to the United States: the probability of serious interstate disputes.

Analytic Foundations

The democratic peace literature advances two explanations for the distinctive behavior of democracies. One is based on norms, the other on checks and balances. In this section, we argue that neither provides a compelling explanation of the peace that is said to prevail between democracies.[6]

NORMS

Norms are "rules for conduct that provide standards by which behavior is approved or disapproved."[7] The democratic peace literature assigns the principal explanatory role to the norm that defines acceptable methods of conflict resolution. In democratic states, acceptable methods include "adjudication and bargaining," whereas the "use of force is disdained."[8] This norm is said to explain peace not only within but also between democracies because states "externalize . . . the norms of behavior that are developed within and characterize their domestic political processes and institutions."[9] Thus, if a norm regulates conflict resolution within two states, it will also regulate the process of conflict resolution between them.

In the extensive literature on norms, norms are defined in two ways. Norms may be regarded as *"ex ante* sources of action." As such, they are not "merely *ex post* rationalizations of self interests," but reflect the internalization of values.[10] Norms have also been interpreted, however, as reflections of interests.[11]

Contributors to the democratic peace literature define norms as sources of action independent of interests. Thus, they regard adherence to peaceful methods of conflict resolution as the product of internalized values. Yet adherence to this norm is of enormous instrumental value: it secures the social order that

---

6. Part of this section draws on material developed in further detail in Joanne Gowa, "Democratic States and International Disputes," *International Organization*, Vol. 49, No. 3 (Summer 1995).
7. Michael Hechter, *Principles of Group Solidarity* (Berkeley: University of California Press, 1987), p. 62.
8. Morgan, "Democracy and War," p. 198.
9. Maoz and Russett, "Normative and Structural Causes."
10. Jon Elster, *The Cement of Society: A Study of Social Order* (Cambridge: Cambridge University Press, 1989), p. 125.
11. See, e.g., John Finley Scott, *The Internalization of Norms: A Sociological Theory of Moral Commitment* (Englewood Cliffs, N.J.: Prentice Hall, 1971).

is the basis of any organized society. It therefore serves the private interest of leaders and the collective interests of those they rule. This implies that norms regulating conflict resolution can be very difficult to distinguish from interests.

This suggests, in turn, that whether the parties to an interstate dispute resort to violence also may depend upon interests rather than norms. In the context of international disputes, it does not seem logical to impute to democracies alone an interest in non-violent means of conflict resolution. Because war is more costly than bargaining, it seems more reasonable to impute a preference for negotiation over war to *all* potential belligerents.[12] As a result, the value added by describing a preference for peaceful methods of conflict resolution as a norm rather than an interest is not obvious.

The empirical foundations of the norms argument are no more compelling. The central problem is that there are no measures of norms or their effectiveness that are independent of interests. For example, Maoz and Russett use both the incidence of violent domestic disputes and the duration of regimes as proxies for the effectiveness of domestic norms.[13] As noted above, peaceful resolution of domestic disputes is quite likely to serve the interests of both leaders and the general populace. Thus, a low incidence of violent disputes domestically might well reflect interests rather than norms.

Using regime duration suffers from much the same flaw. Compliance with a norm of peaceful dispute resolution may be directly related to the tenure of a regime in office. The causal relationship, however, may be due to an increase in the efficacy of sanctions; presumably, the longer regimes endure, the better they learn to cope with violent opposition. In this case, again, increases in compliance may reflect interests induced by the stronger deterrent effect of more effective sanctions.

In the end, any explanation of the distinctiveness of democratic foreign policies based on the distinctiveness of the norms underlying them is not testable. This is because no direct measures of norms related to interstate disputes exist. Proxy measures are not adequate substitutes because their use requires the assumption that they are, in fact, linked to norms governing interstate disputes, rather than merely reflecting underlying interests.

---

12. James D. Fearon, "Threats to Use Force: Costly Signals and Bargaining in International Crises," (Ph.D. dissertation, University of California, Berkeley, 1992).
13. Maoz and Russett, "Normative and Structural Causes."

CHECKS AND BALANCES

The premise of the checks-and-balances argument is that constraints on would-be renegade leaders are much more effective in democratic than in autocratic polities.[14] This is at odds, however, with the conventional finding that, while democracies seem to fight with each other less frequently than do other country pairs, they are just as likely to wage war as are other polities.[15]

In addition, the checks and balances characteristic of democratic polities do not seem to protect the public from politicians maximizing their own interests rather than social welfare in widely varied policy areas. For example, tariffs exist in most democracies despite their negative effects on real income. Their existence is partly the product of the concentrated benefits and diffuse costs of a tariff. As a result of this distribution of cost and benefits, welfare-maximizing politicians gain some freedom to maneuver, at a cost to aggregate social welfare.[16]

The question raised by the case of tariffs is whether a fundamentally different policy process prevails in the case of war. As is true of tariffs, the benefits from war are concentrated, while its costs are diffuse. As a result, defense contractors are likely to be more effective political actors than is the population at large. Moreover, evidence from the United States suggests that the costs of war tend to fall disproportionately on low-income constituents, whose rates of political participation are relatively low.[17] The net effect, again, is to endow political officials with some freedom to maximize their own interests rather than social welfare.

---

14. T. Clifton Morgan and Sally Howard Campbell, "Domestic Structure, Decisional Constraints, and War: So Why Kant Democracies Fight?" *Journal of Conflict Resolution*, Vol. 35, No. 2 (June 1991), pp. 187–211. For a somewhat different argument that reaches the same conclusion, see David A. Lake, "Powerful Pacifists: Democratic States and War," *American Political Science Review*, Vol. 86, No. 1 (March 1992), pp. 24–37.

15. Bruce Bueno de Mesquita and David Lalman, *War and Reason: Domestic and International Imperatives* (New Haven: Yale University Press, 1992); Chan, "Mirror, Mirror on the Wall"; Doyle, "Liberalism and World Politics"; Levy, "Domestic Politics and War"; T. Clifton Morgan and Valerie L. Schwebach, "Take Two Democracies and Call Me In the Morning: A Prescription for Peace?" *International Interactions*, Vol. 17, No. 4 (1992), pp. 305–320; R.J. Rummel, "The Relationship between National Attributes and Foreign Conflict Behavior," in J. David Singer, ed., *Quantitative International Politics: Insights and Evidence* (Englewood Cliffs, N.J.: Prentice Hall, 1968).

16. For a more complete analysis of the political processes that lead to the adoption of tariffs, see, e.g., Susanne Lohmann and Sharyn O'Halloran, "Divided Government and U.S. Trade Policy: Theory and Evidence," *International Organization*, Vol. 48, No. 4 (Autumn 1994), pp. 595–632.

17. Richard V.L. Cooper, "Military Manpower Procurement: Equity, Efficiency, and National Security," in Martin Anderson, ed., *Registration and the Draft* (Stanford, Calif.: The Hoover Institution, 1982), pp. 343–376.

We do not mean to suggest that there are no differences between the policy processes that produce tariffs and those that produce wars. For example, these processes are much more likely to resemble each other in the case of small than of large wars. However, we do want to suggest that there is no *a priori* reason to believe that checks and balances work as intended in the case of wars, since it is clear that they do not do so in other policy areas.

This implies that there may be a smaller gap between democratic and other polities with respect to the autonomy of would-be renegade leaders than is conventionally assumed. Other factors point in the same direction. For example, informal checks and balances are in effect in non-democratic polities,[18] such as the dependence of their leaders of non-democratic societies on the coalition of interests that supports them.[19]

More generally, the most potent deterrent to war may not be the existence of *ex ante* formal or informal checks and balances, but the *ex post* ability of constituents to sanction their leaders.[20] The resort to war creates a risk to incumbency that can tightly constrain heads of states of autocracies as well as democracies.[21]

In summary, neither the norm-based argument nor the one based on checks and balances is completely convincing. We turn next to an analysis of the evidence.

Sample Definition and Central Measures

The sample for our analysis consists of all countries that were members of the interstate system at any time from 1816 to 1980. We adopt the definition of membership in the interstate system that Melvin J. Small and J. David Singer

18. This also suggests one reason why empirical analyses of the relationship between formal constraints and dispute involvement have not found any statistically significant effects (see, e.g., Morgan and Campbell, "Domestic Structure"). Whether or not *de jure* constraints exist may not matter as much as the presence or absence of *de facto* constraints.
19. Bueno de Mesquita and Lalman argue that "the mean ratio of expected political costs from using force to the expected benefits from a negotiated resolution of a dispute" is higher for democracies than for other states. Bueno de Mesquita and Lalman, *War and Reason*, p. 153. This would imply that checks and balances are more effective in democracies than in non-democracies. The empirical basis of this claim is not clear, however.
20. Bruce Bueno de Mesquita, Randolph Siverson, and Gary Woller, "War and the Fate of Regimes: A Comparative Analysis," *American Political Science Review*, Vol. 86, No. 3 (1992), pp. 638–646.
21. Morgan and Campbell, "Domestic Structure," p. 191. Those to whom leaders are accountable differ: democratic leaders are accountable to voters at large; autocrats are not. But this difference may not matter: any war fought in the private interest of the leader will, by definition, arouse opposition among those to whom he is accountable, whether that group is small or large.

use.[22] Thus, a nation qualifies as a member of the interstate system before World War I if and only if it had a minimum population of 500,000, and it had British and French representation on its soil "at or above the rank of *chargé d'affaires*."[23] After World War I, a nation so qualified if it was either "a member of the League or the United Nations at any time during its existence," or it "met the half million population minimum and received diplomatic missions from *any two* . . . major powers."[24]

We use a dyad-year as the unit of observation to address the question of whether the probability of war, or of disputes short of war, is lower between the members of pairs of democratic states than between those of other pairs. Thus, our basic sample consists of 284,602 dyad-years for which we have complete data on the required variables over the entire period from 1816 through 1980.[25]

POLITY TYPE

We define and measure our independent variables in the same ways as many contributors to the existing literature do. Thus, we use Ted Robert Gurr's Polity II data set to define autocratic, democratic, and anocratic regimes.[26] Gurr defines autocracies as systems in which tight constraints on political participation exist; only members of the political elite select the chief executive, and institutions do not constrain the leader's power. In contrast, in democracies, individuals can "express effective preferences about alternative policies and

---

22. Melvin J. Small and J. David Singer, *Resort to Arms: International and Civil Wars, 1816–1980* (Beverly Hills, Calif.: Sage, 1982).
23. This was sufficient to signal international recognition, because "as Britain and France went, so went the majority" of other nations. Ibid., p. 40.
24. Ibid., pp. 40–41, emphasis original.
25. By including every possible dyad-year for which we have complete data on both members, we are including many dyad-years whose members are very unlikely to have meaningful contact of any kind, let alone to form an alliance or have a military dispute. One approach, used by Maoz and Russett, "Normative and Structural Causes," is to include only dyad-years whose members are contiguous or that have at least one major power as a member. While it is true that noncontiguous dyad-years with no major powers have much lower alliance and dispute rates, there are more than a few alliances and disputes involving such dyad-years. Thus we include all dyad-years and control explicitly for contiguity and major-power status. We have also repeated all of the analyses in this study using the restricted sample of dyad-years, and the results are qualitatively similar.
26. Ted Robert Gurr, "Polity II: Political Structures and Regime Change, 1800–1986 [Computer File]" (Boulder, Colo.: Center for Comparative Politics, 1990). Some studies have used Gurr's and another data set to assess polity types; e.g., A.S. Banks, *Cross-Polity Time Series Data* (Cambridge, Mass.: The MIT Press, 1971); Chan, "Mirror, Mirror on the Wall." See, e.g., Bremer, "Dangerous Dyads"; Maoz and Russett, "Normative and Structural Causes."

leaders"; institutionalized constraints limit the leader's power; and guarantees of civil liberties exist.[27] Gurr constructs two discrete eleven-point scales (0 to 10) to measure the degree of autocracy and democracy in each state annually.[28] The scores a polity receives are composite measures that reflect, *inter alia*, the method of executive recruitment, the competitiveness of party politics, and the range of political participation. Gurr labels as "anocratic" those polities that receive "middling scores on both Autocracy and Democracy scales."[29] We use Gurr's scales to categorize each regime as democratic, autocratic, or anocratic. More specifically, we categorize a regime as democratic if it receives a score of six or higher on Gurr's democracy scale; as autocratic if it scores five or higher on Gurr's autocracy scale; and as anocratic if it is categorized as neither a democracy nor an autocracy.[30]

The first column of Table 1 contains a breakdown of regime type for the 10,757 observations on system-member states across the 1816–1980 period for which the Gurr data set has complete information on regime type. This breakdown shows that roughly half of the country-years are classified as autocracies, with the other half evenly split between democracies and anocracies.

This tabulation masks a substantial change over time in the composition of the interstate system. Columns 2 through 4 of Table 1 contain breakdowns of regime type for three sub-periods: 1) pre–World War I (1816–1913); 2) World War I through World War II (1914–45); and 3) post–World War II (1946–80). The central result is clear and consistent with conventional wisdom: democracies have become substantially more common since 1914.

Two other points are worth noting. First, a decline in the relative frequency of anocracies has accompanied the growth of democracies. In contrast, autocracies are as common after World War II as they were before World War I.

---

27. Gurr, "Polity II," p. 38.

28. There are three types of cases that Gurr codes as missing and which we, as a result, omit from our analysis. "Interruptions" are cases in which a wartime occupation temporarily disrupts an existing polity. The other two cases are "transitions," defined as periods of change from one regime type to another, and "interregnums," defined as periods during which no central government exists.

29. Gurr, "Polity II," p. 38. More intuitively, an anocracy is a polity in which the state "had minimal functions, an uninstitutionalized pattern of political competition, and executive leaders constantly imperiled by rival leaders. Anocracy . . . means literally the absence of power or control," although it is used "to signify states which approach but do not reach the extreme conditions." Gurr, "Persistence and Change in Political Systems, 1800–1971," *American Political Science Review*, Vol. 68, No. 4 (December 1974), p. 1487, n. 11.

30. These rules do not generate any inconsistencies. Specifically, there are no regimes that satisfy both the requirement for a democracy and the requirement for an autocracy. The simple correlation between Gurr's autocracy and democracy scales is –0.83.

Table 1. Frequency Distribution of Regime Type by Time Period, Number of Dyad-Years.

Regime Type	Time Period			
	All	Pre-1914	1914–45	1946–80
Autocracy	5,151	2,644	669	1,838
	(47.9)	(52.1)	(33.8)	(49.6)
Anocracy	2,736	1,610	554	572
	(25.4)	(31.8)	(28.0)	(15.4)
Democracy	2,870	817	756	1,297
	(26.7)	(16.1)	(38.2)	(35.0)
Total	10,757	5,071	1,979	3,707

NOTE: The numbers in parentheses are column percentages.

Second, the distribution of regime types in the middle period (1914–45) does not lie between the earlier and later distributions. The relative frequency of autocracies was lower during this period than it was earlier or later. It also appears that the growth in the relative frequency of democracies was completed by World War II.[31]

WAR

We use the Correlates of War (COW) data set to define and measure interstate war;[32] therefore we define a war as a clash that involves "one or more system members" and that leads "to a minimum of 1,000 battle fatalities among all of the system members involved." A member of the international system is defined as a belligerent only if it either committed 1,000 troops to battle or suffered at least 100 casualties.[33]

Our basic sample of 284,602 dyad-years contains 604 dyad-years (0.21 percent) at war, distributed across 62 interstate wars.[34] Contributors to the existing literature usually code all 604 dyad-years as war observations.[35] This treats the

---

31. A finer breakdown than that presented in Table 1 reveals that the growth in the relative frequency of democracies began earlier than 1914 and was completed by 1939.
32. Small and Singer, *Resort to Arms*. The data are taken directly from the public use version of the COW war data set, which is part 1 of ICPSR Study Number 9044.
33. Small and Singer, *Resort to Arms*, p. 55.
34. The COW data set actually contains 67 wars. However, we had to drop five wars from our analysis because of missing polity data on at least one country in every dyad involved in the war.
35. See, e.g., Chan, "Mirror, Mirror on the Wall," p. 621.

onset and the continuation of wars between countries identically. However, given that the issue of central importance is the *incidence*, rather than duration, of war between pairs of states, a more useful measure would count each war between pairs of states as only a single war observation. We use this more restrictive measure.

Thus, we code as a war outcome only the first year a dyad is involved in a particular war, irrespective of whether its members initiated or joined a war.[36] We delete from the sample all subsequent years the dyad is involved in the same war. The years in which a dyad is at peace are coded as non-war observations. For example, the less restrictive measure records the 1877–78 war between Russia and Turkey as two dyad-years at war; we record the war as only one dyad-year at war (1877), and we exclude the remaining dyad-year (1878). The reduced sample based on our measure contains 284,221 dyad-years, of which 223 are dyad-years at war (0.08 percent).[37]

The treatment of war in our analysis differs from other studies in two additional ways: 1) we distinguish between general and other wars; and 2) we include all wars recorded by Small and Singer for which information on polity type exists for at least one dyad involved in the war.

GENERAL AND OTHER WARS. A distinction between general and other wars is common, although not universal, in the larger literature on war.[38] It is based on the fact that general wars create *ex ante* "a reasonable probability of a decisive victory by at least one side that could lead to the emergence of a new dominant or leading power and hence to the structural transformation of the system."[39]

Because there are only two general wars (World War I and World War II) in the 1816–1980 period, it is impossible to test whether there is a difference between these and other wars. As a result, any decision about whether or not

---

36. Cf. Stuart Bremer, "Are Democracies Less Likely to Join Wars?" paper prepared for presentation at the 1992 annual meeting of the American Political Science Association.
37. We have also analyzed the data using all dyad-years at war. The results are qualitatively unchanged.
38. See, e.g., Robert Gilpin, *War and Change in the International System* (Princeton: Princeton University Press, 1981; Jack Levy, *War in the Modern Great Power System, 1495–1975* (Lexington: University of Kentucky, 1983); Manus Midlarsky, *The Onset of World War* (Boston: Unwin Hyman, 1988); William R. Thompson, "Cycles of General, Hegemonic, and Global War," in Urs Luterbacher and Michael D. Ward, eds., *Dynamic Models of International Conflict* (Boulder, Colo.: Lynne Rienner, 1985); Thompson, "The Size of War, Structural and Geopolitical Contexts, and Theory Building/Testing," *International Interactions*, Vol. 18, No. 3 (1993), pp. 183–200; John A. Vasquez, *The War Puzzle* (Cambridge: Cambridge University Press, 1993). For an argument that "big" wars should not be treated differently, see Bruce Bueno de Mesquita, "Big Wars, Little Wars: Avoiding Selection Bias," *International Interactions*, Vol. 16, No. 3 (1990), pp. 159–171.
39. Jack S. Levy, "Theories of General Wars," *World Politics*, Vol. 37, No. 3 (April 1985), p. 364.

to distinguish between the two types depends upon judgments about whether the causes and evolution of general and other wars differ.[40] It also depends upon the precise question that is under investigation.[41] We employ both criteria to decide whether to treat general and other wars differently.

First, it seems to us that a strong argument supports the view that the causes of general and other wars differ. As John A. Vasquez observes, although most wars "can be understood primarily in terms of the interactions that lead to them," general wars "need to be understood also in terms of the context in which they are fought and the systemic conditions associated with them."[42] Of particular concern is the fit between the underlying distribution of power in the extant international system and the existing status quo.[43]

Second, the question we address here is whether members of pairs of democratic nations are less likely to wage war against each other than are members of other pairs of states: thus, interactions *within* dyads are of central concern. The dynamics of general wars, however, render a dyad a substantively meaningless unit of observation. For example, a dyad-based measure cannot capture the attempts to "pass the buck" that dominated the periods immediately before both World War I and World War II.[44] These attempts are crucial to explaining the outbreak of these wars; however, in their absence, deterrence might have succeeded.

Nor can measures based on dyads capture the evolution of general wars. When belligerents entered World War I and World War II, they did not do so as discrete pairs. Consequently it is not theories and measures based on dyads but theories and measures based on the diffusion of war that apply to these wars.[45]

Both pre-war and war-time patterns of interaction among the great powers in World War I and World War II, then, render a dyad-based measure incapable

---

40. Thompson, "The Size of War," p. 184. Edward Mansfield, however, has shown that growth in military expenditures and personnel departs from Gibrat's Law for the major powers *only* during the periods clustered around World War I and World War II. This provides some evidence that the processes leading to general wars differ from those of other wars. Mansfield, *Power, Trade, and War* (Princeton: Princeton University Press, 1994), p. 225.

41. Jack Levy, "Big Wars, Little Wars, and Theory Construction," *International Interactions*, Vol. 16, No. 3 (1990), pp. 215–224.

42. Vasquez, *The War Puzzle*, p. 225.

43. Gilpin, *War and Change*; Robert Powell, "Stability and the Distribution of Power," *World Politics*, forthcoming.

44. Barry R. Posen, *The Sources of Military Doctrine: France, Britain, and Germany between the World Wars* (Ithaca, N.Y.: Cornell University Press, 1984).

45. See, e.g., Randolph M. Siverson and Harvey Starr, *The Diffusion of War: A Study of Opportunity and Willingness* (Ann Arbor: University of Michigan Press, 1991).

of capturing their underlying dynamics. Any attempt to disaggregate either war in terms of its constituent dyads risks distorting the relationship between and among the belligerent states. It also denies the existence of any cross-dyad interdependence. As a consequence, we do not believe that data drawn from general wars are relevant to a study of dyadic relationships.[46]

Although we initially analyzed the relationship between regime type and probability of war for all years in our sample, we subsequently excluded the periods of both World Wars (1914–18 and 1939–45) from our analysis. Note that this is not a trivial change in sample. These periods contain not only the two World Wars (99 dyad-years at war), but also three small wars (four dyad-years at war) which are also lost from the analysis. The periods of the two World Wars together make up only 4.21 percent of the dyad-years in the sample, but they account for fully 46.2 percent of the dyad-years at war (103 of 223). Indeed, that the two World Wars account for almost half of the war observations (44.3 percent) is itself another indication that these two wars are not typical.

We drop the time periods that include these wars rather than simply delete the dyads involved in them. While not a perfect solution to the problem of how to examine only non-general wars, dropping the time periods is preferable to dropping a dyad-year simply because that specific dyad was fighting a war in that year. Such a sample-selection rule would run a serious risk of introducing sample-selection bias. Our decision to drop the time periods of the two World Wars drops many more observations not at war (11,851) than observations at war, so that any sample-selection bias induced by dropping these periods is likely to be much less serious than deleting only dyad-years at war.

THE SET OF WARS. We include in our analysis all other wars that Small and Singer code. In contrast, some contributors to this literature exclude, for various reasons, some wars between democratic polities from their analysis.[47] For example, although Finland fought with the Axis powers in World War II, some analysts purge pairs of belligerent states that include Finland from their studies. The effect of doing so in this and other cases is to undercount the number of wars that have occurred between democratic polities. As a result, these

---

46. The same could be said of any multilateral war. The problem is extraordinarily severe in general wars. World War I had 40 dyads at war and World War II 59 dyads at war. In contrast, the majority of wars (39) involved only one dyad; nine wars had two dyads at war; and four wars had three dyads at war. Other than the two World Wars, only one war (the Korean War) had more than ten dyads at war.

47. E.g., Chan, "Mirror, Mirror on the Wall"; Maoz and Abdolali, "Regime Types and International Conflict"; Russett, *Grasping the Democratic Peace*.

exclusions systematically bias analyses toward the finding that democratic states are less likely to fight with each other.

The explanations offered to explain the exclusion of wars vary. Sometimes the explanation is that one or both members of the dyad were not "really" democratic (e.g., Spain in 1898).[48] Sometimes it is that the members of a dyad were only nominally at war. For example, those who exclude the case of Finland argue that the country was a belligerent against the Western allies in name only: it engaged only Soviet troops in battle during World War II.[49] These explanations of the exclusions are plausible. This does not mean that the exclusions themselves are defensible, however. Decisions to redefine either outcomes or key explanatory measures (e.g., polity type) can be defended if and only if they are the product of the application of the same standard to *all* cases.[50] Redefinition of variables for other reasons will almost certainly lead to biased inferences. In the case of the existing literature on democracy and war, the bias is in the direction of finding that democratic polities are relatively unlikely to fight with each other. Thus, we include all of the wars in the COW data set.

LOWER-LEVEL MILITARIZED INTERSTATE DISPUTES

As in the case of wars, we rely on the COW project to define and measure militarized interstate disputes (MIDs).[51] To be categorized as a MID, a dispute had to involve: "threats to use military force, displays of military force, or actual uses of force"; and a "threat or deployment of military forces" that is "explicit, overt, nonaccidental, and government sanctioned."[52]

There are 961 disputes recorded in the MID data set, which begins in 1817 and ends in 1976. For each country involved in any given MID, Small and Singer record the most severe hostility level reached: 1) threat to use force; 2) display of force; 3) use of force; or 4) outbreak of war (defined above).

---

48. James Lee Ray, "Wars between Democracies: Rare or Nonexistent?" *International Interactions*, Vol. 18, No. 3 (1993), pp. 251–276; Russett, *Grasping the Democratic Peace*.
49. E.g., Russett, *Grasping the Democratic Peace*, p. 18.
50. Despite his *ad hoc* isolation of some wars, Ray acknowledges this problem in Ray, "Wars Between Democracies," p. 269, as does Bremer in "Dangerous Dyads."
51. These data are taken directly from the public use version of the COW militarized interstate dispute data set, which is part 3 of ICPSR Study Number 9044. They are described in more detail by Charles S. Gochman and Zeev Maoz, "Militarized Interstate Disputes, 1816–1976," *Journal of Conflict Resolution*, Vol. 28, No. 4 (December 1984), pp. 585–615.
52. Ibid., p. 587.

Two aspects of the MID data set are worth noting. First, because the only information coded is the maximum level of hostility reached by each participant considered individually, it is impossible to examine the level of hostility reached by specific pairs of countries in a multilateral dispute. Second, the MID data set does not include all wars in the COW interstate war data set, although the relevant documentation suggests that the latter should be a proper subset of the former. More specifically, of the 223 dyad-years at war in the COW wars data set, the MID data set omits 34.[53]

Using the MID data, we create a variable that indicates for each dyad-year in our sample whether or not the two countries in that dyad were on opposite sides of at least one dispute in that year.[54] In the sample are 2,169 dyad-years with disputes, representing 1,372 pairs of countries. The difference between these numbers represents multi-year disputes.

To measure the level of hostility focused on the opposing member of the dyad, we record the level of hostility of each member of a disputing dyad.[55] We code as lower-level MIDs all disputes where neither member of a dyad is coded as having a level of hostility equal to a Small and Singer war.[56] Of the 1,372 disputing dyads, 1,102 are coded as having lower-level disputes. Fully 471 of these are potentially miscoded due to missing data on the level of hostility. However, because only five of these 471 dyad-years are listed in the COW wars data set and all of them occurred during World War II, it is unlikely that substantial numbers of warring dyads are included in our lower-level-disputing dyad sample.

For reasons discussed above, we include only the first year of each dispute for each dyad in our analysis. These are the initial years of the 1,102 disputing dyads referred to in the previous paragraph. The initial years of disputes constitute 0.44 percent of the 252,058 dyad-years from 1817 through 1976. We delete subsequent years from the analysis. As before, we also delete the periods

---

53. Most of these are dyads involved in the two World Wars. Only 12 of the 124 non-general war dyads in the COW wars data set do not appear in the MID data set.
54. Note that there are cases where two countries are involved in more than one dispute with each other in a particular year. Gochman and Maoz, "Militarized Interstate Disputes," describe in detail how disputes are defined and demarcated.
55. As discussed above, however, there is no guarantee in the case of multilateral disputes that the level of hostility coded applies to every dyad involved in that dispute.
56. Where there is more than one dispute involving a specific dyad in a given year, we code the level of hostility of each side as the maximum level of hostility reached by that side in any dispute involving both members of the dyad that year.

of the two general wars. These periods account for 145 (13 percent) of the 1,102 disputing dyads.

The Central Results

We analyze the incidence of wars, as well as the incidence of lower-level MIDs. Some contributors to the democratic peace literature analyze only wars; others also examine MIDs. We believe that both are relevant to the issue of the relationship between regime type and serious interstate disputes. As Bruce Russett argues with respect to MIDs, democracies have conflicts of interest with each other, but, "much more often than other states, they settle their disagreements by mediation, negotiation, or other forms of peaceful diplomacy." Thus, he concludes, analyzing lower-level MIDs "constitutes a logical extension of the research program that began nearly two decades ago with wars."[57]

REGIME TYPE AND THE PROBABILITY OF WAR

The rarity of war raises difficult questions of appropriate statistical techniques, particularly in a multivariate analysis. War is such a low-probability event that there are likely to be configurations of the independent variables where there is no variation in outcomes for a specific value of a dichotomous independent variable. For example, there are no wars within democratic dyads after World War II. We term this the "empty-margin" problem.

There are several standard approaches to estimating models with discrete outcomes, including linear probability models, latent variable models (e.g., logit or probit), and Poisson models. In the context of our analysis, shortcomings afflict each of these three models. The linear probability model is known to be particularly problematic when used for the analysis of very rare events. The latent variable models and the Poisson model yield unbounded parameter estimates where there are empty margins.[58]

To analyze war, we thus take the very simple approach of computing Pearson χ^2 statistics from two-way breakdowns of regime type by war, and we use these

57. Bruce M. Russett, "Correspondence: The Democratic Peace: 'And Yet It Moves'," *International Security*, Vol. 19, No. 4 (Spring 1995), pp. 164–175.
58. The unbounded parameter estimates result from attempting to make the predicted probability of war zero. In latent variable and Poisson models, this is the case as the relevant parameter approaches $-\infty$. Bremer applies a Poisson model to the analysis of democracy and conflict, and he avoids the empty margin problem by aggregating across time periods. Bremer, "Dangerous Dyads"; Bremer, "Democracy and Militarized Interstate Conflict."

χ^2 statistics to test the hypothesis of independence of conflict and regime type.[59] The strength of this approach is that it is straightforward and robust to underlying distributional assumptions.

A weakness of the bivariate approach is that important variables may be omitted that could bias the estimated relationship between regime type and the probability of conflict; in this case, they might include alliance status, wealth, major-power status, and geographic contiguity.[60]

Using alliance status as an explanatory variable is problematic. Both alliances and serious disputes are likely to be affected by a common set of unmeasured variables (e.g., variables measuring the congruence of interests). As a result of these omitted variables, the use of alliances as an independent variable in a multivariate regression analysis of disputes will create biased parameter estimates.[61] Different problems preclude the use of wealth: consistent and reliable data are not available for the entire period from 1816 through 1980.

Two other variables—major-power status and geographic contiguity—are not plagued by problems of simultaneity or lack of data, and both are strongly related to interstate conflict. We have repeated all of the analyses in this section separately by the number of major powers in each dyad (0, 1, or 2), and separately for contiguous and noncontiguous states. We use the classification of states as major powers developed by Small and Singer, and we code contiguity using the data in Siverson and Starr.[62] The Siverson and Starr data are complete through 1965; we extended the data set to 1980. Dyad members can be contiguous in one of three ways: directly territorially contiguous; contiguous across less than 200 miles of water; or contiguous on the basis of shared colonial

---

59. Caution is required in testing hypotheses regarding such rare events as war. However, the Pearson χ^2 statistic is generally recognized to be appropriate as long as the *expected* cell sizes under the null hypothesis of independence are all greater than one. Stephen E. Fienberg, *The Analysis of Cross-Classified Categorical Data* (Cambridge, Mass.: The MIT Press, 1980), p. 170. In our study the minimum expected cell size (the expected number of wars between democracies) is always larger than one, so that the conditions for appropriate use of the Pearson χ^2 statistic are met throughout.
60. See, e.g., Bremer, "Dangerous Dyads"; Bremer, "Democracy and Militarized Interstate Conflict"; Maoz and Russett, "Normative and Structural Causes."
61. For further discussion, see Henry S. Farber and Joanne Gowa, "Common Interests or Common Polities? Reinterpreting the Democratic Peace," *National Bureau of Economic Research Working Paper No. 5005* (February 1995), pp. 4–7 and 34–35.
62. Small and Singer, *Resort to Arms*; Siverson and Starr, *The Diffusion of War*. Siverson and Starr record as an event additions and removals of a boundary of a given type (e.g., colonial), but they do not record whether *all* boundaries of a given type are removed when a removal is recorded. Thus, possible inaccuracies are inherent in these data if, after the last recorded removal of a boundary of a given type (e.g., colonial), there remain existing boundaries of that type.

borders. If they are not contiguous in any of these three ways, we classify them as non-contiguous.

Despite problems associated with the use of linear probability models, we computed estimates of these models of the probability of war as a function of regime type, contiguity, and major-power status. We also computed logit models of the probability of war as a function of the same variables for all periods where there was not an empty margin problem.[63] The results of these analyses are qualitatively identical to the results derived from the two-way breakdowns of war by regime-type. In the interest of simplicity, therefore, we present only the bivariate analysis.[64]

In order to verify that our data yield results consistent with those of previous studies, we first examined the evidence using *all* observations in the entire 1816–1980 period. This includes 284,221 dyad-years. War occurs in only 223 of these dyad-years, making it clear that interstate war is a rare event. In addition, of the 67 wars in the COW data set, there are only two in which war between democracies occurs, involving seven dyads. Six of these involve Finland paired with various nations in World War II. The seventh is Spain fighting the United States in the Spanish-American War.

It is clear, therefore, that any analysis cannot rely on finding substantial numbers of wars between democratic states. Instead, we examined whether there is consistent evidence over time of a statistically significant difference in the probability of war between the members of pairs of democratic states and the members of other pairs of polities. The issue of statistical significance is central. Because both war and democracies are relatively rare, we observe few wars between democracies to date. Yet the underlying probability of war between democracies might in fact be as high as the underlying probability of war of other dyads.[65]

---

63. A logit model is an alternative to OLS regression appropriate for multivariate analysis when the dependent variable is dichotomous. The underlying assumption is that the log-odds of a war is a linear function.

64. See Farber and Gowa, "Common Interests or Common Politics," for a list of the relationship between democracy and war that accounts for contiguity and major power status.

65. This point is recognized by David E. Spiro, "The Insignificance of the Liberal Peace," *International Security*, Vol. 19, No. 2 (Fall 1994), pp. 50–86. Spiro asks whether zero wars occur by chance between members of democratic dyads for each year from 1816 to 1980. He finds that it was only during World War I that a zero incidence of wars between democracies was unlikely to have arisen by chance. Then, in order to address the fact that analyses of a single year bias his findings toward the null hypothesis, he analyzes longer time periods. His substantive results are unchanged. However, Spiro includes in these longer time periods only those states that existed for the entire time period and only those democracies that were democratic for the entire period. For further discussion of the Spiro article, see Russett, "Correspondence: The Democratic Peace."

The results of our preliminary analysis conform to those of other studies in two important ways. First, we find that democracies are no less war-prone than are other polities. We use the sample of country-year (as opposed to dyad-year) data to compute the probability that a country is at war with any other country in a given year. Analyzing the 10,445 country-years for which we have complete data, we find war probabilities of 0.0191 for non-democracies and 0.0189 for democracies. The difference between these probabilities is not statistically significant (p-value of χ^2 statistic for test of independence = 0.937).

Second, we find that war between democracies occurs at a significantly lower rate than does war between members of other pairs of states. The probability of war between democracies is 0.02 percent compared with a probability of war of 0.09 percent for all other dyads. A Pearson χ^2 test of independence of regime type and the probability of war clearly rejects independence (p-value < 0.0005). Both this and the preceding finding are consistent with existing research.

Next we examined whether the difference between war probabilities is consistent across time. To address this issue, we break the data into five time periods: 1) pre–World War I (1816–1913); 2) World War I (1914–18); 3) the interwar years (1919–38); 4) World War II (1939–45); and 5) post–World War II (1946–80).

We disaggregate the data in this way for two reasons. First, both theoretical and empirical analyses suggest that there are important differences between the pre–World War I and the post–World War II periods. Theorists point to the major changes in international politics induced by the advent of bipolarity and nuclear weapons.[66] Empiricists point to the differences between the nineteenth and twentieth centuries (e.g., in the processes leading to alliance formation and war outbreak).[67]

Second, in the interests of full disclosure, we include an analysis of both World War I and World War II. For the reasons we describe above, however, we do not believe that general wars generate observations that are appropriate to a test of whether peace is more likely to prevail between members of pairs of democratic states than between those of other pairs. We therefore report, but do not discuss, the results of the analyses of the periods 1914–18 and 1939–45.

Table 2 contains the probability of war by regime type for each of the five periods. The table also contains Pearson χ^2 statistics for tests of independence of regime type and the probability of war. These results show that there is no

---

66. Kenneth N. Waltz, *Theory of International Politics* (Reading, Mass.: Addison-Wesley, 1979).
67. Chan, "Democracy and War," p. 210.

Table 2. Probability of War by Regime Type and Time Period, Number of Dyad-Years.

Time Period	Regime Type Democratic-Democratic	Other	χ^2 statistic	p-value
1816–1913	0.0007 (1,475)	0.0010 (50,119)	0.18	0.671
1914–18 (World War I)	0.0 (353)	0.0136 (2,937)	4.87	0.027
1919–38	0.0 (5,919)	0.0003 (28,039)	1.90	0.168
1939–45 (World War II)	0.0084 (718)	0.0071 (7,946)	0.13	0.721
1946–80	0.0 (22,498)	0.0004 (164,217)	7.95	0.005

NOTE: The numbers in parentheses are the number of dyad-years. The χ^2 statistics are the Pearson statistics for tests of independence of regime type and the probability of war for each period.

consistency across time in the relationship between regime type and the probability of war. In three of the five time periods (pre–1914; 1919–1938; and 1939–45), no statistically significant relationship exists (p-value of joint test of independence (χ^2 with 3 degrees of freedom) = 0.53). Moreover, pooling these three periods does not change these results (p-value of pooled test of independence (χ^2 with 1 degree of freedom = 0.23). It is only during World War I and after 1945 that a statistically significant relationship exists.[68] We exclude the periods of the two World Wars from our discussion in the rest of this article.

The most interesting contrast in Table 2 is between the pre–1914 and the post–1945 periods.[69] Before World War I, *no* significant relationship exists

68. All six of the democratic-democratic warring dyads in World War II involve Finland. If these dyads are deleted, there is a significant relationship between regime type and the probability of war (p-value = 0.023) during World War II. Because this deletion is not the product of a systematically-applied standard, however, we include the Finnish dyads in our analysis.

69. An analysis of the nineteenth-century data yields the same result as analysis of the data for the pre–World War I period. We also pooled data from the interwar years (1919–38) with the pre–World I period. Using a logit model and taking account of the lower overall rate of war during the interwar period, this pooling had no effect on the finding reported here of no significant difference in war rates by regime type before 1946. In the interests of clarity, therefore, the analysis we report upon contrasts the pre–World War I period with the post–World War II period and excludes the interwar period.

between regime type and the probability of war (p-value = 0.671). This result does not depend on whether Spain is classified as a democracy.[70] After World War II, however, there is a significant relationship (p-value = 0.005) between regime type and the probability of war, with democratic dyads being significantly less likely to fight. In short, these results indicate that what seems to have become the conventional wisdom about the relationship between democracies and war applies, in fact, *only* to the Cold War years.

REGIME TYPE AND THE PROBABILITY OF LOWER-LEVEL MIDS

We also analyzed whether MIDs short of war are less likely to occur between democracies than between other countries, using the data on disputes short of war that we describe above.[71] We begin by presenting the results of bivariate analyses of regime type and low-level MIDs analogous to the analyses of war presented in the preceding sub-section. However, since lower-level MIDs are substantially more common than wars, the problem of empty margins is not relevant. Thus, we were able to carry out a multivariate logit analysis of lower-level MIDs, controlling for contiguity and number of major powers along with regime type, and we present these results below.

As with wars, we first analyzed low-level disputes across the entire 1817–1976 period. Consistent with earlier analyses, we find that low-level disputes between democracies occur at a significantly lower rate than do low-level disputes between members of other pairs of states. The probability of low-level disputes between democracies is 0.30 percent compared with a probability of 0.45 percent for all other dyads. A Pearson χ^2 test of independence of regime type and the probability of war clearly rejects independence (p-value < 0.0005).

Next we examine whether the difference between low-level dispute probabilities is consistent across time. Once again we break the data into five time periods: 1) pre–World War I (1817–1913); 2) World War I (1914–18); 3) the interwar years (1919–38); 4) World War II (1939–45); and 5) post–World War II (1946–76). Table 3 contains the probability of low-level disputes by regime type for each of the five periods. The table also contains Pearson χ^2 statistics for tests

70. If Spain is reclassified as a non-democracy, the p-value of the χ^2 statistic testing independence of regime type and the probability of war is 0.21.
71. While we do not present the results, we also carried out an analysis of militarized interstate disputes that included wars as well as low-level disputes. The results of this analysis are qualitatively similar to those reported in this section for low-level disputes, and similar to those reported by Maoz and Abdolali, "Regime Types and International Conflict," for MIDs generally. This is because wars make up only a small fraction of militarized interstate disputes, so the data are dominated by the MIDs.

Table 3. Probability of Low-Level Disputes by Regime Type and Time Period, Number of Dyad-Years.

| | Regime Type | | | |
| | Democratic-Democratic | Other | χ^2 statistic | p-value |
Time Period				
1817–1913	0.0177 (1,470)	0.0074 (49,767)	20.08	<0.005
1914–18 (World War I)	0.0114 (351)	0.0183 (2,893)	0.87	0.351
1919–38	0.0032 (5,913)	0.0033 (27,983)	0.008	0.927
1939–45 (World War II)	0.0014 (731)	0.0111 (7,853)	6.21	0.013
1946–76	0.0017 (19,198)	0.0031 (135,865)	11.93	0.001

Note: The numbers in parentheses are the number of dyad-years. The χ^2 statistics are the Pearson statistics for tests of independence of regime type and the probability of low-level disputes for each period.

of independence of regime type and the probability of low-level disputes. As with war, these results show that there is no consistency across time in the relationship between regime type and the probability of low-level disputes.

The most striking finding in Table 3 is that the probability of low-level disputes is actually significantly higher for democratic-democratic dyads than for other type of dyads prior to World War I (p-value < 0.0005).[72] It is lower in all subsequent periods; however, the difference is statistically significant only during World War II (p-value = 0.013) and the Cold War (p-value = 0.001).

Again we focus on the results for the pre-1914 and the post-1945 periods. The contrast could not be more stark. Democracies were indeed distinctive prior to World War I, but that distinctiveness seems to have resulted in a *higher* probability of lower-level disputes between them.[73] In part, this reflects the fact

72. This result is entirely due to a higher probability of low-level MIDs in geographically contiguous democratic dyads than in contiguous dyads of other types. There is not a significant difference in the probability of low-level MIDs between non-contiguous democratic dyads and non-contiguous dyads of other types. This is the one exception to the generalization that the substantive results of our study are qualitatively identical when contiguity is controlled for.
73. The United Kingdom is classified as a democracy since 1837 by our coding scheme. The United States is classified as a democracy throughout.

Table 4. Logit Analysis of Probability of Low-Level Disputes.

Variable	Time Period			
	Pre-1914	Pre-1914	Post-1945	Post-1945
Constant	−4.91 (93.5)	−6.02 (60.7)	−5.77 (118.4)	−6.65 (89.4)
Democratic	0.888 (4.34)	0.336 (1.60)	−0.624 (3.40)	−1.28 (6.68)
Contiguous	—	1.97 (17.1)	—	3.15 (30.8)
1 major power	—	0.702 (5.87)	—	0.789 (7.13)
2 major powers	—	1.49 (8.85)	—	2.54 (11.7)
Log-likelihood	−2293.3	−2015.4	−3094.8	−2517.4
Sample Size	51,237	51,237	155,063	155,063

NOTE: The numbers in parentheses are absolute values of asymptotic t-statistics. The base category consists of dyads that are non-democratic/democratic, non-contiguous, and with no major powers. All variables are 0–1 indicators.

that two democracies (the United States and the United Kingdom) are the two most dispute-prone nations in the MID data set as a whole.[74]

Table 4 contains logit analyses, separately for the pre-1914 and post-1945 periods, of the probability of low-level MIDs that control for regime type, number of major powers in the dyad, and contiguity. The first and third columns of Table 4 contain estimates for the two time periods that include only a constant and a dummy variable indicating democratic-democratic dyads. These estimates reproduce the significantly higher probability of lower-level MIDs for democratic dyads in the earlier period and the significantly lower probability of lower-level MIDs for democratic dyads in the later period. The second and fourth columns of Table 4 include additional controls for geographic contiguity and for the number of major powers in the dyad.

These additional factors are clearly strongly related to the probability of conflict. Contiguous dyads are substantially more likely to come into conflict. Dyads with one major power are substantially more likely to be involved in

---

74. Gochman and Maoz, "Militarized Interstate Disputes," p. 609.

disputes than are dyads with no major powers. Dyads with two major powers are even more likely to be involved in disputes than are dyads with one major power. These results hold in both time periods.

With regard to regime type, the basic results are the same as those of the bivariate analysis. Prior to World War I, democratic dyads were marginally significantly more likely to be involved in disputes than were other types of dyads (p-value = 0.10). After World War II, there was a marked and statistically significant lower probability of disputes short of war between democracies (p-value < 0.0005).[75] As was true of war, then, these results indicate that the conventional wisdom about the effect of democratic dyads on the probability of disputes holds only for the post–World War II world. Also in sharp contrast to the existing literature is the finding that democracies are more likely to engage in disputes with each other before 1914.

Conclusion

The evidence we analyzed suggests that the democratic peace is of relatively recent origin. Indeed, it coincides with the Cold War. Whether the post-1945 result is the product of common polities is, at best, unclear. The onset of the Cold War precipitated strong common interests among a relatively large number of democratic states. Alliance patterns reflect this: after 1945, democratic states were more likely to join defense pacts with each other than were nondemocracies. That this is far from typical is clear from the pre–World War I pattern: During the century before 1914, members of democratic dyads were less likely to join defense pacts with each other than were members of other dyads.[76] Thus, it is difficult to conclude that it is common polities, rather than common interests, that explain the relatively low incidence of disputes between democracies during the Cold War.

This finding is central to a long-standing debate in international relations about the relative importance of "Second Image" (domestic political) and "Third Image" (systemic) variables. The existing democratic peace literature suggests that Second Image variables play an essential role in explaining the incidence of war and disputes short of war, but our analysis does not support this conclusion.

---

75. Maoz and Russett, "Normative and Structural Causes," established the post-1945 result earlier.
76. For further discussion of the alliance issue and the relevant statistical evidence, see Farber and Gowa, "Common Interests or Common Polities," pp. 4–13.

Our analysis also suggests that the Clinton administration's foreign-policy strategy of "enlargement" may be misguided. On the basis of the historical record, it is not clear that the spread of democracy in and of itself will exert much influence on the incidence of serious interstate conflict. Although a policy of supporting the emergence of democratic regimes may be desirable on other grounds, there does not seem to be convincing evidence that enlarging the world's community of democracies will reduce the danger of international conflict. Instead, the analysis here suggests that the Clinton administration foreign policy will be more successful if it focuses on encouraging the emergence of common interests.

The Subjectivity of the "Democratic" Peace

Ido Oren

Changing U.S. Perceptions of Imperial Germany

Few claims about international relations are as widely accepted as the claim of a democratic peace. Many scholars are convinced, along with President Clinton, that "democracies rarely wage war on one another."[1] This proposition provides an important rationale for promoting "democratization" as a pillar of American foreign policy: "ultimately the best strategy to insure our security and to build a durable peace is to support the advance of democracy elsewhere."[2]

However, the search for a democratic peace, scientific though it may be, is not value-free. I argue that the democratic peace claim is not about democracies *per se* as much as it is about countries that are "America-like" or of "our kind." The apparently objective coding rules by which democracy is defined in fact represent current American values.

The democratic peace claim is ahistorical; it overlooks the fact that these values have changed over time. In no small part, this change has been influenced by changing international political realities. The values embodied in the current definition of democracy were historically shaped by the need to distance America from its adversaries. They are products, more than determinants, of America's past foreign political relations. The reason we do not fight "our kind" is not that "likeness" has a great effect on war propensity, but rather that we from time to time subtly redefine our kind to keep our self-image consistent with our friends' attributes and inconsistent with those of our adversaries.

Ido Oren is Assistant Professor of Political Science at the University of Minnesota. He is currently an SSRC–MacArthur Foundation Fellow on Peace and Security in a Changing World.

I thank the following individuals (some of whom disagreed with my argument) for helpful counsel: William Dixon, Geoff Eley, Scott Gates, Jeff Legro, Rhona Leibel, Yair Magen, John Mearsheimer, Andy Moravcsik, Dick Price, Diana Richards, Bruce Russett, Marc Trachtenberg, Stephen Van Evera, Bill Wohlforth, Amy Zegart, two anonymous referees, and especially Raymond Duvall and James Farr. Ethan Cherin and Luigi Cocci extended excellent research assistance.

1. William Clinton, *Confronting the Challenges of a Broader World* (Washington, D.C.: U.S. Department of State, 1993).
2. President Clinton's State of the Union Message, January 1994, quoted in John M. Owen, "How Liberalism Produces Democratic Peace," *International Security*, Vol. 19, No. 2 (Fall 1994), p. 87.

International Security, Vol. 20, No. 2 (Fall 1995), pp. 147–184
© 1995 by the President and Fellows of Harvard College and the Massachusetts Institute of Technology.

In 1917 President Wilson denounced German autocracy, and declared war on Germany to "make the world safe for democracy." Wilson's legacy is embraced by the present proponents of the democratic peace theory.[3] I show, however, that as a political scientist Wilson viewed Germany not as an autocracy, but as a most advanced constitutional state, and that he admired Prussia's statism, administration, and its unequal suffrage. In the 1890s Wilson's political values were different from those currently associated with "democracy," and Germany as he perceived it was significantly more "normal" by his standards at the time than it appears by present norms. Only after U.S.-German political rivalry developed did Wilson begin to differentiate a democratic America from an autocratic Germany. Indeed, America's very self-portrayal as a democracy and the norms by which it defines democracy were in part shaped by the conflict with Imperial Germany. These norms, I argue, came to be selected because the difference between America's political system and its adversary's was greatest when measured against them.

In the following section I criticize the democratic peace literature and elaborate my argument. Then, I reconstruct the political theories and perceptions of Germany held by two prominent political scientists of the late nineteenth century: Woodrow Wilson, later U.S. president, and John Burgess, founder of the first graduate program in political science in the United States. I conclude with the theoretical and policy implications of the argument, especially that "democratization" provides but a frail foundation for U.S. security policy. The democratic character of foreign countries depends on the peacefulness of their foreign policies, no less than their foreign policies toward the United States depend on their democratic character.

The Appearance of a Democratic Peace

A remarkable finding emerged from recent empirical research in international relations: democracies do not wage war on one another.[4] In these studies,

---

3. For example, the motto of chapter 1 in Bruce Russett, *Grasping the Democratic Peace: Principles for a Post-Cold War World* (Princeton: Princeton University Press, 1993), is excerpted from Wilson's 1917 war message to Congress.
4. Key studies include: Michael Doyle, "Liberalism and World Politics," *American Political Science Review*, Vol. 80, No. 4 (December 1986), pp. 1151–1169; Zeev Maoz and Nasrin Abdulali, "Regime Types and International Conflict, 1815–1976," *Journal of Conflict Resolution*, Vol. 33, No. 1 (March 1989), pp. 3–35; T. Clifton Morgan and Valerie L. Schwebach, "Take Two Democracies and Call Me in the Morning: A Prescription for Peace?" *International Interactions*, Vol. 17, No. 4 (1992), pp. 305–320; William Dixon, "Democracy and the Settlement of International Conflict," *American Political*

polities are coded on a scale that typically takes competitiveness and fairness of electoral processes, as well as constraints on the freedom of executive action, as the defining empirical features of democracy.[5] It is then shown statistically that, controlling for other variables, the likelihood of war between democratic countries is significantly smaller than between non-democracies or between democracies and non-democracies.

There is no consensus on explaining this finding. Two lines of explanation have emerged: one highlights the normative respect that democracies harbor toward each other,[6] while the other focuses on institutional features characteristic of democratic regimes.[7] The differences between these two strands notwithstanding, their proponents use essentially identical rules for coding regimes.[8] I question the objectivity and trans-historical validity of these coding rules, and hence my argument does not discriminate between the two explanations. It is the empirical claim of a democratic peace that I challenge, whatever its explanation.

Science Review, Vol. 88, No. 1 (March 1994), pp. 14–32; Zeev Maoz and Bruce Russett, "Normative and Structural Causes of Democratic Peace, 1946–1986," American Political Science Review, Vol. 87, No. 3 (September 1993), pp. 624–638; and Russett, Grasping the Democratic Peace. The recent studies by Russett and his collaborators are indicative of the high methodological sophistication attained by the literature. The technical quality of the statistical studies is not challenged here.
5. These features are central to Ted Robert Gurr's coding scheme, which is the most widely used in studies of the democratic peace. See Ted R. Gurr (Principal Investigator), Polity II: Political Structures and Regime Change, 1800–1986 (Codebook) (Ann Arbor: ICPSR No. 9263, 1990). Gurr's data are used, for example, by Dixon, Maoz and Abdulali, and Maoz and Russett (see fn. 4). Other researchers employ coding schemes that assign greater weight to indicators of civic, political, and economic freedom (e.g., Doyle, "Liberalism and World Politics," p. 1164). But despite the lack of definitional uniformity, the assignment of countries to the democratic/liberal or to the autocratic/illiberal ends of the continuum must be consistent across the various studies or else the consensus on the robustness of the democratic peace finding would not have been as strong as it is.
6. See, e.g., Doyle, "Liberalism and World Politics"; Dixon, "Democracy and the Settlement of International Conflict;" Maoz and Russett, "Normative and Structural Causes of the Democratic Peace." For a helpful review of the theoretical debate see T. Clifton Morgan, "Democracy and War: Reflections on the Literature," International Interactions, Vol. 18, No. 3 (1993), pp. 197–203.
7. See, e.g., Morgan and Schwebach, "Take Two Democracies and Call Me in the Morning." Much of the work on the structural-institutional explanation of the democratic peace is formal-deductive, most notably: Bruce Bueno de Mesquita and David Lalman, War and Reason: Domestic and International Imperatives (New Haven: Yale University Press, 1992), chap. 5; David Lake, "Powerful Pacifists: Democratic States and War," American Political Science Review, Vol. 86, No. 1 (March 1992), pp. 24–37. These formal studies are imaginative, and their normative content—residing in the axiomatic assumptions—is less opaque than in the verbal explanations. Still, to verify their implications the formal studies rely on the same data used by the purely statistical studies.
8. For example, Gurr's Polity data are employed both by Morgan and Schwebach, "Take Two Democracies and Call Me in the Morning," and by Maoz and Russett, "Normative and Structural Causes of the Democratic Peace," proponents of the structural-institutional and of the normative arguments respectively.

CRITIQUE

The appearance of a democratic "zone of peace" is the product of three inter-related biases. First, the scientific claim of peace among democracies, let alone the claim's articulation by policy makers, is not value-free. This is hinted by the fact that in all studies America receives virtually perfect scores on the democracy scale.[9] America is the norm against which other polities are measured. American scholars are busier searching for a democratic peace rather than, say, a Moslem peace not least because democracy enjoys strong normative approval in present-day America. Furthermore, the selection of the empirical criteria by which this abstract concept is described—primarily fair electoral processes and executive responsibility—is consistent with the dominant image of democracy in current American culture.

The second bias of the democratic peace literature is betrayed by the fact that America's perfect democracy scores are applied to its past as much as to its present.[10] Current American values are projected backward and other polities, past and present, are ahistorically compared to the present American ideal. Considerable historical experience suggesting that political norms are elastic over time is ignored.[11] Thus, the tastes of present researchers, disguised as impartial coding rules, are conflated with the rather different tastes of past (and arguably of future) actors.[12]

Third, the studies of the democratic peace not only disguise elastic values as fixed coding rules; they risk mistaking the cause of these values for their effect. In postulating "regime type" as an independent variable, they rule out *a priori*

9. In Gurr's Polity II data set, for example, the United States receives a perfect score on the democracy scale and the lowest score on the autocracy scale. See Gurr, *Polity II*. Interestingly, on an alternative scale of democracy constructed by a Finnish author (*not* used in democratic peace studies), it is Finland that scores the highest, far higher than the United States. See Tatu Vanhanen, *The Process of Democratization: A Comparative Study of 147 States* (New York: Crane Russak, 1990). I thank Chris Lindborg for calling my attention to the book.
10. In Doyle's data set the United States (north of the Mason-Dixon line) is one of only two countries that are classified as "liberal regimes" continuously from the eighteenth century (the other is Switzerland). In Gurr's Polity II data set the United States is the only great power that consistently receives perfect democracy scores for the pre–World War I period. See Doyle, "Liberalism and World Politics," p. 1164; Gurr, *Polity II*.
11. Terrence Ball, James Farr, and Russell Hanson, eds., *Political Innovation and Conceptual Change* (New York: Cambridge University Press, 1989). The essays in that volume document how both the empirical meanings and the moral signs attached to concepts such as democracy, the state, and representation have changed in time.
12. I fully share John Owen's belief that we must examine how actors "coded" each other *at the time*. Such historical awareness makes his analysis richer and more nuanced than the statistical ones. But my critique is more radical than Owen's in emphasizing the historical change of the actors' perception of *themselves* (which Owen assumes constant). See Owen, "How Liberalism Produces a Democratic Peace."

the possibility that democratic norms are the products, as much the determinants, of America's past foreign relations.

THE ARGUMENT

Following these three critiques, my argument is in three steps concerning the "normalizing," historicizing, and endogenizing of the concept of democracy. First, I argue, "democracy" must be "normalized." The democratic peace proposition is not about democracy *per se;* rather, it should be understood as a special case of an argument about peace among polities that are similar relative to some normative benchmarks. What is special about the benchmarks represented by the coding rules of "democracy" is that they are American. They represent "our kind."

Second, I contend that "our kind" changes over time. Both the normative and empirical content attached to "democracy" by American elites changed notably over the past two centuries. In the nineteenth century, democracy was associated with socialism more than with liberalism. It was understood as the rule of a particular class, the working *demos.* Democracy was thus deplored by most American intellectuals, who feared that the untamed rule of mass majorities would lead to tyranny and subvert individual liberty.[13] Therefore, in the nineteenth century American elites were reluctant to identify America as a democracy, and instead associated America with republicanism, constitutionalism, liberty, and even Teutonism. It was only around the turn of the century that the moral sign of democracy was reversed. The reversal was facilitated by a re-conceptualization that cleansed democracy of its class connotation. By marrying it to the Prussian science of administration and thus insulating wide areas of decision making from the immature masses, democracy was made safe for the world before the world could be made safe for democracy.[14] Indeed, making democracy safe was precisely the project in which the statist political science of Woodrow Wilson and his generation was engaged in the 1890s. Still,

---

13. Russell Hanson, "Democracy," in Ball, Farr, and Hanson, *Political Innovation and Conceptual Change,* pp. 68–89; Charles S. Maier, "Democracy Since the French Revolution," in John Dunn, *Democracy: The Unfinished Journey, 508 BC to AD 1993* (New York: Oxford University Press, 1992), pp. 125–154; James Farr, "From Modern Republic to Administrative State: American Political Science in the Nineteenth Century," in David Easton, John Gunnell, and Michael Stein, *Regime and Discipline: Democracy and the Development of Political Science* (Ann Arbor: University of Michigan Press, 1995), pp. 131–168. A similar sentiment was expressed earlier by the Prussian philosopher Immanuel Kant, whose legacy is currently invoked by proponents of the democratic peace: "*Democracy* is necessarily *despotism,* as it establishes an executive power contrary to the general will; all being able to decide against one whose opinion may differ." See Kant, *Perpetual Peace* (New York: Columbia University Press, 1939), p. 15. Emphasis original.
14. Charles Maier, "Democracy Since the French Revolution," pp. 126 and 140.

the *New York Times* continued to contrast authoritarianism against "republic" or "constitutional government" (read: America) until 1917; only thereafter did "democracy" become America's chief self-portrayal.[15]

"Democracy" remains a moving target. Today the association of democracy with a set of classless electoral practices seems to dominate American culture—and, by extension, the scientific coding rules—but this image is not uncontested. It is challenged by the successors of "Students for a Democratic Society" and the New Left who wish to re-associate democracy with class, advocating greater participation of the *demos*.[16] Equally critical, if less radical, are political economists fearful of the atrophy of democracy into "demosclerosis" due to the malignant effect of "special interests."[17] And critics on the right wish to emancipate the people from "big government," i.e., the very administrative bureaucracy erected in order to make democracy safe for the world. Historical experience cannot tell us which challenge to the present vision of democracy will succeed, but from it we can draw two more modest lessons: that the present vision is not permanent—the future may bring different understandings of democracy or even a renewed disapproval of the concept—and that the future direction of "democracy" (or "our kind") will not be independent of the course of America's foreign relations, the third step of my argument.

The process by which the definition of "our kind" changes in time is not entirely an internal one. To a considerable degree it is influenced by foreign affairs. America's identity has historically developed in ways that made political enemies appear subjectively further and friends subjectively closer to it. The estrangement of democracy from the *demos* can be better understood if we recognize that many of America's enemies in the twentieth century identified themselves as "people's democracies." By the same token, the reason why after World War I "constitutionalism" has become less central to America's self-definition must be related to the fact that Imperial Germany was widely

---

15. See Ithiel de Sola Pool with Harold D. Lasswell and Daniel Lerner, *Symbols of Democracy* (Stanford: Stanford University Press, 1952), p. 27.

16. See Hanson, "Democracy," pp. 83–84.

17. See Maier, "Democracy Since the French Revolution," p. 147. For a forceful articulation of this critique see Mancur Olson, *The Rise and Decline of Nations: Economic Growth, Stagflation, and Social Rigidities* (New Haven: Yale University Press, 1982). Interestingly, the "Asian tigers" appear to be Olson's normative model in that book. For an indication of Olson's influence outside academia see Peter Passell, "Democracy's Hardened Arteries and Washington's Problems," *New York Times*, June 2, 1994, p. C2. The term "demosclerosis" is from the latter article.

regarded as an advanced constitutional state. America's Aryan and Teutonic identities were purged for the same reason.[18]

Current American social science is not insulated from this process. Polities have numerous objective dimensions by which they can be measured. The dimensions captured by the current empirical measures of democracy came to be selected through a subtle historical process whereby objective dimensions on which America resembled its enemies were eliminated, whereas those on which America differed the most from its enemies became privileged. Thus, the coding rules defining democracy are better understood as a time-bound product of America's historical international circumstances than as the timeless exogenous force that they are presumed to be.

THE CHANGING "CODING" OF IMPERIAL GERMANY

The contrast between the present and past "coding" of Imperial Germany by American political scientists provides a case in point. Examination of Polity II scores for the pre-1914 period shows that England and France are ranked close behind the United States (i.e., the norm) on the democracy scale, whereas Imperial Germany is significantly behind them, and Austria-Hungary and Russia are even further behind. Alas, the predecessors of today's coders, the political scientists of 100 years ago, subscribed to a different concept of the "good state." To them, Imperial Germany was a member of a select group of states—modern, constitutional, administrative, cohesive nation-states—that were politically the most developed on earth. The difference in political development between this select group (whose chief members included the United States, France, Germany, and England) and the rest of humanity was perceived as far greater than the differences among members of the group themselves. Certainly, members of this group, Germany included, were considered superior in their political development to countries such as Greece, Italy, Argentina, and Chile that are listed by Michael Doyle as members of the liberal club for the pre–World War I period.[19] Within the group of "modern constitutional states," Germany was not necessarily the farthest from the ideal. John Burgess's belief in the superiority of the German polity and culture was fairly close to the views of ardent German nationalists such as Treitschke and Droysen. And Woodrow Wilson's more Anglophile disposition did not exclude Germany from the small

---

18. On the search for America's Aryan and Teutonic heritage by nineteenth century intellectuals, see Dorothy Ross, *The Origins of American Social Science* (New York: Cambridge University Press, 1991), chap. 3.
19. Doyle, "Liberalism and World Politics," p. 1164.

circle of the most modern nations, nor did it preclude high regard for important features of the German system. To Wilson circa 1890, for example, the Prussian administrative model was superior to the French one (not to mention Anglo-American administrative impotency); the Prussian constitutional state was preferable to the immature democracy of France; and Prussian local government was *the* shining model of "self-government" not despite but partly *because* of its three-class voting system. If any West European country deviated from Wilson's norms it was France, not Germany.

The "re-coding" of Imperial Germany cannot be attributed to the discovery of new facts regarding the nature of its political system. The political scientists of the late nineteenth century knew the facts full well since most of them trained in Germany, and they all read German. The disagreement between the current coders and their predecessors is rather about the *selection* of the facts. Imperial Germany, like any polity, was a complex multidimensional creature. What changed over time was not the objective creature as much as the dimensions by which it came to be defined. The selection of such defining dimensions is a subjective, normative exercise, and it fundamentally affects the classification of the creature relative to others: if one selects "constitutionalism," "rule of law," or "federalism," Imperial Germany appears "normal" relative to America; select "efficient administration," "progressive social legislation," or "academic freedom," and it becomes *the* norm; set the norm to Prussia and "one-person, one vote," and Germany becomes "abnormal" (although not so different from the United States if the latter's disfranchised black population is properly accounted for). Social scientists must recognize that their coding rules constitute such summary measurement *norms,* and that norm selection is not unaffected by the scientist's historical context.

The present coding of regime types in general, and of the Imperial German regime in particular, cannot be understood outside the context of the history of German-American political relations. Whereas in the 1870s and 1880s friendship between the United States of America and "the United States of Germany" was taken as axiomatic, around the turn of the century diplomatic tensions began to mount as both nations were simultaneously emerging on the global imperial scene (the focal points that triggered the tension included Samoa, the Philippines, and Venezuela).[20] The rising tension brought about a gradual

---

20. See Manfred Jonas, *The United States and Germany: A Diplomatic History* (Ithaca: Cornell University Press, 1984).

erosion of Germany's positive image in America.[21] America's entry into the war in 1917 led to a more radical change in its image of Germany, including a re-characterization of the German political system. It was then that the sharp dichotomy between "autocratic" Germany and democratic America was born. Colleges across the country hastily introduced patriotic "War Issues" courses whose subject matter "presented itself as a clear-cut contest between the forces of light and the forces of darkness."[22] Not only did American social scientists bring war propaganda into their classrooms, some of them also participated in the administration's propaganda effort abroad.[23] Those who dared to take issue with the anti-German hysteria risked their jobs and professional reputation. For example, the chairman of the University of Minnesota's department of political science, William Schaper, was summarily dismissed by the university's regents for insisting that the blame for the war did not rest wholly upon Germany.[24] John Burgess, the father of the discipline of political science in America, is virtually forgotten today in part because of his unrelenting pro-Germanism.[25]

---

21. In the prewar years the stellar reputation of German scholarship began sagging, and anti-German books began to supplant the more sympathetic literature of years past. See Konrad H. Jarausch, "Huns, Krauts, or Good Germans? The German Image in America, 1880–1980," in James F. Harris, *German-American Interrelations: Heritage and Challenge* (Tübingen: Tübingen University Press, 1985), pp. 146–149; Frank Trommler, "Inventing the Enemy: German-American Cultural Relations, 1900–17," in Hans-Jurgen Schröder, *Confrontation and Cooperation: Germany and the United States in the Era of World War I, 1900–1924* (Providence: Berg Publishers, 1993), pp. 99–126.
22. David M. Kennedy, *Over Here: The First World War and American Society* (New York: Oxford University Press, 1980), pp. 53–59; quotation, p. 58. The "War Issues" courses evolved after the war into the "Contemporary Civilization" curricula. See "Columbia to Celebrate 75 Years of Great Books," *New York Times*, November 16, 1994, p. B9. For a contemporary condemnation of the hysterical "coalescence of the intellectual classes in support of the military programme" see Randolph Bourne, "The War and the Intellectuals," *The Seven Arts*, Vol. 2 (1917), pp. 133–136, reprinted in David F. Trask, *World War I at Home* (New York: Wiley, 1970), pp. 73–80.
23. For example, University of Chicago political scientist Charles Merriam served as chief American "publicist" in Italy. See Ross, *The Origins of American Social Science*, p. 454. On the role of leading historians in the propaganda effort at home and abroad, see George T. Blakey, *Historians on the Homefront: American Propagandists For the Great War* (Lexington: University Press of Kentucky, 1970). See also Jarausch, "Huns, Krauts, or Good Germans?" p. 150.
24. Charles McLaughlin, *A Short History of the Department of Political Science* (Minneapolis: University of Minnesota, 1977). At the University of Minnesota, recording machines were placed in classrooms, and the desks of allegedly unpatriotic professors were rifled at night. See Robert Morlan, "The Reign of Terror in the Middle West," in Arthur S. Link, *The Impact of World War I* (New York: Harper and Row, 1969), p. 76. On the dismissal and intimidation of professors at Columbia and elsewhere, see "The Case of the Columbia Professors," *Nation*, October 11, 1917, pp. 388–389, reprinted in Trask, *World War I at Home*, pp. 159–162.
25. See Albert Somit and Joseph Tanenhaus, *The Development of American Political Science: From Burgess to Behavioralism* (Boston: Allyn and Bacon, 1967), p. 3.

It is the 1917 image of Germany, greatly magnified by the experience of 1933–45, that pervades current American social science.[26] The coding rules employed by the democratic peace literature are heavily influenced by this image. Gurr's democracy/autocracy scales are explicitly informed by the notion that "the empires of Central and Eastern Europe—Germany, Russia, Austro-Hungary—implemented the trappings but not the substance of effective democratic participation in the late nineteenth and early twentieth centuries."[27] Now not only is it curious that a "scientific" data set relies so heavily on a particular *interpretation* of "trappings" versus "substance," it must also be recognized that this interpretation is ahistorical. For Wilson and the political scientists of a century ago did *not* consider Germany an autocracy, did *not* lump the German and Russian regimes in the same category (Russia *was* an autocracy), and were remarkably ambivalent as to whether mass electoral processes were the substance, as opposed to "mere trappings," of effective democratic participation. In sum, the perception of Imperial Germany imprinted in the present coding rules is grossly colored by hindsight and by contemporary values, which in no small part became our values because of the benefit of hindsight.

While the present definition of "democracy" was shaped by the social reality of past U.S.-German enmity, its endurance and universal appeal derive from

---

26. Three classics of American social science, their differences aside, single out Germany as a country whose political and economic development sharply diverged from the Anglo-American "norm": Thorstein Veblen, *Imperial Germany and the Industrial Revolution* (New Brunswick, N.J.: Transaction Publishers, 1990 [1915]); Alexander Gerschenkron, *Economic Backwardness in Historical Perspective* (Cambridge: Harvard University Press, 1962); Barrington Moore, Jr., *Social Origins of Dictatorship and Democracy* (Boston: Beacon Press, 1966), esp. chap. 8. In the 1960s and 1970s these social-scientific models influenced the writings of German historians who sought to combat the impulse to downplay German guilt for the horrors of Nazism. See, e.g., Hans-Ulrich Wehler, *The German Empire, 1871–1918* (Dover, N.H.: Berg Publishers, 1985 [1973]). More recently, English historians led by David Blackbourn and Geoff Eley sought to correct what they regarded as the ahistorical quality of the "special path" interpretation of German history. They argued that the emphasis on past German peculiarity is overly colored by hindsight, that Imperial Germany tends to be judged by the standards of idealized images of the Anglo-American past, and that the German past might look more "normal" if compared to the experience of continental Europe rather than to England. The present essay, inasmuch as it shows that past American scholars regarded Imperial Germany as more normal than do present scholars, provides support for this critique. See David Blackbourn and Geoff Eley, *The Peculiarities of German History: Bourgeois Society and Politics in 19th Century Germany* (New York: Oxford University Press, 1984); David Blackbourn, *Populists and Patricians: Essays in Modern German History* (London: Allen and Unwin, 1987); Geoff Eley, "Liberalism, Europe, and the Bourgeoisie, 1860–1914," in David Blackbourn and Richard Evans, *The German Bourgeoisie: Essays on the Social History of the German Middle Class from the Late 18th to the Early 20th Century* (London: Routledge, 1991). For helpful reflections on the debate, see Peter Paret, "Some Comments on the Continuity Debate in German History," in James Harris, *German-American Interrelations*, pp. 83–88.
27. Gurr, *Polity II*, pp. 36–37.

the *material* reality of America's triumph. America's military victories established it as the world's leading military, economic, and *academic* power. But consider, as a counterfactual, the possibility of a German victory in 1917–18. Would Heidelberg not have remained more prestigious than Princeton or Oxford? Would it be common knowledge that Imperial Germany was autocratic, or would we instead remember Victorian England as the imperialistic "autocrat of the sea," as John Burgess described it in 1915? Would articles on peace among "our kind" have sprouted in American political science journals, or rather in German *Staatswissenschaft* periodicals? And would "our kind" not have been defined in terms of, say, powerful professional bureaucracies insulated from mass public caprice?

The science of the democratic peace is an *American* social science.[28] Citizens of small, vulnerable countries tend to be acutely aware of the historical contingency of their present circumstances, but from the perspective of an extraordinarily secure, triumphant superpower, counterfactuals such as the above are almost unimaginable. It is a social science written from the latter perspective that typically assumes away the historical contingency of the present. And it is from such a perspective that particular time-bound values can be mistaken for universal timeless truths.

The bulk of what follows is devoted to reconstructing the political theories and views of Germany held by two leading American political scientists, John Burgess and Woodrow Wilson. But first, two methodological issues must be addressed: why focus on political scientists, and, among them, why these two?

METHODOLOGICAL CONSIDERATIONS
The political scientists of the gilded age generally shared the socioeconomic background of contemporary American political elites. Whether by birth or by education, they belonged to a cosmopolitan gentry class that was mostly northeastern in residence, liberal or heterodox in religion, and whiggish in outlook.[29] But the socioeconomic affinity of academic and political elites cannot alone justify selecting political scientists to represent "America's" perception

---

28. On this theme, see Stanley Hoffmann, "An American Social Science: International Relations," *Daedalus*, Vol. 106, No. 3 (1977), pp. 41–60; Ekkehart Krippendorf, "The Dominance of American Approaches in International Relations," *Millennium*, Vol. 16, No. 2 (Summer 1987), pp. 207–214.
29. Ross, *The Origins of American Social Science*, chap. 3. Ross's book provides excellent guidance on the intellectual history of American political science, as does (in a more stylized fashion) Farr, "From Modern Republic to Administrative State."

of Germany; academics, after all, exerted little direct influence over American diplomacy.

There are, however, two other important reasons for focusing on the views of past political scientists. First, they constitute the most appropriate "control group" for today's democratic peace theorists who are also mostly political scientists. Early American political scientists were deeply committed to inductive, if unimaginative, science "firmly bottomed on fact and experience."[30] They prized precision of definition and measurement no less than their successors.[31] Therefore, inasmuch as their account of Germany differs from the present account the difference cannot be attributed to pre-scientific idle speculation. Second, while political scientists *qua* academics had no direct control of the levers of government, one prominent member of the profession did go on to make a crucial mark on U.S. foreign policy: the relevance of Woodrow Wilson's scholarship to assessing the democratic peace proposition need not be rehearsed.

An examination of the political theory of John Burgess in addition to Wilson's makes the "sample" more representative of early American political science. Wilson and Burgess represent two distinct, if immediately successive, professional generations. Burgess was the most prominent member of the German-trained generation that founded professional political science in America, whereas Wilson belonged to the first Ph.D. cohort "minted in America." The two scholars also represent two distinct institutional settings. Burgess founded the graduate school in political science at Columbia University (1880)—the first, and for many years the leading, political science graduate program in the country.[32] Wilson was trained (1883–85) and for several years

---

30. Woodrow Wilson, "Of the Study of Politics," November 25, 1886, in Arthur Link, *The Papers of Woodrow Wilson*, Vol. 5 (Princeton: Princeton University Press, 1968), p. 400. (Below, this invaluable comprehensive collection of Wilson's papers is referred to as *PWW*, followed by volume number.) On the disdain for writing that is unsupported by evidence, which Wilson absorbed as a graduate student at Johns Hopkins, see "Editorial Note to 'The Modern Democratic State'," *PWW* 5, p. 55. On John Burgess's strong belief in modeling the social after the natural sciences, see Somit and Tanenhaus, *The Development of American Political Science*, p. 28.

31. What separates the current coders of the democratic peace from their predecessors is the inferential statistical tools that are available to them, more than the very commitment to rigorous empirical science. The common belief that a "scientific revolution" swept political science in the mid-twentieth century unfairly understates the scientific aspirations of earlier generations. See Ido Oren, "Perceptions of Germany in Early American Political Science," paper delivered at the 1994 annual meeting of the American Political Science Association, New York.

32. Somit and Tanenhaus, *The Development of American Political Science*, pp. 7–21. See also Wilfred McClay's introduction to the recent re-issue of John Burgess, *The Foundations of Political Science* (New Brunswick, N.J.: Transaction Books, 1994 [1933]); and Daniel T. Rodgers, *Contested Truths: Keywords in American Politics Since Independence* (New York: Basic Books, 1987), pp. 164–168.

taught at Johns Hopkins University, then Columbia's rival for the discipline's leadership.[33] Burgess was a Germanophile, while Wilson's cultural and sentimental compass was more oriented toward England. Burgess and Wilson epitomize different shades of the theoretical concerns, political views, and professional experiences of mainstream American political scientists in the late nineteenth century.

Another reason for the inclusion of Burgess in this study is theoretical as much as methodological. There is one key contrast between Burgess and Wilson that is more than a matter of shade or nuance. Whereas Wilson's characterization of Germany changed radically in time, Burgess's positive view of Imperial Germany withstood the worsening of U.S.-German relations and even the hysteria of 1917–18. To the end of his life in 1931, Burgess regarded the German-American conflict, which he considered an intra-Teutonic one, as a calamitous error. The variation between the shifting views of one individual and the steadfastness of the other's elucidates an important theoretical point, namely that my argument operates at the *social* level more than the individual one. The contrast between Wilson and Burgess, in other words, suggests that a *sociology* rather than a psychology of knowledge may be appropriate if we wish to understand the process by which values and "coding" of nations change in time. Burgess's case demonstrates that individual scholars are not necessarily puppets in the hands of historical forces, nor do they readily revise their attitudes to accommodate changing political realities. But it also shows that the knowledge generated by, and clung to, by such individual scholars is liable to being forgotten by future *communities* of scholars. John Burgess was arguably the most important political scientist of his time, and yet few present political scientists recognize his name, let alone are familiar with his theory. Woodrow Wilson's legacy, on the other hand, is well remembered by present political scientists, notably by democratic peace theorists. But even in Wilson's case, collective historical memory is selective. It is the 1917 image of Wilson deploring German autocracy that is etched in the present recollection rather than the earlier Wilson who detested French "democracy," approved German constitutionalism, and admired Prussian statism.

---

33. For a concise factual account of Wilson's academic career see August Heckscher, *Woodrow Wilson: A Biography* (New York: Collier Books, 1991), chaps. 2–3. Henry W. Bragdon, *Woodrow Wilson: The Academic Years* (Cambridge, Mass.: Belknap, 1967), if somewhat dated, remains an excellent biographical source on Wilson's pre-political career.

The Nationalist Theory of John W. Burgess

Two episodes that critically shaped the life of John Burgess can also be said to have shaped the origins of academic political science in America: the Civil War and the encounter with Germany. The traumatic experience of disunion and Civil War "provided American political science at the moment of its birth with a compelling *raison d'etre* and a proximate task: formulating the grounds for an enduring and cohesive national political unit."[34] Of the members of his generation, John Burgess was the most effective in providing the nationalist postwar impulse with a "complete and scientific" theoretical foundation.[35]

Born in Tennessee in 1844 into a family that upheld firm Unionist principles, Burgess enlisted in the Federal army, and observed the horrors of the Civil War first hand.[36] When he graduated from Amherst College after the war there was virtually no academic institution in America that offered rigorous graduate training in the social sciences. Like thousands of other young Americans, Burgess was drawn to Germany, whose universities were the most advanced in the world.[37]

Virtually all the founders of academic social science in America studied in Germany. John Burgess earned his Ph.D. there in the 1870s, and the three young scholars he recruited in 1880 to join him at Columbia had also studied in Germany.[38] Herbert B. Adams, who was to lead the program in history and political science at Johns Hopkins and to supervise Woodrow Wilson's studies there, trained in Germany, as did Wilson's two other teachers.[39] Upon their return to the United States these scholars sought to emulate the model of the

---

34. McClay, "Introduction," p. vii.
35. Charles Merriam, *A History of American Political Theories* (New York: Macmillan, 1903), p. 299. The preoccupation with national cohesion was shared by American elites in general; it was not limited to political scientists alone. See Trommler, "Inventing the Enemy," p. 110.
36. McClay, "Introduction," pp. xiii–xv.
37. During the nineteenth century about 9,000 American students flocked to German universities, most of them after 1870. Berlin, the national Prussian university, was the most popular destination, with American enrollment totalling 1300 for the 1880s. See Ross, *The Origins of American Social Science*, p. 55; Somit and Tanenhaus, *The Development of American Political Science*, pp. 15–16; Jarausch, "Huns, Krauts, or Good Germans," p. 148; Jurgen Herbst, *The German Historical School in American Scholarship, 1800–1870* (Port Washington, N.Y.: Kennikat Press, 1972), chap. 1.
38. Somit and Tanenhaus, *The Development of American Political Science*, p. 17.
39. Richard Ely instructed Wilson in political economy and George S. Morris in philosophy. See Niels A. Thorsen, *The Political Thought of Woodrow Wilson: 1875–1910* (Princeton: Princeton University Press, 1988), chap. 4; John M. Mulder, *Woodrow Wilson: The Years of Preparation* (Princeton: Princeton University Press, 1978), pp. 75, 83.

German research university.[40] Students in their German-style graduate seminars were required to master the German language, since German scholarship was held in the highest esteem.[41]

But Germany's appeal was not limited to academic excellence. Germany also provided a powerful model of national reunion and consolidation. Upon arriving in Berlin in 1871 Burgess witnessed the victory parade of the troops returning from the Franco-Prussian war, and compared it favorably to "the march of the Grand Army of the Republic through Washington six years before."[42] This personal experience foreshadowed a lifelong love affair with German institutions and culture.

NATION, STATE, LIBERTY, GOVERNMENT

The major theoretical work of John Burgess, *Political Science and Comparative Constitutional Law* (pub. 1890) contains four sections: "the nation," "the state," "liberty," and "Government."[43] The first section opens with a "German," i.e., exact and scientific, definition: "A population of an ethnic unity, inhabiting a territory of a geographic unity, is a nation."[44]

Nations are not born equal, Burgess argued. They have talents latent in their character, largely determined by the racial composition of their population. At the bottom of the racial hierarchy are the peoples of Asia, Africa, and Latin America (who do not even merit "scientific treatment"), while the middle ranks are populated by the non-Teutonic European races. The Greek and the Slavonic races excel in the arts, philosophy, and religion, but their form of political organization "manifests a low order of political genius." The Celts "have never manifested any consciousness of political principles or developed any constancy in political purpose." The Romans have a gift for building empires. The most advanced polities were formed by "those nations that may be termed the political nations *par excellence*, viz, the Teutonic; and if the peculiar creations of these nations may be expressed in a single phrase it must be this: that they are

---

40. Somit and Tanenhaus, *The Development of American Social Science*, pp. 34–38.
41. Wilson, for example, characterized German scholarship as exceptionally "diligent" and "learned." See "A Book Review," April 17, 1887, *PWW* 5, p. 494.
42. McClay, "Introduction," p. xvi.
43. In later years Burgess prepared an abridged version of the book, but a contract to publish it was rescinded during World War I because of the author's pro-German sympathy. That version was published only in 1933, posthumously, as *The Foundations of Political Science*. My discussion below draws on the 1994 re-issue of the latter book, which I refer to as *Foundations*.
44. *Foundations*, p. 3.

the founders of national states." For Burgess, thus, the nation-state is the highest form of political development, a form that only the Teutonic nations are capable of approaching.[45] Fortunately, in America "an amalgamated Teutonic race is the dominant factor," although the Teutonic elements, "the Anglo-Americans, the Germans, and Scandinavians do not yet mingle their blood completely."[46] Also Teutonic were Germany, England, Holland, Switzerland, the Scandinavian nations, and France (although French blood is diluted by Iberian, Celtic, and Roman elements).[47]

Burgess subscribed to an idealist conception of "the state," subject of the second section of his treatise. The state is not the aggregate product of a contract among free individuals,[48] but an *organic* body that grows in historical time toward the ideal of the perfect state.[49] Along the state's evolutionary growth path, the creation of a national monarchy signals "the beginning of the modern political era." Then, "a large proportion of the population is awakened to the consciousness of the state, and feels the impulse to participate in the work of its objective realization." They "gather about their king" and "make him but the first servant of the state."[50] Once the king turns into a mere office-holder, subordinate to popular sovereignty, the state can be said to be democratic. Democracy is embodied in a revolutionary popular act of constitution-making, and is conditional upon national harmony and cohesion: "the democratic state must be a national state, and the state whose population has become truly national will inevitably become democratic."[51]

On this historical path, Burgess found both Germany and the United States in the most advanced category of (Teutonic) popular democratic states. For Burgess, the German process of constitution-making was no less revolutionary and progressive than its counterpart, a century earlier, in America. In both cases the people consciously formed a modern national state.[52] Moreover, Burgess

---

45. *Foundations*, pp. 31–38. On the popularity and legitimacy of racialist ideas in the intellectual discourse of late nineteenth-century America, see Rogers M. Smith, "Beyond Tocqueville, Myrdal, and Hartz: The Multiple Traditions in America," *American Political Science Review*, Vol. 87, No. 3 (September 1993), pp. 558–560; John Higham, *Strangers In the Land: Patterns of American Nativism, 1860–1925*, 2nd ed. (New Brunswick: Rutgers University Press, 1988), chap. 6.
46. *Foundations*, p. 20.
47. *Foundations*, p. 16.
48. *Foundations*, p. 66.
49. *Foundations*, chap. 5.
50. *Foundations*, p. 70.
51. *Foundations*, pp. 85–86.
52. The analogy between the German and American experience is most evident in John Burgess, "Laband's Public Law of the German Empire," *Political Science Quarterly*, No. 1 (March 1888), esp. pp. 124–126.

identified the Prussian monarch, whether in his capacity as king of Prussia or as emperor of Germany, as a constitutional office holder,[53] a signal of the formation of the modern popular democratic state.

Burgess was a staunch defender of individual liberties, and he regarded the constitutional state as the ultimate guarantor of liberty; it protects individuals both from the incursion of government and from the tyranny of majorities. While in all modern nation-states individuals enjoy similar freedoms, it is in the United States that these freedoms are protected best. In America the fundamental principles of freedom "are written by the state in the constitution; the power to put the final and authoritative interpretation upon them is vested by the state in a body of jurists, holding their offices independently of the political departments of the government."[54]

How do the other modern democratic nation-states measure up? "Of the three chief European constitutions only that of Germany contains, in any degree, the guarantees of individual liberty which the constitution of the United States so richly affords." As much as Germany falls short of the American ideal, its system is superior to France where "there is not the slightest trace of a constitutional guaranty of individual liberty," or to England where the trouble is "that the whole power of the state is vested in the government, and that no sufficient distinction is made between the state and the government." As far as constitutional liberty is concerned, then, Germany is more America-like than either France or England (not to mention countries such as Italy and Greece which are currently coded as having been "liberal" at the time).[55]

John Burgess went to a great length to distinguish "the state"—an abstract organic concept—from the actual government. In fact, the form of the state and the form of the government need not necessarily be in harmony. "It is difficult to see why the most advantageous political system, for the present, would not be a democratic state with an aristocratic government, provided only the aristocracy be that of real merit, and not of artificial qualities. If this be not the real principle of the republican [read: American] form of government then I must confess that I do not know what its principle is."[56] In expressing a preference for a democratic state with a meritocratic government, Burgess

---

53. John Burgess, "Tenure and Powers of the German Emperor," *Political Science Quarterly*, No. 2 (June 1888), p. 335.
54. *Foundations*, p. 106.
55. *Foundations*, pp. 106, 108, 109 respectively. Italy and Greece in the late nineteenth century are listed as liberal countries by Doyle, "Liberalism and World Politics," p. 1164.
56. *Foundations*, pp. 75–76.

anticipated the program of Woodrow Wilson and his generation—who sought to erect an efficient administrative state in the service of the nation—but he himself stopped short of fully articulating this agenda.

Having elaborated the distinction between state and government, Burgess ends his treatise by assessing the merits of various forms of government. A "representative government" is only good if it is constitutionally limited, i.e., "if the state confers upon the government less than its whole power, less than sovereignty, either by enumerating the powers of government, or by defining and safeguarding individual liberty against them." On the other hand, "if the state vests its whole power in the government, and reserves no sphere of autonomy for the individual, the government is unlimited; it is despotism in theory, however liberal and benevolent it may be in practice."[57] From Burgess's earlier discussion of liberty, the identity of the good and bad prototypes of representative government is unmistakable. The English system where "the whole power of the state is vested in the government" epitomizes the bad unlimited representative government; it is despotic in theory and there are no firm guarantees that would arrest a potential slide toward despotism in practice. The United States is the good limited representative state, and from Burgess's earlier discussion of liberty it can be inferred that Germany is closer to this ideal than either England or France.

Another interesting distinction in Burgess's taxonomy of governments concerns "the tenure of the persons holding office or mandate. Viewed from this standpoint, the government is either *hereditary* or *elective*." Burgess makes no normative judgment whatsoever regarding the superiority of one system relative to the other. Discerning four alternative hereditary principles, he concludes that "primogeniture in the male line appears the most useful and successful."[58] That this is precisely the Prussian principle should come as no surprise.[59]

Burgess also made a distinction between presidential and parliamentary government. In presidential systems "the state, the sovereign, makes the executive independent of the legislature, both in tenure and prerogative, and furnishes him with sufficient power to prevent the legislature from trenching upon the sphere marked out by the state as executive independence and prerogative." Burgess has high praise for presidential government: "it is con-

---

57. *Foundations*, p. 114 (both quotations).
58. *Foundations*, pp. 121–122.
59. See Burgess, "Tenure and Power of the German Emperor," p. 337.

servative. It fixes the weight of responsibility upon a single person; and there is nothing like this to produce caution, deliberation, and an impartial regard for all interests concerned."[60]

Now one naturally associates the United States with presidential government, but Imperial Germany was also squarely a member of Burgess's "presidential club." In his essay on the "Tenure and Powers of the German Emperor," he refers repeatedly to the kaiser as the president of the German union or "president of a republic."[61] That the king of Prussia was the president of Germany was written in the German constitution, and for Burgess to have referred to him as such (accepting the form of the constitution as its substance) was entirely uncontroversial in 1888. The kaiser's lack of electoral approval did not matter to Burgess at all (the kaiser, after all, inherited the crown through the best hereditary principle); and if one "president of a republic" should emulate the other, then it was probably the American executive who could learn from his more powerful German counterpart. Burgess's comment about the emperor's veto power in his capacity as king of Prussia is instructive: "These are very wise provisions under existing conditions. I do not see how the Emperor would be able to discharge his great duties to the nation without them."[62]

Parliamentary government was regarded by Burgess as inferior to presidential government. Conspicuously alluding to England, Burgess suggested that the successful operation of parliamentary government depended upon peculiar conditions: a hereditary kingship "possessing the most sincere devotion and loyalty of the masses," a national religion that preserves "the morality of the masses," and "limited suffrage through which the intelligent, conservative and moderate classes shall be the bearers of the political power." The extension of the franchise was threatening to undermine the system. For "how with the present degree of popular intelligence in even the most advanced states can these qualities [stability, civility] be secured in a legislature whose members are chosen by an universal or a widely extended suffrage?"[63] To the extent that Burgess liked liberal England, then, it was the England envisioned by conservative whiggish liberals such as Walter Bagehot, rather than the increasingly democratic England of the late nineteenth century.

---

60. *Foundations*, p. 124.
61. See pp. 334, 335, 347.
62. Burgess, "Tenure and Powers of the German Emperor," p. 349.
63. *Foundations*, pp. 127–128.

In sum, for John Burgess, Germany, England, and France were all closer to the American ideal than Italy, Greece, and the Slavic countries, let alone the colonial world, and among the ranks of those most advanced nation-states, Germany was clearly at the top.

GERMANY: EUROPE'S BEST GUARANTEE OF PEACE

In "Tenure and Powers of the German Emperor," Burgess discussed the emperor's powers in the area of foreign affairs. The emperor was constitutionally empowered to make "alliances with foreign powers, and to declare [defensive] war and make peace." But he was "most heavily handicapped in the exercise of the power of declaring offensive war" since for such an act "the consent of the Federal Council is necessary." As king of Prussia, the kaiser controlled 17 seats in the Federal Council, yet in order to muster the 30 votes necessary to declare war, he needed "an agreement between the princely heads of at least three states besides Prussia." The German princes are not only "old" and "conservative," they are also "hostile to centralization of power in the Imperial government, and they know that war tends to that." Hence, the German constitution provides the best "safeguards against arbitrary, ill-considered, unnecessary declarations of war" that one could possibly devise.[64]

Burgess closes the essay with the following evaluation of the character of the German *imperium*:

It is full of the spirit of conservatism, and well regulated by law. Its constitution guards it well against personal arbitrariness or vacillation on the part of the Emperor or the princes, or fickleness and violence on the part of the people. It is Europe's best guaranty of peace through the power to enforce peace. In a sentence, it is a constitutional presidency; and if it needs any reform, it is in the direction of more strength rather than less.[65]

BRITAIN: "AUTOCRAT OF THE SEA"

John Burgess remained an unwavering Germanophile even after the turn of the century, when the mainstream of political science was beginning to moderate its German accent. His remarks before the Germanic society of America in 1908 betray a feeling of unease about the erosion of German-American amity.[66] In 1914 Burgess, who had retired from Columbia in 1912, was not alone in sympathizing with the German side. But on balance, when Burgess publish-

---

64. Burgess, "Tenure and Powers of the German Emperor," pp. 345–347.
65. Ibid., p. 357.
66. John Burgess, *Germany and The United States* (New York: The Germanistic Society of America, 1908).

ed *The European War of 1914,* he was swimming against the stream of public opinion.[67] Attempting to avert a German-American conflict, Burgess pulled no punches in venting his pro-German and vehemently anti-British views. He not only depicted England as "despotic" and "navalistic-militaristic," but also drew a most unflattering comparison between the "autocrat of the sea" and the "autocrat of the land" (Russia). Germany, however, Burgess proclaimed to be Britain's "opposing counterpart":

Its economic system is by far the most efficient, most genuinely democratic, which exists at the present moment in the world, or has ever existed. There is no great state in the world today in which there is so general and even a distribution of the fruits of civilization as in the United States of Germany. And there is no state, great or small, in which the plane of civilization is so high.[68]

The Statist Theory of Woodrow Wilson

Born in the South in 1856, young Woodrow Wilson shared his father's Confederate sympathy, but as an adult he came to support the Union's cause.[69] The Civil War experience cast a shadow on Wilson's thought no less than it did on the older Burgess; one theme that recurs throughout Wilson's writings is the concept of an organic, cohesive nation-state. Yet whereas for Burgess the state remained an abstract expression of the nation, Wilson sought to endow the nation with a concrete, efficient, administrative state.[70]

Woodrow Wilson was a well-published political scientist, but he never completed *The Philosophy of Politics,* the treatise he hoped would become his definitive theoretical book. According to the editors of Wilson's papers, the book would have consisted of a series of essays or addresses on "the modern democratic state," the historical chapters of his book *The State,* and above all, Wilson's notes for his lectures on administration, law, and jurisprudence.[71]

---

67. Burgess, *The European War of 1914: Its Causes, Purposes, and Probable Results* (Chicago: A.C. McClury, 1915).
68. Ibid., pp. 92–94.
69. Upon entering Princeton College, Wilson identified himself as a supporter of Southern secessionism. The reason for the subsequent alteration in his view had more to do with nationalism than with concern for racial justice. See Bragdon, *Woodrow Wilson: The Academic Years,* pp. 11–12, 21.
70. On the shift in the focus of late nineteenth-century political science from the issue of "nation" to that of "state," see Farr, "From Modern Republic to Administrative State."
71. "Editorial Note: Wilson's First Treatise on Democratic Government," *PWW* 5, p. 58. Wilson, *The State: Elements of Historical and Practical Politics* (Boston: D.C. Heath, 1889). Perusing Wilson's papers from his academic years, one is struck by the thoroughness of his course notes. They read more like preliminary book drafts than skeletal lecture outlines, and thus they provide an invaluable insight into Wilson's thought.

These materials were produced mostly in the decade subsequent to Wilson's receipt of the Ph.D. (1886), during which he taught at Bryn Mawr College, at Wesleyan College, and from 1890 onward at Princeton.[72] My analysis focuses primarily on Wilson's writings and notes from that period because they constitute the core of his never-completed big book, because the book he did complete during that period (*The State*, 1889) is considered his "greatest scholarly achievement," and because it was the period of Wilson's greatest productivity as a political scientist. (In later years he increasingly turned to popular, largely historical, writing and speaking and to academic administration.)[73]

Before turning to Wilson's *Philosophy of Politics*, a few comments are in order with regard to his earlier writings. Woodrow Wilson is rightly remembered as an Anglophile. His family maintained a strong sentimental attachment to their Anglo-Scottish ancestry,[74] and the young Wilson advocated the adoption of the parliamentary system in the United States.[75] The fascination with England did not indicate an anti-German attitude, though. Bismarck in particular was the subject of Wilson's admiration. The chancellor was not above intrigue and deceit, Wilson wrote, but he was nevertheless a most "creative," "insightful," and "energetic" statesman. "We can find on record few instances in which a comparatively small and virtually dependent kingdom has been raised in eight years to the proud place of a first class power by the genius of a single man."[76]

But even more important is the fact that from his earliest writings Wilson had displayed extraordinary animus toward France. In his unpublished essay on "Self-Government in France," Wilson argued that the French people were

72. During 1888–95 Wilson also returned to Johns Hopkins annually to teach administration, thus maintaining a vital connection with a graduate research environment. See Bragdon, *Woodrow Wilson*, chaps. 8–10.

73. *The State* was a textbook that made available in English vast amounts of knowledge that were formerly accessible only to advanced scholars. It was very successful, and was revised in 1898 and 1910. The first part of the book is historical, while the second part consists of comparative "country chapters." In writing the comparative chapters Wilson relied heavily on "the great" *Handbuch des Oeffentlichen Rechts der Gegenwart*, an encyclopedic comparative survey of the theoretical principles and practice of politics and administration. See "Editorial Note: Wilson's 'The State'," *PWW* 6, p. 245. *The State* was translated into several foreign languages one of which, ironically, was German. See Bragdon, *Woodrow Wilson*, pp. 173–178. The opinion that the book was "probably Wilson's greatest scholarly achievement" is due to his biographer Arthur Link, quoted in Mulder, *Woodrow Wilson*, p. 103.

74. Bragdon, *Woodrow Wilson*, chap. 1.

75. See especially *Congressional Government*, which was published in 1885 as a successful book and was later accepted as Wilson's dissertation. The book is fully reproduced in *PWW* 4, pp. 13–179.

76. "Prince Bismarck," November 1877, *PWW* 1, p. 313. See also "Congressional Government," *PWW* 4, pp. 42–43, for a description of Gladstone's status in Parliament as similar to Bismarck's status in the *Reichstag*.

not ready for self-government.[77] French peasants are "almost hopelessly ignorant" and "acquiescent" (p. 529), while members of the bourgeoisie are "not of
the stuff of which trustworthy citizens are made" (p. 527). Inspired by Edmund
Burke, Wilson complains that the French are impetuous.[78] They try to install
methods of self-government by way of revolution, methods that can only be
applied successfully in England and America, where they evolved naturally
over time. "The history of France since the opening of the Revolution has been
little more than a record of the alternation of centralized democracy with
centralized monarchy, or imperialism, in all cases of the sway of a virtual
despotism" (p. 523). The parliamentary system fits France "as ill as independence of parental authority fits a child" (p. 524); "for more than a century
its *forms* have been observed" (p. 533; emphasis original).

In various subtle ways, the derogatory language of the essay reappears in
Wilson's later writings. Throughout his more mature scholarship, references to
the French polity are laced with terms like "intoxicated," "poisonous," "me-
chanical," "unstable," and "impetuous."[79] The view of the French political
system as dissonant with French national character, of France as a democracy
in form only, and of French administration as inferior to Prussia's is a virtual
constant in Wilson's "philosophy of politics." Unlike current social scientists
who tend to single Germany out as an aberrant case of political development,
Wilson rather considered France the "abnormal" case. In his political theory
Germany was in the proper place in its natural trajectory of political development; "impetuous" France was not.

Let us now turn to Wilson's "philosophy of politics," written in fragments
at a time when Wilson had conquered the German language, and when his
intellectual horizon expanded to cover foreign polities other than England
alone.[80] Wilson's scholarship was typical of his generation in combining a

---

77. September 4, 1879, *PWW* 1, pp. 515–538. Page numbers in the text refer to this essay.
78. In later years Wilson adopted Burke as his chief mentor; see Mulder, *Woodrow Wilson*, pp. 126–
127.
79. French democracy is described as a "quick intoxicant or a slow poison" in "The Modern
Democratic State," December 1885, *PWW* 5, p. 63. "Intoxication" is also attributed to France in
"Democracy and Efficiency," October 1900, *PWW* 12, p. 6. For reference to "unstable" constitutionalism" in France see "An Outline of the Preface to 'The Philosophy of Politics'," January 12, 1891,
PWW 7, p. 98. In the same outline Wilson also refers to French political development as "mechani-
cally homogenous" (p. 101) and "impetuous" (p. 102). Both terms carry a negative connotation
from the perspective of Wilson's notion of "normal" organic political development.
80. On Wilson's struggle with the German language see "WW to Edwin R.A. Seligman," April 19,
1886, *PWW* 5, p. 163. That he won the struggle and read widely in German *Staatswissenschaft*,
philosophy, and political economy is most evident from Wilson's "Working Bibliography, 1883–90,"
PWW 6, pp. 562–611. Wilson's writings and lecture notes are loaded with citations of leading
German scholars.

historical account of political development with a current cross-national comparison.

Wilson's theory of political development is reminiscent of Burgess's in that it is racialist-hierarchical in nature. To understand the origins of modern government, Wilson wrote, one need not study the "savage" traditions of "defeated" primitive groups but rather the contributions of the "survived fittest," primarily the groups comprising the Aryan race.[81] From the infancy of Slavonic village communities,[82] Wilson traces the Aryan path to political maturity through the history of the Greeks and Romans, the Germanic tribes, and the English people. Each group adopted the positive practices of its predecessor and added the ingredients consistent with its own character. The Teutons "brought about that fusion of German customs with Roman law and conception which . . . was to produce the conditions of modern political life."[83] They also bequeathed to England "the principle of representation."[84] In England, "out of the freehold and local self-government grew the constitutional state; out of the constitutional state grew that greatest of political developments, the free, organic, self-conscious, self-directing nation, with its great organs of popular representation and its constitutional guarantees of liberty." Finally the English nation "gave birth to America."[85] In sum, the Aryan race left behind more backward races and embarked on a slow march toward political progress. At the pinnacle of Aryan political development is the organic, free, constitutional nation-state, and America is its best exemplar.

Wilson stressed even more emphatically than Burgess the organic nature of the nation-state.[86] The state is "an abiding natural relationship"; it is the eternal "expression of a higher form of life than the individual, namely the common life which gives leave to individual life."[87] The embodiment of the most fully-grown modern nation-state is the constitutional state: "a self conscious, adult, self-regulated (democratic) state."[88] This definition is important, for it suggests that the "democratic state" was a sub-type, the most radical form of

---

81. Wilson, *The State*, p. 2. The Aryan theme is from the British scholars Sir Henry Maine and William Hearn, while the Darwinian theme is from Herbert Spencer; see bibliography in *The State*, p. 15. All references below to *The State* are to the 1889 (first) edition, unless noted otherwise.
82. *The State*, pp. 4–5.
83. *The State*, p. 154.
84. *The State*, p. 580.
85. *The State*, p. 577.
86. Wilson thoroughly rejected the social contract theory of the state. See *The State*, pp. 11–15.
87. "Notes for Lectures at the Johns Hopkins," 1891–94, *PWW* 7, p. 124.
88. "Notes for Lectures on Public Law," 1894–95, *PWW* 9, p. 12.

the most advanced political form, the constitutional state. Constitutional states are characterized by four elements: first, that "the people have some form of representation. It does not make any difference what the representation is, as long as it be broad enough";[89] second, administration subject to the laws; third, an independent judiciary with independent tenure; and fourth, a more or less complete formulation of the rights of individual liberty.[90]

There is absolutely no doubt that Wilson regarded both the German Federation and its chief member, Prussia, as members of this elite group of "constitutional states," along with England, the United States, France, Switzerland, Sweden-Norway, and Austria-Hungary. These are the states that are the subjects of "country chapters" in *The State* and that are most often used by Wilson to illustrate his arguments on constitutional law and administration. The most important of them in Wilson's eyes appear to have been England, the United States, Prussia/Germany, France, and Switzerland, whose constitutions Wilson explicitly compares to the U.S. constitution in his lecture on the "modern constitutional state." These constitutions are not precisely alike; they should not be, because "they originated in the circumstances of the time." Their differences notwithstanding, none is inferior to the others. All of these countries possess the four elements characteristic of the modern constitutional state, and in all of them the constitution is supreme. For example, "the King of Prussia cannot change the constitution made by him: it is held fast in its place by the feeling that it would be unsafe to play with it. Once given forth, it cannot be withdrawn."[91]

Wilson's theory of organic political development stressed the importance of harmony between actual legal and political institutions and the readiness of the national "habit" to benefit from such institutions. Consider Wilson's commentary on the then new Japanese constitution, "copied, in the main, [from] the Constitution of Prussia." The chief point of resemblance between the two is that "the ministers are responsible to the Emperor, not to the legislature. . . . Here the model is not one of responsible government in the English, French, Italian sense." Now, from a present perspective this sounds like a serious indictment of the Prussian and Japanese arrangements, but Wilson says that "considering the stage of development in which Japan now finds itself, the

---

89. "Report of a Lecture at the New York Law School," March 11, 1892, *PWW* 7, p. 477.
90. "Notes for Lectures on Public Law," *PWW* 9, p. 13. See also "Report of a Lecture at the New York Law School," *PWW* 7, pp. 477–479.
91. Ibid., p. 474.

Prussian constitution was an excellent instrument to copy. Her choice of it as a model is but another proof of the singular sagacity, the singular power to see and learn, which is Japan's best constitution and promise of success."[92] Notice that this is not only a direct endorsement of the Japanese constitution but also an indirect approval of the Prussian one. Prussia is not indicted for deviating from the English norm, but rather praised precisely for not copying it mindlessly. Prussia's legal institutions are properly consonant with its national "habit." In contrast, the history of France illustrates the perils of copying English arrangements in form only and of adopting legal institutions "not sustained by habit."[93]

THE DEMOCRATIC STATE

As noted earlier, in Wilson's thought the "democratic state" is a sub-category of the "modern constitutional state." The membership of this category is extremely limited: it includes the United States, Switzerland, Australia, and to a lesser degree England, where there remain "some rebellious pulses" and "the drill of liberty has not extended to all classes." (Fortunately, though, "it was [England's] drilled classes that she sent to America.") France would not become a democracy unless "she shall have . . . [a] few more hard lessons in self-control."[94] To both France and Spain, moreover, democracy is a "slow poison" and South America suffers from a "maddening drought" of democratic institutions.[95]

While Wilson used "democracy" with approval, his understanding of the term was quite unlike its present meaning. First, the concept of democracy was as attached to the notion of organic national development as the wider category of "constitutional state" was. Democracy and "nation" were inseparable, for democracy is only possible when the nation is ripe for it. Thus, Wilson did not denounce the continental states for not being democratic enough, since he recognized that they were disadvantaged by their "hazardous" geographical and historical circumstances.[96] The English race was fortunate (like "closeted" Switzerland) to be insulated from the "fierce contests of national rivalries" that characterized the continental experience. For the continental countries prema-

---

92. All quotations are from "WW to Daniel Coit Gilman," April 13, 1889, *PWW* 6, pp. 169–172.
93. "Minutes of the Johns Hopkins Seminary of Historical and Political Science," March 15, 1889, *PWW* 6, p. 153.
94. "A Lecture on Democracy," December 5, 1891, *PWW* 7, p. 358.
95. "The Modern Democratic State," December 1, 1885, *PWW* 5, p. 63.
96. "A Lecture on Democracy," December 5, 1891, *PWW* 7, p. 358.

turely to adopt institutions which developed slowly and organically in the English-speaking world would be a greater sin than to remain less democratic yet in national habit. France was the impetuous sinner, whereas Germany's institutions were in harmony with her organic development.[97]

Second, Wilson greatly downplayed the role of elections as the proper touchstone of democracy. A democracy is properly ruled by "the men of the schools, the trained, instructed, fitted men." As long as these men get a fair opportunity to govern—through ballot or through civil service examinations—the requirements of democracy are met. The civil service method of selection is "eminently democratic" since "it draws all the governing material . . . from such part of the people as will fit themselves for the function." Selection by merit "is but another form of representation."[98] In Wilson's eyes, then, democracy was not an electoral process as much as a meritocracy. Indeed, one is struck by how little Wilson expressed concern about electoral equality: "Not universal suffrage constitutes democracy. Universal suffrage may confirm a *coup d'état* which destroys liberty."[99] He had little moral problem with the fact that the U.S. Senate was not popularly elected or with the disfranchisement of blacks in the South. In *The State* he reviewed the details of the unequal three-class voting system of Prussia in a purely factual manner without moral condemnation. At the municipal level he unambiguously endorsed this very voting scheme for the United States.[100] Moreover, a democracy *qua* meritocracy—the rule of the educated and trained—was for Wilson a bulwark against the ignorance of the masses. As much as he championed the forces of public opinion, his view of the mass public was very unflattering. The average citizen's mind is fickle: "you cannot expect him to have a 'sound conviction' on the silver question,

---

97. "The Modern Democratic State," *PWW* 5, p. 63. Elsewhere Wilson wrote that England was fortunate to be geographically separated from "the fell sweep of European wars and revolutions." But it was not Germany's fate that England was spared from, as much as the "international compulsion which forced France to become a centralized military despotism." Protected by their natural boundaries, the English "were in every way much more German [read: better] than the Franks." See "The English Constitution," 1890–91, *PWW* 7, pp. 12–14.

98. "A Lecture on Democracy," *PWW* 7, p. 356. For the argument that meritocracy is a form of democracy, see also "Notes on Administration," 1892–95, *PWW* 7, pp. 392–393. In later years Wilson used the Catholic Church of the Middle Ages as an example of an "absolutely democratic organization," since its ranks were open to any qualified man, regardless of his class. See "Address at the Inauguration of the President of Franklin and Marshall College," January 7, 1910, *PWW* 19, p. 743, and class notes taken by Homer Zink, a student in Wilson's course in 1904, at the manuscript library of Princeton University, Woodrow Wilson collection, Box 6.

99. "The Modern Democratic State," *PWW* 5, p. 85.

100. The three-class system is described in *The State*, p. 285. For an approval of that system in city government see *The State*, p. 296; see also "Notes for Public Lecture at the Johns Hopkins," March 16, 1888, *PWW* 5, pp. 713–714.

substantial views on the Behring Sea controversy, or original ideas on the situation in Brazil."[101]

Thus it is not surprising that Wilson approved of insulating foreign affairs from the scrutiny of popular assemblies. Noting that the House of Commons exercised but minimal control over the conduct of British foreign policy, Wilson opined that some matters are "of too delicate a nature to be publicly discussed in Parliament; some plans, particularly of foreign policy, would be simply frustrated by being prematurely disclosed. . . . A certain wide discretion must be allowed the Ministers as to the matters they will make public."[102]

In short, Wilson is better interpreted as a Burkean conservative than as a champion of mass electoral democracy. His aim was to purify the concept of democracy from its association with (French) revolution, Jacksonian populism, and the rule of the unenlightened *demos*. Electoral equality was good "only up to the point where all are equal in capacity to judge," but since that point can at best be only "roughly approximated," government must be entrusted to an educated, not necessarily elected, administrative elite.[103] Enter Prussia, a model of rational administration.

WILSON ON ADMINISTRATION

At the turn of the century, "public administration"—local and federal—was at the center of the agenda of American political science. Woodrow Wilson was among the pioneers of the academic study of administration. In his first essay on the subject, published in 1887, Wilson lamented "the poisonous atmosphere of city government, the crooked secrets of state administration," and federal "corruption," which "forbid us to believe that any clear conceptions of what constitutes good administration are as yet widely current in the United States."[104] The solution was to study the science of administration "developed by French and German professors." In France, administrative machinery was perfected by Napoleon. In Prussia, an "admirable system" of administration was "most studied and most nearly perfected"[105] by great kings and reformers who "transformed arrogant and perfunctory bureaux into public spirited in-

---

101. "A Lecture on Democracy," *PWW* 7, p. 354.
102. "The English Constitution," 1890–91, *PWW* 7, pp. 36–37. On the lack of popular control of the Foreign Office, see Zara Steiner, *The Foreign Office and Foreign Policy, 1898–1914* (New York: Cambridge University Press, 1969).
103. Zink notes.
104. "The Study of Administration," *PWW* 5, p. 363.
105. Ibid., pp. 365–366.

struments of just government."[106] The English race, on the other hand, "has exercised itself much more in controlling than in energizing government."[107] Americans must learn from continental administrative wisdom, and "distill away its foreign gases" to suit the American system.[108]

In the following years, as Wilson's knowledge of the German language and of the continental literature improved, he mitigated his view that the continent was "foreign gas." Especially in the area of city government, Wilson was to determine that the Prussian system was not foreign as much as "Pan-Teutonic" in nature, and that it was the highest form of self-government.[109] He was to discover, furthermore, that to the extent that continental ideas contained foreign gases, the French ideas were more lethal than the Prussian.

The administrative state envisioned by Wilson was not the "night watchman" of the English liberal model but was rather patterned after the statist German model. It was a state that fulfilled many tasks that as far as Washington was concerned still lay in the far future: "poor relief, insurance (pensions and other); savings banks; forestry, game and fishing laws"; promoting the "economic and other activities of society by means of . . . posts, telegraphs, telephones, etc.; Maintenance and supervision of railways; . . . Establishing of institutions of credit" and so on.[110] Furthermore, Wilson admired the model of the University of Berlin—a university harnessed in the service of the nation.[111] In sum, Wilson was an admirer of German statism, and in regard to the functions of the state he unambiguously wished that the United States would become more like Germany than England.[112] He was by no means a maverick within the ranks of American political science at the time.

Turning now from the functions of administrative states to their governmental structure, Wilson customarily classified states into three classes based on their "type of headship." In "autocratic" polities such as Russia and Turkey, "there is an entire absence of any constitutional means of controlling the acts of the head of the state." In "republican" polities such as the United States,

---

106. Ibid., p. 376.
107. Ibid., p. 367.
108. Ibid., p. 378.
109. In the 1887 essay it was described as "not fully" self-government; see ibid., p. 380.
110. "Notes for Lectures on Public Law," 1894–95, *PWW* 9, p. 24.
111. See "Random Notes for 'The Philosophy of Politics'," January 25, 1895; *PWW* 9, p. 130.
112. See for example "A Newspaper Report of a Lecture at Brown University," November 12, 1889, *PWW* 6, pp. 417–423. See also "Marginal Note to 'The Labor Movement in America' by Richard Ely" and "Socialism and Democracy," August 22, 1887, both in *PWW* 5, pp. 560 and 560–563 respectively.

France, and Switzerland, "the Head of the State is made subject to complete subordination to the laws, and is besides held to a personal responsibility for his observance of them." In the third category—"constitutional" systems—the head of state is subjected to "constitutional control" while "there is no personal liability on his part to arrest or other punishment." Interestingly, both England and Prussia exemplify the latter category (as do Bavaria, Spain, and Italy). In constitutional states, royal sovereignty "is nowadays mediate; and mediate sovereignty is no sovereignty at all. The modern monarch is, consequently sovereign only representatively and by reason of his participation in the determinations of the highest body of the State."[113]

To learn about the status of the head of the "Federal State," Wilson compared the United States to Germany. The U.S. head of state is "the executive agent of the central government," whereas in Germany he is "member of the sovereign body [*Bundesrat*] as head of a presiding member state [Prussia]." Yet, "in all these cases the head of the State is strictly *subject* to the laws, to *constitutional rule and procedure*, though in some cases the responsibility is direct and personal, while in others it is only through ministerial proxy."[114] What the latter phrase shows is that in 1894 Wilson perceived the German emperor as an indirectly responsible executive. Overall, from Wilson's lectures and from *The State*, the picture arises of the kaiser as a hereditary chief executive who "possesses no slight claim to be regarded as the most powerful ruler of our time" yet who is nonetheless bound by a fine constitutional machinery. "There are distinct limits to his power as Emperor, limits which mark and emphasize the federal character of the Empire and of it a state governed by law, not by prerogative."[115]

Nowhere in Wilson's writings from that period was I able to find references to the emperor—whether in his capacity as federal president or king of Prussia—as an autocrat. The adjective "autocrat" was reserved for absolutist tsars and caliphs, and it was not counterposed to democratic rule but rather to republican and constitutional forms of government.

Wilson was as interested in local as in national government, for the "local organs of self-government are . . . after all, the most important to the life and

---

113. All quotations are from "Notes For Lectures on Public Law," September 1894, *PWW* 9, pp. 26–27. One must remember that at the time the English crown, held by Victoria, did not appear as lame as it does today, and that the negative image of King/Kaiser Wilhelm was yet to fully crystalize in the future.
114. Ibid., p. 27. Emphasis original.
115. *The State*, p. 254.

vigor of political liberty."[116] American city government lacks vitality and "is conspicuous chiefly because of its lack of system."[117] In France, centralized "interference in local affairs . . . more and more minute and inquisitive, results in the strangulation of local government."[118] Prussia offers by far the best model of local self-government. Whereas the highly centralized French system "misses the principle of life, which is not uniformity but variety," the Prussian model of "concentration" (centralized oversight, but not control of local government) secures "local variety and vitality without loss of vital integration."[119] In a framework such as Wilson's which emphasizes organic national life, the term "vitality" is the ultimate compliment.

Self-government is not about mass voting, but rather "consists in taking part in the government: If we could give, say, to the better middle class the whole power of government then we should have discovered self government. . . . What we should seek is a way to harness the people to the great wagon of state and make them pull it."[120] Wilson regarded Berlin—"the most perfect flower of the Prussian municipal system"[121]—as the best example of this ideal system, where the "better" citizens (but not the *demos*) actively participate in administration, and where rights are tied to service. In Berlin "over 10,000 people [are] associated in the Government, besides the paid officers of the civil service." They must serve without pay "or else lose [their] franchise and have [their] taxes raised." Berlin's electoral system is "characteristic of the Prussian system. The voters are divided into three classes, according to their contribution to the taxes." Although unequal in size, "each of these classes elects an equal number to the Board of Alderman."[122] These facts are recounted with Wilson's highest stamp of approval, namely with a certification of English origins. Berlin was not a foreign example but "just as truly an English example. It is a Pan-Teutonic example of processes that seemed to inhere in the ancient policy of the people to which we belong . . . so we shall not find ourselves on unfamiliar ground by going back to Berlin."[123] Berlin, in sum, embodied the

116. "The English Constitution," October 1890, *PWW* 7, p. 41.
117. "A Newspaper Report of a Lecture on 'Systems of City Government'," April 8, 1890, *PWW* 6, pp. 612–613.
118. "Notes for a Classroom Lecture," February 14, 1889, *PWW* 6, p. 91.
119. "Notes for Lectures at the Johns Hopkins," February 1892, *PWW* 7, pp. 388–391.
120. "A Newspaper Report of a Lecture on Municipal Government," January 19, 1889, *PWW* 6, p. 53.
121. "Note for a Public Lecture at the Johns Hopkins," March 16, 1888, *PWW* 5, p. 712.
122. "A Newspaper Report of a Lecture on Municipal Government," January 19, 1889, *PWW* 6, p. 54.
123. Ibid., pp. 53–54.

highest form of "self-government": a most successful blend of popular participation with great administrative efficiency, a shining model to be emulated by American reformers.

Conclusion: Implications for Theory and Policy

The claim that democracies do not fight one another is not about democracies *per se;* it is better understood as a claim about peace among countries conforming to a subjective ideal that is cast, not surprisingly, in America's self-image. Democracy is "our kind," and the coding rules by which it is defined are but the unconscious representations of current American political values. These values are elastic over time, and their historical change is influenced by America's changing international circumstances. The normative standards embodied in the present definition of democracy were selected by a subtle historical process whereby standards by which America resembled its adversaries have been excluded, while those that maximized the distance between America and its rivals have become privileged. In the process, not only has the perception of friends and adversaries changed, but so has America's own self-perception. Democracy, therefore, is not a determinant as much as a *product* of America's foreign relations. The reason we appear not to fight "our kind" is not that objective likeness substantially affects war propensity, but rather that we subtly redefine "our kind."

American political scientists do not stand apart from this historical process. The political values espoused by scholars a century ago were rather different than present values. John Burgess's ideal political system was a Teutonic, national, "democratic [read: constitutional] state with an aristocratic government."[124] Woodrow Wilson was as fearful as Burgess of the untamed rule of the *demos,* and by purifying the concept of democracy of its radical French content he sought to make it safe for the world long before vowing to do the converse. Wilson's ideal polity was a constitutional (Aryan) state administered efficiently by a selected, not necessarily elected, educated elite, insulated from the ignorant masses. Relative to contemporary ideals, Imperial Germany appeared more "normal" than relative to present norms, which prize fair electoral process and executive responsibility. For both Burgess and Wilson, Germany was a member of a select group of the most politically advanced countries, far

---

124. *Foundations,* p. 76.

more advanced than some of the nations that are currently coded as having been "liberal" during that period.[125] And within this group Germany was ranked either as second only to the United States itself (Burgess), or as positioned below England yet above France (Wilson). What has changed since the 1890s was not the objective nature of the (Imperial) German polity as much the nature of its political relations with America and, subsequently, the subjective norms by which it came to be measured. American social scientists are deluding themselves if they believe that their scientific definitions are value-free, or that their values are fixed in time and place. It is only from the perspective of a secure and overwhelmingly victorious country that a time-bound illusion can so easily be taken for a universal truth.

THE THEORETICAL CONTEXT

In the late 1930s, E.H. Carr was inspired by Mannheim's sociology of knowledge to expose the idealist foundations of the young English science of international relations. Building upon "the outstanding achievement of modern realism"—revealing "the relative and pragmatic character of thought"—he criticized the Wilsonian-liberal paradigm of the harmony of interests as the unconscious product of the peculiar historical and geographic circumstances of the English-speaking countries. Beneath the veneer of the objective concept of international harmony, Carr argued, lay a *post-hoc* ideological justification of Anglo-American mastery.[126]

By the dawn of the Cold War era, international relations has become a predominantly American science.[127] To Hans Morgenthau and fellow realists, whose agenda was shaped by the lesson of Munich, Carr's thought held only a partial appeal, for as much as they admired his analysis of the bankruptcy of liberal thought, they were justly reluctant to accept the policy conclusion the analysis led him to: support of appeasement.[128] Later, while the Cold War was evolving into a "long peace," the attraction of Carr's historical realism eroded further as a generation of "neo-realists" understandably found the analytical

125. E.g., Greece, Chile, Argentina, Italy; see Doyle, "Liberalism and World Politics," p. 1164.
126. Edward H. Carr, *The Twenty Years Crisis, 1919–1939*, 2nd ed. (New York: Harper and Row, 1964 [1946]), esp. chap. 5. Quotations are from pp. 67–68. The influence of Karl Mannheim's *Ideology and Utopia* is acknowledged in Carr's preface, p. ix.
127. Hoffmann, "An American Social Science," pp. 44–45.
128. See Hans Morgenthau, "The Political Science of E.H. Carr," *World Politics*, Vol. 1, No. 1 (October 1948), pp. 127–134. I thank Charles Lipson for bringing Carr's pro-appeasement attitude to my attention.

tools of microeconomics more suitable for making sense of "the stability of a bipolar world,"[129] and for designing "deterrence" of a conveniently fixed adversary. Indeed, in recent decades Carr's legacy has not been upheld by realists (or neo-realists) as much as by critical theorists, who were attracted to Carr's historicist-sociological approach.[130]

Now that the stability of the Cold War has given way to greater fluidity, and so long as the new multipolarity does not yet seem to coincide with major war, neo-realist theory appears out of alignment with the times. Its appeal is diminishing precisely when Wilsonian internationalism is re-issuing a formidable challenge to realist pessimism in the form of the democratic peace claim. The scientific, ahistorical tool kit of neo-realism is ill equipped to deal effectively with the equally ahistorical and ostensibly more scientific neo-Wilsonian challenge. Engaging democratic peace theory on its own scientific ground—quibbling over particular coding decisions, the significance of statistical coefficients, or the details of diplomatic cases—may usefully bruise it but does not critically damage it.[131] Instead, it may be time for realists to offer a more fundamental *critical* exposition of the limits of the very ground. It is time for pessimists to re-acquaint themselves with Carr's historical sociology of knowledge.[132] This is the path I attempted to follow here.

---

129. Kenneth Waltz, "The Stability of a Bipolar World," *Daedalus*, Vol. 93, No. 3 (Summer 1964), pp. 881–909; and Waltz, *Theory of International Politics* (New York: Random House, 1979).

130. Perhaps the most lucid statement of the nature of critical international relations theory, and one which acknowledges Carr's influence, is Robert Cox, "Social Forces, States, and World Orders: Beyond International Relations Theory," in Robert Keohane, *Neorealism and Its Critics* (New York: Columbia University Press, 1986), pp. 204–254.

131. E.g., David Spiro, "The Insignificance of the Liberal Peace," *International Security*, Vol. 19, No. 2 (Fall 1994), pp. 50–86; Christopher Layne, "Kant or Cant: The Myth of the Democratic Peace," ibid., pp. 5–49.

132. To the extent that realists re-adopt Carr's historicist thought, they may find themselves sharing some common ground with critical theorists. Of the variety of critical approaches currently applied to international relations, this essay, in focusing on how an international interaction led to "identity-change," has an affinity with the social construction approach articulated by Alexander Wendt; see Wendt, "Anarchy is What States Make of It: The Social Construction of Power Politics," *International Organization*, Vol. 46, No. 2 (Spring 1992), pp. 391–425. My analysis differs from Wendt's approach in two ways, though. First, inasmuch as it centers on the construction of knowledge by a community of scholars, my approach is more faithful to the label "social" (whereas Wendt maintains the assumption that states are unitary actors; ibid., p. 21, note 2). Second, whereas "constructivists" such as Wendt tend to discount the role of material capabilities (relative to social interaction) in the construction of identities, my argument suggests that material power may be very important. At minimum, it is a necessary condition for the interaction process. Had Germany, for example, not possessed the material capability to challenge the U.S. Navy in Manila Bay, and had the United States not possessed the capability to send a massive army to fight Germany across the Atlantic, America's identity would not have been affected by Germany more radically than it has been shaped by, say, Luxembourg. More importantly, it is the very material fact of America's

OTHER CASES AND POLICY IMPLICATIONS

Germany may not be the only nation that underwent a substantial transformation in the American mind, for in the twentieth century America faced two other bitter enemies: Russia and Japan.

Several times in the past century Americans have come to believe that Russia was closer to their ideals than they previously thought. In 1917–18 the United States and Russia's new Menshevik government were allied against Germany. Woodrow Wilson then declared that "Russia was known by those who knew it best to have been *always* in fact democratic at heart, in all the vital habits of her thought." Wilson himself apparently was not among those who knew Russia best, since in his past writings he had never described it as anything but a backward autocracy. In 1917, though, he discovered that autocracy, "terrible as was the reality of its power, was not in fact Russian in origin, character, or purpose."[133] A writer in the *American Political Science Review* struck similar themes when he sought to refute the myth that the Russians were "Asiatic" (read: inferior), to establish that "Russian Slavs in the early periods of their national existence were democratic," and to attribute the excesses of Russian despotism to pervasive German influence.[134]

Russia's image in America, tarnished following Wilson's anti-Bolshevik military intervention, improved again in the early 1930s. Against the backdrop of deep capitalist crisis many liberal intellectuals (and not just "fellow travelers") looked to Russia for inspiration. Not only were they awed by Russia's rapid economic growth (contrasting sharply with America's stagnation), they were especially enamored of Soviet centralized planning.[135] With the rise of the Fascist threat and the formation of the popular front in 1935, Russia's attraction had grown so much that many liberal intellectuals were all too willing to apologize for Stalin's atrocities. Perhaps the most cogent philosophical justification of "progressive" unity against Fascism was provided by political scientist and popular commentator Frederick Schuman. Liberalism and communism, he

---

battlefield victory that accounts for the universal appeal of the identity known as "democracy." As noted earlier, had Germany won World War I, American scholars might have been busy searching for peace among countries ruled by selfless professional bureaucracies and autonomous chief executives, rather than among "democracies."

133. Quotations from N. Gordon Levin, Jr., *Woodrow Wilson and World Politics* (London: Oxford University Press, 1968), pp. 42–43. Emphasis added to first quotation.

134. Simon Litman, "Revolutionary Russia," Vol. 12, No. 2 (May 1918), pp. 181–191. Quotations are from p. 187 and 182 respectively.

135. Stalin's first five-year plan was praised even by the conservative *New York Times*. See Frank A. Warren, *Liberals and Communism: The "Red Decade" Revisited*, 2nd ed. (New York: Columbia University Press, 1993), chap. 4.

argued in 1936, shared common philosophical roots, and were both on the "democratic" side; Russia and America were both democracies, and they might become even more alike as the Russians moved toward greater political liberty while America progressed toward greater economic equality.[136]

The positive image of Russia receded in 1939 as a result of the Nazi-Soviet pact, only to be revived in 1941. The uncritical depiction of Russia and "Uncle Joe" Stalin during the wartime alliance was not limited to the mass media. Harvard sociologist Pitirim Sorokin attributed the friendship between Russia and America to the compatibility of their fundamental values and their socio-cultural similarity.[137] Harvard philosopher Ralph Barton Perry found that the Soviets were moving away from Marxism "in the direction of ideas that we can call, in very broad terms, democratic." And theologian Reinhold Niebuhr echoed Schuman's view when he wrote that "we have, on the whole, more liberty and less equality than Russia has. Russia has less liberty and more equality. Whether democracy should be defined primarily in terms of liberty or equality is a source of unending debate."[138] The "unending debate" ended abruptly with the outbreak of the Cold War. Not surprisingly, it was resolved in favor of American liberty, against socialist equality, thus opening the door to a historic reconciliation between the formerly contentious ideas of democracy and free market capitalism.[139]

After the end of the Cold War, Americans again rushed to embrace Russia's "transition" toward American democratic ideals (now wedded to free market ideals). American economists hurried to advise the Russians how to dismantle their previously admired planned economy, while lawyers and political scientists were eager to help remake Russian legal and political institutions. In those euphoric days Americans widely agreed that if Russia were not a mature democracy yet, it surely was a nascent one. At the present moment, however, many Americans are far less certain of Russia's democratic credentials. Why? Has the Russian Parliament been shut down or the constitution suspended? Has the president been violently overthrown? No, what has changed is not the objective nature of the Russian political system as much as Russia's external behavior. The recent change in the American perception of the Russian polity has been driven by an erosion of trust in Russia's commitment to political

---

136. Ibid., pp. 109–110.
137. Pitirim Sorokin, *Russia and the United States* (New York: E.P. Dutton, 1944).
138. Quotations are from pp. 39 and 37 respectively in John Lewis Gaddis, *The United States and the Origins of the Cold War, 1941–47* (New York: Columbia University Press, 1972).
139. Maier, "Democracy Since the French Revolution," pp. 146–147.

cooperation more than by a genuine erosion of Russian "democracy." Another Chechnya, another demonstration of Russian foreign policy assertiveness, and those voices that currently invoke the "nascent democracy" image of Russia might also turn silent.[140]

The practical moral of the story is straightforward. If history is any guide, the American view of the democratic or non-democratic identity of Russia (or the other formerly communist countries of Europe) will continue to depend on the peacefulness of their foreign policies more than their foreign policies will depend on their democratic identity. The current American policy of "democratization" may be good for other reasons, but as a pillar of international peace and security it is extremely shaky, for it lacks solid historical foundations.

As for Japan, given that in the late nineteenth century its leaders emulated the Prussian model, and that it later fought alongside Germany against America, it is not surprising that Japan's image in America underwent a transformation similar to Germany's. As noted above, Japan's adoption of Prussian constitutionalism was hailed by Woodrow Wilson in 1889 as proof of her "singular sagacity." As Japan turned to external aggression, the notion of her distinctiveness lingered but the moral sign attached to it shifted from positive "singularity" to negative peculiarity. This view is echoed, for example, by Barrington Moore, a prominent social scientist who assigned Imperial Japan (with Germany) to the "capitalist and reactionary" category of political development.[141] As Japan was remade by the American victors after 1945, a distinction was drawn between its deviant past and its more normal present.[142] Indeed, by the coding rules used by students of the democratic peace, Japan is presently a democracy, which is reflective of the mainstream view of Japan in America today. But there is also a dissenting account of Japan, depicting it as democratic in form only (like France in Wilson's eyes). Proponents of this minority view stress the enormous power wielded by unelected Japanese bureaucrats and argue that in Japan "the idea of 'citizen' as distinct from 'subject' is hardly understood. Pluralist representation exists on paper, of course, but to believe that this informs Japanese practice is taking very much

---

140. Russian diplomats appear to understand this logic better than their Western counterparts. Foreign Minister Andrei Kozyrev stated recently that "if Russia agrees with the West it is assumed to be a new democracy. If not, it is assumed to be going back to the old days." Quoted in "Foreign Minister Defends Russia's Policies," *St. Paul Pioneer Press*, April 29, 1995, p. B7.
141. Moore, *Social Origins of Dictatorship and Democracy*, p. 433.
142. On the postwar transformation of Japan's image in America, see Akira Iriye, "War, Peace and U.S.-Japanese Relations," in Akira Iriye and Warren Cohen, *The United States and Japan in the Postwar World* (Lexington: University Press of Kentucky, 1989), pp. 191–208.

on faith."[143] Which of the competing views is more accurate, I do not know. But what I do know is that if America ever fights Japan again, the current mainstream and the minority views will trade places. This is what happened to Imperial Germany (and probably to Japan itself). If, however, America and Japan ever find themselves fighting a common enemy, Japan will be happily vindicated from the charge that it is democratic in form only. This is exactly what happened to France. Either way, the theory that "our kind do not fight each other" will be safely salvaged.

---

143. Karel van Wolferen, *The Enigma of Japanese Power: People and Politics in a Stateless Nation* (New York: Knopf, 1989), p. 22. See also Chalmers Johnson and E.B. Keehn, "A Disaster in the Making: Rational Choice and Asian Studies," *The National Interest*, No. 36 (Summer 1994), pp. 14–22.

Democratization and the Danger of War

Edward D. Mansfield and Jack Snyder

One of the best-known findings of contemporary social science is that no democracies have ever fought a war against each other, given reasonably restrictive definitions of democracy and of war.[1] This insight is now part of everyday public discourse and serves as a basis for American foreign policymaking. President Bill Clinton's 1994 State of the Union address invoked the absence of war between democracies as a justification for promoting democratization around the globe. In the week following the U.S. military landing in Haiti, National Security Adviser Anthony Lake reiterated that "spreading democracy . . . serves our interests" because democracies "tend not to abuse their citizens' rights or wage war on one another."[2]

It is probably true that a world where more countries were mature, stable democracies would be safer and preferable for the United States. However, countries do not become mature democracies overnight. More typically, they go through a rocky transitional period, where democratic control over foreign policy is partial, where mass politics mixes in a volatile way with authoritarian elite politics, and where democratization suffers reversals. In this transitional phase of democratization, countries become more aggressive and war-prone, not less, and they do fight wars with democratic states.

Edward D. Mansfield is Associate Professor of Political Science at Columbia University and author of Power, Trade, and War *(Princeton University Press, 1994). Jack Snyder is Professor of Political Science and Director of the Institute of War and Peace Studies at Columbia University. His most recent book is* Myths of Empire: Domestic Politics and International Ambition *(Cornell University Press, 1991).*

The authors thank Sergei Tikhonov for assistance with computer programming; Liv Mansfield for preparing the figures; Richard Betts, Miriam Fendius Elman, David Lake, Bruce Russett, Randall Schweller, David Spiro, Randall Stone, Celeste Wallander, and participants at seminars at Harvard and Columbia for helpful comments; and the Pew Charitable Trusts for financial support.

1. Michael Doyle, "Liberalism and World Politics," *American Political Science Review*, Vol. 80, No. 4 (December 1986), pp. 1151–1169; Bruce Russett, *Grasping the Democratic Peace* (Princeton: Princeton University Press, 1993). For skeptical views, see David E. Spiro, "The Insignificance of the Liberal Peace," *International Security*, Vol. 19, No. 2 (Fall 1994), pp. 50–86; and Christopher Layne, "Kant or Cant: The Myth of the Democratic Peace," *International Security*, Vol. 19, No. 2 (Fall 1994), pp. 5–49. They are rebutted by Bruce Russett, "The Democratic Peace: 'And Yet It Moves'," *International Security*, Vol. 19, No. 4 (Spring 1995), pp. 164–175.
2. "Transcript of Clinton's Address," *New York Times*, January 26, 1994, p. A17; Anthony Lake, "The Reach of Democracy: Tying Power to Diplomacy," *New York Times*, September 23, 1994, p. A35.

International Security, Vol. 20, No. 1 (Summer 1995), pp. 5–38
© 1995 by the President and Fellows of Harvard College and the Massachusetts Institute of Technology.

The contemporary era shows that incipient or partial democratization can be an occasion for the rise of belligerent nationalism and war.[3] Two pairs of states—Serbia and Croatia, and Armenia and Azerbaijan—have found themselves at war while experimenting with varying degrees of partial electoral democracy. Russia's poorly institutionalized, partial democracy has tense relationships with many of its neighbors and has used military force brutally to reassert control in Chechnya; its electorate cast nearly a quarter of its votes for the party of radical nationalist Vladimir Zhirinovsky.

This contemporary connection between democratization and conflict is no coincidence. Using the same databases that are typically used to study the democratic peace, we find considerable statistical evidence that democratizing states are more likely to fight wars than are mature democracies or stable autocracies. States like contemporary Russia that make the biggest leap in democratization—from total autocracy to extensive mass democracy—are about twice as likely to fight wars in the decade after democratization as are states that remain autocracies. However, reversing the process of democratization, once it has begun, will not reduce this risk. Regimes that are changing toward autocracy, including states that revert to autocracy after failed experiments with democracy, are also more likely to fight wars than are states whose regime is unchanging.

Moreover, virtually every great power has gone on the warpath during the initial phase of its entry into the era of mass politics. Mid-Victorian Britain, poised between the partial democracy of the First Reform Bill of 1832 and the full-fledged democracy of the later Gladstone era, was carried into the Crimean War by a groundswell of belligerent public opinion. Napoleon III's France, drifting from plebiscitary toward parliamentary rule, fought a series of wars designed to establish its credentials as a liberal, popular, nationalist type of empire. The ruling elite of Wilhelmine Germany, facing universal suffrage but limited governmental accountability, was pushed toward World War I by its escalating competition with middle-class mass groups for the mantle of German nationalism. Japan's "Taisho democracy" of the 1920s brought an era of mass politics that led the Japanese army to devise and sell an imperial ideology

---

3. Zeev Maoz and Bruce Russett, "Normative and Structural Causes of the Democratic Peace, 1956–1986," *American Political Science Review*, Vol. 87, No. 3 (September 1993), pp. 630, 636; they note that newly created democracies, such as those in Eastern Europe today, may experience conflicts, insofar as their democratic rules and norms are not adequately established. See also Russett, *Grasping the Democratic Peace*, p. 134, on post-Soviet Georgia.

with broad-based appeal.[4] In each case, the combination of incipient democratization and the material resources of a great power produced nationalism, truculence abroad, and major war.

Why should democratizing states be so belligerent? The pattern of the democratizing great powers suggests that the problem lies in the nature of domestic political competition after the breakup of the autocratic regime. Elite groups left over from the ruling circles of the old regime, many of whom have a particular interest in war and empire, vie for power and survival with each other and with new elites representing rising democratic forces. Both old and new elites use all the resources they can muster to mobilize mass allies, often through nationalist appeals, to defend their threatened positions and to stake out new ones. However, like the sorcerer's apprentice, these elites typically find that their mass allies, once mobilized, are difficult to control. When this happens, war can result from nationalist prestige strategies that hard-pressed leaders use to stay astride their unmanageable political coalitions.[5]

The problem is not that mass public opinion in democratizing states demonstrates an unvarnished, persistent preference for military adventure. On the contrary, public opinion often starts off highly averse to war. Rather, elites exploit their power in the imperfect institutions of partial democracies to create *faits accomplis*, control political agendas, and shape the content of information media in ways that promote belligerent pressure-group lobbies or upwellings of militancy in the populace as a whole.

Once this ideological connection between militant elites and their mass constituents is forged, the state may jettison electoral democracy while retaining nationalistic, populist rhetoric. As in the failure of Weimar and Taisho democracy, the adverse effects of democratization on war-proneness may even heighten after democracy collapses. Thus, the aftershock of failed democratization is at least one of the factors explaining the link between autocratization and war.

---

4. Asa Briggs, *Victorian People*, rev. ed. (Chicago: University of Chicago, 1970), chaps. 2–3; Geoff Eley, *Reshaping the German Right* (New Haven: Yale University Press, 1980); Alain Plessis, *De la fête impériale au mur des fédérés, 1852–1871* (Paris: Editions du seuil, 1973), translated as *The Rise and Fall of the Second Empire, 1852–1871* (Cambridge: Cambridge University Press, 1985); Jack Snyder, *Myths of Empire: Domestic Politics and International Ambition* (Ithaca: Cornell University Press, 1991), chaps. 3–5.
5. Hans Ulrich Wehler, *The German Empire, 1871–1918* (Dover, N.H.: Berg, 1985); Jack S. Levy, "The Diversionary Theory of War: A Critique," in Manus Midlarsky, ed., *Handbook of War Studies* (Boston: Unwin Hyman, 1989), pp. 259–288.

In developing these arguments, we first present our statistical findings showing that democratizing states have been disproportionately likely to fight wars. We then explain why democratizing states are so war-prone, drawing illustrations from the history of the great powers. Finally, we offer suggestions for reducing the risks of transitions to democracy.

Quantitative Analysis: Definitions, Measures, and Techniques

Much of the research on the democratic peace has relied on statistical tests, which indicate that democracies become involved in wars about as frequently as other states, but that by reasonably restrictive definitions, they have never fought each other. Using similar methods and the same databases (covering the period from 1811 to 1980), we find that *democratizing* states—those that have recently undergone regime change in a democratic direction—are much more war-prone than states that have undergone no regime change, and are somewhat more war-prone than those that have undergone a change in an autocratic direction. In this section, we distinguish between *democratic* and *democratizing* regimes and explain how we set up our statistical tests. We then report our statistical findings.

Definitional issues have been central to the debate on the democratic peace. Even fairly minimal definitions of democracy require periodic elections between candidates who compete fairly for the votes of a substantial portion of the adult population, and whose outcome determines who makes state policy, including foreign and military policy.[6] Thus, the War of 1812 does not count as a war between democracies because Britain's suffrage was too narrow. Conversely, although the German Reichstag of 1914 was elected by universal suffrage with voter turnout over 90 percent, the war between France and Germany is excluded because German cabinet officials were chosen by the Kaiser. Nonetheless, in light of the current enthusiasm about the prospects for promoting peace by encouraging democratization, it is important not simply to discard cases that are not yet mature democracies, but to analyze democratization as a significant category in its own right.

Ted Robert Gurr's Polity II database on regime characteristics is commonly used to study the democratic peace, and is especially well-suited to measuring

---

6. Joseph Schumpeter, *Capitalism, Socialism, and Democracy*, 2d ed. (New York: Harper, 1947); Samuel P. Huntington, *The Third Wave: Democratization in the Late Twentieth Century* (Norman: University of Oklahoma Press, 1991), pp. 5–13, esp. p. 6; see also Russett, *Grasping the Democratic Peace*, pp. 16–18, and Michael Doyle, "Liberalism and World Politics," esp. p. 1164.

gradations of regime change toward or away from democracy.[7] Gurr created measures of democracy and autocracy (with values from 0 to 10) based on the competitiveness of political participation, the strength of the rules regulating participation in politics, the competitiveness of the process for selecting the chief executive, the openness of executive recruitment, and the strength of the constraints on the chief executive's power. Bruce Russett has combined these measures to develop a composite index of a state's regime type.[8] Based on this index and following Gurr, Russett distinguishes among democracies, autocracies, and "anocracies," political systems in which democratic and autocratic features are mixed, or in which very little power is concentrated in the hands of public authorities.[9] Some of the anocracies discussed by Russett include Iran under Mossadegh, Indonesia after Sukarno's first election, Goulart's Brazil, and Allende's Chile.[10] Victorian Britain is coded as close to fully democratic on some dimensions, but anocratic on others.[11]

We consider states to be *democratizing* if, during a given period of time, they change from autocracy to either anocracy or democracy, or if they change from anocracy to democracy. Conversely, states are *autocratizing* if they change from democracy to autocracy or anocracy, or from anocracy to autocracy.

We conduct separate analyses based on the composite index of regime change and on three of its components, because we are interested in both their combined and their separate effects on war. The first of these components is the openness of executive recruitment. In Gurr's definition, "recruitment of the chief executive is 'open' to the extent that all the *politically active* population has an opportunity, in principle, to attain the position through a regularized process."[12] The second component, executive constraints, measures "the insti-

7. Ted Robert Gurr, *Polity II: Political Structures and Regime Change, 1800–1986*, Inter-University Consortium for Political and Social Research No. 9263 (1990).
8. Russett, *Grasping the Democratic Peace*, p. 77; see also Maoz and Russett, "Normative and Structural Causes of the Democratic Peace, 1956–1986." This index is: PCON(DEM − AUT), where DEM is a state's score on the summary measure of democracy, AUT is a state's score on the summary measure of autocracy, and PCON is a measure of the extent to which power in a regime is monopolized by state authorities, which takes on values ranging from 0 to 10. This index therefore takes on values ranging from 100 (maximal democracy) to −100 (maximal autocracy).
9. More specifically, Russett classifies as democracies those states with values of the index of regime type described in footnote 8 ranging from 30 to 100, those with scores ranging from −25 to −100 as autocracies, and those with scores ranging from −24 to 29 as anocracies. See Russett, *Grasping the Democratic Peace*, p. 77; and Ted Robert Gurr, "Persistence and Change in Political Systems," *American Political Science Review*, Vol. 68, No. 4 (December 1974), pp. 1482–1504.
10. Russett, *Grasping the Democratic Peace*, pp. 121–122.
11. Gurr, *Polity II*, p. 11.
12. Gurr, *Polity II*, p. 11; emphasis in original. This variable is coded, based on a four-point scale ranging from closed to open. Closed regimes and regimes in which the recruitment of executives

tutionalized constraints that exist on the decision-making powers of chief executives, whether individuals or collectivities."[13] The greater these constraints, the more democratic is the polity.[14] The third component, the competitiveness of political participation, "refers to the extent to which alternative preferences for policy and leadership can be pursued in the political arena."[15] The greater the competitiveness, the more democratic is the polity.[16]

Although Gurr's selection of indicators and his classification of cases are not beyond dispute, they are generally considered to be better documented and more discriminating than other compilations.[17] Moreover, by using Gurr's data, we insure that none of the cases included in our analysis were coded with an eye toward confirming the hypothesis that democratization promotes war.

Like most research on the democratic peace, we rely on the Correlates of War (COW) Project data on war.[18] Most of these studies have focused on wars

---

is unregulated were coded autocratic; regimes characterized by hereditary succession and an executive chief minister chosen by either "executive or court selection" or "electoral selection" were coded anocratic; and open regimes were coded democratic. This sometimes leads to counterintuitive coding of cases. Partly for this reason, Britain's composite score remains anocratic until 1922. However, recoding cases piecemeal would be fraught with dangers. Rather than dealing with possible validity problems through recoding, we checked for the impact of any particular coding quirks by running separate tests for the various component indices and for different time periods. The fact that we obtained roughly parallel results from these various tests suggests that possible biases in the coding of specific regimes or the measurement of specific indicators were not decisively influencing our findings.

13. Gurr, *Polity II*, p. 15.

14. Regimes are coded using a seven-point scale. Polities in which executives are vested with unlimited authority and those classified as falling between these regimes and those in which limited constraints exist on the executive are coded autocratic. Polities in which "accountability groups have effective authority equal to or greater than the executive in most areas of activity" (Gurr, *Polity II*, p. 16), and those classified as falling between these regimes and those in which substantial constraints exist on executive authority, are coded democratic. All polities falling between these extremes are coded anocratic.

15. Gurr, *Polity II*, p. 18.

16. The competitiveness of political participation is coded on a five-point scale ranging from "suppressed competition" to "competitive competition." We code the former polities as autocratic, the latter polities as democratic, and all polities in between these extremes as anocratic.

17. We are unaware of any data set that is better suited to our purposes. For example, Michael Doyle's data on democracies emphasize normative features of a polity rather than the institutional features on which we focus. Further, since these data do not distinguish among the regime types of non-democracies, it is not possible to identify countries that underwent periods of democratization but failed to become mature democracies. Arthur Banks's data do not tap the institutional factors emphasized in our analysis as well as the Polity II data developed by Gurr. And, as Russett points out, although measures of regime type based on Gurr's and Banks's data are moderately related to one another, Banks's "simpler categorization, compiled earlier than that of Gurr et al. and less fully documented, is probably less discriminating." See Russett, *Grasping the Democratic Peace*, p. 78; Doyle, "Liberalism and World Politics"; and Banks, *Cross-Polity Time-Series Data* (Binghamton: State University of New York, Center for Comparative Political Research, 1986).

18. See Melvin Small and J. David Singer, *Resort to Arms: International and Civil Wars, 1816–1980* (Beverly Hills, Calif.: Sage Publications, 1982).

between states. However, we also assessed whether democratizating states fight non-state actors, as in a colonial war.[19] Consistent with the COW definition, we consider as a war any military conflict that led to at least 1,000 battle fatalities.[20]

Because we view democratization as a gradual process, rather than a sudden change, we analyze whether democratization during periods of one, five, and ten years is associated with involvement in war over subsequent periods of one, five, and ten years, respectively. Insofar as the effects of democratization on domestic coalitions, interest groups, and ideologies might unfold gradually after the initial political opening, the likelihood of war might increase gradually over the following decade. We compare the first and last year of each time period to identify cases of democratization, autocratization, and no regime change. We then examine whether a war involving that state began in the subsequent period. We carry out this analysis for each measure of democratization discussed above, and for both interstate wars and all wars, during the period from 1811 to 1980, the only era common to Gurr's Polity II data and the COW data.[21]

---

19. Since the correlation between the COW data sets of interstate wars and all wars is quite modest, the relationship between democratization and all wars need not be similar to that between democratization and interstate wars. See Edward D. Mansfield, *Power, Trade, and War* (Princeton: Princeton University Press, 1994), chap. 2. Most of the literature on the democratic peace, especially that which focuses on the role of norms, is cast at the dyadic level of analysis and therefore analyzes wars between pairs of states. Thus, it necessarily ignores wars between states and non-state actors. Our tests, however, are not dyadic, but rather address the characteristics of individual states. We will analyze dyadic relationships of democratizing states in a subsequent study.

20. To be counted as a participant, each state involved in an interstate war must have suffered at least 100 fatalities or sent at least 1,000 troops into active combat. States involved in wars against non-state actors must have sustained (in combination with any allies) at least 1,000 deaths in battle during each year of the conflict. On these coding procedures, see Small and Singer, *Resort to Arms*, pp. 55–57.

21. The COW data on war cover the period from 1816 to 1980, whereas Gurr's data cover the period from 1800 to 1986. As a result, our analysis based on one-year periods begins in 1815, and our analyses based on five-year and ten-year periods begin in 1811. In the case of five-year periods, the first observation measures democratization between 1811 and 1815 and war between 1816 and 1820. In the case of ten-year periods, the first observation measures democratization from 1811 to 1820 and war from 1821 to 1830. In order to observe the need for statistical independence among the observations, non-overlapping periods are used in each set of analyses. Certain countries were formed during this period (e.g., Italy, Germany, the Soviet Union), whereas others dissolved (e.g., Austria-Hungary, the Ottoman Empire, Serbia, Germany). Small and Singer agree with Gurr that some countries should be treated separately (Austria-Hungary and Austria; Russia and the Soviet Union; Germany, West Germany, and East Germany; the United Arab Republic and Egypt; Cambodia and Kampuchea; and Tanganyika and Tanzania). We therefore follow this procedure in our analyses. In other cases, however, Small and Singer disagree with Gurr. We analyzed these countries in two ways. First, the Ottoman Empire and Turkey, Sardinia and Italy, Prussia and Germany, and Serbia and Yugoslavia were considered a single country during the period from 1811 to 1980. Second, we treated each country in every pair separately. Since there was little

To assess the strength of the relationship between regime change and war, we construct contingency tables to determine whether democratization and autocratization are each statistically independent of a state's subsequent involvement in war. The null hypothesis is that the probabilities are identical that a democratizing state, an autocratizing state, and a regime with no change will become involved in a war. To test this hypothesis, we calculate the expected frequency of each outcome (democratization and war, democratization and no war, autocratization and war, autocratization and no war, no regime change and war, no regime change and no war) assuming that the probability of war is the same, whether the regime changes or not. We then compare these expected frequencies to the corresponding observed frequencies. A Pearson chi-square statistic (χ^2) is calculated, the value of which indicates the extent of the difference between these frequencies.[22] The greater the value of this statistic, the lower is the probability that regime change and war are statistically independent.[23]

DEMOCRATIZATION AND WAR: STATISTICAL FINDINGS
We found that democratizing states were more likely to fight wars than were states that had undergone no regime change. As shown in Figures 1 and 2, the probability of war for democratizing states always exceeds that for states undergoing no regime change. On average, democratizing states were about two-thirds more likely to go to war than were states that did not experience a regime change. For example, during any given ten-year period, a state that had not experienced a regime change during the previous decade had about one chance in six of fighting a war; in the decade following democratization, a state's chance of fighting a war was about one in four. The relationship between

---

difference in the results based on these two sets of tests, we report the results based on the latter procedure, which is consistent with that of Gurr.
22. More formally, $\chi^2 = \Sigma[(f - e)^2/e]$, where f is the observed frequency for each outcome, e is the expected frequency for each outcome, and sigma (Σ) refers to the summation of this value for all outcomes.
23. The null hypothesis of statistical independence is rejected if $\Sigma[(f - e)^2/e] > \chi^2_{.05}$, if we rely on the .05 level of statistical significance. This statistic has degrees of freedom equal to $(r - 1)(c - 1)$, where r refers to the number of rows and c refers to the number of columns in the contingency table. The use of this statistic is appropriate only if the expected frequency for each outcome exceeds one, a condition which is met in all of the following tests. Indeed, the expected frequency of war usually exceeds five when five-year and ten-year periods are analyzed. On this issue, see Stephen E. Fienberg, *The Analysis of Cross-Classified Categorical Data* (Cambridge, Mass.: The MIT Press, 1980), p. 170.

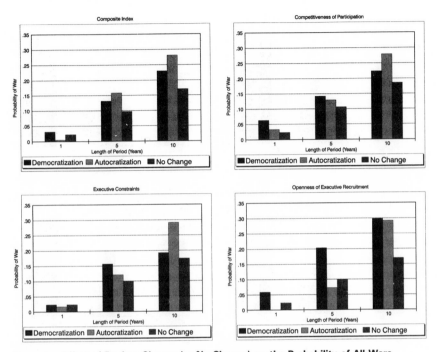

Figure 1. Effect of Regime Change (or No Change) on the Probability of All Wars.

democratization and war was strongest for ten-year periods and weakest for one-year periods.

These findings are not very sensitive to our decision to distinguish autocratizing regimes from those experiencing no change. When we compared the probability of war for democratizing states with that of all countries that were not democratizing (i.e., autocratizing countries and those experiencing no change), democratization gave rise to a higher probability of war than the absence of democratization in every instance. Democratizing states were, on average, about 60 percent more likely to go to war than states that were not democratizing.

Although our results provide strong support for the hypothesis that democratization promotes war, the strength of this relationship differs depending on the measure of democratization used and the length of time that is analyzed.

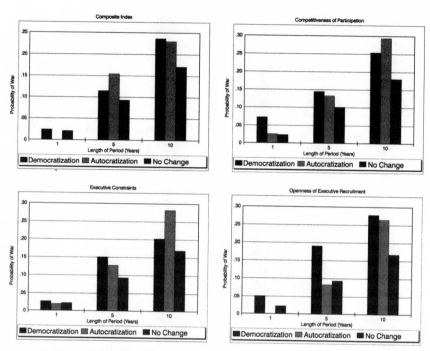

Figure 2. **Effect of Regime Change (or No Change) on the Probability of Interstate Wars.**

Based on the composite index, states undergoing democratization were, on average, about one-third more likely to go to war than states experiencing no regime change, regardless of whether all wars or interstate wars are considered. The effects of democratization were somewhat stronger when the three components of regime change (discussed earlier) are analyzed separately. Based on the openness of executive recruitment, the probability of both interstate wars and all wars was, on average, about twice as large for states in the process of democratization as for states undergoing no regime change. Based on the competitiveness of political participation, the probability that democratizing states would fight any type of war was, on average, about 75 percent greater than for states undergoing no regime change. The probability of interstate wars for countries in the process of democratization was, on average, about twice as large as for countries experiencing no regime change. Based on the constraints placed on a chief executive, states undergoing democratization were, on average, about 35 percent more likely to become engaged in both interstate wars and all wars than states experiencing no regime change.

The strength of the relationship between democratization and war also varies depending on the length of time that is analyzed. Our results were statistically significant in three out of eight tests based on one-year periods; in four out of eight tests based on five-year periods; and in six out of eight tests based on ten-year periods.[24] (The latter results are presented in Table 1.) Further, based on the composite index, the percentage change in the probability of war associated with democratization and that associated with the absence of regime change increases as the period of time analyzed becomes longer: it is greatest based on ten-year periods and lowest based on one-year periods.

These results are quite robust. Our findings about democratization and war did not change significantly when we excluded changes from autocracy to anocracy from the category of democratization; when we excluded changes from democracy to anocracy from the category of autocratization; when we excluded states that underwent transitions in both directions, toward democracy and autocracy, in a given five-year or ten-year period; when we analyzed the periods before and after World War I separately; nor when we analyzed great powers and other states separately.[25]

---

24. Only our results based on the competitiveness of participation fail to conform to this tendency for the strength of the relationship between regime change and war to increase as the period of time we analyzed becomes longer. In this case, however, our results are statistically significant only when one-year periods are considered (for all wars, $\chi^2 = 5.44$ ($p < .10$); for interstate wars, $\chi^2 = 7.54$ ($p < .05$)) and, for interstate wars, when ten-year periods are analyzed (see Table 1).

25. For a description of the criteria used to code states as great powers and a list of these states, see Small and Singer, *Resort to Arms*, pp. 44–45. One reason that we conducted separate tests based on pre–World War I cases is that a few of the cases of democratizing states that went to war in the period after World War I seemed on the surface to be causally questionable. For example, after World War II, Greece became democratic and subsequently became involved in the Korean War. Though events in Greece and Korea were connected through the larger contest between democratic and communist states, it hardly seems correct to say that Greek democratization caused the Korean War. Rather than throwing out such cases in *ad hoc* manner, we checked to see whether these cases were substantially influencing our overall findings by examining the seemingly less problematic pre-1914 cases separately. In addition, we checked whether states initially autocratized and subsequently, during the following five or ten years, democratized to a sufficient extent that the state was coded as democratizing. Under these circumstances, we would not be able to determine whether to attribute a war to the initial autocratization or the subsequent democratization. Fortunately, there were few cases in which multiple fluctuations occurred within a given period, and they did not noticeably influence our results. To analyze their influence, we first omitted these periods, and then coded them on the basis of the last fluctuation that occurred in each period. The only marked changes in our results due to multiple fluctuations occurred when the composite index and ten-year periods were analyzed. In these cases, the results became substantially stronger (for all wars, $\chi^2 = 11.54$ ($p < .01$); for interstate wars, $\chi^2 = 7.75$ ($p < .05$)).

Table 1. Contingency Tables of the Relationships Between Regime Change and War, Based on Ten-Year Periods, 1811–1980.

Regime Change	War	No War	Total
A. All Wars			
Composite Index (χ^2 = 7.99**)			
Democratization	22 (17.8)	62 (66.2)	84
Autocratization	25 (16.6)	53 (61.4)	78
No Change	142 (154.6)	586 (573.4)	728
Total	189	701	890
Openness of Executive Recruitment (χ^2 = 9.10**)			
Democratization	17 (10.4)	33 (39.6)	50
Autocratization	10 (6.2)	20 (23.8)	30
No Change	140 (150.4)	584 (573.6)	724
Total	167	637	804
Competitiveness of Participation (χ^2 = 3.09)			
Democratization	14 (12.2)	41 (42.8)	55
Autocratization	14 (9.7)	30 (34.3)	44
No Change	137 (143.1)	510 (503.9)	647
Total	165	581	746
Executive Constraints (χ^2 = 6.17**)			
Democratization	14 (13.4)	50 (50.6)	64
Autocratization	20 (12.6)	40 (47.4)	60
No Change	135 (143.0)	548 (540.0)	683
Total	169	638	807
B. Interstate Wars			
Composite Index (χ^2 = 3.51)			
Democratization	20 (15.4)	64 (68.6)	84
Autocratization	18 (14.3)	60 (63.7)	78
No Change	125 (133.3)	603 (594.7)	728
Total	163	727	890
Openness of Executive Recruitment (χ^2 = 5.58*)			
Democratization	14 (9.0)	36 (41.0)	50
Autocratization	8 (5.4)	22 (24.6)	30
No Change	122 (129.7)	602 (594.3)	724
Total	144	660	804
Competitiveness of Participation (χ^2 = 4.92*)			
Democratization	14 (10.6)	41 (44.4)	55
Autocratization	13 (8.5)	31 (35.5)	44
No Change	117 (124.9)	530 (522.1)	647
Total	144	602	746
Executive Constraints (χ^2 = 5.03*)			
Democratization	13 (11.6)	51 (52.4)	64
Autocratization	17 (10.9)	43 (49.1)	60
No Change	116 (123.6)	567 (559.4)	683
Total	146	661	807

NOTE: Cell entries are observed frequencies of war and no war with expected frequencies in parentheses. χ^2 is the Pearson chi-square statistic for tests of statistical independence. In all cases, there are two degrees of freedom. The total number of observations differs among the tables due to variations across states in the availability of data on the features of regime change analyzed here.
* Significant at the .10 level.
** Significant at the .05 level.

We also analyzed whether the relationship between democratization and war depends on either a state's regime type prior to this transition or the magnitude of the regime change. To do this, we computed the probability of war separately for each of the three types of regime change in a democratic direction: that is, from anocracy to democracy, autocracy to democracy, and autocracy to anocracy. Likewise, we computed separately the probability of war for states that, during a given period of time, remained autocracies, anocracies, and democracies. Consistent with our other findings, democratization increased the probability of both interstate wars and all wars, especially based on five-year and ten-year periods. Consistent with the findings of other scholars,[26] stable democracies were, on average, no more and no less likely to go to war than other states. In addition, the probability of war for regimes that remained autocracies, anocracies, or democracies during a given period of time was roughly similar.

Our findings based on ten-year periods are presented in Table 2. Depending on which index is used to measure democratization, a change from anocracy to democracy increased the probability of any type of war by roughly 15 to 100 percent, and of interstate war by roughly 35 to 115 percent, compared to a state that remained anocratic. A change from autocracy to democracy increased the probability of any type of war by approximately 30 to 105 percent, and of interstate war by approximately 50 to 135 percent, compared to a state that remained autocratic. A change from autocracy to anocracy increased the probability of war by about 70 percent compared to states that remained autocratic, based on the openness of executive recruitment, whereas it slightly decreased the likelihood of war based on the other three indices. Moreover, on average, the percentage increase in the probability of war was smallest for countries making transitions from autocracy to anocracy and greatest for countries making the dramatic leap from autocracy to democracy. More dramatic transitions toward democracy therefore seem more likely to promote wars than do less profound changes of this sort.

---

26. See, for example, Bruce Bueno de Mesquita and David Lalman, *War and Reason: Domestic and International Imperatives* (New Haven: Yale University Press, 1992); Steven Chan, "Mirror, Mirror on the Wall . . . Are the Freer Countries More Pacific?" *Journal of Conflict Resolution*, Vol. 28, No. 4 (December 1984), pp. 617–648; Jack S. Levy, "Domestic Politics and War," in Robert I. Rotberg and Theodore K. Rabb, eds., *The Origin and Prevention of Major Wars* (New York: Cambridge University Press, 1989), pp. 83–88; Zeev Maoz and Nasrin Abdolali, "Regime Types and International Conflict, 1816–1976," *Journal of Conflict Resolution*, Vol. 33, No. 1 (March 1989), pp. 3–35; and Melvin Small and J. David Singer, "The War-Proneness of Democratic Regimes," *Jerusalem Journal of International Relations*, Vol. 1, No. 1 (Summer 1976), pp. 50–69.

Table 2. Probability of War for Autocracies, Anocracies, Democracies, States Undergoing Democratization, and States Undergoing Autocratization, Based on Ten-Year Periods, 1811–1980.

	Composite Index	Openness of Executive Recruitment	Competitiveness of Participation	Executive Constraints
A. All Wars				
No Change in Regime Type				
Autocracy	.24	.22	.27	.21
Anocracy	.16	.31	.20	.16
Democracy	.19	.16	.20	.23
Democratization				
Autocracy to Anocracy	.22	.38	.21	.20
Anocracy to Democracy	.33	.39	.27	.18
Autocracy to Democracy	.33	.29	.50	.43
Autocratization				
Democracy to Anocracy	.25	.25	.13	.20
Anocracy to Autocracy	.32	.50	.35	.37
Democracy to Autocracy	.67	.28	.50	.33
B. Interstate Wars				
No Change in Regime Type				
Autocracy	.21	.19	.23	.18
Anocracy	.14	.23	.16	.14
Democracy	.19	.15	.20	.19
Democratization				
Autocracy to Anocracy	.20	.25	.21	.17
Anocracy to Democracy	.30	.31	.27	.18
Autocracy to Democracy	.33	.29	.50	.43
Autocratization				
Democracy to Anocracy	.17	.25	.13	.20
Anocracy to Autocracy	.24	.50	.35	.34
Democracy to Autocracy	.33	.17	0	.11

AUTOCRATIZATION AND WAR: STATISTICAL FINDINGS

Although democratization increases the probability of war, autocratization is also dangerous. Autocratizing states were more likely to go to war than countries experiencing no regime change, based on the results of 16 out of 24 tests, which are presented in Figures 1 and 2. However, autocratization tends to be a somewhat less combustible process than democratization. States in the process of democratization are more likely to go to war than those in the process of autocratization, based on the results of 17 out of 24 tests that we conducted.

Like the effects of democratization on war, the effects of autocratization vary across the different indices and periods of time that we analyzed. For example, on average, autocratization yields about a 35 percent greater likelihood of war than does the absence of regime change, when we focus on a state's competitiveness of participation, and about a 25 percent increase in the probability of war, when we focus on a polity's constraints on its executive. In contrast, autocratization decreases the likelihood of war in many cases compared to a country that experienced no regime change, based on the composite index and on the openness of executive recruitment.

Our findings also indicate that autocratization is less likely to lead to war over the short run than in the long run. Regardless of whether all wars or interstate wars are analyzed, autocratization occurring over a one-year period substantially decreases the probability of war compared to states experiencing no regime change, based on every measure except the competitiveness of participation. In contrast, as the results in Table 1 show, autocratization over a ten-year period yields a marked percentage increase in the probability of war in every instance.

The results in Table 2 likewise show that autocratization over a ten-year period is associated with an increased probability of war. States making the large change from democracy to autocracy were especially likely to fight in all wars, compared to countries that remained democratic. States changing from anocracy to autocracy were especially likely to fight interstate wars. However, states changing from democracy to anocracy were not especially war-prone at all. In combination with our earlier results, these findings suggest that the biggest leaps in democratization disproportionately increase the likelihood that a country will engage in an *interstate* war, whereas the most dramatic types of autocratization disproportionately increase the likelihood that a state will fight *non-state opponents*.

In short, although democratizing states are, on average, somewhat more likely to engage in war than their autocratizing counterparts, states experiencing either type of change run a greater risk of war than those experiencing no change.

How Democratization Causes War

Why are democratization and autocratization associated with an increased chance of war? What causal mechanism is at work? Based on case studies of four great powers during their initial phases of democratization, we argue that threatened elites from the collapsing autocratic regime, many of whom have parochial interests in war and empire, use nationalist appeals to compete for mass allies with each other and with new elites. In these circumstances, the likelihood of war increases due to the interests of some of the elite groups, the effectiveness of their propaganda, and the incentive for weak leaders to resort to prestige strategies in foreign affairs in an attempt to enhance their authority over diverse constituencies. Further, we speculate that transitional regimes, including both democratizing and autocratizing states, share some common institutional weaknesses that make war more likely. At least in some cases, the link between autocratization and war reflects the success of a ruling elite in using nationalist formulas developed during the period of democratization to cloak itself in populist legitimacy, while dismantling the substance of democracy. In explaining the logic behind these arguments, we draw on some standard theories about the consequences of different institutional arrangements for political outcomes.

We illustrate these arguments with some contemporary examples and with cases drawn from four great powers at early stages in the expansion of mass political participation: mid-Victorian Britain, the France of Napoleon III, Bismarckian and Wilhelmine Germany, and Taisho Japan. In each of these cases, elections were being held and political leaders were paying close attention to public opinion in the making of foreign policy, yet some key aspects of democratic control over policy were absent or distorted. We do not claim that these four cases constitute a systematic test of our hypotheses. Our definition of democratization is a broad one, and these are not the only instances of democratization among the great powers. France has been "democratizing" in fits and starts between 1789 and the Fifth Republic, sometimes fighting wars linked to surges of democratization and sometimes not. Moreover, there are cases where great powers democratized peacefully when circumstances were propitious: for example, West Germany and Japan after 1945. Though the qualitative part of our study does show that democratization and war have often been linked in the history of the great powers, its main task is less to test the strength of this relationship than to trace how democratization and war were linked in several important cases.

Nor do we claim that these great powers are necessarily representative of all democratizing states. However, as mentioned earlier, in order to assess the robustness of our statistical results, we analyzed separately the relationship between democratization (and autocratization) and war for great powers, and for other states. We found few significant differences between the results based on great powers and those based on other states. Further, it is especially important to have a theory about democratizing great powers, because they have such a huge impact on world politics, and because Russia—and perhaps soon China—is in a democratizing phase.

The features of democratization captured in Gurr's data are echoed in the arguments we derive from the case studies, but they do not correspond in every respect. In discussing the case studies, we used concepts that seemed most useful in illuminating the patterns we found, rather than strictly applying Gurr's categories. Sometimes the fit between Gurr's concepts and our own is quite close. For example, Gurr's category of "factional competition," which is the mid-point on his scale of the competitiveness of a country's political participation, is similar to our concept of interest-group jockeying and logrolling in a democratizing setting. In contrast, however, elements such as ideology play a large role in our argument, but are ignored in Gurr's data.

In the following sections, we first explain why the institutional structures of democratizing states produce a different pattern of policy outcomes than in fully democratic states. We then show how this affects the strategies of domestic interest groups, patterns of coalition politics, and foreign policy outcomes in the context of the collapse of an autocratic state.

Democratic versus Democratizing Institutions

Well-institutionalized democracies that reliably place ultimate authority in the hands of the average voter virtually never fight wars against each other. Moreover, although mature democracies do fight wars about as frequently as other types of states, they seem to be more prudent: they usually win their wars; they are quicker to abandon strategic overcommitments; and they do not fight gratuitous "preventive" wars.[27] Explanations for these tendencies focus variously on the self-interest of the average voter who bears the costs of war, the norms of bargaining and conflict resolution inherent in democracy, the moderating impact of constitutional checks and balances, and the free market-place of ideas.[28]

---

27. David Lake, "Powerful Pacifists," *American Political Science Review*, Vol. 86, No. 1 (March 1992), pp. 24–37; Snyder, *Myths of Empire*, pp. 49–52; Randall Schweller, "Domestic Structure and Preventive War: Are Democracies More Pacific?" *World Politics*, Vol. 44, No. 2 (January 1992), pp. 235–269.
28. Russett, *Grasping the Democratic Peace*; Miles Kahler, "Introduction," in Miles Kahler, ed., *Liberalization and Foreign Policy* (forthcoming); Jack Snyder, "Democratization, War, and Nationalism in the Post-Communist States," in Celeste Wallander, ed., *The Sources of Russian Conduct after the Cold War* (Boulder: Westview, forthcoming).

However, these happy solutions typically emerge only in the very long run. In the initial stages of expanding political participation, strong barriers prevent the emergence of full-fledged democratic processes and the foreign policy outcomes associated with them. The two main barriers are the weakness of democratic institutions and the resistance of social groups who would be the losers in a process of full-fledged democratization.

Popular inputs into the policymaking process can have wildly different effects, depending on the way that political institutions structure and aggregate those inputs.[29] It is a staple of political science that different institutional rules —for example, proportional representation versus single-member districts, or congressional versus executive authority over tariffs—can produce different political outcomes, even holding constant the preferences of individual voters. In newly democratizing states, the institutions that structure political outcomes may allow for popular participation in the policy process, but the way they channel that input is often a parody of full-fledged democracy. As Samuel Huntington has put it, the typical problem of political development is the gap between high levels of political participation and weak integrative institutions to reconcile the multiplicity of contending claims.[30] In newly democratizing states without strong parties, independent courts, a free press, and untainted electoral procedures, there is no reason to expect that mass politics will produce the same impact on foreign policy as it does in mature democracies.

In all of the democratizing great powers, public inputs were shaped and aggregated in ways that differed from those of mature democracies. In mid-Victorian Britain, rural areas had greater representation than urban areas, the ballot was not secret, and only propertied classes could vote.[31] In rural France under Napoleon III, the local prefect, appointed in Paris, stood at the ballot box and exercised control over voters' choices.[32] In Wilhelmine Germany, the parties that won the elections could not name governmental ministers; rather, they had to use their limited powers over the budget to bargain over policy with ministers named by the kaiser.[33] In Taisho Japan, the electoral franchise

29. Kenneth Shepsle, "Studying Institutions: Some Lessons from the Rational Choice Approach," *Journal of Theoretical Politics*, Vol. 1, No. 2 (April 1989), pp. 131–147.

30. Samuel Huntington, *Political Order in Changing Societies* (New Haven: Yale University Press, 1968).

31. D.C. Moore, "The Other Face of Reform," *Victorian Studies*, Vol. 5, No. 1 (September 1961), pp. 7–34.

32. Theodore Zeldin, *The Political System of Napoleon III* (New York: Norton, 1958), pp. 84–85, 91–94, 135.

33. Wehler, *German Empire*.

was widened, but the choice of who would govern was left to the oligarchs who had founded the Meiji state.[34] And in Russia today almost none of the major institutions of representative government work in a reliable way: constitutional rules change to fit the needs of the moment; constitutional courts take sides on transparently political grounds; elections are postponed or announced on short notice; and political parties are transitory elite cliques, not stable organizations for mobilizing a mass coalition. Moreover, in all of these cases, the political press was to some degree bribed or censored by the government or had not yet institutionalized the objectivity, knowledge, and professionalism needed to create a full and fair public debate.[35]

As a result of these institutional deformations, ruling circles in these democratizing great powers were only haphazardly accountable to the electorate. Typically, elite groups reached out intermittently and selectively for mass support but were able to buffer themselves from systematic accountability through the ballot box. In Britain both the Whig and Tory parties were still dominated by landed oligarchs, who refused to entertain the notion of anything more than issue-specific alignments with the parliamentary representatives of middle-class radical opinion. Similarly, in Wilhelmine Germany the ruling elite bargained with mass groups like the Catholic Center Party over specific horse-trades, for example, exchanging support on the naval budget for concessions on Catholic rights. The Center Party was not, however, offered ministerial portfolios.

As a consequence, public groups in all of these polities tended to organize as narrow pressure groups or single-issue lobbies, such as the Anti-Corn Law League in Britain in the 1840s, or the Navy and Agrarian Leagues in pre-1914 Germany. These groups often worked outside the electoral system, making direct demands on public authorities, since the democratic path to power was rigged against them. This tendency toward direct action in the streets or in smoke-filled back rooms rather than through the ballot box is typical of what Huntington calls the "praetorian society," where pressures for participation are strong but institutions for effective participation are weak.[36]

---

34. Peter Duus, *Party Rivalry and Political Change in Taisho Japan* (Cambridge, Mass.: Harvard University Press, 1968).
35. Lynn M. Case, *French Opinion on War and Diplomacy during the Second Empire* (Philadelphia: University of Pennsylvania Press, 1954), pp. 2–6; Stephen Koss, *The Rise of the Political Press in England* (London: Hamish Hamilton, 1981), pp. 72–80.
36. Patricia Hollis, ed., *Pressure from Without in Early Victorian England* (London: Edward Arnold, 1974); Huntington, *Political Order in Changing Societies*, pp. 78–92.

To some extent this weakness of democratic institutions simply reflects the difficulty of building effective structures from scratch. Well-developed organizations, skilled cadres to staff them, and habits of democratic action are not acquired overnight by journalists, parliamentarians, judicial officials, and party politicians. Nor is trust in the efficacy and objectivity of such institutions easily acquired. As rational-choice analysts of the creation of institutional structures have convincingly and repeatedly shown, "transaction costs" and dilemmas of collective action hinder the emergence of institutions to facilitate bargaining that would make everyone better off.[37]

Of course, the development of efficient democratic institutions is hindered further by the fact that everyone is *not* made better off by effective democratic reforms. Many social groups, including many powerful ones, are likely to be losers from the strengthening of democratic institutions.[38] These include the autocratic rulers themselves, state bureaucrats of the old regime who might fear that their function would lose its importance in a transformed polity, social and economic elites whose privileges might diminish in a more open system, or even mass special interest groups who would lose from reforms that the average voter might find attractive. In the nineteenth and early twentieth centuries, constituencies having an interest in holding back full democratization typically included kings, nobles, landowners, owners of industrial capital, militaries that were closely tied to old elites or the old regime, and artisans and other middle-class groups that benefited from the guild-type economic restrictions backed by the old regime.[39] In contemporary post-communist states, the analogous cast of characters has, in one place or another, included national and local former Communist party officials, the military, ministries or firms controlling obsolete industrial capital, workers in such sectors, and people living and working in the regions where such sectors predominate.

The strength of these groups' incentives to hold back democratic change depends in large part on the mobility of their assets and skills. British landowners were comparatively relaxed about the expansion of democratic rights: the relative mobility of their substantial commercial investments allowed many

---

37. Todd Sandler, *Collective Action* (Ann Arbor: University of Michigan, 1992); Robert Keohane, *After Hegemony: Cooperation and Discord in the World Political Economy* (Princeton: Princeton University Press, 1984).

38. For a rational choice perspective emphasizing distributional issues, see Jack Knight, *Institutions and Social Conflict* (Cambridge: Cambridge University Press, 1992).

39. The classic study is Barrington Moore, Jr., *Social Origins of Dictatorship and Democracy* (Boston: Beacon, 1966).

of them to accept the end of agricultural protection and to profit from a liberalizing, free-trading political alliance with the commercial middle classes. In contrast, Germany's Junker landowning elite, who largely staffed the Prussian state, had very few attractive economic prospects outside of their relatively inefficient agricultural holdings, and thus had a larger stake in using state-backed protectionism and political repression to maintain their social position.[40] In Russia today, some former Communist elites have shown agility in adapting to a privatized economy, where they have devised ways to maintain control over or profit from the disposal of many of the elite's economic assets. However, the military has suffered greatly in status and organizational cohesion from the opening of the political system. And even the elites who *are* doing well in the transition have a stake in making the transition a controlled, partial one, where profiteering is not too fettered by democratic scrutiny or rule of law.

Both in the nineteenth century cases and in the contemporary post-communist ones, it is striking that many of the groups with an interest in retarding democratization are also those with a parochial interest in war, military preparation, empire, and protectionism. This is not accidental. Most of the benefits of war, military preparations, imperial conquest, and protectionism—e.g., in career advancement or in protection from foreign economic competition—are disproportionately concentrated in specific groups.[41] Any special interest group, including the military, that derives parochial benefits from a public policy has to feel wary about opening up its affairs to the scrutiny and veto of the average voter, who pays for subsidies to special interests. Whenever the costs of a program are distributed widely, but the benefits are concentrated in a few hands, democratization may put the program at risk.

When autocratic states start to democratize, many of the interests threatened by democratization are military in nature. As Charles Tilly says, "war made the state and the state made war."[42] In early modern Europe, military organizations occupied a privileged position in the state, which was built to serve their needs. Moreover, ruling aristocracies were intertwined with military in-

---

40. In addition to Moore, *Social Origins*, see David Spring, ed., *European Landed Elites in the Nineteenth Century* (Baltimore: Johns Hopkins University Press, 1977); and Robert Moeller, ed., *Peasants and Lords in Modern Germany* (Boston: Allen & Unwin, 1986).
41. Snyder, *Myths of Empire*, pp. 32–35, 49–52; Lance Davis and Robert Huttenback, *Mammon and the Pursuit of Empire: The Political Economy of British Imperialism, 1860–1912* (Cambridge: Cambridge University Press, 1986).
42. Charles Tilly, "Reflections on the History of European State-Making," in Charles Tilly, ed., *The Formation of National States in Europe* (Princeton: Princeton University Press, 1975), p. 42.

stitutions, so democratization inherently challenged the vested social, economic, and bureaucratic interests of an old elite that was at its core a military elite. Joseph Schumpeter constructed a whole theory of imperialism on the atavistic interests of the military-feudal aristocracy.[43] It is true that middle-class reformers sometimes wanted to build up the state's military power: this was a rallying cry of English radicals in the Crimean War, and of German middle-class officers before 1914. However, they wanted to replace aristocratic deadwood with middle-class rationalizers. Democratization led by proponents of military power was thus nearly as much of a threat to the old army as democratization led by pacifists like Richard Cobden.[44]

THE POLITICAL IMPASSE OF DEMOCRATIZATION
This situation of social change, institutional weakness, and threatened interests tends to produce a political impasse along the route toward democracy: it becomes difficult to form stable political coalitions with coherent policy platforms and sufficient support to stay in power. This impasse, which breeds the kind of short-run thinking and reckless policymaking that lead to war, occurs for four reasons.

WIDENING THE POLITICAL SPECTRUM. First, the social changes impelling democratization create a wider spectrum of politically significant groups with diverse, incompatible interests. Kings, aristocrats, peasants, and artisans may share the historical stage with industrialists, an urban working class, and a middle-class intelligentsia. Or in the contemporary post-communist cases, former party apparatchiks, atavistic heavy industrialists, and downwardly mobile military officers may share the stage with populist demagogues, free-market entrepreneurs, disgruntled workers, and newly mobilized ethnic groups. In principle, a fully institutionalized democracy can integrate even the widest spectrum of interests through party competition for the favors of the median voter. But where democracy is only incipient and partial, the wide spread of politically mobilized social interests characteristic of a transition to democracy may make the formation of stable coalitions extremely difficult.

For example, in Britain during the period leading up to the Crimean War, neither Whigs nor Tories could form a governing coalition that was more than temporary, because so many groups refused to enter into stable political alli-

43. Joseph Schumpeter, *Imperialism and Social Classes* (New York: Kelly, 1950; orig. ed. 1919).
44. Olive Anderson, *A Liberal State at War: English Politics and Economics during the Crimean War* (New York: St. Martin's, 1967).

ances with each other. None of the old elites would coalesce with the parliamentary bloc of radicals elected by British urban middle-class and Irish voters. Moreover, protectionist Tories would not unite with free-trading Tories or Whigs. Thus, the social and political mid-Victorian "equipoise" between traditional and modern Britain created a temporary political stalemate, as groups found it impossible to compromise vital interests in the construction of a ruling coalition.[45]

An even more serious example is the stalemate in Wilhelmine-era electoral politics. In principle, coalitions of the left and the right might have formed to vie for the median voter, thus driving policy in a moderating direction. In fact, both the left and the right were too divided internally to mount effective coalitions with internally consistent policies. Progressives dreamed of a bloc extending "from Bassermann to Bebel," from the liberal-democratic middle classes through the Marxist working classes, but the differences between labor and capital chronically barred this development. Conservatives had more success in forging a "marriage of iron and rye," but fundamental differences between military-feudal Junkers and Ruhr industrialists, ranging from the distribution of tax burdens to military strategy, made their policies incoherent. Germany wound up with plans for a big army, a costly navy, and nobody willing to pay for it.[46]

In more recent times, incipient democratization has caused political impasse by widening the political spectrum to include too many irreconcilable political forces. In the final days of Yugoslavia, efforts by moderates like Ante Markovic to promote compromise on a federalist, democratic, economic reformist platform were hindered not only by ethnic divisions but also by the cleavage between market-oriented business interests, on the one hand, and party bosses and military officers, on the other.[47]

INFLEXIBLE INTERESTS AND SHORT TIME HORIZONS. Groups threatened by social change and democratization, including still-powerful elites, are often compelled to take a very inflexible view of their own interests, especially when their assets cannot be readily adapted to changing political and economic

---

45. W.L. Burn, *The Age of Equipoise* (London: George Allen & Unwin, 1964).

46. Eckart Kehr, *Economic Interest, Militarism, and Foreign Policy* (Berkeley: University of California Press, 1977); David D'Lugo and Ronald Rogowski, "The Anglo-German Naval Race and Comparative Constitutional 'Fitness'," in Richard Rosecrance and Arthur Stein, eds., *The Domestic Bases of Grand Strategy* (Ithaca: Cornell University Press, 1993), pp. 65–95, esp. 81–83.

47. V.P. Gagnon, Jr., "Ethnic Nationalism and International Conflict: The Case of Serbia," *International Security*, Vol. 19, No. 3 (Winter 1994/95), pp. 130–166; Branka Magas, *The Destruction of Yugoslavia: Tracking the Break-Up, 1980–1992* (London: Verso, 1993).

conditions. In extreme cases, there may be only one solution that will maintain the social position of the group. For the Prussian landowners, it was agricultural protection in a non-democratic state; for the Japanese military, organizational autonomy in an autarkic empire; for the Serbian military and party elites, a Serbian nationalist state. Compromises that may lead down the slippery slope toward social extinction or irrelevance have no appeal, despite the danger that taking an intransigent stance might provoke a hostile encirclement by great-power opponents. This adds to the difficulty of finding an exit from the political impasse.

COMPETITIVE MASS MOBILIZATION. In a period of democratization, threatened elite groups have an overwhelming incentive to mobilize allies among the mass of people, but only on their own terms, using whatever special resources they still retain. These have included monopolies of information (e.g., the German Navy's unique "expertise" in making strategic assessments); propaganda assets (the Japanese Army's public relations blitz justifying the invasion of Manchuria); patronage (British Foreign Secretary Palmerston's gifts of foreign service postings to the sons of cooperative journalists); wealth (Krupp steel's bankrolling of mass nationalist and militarist leagues); organizational skills and networks (the Japanese army's exploitation of rural reservist organizations to build a social base); and the ability to use the control of traditional political institutions to shape the political agenda and structure the terms of political bargains (the Wilhelmine ruling elite's deal with the Center Party, eliminating anti-Catholic legislation in exchange for support in the Reichstag on the naval budget).[48]

This elite mobilization of mass groups takes place in a highly competitive setting. Elite groups mobilize mass support to neutralize mass threats (e.g., patriotic leagues to counter workers' movements) and to counter other elite groups' successful efforts at mass mobilization (e.g., the German Navy League, as a political counterweight to the Junker-backed Agrarian League). Thus, the elites' resources allow them to influence the direction of mass political participation, but the imperative to compete for mass favor makes it difficult for a single elite group to control the outcome of this process. For example, mass groups that gain access to politics through elite-supported nationalist organizations often try to outbid their erstwhile elite sponsors. By 1911, German popular nationalist lobbies were in a position to claim that if Germany's foreign

---

48. Snyder, *Myths of Empire*, pp. 103, 140–141, 205; Louise Young, "Mobilizing for Empire: Japan and Manchukuo, 1931–1945," Ph.D. dissertation, Columbia University, 1992.

foes were really as threatening as the ruling elites had portrayed them, then the government had sold out German interests in reaching a compromise settlement of the Moroccan dispute with France.[49] In this way, the process of elite mobilization of the masses adds to the ungovernability and political impasse of democratizing states.

Ideology takes on particular significance in the competition for mass support. New participants in the political process may be uncertain of where their political interests lie, because they lack established habits and good information, and are thus fertile ground for ideological appeals. Ideology can yield particularly big payoffs, moreover, when there is no efficient free marketplace of ideas to counter false claims with reliable facts. Elites try out all sorts of ideological appeals, depending on the social position that they need to defend, the nature of the mass group that they want to recruit, and the type of appeals that seem plausible in the given political setting. A nearly universal element in these ideological appeals is nationalism, which has the advantage of positing a community of interest that unites elites and masses, thus distracting attention from class cleavages.

Nationalist appeals have often succeeded even though the average voter was not consistently pro-war or pro-empire. For example, the French public was not keen to enter the Crimean War when it began in January 1854, and after sustaining 100,000 war-related deaths by 1855, the public's war-weariness led Napoleon to make concessions to Russia at the bargaining table. Likewise, the French public was initially opposed to participation in the Italian and Austro-Prussian Wars, fearing a disruption of the economy.[50] Mass opinion was similarly pacifist and anti-imperial in Britain during the high tide of Richard Cobden's Anti-Corn Law League, which succeeded in linking foreign military intervention and military budgets to the popular issues of free trade and democracy.[51] In Japan, too, the Naval Arms Limitation Treaty of 1930 was initially popular with the public.[52] And even in Germany, where public opinion was more consistently bellicose, the two largest mass parties, the Social Democrats and the Catholic Center Party, had no interest in imperialism. Though the

49. Eley, *Reshaping the German Right*, chap. 10.
50. William E. Echard, *Napoleon II and the Concert of Europe* (Baton Rouge: Louisiana State University Press, 1983), pp. 31, 37, 49; Case, *French Opinion*, pp. 54–56, 64–65, 71, 273.
51. Peter Cain, "Capitalism, War and Internationalism in the Thought of Richard Cobden," *British Journal of International Studies*, Vol. 5 (October 1979), pp. 229–247.
52. Tatsuji Takeuchi, *War and Diplomacy in the Japanese Empire* (Garden City, N.Y.: Doubleday, 1935), pp. 303–304.

German leaders' strategy is often called "social" imperialism, its appeal was almost entirely to the middle classes, not the workers. And Catholics backed the fleet not out of conviction, but to get side-payments on domestic issues.[53]

Since mass opinion was typically mobilized into politics by elite interest groups rather than by broad-based parties competing for the median voter, mass voices tended to reinforce the pattern of elite interests, rather than to check them: in Germany, the Agrarian League clamored for grain tariffs, the Navy League for a fleet, the imperial groups for settler colonies abroad, and the Pan-German League for a bigger army. In cases where mass opinion has been articulated through different channels, such as the institutionalized two-party competition in twentieth century Britain and the United States, its impact on foreign policy has been very different.

THE WEAKENING OF CENTRAL AUTHORITY. The political impasse and recklessness of democratizing states is exacerbated further by the weakening of the state's authority. Autocratic power is in decline *vis-à-vis* both the elite interest groups and mass groups, but democratic institutions lack the strength to integrate these contending interests and views. Parties are weak and lack mass loyalty. Elections are rigged or intermittent. Institutions of public political participation are distrusted, because they are subject to manipulation by elites and to arbitrary constraints imposed by the state, which fears the outcome of unfettered competition.

In each of the historical great-power cases, the problem was not excessive authoritarian power at the center, but the opposite. The Aberdeen coalition that brought Britain into the Crimean War was a makeshift cabinet headed by a weak leader with no substantial constituency. Likewise, on the eve of the Franco-Prussian War, Napoleon III's regime was in the process of caving in to its liberal opponents, who dominated the parliament elected in 1869. As Europe's armies prepared to hurtle from their starting gates in late July 1914, Austrian leaders, perplexed by the contradictions between the German Chancellor's policy and that of the German military, asked "Who rules in Berlin?" The 1931 Manchurian Incident was a *fait accompli* by the local Japanese military; Tokyo was not even informed.[54] Today, the return to imperial thinking in

---

53. Jonathan Steinberg, *Yesterday's Deterrent* (London: Macdonald, 1965), pp. 190–191; David Blackbourn, *Populists and Patricians* (London: Allen & Unwin, 1987), pp. 161–162, 190, 211.
54. J.B. Conacher, *The Aberdeen Coalition, 1852–1855* (London: Cambridge University Press, 1968); Zeldin, *The Political System of Napoleon III*, pp. 3, 135; Gerhard Ritter, *The Sword and the Sceptre: The Problem of Militarism in Germany*, Vol. 2 (Coral Gables: University of Miami Press, 1969), pp. 257–263; Sadako Ogata, *Defiance in Manchuria* (Berkeley: University of California Press, 1964).

Moscow is the result of Yeltsin's weakness, not his strength. As Sergei Kara-ganov has recently argued, the breakdown of the Leninist state "has created an environment where elite interests influence [foreign] policy directly."[55] In each of these cases, the weak central political leadership resorts to the same strategies as do the more parochial elite interests, using nationalist ideological appeals and special-interest payoffs to maintain their short-run viability, de-spite the potential long-run risks associated with these strategies.

IMPLICATIONS FOR WAR-PRONENESS

Political leaders in the great powers resorted to a typical syndrome of expedi-ents in their attempts to deal with the political impasse of democratization. These tactics—logrolling, squaring the circle, and prestige strategies—tended to breed recklessness in foreign relations and the resort to war.

LOGROLLING. In these democratizing states, the power of elite groups was strengthened relative to the weakened autocratic center, yet the power of mass groups was not yet institutionalized as in a mature democracy. This created the incentive to make policy by logrolling among elite interest groups. Elite log-rolling often yielded policies of war, military preparation, and imperial expan-sion, in part because many of the interest groups created in the process of weakening and breaking up the autocratic state were its military-feudal detri-tus: the army, the navy, and the aristocratic elites that staffed them. Similar military interest groups also figure in some of the post-communist cases, especially Yugoslavia and Russia. Militaries do not necessarily favor war, es-pecially when they feel unprepared to win quickly and decisively. However, because of militaries' typically zero-sum view of security, they often recom-mend offensive military strategies that inadvertently lead the state down the path toward war.[56]

Moreover, logrolling works by giving each group what it wants most, so that even if only some of the groups in the coalition favored policies leading to war

---

55. Sergei A. Karaganov, "Russia's Elites," in Robert Blackwill and Sergei A. Karaganov, eds., *Damage Limitation or Crisis? Russia and the Outside World* (Washington, D.C.: Brassey's, 1994), p. 42; see also Robert Legvold, "The Russian Question," in Vladimir Baranovsky, ed., *Russia and Europe: Emerging Security Agenda* (N.Y.: Oxford University Press, forthcoming in 1995).
56. Stephen Van Evera, "Causes of War," Ph.D. dissertation, University of California at Berkeley, 1984. This does not seem to apply in cases of military dictatorship. Rather, it is when the military acts as a cartel in political logrolling or as an actor in the politics of the democratization process that the military's political role makes war more likely. See Stanislav Andreski, "On the Peaceful Disposition of Military Dictatorships," *Journal of Strategic Studies*, Vol. 3, No. 3 (December 1980), pp. 3–10.

and expansion, that would be enough to make their adoption likely. The classic example is the Wilhelmine iron-and-rye logroll, where the navy and heavy industry insisted on a fleet that alienated Britain, the Junkers got grain tariffs that sowed discord with Russia, and the army got the offensive Schlieffen Plan, which threatened all of Germany's neighbors. Another instance is the logroll between the Japanese imperial army and navy, which overtaxed the economy and embroiled Japan with enemies on all azimuths.[57]

SQUARING THE CIRCLE, OR INTEGRATING OPPOSITES. Since democratizing states typically comprise such a broad spectrum of social interests, would-be ruling coalitions must often be cobbled together from diverse or even contradictory bases of support. For this reason, one of the characteristic problems of the leadership of transitional, democratizing states is explaining away the self-contradictory aspects of a coalition or policy that must integrate antithetical elements. In foreign affairs, this often means sweeping tough trade-offs under the rug, pretending that contradictory policies actually make sense or cannot be avoided. As a consequence, the foreign policies of democratizing states are often overcommitted, provoking too many enemies at the same time, while claiming that the resulting conflicts are due to the others' inherent hostility. For example, Wilhelmine iron-and-rye policies leading to a hostile encirclement of Germany were explained away in two ways: first, that the hostility was inherent in the nature of Germany's opponents, and that German policy had done nothing to provoke it; and second, that the way to break apart the hostile coalition was to issue threats, rather than to make concessions that would have jeopardized the policies of the iron-and-rye coalition.[58]

Palmerston and Louis Napoleon faced a somewhat different problem of integrating opposites. Their strategies required winning over substantial middle-class backers to a strategy of social conservatism to safeguard the interests of old elites in an era of mass politics. In part, the rise of the working-class threat made this alliance possible. But in order to win converts from middle-class radicalism, Palmerston and Napoleon both had to show that their conservative policies were somehow actually liberal. The simplest way to do this was to back liberal goals abroad, such as national self-determination and the expansion of commercial opportunities, while fighting a rear-guard action against them at home. This was convenient because liberal goals abroad could easily

---

57. Michael Barnhart, *Japan Prepares for Total War: The Search for Economic Security, 1919–1941* (Ithaca: Cornell University Press, 1987).
58. Snyder, *Myths of Empire*, pp. 85–89.

be made to dovetail with geopolitical goals that Palmerston and Napoleon wanted to pursue anyway.[59] However, liberals were not completely passive dupes of this strategy. In Britain, for example, they used the Crimean War to force an opening of the administration of the war office to middle-class rationalizers, a move that Palmerston could hardly prevent in light of the way he had justified his foreign policy.[60]

In Russia today, foreign policy is likewise providing glue for an emerging "red-brown" coalition of nationalists and neo-communists. The Soviet system created organized vested interests in a particular pattern of industrial investment, a large military establishment, a working class protected from market forces, a local elite that served as a substitute for the market in administering the economy, and a division of labor on an imperial scale. The collapse of the Marxist-Leninist state took away the ideological underpinnings of this collection of interests, but many of these interests remain in place. The doctrines of nationalism and of the distinctiveness of Russia from the liberal West provide natural ideological justification for reasserting imperial control and retaining at least some of the strong-state, limited-market tendencies from Russia's past. It may also help to justify a truncated approach to democratization, which would help secure these traditional elite interests.

PRESTIGE STRATEGIES. One of the simplest but most risky strategies for a hard-pressed regime in a democratizing country is to shore up its prestige at home by seeking victories abroad. Johannes Miquel, who revitalized the iron-rye coalition at the turn of the century, argued that "successes in foreign policy would make a good impression in the Reichstag debates, and political divisions would thus be moderated."[61] The domestic targets of such strategies often share this view. Cobden, for example, argued that military victories abroad would confer enough prestige on the military-feudal landed elite to allow them to raise food tariffs and snuff out democracy: "Let John Bull have a great military triumph, and we shall have to take off our hats as we pass the Horse Guards for the rest of our lives."[62]

Prestige strategies make the country hypersensitive to slights to its reputation. As the kaiser found out in the First and Second Moroccan Crises, stiff foreign resistance can produce not cheap victories but embarrassing defeats,

---

59. Plessis, *De la fête*, p. 189; Snyder, *Myths of Empire*, pp. 180–183.
60. Anderson, *A Liberal State at War*.
61. J.C.G. Rohl, *Germany without Bismarck* (Berkeley: University of California, 1967), p. 250.
62. Letter to John Bright, October 1, 1854, quoted in John Morley, *The Life of Richard Cobden*, abridged ed. (London, n.d.), pp. 311–312.

which further complicate domestic governance. In another instance, Napoleon III was easily goaded into a fateful declaration of war in 1870 by Bismarck's insulting editorial work on a leaked telegram from the kaiser.[63]

If the public itself is wary of war, the prestige-enhancing venture may have to be mounted in the face of initial domestic opposition. Nonetheless, the gamble may be worth it. The Crimean victory created the conditions for what is acknowledged to be the high point of Napoleon III's rule, despite the popular reluctance and war-weariness that accompanied it.[64] Napoleon learned this lesson well, and tried to recapitulate his success when he saw his popularity waning in January 1859. On the eve of French military intervention in the Italian struggle with Austria, Napoleon told his cabinet, "On the domestic front, the war will at first awaken great fears; traders and speculators of every stripe will shriek, but national sentiment will [banish] this domestic fright; the nation will be put to the test once more in a struggle that will stir many a heart, recall the memory of heroic times and bring together under the mantle of glory the parties that are steadily drifting away from one another day after day."[65] Napoleon was trying to lead public opinion to become bellicose, not just to follow opinion, but in order to stir a national feeling that would enhance the state's ability to govern a split and stalemated political arena.

Autocratization and Great Power War

Though democratization has been a cause of great power war, reversing that process is not an effective antidote. At least four times, great powers have undergone sharp reversals of incipient democratization: France under Napoleons I and III, Nazi Germany, and Japan in the 1930s. Each then embarked on an aggressive foreign adventure. It is true that the reassertion of traditional autocracy under the Concert of Europe after 1815 produced a period of comparative peace. However, this merely postponed domestic and international conflicts, which returned with the democratizing trend after the revolutionary uprisings of 1848.[66]

---

63. Case, *French Opinion*, p. 267.
64. Thompson, *Louis Napoleon*, pp. 144–145.
65. Alain Plessis, *The Rise and Fall of the Second Empire, 1852–1871* (Cambridge: Cambridge University Press, 1985), pp. 146–147.
66. Charles A. Kupchan and Clifford A. Kupchan, "Concerts, Collective Security, and the Future of Europe," *International Security*, Vol. 16, No. 1 (Summer 1991), pp. 114–161.

How should the link between autocratization and war be interpreted? It is possible that any regime change increases the likelihood of war, whether it is on the dimension of democratization and autocratization, or on any other dimension. Regime change more generally may lead to some of the same war-causing pathologies that are present in democratizing states, including policy stalemates, threatened elites, and other social groups with shortened time horizons. Since political scientists have barely begun to address this question, this interpretation cannot be ruled out.[67]

However, at least some wars of autocratization can be best understood as wars of failed or perverted democratization. In each of these great power cases, the autocratizing ruler's foreign policy was either a tool that helped him to overcome the political impasse of the democratizing regime, or else it grew out of ideas that had arisen in the political context of the preceding period of democratization. For example, explanations of Nazi foreign policy can be grouped into two general categories: "structuralist" ones that see Nazi policies as functional responses to the political impasse of Weimar society, and "intentionalist" ones that see such policies as the implementation of racist, nationalist ideas spawned in the coffeehouses of the late Wilhelmine and Weimar periods.[68] In either case, the warlike character of the new autocracy grew out of a flaw in the democratizing society that preceded it.

These new autocrats, unlike traditional monarchs, all claimed to rule in the name of people, while shutting down democratic institutions. Napoleon I exploited the popular nationalism of the French Revolution, promising to spread its ideals throughout Europe even as he extinguished them in France. The Japanese army invented a populist ideology, rooted in the nation's imperial myths, designed to solidify the army's links to a rural mass constituency and to denigrate the commercially-oriented Taisho democrats. Thus, the foreign policy of these autocratizing states was at least partially shaped by the character of the democratic political system that they were escaping. In some cases, it was a means for accomplishing that escape. In this sense, the wars of re-autocratization can be seen as part of the larger phenomenon of wars of democratization.

---

67. Addressing one aspect of this question is Zeev Maoz, "Joining the Club of Nations: Political Development and International Conflict, 1816–1976," *International Studies Quarterly*, Vol. 33, No. 2 (June 1989), pp. 199–231.
68. John Hiden and John Farquharson, *Explaining Hitler's Germany: Historians and the Third Reich* (Totowa, N.J.: Barnes and Noble, 1983).

Implications for Policy

In light of these findings, it would be hard to maintain a naive enthusiasm for spreading peace by promoting democratization. Pushing nuclear-armed great powers like Russia or China toward democratization is like spinning a roulette wheel, where many of the potential outcomes are likely to be undesirable. However, in most cases the initial steps on the road to democratization will not be produced by the conscious policy of the United States, no matter what that policy may be. The roulette wheel is already spinning for Russia, and perhaps China, regardless of what the West does. Moreover, reversals of democratization are nearly as risky as democratization itself. Consequently, the international community needs a strategy not so much for promoting or reversing democratization as for managing the process in ways that minimize its risks and facilitate smooth transitions.

What might be some of these mitigating conditions, and how might they be promoted? The association of democratization with war is probabilistic. Democratization can lead either to war or to peace, depending on a variety of factors, such as the incentives facing the old elites during the transition process, the structure of the marketplace of foreign policy ideas, the speed and thoroughness of the democratic transition, and the character of the international environment in which democratization occurs. Some of these features may be subject to manipulation by astute democratic reformers and their allies in the international community.

One of the major findings of scholarship on democratization in Latin America is that the process goes most smoothly when elites that are threatened by the transition, especially the military, are given a "golden parachute."[69] Above all, they need a guarantee that if they relinquish power they will not wind up in jail. The history of the democratizing great powers broadens this insight. Democratization was least likely to lead to imprudent aggression in cases where the old elites saw a reasonably bright future for themselves in the new social order. British aristocrats, for example, had more of their wealth invested in commerce and industry than they did in agriculture, so they had many interests in common with the rising middle classes. They could face democratization with relative equanimity. In contrast, Prussia's capital-starved, small-

---

69. On the importance of bargaining with and co-opting old elites (giving them incentives, a "golden parachute," to depart from power), see the literature summarized in Doh Chull Shin, "On the Third Wave of Democratization: A Synthesis and Evaluation of Recent Theory and Research," *World Politics*, Vol. 47, No. 1 (October 1994), pp. 135–170, esp. 161–163.

scale Junker landholders had no choice but to rely on agricultural protection and military careers.

In today's context, finding benign, productive employment for the erstwhile Communist *nomenklatura*, military officer corps, nuclear scientists, and smokestack industrialists ought to rank high on the list of priorities. Policies aimed at giving them a stake in the privatization process and subsidizing the conversion of their skills to new, peaceful tasks in a market economy seem like a step in the right direction. According to some interpretations, Russian Defense Minister Pavel Grachev was eager to use force to solve the Chechen confrontation in order to show that Russian military power was still useful and that increased investment in the Russian army would pay big dividends. Instead of pursuing this reckless path, the Russian military elite needs to be convinced that its prestige, housing, pensions, and technical competence will rise if and only if it transforms itself into a western-style military, subordinate to civilian authority and resorting to force only in accordance with prevailing international norms. Moreover, though old elites need to be kept happy, they also need to be kept weak. Pacts should not prop up the remnants of the authoritarian system, but rather create a niche for them in the new system.

A top priority must also be placed on creating a free, competitive, yet responsible marketplace of ideas in the newly democratizing states. Most of the war-prone democratizing great powers had pluralistic public debates, but the terms of these debates were skewed to favor groups with money, privileged access to the media of communication, and proprietary control over information, ranging from historical archives to intelligence about the military balance. Pluralism is not enough. Without an even playing field, pluralism simply creates the incentive and opportunity for privileged groups to propound self-serving myths, which historically have often taken a nationalist turn. One of the rays of hope in the Chechen affair was the alacrity with which Russian journalists exposed the true costs of the fighting and the lies of the government and the military about it. Though elites should get a golden parachute in terms of their pecuniary interests, they should be given no quarter on the battlefield of ideas. Mythmaking should be held up to the utmost scrutiny by aggressive journalists who maintain their credibility by scrupulously distinguishing fact from opinion and tirelessly verifying their sources. Promoting this kind of journalistic infrastructure is probably the most highly leveraged investment that the West can make in a peaceful democratic transition.

Our research offers inconclusive results about the wisdom of speed and thoroughness in transitions to democracy. On the one hand, we found that states making the big jump from autocracy to democracy were much more war-prone than those moving from autocracy to anocracy. This would seem to favor a strategy of limited goals. On the other hand, the experience of the former Communist states suggests that those that have gone farthest and fastest toward full democracy are less nationalistic and less involved in militarized quarrels. This is a question that needs more research.

Finally, what kind of ruling coalition emerges in the course of democratization depends a great deal on the incentives that are created by the international environment. Both Germany and Japan started on the path toward liberal, stable democratization in the mid-1920s, encouraged in part by abundant opportunities for trade and investment from the advanced democracies and by credible security treaties that defused nationalist scare-mongering in domestic politics. But when the international supports for free trade and democracy were yanked out in the late 1920s, their liberal coalitions collapsed. Especially for the case of contemporary China, whose democratization may occur in the context of sharply expanding economic ties to the West, the steadiness of the Western commercial partnership and security presence is likely to play a major role in shaping the incentives of proto-democratic coalition politics.

In the long run, the enlargement of the zone of stable democracy will probably enhance the prospects for peace. But in the short run, there is a lot of work to be done to minimize the dangers of the turbulent transition.

Part III:
Point and Counterpoint

The Democratic Peace—And Yet It Moves

Bruce Russett

In their introduction to the Fall 1994 issue on the democratic peace, the editors of *International Security* called it (p. 3) "the conventional wisdom."[1] If it has become conventional wisdom, or seems likely to do so, we should expect to see challenges to it. The theoretical edifice of realism will collapse if attributes of states' political systems are shown to have a major influence on which states do or do not fight each other. The dialectic of proposition and attempted refutation is a healthy necessity for developing any kind of scholarly understanding. The critiques published in this journal argue that the new "conventional wisdom" is, in terms of the old Scottish verdict, "not proven." But that "conventional wisdom" is not dispelled by either critique: the logic of their contents fails to match their snappy titles.

Christopher Layne and David Spiro offer three major objections:

1) To be valid, democratic peace theory (Layne, p. 13) "must account powerfully for the fact that serious crises between democratic states ended in near misses rather than in war," and cannot do so.

2) The number of wars between democracies is somewhat higher than proponents of democratic peace admit, because they engage in "intellectual suppleness" with "continual tinkering with definitions and categories" (Layne, p. 40), or "selectively adopt definitions of key variables so that data analysis yields the results they seek" (Spiro, p. 55).

3) Wars are rare phenomena, and through most of modern world history, democracies are also rare. Thus the number of wars to be expected between democracies is so small that no statistical test can distinguish the actual number (zero, or very low, depending on who counts) from the very low number that would be predicted by chance. This argument—the main burden of Spiro's piece, seconded by Layne (p. 39)—does *not* claim to have disproved the hy-

---

Bruce Russett is Dean Acheson Professor of International Relations and Political Science at Yale University. He thanks Don Green, Gary King, Zeev Maoz, Barry O'Neill, James Ray, Dan Reiter, R.J. Rummel, and Spencer Weart for comments, and Soo-Yeon Kim for computations.

---

1. "Editors' Note," *International Security*, Vol. 19, No. 2 (Fall 1994), p. 3; Christopher Layne, "Kant or Cant: The Myth of Democratic Peace," ibid., pp. 5–49; David Spiro, "The Insignificance of the Liberal Peace," ibid., pp. 50–86.

International Security, Vol. 19, No. 4 (Spring 1995), pp. 164–175
© 1995 by the President and Fellows of Harvard College and the Massachusetts Institute of Technology.

pothesis of democratic peace. It says only that the evidence is so sparse that statistical tests cannot confirm the hypothesis.

John Owen's article in the same issue in part considers the first two objections, so they require less attention here.[2] But since Owen does not address the third, it needs more extensive discussion, which I offer below. I conclude with some new analyses, stimulated by the critiques, that strongly support the democratic peace proposition.

Near Misses, and Dogs that Didn't Bark

We begin with the matter of why in particular instances democratic states have not fought each other. Layne argues (p. 38) that whereas "democratic peace theory identifies a correlation between domestic structure and the absence of war between democracies, it fails to establish a causal link." Yet certainly the literature on the democratic peace has gone well beyond correlation, and has postulated a variety of causal mechanisms, involving perceptions of shared norms, institutional constraints, and strategic behavior.[3] What Layne presumably means is that until recently, the democratic peace literature was light on the kind of in-depth case study analysis that would establish with reasonable force that the considerations identified in one variant or another of the theory actually were important motivators of individual and state behavior. To correct this omission he examines four crises between democratic states. He then looks at a selection of statements by major figures in government or affecting governments, and finds that although the crises ended without war, the participants' calculations were exclusively concerned with matters central to realism's focus on power and strategic interest, and claims (p. 38) that "democratic peace theory indicators appear not to have played *any* discernible role in the outcome."

---

2. John M. Owen, "How Liberalism Produces Democratic Peace," ibid., pp. 87–125.
3. Bruce Russett, *Grasping the Democratic Peace: Principles for a Post–Cold War World* (Princeton, N.J.: Princeton University Press, 1993), chap. 2, discusses two sets of causal propositions at length; Zeev Maoz and Bruce Russett, "Normative and Structural Causes of Democratic Peace," *American Political Science Review*, Vol. 87, No. 3 (September 1993), pp. 624–638, give a slightly different version. Bruce Bueno de Mesquita and David Lalman, *War and Reason* (New Haven, Conn.: Yale University Press, 1992), develop and test an elaborate game-theoretic explanatory process, as does D. Marc Kilgour, "Domestic Political Structure and War: A Game-Theoretic Approach," *Journal of Conflict Resolution*, Vol. 35, No. 2 (June 1991), pp. 266–284. See also R.J. Rummel's five-volume *Understanding Conflict and War* (Newbury Park, Calif.: 1975–81); and David Lake, "Powerful Pacifists: Democratic States and War," *American Political Science Review*, Vol. 86, No. 1 (March 1992) pp. 24–37.

Process-tracing of decision-making can be enlightening, and not enough of it has been done on this topic. Layne's effort is welcome, but his conclusions are not beyond contest. A poststructuralist, for instance, would have serious reservations about the ability of an observer to penetrate the self-justificatory and mythological functions of decision-makers' texts to discern "real" motivations. Since I am no poststructuralist I would not push the objection that far. Nonetheless, serious problems of interpretation are unavoidable, and difficulties regarding which statements are reported and which are not, and of obtaining agreement among observers, must not be evaded.[4] Owen, for example, interprets two of Layne's crises, notably the 1895–96 Anglo-American confrontation, differently.[5] He finds substantial evidence that considerations consistent with the expectations of democratic peace did appear, and made a difference. Furthermore, Layne does not explain why Britain decided that its strategic interests lay in accommodation with the United States, in the first instance, and France, in the second, rather than with Germany. Why did the British not consider America "another enemy," a threat along with other rivals like Germany, since they certainly (Layne, p. 15) considered the United States a latent "world power"? The calculus of strategic interest is not obvious without asking why some states were regarded as intrinsically more desirable and trustworthy friends.

But suppose we were to concur entirely with Layne that democratic peace considerations really were invisible, or nearly so. Indeed, from my own research I conceded much of the case that Layne makes for realism as applied to the Venezuela and Fashoda crises.[6] In each of Layne's cases, power and strate-

---

4. "1) Decision makers may not fully understand their own (often unconscious) motives or intentions. 2) If they do, they may not articulate them. 3) Over the duration of a crisis, there may be a change in their motives and intentions . . . that is not being articulated. 4) They may articulate conflicting expressions of intentions . . . 5) They may deliberately disguise their true motives and intentions." Paul Huth and Bruce Russett, "Testing Deterrence Theory: Rigor Makes a Difference," *World Politics*, Vol. 47, No. 4 (July 1990), p. 481.

5. For interpretations of Fashoda giving more credit to democratic peace intepretations, see James Lee Ray, *Democracy and International Conflict* (Columbia: University of South Carolina Press, 1995), chap. 5, and Spencer Weart, *Never at War: Why Democracies Will Not Fight One Another* (forthcoming 1995), chap. 13.

6. Respectively, "although important in preventing an Anglo-American war over this bagatelle, British strategic interests do not deserve all the credit for avoiding war"; "Considerations of any norm that these two nations should not fight each other were well in the background on both sides; war was avoided primarily for other reasons." Russett, *Grasping the Democratic Peace*, pp. 6, 8. I do contend, however, that the experience of near war stimulated in each case intense reconsideration about interests and the direction of foreign policy, in which the previous antagonists' views of the democratic norms and institutions they shared played a major role in changing the way they behaved toward each other.

gic considerations *were* predominant. No vital issues were at stake over *Trent* and Venezuela, and in Fashoda and the Ruhr the weaker side had no hope of prevailing in war. Does that concession give away the game? It would if democratic peace proponents claimed that shared democracy is the *only* influence permitting states to avoid war—but that is nonsense. I am happy to grant that power and strategic interest greatly affect the calculations of all states, including democracies. States sometimes start wars they think they can profit from, and usually avoid those where a cost-benefit calculation indicates they will lose, or win but at unacceptable cost. They do not, however, always initiate a war just because they think they could win at some acceptable price.[7]

Neither an unfavorable strategic cost-benefit evaluation nor shared democracy is a *necessary* condition for avoiding war. But, allowing for some possibility of irrationality or misconception, either may well constitute a virtually *sufficient* condition. For this reason, conceding most—or even all—of Layne's argument does not gain him the day on the larger issue of whether democratic peace exists. Extending that argument commits the logical fallacy of inducing a principle of universal non-existence merely by finding a few cases of non-existence. Even if there were no evidence for democratic peace considerations in four cases, that would prove nothing about their putative absence in other instances.

Now, at some point after examining very many cases my objection would become rather silly, at least for an influence—shared democracy—which I contend really is important in international affairs. But we have Owen's good case studies (twelve of them in his dissertation cited on pp. 88–89 of his article, not just the four discussed at length in the article), many of which find more evidence for democratic peace considerations. That is noteworthy because Owen's cases are all from the period between 1794 and 1917, an era during which, I believe, such considerations were much less influential than they later became.[8]

Moreover, *any* research design focusing on crises misses all the dogs that did not bark—the crises that never erupted or never brought the participants to

---

7. In the formal expected-utility calculation of Bueno de Mesquita and Lalman, *War and Reason,* positive expected utility for war is a necessary condition for a state to start a war but is far from a sufficient condition.

8. Russett, *Grasping the Democratic Peace,* p. 22. One important reason may be the denial of the franchise to women in the nineteenth century. There are no public opinion data on the earlier era, but over the past fifty years both American and British women have been much more averse than men to using military force. Lisa Brandes, *Public Opinion, International Security Policy, and Gender: The United States and Britain since 1945,* Yale University, Ph.D. dissertation, 1994.

the brink of war. What about the many conflicts of interest between democracies that were settled amicably, without threatening war—even though considerations of power and strategic interest might well have argued against such a settlement? The Venezuelan and Fashoda crises were the last of their type between these two pairs of states. Never since has Britain engaged in a diplomatic crisis with a democratic France or the United States that even remotely approached a likely step to war itself. Why? Might shared democratic norms and institutions possibly have something to do with it?

Who Is the Supplest of Them All?

Layne and Spiro's charge of "intellectual suppleness" is perhaps the most colorful but not the most important item in dispute. Owen says (p. 88) that "most democratic peace theorists are meticulous in their definitions"; readers can look, for example, at my criteria or James Lee Ray's and make up their own minds.[9] But neither critic is above suspicion himself. Layne avoids tinkering with a definition by the simple expedient of never giving us an explicit one. The closest he comes is the statement (p. 43), "In the realm of foreign policy, France and Britain were no more and no less democratic than the Second Reich [Imperial Germany]," with the explanation (p. 42) that in all three countries "crucial foreign policy decisions were taken without consulting Parliament." One might conclude from this that virtually no countries had democratically-controlled foreign policy. (Would the United States pass this test in most of the twentieth century?) If so, there would not have been much opportunity for any wars between "democracies," and hence there could be no democratic peace! But he seems instead to want to include Imperial Germany among the ranks of democratic powers (p. 44), an idiosyncratic view, rejected even by Spiro (p. 69).

Spiro, however, wants to count Finland's role on the Axis side in World War II as war against four or five democracies in each of the years 1941–44. In doing so he seeks consistency in applying a definition—reasonable enough, but at some cost in good sense. His argument is that other democracies declared war on democratic Finland, and that those pairs of "warring" democracies

---

9. Russett, *Grasping the Democratic Peace*, chap. 1; James Lee Ray, "Wars between Democracies: Rare, or Non-Existent?" *International Interactions*, Vol. 18, No. 3 (1993), pp. 251–276. Spiro says (p. 56) that various researchers have used different criteria for democracy, and implies that this weakens the case. Rather, the fact that essentially the same results hold across a range of definitions is evidence that the findings are robust.

should thus count. I thought it grotesque to count them. So far as I can tell there is no record of combat casualties between Finland and any democracy during World War II. The definition used by the Correlates of War Project from which both Spiro and I drew our data is to count a "warring" state as part of a multilateral war only if it has at least 1000 troops in combat or suffers at least 100 battle-related fatalities.[10] Spiro seems to mean that we could properly exclude Finland only if we also looked carefully at all other multilateral wars to see if there are other instances where a particular pair of states (presumably, for his argument, not a democratic pair) were identified as participants in a multilateral war but really inflicted few if any fatalities *on each other*. That might be a good way to proceed, but it would be a lot of work, so instead poor Finland is made to count 17 times.[11]

Spiro further defends this decision on grounds of consistency and deference to the data's originators (p. 74): "Singer and Small coded Finland as at war with the liberal alliance during World War II, and so should studies that use the data set." He does not always find it convenient, however, to be consistent and deferential: he chooses to drop Mecklenburg-Schwerin in 1866, and all but four states during the Korean War, because they suffered fewer than 1000 fatalities. This allows him to cut the number of warring dyads (warring pairs of states) from 29 to 21 in 1866, and from 28 to 4 in each year from 1950 to 1953. Since all these dyads are non-democratic, their deletion greatly raises the likelihood that he will fail to reject the null hypothesis. Without the deletion, the four Korean War years would support the democratic peace by rejecting the null hypothesis at the .056 level or less. (Reversing his Mecklenburg-

---

10. Melvin Small and J. David Singer, *Resort to Arms: International and Civil Wars, 1816–1980* (Thousand Oaks, Calif.: Sage, 1982), p. 67.

11. Spiro decides (p. 74) that Finland "threw in its lot with those of fascist powers against other liberal democracies." He does not dispute my statement about no casualties, though he refers (p. 61) to Ohto Manninen, "Operation Barbarossa and the Nordic Countries," in Henrik S. Nissen, ed., *Scandinavia in the Second World War* (Minneapolis: University of Minnesota Press, 1983). On p. 166 (not p. 85), Manninen reports that some Royal Navy planes bombed Finnish territory on July 30, 1941. Spiro does not mention Manninen's statement on the next overleaf (p. 168) that subsequent "declarations of war did not mean at any stage of the Second World War that Finland had become involved in real hostilities with the Western allies." This raid was four months before Britain, under great pressure from Stalin, reluctantly declared war on Finland; Winston S. Churchill, *The Grand Alliance* (Boston: Houghton Mifflin, 1951), pp. 526–535. The target was a German-operated nickel-mining operation in northern Finland; Weart, *Never at War*, Appendix. Finland took no hostile action against any Western ally, nor during the period of declared war did the Western allies shoot Finns. (Australia, Canada, and New Zealand joined Britain in a formal declaration of war lasting from December 1941 to 1944; the non-elected Free French government was briefly at war with Finland in 1944.)

Schwerin adjustment brings the 1866 level down too, but only to .29.) In massaging the data, he tosses aside the very coding rules of Singer and Small noted above; i.e., the 1000 troops/100 fatalities minimum for participation. Has the fate of realism come to hang on such manipulations?

Insignificant Insignificance

All of this might sound a wee bit *récherché* but for two considerations. A few democratic peace proponents have maintained the strong proposition that democracies *never* fight each other. I do not wish to defend that position here, partly because of my own doubts about its evidentiary basis and partly because it invites eternal nit-picking discussions that do not greatly interest me. It is enough to say, first, that wars between democracies are at most extremely rare events, and second, that even violent conflicts between democracies that fall short of war are also very rare. Application of the proposition to violent conflicts well short of war is useful in expanding the number of "events" that can be analyzed, and, more important, is integral to the theory.

Neither Finland nor Imperial Germany would make much difference save for the matter of few wars and few democracies, leading to the third allegation, that it is difficult to find enough cases to distinguish zero as a statistically significant number. Even so, the notion that the data do not support the democratic peace proposition becomes possible only by procedures that make it impossible to find statistically- significant results, even with zero democratic wars.

Spiro's statistical analysis has many dubious and inconsistent assumptions. If we scrutinize that analysis, and examine some alternatives, it will be clear the lengths to which one must go to support the "finding" of non-significance. His major effort—comprising 12 pages of text, Appendix table, and graph—is devoted to chopping the data into yearly intervals and doing 165 separate year-by-year analyses to discover whether the frequency of democratic dyads actually at war was significantly different from zero.[12] In only 6 of the 165 years

---

12. Spiro performs his test using a hypergeometric distribution. In simple English, he is usually asking what is the *exact* probability that one will find no liberal (democratic) dyads at war. Yet consistent with my position above, the correct hypothesis is only that liberal dyads have a lower propensity to engage in war. In 1941 through 1943 he computes the probability of finding exactly 4 (5 in 1944) democracies at war, to conform with his argument that Finland and the Western allies constitute warring democratic dyads. For those years, however, he should instead have computed the probability of the observed outcome of 4 (or 5), or fewer. Thus in 1941 it would be not just the probability of observing 4 democratic wars, but the sum of the probabilities of observing 4, 3, 2,

does he find the difference statistically significant, as democratic peace theory would predict. (He avoids finding statistical significance for 8 other years by the way in which he defines a warring dyad.)[13] Thus he fails to reject the hypothesis that democratic dyads are no different from other dyads. But of course; by splitting the data into small enough parts, he has guaranteed a low rate of war outbreak in each year, so most of the tests he runs will have zero statistical power. Even though there are never (except for Finland) any wars between democracies, with so few wars in any one year it is almost always mathematically impossible to reject the hypothesis of no relationship. He might as well have broken the time periods down into even finer units, like the month or week.

Any proposed correlate of peace, however strong, could be discarded through such a divide-and-conquer approach. Realism's assumption—that states' internal characteristics are irrelevant to peace—would thus be safe. Imagine a trial judge instructing the jury to divide the evidence into 165 pieces, and then to deliberate whether each fraction alone warrants a conviction. Someone could get away with murder. A juror should decide on the aggregate of the evidence presented, and so should the international relations scholar. This requirement to use "total evidence" was enunciated by Jakob Bernoulli in 1713, at the birth of our concept of probability.[14]

An obvious question to ask is: what is the probability, assuming independence over many trials, of consistently finding zero (or 4 or 5 in the Finland years) democracies at war. Instead of taking each individual-year "test" in isolation, what is the probability of producing this finding *year after year?* The answer requires multiplying the probabilities in each year; for example, the probability of finding no liberal dyads at war in 1980 is, from Spiro's table, .829; in 1979 .704, etc., so the calculation is .829 times .704, etc. The joint prob-

---

1, and 0 wars. This would give significance levels of .437, .719, .691, and .660 for 1941 through 1944. These are higher than in column 8 of his Appendix (p. 85), and would have made his null hypothesis fare even better. This is the same as Fisher's Exact Test (one-tailed), which compares the test statistic with the hypergeometric distribution. In years with no wars between democracies, Spiro's method does not differ from the method used here.

13. In 4 years of World War I, and in 1940 and 1945, the results are statistically significant as I predict. For 1941–44 they in the wrong direction. That is solely due to calling Finland "at war" with democracies; otherwise these 4 years would be significant in the theoretically predicted direction. His revision of the Korean War data avoids showing another 4 years as statistically significant. During the 66 years when no dyads at all were at war, the probability of no war between democracies in these 66 years was *a priori* 100 percent.

14. Rudolf Carnap, *Logical Foundations of Probability*, 2nd ed. (Chicago: University of Chicago Press, 1971).

ability over 165 years is .000000000000000000002, which would appear to be impressive evidence for democratic peace.

Spiro does not do that, because it requires assuming that each year constitutes a test fully independent of every other year. The very factors that produce peace between two states in one year are likely to make them peaceful the next; indeed expectations built upon past peace encourage its perpetuation. Likewise, a war begun last year may well carry over. Yet to acknowledge this exposes a contradiction in how to interpret Spiro's repeated year-by-year tests. When he treats 1967 as one test of the proposition and 1968, 1969, and so on as quite different tests, he ignores the fact that most of the warring dyads are continuing participants in the Vietnam War. This makes a big difference on the impact that multi-state multi-year wars have on the analysis. Finland again is an example. So too are the continuities from World War I to World War II in what has been called the Thirty-Years War for German Hegemony. By this reasoning, year-by-year tests are not at all independent of each other, and multiplying probabilities is not permissible. But if so, just what does it mean to take 165 different "samples"? If one year's sample is much like the next, how persuasive is it to say that all those repetitions failed to turn up support for democratic peace?

Subsequently Spiro offers to aggregate the years in another way. Exact results for periods longer than a year are not reported, either in numbers or graphs. It is evident, however, that his procedure (pp. 74–75) does not enlarge the "sample" sizes, but rather is guaranteed to keep them small. He includes only countries that were continuously in existence over the longer period, and continuously liberal. The samples shrink as the time period is extended. In the longest (150-year period), the sample is reduced to only 12 countries (3 of them liberal). He says the results confirm the "no different than random chance would predict" model, especially in the longer periods, and (p. 75) that "the results are not at all what one would expect." Given such reductions in the sample size, who should be surprised?

By contrast, consider some support for the democratic peace proposition. I use my own work as an example, but related work reaches nearly identical conclusions.[15] Start with the recognition that not all dyads have an equal

15. Russett, *Grasping the Democratic Peace*, chap. 4; Maoz and Russett, "Normative and Structural"; also Stuart Bremer, "Dangerous Dyads: Conditions Affecting the Likelihood of Interstate War, 1816–1965," *Journal of Conflict Resolution*, Vol. 36, No. 2 (June 1992), pp. 309–341; and Bremer, "Democracy and Militarized Interstate Conflict, 1816–1965," *International Interactions*, Vol. 18, No. 3 (1993), pp. 231–250. Bremer's work is important not only because we replicate each other's

probability of being at war. A few states are great powers, with interests all over the globe, and the ability to land troops, naval bombardments, or nuclear weapons anywhere. For dyads that include great powers, war is in principle possible. War is also possible between neighboring states or near-neighbors. As Layne recognizes (p. 39), but Spiro does not, "only dyads meeting these preconditions are part of the appropriate universe of cases from which democratic peace theory can be tested." Most dyads (e.g., Ghana and Burma) are politically irrelevant—too far apart to have border conflicts or to be much involved in each other's affairs, and too weak to project power over long distances. On occasion—as in the World Wars and the Korean War—they may be drawn into conflict with distant states. But under nearly any other other circumstance it is pointless to include them in an empirical test of potential war adversarsies. Thus we should concentrate on the roughly 12 percent of dyads in the international system for whom war is a real possibility.[16]

Furthermore, we do not begin with total ignorance (the equivalent of Spiro's random model for all dyads in the international system) about what kinds of countries go to war with each other. In addition to the effect of geographical proximity, good theory (much of it straight out of realism) suggests that rich countries are unlikely to fight each other, as are countries whose economies are growing rapidly; that states of relatively equal power are more likely to fight each other than are states of widely disparate military capabilities; and that states which share ties of military alliance do not have the same incentives to

findings, but because it covers the long period of Spiro's analysis. Spiro's treatment of this research is misleading. He says (p. 77) that Maoz and Russett did not analyze the earlier period "presumably because they suspected that democracy would not be statistically significant." But I knew from a copy of Bremer's first manuscript in mid-1991, before the Maoz-Russett multivariate analysis, that the effect of democracy *was* significant over the long time-span. Spiro also identifies (p. 76) "many" studies as showing, "at best, a very weak correlation between democracy and peace." He cites two from 1984 and one from 1989, neglecting to say that all three authors later decided the correlation is robust. See Steve Chan, "Democracy and War: Some Thoughts on Future Research Agenda," *International Interactions,* Vol. 18, No. 3 (1993), pp. 197–213; William Dixon, "Democracy and the Management of International Conflict," *Journal of Conflict Resolution,* Vol. 37, No. 1 (March 1993), pp. 42–68; Erich Weede, "Some Simple Calculations on Democracy and War Involvement," *Journal of Peace Research,* Vol. 29, No. 4 (November 1992), pp. 377–383. Whereas Rummel's early empirical work was limited to a short time-period, his subsequent review of five other studies showed robust support for the democratic peace. R.J. Rummel, "Libertarian Propositions on Violence within and between Nations: A Review of Published Research Results," *Journal of Conflict Resolution,* Vol. 29, No. 3 (September 1985), pp. 441–442.

16. Maoz and I discuss analyzing "politically relevant dyads" at length in our publications. Whereas doing so misses some conflicts (and a few wars) between dyads not politically relevant by these criteria, it picks up a greater proportion of conflicts and wars between democratic dyads than between non-democratic ones. Hence it does not bias the results in favor of our hypothesis. See Russett, *Grasping the Democratic Peace,* p. 74.

fight one another as do states not so allied. One should incorporate this knowledge into a test, controlling for the influence of these variables as well as of democracy. By doing so we make it *harder* to find an independent causal relationship for democracy, since many democracies also are wealthy, allied, etc. Nevertheless, we do still find it.

Equally important is the proposition that, not only are wars between democracies rare or non-existent, but democracies are more likely to settle mutual conflicts of interest (and there surely are such) short of the threat or use of any military force. Conflicts of interest arise, but democracies rarely escalate those disputes to the point where they threaten to use military force against each other, or actually use force at all (even at a level of violence far below the threshold at which we would call it a war). Much more often than other states, they settle their disagreements by mediation, negotiation, or other forms of peaceful diplomacy. This integral element of democratic peace theory constitutes a logical extension of the research program that began nearly two decades ago with wars. By ignoring it, Spiro is more than five years behind the curve.[17]

With these specifications, Zeev Maoz and I analyzed the year-by-year behavior of all politically-relevant dyads in militarized disputes (if any) during the period 1946–86. The result was that democratic dyads were significantly (statistically) less likely to engage in conflict—whether wars or minor disputes—than were pairs of states where one or both members were not democratic, even allowing for the effect of the control variables.

Spiro, however, objects (pp. 77–79) to anything that combines 41 years of observations into a single analysis, because aggregating years violates the assumption of independence between observations. He does identify a well-known problem in the statistical procedure, known as pooled-time series analy-

---

17. See Zeev Maoz and Nasrin Abdolali, "Regime Types and International Conflict, 1816–1976," *Journal of Conflict Resolution*, Vol. 33, No. 1 (March 1989), pp. 3–36. For the most recent extension, to democracies' use of negotiation and third-party mediation, see Dixon, "Democracy and the Management of International Conflict"; Russell Leng, "Reciprocating Strategies and Success in Interstate Crisis Bargaining," *Journal of Conflict Resolution*, Vol. 31, No. 1 (March 1993), pp. 3–41; Gregory Raymond, "Democracies, Disputes, and Third-Party Intermediaries," *Journal of Conflict Resolution*, Vol. 38, No. 1 (March 1994), pp. 24–42. Spiro says (p. 78) that Russett shifts to militarized international disputes from war although he "proposed to study the latter in his introductory chapter." Not so. Although that chapter begins with the extreme case (war), pp. 20 ff. and the theory in chap. 2 consider the full range of threats and use of interstate violence. Layne (p. 14) recognizes that realism, unlike the democratic peace literature, expects democracies to use "threats, ultimata, and big-stick diplomacy against another democracy." James Fearon, "Domestic Political Audiences and the Escalation of International Disputes," *American Political Science Review*, Vol. 88, No. 3 (September 1994), pp. 585–586, offers a formal explanation for why democracies are less likely to escalate disputes with each other.

sis, which we used.[18] We acknowledged that patterns of behavior in one year depend *in part* on behavior in the previous year, and took the standard methodological precautions to minimize the effects. There is no perfect statistical solution; the observations are neither completely independent nor so dependent that one need restrict the evidence just to what can be shown on a year-by-year basis. One important mitigation of the independence problem would be, unlike Spiro, to include a dispute only in the year it began, or if it subsequently escalated to a higher level of violence on our scale, to include it in the year of escalation. This would avoid counting wars or disputes which are merely continuations of the past.[19]

New Looks

If we grant that dependence between years does raise some problems for pooled time-series, other analyses—not previously reported—are still possible. Instead of using the dyad-year as a unit of analysis, take the whole *regime-dyad* as the unit of analysis. For example, the United States and Costa Rica constitute an always-democratic dyad. The United States and the USSR are an always non-democratic dyad. The United States and Argentina are a democratic dyad in the years 1966–72 and 1983–86; in all our other years they constitute a non-democratic dyad because of the character of the Argentine regime. (For simplicity I treat all democratic dyad-years as a single unit even if the years were interrupted; ditto for non-democratic years.) For each of these regime dyads then ask: did they ever initiate a dispute, or escalate one? We are not counting the number of disputes or escalations within each regime-dyad; we are only asking if a dyad experienced at least one. The result is 1251 units for comparison, one for each dyad over time. We then can ask, very simply, whether democratic dyads are less likely than non-democratic dyads, over their whole "lifetimes" (up to 41 years in these data), to begin or escalate disputes.

The answer, shown in Table 1, is overwhelmingly clear: yes. Comparing percentages in the last column, non-democratic dyads were "infinitely" more

---

18. His discussion, however, is confused. The first two reasons or problems he identifies are one and the same. His only objection to "enlarging the number of observations" is that the observations are not fully independent. Nor are we "sure of finding significant results" (p. 78) by pooling observations—we merely have not cut the data into so many small parts as to guarantee not finding significant results.
19. This distinction informed the presentation in chap. 1 of my book, although not the multivariate analysis. It cannot correct for non-independence among dyads at peace.

Table 1. Dispute Behavior with Regime-Dyad as the Unit of Analysis, 1946–86.

	War	No War	Percent with War
Democracy	0	169	0
Not Democracy	37	1045	3.4
	Use of Force	No Use of Force	Percent Using Force
Democracy	8	161	4.7
Not Democracy	229	853	21.2
	Any Dispute	No Dispute	Percent with Dispute
Democracy	12	157	7.1
Not Democracy	257	825	23.8

likely to make war on each other. They were four-and-a-half times more likely to use force against each other than were democratic dyads. As for disputes, non-democratic dyads were more than three times as likely as democratic dyads to engage in any sort of militarized dispute. These big differences confirm that the inhibition against violence between democracies applies at all levels, and that it is most powerful as a restraint on war. Statistical tests are fully appropriate, and these differences are highly significant: at the .004 level for wars, and the .0000001 level for use of force and for all disputes. This is powerful evidence for the relatively pacific behavior of democratic dyads.[20]

Now the *coup de grace*. Take our data, but otherwise replicate Spiro's year-by-year analysis, using the same .20 probability level and, for comparison, counting disputes that continued from the past year. We know wars are too rare for us to expect significant results on a year-to-year basis, but uses of force and all disputes are much more common. I created 41 two-by-two tables (one for each year), with the number of all democratic dyads which did not use force against each other, the number of democratic dyads which did use force, and the number of all other dyads with and without use of force. I then did the same thing for disputes at all levels. Table 2 gives the results. Using Spiro's

---

20. Zeev Maoz has performed an analysis like this on the entire 1816–1986 period, with very similar results to be reported elsewhere. It is essential to distinguish new or escalated disputes from continuing ones, since if a regime changes from democratic to non-democratic, or vice versa, one would not want to blame the new regime for simply inheriting an old dispute from its predecessor. Here and below I use Maoz's recently refined data-set; the results would not be substantively different using data employed for my book. Fisher's Exact Test gives the probability that the difference is attributable to chance. As explained in footnote 12, this test is *less* likely than Spiro's to reject the null hypothesis when there actually are disputes between democracies.

Table 2. Year-by-Year Tests of Disputes and Use of Force by Politically Relevant Dyads, 1946–86.

	Democracies Significantly Lower	No Significant Difference
Use of Force	32	9
Any Dispute	34	7

own method of analysis, more than four-fifths of the years showed the predicted statistically significant difference between democratic dyads and non-democratic ones.[21] None showed a difference—significant or not—opposite to what democratic peace theory predicts.

By raising new objections to the evidence for the democratic peace, Spiro forced me to devise new tests. The result is that the evidence for the democratic peace is stronger and more robust than ever. I am grateful for the challenge.

Conclusion

There is no need to jettison the insights of realism which tell us that power and strategic considerations affect states' decisions to fight each other. But neither should one deny the limitations of those insights, and their inability to explain many of the instances when liberal states have chosen not to fight or threaten one another. The danger resides in "vulgar realism's" vision of war of all against all, in which the threat that other states pose is unaffected by their internal norms and institutions. The challenges posed in this journal to the theory of democratic peace, and to the fact of democratic peace, hardly compare with the force of the Inquisition. Nevertheless, Galileo's response works here: *"Epure si muove."*

---

21. Deleting non-escalating disputes after the year of initiation avoids the problem of non-independence of conflicts over time, but it also cuts the number of events by one-third, reducing the ability to achieve statistical significance. Even so, 60 percent of the years still show a significant difference.

The Liberal Peace— And Yet It Squirms

David E. Spiro

The debate between Professor Bruce Russett and me is about the causes of peace. Russett's recent work aims to support a commonly-accepted theory—the Liberal Peace—which argues that democracies do not fight one another. My article directly challenges this theory by demonstrating that the number of wars between democracies is not statistically different from what random chance would predict. Both wars and democracies are rare, and that is why there are not many wars between democracies.

My article did not try to "disprove" liberal theory. Instead, I showed that, in statistical tests, random chance accounts for the Liberal Peace better than regime-type. Since random chance, which we know does not explain peace or war, is statistically more significant than regime-type, it follows that the absence of wars between democracies is not empirical confirmation for liberal theory. Furthermore, I argued that the reason some studies find statistically significant results is that the authors have biased the results by selectively choosing definitions and methods.

Russett's critique is lengthy and detailed, but I am confident that I have answers to all of his points. Because of space limitations, however, I will address only his four principal criticisms.

Definitions

Russett charges that my case against the Liberal Peace rests on manipulating data sets. He specifically objects to my exclusion of Mecklenburg-Schwerin from the Seven Years War in 1866 and of twelve minor participants (such as Belgium and Ethiopia) from the Korean Conflict. At the same time, he wants me to alter the original data sets so that Finland is not considered at war against the allied democracies during World War II. His objections are curious, since his own work does not include World War II at all, and he himself excluded 10 of those same 12 minor participants in the Korean Conflict. I agree, however, that how we define participation in the World War II and the Korean Conflict

David E. Spiro is Assistant Professor of Political Science at the University of Arizona. He is the author of Hegemony Unbound: Petrodollar Recycling and the De-legitimization of American Hegemony (Cornell University Press, forthcoming). He thanks Michael Desch, John Mearsheimer, Edward Muller, Tom Volgy, and Steven Weber for their comments.

International Security, Vol. 19, No. 4 (Spring 1995), pp. 177–180

is important, because it determines whether the Liberal Peace is significant during two of the biggest wars in recent history.

It is indeed difficult to decide how to define certain wars. Russett makes a reasonable argument for excluding Finland, even though it allied with the fascist powers; was formally at war with Australia, Britain, Canada, and New Zealand; and was bombed at least once by the RAF. He also argues for including nations such as Belgium in the Korean Conflict even though it suffered fewer than 25 casualties each year in combat, fewer Belgians than succumbed to falls from ladders.

My main point was that the issue of how to treat the data is quite contestable. Russett himself cannot decide whether to criticize me for excluding nations or for including too many nations. On page 168 [p. 341 in this volume, eds.] of his response I include too many and on pages 168–169 [pp. 341–342] too few, then on page 171 [p. 345] "reductions in the sample size" lead to my results and on the next page my failure to reduce the sample size leads to my results. His response is empirical confirmation that these issues are not clearcut.

What is most important, and what Russett conveniently ignores, is that his case for the significance of the Liberal Peace rests *heavily* on these definitional issues. These are issues over which Russett himself demonstrates confusion and inconsistency. If Russett were to change his mind about any single one of these highly contestable definitions, his results would no longer be significant. The argument for the Liberal Peace completely depends upon this selective choice of definitions.

Slicing Up the Data

Russett protests that the analysis I did for one-year periods makes it impossible to prove significance, because "by splitting the data into small enough parts [I] guarantee a low rate of war outbreak in each year." This objection represents a serious misunderstanding of my methodology, and of the difference in statistical analysis between analyzing a sample and analyzing the entire population.[1] I looked at all nations (not a sample), and I compared the proportion that

---

1. In another objection, Russett uses my results to calculate a joint probability of peace year after year, and then points out that the years are not independent from one another (which I knew, and which was why I did not calculate a joint probability). Then he criticizes his own assumption of independence, recognizes "a contradiction" in the way he interprets my analysis of one-year periods, and blames *me* for ignoring historical context. I find it difficult to respond to someone who presents an argument that I did not make, rebuts that argument, and then criticizes me for inconsistency.

were at war to the proportion that were democratic during a set period of time. The length of the time-period is irrelevant to the number of nations that are at war, unless the wars we are studying were extraordinarily short and trivial.

Russett seems to be hung up on my analysis of one-year periods, but I also examined all of the possible 5, 10, 20, 30, 40, 50, 60, 70, 80, 90, 100, 110, 120, 130, 140, and 150-year periods between 1816 and 1982. He chooses to ignore my many analyses of longer periods, which support the argument that the absence of wars between democracy is statistically insignificant.[2] The reader might wonder, if Russett's primary objection to my article was the analysis of one-year periods, why my results for multi-year periods also contradict his work. Russett gives the reason in his response. His results depend upon a pooled time-series analysis, which means that he takes one-year observations and mixes them all together. (The dyad between the United States and Canada, for example, counts 41 separate times.) I pointed out in my article that there is no logical rationale for presenting data this way, and furthermore it violates several rules for proper statistical methods. Russett responds that my article identified "a well-known problem in the statistical procedure," and "there is no perfect statistical solution" to this problem. Having misunderstood my methodology, and having conceded that his own data analysis was faulty, Russett is forced to present entirely new data analysis instead of standing by his previous work.

Restricting the Data to Relevant Dyads

Russett's pooled time-series analysis considered only dyads that he defined as "politically relevant." No one can be sure of what criteria Russett used for political relevance, because he has not made the decision-rules or his data publicly available. The criteria seem to be based on whether nations and their colonies are contiguous or bordering the same body of water, and whether one of them is a great power. The result is that his analysis leaves out 78 percent of all dyads between nations.

In principle, it seems like a good idea to consider only nations that have the possibility of war. In practice, however, this is a difficult idea to implement. According to Russett, the dyads of nations that he does not consider relevant

---

2. Russett says that I did not provide the detailed results of these analyses, but as I wrote in my article, all of the data, the computer programs, and the results are available to anyone on the Internet. In fact, it appears that Russett himself took advantage of this public access, since he quotes results that I did not have space to report in my article. "Spiro.exe" (a self-extracting zip file) is available from haavelmo.harvard.edu via anonymous ftp or gopher.

occasionally go to war with one another; and those "occasions" include "the World Wars and the Korean War" (p. 171) [p. 346]. These dyads cannot be very "politically relevant" if the criteria for choosing them does not allow consideration of the major conflicts of this century.

I also grappled with a problem of how to define relevant dyads. Since the issue is the endurance of peace over time, when I analyzed (for example) a forty-one year period, I examined only nations that existed for the entire time.[3] Russett includes a war between two nations, even if they existed for only one day during the single forty-one year period he examines. Because I examined every possible period for every possible time-frame, I am sure that the way I selected the data did not bias my results.

I believe the way I defined relevant dyads is correct. But even if I am wrong, the point remains that the case for the Liberal Peace is entirely dependent on tricky and highly contestable definitional issues. Russett consistently and across the board chooses definitions of key concepts and data and methods so that they always yield results favoring the Liberal Peace. My article pointed to problems with definitional issues, and reported results for both sides of each issue.

New Data Analysis

Russett has addressed the theory of the Liberal Peace in at least two books and three articles, and thus has had ample opportunity to present convincing arguments in its support. But rather than stand by this work, he now presents new data analyses, calling them a *"coup de grace."* Has he delivered the definitive proof of the Liberal Peace? Who knows? There are no citations on where the new data come from or how he manipulated it. There are no descriptions of the statistical tests or methods used, and no detailed results. This seems less like a *coup de grace* than a desperate *coup de theatre.* If Professor Russett publishes his results in an appropriate form, making his data, methods, and results publicly available for replication, we will be able to evaluate this *ad hoc* argument for the Liberal Peace.

---

3. I devised my tests for the endurance of the Liberal Peace at the suggestion of Michael Doyle, who had commented on an early draft of the article. Before either Doyle (whose work established modern study of the Liberal Peace) or I had the idea of what tests of longer periods woulds show, we agreed that it would be appropriate to include only dyads that existed for the entire period. To include dyads of nations that existed for only part of the period, as Russett wants to do, is not a proper test of endurance.

On the Democratic Peace

Christopher Layne

Because of space constraints, my response to Professor Russett is confined to three central points of disagreement: (1) he imputes to me the position that democratic peace theory is nothing more than statistical correlation; (2) he criticizes my research design on the grounds that my case studies cannot account for instances where "the dog did not bark"; and (3) he questions the reliability of the historical evidence on which my (or any) process-tracing cases studies are based.

Professor Russett notwithstanding, it plainly is not the case that my article dismisses democratic peace theory as mere statistical correlation. On the contrary, the main thrust of my article is precisely my detailed examination of democratic peace theory's causal logic. As I demonstrate, democratic peace theory relies on two asserted causal explanations: (a) institutional constraints and (b) democratic norms and culture. After demonstrating that institutional constraints do not explain the democratic peace, I test the explanatory power of democratic norms and culture, and conclude that this causal logic does not hold up when examined in four key cases where it should apply. Once democratic peace theory's causal logic is shown to be threadbare, then, indeed, little is left but statistical correlations; democratic peace theory offers no convincing explanation of *why* democracies purportedly do not fight each other.

Next, invoking the "dog that did not bark" argument, Professor Russett claims (pp. 165–167) [pp. 338–341 in this volume, eds.] that I commit the "logical fallacy of inducing a principle of universal non- existence merely by finding a few cases of non-existence. Even if there were no evidence for democratic peace considerations in four cases, that would prove nothing about their putative absence in other instances." Professor Russett asserts that my methodological focus on near misses overlooks "the crises that never erupted or never brought the participants to the brink of war." This criticism simply misses the point: nothing can be learned from mute dogs because it is difficult (if not impossible) to prove why a non-event did not happen. The only way we can test democratic peace theory's causal explanations—and thereby determine what factors influence states to remain at peace—is precisely to examine instances where they have come to the brink of war without going over it, that

Christopher Layne is an unaffiliated scholar in Los Angeles. He is presently a consultant to the government contracts practice group of Hill, Wynne, Trop, and Meisinger, which represents major firms in the defense industry.

International Security, Vol. 19, No. 4 (Spring 1995), pp. 175–177

is, crises. Professor Russett clearly wants to believe that democratic peace theory explains the "non-barking dogs" but there is no evidence to substantiate his belief.[1]

Professor Russett also attacks my case studies on post-modernist grounds, implying that the historical evidence of what and why decision-makers did what they did is inherently unreliable. Lawyers and historically-trained IR theorists (I have been trained in, and practiced, both professions) know that evidence must always be sifted painstakingly to determine its probative value. One learns to look carefully at archives, diaries, memoirs, and policy statements to determine whether the evidence is consistent and corroborative. Historical evidence of this type is the fundamental data base for studying international politics. We are properly enjoined that such evidence must be used punctiliously. It is something rather different, however, to suggest—as Professor Russett comes perilously close to doing—that the historical record must be discarded entirely because it is fundamentally untrustworthy. "Post-modernism" may have a place in art museums but it should be kept out of the study of international relations.

In reality, rather than attacking my conclusions, Russett admits (p. 166) [pp. 339–340] that, in the cases I studied, "power and strategic considerations were predominant." While this admission reflects well on Professor Russett's social scientific rigor, it also leaves him in a bind. He says that his concession does not give the game away. In fact, it ends the game decisively. Unable to demonstrate that democratic peace theory explains the avoidance of war in near-miss crises, he is left only with his weak "non-barking dogs" argument.

Whatever else it may be, democratic peace theory is not a compelling explanation of international political outcomes. It is, however, a dangerous retrogression to the kind of "normative international relations theory" (itself an oxymoron) so popular in Britain and America after World War I. Indeed, in

---

1. Illustrative is Russett's contention that democratic peace theory factors played an important role in explaining why, *circa* 1900, Britain pursued rapprochement with the United States rather than with Germany. In fact, between 1898–1901, Britain and Germany tried to form an alliance. The effort did not materialize because London and Berlin could not reconcile their conflicting strategic interests. Domestic political factors had little, if anything, to do with the outcome. Britain subsequently focused on the German threat, rather than on the (geographically and temporally) more distant American one for geopolitical reasons. Specifically, British policymakers recognized that Germany, the dominant land power on the continent, which possessed a powerful and growing navy, fit the classic mold of a potential European hegemon that could threaten Britain's security. These points are not controversial.

Grasping the Democratic Peace (p. 136), Professor Russett gives the game away again when he says:

Understanding the sources of democratic peace can have the effect of a self-fulfilling prophecy. Social scientists sometimes create reality as well as analyze it. Insofar as norms do guide behavior, repeating those norms helps to make them effective. *Repeating the norms as descriptive principles can help to make them true.* (Emphasis added.)

We are all entitled to our value preferences. However, these should never be conflated with the rigorous theory building and testing that must constitute the intellectual foundation of the study of international relations.

Reflections on the Liberal Peace and Its Critics

Michael W. Doyle

The collection "Give Democratic Peace a Chance?"[1] is remarkable evidence for the progressive development of the liberal research program. Christopher Layne offers a valuable exploration of hard cases, where war nearly occurred; David Spiro challenges the significance of the statistical regularity that liberal states are unlikely to go to war with each other; and John Owen takes a large step toward the deepening of the liberal paradigm by showing how the process of the liberal peace might have worked. What other research program in international relations displays its proponents and critics contesting on the same playing field, producing social science of this quality and drawing upon both statistical testing and case studies? Together, they point the way forward for further development, illustrating the importance but also the limitations of either case studies or statistical tests, considered alone.

I wrote "Kant, Liberal Legacies and Foreign Affairs," published in two parts in *Philosophy and Public Affairs* (Summer and Fall 1983) in order to show how Immanuel Kant's 1795 essay, "Perpetual Peace," could be constructed as a coherent explanation of two important regularities in world politics: the tendencies of liberal states simultaneously to be peace-prone in their relations with each other and unusually war-prone in their relations with nonliberal states. Republican democratic representation, an ideological commitment to fundamental human rights, and trans-national interdependence (to rephrase Kant's three "definitive articles" of the hypothetical peace treaty he asked states to sign) could, I argued, be seen as three necessary and, together, sufficient causes of the two regularities taken together. This causal structure distinguished Kantian liberal theory from the international implications of nonliberal democracy, commercial pacifism, and mixed republicanism.[2] (It also gave rise to difficult determinations of what did or did not constitute a liberal regime.) The first

Michael W. Doyle is Professor of Politics and International Affairs at the Center of International Studies, Princeton University.

---

1. Christopher Layne, "Kant or Cant: The Myth of the Democratic Peace," *International Security*, Vol. 19, No. 2 (Fall 1994), pp. 5–49; David Spiro, "The Insignificance of the Liberal Peace," ibid., pp. 50–86; and John M. Owen, "How Liberalism Produces Democratic Peace," ibid., pp. 87–125. My views on these issues have benefited from discussions with George Downs.
2. I have reexamined the imperial, isolationist, pacifist, and internationalist implications of various forms of democracy, both "realist" and "liberal," in Doyle, "Voice of the People: Political Theorists

International Security, Vol. 19, No. 4 (Spring 1995), pp. 180–184
© 1995 by the President and Fellows of Harvard College and the Massachusetts Institute of Technology.

part of the essay focused on the liberal peace and its Kantian sources. The second part focused on exposing the dangers of liberal imperialism, liberal aggression, and liberal appeasement.

Christopher Layne's article raises serious and important issues that question the liberal argument I discussed. He chose as his cases "near misses"—episodes when supposed liberals came close to war. In those cases, he argues, the logic of power replaced the liberal logic of accommodation. At the minimum, he succeeds in warning liberals of the dangers of imperial pursuits of principled settlements (the Venezuelan Dispute), unprincipled and punitive peace settlements (the Ruhr Crisis), and the contest over undefined colonial assets (Fashoda). In addition to their strategic significance, each of these disputes was problematic from a liberal point of view; liberal interests—both ideal and material—were also at odds. But Layne's tests have problems.

First, case studies designed to test a theory should be selected not by outcomes (in this case peace or war), as Christopher Layne does when he seeks out near-wars in which to test decision processes, but according to the hypothetical causes: liberal republics and non-liberal states. Hard cases, such as those for which he searches, are useful to generate alternative hypotheses or to test and, when met, to confirm theories, but they are not the best tests to invalidate anything but iron laws. (Most advocates of liberal theory took the trouble to point out exceptions to the peace-proneness of liberal republics or democracies.) A fairer set of case studies, for example, would include a small random sample of liberal dyads, liberal-nonliberal dyads, and nonliberal dyads, and examine whether liberalism makes a difference and the liberal thesis was confirmed or disconfirmed.

And, second, in the next round of theory testing, case studies should not be as dependent on secondary literature as Layne's are. Historians, like the rest of us, write with a purpose in mind. They are not simple chroniclers. Those purposes shape their presentation of events, giving rise to the well-known disputes between radical and conservative historians on, for example, German policy before World War I. We cannot resolve an issue by quoting conservative historians against supposed liberal ones on, in his example, the authoritarian aspects of pre–World War I Germany. None of the historians wrote to probe

---

on the International Implications of Democracy," in Geir Lundestad, ed., *The Fall of Great Powers: Peace, Stability and Legitimacy* (London: Scandinavian University Press/Oxford University Press, 1994), pp. 283–310; and in Doyle, *Ways of War and Peace* (New York: W. W. Norton, forthcoming).

these issues and their treatment is consequently incomplete. (The radical historians, for example, would not necessarily agree with the liberal thesis, nor the conservative ones with a balance-of-power interpretation.) Instead, while prior historiography will serve as a useful guide and check, we will need to examine the primary sources with our new questions in mind. To test the liberal thesis on decision-making, moreover, we will need a wider investigation than is typical of conventional diplomatic history, tracing decision processes outside cabinets, through parliaments and pressure groups, to, sometimes, the public. We will need to look for distinctions between informed and uninformed publics (often aroused by crises), axiomatic and articulated assumptions,[3] and issues on or absent from the policy agenda.

If further investigation sustains Layne's view of the crises he examined, we need to go a step further and note that the liberal failure not only took place in the inability to control the crisis, it also, and more importantly, preceded the crisis. When a liberal state is expecting war, it *should* look to its power. One of the signs of liberalism at work will be, not the war-crises resolved, but the issues and crises that did not arise. The thesis I drew from Kant focused on a *state* of peace distinguishing liberal relations from the *state* of war characterizing liberal-nonliberal and nonliberal-nonliberal relations. Kant, of course, was drawing on Hobbes's famous realist description of international relations not as war, but as a "state of war," which is "a tract of time, wherein the will to contend by battle is sufficiently known. "For," Hobbes continued, "as the nature of foul weather, lieth not in a shower or two of rain; but in an inclination thereto of many days together: so the nature of war, consisteth not in actual fighting; but in the known disposition thereto, during all the time there is no assurance to the contrary." War or peace are thus merely indicators of the "states" that permit them. States of war and peace are well-captured in studies such as those conducted by Anne-Marie Slaughter Burley, who focused on the differing treatments accorded to liberal and nonliberal states in American courts, and by William Dixon, who examined the management of conflict prior to the outbreak of a crisis.[4]

---

3. Ernest May, *"Lessons" of the Past: The Use and Misuse of History in American Foreign Policy* (New York: Oxford University Press, 1973).
4. Anne-Marie Slaughter Burley, "Law Among Liberal States: Liberal Internationalism and the Act of State Doctrine," *Columbia Law Review*, Vol. 92, pp. 1907–1996; and William Dixon, "Democracy and the Management of Conflict," *Journal of Conflict Resolution*, Vol. 37, No. 1 (March 1993), pp. 42–68.

If the liberal thesis is anything like normal social science, we will discover exceptions—interliberal wars or interliberal crises—with some of the latter resolved by (from the liberal view) luck rather than by principled respect, institutional restraint, and commercial interest. Erik Yesson's study of Fashoda, using primary sources, came to just such a conclusion: the liberals were lucky, not effective.[5] Passions, colonial uncertainty, and a long history of rivalry overwhelmed liberal restraint; peace was rescued by the balance of power. In many other instances, as liberals suggest (and as Dixon and Slaughter Burley found), differences will be managed long before they become violent disputes in the public arena. Rather than writing case after case of non-events, however, this is where the utility of statistically testing the significance of the liberal thesis will make itself clear.

What is the best statistical measure of the political significance of international liberalism? The test should probe whether liberalism makes a difference. Following a revolution in which a liberal state replaces a nonliberal state, would the liberal state in its foreign relations with other liberals and nonliberals behave in the same way, in the same circumstances, for as long as would have a continuing nonliberal state, and vice versa? Such a question is not readily testable. The keys are regime and position and duration. We can control for contiguity, income, etc., across an entire sample as, for example, Zeev Maoz and Bruce Russett did,[6] but not for all those factors together with geopolitical position. Geopolitical position clearly counts: regions are not the same and some (such as Europe) have been much more dangerous than others. If we cannot test all these at once, we will need to settle for something less. One valuable research strategy is, as suggested above, to expand the dependent variables to events other than war: court cases, crises, trade treaties, secret intelligence-sharing arrangements, war plans, and alliances. The unit of time by which we measure duration is, moreover, inherently ambiguous. How long does it take to decide or to preclude, to avoid or to embark on war? A year,

---

5. Erik Yesson, *Power and Identity in World Politics*, Ph.D. Dissertation, Department of Politics, Princeton University, 1992. Other difficulties for the liberal thesis are raised by Hongying Wang, "Liberal Peace? A Study of the Fashoda Crisis of 1898," paper presented at the annual conference of the American Political Science Association (APSA), 1992. But for a contrast favoring liberal explanations over realist in the Fashoda and Spanish-American War crises, see James Lee Ray, "Comparing the Fashoda Crisis and the Spanish American War," APSA, March 1994.
6. Zeev Maoz and Bruce Russett, "Alliance, Contiguity, Wealth and Political Stability: Is the Lack of Conflict Among Democracies a Statistical Artifact?" *International Interactions*, Vol. 17, No. 3 (1992), pp. 245–268.

month, or week? (The Cuban Missile Crisis was resolved in "21 Days"; the Cold War took 45 years.) Each measure affects the level of statistical significance of the inter-liberal peace, as David Spiro points out. David Spiro usefully tries out year-by-year and decade-by-decade comparisons, putting aside the positional issue. Another useful (but also very incomplete) test would be to compare for each country its war experience during its liberal periods to that during nonliberal periods. John Owen uses case studies to address (at least partially) just this geopolitical issue by comparing U.S. relations with Britain and France under liberal and nonliberal regimes. History, as Spiro confirms, also provides its own test during world wars, when states are forced to choose on which side of an impending conflict they will fight; interestingly, liberals tend to wind up on the same side (with a few anomalies).

Can we rely on statistical data sets to decide anomalies? Finland's formal status as a belligerent of the Allies in World War II is driving much of the recent statistical differences. Ruling Finland out of the war data set by the 1000-battle-deaths criterion of Singer and Small is a useful statistical convenience, but does not resolve the issue.[7] If today the United States and Britain suddenly attacked each other, and stopped before sustaining 1000 casualties, no advocate of the liberal thesis should regard the theory as vindicated. Here is where we need careful case studies. A good place to begin would be Allied and Nazi relations with Finland. Was Finland regarded as an enemy by the Allies and, if so, in a way similar to how the other enemy states were regarded? If yes, then it should be regarded as a disconfirming case; if not, not.

In the end, as with most theoretical disputes, the debate will turn on the alternatives. Liberal theory should not be compared to the statistical residual or to a richly described case study, but to the comparative validity of other theories of similar scope. Then we might be able to determine whether liberal internationalism is but a spurious correlation of some other causal model. To do this we will need to develop disconfirmable versions of at least the two other leading modern candidates for a general theory of world politics, realism and Marxism. The present difficulty of such a comparison lies in the current condition of the rivals. The most popular and developed current versions of realism see the theory confirmed by international systemic hierarchy (hegemony) or by equilibrium, by bandwagoning or by balancing behavior, all without offering us clear ways of distinguishing when we should expect one and when the other of those opposites. Marxism is confirmed for its adherents in equally

---

7. J. David Singer and Melvin Small, "Wages of War, 1816–1980," ICPSR Study 19044.

confusing ways, depending on whether the theorists regard the mode of production (ownership) or rather the mode of exchange (market) as the more fundamental feature of modern capitalism. For some, existing communist states were (are) a rejection of capitalism; for others they are an integral part of world capitalism.

In short, before we can truly engage in a debate over a general theory in international politics, other traditions will need to catch up to the kind and quality of work represented in the Fall 1994 issue of *International Security*. If the liberal theory is to have its chance, the other traditions also need to be put to their chance.

Michael Doyle on the Democratic Peace— Again

Michael W. Doyle

Liberalism is now widely regarded as having an important connection to international security. Liberal democratic republics do not seem to go to war with each other. They seem to be as war prone as any other regime, but they do not (with a very few exceptions) fight with each other. This apparent law also seems connected to the great global changes of our time. The end of the Cold War fits with the democratization of Russia.[1] And in many local contests—such as the Falklands or Gibraltar—the dampening of once bitter or violent conflict coincides with the emergence of mutual liberal democratic respect. The liberal peace, furthermore, takes on even greater significance as we observe the worldwide spread of democratic forms to every continent and region.

None of this has escaped the politicians. Drawing on Wilsonianism, Roosevelt's Four Freedoms, the Truman Doctrine and, more recently, addresses by Presidents Reagan and Bush, President Bill Clinton's 1994 "State of Union Address" affirmed that "democracies don't attack each other."[2] "Democratic Enlargement" has become the doctrinal centerpiece of the administration's foreign policy.

But the concern of social scientists is special. That significance was well expressed by Jack Levy who observed a few years ago that "the absence of war between democracies comes as close as anything to an empirical law in international relations."[3] Liberalism is thus emerging as a powerful paradigm in the social scientific sense. Unusually— for international relations—it is a testable, causal theory. It has a causal argument that can generate law-like hypotheses capable of being specified in such a way that they can, in principle, be disconfirmed.

One sign of the health of such a research program is that it attracts serious critical attention. By this measure the "Liberal Democratic Peace" is flourishing.

Michael W. Doyle is Professor of Politics and International Affairs at the Center of International Studies, Princeton University.

I would like to thank George Downs and Bruce Russett for their valuable advice.

1. See James Lee Ray and Bruce Russett, "The Future as Arbiter of Theoretical Controversies: Predictions, Explanations, and the End of the Cold War," *British Journal of Political Science* (forthcoming).
2. In the *New York Times,* January 26, 1994, p. A17.
3. Jack Levy, "Domestic Politics and War," *Journal of Interdisciplinary History* Vol. 18, No. 4, (Spring 1988), pp. 653–673.

The core association between peace and democracy has been extensively criticized and then defended, both in statistical and case study tests, both in this volume and elsewhere

Where should the debate go from here? I would recommend that we direct our efforts in three areas. We should elaborate—as a means of testing—the potential outcomes, or dependent variables. We should reexamine the causal model, adopting more careful ways to test it against relevant alternatives. And we should revisit its policy implications.[4]

Elaborate the Dependent Variables

An absence of war is not the same as a state of peace. A state of peace is the expectation that war is not a legitimate or likely recourse. That is what the liberal model seeks to explain and what Immanuel Kant envisaged in his *Perpetual Peace* written just 200 years ago. A state of peace thus is not the same as successful deterrence. It is a condition that should change expectations, attitudes, and give rise to more extensive forms of dispute avoidance and international collaboration. This is hard to measure. Recent valuable extensions—I can't name them all—have explored disputes short of war (Bremer); internal violence (Rudolph Rummel); peaceful territorial change (Arie Kacowicz); and great power cooperation (Benjamin Miller).[5] We should be expanding on the research in political economy, examining whether liberal ideas, institutions and interests make a difference in trade, investment, and financial disputes. Liberal institutions, principles and interests should also provide a firm foundation for international law, leading liberal states to abide by international law more reliably in dealings with each other than do other pairs of states.

To those areas, we should add studies of: Defense policies—which way do the weapons point and why? Intelligence cooperation—do liberals resist better the temptation to engage in covert activity (was the recent squabble with

---

4. These suggestions, of course, draw on Imre Lakatos, "Falsification and the Methodology of Scientific Research Programs," in I. Lakatos and A. Musgrave, eds., *Criticism and the Growth of Knowledge* (Cambridge: Cambridge University Press, 1970).
5. Stuart Bremer, "Democracy and Militarized International Disputes, 1816–1965," *International Interactions* Vol. 18, No. 3 (1992), pp. 23–50; Rudolph Rummel, *Death By Government* (New Brunswick, N.J.: Transaction Publishers, 1994); Arie Kacowicz, *Peaceful Territorial Change* (Columbia, SC: University of South Carolina Press, 1994); and Benjamin Miller, *When Opponents Cooperate* (Ann Arbor: University of Michigan Press, 1995).

France the norm or an exception)? Foreign aid—is there a "democratic difference" discriminating, other things equal, in favor of fellow democracies?

Liberal Democracy should make some difference over and beyond war. Does it?

Causal Argument and Testing

One additional reason to expand our view of potential outcomes is (I suspect) that our current statistical tests of the "democratic peace" are full of false positives and false negatives. False negatives (absolving liberalism) arise from the fact that there are many reasons not to go to war other than liberalism. Distance, exhaustion or deterrence resulting from an expectation that one will lose or that the costs of victory are too high are some of the obvious candidates. False positives (condemning liberalism) arise from the circumstance that it is not at all clear that most lists of participatory polities—including my own list—are all liberal republics. Many or some of the "democratic" conflicts and disputes may be among participatory polities, but not among "liberal republics."

Kant's theory held that a stable expectation of peace among states would be achieved once three conditions were met. Together they constitute a liberal republic. We can rephrase them as:

1. *Representative, republican government.* That includes an elected legislative, separation of powers and the rule of law. Kant argued that together those institutional features lead to caution because the government is responsible to its citizens. This does not guarantee peace. It should select for popular wars.

2. *A principled respect for nondiscriminatory human rights.* This should produce a commitment to respect the rights of fellow liberal republics (because they represent free citizens, who as individuals have rights that deserve our respect) and a suspicion of nonrepublics (because if those governments cannot trust their own citizens, what should lead us to trust them?).[6]

3. *Social and economic interdependence.* Trade and social interaction generally engender a mix of conflict and cooperation. Liberalism produces special material incentives for cooperation. Among fellow liberals, interdependence should

---

6. The individual subjects of autocracies, of course, do not lose their rights. It's just that the autocrats cannot legitimately claim to speak for their subjects. Subjects retain basic human rights, such as the rights of noncombatants in war. The terror bombing of civilians—as in the bombings of Dresden, Tokyo, Hiroshima and Nagasaki—constitute, in this view, violations of these rights and of liberal principles and demonstrate weaknesses of liberal models in these cases.

not be subject to security-motivated restrictions and, consequently, tends to be more varied, less dependent on single issues and less subject to single conflicts.[7]

Kant suggested that each condition was necessary and together they were sufficient to establish a secure expectation of peace. The first principle specifies representative government responsible to the majority; the second and third specify the majority's ends and interests. Together the three generate an expectation of peaceful accommodation among fellow liberals and hostility toward nonliberals.

Not all participatory polities would meet his criteria. Kant distrusted unfettered, democratic majoritarianism and his argument offers no support for a claim that participatory polities—democracies—should be peaceful either in general or between fellow democracies. Many participatory polities have been nonliberal. For 2000 years before the modern age, popular rule was widely associated with aggressiveness (by Thucydides) or imperial success (Machiavelli). Today, a list of Kantian republics would not include, for example, institutionalized representative democracies that are motivated by a public culture of indiscriminate empire-mongering, or racism or ethnic purity. The decisive preference of their median voter might well include "ethnic cleansing" against other democratic polities. Nor would they include autocracies, however enlightened and liberal, because the autocrats are not constrained by representative legislatures and the rule of law.[8] Their rule would not generate a stable expectation of liberal respect. Nor would they include autarkic democracies which lack the material and social foundations of interdependent interests that can generate mutual knowledge and egoistic incentives in support of moral commitments.[9]

How weed out the false positives? One way is a better data set of liberal polities that excludes nonliberal republics, which may be generating cases of the "interliberal" conflict. How weed out the false negatives, where the liberal model may be getting undue credit for peace? Distinguishing liberal peace from peace by nonliberal means calls for process tracing case studies and

---

7. These three points are all developed above in "Liberal Legacies."
8. Kant himself had a weakness for seeing pacific potential in some enlightened despots, a point drawn to my attention by Dr. Dominique Leydet. Kant appears to hope that enlightened despots will begin the process of establishing peace, even if despotic governments cannot sustain a secure peace.
9. Kant's is a testable proposition. All three may not be necessary, and we might be able to develop a more parsimonious theory of democratic peace than the one he offers. But it appears to be the case in the modern period that there is a strong tendency for stable democracies to be liberal and interdependent.

comparisons that weigh the liberal model against nonliberal theories of a similar scope.

Case studies that probe the processes and considerations underlying policy are growing and include in this volume Owen, Layne and Oren as well as others elsewhere. Ido Oren's study[10] effectively illustrates both the dependence of the liberal peace on multiple sources for its effective operation and the importance of intersubjective indicators for social scientific assessment. One cannot rely on good will alone to produce peace. Liberal regimes appear conflict–prone, inclined to excess suspicion in dealings with powerful nonliberal states and imperial crusading against weak nonliberal societies. These tendencies can lead to morally disastrous outcomes. Liberal intellectuals and leaders, moreover, have interpreted political regimes in a biased fashion, as do Oren's examples of Burgess and Wilson. Double standards abound. Left-wing liberals have found democratic mandates in revolutionary dictatorships; Stalin became, briefly, "Uncle Joe." Right-wing liberals have found liberal potential in anti-communist, capitalist dictatorships.[11]

If the liberal peace rested on enlightened liberal intellectuals alone, its salience would presumably be much less. Constraining leaders, however, and contributing to the public reliability of the peaceful expectation are institutions of representative government and material interests which can control individual biases. Each of the three Kantian conditions can be conceived of as a potential back-up to each of the others. The system can allow for an occasional imperialist or racist or ethnocentric or simply erratic leader, provided his or her success and tenure in office rest on a calculation of what the interests of the represented majority will bear. Similarly, mass racism or ethnocentrism can be temporarily mitigated by liberal statesmanship or commercial interests.

When it comes to testing the validity of the liberal peace, therefore, we need to measure regimes better than some of the actual democratic leaders do, if only to identify where they may have made a mistake and mistook favored or "like" regimes for "liberal" ones. This is because ideologies are not the only source of the peace and because we will want to discover where their particular ideologies may have led them astray. Intersubjective measures play a particularly useful check on subjective interpretation in this connection, since they go

---

10. Ido Oren, "The Subjectivity of the "Democratic" Peace?" *International Security* Vol. 20, No. 2, (Fall 1995), pp. 147–184.
11. "Liberal Legacies, Part 2" pp. 205–235.

beyond the views of a single intellectual, statesman, or country.[12] It may be the case that the liberal peace is systematically misinterpreted and spurious and that it really is instead a "Teutonic," "Aryan," or "Anglo-Saxon"—or today "capitalist"—condominium resulting from "Anglo-Saxon" virtue or simple profit-mongering, as some of the politicians and intellectuals of earlier and current times may have thought or think. The best way to find out is to test the counterproposition. Is there any evidence that the "Teutons" hang together? Have the capitalists?

What will also help is comparing liberal paradigms to other general theories of international relations of a similar scope, such as Realism and Marxism. Other theories need some catching up, such that they develop explanatory models that can generate testable general hypotheses, derived from their core propositions, that are subject to potential disconfirmation. How should we identify when classes are engaged in international class warfare? How do we weigh the balance of power such that we can tell when states actually balance power against power, capability against capability? When states balance, will we find that they then devote equivalent or proportional efforts to security (internal balancing)? Will they form alliances that maximize the prospect of minimizing threats (external balancing against threats, defined in terms of capabilities)?

Once these tests are done, we can compare these outcomes to liberal concepts of alliances—such as the proposition that there should be no alliances against fellow liberals—highlighting cases which two or three theories explain, one explains better, or none do well. Then one can assess the liberal research program comparatively—how does it measure against, not perfection, but other research paradigms?

The article by Henry Farber and Joanne Gowa presents a valuable attempt at a more refined statistical testing of the "democratic peace" proposition. Drawing on evidence from 1816 to 1980,[13] they confirm the three major propositions: that "democracies" are as likely as any other regime to get into war;

12. For example: proportion of the citizenry who can vote; proportion of the society open to international trade, investment and travel; the degree of control exercised by the legislature over public decisions, including foreign affairs; the condition of personal and civic rights and the attitudes of the citizenry on questions of human rights: all can be studied intersubjectively and should be. My list of liberal regimes is a very rough approximation of such a measure, "Liberal Legacies, I," pp. 236–266.

13. Henry S. Farber and Joanne Gowa, "Polities and Peace," *International Security* Vol. 20, No. 2, (Fall 1995) pp. 108–132.

that they are significantly less likely to go to war with each other; and that they are less likely to get into militarized disputes with each other.[14] (The authors follow much of the literature in including all participatory polities irrespective of whether they are liberal or not.)

The authors then proceed to segment the dependent variable—both war and dispute data—into five periods: "1) pre-World War I (1816–1913); 2) World War I (1914–18); 3) the interwar years (1919–38); 4) World War II (1939–45); and post-World War II (1946–80)."[15] Doing so, they discover that before 1914, although democratic states were less likely to engage in war with each other, this result is no longer statistically significant (it could have occurred by chance). (The democratic probability of war is lower in every period but World War II, but the relationship is statistically powerful only during World War I and the Cold War.) Democratic states, moreover, before World War I are more, not less, likely to get into low-level disputes with each other than are nondemocratic states with other nondemocratic states. (Democratic states are less likely to get into disputes in every period but the pre-1914 period, but only the periods of World War II and the Cold War are statistically significant.) The results are interesting.

The reasons for segmenting the data, however, are less than clear. Segmenting the data in that fashion makes no more sense than picking or choosing a single year or random set of decades or half centuries, unless one is testing the democratic or liberal model against some other model. It is worth paying some attention to their justifications

The authors offer two reasons for breaking up the data set of democratic peace and war. First, they argue that general wars such as World War I and World War II are different from dyadic wars. These wars are seen to involve systemic effects and attempts to "pass the buck" that operate over and above dyad-specific, or domestic regime effects.[16] This may be so; but, if so, these

---

14. Ibid., pp. 119 and 121. The authors are raising issues that should concern liberals. Even if democracies get into fewer disputes, why democracies get into militarized disputes at all is a problem worth more attention. Perhaps they are more commercially interdependent—and thus have much to dispute about? Their disputatiousness may also be an ironic product of their success in avoiding war—militarized signaling may be employed simply because neither party assumes real war will result. Thus the Anglo-Icelandic Cod War, one of the most serious liberal disputes of the Cold War period, which involved naval intimidation and bumping and may have resulted in a casualty, could have been a product of the assumption that the dispute would never go as far as real war. In this respect it resembles perhaps the bumping games (constrained by nuclear deterrence) that US and Soviet submarines played during the Cold War.
15. Ibid., p. 119.
16. Ibid., p. 114.

periods of general war should constitute an especially difficult time for liberal cooperation. General systemic wars constitute especially severe tests of dyadic conceptions of war as states are pressured to choose sides on strategic alliance criteria ("enemy of my enemy is my friend") rather than regime criteria. In World War II, this produced the well-known anomaly of the formal state of war existing between the liberal Allies and liberal Finland, because Finland was an enemy of the nonliberal Soviet Union, which was allied to the US and Britain. Nonetheless, liberal logic should resist systemic logic and hold up here. Why exclude those challenges?

A second reason offered for separating pre-World War I data from post-World War II data are unspecified differences in "processes underlying alliance formation (and) war outbreak," on the one hand, and "bipolarity and nuclear weapons" on the other. First, it is, of course, just these "processes" that we seek to test—what is the alternative set of processes? Second, one could and should test the liberal or democratic model against other theories such as international structure—bipolarity and multipolarity, nuclear or conventional weapons. Indeed, there have been—so far—no wars between atomic or nuclear-armed powers.[17] Nuclear deterrence thus might account for peace among the United States, Britain, and France in the Cold War and it widens the argument to incorporate U.S.-Soviet relations. Does it also account for fewer militarized disputes and as extensive cooperation? Doesn't it leave the pre-atomic peace among liberal republics unaccounted for? More promisingly, do multipolar alliances perhaps generate inter-allied strife and bipolar alliances inter-allied peace? Perhaps common security interests are stronger in alliances in bipolar systems or perhaps the bipolar hegemons preserve the peace by policing the weaker allies. It would be worth testing whether bipolar peace is the true underlying cause of the peace among democracies in the U.S. Bloc of the Cold War—and, presumably, an equivalent peace among communist republics in the Soviet Bloc?

As it is, the data on democratic wars and democratic disputes could just as well be a product of measurement error (the participatory polities were not liberal) or uncontrolled factors—greater commerce, perhaps, among democracies. Interdepence is a source both of conflict and for liberals (by argument),

---

17. Kenneth Waltz has elaborated the reasons for nuclear peace in Scott D. Sagan and Kenneth N. Waltz, *The Spread of Nuclear Weapons: A Debate* (New York: Norton, 1995). One exception to the nuclear peace might be the conflicts between the USSR and the People's Republic of China along the Ussuri River border. But casualty figures are uncertain in that conflict and so was the status of China's deliverable nuclear weapons.

peace. If one controls for commerce does the relationship between democracies and disputes change?[18] Or, perhaps, segmenting the data by neutral time periods (decades), the pre-1900 disputatiousness of democracies is due to the incompleteness of liberal democracy in the earlier era when the franchise was limited (*inter alia*: women were denied the franchise) and democratic principles were new? The best we can do is test theoretical models against each other. Until we have an alternative model, segmenting the data does not produce meaningful results.

The authors conclude by suggesting that the US abandon the pursuit of "democratic enlargement" and instead recognize that states in fact pursue "common interests" over "common polities."[19] But "common interests" does not constitute an alternative model. The debate is not about whether states pursue their interests; it is about how to define and judge the interests of states. Realists (of a structural persuasion) see those interests in terms of the balance of power; liberals in terms of liberal accommodation; Marxists in terms of class warfare and solidarity. When we have to choose, is democratization a better long-term strategy for the US than enhancing our position in the balance of power? It is over choices such as these that the debate should continue.

Policy

Even if your answer favors democratization, Edward Mansfield and Jack Snyder warn us that democratization is not enough.[20] Given all the instabilities of regime change, democratization may provoke more war. Their statistical analysis has recently been challenged and the evidence is still in dispute.[21] But if Mansfield and Snyder are correct, liberals have little to be surprised about, but much to worry about. Without liberal principles and international interdependence—all of which take time—democratizing regimes may well be war-prone.

We have here a useful warning. Yet in the long run liberalization across nations seems to hold great promise. How does one get from here to there? "Golden parachutes" for ex-dictators and the military is one idea with a

18. John Oneal, Frances Oneal, Zeev Maoz and Bruce Russett in "The Liberal Peace: Interdependence, Democracy and International Conflict, 1950–1985," *Journal of Peace Research* (February 1996) examine these questions and find that both interdependence and democracy contribute to peace.
19. Farber and Gowa, p. 122.
20. Edward D. Mansfield and Jack Snyder, "Democratization and the Danger of War," *International Security* Vol. 20, No. 1 (Summer 1995), pp. 5–38.
21. Andrew Enterline, "Driving While Democratizing: A Rejoinder to Mansfield and Snyder," *International Security*, Vol. 20, No. 4 (Spring 1996).

considerable history that may contribute to at least short-run stability.[22] Extending international institutions, or enhancing them, may be another answer.[23] Can the promise of European Union membership and the presence of assistance and association be an institutional bridge over a difficult transition? Can similar institutional mechanisms become operative in Africa and Asia? These questions are well-worth our attention.

Liberalism at twentieth century's end looks remarkably robust. Ironically, so it did at the beginning. But if nothing else we should have learned something about peace, war and cooperation from our very bloody 20th century. We have paid a high tuition; let us hope we have learned that liberal democracy is worth defending. The promise of peace may well be one more reason for doing so.

---

22. Mansfield and Snyder, "Democratization and the Dragon of War," p. 36.
23. See Jack Snyder, "Averting Anarchy in the New Europe," *International Security*, Vol. 14, No. 4, (Spring 1990), pp. 5–41. The most impressive of the early studies of the "democratic peace" proposition also stressed the importance of institutionalizing democratic cooperation for security. Clarence Streit, Union Now: A Proposal for a Federal Union of the Leading Democracies (New York: Harpers, 1938), pp. 88 and 90–92, seems to have been the first to demonstrate (in twentieth century foreign relations) the empirical tendency of democracies to maintain peace among themselves, and he made this the foundation of his proposal for a (non-Kantian) federal union of the fifteen leading democracies of the 1930's.

Suggestions for Further Reading

$\mathbf{T}$here has been a vast outpouring of research and writing on the democratic peace since the early 1980s. Some of the more significant contributions to this literature are listed below. The list is by no means exhaustive. Readers should refer to the footnotes of the essays included in this volume for additional references.

Kant, Perpetual Peace, and the Democratic Peace

Many books and articles have analyzed Kant's political philosophy. Listed below are some of the most accessible volumes that contain Kant's 1795 essay "Perpetual Peace," as well as several important commentaries on Kant's contribution to international relations theory. Michael Doyle's essay, "Kant, Liberal Legacies, and Foreign Affairs," in this volume also discusses Kant's ideas in detail.

Kant, Immanuel. "Perpetual Peace." In *Kant's Political Writings,* 2nd ed. Ed. Hans Reiss, trans. H.B. Nisbet. Cambridge: Cambridge University Press, 1991.

Kant, Immanuel. "Perpetual Peace." In *The Philosophy of Kant.* Ed. Carl J. Friedrich. New York: Modern Library, 1949.

Kant, Immanuel. "To Perpetual Peace: A Philosophical Sketch." In *Perpetual Peace and Other Essays.* Trans. Ted Humphrey. Indianapolis: Hackett, 1983, pp. 107–143.

Bourke, John. "Kant's Doctrine of 'Perpetual Peace.'" *Philosophy,* Vol. 17, No. 68 (November 1942), pp. 324–333.

Brown, Chris. *International Relations Theory: New Normative Approaches.* New York: Columbia University Press, 1992.

Gallie, W.B. *Philosophers of Peace and War: Kant, Clausewitz, Marx, Engels and Tolstoy.* Cambridge: Cambridge University Press, 1978, chap. 2.

Hinsley, F.H. *Power and the Pursuit of Peace: Theory and Practice in the History of Relations Between States.* Cambridge: Cambridge University Press, 1963, chap. 4.

Hoffmann, Stanley. *The State of War: Essays on the Theory and Practice of International Politics.* New York: Praeger, 1965, chap. 3.

Riley, Patrick. *Kant's Political Philosophy.* Totowa, N.J.: Rowman and Littlefield, 1983, chap. 6.

Sorenson, Georg. "Kant and Processes of Democratization: Consequences of Neorealist Thought." *Journal of Peace Research,* Vol. 29, No. 4 (November 1992), pp. 397–414.

Waltz, Kenneth N. "Kant, Liberalism, and War." *American Political Science Review,* Vol. 56, No. 2 (June 1962), pp. 331–340.

Early Articulations of the Democratic Peace

In addition to the two-part Doyle article reprinted in this volume, the following works were among the first to propound and call attention to the possibility and existence of a democratic peace. Kant's "Perpetual Peace" deserves pride of place among the initial versions of the democratic peace proposition, of course, but several more recent works helped to revive interest in the general question of democracies and war. Most of the early works in the recent wave of scholarship on the democratic peace are listed below. Not all of them, however, received much attention until other scholars had begun to explicate and test the democratic peace proposition in the mid-1980s.

Babst, Dean. "A Force for Peace." *Industrial Research,* April 1972, pp. 55–58. Originally published as "Elective Governments — A Force for Peace." *The Wisconsin Sociologist,* Vol. 3, No. 1 (1964), pp. 9–14.

Rummel, R.J. *Understanding Conflict and War: Vols. 1–5.* Los Angeles: Sage, 1975–1981.

Russett, Bruce, and Harvey Starr. *World Politics: The Menu for Choice,* 1st ed. New York: W.H. Freeman, 1981.

Wallensteen, Peter. *Structure and War: On International Relations 1820–1968.* Stockholm: Raben and Sjogren, 1973.

Books on the Democratic Peace

Most of the research on the democratic peace has been published in article form. The following works are among the few books on the subject as this volume goes to press. Each addresses topics in several of the categories into which the articles listed afterward are grouped.

Ray, James Lee. *Democracy and International Conflict: An Evaluation of the Democratic Peace Proposition.* Columbia: University of South Carolina Press, 1995.

Russett, Bruce. *Grasping the Democratic Peace: Principles for a Post-Cold War World.* Princeton, N.J.: Princeton University Press, 1993.

Quantitative Studies on Democracies, War, and Peace

The following articles assess two propositions: that democracies are less war-prone than other states in general; and that democracies are less likely to wage war against one another. The articles by Small and Singer, Chan, and Weede find that democracies are no less likely to go to war than are other types of states. They do not challenge the claim that democracies rarely fight one another. Rummel, however, argues that libertarian states are less war-prone. Bremer, as well as Maoz and Abdolali, find that pairs of democratic states rarely, if ever, go to war with one another. They argue that this finding is statistically robust.

Bremer, Stuart A. "Dangerous Dyads: Conditions Affecting the Likelihood of Interstate War, 1816–1965." *Journal of Conflict Resolution*, Vol. 36, No. 2 (June 1992), pp. 309–341.

Bremer, Stuart A. "Democracy and Militarized Interstate Conflict, 1816–1965." *International Interactions*, Vol. 18, No. 3 (1993), pp. 231–249.

Chan, Steve. "Mirror, Mirror on the Wall . . . Are the Freer Countries More Pacific?" *Journal of Conflict Resolution*, Vol. 28, No. 4 (December 1984), pp. 617–648.

Maoz, Zeev, and Nasrin Abdolali. "Regime Type and International Conflict." *Journal of Conflict Resolution*, Vol. 33, No. 1 (March 1989), pp. 3–35.

Rummel, R.J. "Libertarianism and International Violence." *Journal of Conflict Resolution*, Vol. 27, No. 1 (March 1983), pp. 27–71.

Small, Melvin, and J. David Singer. "The War-proneness of Democratic Regimes, 1816–1965." *Jerusalem Journal of International Relations*, Vol. 1, No. 4 (Summer 1976), pp. 50–69.

Weede, Erich. "Democracy and War Involvement." *Journal of Conflict Resolution*, Vol. 28, No. 4 (December 1984), pp. 649–664.

Weede, Erich. "Some Simple Calculations on Democracy and War Involvement." *Journal of Peace Research*, Vol. 29, No.4 (November 1992), pp. 377–383.

Norms and Structures: The Causal Logic of the Democratic Peace

The following works explicate and, in some cases, test competing explanations of why democracies rarely fight one another. The articles by Burley, Dixon, Doyle, Ember, Ember and Russett, Moravcsik, Raymond, and Weart emphasize the role of liberal and democratic norms in preventing wars between democracies. Lake, Mintz and Geva, Morgan and Campbell, Morgan and Schwebach, and Schweller focus on how democratic institutions structurally constrain decision-makers who might opt for war. Russett and Maoz explicate and test both explanations, concluding that the normative argument is more powerful. Bueno de Mesquita and Lalman, as well as Starr, endorse an expected-utility model that essentially argues that democracies recognize one another as "dovish" states and that such states have no incentives to wage war on one another. Their approach is closest to the structural explanation.

Bueno de Mesquita, Bruce, and David Lalman. *War and Reason: Domestic and International Imperatives.* New Haven, Conn.: Yale University Press, 1992.

Burley, Anne Marie Slaughter. "Law among Liberal States: Liberal Internationalism and the Act of State Doctrine." *Columbia Law Review*, Vol. 92, No. 8 (1992), pp. 1907–1996.

Dixon, William J. "Democracy and the Peaceful Settlement of International Conflict." *American Political Science Review*, Vol. 88, No. 1 (March 1994), pp. 14–32.

Doyle, Michael W. "Liberalism and World Politics." *American Political Science Review*, Vol. 80, No. 4 (December 1986), pp. 1151–1169.

TRANSACTION SLIP

SELLER   YELLOW COPY
BUYER   PINK COPY

AUTHORIZATION NO. | CLERK

DATE

CARDHOLDER ACCOUNT NO. (BUYER)

CARDHOLDER NAME

SERVICE ESTABLISHMENT ACCOUNT NO. (SELLER)

SELLER NAME

DESCRIPTION / INVOICE NO. | AMOUNT

SALES TAX

TOTAL $

USA

24 HOURS AUTHORIZATION (770) 592-6767
FOR AUTHORIZATIONS CALL (770) 591-4943
White copy must be received by TBC within
seven (7) days after transaction.

Cardholder acknowledges receipt of goods and/or
service in the amount of total shown herein and
agrees to perform the obligations set forth in the
Cardholder's Contract with the issuer.

CARDHOLDER'S SIGNATURE

X

GRATUITIES MINIMUM 15% CASH

Ember, Carol, Melvin Ember, and Bruce Russett. "Peace Between Participatory Polities: A Cross-Cultural Test of the 'Democracies Rarely Fight Each Other' Hypothesis." *World Politics*, Vol. 44, No. 4 (July 1992), pp. 573–599.

Lake, David A. "Powerful Pacifists: Democratic States and War." *American Political Science Review*, Vol. 86, No. 1 (March 1992), pp. 24–37.

Mintz, Alex, and Nehemia Geva. "Why Don't Democracies Fight Each Other? An Experimental Assessment of the 'Political Incentive' Explanation." *Journal of Conflict Resolution*, Vol. 37, No. 3 (September 1992), pp. 484–503.

Moravcsik, Andrew. "Liberalism and International Relations Theory." Working Paper 92–6. Center for International Affairs, Harvard University, 1992.

Morgan, T. Clifton, and Sally H. Campbell, "Domestic Structure, Decisional Constraints and War: So Why Kant Democracies Fight?" *Journal of Conflict Resolution*, Vol. 35, No. 2 (June 1991), pp. 187–211.

Morgan, T. Clifton, and Valerie L. Schwebach. "Take Two Democracies and Call Me in the Morning: A Prescription for Peace?" *International Interactions*, Vol. 17, No. 4 (Summer 1992), pp. 305–320.

Raymond, Gregory. "Democracies, Disputes, and Third-Party Intermediaries." *Journal of Conflict Resolution*, Vol. 38, No. 1 (March 1994), pp. 24–42.

Russett, Bruce, and Zeev Maoz. "Normative and Structural Causes of Democratic Peace." *American Political Science Review*, Vol. 87, No. 3 (September 1993), pp. 642–638.

Schweller, Randall L. "Domestic Structure and Preventive War: Are Democracies More Pacific?" *World Politics*, Vol. 44, No. 2 (January 1992), pp. 235–269.

Starr, Harvey. "Democracy and War: Choice, Learning and Security Communities." *Journal of Peace Research*, Vol. 29, No. 2 (May 1992), pp. 207–213.

Starr, Harvey. "Why Don't Democracies Fight One Another? Evaluating the Theory-Findings Feedback Loop." *Jerusalem Journal of International Relations*, Vol. 14, No. 4 (December 1992), pp. 41–59.

Weart, Spencer. "Peace Among Democratic and Oligarchic Republics." *Journal of Peace Research*, Vol. 31, No. 3 (August 1994), pp. 299–316.

Critiques of the Democratic Peace Proposition

In addition to the essays by Layne, Spiro, Farber and Gowa, and Oren in this volume, there is a small but growing literature that takes issue with the claim that democracies rarely fight one another. Cohen contends that the apparent existence of the democratic peace reflects questionable definitions of "democracy" and "war." In his view, there is only a security community in the North Atlantic and West European regions, not a general peace among democracies. Kacowicz makes a similar argument, claiming that many factors explain why democracies tend to be satisfied powers. Gowa critiques the various explanations of the democratic peace, and finds that none is convincing. As realists, Mearsheimer and Waltz both argue that the international behavior of democracies reflects systemic imperatives. Democracies are no more peace-loving than other types of states; democracies have not fought one another often because they have been rare and far apart geographically. Mueller argues that the absence of war between democracies reflects the fact that war in general is becoming obsolete. As some of the most advanced states, democracies happened to be among the first to grasp this idea. Porter questions the existence of the democratic peace, but expresses graver doubts about the durability of democratic regimes. Vincent presents evidence that undermines R.J. Rummel's claim that libertarian states are more pacific.

Cohen, Raymond. "Pacific Unions: A Reappraisal of the Theory that 'Democracies do not go to War with Each Other." *Review of International Studies*, Vol. 20, No. 3 (July 1994), pp. 207–223.

Gowa, Joanne. "Democratic States and International Disputes." *International Organization*, Vol. 49, No. 3 (Summer 1995), pp. 511–522.

Kacowicz, Arie M. "Explaining Zones of Peace: Democracies as Satisfied Powers?" *Journal of Peace Research*, Vol. 32, No. 3 (August 1995), pp. 265–276.

Mearsheimer, John J. "Back to the Future: Instability in Europe After the Cold War." *International Security*, Vol. 15, No. 1 (Summer 1990), pp. 5–56 at 48–51.

Mueller, John. *Quiet Cataclysm: Reflections on the Recent Transformation of World Politics.* New York: HarperCollins, 1995, chap. 10.

Porter, Bruce D. "Is the Zone of Peace Stable? Sources of Stress and Conflict in Industrial Democracies of Post–Cold War Europe." *Security Studies*, Vol. 4, No. 3 (Spring 1995), pp. 520–551.

Vincent, Jack. "Freedom and International Conflict: Another Look." *International Studies Quarterly*, Vol. 31, No. 1 (March 1987), pp. 102–112.

Waltz, Kenneth N. "America as Model for the World? A Foreign Policy Perspective." *PS: Political Science and Politics*, Vol. 24, No. 4 (December 1991), pp. 667–670.

Responses, Reflections, and Refinements: The Future of the Democratic Peace Proposition

Several scholars have begun to reflect on the various waves of research on the democratic peace. Doyle's concluding contribution to this volume is one example. Chan and Morgan present overviews of the literature on democracy and peace and suggest avenues for future research. Maoz and Russett argue that the empirical evidence for the democratic peace is statistically robust even when one controls for other factors that increase the likelihood of war. Ray enumerates the alleged cases of wars between democracies, including the Spanish-American War, the War of 1812, and the U.S. Civil War, and argues that not a single case should be classified as a war between democracies.

Chan, Steve. "Democracy and War: Some Thoughts on Future Research Agenda." *International Interactions*, Vol. 18, No. 3 (1993), pp. 205–213.

Maoz, Zeev, and Bruce Russett. "Alliance, Contiguity, Wealth, and Political Stability: Is the Lack of Conflict among Democracies a Statistical Artifact?" *International Interactions*, Vol. 17, No. 3 (1992), pp. 245–267.

Morgan, T. Clifton. "Democracy and War: Reflections on the Literature." *International Interactions*, Vol. 18, No. 3 (1993), pp. 197–203.

Ray, James Lee. "Wars Between Democracies: Rare, or Nonexistent?" *International Interactions*, Vol. 18, No. 3 (1993), pp. 251–276.

The Spread of Democracy and U.S. Foreign Policy

Virtually all studies agree that there has been a long-term increase in the number of democracies in the world. The democratic peace proposition suggests that the spread of democracy will reduce international conflict. Many authors have thus argued that the United States should adopt global democratization as its mission in the post–Cold War world. The following books and articles consider the spread of democracy, its international implications, and how the United States might best promote democracy. Many scholars have written on the political, social, and economic conditions for democracy and on how states become democracies. Shin's review essay provides a recent overview of research in this area. Smith's article reviews recent research on the feasibility and desirability of U.S. efforts to spread democracy.

Allison, Graham T. and Robert P. Beschel. "Can the United States Promote Democracy?" *Political Science Quarterly*, Vol. 107, No. 1 (Spring 1992), pp. 81–98.

Diamond, Larry. "Promoting Democracy." *Foreign Policy*, No. 87 (Summer 1992), pp. 25–46.

Huntington, Samuel P. *The Third Wave: Democratization in the Late Twentieth Century*. Norman: University of Oklahoma Press, 1991.

Muravchik, Joshua. *Exporting Democracy: Fulfilling America's Destiny*. Washington, D.C.: AEI Press, 1991.

Singer, Max, and Aaron Wildavsky. *The Real World Order: Zones of Peace/Zones of Turmoil*. Chatham, N.J.: Chatham House, 1993.

Shin, Doh Chull. "On the Third Wave of Democratization: A Synthesis and Evaluation of Recent Theory and Research." *World Politics*, Vol. 47, No. 1 (October 1994), pp. 135–170.

Smith, Tony. *America's Mission: The United States and the Worldwide Struggle for Democracy in the Twentieth Century*. Princeton. N.J.: Princeton University Press, 1994.

Smith, Tony. "Making the World Safe for Democracy." *The Washington Quarterly*, Vol. 16, No. 4 (Autumn 1993), pp. 197–214.

International Security

Center for Science and International Affairs
John F. Kennedy School of Government
Harvard University

Articles in this reader were previously published in **International Security**, a quarterly journal sponsored and edited by the Center for Science and International Affairs at the John F. Kennedy School of Government at Harvard University, and published by MIT Press Journals. To receive subscription information about the journal or find out more about other readers in our series, please contact MIT Press Journals at 55 Hayward Street, Cambridge, MA, 02142.